Statutes, Regulations and Case Law Protecting Individuals with Disabilities

"This publication is designed to provide accurate and authoritative information in regard to the subject matter covered. It is sold with the understanding that the publisher is not engaged in rendering legal, accounting or other professional service. If legal advice or other expert assistance is required, the services of a competent professional person should be sought."—from a Declaration of Principles jointly adopted by a Committee of the American Bar Association and a Committee of Publishers and Associations.

Published by
Data Research, Inc.
P.O. Box 490
Rosemount, Minnesota 55068

OTHER TITLES PUBLISHED
BY DATA RESEARCH, INC.:

Deskbook Encyclopedia of American School Law
Students with Disabilities and Special Education
Private School Law in America
U.S. Supreme Court Education Cases
Deskbook Encyclopedia of American Insurance Law
Deskbook Encyclopedia of Public Employment Law
U.S. Supreme Court Employment Cases
Deskbook Encyclopedia of Employment Law

Copyright © 1994 by Data Research, Inc.

Library of Congress Cataloging-in-Publication Data

Statutes, regulations, and case law protecting individuals with disabilities.
p.   cm.
Includes index.
ISBN 0-939675-39-0
1. Handicapped--Legal status, laws, etc.--United States.
2. Discrimination against the handicapped--Law and legislation--United States
KF480.S68   1994
346.7301'3--dc20
[347.30613]   93-39443
                                                                          CIP

PREFACE/ USER GUIDE

This book is a compilation of federal statutes and regulations that affect the rights of disabled Americans. The statutes include the Individuals with Disabilities Education Act (the "IDEA," formerly known as the Education of the Handicapped Act), the Rehabilitation Act of 1973, and the Americans with Disabilities Act of 1990 (ADA). Also included are federal regulations enacted by some of the agencies that enforce these acts. This book is intended to complement other Data Research titles by providing easy access to federal statutes and regulations that may not be readily available to employers and educators.

The ADA, IDEA and Rehabilitation Act of 1973 are civil rights acts designed to protect the rights of disabled persons. The most basic, important civil right protected by these statutes is *access* — the right of persons with disabilities to be integrated into society through the removal of societal and architectural barriers. As stated by the Department of Justice in the analysis of its ADA regulations (found at 28 CFR Part 36, *et seq.* and included in this book): "Integration is fundamental to the purposes of the Americans with Disabilities Act. Provision of segregated accommodations and services relegates persons with disabilities to second-class status." The IDEA also requires schools to integrate students with disabilities by "mainstreaming" them into general student populations to the maximum extent possible. The Rehabilitation Act of 1973 was the first comprehensive congressional action that attempted to address the removal of societal barriers to disabled Americans. It established the Rehabilitation Services Administration and authorized federal grants to states to assist them in providing vocational rehabilitation service with a focus on comprehensive vocational rehabilitation and independent living programs. It sought to promote employment opportunities for disabled persons and to remove societal and architectural barriers which made access difficult for them. Although the Rehabilitation Act includes many sections, only § 504 (29 U.S.C. § 794) and § 501 (29 U.S.C. § 791) are significant for this book. They account for almost all of the litigation under the Rehabilitation Act.

The terms "disabled" and "handicapped" appear throughout this book and have the same meaning under federal law. Although Congress and federal agencies have made efforts in recent years to replace the term "handicapped" with "disabled" in statutes and regulations, Rehabilitation Act regulations have not yet been so revised. Of course, almost every court employed the term "handicapped" until the term "disabled" came into common usage in recent years, and some continue to do so. As explained by the U.S. Department of Justice in the analysis following ADA Title II regulations (28 CFR Part 36, *et seq.*), the terms "handicap" and "disability" and "individual with handicaps" and "individual with a disability" have the same definition. "In enacting the Americans with Disabilities Act, Congress concluded that it was important for the current legislation to use terminology most in line with the sensibilities of most Americans with disabilities. No change in definition or substance is intended nor should one be attributed to this change in phraseology." Congress explicitly intended the case law definition of "handicap" developed under the Rehabilitation Act to apply to the ADA's term "disability." See the Appendix to 29

CFR Part 1630.2(g), which appears in the **Federal Regulations Under the Americans with Disabilities Act of 1990** section of this book.

Where possible, this book avoids use of the terms "handicap" and "individual with handicaps." However, since these terms have been in use over the past 20 years in Rehabilitation Act and IDEA/EHA jurisprudence, and are in fact still in use in federal regulations and by some courts, these terms are used in the Rehabilitation Act and IDEA portions of this book. By doing so, Data Research, Inc. does so in order to faithfully report the activity of the courts and federal agencies which interpret this legislation and its regulations, and not to reinforce discriminatory, patronizing or stereotypical attitudes.

Until the passage of the ADA in 1990, section 504 was probably the most important law protecting the rights of disabled Americans. In fact, the ADA originated as a proposal by the National Council on Disability, which was itself formed under the Rehabilitation Act (29 U.S.C. § 701, *et seq.*). Because the ADA's legislative content is firmly rooted in Rehabilitation Act § 504 (29 U.S.C. § 794), an understanding of the Rehabilitation Act is essential to the study of disabled Americans' civil rights. According to the Department of Justice, (in its analysis of ADA regulations found at 36 CFR Part 28, *et seq.*, included in this book): "Standards for title I of the ADA and section 504 of the Rehabilitation Act are for the most part identical because title I of the ADA was based on requirements set forth in regulations implementing section 504."

Persons interested in assessing the impact of the ADA are strongly urged to review the Rehabilitation Act and its legal precedents, because the courts are mandated to apply the same legal analysis in ADA cases as that used in considering § 504 cases. The difference between the acts is in scope and application, rather than in substance and effect. Whereas § 504 applies only to programs or activities receiving federal funds, the ADA is far broader in scope, applying to a multitude of public and private entities. It is also noteworthy that the ADA and Rehabilitation Act are primarily enforced by the same federal agencies, the Department of Justice and the Equal Employment Opportunity Commission. According to the official comment to 28 CFR Part 35, the ADA imposes additional responsibilities upon public school systems which may exceed their obligations under the Individuals with Disabilities Education Act (IDEA). Examples given are "programs open to parents or to the public, graduation ceremonies, parent-teacher organization meetings, plays and other events open to the public, and adult education classes. Public school systems must comply with the ADA in all of their services, programs, or activities, including those that are open to parents or to the public." Users of this book are urged to study the cases of *Coleman v. Zatechka,* 824 F.Supp. 1360 (D.Neb.1993), and *Galloway v. Sup. Court of Dist. of Columbia,* 816 F.Supp. 15 (D.D.C.1993), which appear in the **Case Law Guide for the Americans with Disabilities Act** section of this book. In these cases, the complaining parties brought successful lawsuits under both the Rehabilitation Act and the ADA, a result which is expressly permitted by the acts.

Organization of this Book

This book is designed as a convenient reference tool and treats each act in a separate section. For each act, there is an explanatory note entitled "Overview," followed by the statute itself, and a caselaw guide to important court interpretations of the act. Following the statute and caselaw guide, each section presents the text of agency regulations published under the authority of the act, and important court decisions interpreting the regulations. The statutory or regulatory overview that precedes the text of each of the statutes and regulations reproduced in this book will explain the most important legal concepts contained therein. Important words and phrases are highlighted in bold print. For a further, brief discussion of many of the bold print words and phrases used in these sections, turn to the Glossary (Appendix A) near the end of this book. Users who require further research will want to study and review the list of important cases found in the Case Law Guide section following each statute and regulation in this book.

In addition to the statutes and regulations themselves, this book contains many of the interpretive guidelines published by the agencies which enforce these enactments. Users of this book are urged to read these generally helpful and readable discussions for further understanding of the statutes and regulations as interpreted by the federal agencies which enforce them.

TABLE OF CONTENTS

PART TWO
AMERICANS WITH DISABILITIES ACT

PART THREE
INDIVIDUALS WITH DISABILITIES EDUCATION ACT

APPENDIX

TABLE OF CASES

TABLE OF CASES

TABLE OF STATUTES CITED

*References are to statutory sections and the page
numbers in this volume where the
statutory sections are cited*

20 U.S.C. §

29 U.S.C. §

42 U.S.C. §

TABLE OF REGULATIONS CITED

*References are to sections of the Code of Federal Regulations
and the page numbers in this volume
where the regulations are cited*

TABLE OF REGULATIONS CITED

PART ONE

REHABILITATION ACT

PARTS 501 AND 504 OF THE REHABILITATION ACT OF 1973
(29 U.S.C. §§ 791, 794)

Rehabilitation Act Overview

It is important for users of this book to have a basic understanding of the following sections of the Rehabilitation Act, because the Americans with Disabilities Act (ADA) is based upon the Rehabilitation Act, its regulations, and its case law precedents. Section 504 of the Rehabilitation Act of 1973 (29 U.S.C. § 794) prohibits discrimination against otherwise qualified individuals with disabilities, solely on the basis of the disabling condition in any program or activity that receives federal funds. Section 504's language is based on Title VI of the Civil Rights Act of 1964 (42 U.S.C. § 2000d). The nondiscrimination principle codified in § 504 (29 U.S.C. § 794) was first proposed to the U.S. House of Representatives as an amendment to Title VI. Congress was concerned not merely with overt discrimination against disabled persons, "but [also with] thoughtlessness and indifference— [with] benign neglect." *Alexander v. Choate,* 469 U.S. 287, 105 S.Ct. 712, 83 L.Ed.2d 661 (1985). An example given by the U.S. Supreme Court in *Alexander v. Choate* was that architectural barriers existing for disabled Americans were not constructed with the idea of excluding them from access to buildings, but had the net result of doing exactly that. An important part of the Rehabilitation Act of 1973 was the creation of the National Council on Disability and the Architectural Barriers Compliance Board. The U.S. Commission of Civil Rights also noted that disabled Americans suffered primarily as a result of apathetic attitudes of non-disabled persons, rather than from affirmative discrimination.

Section 501 of the Rehabilitation Act (29 U.S.C. § 791) is the exclusive remedy for federal employees alleging employment discrimination, as incorporated by Title VII of the Civil Rights Act of 1964. It also applies to federal executive agencies and the U.S. Postal Service. For example, in *Rattner v. Bennett*, 701 F.Supp. 7 (D.D.C.1989), the U.S. District Court for the District of Columbia dismissed claims for intentional infliction of emotional distress and Fifth Amendment violations by an aggrieved federal employee, stating that the Rehabilitation Act was the preemptive remedy for the employee's handicap discrimination complaint, while the Age Discrimination in Employment Act (ADEA) was the exclusive remedy for his age discrimination complaint. The U.S. Court of Appeals, Ninth Circuit, dismissed the § 501 complaint of a hearing-impaired toolmaker employed by a naval shipyard because he had erroneously named the shipyard commander instead of the Secretary of the Navy. The employee's § 504 claim also failed because there is no private cause of action under that section; section 501 is the exclusive remedy of federal employees. *Johnson v. Horne*, 875 F.2d 1415 (9th Cir.1989). See also *DiPompo v. West Point Academy*, 770 F.Supp. 887 (S.D.N.Y.1991).

In order to succeed under § 504, the complaining party must show discrimination "solely by reason" of a disability. See *Norcross v. Sneed*, 755 F.2d 113, 117 (8th Cir.1985), *Harris v. Adams*, 873 F.2d 929, 933 (6th Cir.1990) and *Leckelt v. Bd. of Commissioners of Hospital Dist. No. 1*, 909 F.2d 820, 825 (5th Cir.1990). Next, the complaining party must show ability to perform the "**essential functions**" of the job. See Health and Human Services Department regulations arising under § 504, at 45 CFR Part 84.3(k). The individual must show that she or he is **otherwise qualified** to perform the job. The leading U.S. Supreme Court case which interprets Rehabilitation Act § 504 is *School Board of Nassau County, Florida v. Arline*, 480 U.S. 273, 107 S.Ct. 1123, 94 L.Ed.2d 307 (1987). According to the Supreme Court, Rehabilitation Act § 504 was enacted "to ensure that handicapped individuals are not denied jobs or other benefits because of the prejudiced attitudes or ignorance of others" and "that society's accumulated myths and fears about disability and disease are as handicapping as are the physical limitations that flow from the actual impairment." Other key U.S. Supreme Court cases involving the Rehabilitation Act § 504 include *Alexander v. Choate*, 469 U.S. 287, 99 S.Ct. 2361, 60 L.Ed.2d 980 (1985) and *Southeastern Community College v. Davis*, 442 U.S. 397, 105 S.Ct. 712, 83 L.Ed.2d 661 (1979).

The Rehabilitation Act of 1973 (29 U.S.C. § 701 *et seq.*).

§ 706. Definitions

For the purposes of this chapter:
***

     (2) ***

     (8)(A) Except as otherwise provided in subparagraph (B), the term "individual with a disability" means any individual who (i) has a physical or mental impairment which for such individual constitutes or results in a substantial impediment to employment and (ii) can benefit in terms of an employment outcome from vocational rehabilitation services provided pursuant to subchapters I, II, III, VI, and VIII of this chapter.

     (B) Subject to subparagraphs (C), (D), (E) and (F), the term "individual with a disability" means, for purposes of sections 701, 713, and 714 of this title, and titles

IV and V of this chapter, any person who (i) has a physical or mental impairment which substantially limits one or more of such person's major life activities, (ii) has a record of such an impairment, or (iii) is regarded as having such an impairment.

(C)(i) For purposes of subchapter V of this chapter, the term "individual with a disability" does not include an individual who is currently engaging in the illegal use of drugs, when a covered entity acts on the basis of such use.

(ii) Nothing in clause (i) shall be construed to exclude as an individual with a disability an individual who—

(I) has successfully completed a supervised drug rehabilitation program and is no longer engaging in the illegal use of drugs, or has otherwise been rehabilitated successfully and is no longer engaging in such use;

(II) is participating in a supervised rehabilitation program and is no longer engaging in such use; or

(III) is erroneously regarded as engaging in such use, but is not engaging in such use;

except that it shall not be a violation of this chapter for a covered entity to adopt or administer reasonable policies or procedures, including but not limited to drug testing, designed to ensure that an individual described in subclause (I) or (II) is no longer engaging in the illegal use of drugs.

(iii) Notwithstanding clause (i), for purposes of programs and activities providing health services and services provided under subchapters I, II and III of this chapter, an individual shall not be excluded from the benefits of such programs or activities on the basis of his or her current illegal use of drugs if he or she is otherwise entitled to such services.

(iv) For purposes of programs and activities providing educational services, local educational agencies may take disciplinary action pertaining to the use or possession of illegal drugs or alcohol against any student who is an individual with a disability and who currently is engaging in the illegal use of drugs or in the use of alcohol to the same extent that such disciplinary action is taken against students who are not individuals with disabilities. Furthermore, the due process procedures at 34 CFR 104.36 shall not apply to such disciplinary actions.

(v) For purposes of sections 793 and 794 of this title as such sections relate to employment, the term "individual with a disability" does not include any individual who is an alcoholic whose current use of alcohol prevents such individual from performing the duties of the job in question or whose employment, by reason of such current alcohol abuse, would constitute a direct threat to property or the safety of others.

(D) For the purpose of sections 793 and 794 of this title, as such sections relate to employment, such term does not include an individual who has a currently contagious disease or infection and who, by reason of such disease or infection, would constitute a direct threat to the health or safety of other individuals or who, by reason of the currently contagious disease or infection, is unable to perform the duties of the job.

(E) For the purposes of sections 791, 793, 794 of this title—

(i) for purposes of the application of subparagraph (B) to such sections, the term "impairment" does not include homosexuality or bisexuality; and

(ii) therefore the term "individual with a disability" does not include an individual on the basis of homosexuality or bisexuality.

(F) For the purposes of sections 791, 793, and 794 of this title, the term "individual with a disability" does not include an individual on the basis of—

(i) transvestism, transsexualism, pedophilia, exhibitionism, voyerism, gender identity disorders not resulting from physical impairments, or other sexual behavior disorders;

(ii) compulsive gambling, kleptomania, or pyromania; or

(iii) psychoactive substance use disorders resulting from current illegal use of drugs.

***

(As amended Pub. L. 99-506, Title I, § 103(d)(2)(B), Title X § 1002(e)(4), Oct. 21, 1986, 100 Stat. 1810, 1844; Pub. L. 100-259, § 4, Mar. 22, 1988, 102 Stat. 29; Pub. L. 100-630, Title II, § 206(d), Nov. 7, 1988, 102 Stat. 3312; Pub. L. 102-569, Title I, § 102(p)(32), Title V, § 506, Oct. 29, 1992, 106 Stat. 4360, 4428.)

Statutory Text—Section 504 of the Rehabilitation Act of 1973 (29 U.S.C. § 794) Nondiscrimination under federal grants and programs

(a) Promulgation of rules and regulations

No **otherwise qualified individual** with a **disability** in the United States, as defined in section 706(8) of this title, shall, solely by reason of her or his disability, be excluded from the participation in, be denied the benefits of, or be subjected to discrimination under any program or activity receiving Federal financial assistance or under any program or activity conducted by any Executive agency or by the United States Postal Service. The head of each such agency shall promulgate such regulations as may be necessary to carry out the amendments to this section made by the Rehabilitation, Comprehensive Services, and Developmental Disabilities Act of 1978. Copies of any proposed regulation shall be submitted to appropriate authorizing committees of the Congress, and such regulation may take effect no earlier than the thirtieth day after the date on which such regulation is so submitted to such committees.

(b) "Program or activity" defined

(1)(A) a department, agency, special purpose district, or other instrumentality of a State or of a local government; or

(B) the entity of such State or local government that distributes such assistance and each such department or agency (and each other State or local government entity) to which the assistance is extended, in the case of assistance to a State or local government;

(2)(A) a college, university, or other postsecondary institution, or a public system of higher education; or

(B) a local educational agency (as defined in section 2891(12) of Title 20) system of vocational education, or other school system;

(3)(A) an entire corporation, partnership, or other private organization, or an entire sole proprietorship—

(i) if assistance is extended to such corporation, partnership, private organization, or sole proprietorship as a whole; or

(ii) which is principally engaged in the business of providing education, health care, housing, social services, or parks and recreation; or

(B) the entire plant or other comparable, geographically separate facility to which Federal financial assistance is extended, in the case of any other corporation, partnership, private organization, or sole proprietorship; or

(4) any other entity which is established by two or more of the entities described in paragraph (1), (2), or (3);

any part of which is extended Federal financial assistance.

(c) Significant structural alterations by small providers; exception

Small providers are not required by subsection (a) of this section to make significant structural alterations to their existing facilities for the purpose of assuring program accessibility, if alternative means of providing the services are available. The terms used in this subsection shall be construed with reference to the regulations existing on March 22, 1988.

(d) Standards used in determining violation of section

The standards used to determine whether this section has been violated in a complaint alleging employment discrimination under this section shall be the standards applied under title I of the Americans with Disabilities Act of 1990 (42 U.S.C. 12111 et seq.) and the provisions of sections 501 through 504 and 510, of the Americans with Disabilities Act of 1990 (42 U.S.C. 12201-12204 and 12210), as such sections relate to employment.

***

Cases Interpreting § 504 of the
Rehabilitation Act of 1973

Alexander v. Choate, 469 U.S. 287, 105 S.Ct. 712, 83 L.Ed.2d 661 (1985). This case is significant as an interpretation of the term **reasonable accommodation** by the U.S. Supreme Court. The *Alexander* decision explained *Southeastern Community College v. Davis,* 442 U.S. 397, 99 S.Ct. 2361, 60 L.Ed.2d 980 (1979) as an attempt to balance the statutory rights of disabled persons to be integrated into society with the legitimate interest of federal fund recipients to preserve the integrity of their programs. In *Alexander,* the state of Tennessee sought to reduce Medicaid costs by reducing the number of state reimbursed inpatient hospital days from 20 to 14 per year. State Medicaid recipients filed a class action under § 504, claiming that the state's action was discriminatory and likely to disproportionately affect persons with disabilities. The Court held that Tennessee made the same benefit available to all persons and that the 14-day coverage was equally accessible to all persons. The Court employed a balancing of interests approach, not the disparate impact analysis of Title VI jurisprudence. Tennessee could redefine the Medicaid benefit it would provide as long as the change was neutral on its face and equally accessible to all persons.

Alexopulos v. Riles, 784 F.2d 1408 (9th Cir.1986). The requirements of the Education for All Handicapped Children Act (now designated IDEA) may not be circumvented by filing a complaint under the Rehabilitation Act. Neither act applied retroactively to pre-1973 claims.

Anderson v. Univ. of Wisconsin, 665 F.Supp. 1372, *aff'd,* 841 F.2d 737 (7th Cir.1988). An **alcoholic** law school student was not a **qualified handicapped person** under the Rehabilitation act because he was not academically entitled to continue in school.

Assa'ad-Faltas v. Virginia, 738 F.Supp. 982 (E.D.Va.1989), *aff'd,* 902 F.2d 1564 (4th Cir.1990). A public employee's Rehabilitation Act complaint was dismissed because she was unable to show that her alleged disability was the sole reason for termination of her employment.

Baker v. Bd. of Regents of State of Kansas, 991 F.2d 628, 1056 (10th Cir.1993). The U.S. Court of Appeals, Tenth Circuit, applied Kansas' two-year **statute of limitations** for personal injury to a Rehabilitation Act case, finding an analogy between personal injury actions and civil rights actions filed under § 504. The Rehabilitation Act has no explicit statute of limitations and courts are expected to apply the limitations of local law.

Bentivegna v. U.S. Dept. of Labor, 694 F.2d 619 (9th Cir.1982). A diabetic laborer hired by the City of Los Angeles under the federal Comprehensive Employment and Training Act failed a physical examination because of lack of blood sugar control. A federal district court denied his claim for backpay, and the U.S. Court of Appeals, Ninth Circuit, reversed. There was insufficient evidence that the city's requirement of controlled blood sugar levels did not discriminate against handicapped persons under § 504, because it failed to establish a direct connection between job requirements and "business necessity and safe performance."

Carter v. Casa Cent., 849 F.2d 1048, (7th Cir.1988). A nursing director was denied reemployment after she was diagnosed with multiple sclerosis. The U.S. Court of Appeals, Seventh Circuit, affirmed the district court award of $25,000 in backpay to the director. The court found that she had been denied reemployment solely on the basis of her handicap, where she was **otherwise qualified** for the job and posed no health risk.

Casey v. Lewis, 773 F.Supp. 1365 (D.C.Ariz.1991). A prison was not allowed to arbitrarily exclude inmates from employment in food service because of HIV-positive status. Each inmate was entitled to an individualized determination of the risk of transmitting HIV.

Chalk v. U.S. Dist. Court, Central Dist. of California, 840 F.2d 701 (9th Cir.1988). When a California teacher was diagnosed HIV positive, his employer sought to remove him from the classroom and place him in an administrative position without student contact. The U.S. Court of Appeals, Ninth Circuit, reversed the district court's decision and ruled that the teacher should be permitted a preliminary injunction allowing him to remain in the classroom. Applying the analysis used by the Supreme Court in *School Bd. of Nassau County v. Arline,* the court determined that the teacher was an **otherwise qualified handicapped individual** under Rehabilitation Act § 504 because he did not present a serious risk of infecting others in the classroom.

Chiari v. City of League City, 920 F.2d 311 (5th Cir.1991). A handicapped individual who cannot perform **essential job duties** is not entitled to Rehabilitation Act protection. In this case, a person with Parkinson's disease failed in his lawsuit against a Texas municipality because he could not perform his job without endangering the safety of others or himself. **Reasonable accommodation** is not possible in such situations.

City of Cleburne, Texas v. Cleburne Living Center, 473 U.S. 432, 105 S.Ct. 3249, 87 L.Ed.2d 313 (1985). A non-Rehabilitation Act case involving a Texas zoning ordinance, which is important for the Supreme Court's ruling that mental impairment does not constitute a "suspect classification" requiring strict constitutional scrutiny.

Commonwealth v. Boros, 620 A.2d 1139 (Pa.1993). The Pennsylvania Department of Transportation revoked the licenses of three epileptic school bus drivers. The Pennsylvania Supreme Court held that the Commonwealth Court of Pennsylvania did not have the authority to introduce Rehabilitation Act coverage where none of the complaining parties had raised this issue before the trial court.

Consolidated Rail Corp. v. Darrone, 465 U.S. 624, 104 S.Ct. 1248, 79 L.Ed.2d 568 (1984). Although § 504 jurisprudence is based upon legal precedents set by Title VI of the Civil Rights Act of 1964, 42 U.S.C. § 2000d *et seq.,* the *Darrone* case recognizes distinctions in the two statutes. In *Darrone,* a railroad engineer who suffered severe permanent injuries was rejected for further employment by his former employer. In the employee's § 504 lawsuit, the U.S. Supreme Court held that Conrail was subject to § 504 liability, even though its primary objective was transportation, and not providing employment.

Copeland v. Philadelphia Police Dept., 840 F.2d 1139 (3d Cir.1988). A municipal police department was not required to modify its drug policies to accommodate the drug use of an officer because that was a **"substantial modification"** of essential department functions.

Disabled in Action v. Baltimore, 685 F.2d 881 (4th Cir.1982). An award of attorney's fees was appropriate in a Rehabilitation Act case brought against a city to provide accessible accommodations for disabled fans at the city's ballpark.

Disabled in Action of Pennsylvania v. Sykes, 833 F.2d 1113 (3d Cir.1987), *cert den.,* 485 U.S. 989, 108 S.Ct. 1293, 99 L.Ed.2d 503 (1988). A § 504 case interpreting

U.S. Department of Transportation (DOT) regulations (found at 49 CFR Part 27) which correspond with 1978 Health, Education and Welfare (now Health and Human Services) guidelines published at 45 CFR Part 85 *et seq.*

Doherty v. Southern College of Optometry, 862 F.2d 570 (6th Cir.1988), *cert. den.,* 493 U.S. 810, 110 S.Ct. 53, 107 L.Ed.2d 22 (1989). A disabled student who suffered from retinitis pigmentosa enrolled in an optometry college. During the student's first year of study, the college introduced a proficiency requirement which required the use of special equipment. The student failed his equipment tests and the college board of trustees denied his request for a waiver. The student was consequently unable to obtain a degree. In the lawsuit which followed, the student argued that the test was a pretext for discrimination against him. The U.S. Court of Appeals, Sixth Circuit, ruled that the college could permissibly set competency standards. Section 504 did not require the college to lower its **academic standards** in order to **reasonably accommodate** disabled students.

Graves v. Methodist Youth Serv., Inc., 624 F.Supp. 429 (N.D.Ill.1985). A mentally-disabled counselor employed by a Methodist social services organization had standing to file a Rehabilitation Act lawsuit because the organization received indirect federal funding.

Halasz v. Univ. of New England, 816 F.Supp. 43 (D.Me.1993). Section 504 does not require educational institutions to lower **admission standards** to **reasonably accommodate** handicapped applicants.

Hoyt v. St. Mary's Rehabilitation Center, 711 F.2d 864 (8th Cir.1983). A nursing home resident's "next friend and daily visitor" was without standing to bring a § 504 complaint against the home to compel it to allow unrestricted visits and provide the resident with specified medical and dental care.

Hurry v. Jones, 734 F.2d 879 (1st Cir.1984). The Rehabilitation Act portion of an action brought by parents seeking transportation of their disabled son failed because the claim was properly to be filed under the EAHCA [now IDEA].

Hutchings v. Erie City & County Library Bd. of Dir., 516 F.Supp. 1265 (W.D.Pa.1981). The court held that a **damage award** might be recovered under § 504 in a lawsuit filed by an employee with multiple sclerosis. The employer had attempted to transfer the employee to a new job where she would be required to perform duties which she was not capable of performing due to her disability.

Irving Indep. School Dist. v. Tatro, 468 U.S. 883, 104 S.Ct. 3371, 82 L.Ed.2d 664 (1984). A school district was required under the EHA (IDEA) to provide catheterization for a disabled student, but was not liable for attorney's fees under § 504.

Kaelin v. Grubbs, 682 F.2d 595 (6th Cir.1982). A disabled student expelled for disruptive behavior was entitled to a hearing before the appropriate board to review the relationship between the student's disability and his behavior. **Expulsion constitutes a change in placement** under complementary provisions of the IDEA and Rehabilitation Act.

Kohl by Kohl v. Woodhaven Learning Center, 865 F.2d 930 (8th Cir.1989), *cert. den.* 493 U.S. 892, 110 S.Ct. 239, 107 L.Ed.2d 189 (1989). A federal district court determined that a Missouri private school violated § 504 by refusing to admit a blind, mentally and physically disabled student who had hepatitis B. The court ordered the school to admit the student and to immunize its employees who would regularly have contact with the student. The U.S. Court of Appeals, Eighth Circuit, reversed and remanded the case, finding that the student was not entitled to admission to the school because of the **significant risk of infection** to school staff.

Langon v. U.S. Dept. of Health and Human Services, 749 F.Supp. 1 (D.D.C.1990). **Reasonable accommodation** can only occur when the person seeking accommodation provides the employer, service provider, or agency with information about his or her disabling condition.

Leckelt v. Bd. of Commissioners of Hosp. Dist. No. 1, 755 F.Supp. 1377 (E.D.La.1989), *aff'd*, 909 F.2d 820 (5th Cir.1990). An HIV-positive nurse who refused to provide his test results was permissibly terminated under § 504 because his lack of cooperation made him not **otherwise qualified** to perform his job. He was fired for failure to follow hospital infection control policies, not merely for being HIV positive, and his refusal to disclose information prevented the employer from undertaking a **reasonable accommodation**.

Lucero v. Hart, 915 F.2d 1367 (9th Cir.1990). A county employee was not **otherwise qualified** for a job because she failed to type the required 45 words per minute and the employer had already made attempts to accommodate her.

Marvin H. v. Austin Indep. School Dist., 714 F.2d 1348 (5th Cir.1983). The Rehabilitation Act does not create a private right of action for **damages**, unless the complaining party proves **intentional discrimination**. In this case, a disabled student failed to make the required showing because there was no evidence that the school had intentionally discriminated against him.

Nathanson v. Medical College of Pennsylvania, 926 F.2d 1368 (3d Cir.1992). In order to impose § 504 liability, the agency or program receiving federal funds must have **knowledge** of the complaining party's handicap.

Nelson v. Thornburgh, 567 F.Supp. 369 (E.D.Pa.1983), *aff'd* 732 F.2d 146 (3d Cir.1984, *cert den.*, 469 U.S. 1189, 105 S.Ct. 955, 83 L.Ed.2d 962 (1985). Section 504 of the Rehabilitation Act made a full range of remedies available to plaintiffs, including **damages**, but the 11th Amendment to the U.S. Constitution precluded a damage award by federal courts against states.

Niehaus v. Kansas Bar Ass'n., 793 F.2d 1159 (10th Cir.1986). Because the Kansas Bar Association received no direct **federal funding**, the Rehabilitation Act was inapplicable in a discrimination suit filed against it.

Paralyzed Veterans of America v. U.S. Civil Aeronautics Bd., 804 F.2d 1306 (D.C.Cir.1986). In a case remanded by the U.S. Supreme Court, the U.S. Court of Appeals, District of Columbia Circuit, ruled that § 504 of the Rehabilitation Act applies only to recipients of **direct federal subsidies**.

Parks v. Pavkovic, 753 F.2d 1397 (7th Cir.1985), *cert den.*, 473 U.S. 906, 105 S.Ct. 3529, 87 L.Ed.2d 653 (1985). The Rehabilitation Act does not require states to provide special education programs, but prohibits them from denying benefits to otherwise qualified handicapped individuals in programs or activities receiving federal funds.

Pendleton v. Jefferson Local School Dist., Bd. of Educ, 754 F.Supp. 570 (S.D.Ohio 1989). Although a teacher with multiple sclerosis showed she was an **otherwise qualified handicapped person** under the Rehabilitation Act, the court granted the school district summary judgment where the teacher alleged that the school's principal harassed her, causing her condition to worsen.

Pesterfield v. Tennessee Valley Authority, 941 F.2d 437 (6th Cir.1991). A mentally disabled tool room attendant was a handicapped person under the Rehabilitation Act, but was not **otherwise qualified** because he became extremely anxious and depressed by normal job stress.

Pittsburgh Fed. of Teachers v. Langer, 546 F.Supp. 434 (W.D.Pa.1982). Section 504 creates a private right of action to enforce discrimination cases on the basis of disability, but plaintiffs must show the existence of discrimination by the **federal funding** recipient in order to recover.

Pushkin v. Regents of Univ. of Colorado, 658 F.2d 1372 (10th Cir.1981). A medical doctor with multiple sclerosis had been improperly denied entry into a university program because he was **otherwise qualified** under § 504. The proper **standard in § 504 cases** is whether the plaintiff is otherwise qualified, unlike non-Rehabilitation Act civil rights cases which require a showing of disparate impact.

Rhode Island Handicapped Action Committee v. Rhode Island Public Transit Authority, 718 F.2d 490, 494 (1st Cir.1983). The U.S. Court of Appeals, First Circuit, in finding § 504 "both ambiguous and lacking in specifics" suggested that the federal agency vested with authority to enforce the Rehabilitation Act has the primary responsibility to interpret the Act. See also *Southeastern Community College v. Davis,* 442 U.S. 397, 99 S.Ct. 2361, 60 L.Ed.2d 980 (1979).

Ross v. Beaumont Hosp., 687 F.Supp. 1115 (E.D.Mich.1988). The firing of a narcoleptic public employee could be justified by her history of verbally abusing patients, despite her assertion of handicap discrimination.

School Board of Nassau County v. Arline, 480 U.S. 273, 107 S.Ct. 1123, 94 L.Ed.2d 307 (1986). In *Arline,* a case involving a tubercular teacher in Florida, the Court helped define a standard for determining whether a person is **otherwise qualified** under § 504. The Court held: "A handicapped individual who cannot meet all of a program's requirements is not **otherwise qualified** if there is a factual basis in the record reasonably demonstrating that accommodating that individual would require either a modification of the essential nature of the program, or impose an undue burden." The Court's "individualized inquiry" employed a balancing of interests approach. The case is a landmark because it ruled that a person with a contagious disease (in this case, tuberculosis) could be entitled to the protections of § 504, if the person is otherwise qualified to receive benefits. The *Arline* case paved the way for court decisions in which persons with contagious diseases, including those testing HIV-positive, could be considered **handicapped individuals** under § 504. [On remand, the district court found the teacher otherwise qualified under § 504 and awarded her over $750,000 in front pay. *Arline v. School Bd.,* 692 F.Supp. 1286 (M.D.Fla.1988).]

Severino v. North Fort Myers Fire Control Dist., 935 F.2d 1179 (11th Cir.1991). A Florida firefighter who tested positive for HIV resigned but was reassigned to light duties not involving medical rescue work. The department terminated the firefighter's employment when he failed to return from a 90-day medical leave. The U.S. Court of Appeals, Eleventh Circuit, affirmed the district court's decision that the firefighter, although handicapped under the Rehabilitation Act, was not **otherwise qualified** to return to work as a firefighter.

Shinault v. American Airlines, Inc., 738 F.Supp. 193, 198 (S.D.Miss.1990), *aff'd in part, rev'd in part,* 936 F.2d 796 (5th Cir.1991). Under § 504, monetary **damages** are limited to cases in which the court makes a finding of intentional discrimination.

Simpson v. Reynolds Metals Co., 629 F.2d 1226 (7th Cir.1980). The U.S. Court of Appeals, Seventh Circuit, ruled that an alcoholic employee's case had been properly dismissed by the district court for lack of standing because he failed to show receipt of federal assistance by his employer, which contracted with the government.

Smith v. Barton, 914 F.2d 1330 (9th Cir.1990). Visually-impaired employees of an Idaho state agency were entitled to a jury trial in their Rehabilitation Act case, where they alleged that the agency's failure to promote them constituted constructive discharge and retaliation.

Smith v. Robinson, 468 U.S. 992, 104 S.Ct. 3457, 82 L.Ed.2d 746 (1984). This case led to passage by Congress of the Handicapped Children's Protection Act of 1986 (P.L. 99-372), an amendment to the IDEA which authorized courts to award attorney's fees to prevailing students and parents in IDEA lawsuits. It also legislatively overruled the *Smith* Court's ruling that the IDEA was an exclusive remedy for disabled students. Disabled students are expressly allowed to pursue and combine **available remedies under § 504**, the Civil Rights Act of 1964 and the IDEA.

Southeastern Community College v. Davis, 442 U.S. 397, 99 S.Ct. 2361, 60 L.Ed.2d 980 (1979). This was the first U.S. Supreme Court case which considered Rehabilitation Act § 504 and its implementing regulations. In *Davis*, the court determined that § 504 did not require a college to admit a hearing impaired nursing student where she could not safely perform duties as a registered nurse and the college argued that it would have to make major curricular modifications in order to **accommodate** her disability. The Court also ruled that § 504 did not require education institutions to disregard disabilities, and imposed no affirmative action obligation to accommodate applicant disabilities. Under *Davis,* a **substantial modification** or **fundamental alteration** to a program represented an impermissible attempt to impose an affirmative action obligation. This case is often cited for the proposition that an "**otherwise qualified handicapped individual**" is one who is qualified in spite of handicap, not qualified in all respects, but for the handicap.

Thomas v. Atascadero Unified School Dist., 655 F.Supp. 376 (C.D.Cal.1986). An HIV-positive student was an **otherwise qualified handicapped individual** under the Rehabilitation Act and was entitled to attend regular classes.

Traynor v. Turnage, 485 U.S. 535, 108 S.Ct. 1372, 99 L.Ed.2d 618 (1988). Two disabled veterans who were recovering **alcoholics** were denied an extension of the time to apply for Veterans' Administration (VA) educational assistance benefits under a VA regulation which stated that deliberate drinking of alcohol was considered "willful misconduct." The Supreme Court held that the Rehabilitation Act did not bar an action against the VA, but that the willful misconduct provision found in its regulations was permissible.

Tudyman v. United Airlines, 608 F.Supp. 739 (D.C.Cal.1989). A weightlifter did not qualify as a **handicapped individual** under § 504 despite being rejected for employment because he was over the **employer's weight restriction guidelines**. The weightlifter had no physical impairment and was not substantially limited in any major life activity.

U.S. Dept. of Transportation v. Paralyzed Veterans of America, 477 U.S. 597, 106 S.Ct. 2705, 91 L.Ed.2d 494 (1986). (on remand, see *Paralyzed Veterans of America v. U.S. Civil Aeronautics Bd.,* 804 F.2d 1306 (D.C.Cir.1986)). The U.S. Supreme Court refused to extend § 504 coverage to commercial airlines in a case brought by handicapped persons to enforce § 504 regulations of the Civil Aeronautics Board (14 CFR Part 382). The Rehabilitation Act did not apply to the airlines, despite their indirect **receipt of federal funds** via an airport development trust. Although the air traffic control system was owned and operated by the U.S. government it was not a recipient of federal financial assistance under § 504.

Univ. Interscholastic League v. Buchanan, 848 S.W.2d 298 (Tex.App.-Austin 1993). Learning disabled students who were 19 at the start of their senior years in high school due to disabilities were entitled (as **reasonable accommodation** under § 504) to special consideration by the state athletic association in the application of its rule prohibiting participation in varsity sports by students over 18 years old.

Univ. of Texas v. Camenisch, 451 U.S. 390, 101 S.Ct. 1830, 68 L.Ed.2d 175 (1981). A student with a hearing impairment requested the University of Texas to provide a **sign language interpreter**. The request was refused because the student did not meet university financial assistance guidelines. The student's § 504 lawsuit did not reach the U.S. Supreme Court until after the student had completed his graduate program. He completed his studies under a lower court order which required the university to pay for the interpreter. The U.S. Supreme Court found the case moot, but remanded it for a trial on the issue of which party should be responsible for paying the interpreter.

Wynne v. Tufts Univ. School of Medicine, 976 F.2d 791 (1st Cir.1992). A medical student's § 504 complaint failed because reasonable accommodation of his needs would have imposed an impermissible, **undue hardship** on the university by forcing it to lower its **academic standards**.

Statutory Text—Section 501 of the Rehabilitation Act of 1973 (29 U.S.C. § 791).

§ 791. Employment of individuals with disabilities.

(a) Interagency Committee on Employees who are Individuals with Disabilities; establishment; membership; co-chairmen; availability of other Committee resources; purpose and functions

There is established within the Federal Government an Interagency Committee on Employees who are Individuals with Disabilities (hereinafter in this section referred to as the "Committee"), comprised of such members as the President may select, including the following (or their designees whose positions are Executive Level IV or higher): the Chairman of the Equal Employment Opportunity Commission (hereafter in this section referred to as the "Commission"), the Director of the Office of Personnel Management, the Secretary of Veterans' Affairs, the Secretary of Labor, the Secretary of Education, and the Secretary of Health and Human Services. Either the Director of the Office of Personnel Management and the Chairman of the Commission shall serve as co-chairpersons of the Committee or the Director or Chairman shall serve as the sole chairperson of the Committee, as the Director and Chairman jointly determine, from time to time, to be appropriate. The resources of the President's Committees on Employment of People With Disabilities and on Mental Retardation shall be made fully available to the Committee. It shall be the purpose and function of the Committee (1) to provide a focus for Federal and other employment of individuals with disabilities, and to review, on a periodic basis, in cooperation with the Commission, the adequacy of hiring, placement, and advancement practices with respect to individuals with disabilities, by each department, agency, and instrumentality in the executive branch of Government, and to insure that the special needs of such individuals are being met; and (2) to consult with the Commission to assist the Commission to carry out its responsibilities under subsections (b), (c), and (d) of this section. On the basis of such review and consultation, the Committee shall periodically make to the Commission such recommendations for legislative and administrative changes as it deems necessary or desirable. The Commission shall timely transmit to the appropriate committees of Congress any such recommendations.

(b) Federal agencies; affirmative action program plans

Each department, agency, and instrumentality (including the United States Postal Service and the Postal Rate Commission) in the executive branch shall, within one hundred and eighty days after September 26, 1973, submit to the Commission and to the Committee an affirmative action program plan for the hiring, placement, and advancement of individuals with disabilities in such department, agency, or instrumentality. Such plan shall include a description of the extent to which and methods whereby the special needs of employees who are individuals with disabilities are being met. Such plan shall be updated annually, and shall be reviewed annually and approved by the Commission, if the Commission determines, after consultation with the Committee, that such plan provides sufficient assurances, procedures and commitments to provide adequate hiring, placement, and advancement opportunities for individuals with disabilities.

(c) State agencies; rehabilitated individuals, employment

The Commission, after consultation with the Committee, shall develop and recommend to the Secretary for referral to the appropriate State agencies, policies and procedures which will facilitate the hiring, placement, and advancement in employment of individuals who have received rehabilitation services under State vocational rehabilitation programs, veterans' programs, or any other program for individuals with disabilities, including the promotion of job opportunities for such individuals. The Secretary shall encourage such State agencies to adopt and implement such policies and procedures.

(d) Report to Congressional committees

The Commission, after consultation with the Committee, shall, on June 30, 1974, and at the end of each subsequent fiscal year, make a complete report to the appropriate committees of the Congress with respect to the practices of and achievements in hiring, placement, and advancement of individuals with disabilities by each department, agency, and instrumentality and the effectiveness of the affirmative action programs required by subsection (b) of this section, together with recommendations as to legislation which have been submitted to the Commission under subsection (a) of this section, or other appropriate action to insure the adequacy of such practices. Such report shall also include an evaluation by the Committee of the effectiveness of the activities of the Commission under subsections (b) and (c) of this section.

(e) Federal work experience without pay; non-Federal status

An individual who, as a part of an individualized written rehabilitation program under a State plan approved under this chapter, participates in a program of unpaid work experience in a Federal agency, shall not, by reason thereof, be considered to be a Federal employee or to be subject to the provisions of law relating to Federal employment, including those relating to hours of work, rates of compensation, leave, unemployment compensation, and Federal employee benefits.

(f) Federal agency cooperation; special consideration for positions on President's Committee on Employment of People With Disabilities

(1) The Secretary of Labor and the Secretary of Education are authorized and directed to cooperate with the President's Committee on Employment of People With Disabilities in carrying out its functions.

(2) In selecting personnel to fill all positions on the President's Committee on Employment of People With Disabilities, special consideration shall be given to qualified individuals with disabilities.

(g) Standards used in determining a violation of section

The standards used to determine whether this section has been violated in a complaint alleging nonaffirmative action employment discrimination under this section shall be the standards applied under title I of the Americans with Disabilities

Act of 1990 (42 U.S.C. 12111 et seq.) and the provisions of sections 501 through 504, and 510, of the Americans with Disabilities Act of 1990 (42 U.S.C. 12201-12204 and 12210), as such sections relate to employment.

(Pub. L. 93-112, title V, § 501, Sept. 26, 1973, 87 Stat. 390; Pub. L. 98-221, title I, § 104(b)(3), Feb. 22, 1984, 98 Stat. 18; Pub. L. 99-506, title I, § 103(d)(2)(C), title X, §§ 1001(f)(1), 1002(e)(1), (2)(A), Oct. 21, 1986, 100 Stat. 1810, 1843, 1844; Pub. L. 100-630, Title II, § 206(a), Nov. 7, 1988, 102 Stat. 3311; Pub. L. 102-54, § 13(k)(1)(B), June 13, 1991, 105 Stat. 276; Pub. L. 102-569, Title I, § 102(p)(29), Title V, § 503, Oct. 29, 1992, 106 Stat. 4360, 4424.)

Cases Interpreting § 501 of the
Rehabilitation Act of 1973

Adrain v. Alexander, 792 F.Supp. 124 (D.D.C.1992). The U.S. District Court for the District of Columbia ruled that a quadriplegic person who was unable to perform essential job duties because of his disabilities was not a **qualified handicapped individual** entitled to **reasonable accommodation** under the Rehabilitation Act.

Anderson v. Block, 807 F.2d 145 (8th Cir.1986). **Exhaustion of administrative remedies** case involving time limits for filing administrative action.

Arneson v. Sullivan, 946 F.2d 90 (8th Cir.1991). A social security administration employee claimed that he had apraxia, a condition which required him to work in an environment free from distractions. The U.S. Court of Appeals, Eighth Circuit, reversed a district court decision for the employer, determining that the employer had made no effort to accommodate the employee and that **reasonable accommodation** was feasible.

Black v. Frank, 730 F.Supp. 1087 (S.D.Ala.1990). Section 501 imposed no duty upon postal service to assign light duties to an employee who was disabled by bilateral carpal tunnel syndrome. Employment termination was permissible where the employee had been absent from work for over two years and he could no longer perform **essential job duties**.

Bowen v. American Hospital Ass'n, 476 U.S. 610, 106 S.Ct. 2101, 90 L.Ed.2d 584 (1986). The U.S. Supreme Court declared invalid Health and Human Services regulations under the Rehabilitation Act, 45 CFR Part 84.55. Designated as "procedures relating to health care for handicapped infants," the regulations went beyond the Act's legislative grant of authority, which is to fight **discrimination against the handicapped**. There had been no showing of discrimination by the complaining parties.

Butler v. Thornburgh, 900 F.2d 871 (5th Cir.1990), *cert. den.,* 498 U.S. 998, 111 S.Ct. 555, 112 L.Ed.2d 562 (1990). A former FBI agent who could not continue performing his job duties safely was not entitled to Rehabilitation Act protection, where there was evidence of on-the-job **alcohol abuse**.

Carter v. Bennett, 840 F.2d 63 (D.C.Cir.1988). Sufficiency of evidence case under § 501. The U.S. Court of Appeals for the District of Columbia affirmed a district court decision finding that a blind federal agency employee's **unsatisfactory work performance** and attitude permitted the agency to terminate his employment. The agency had provided reasonable accommodation by providing readers, but the employee's performance continued to be far below the office norm.

Davis v. Meese, 692 F.Supp. 505 (E.D.Pa.1988), *aff'd,* 865 F.2d 592 (1989). A federal district court upheld employment standards which included an entire class of disabling conditions, in this case diabetes, because they related directly to employment **safety and job performance concerns** and would require **"fundamental alteration"** of job descriptions.

Davis v. U.S. Postal Service, 675 F.Supp. 225 (M.D.Pa.1987). A postal service worker hired noncompetitively under a special program for severely handicapped persons was unlawfully paid only half the **wages** earned by nonhandicapped workers, but was not entitled to reassignment under the Rehabilitation Act.

DiPompo v. West Point Academy, 770 F.Supp. 887 (S.D.N.Y.1991). In a case involving the application of a dyslexic applicant to work as a firefighter for a military academy, a federal district court ruled that although § 501 imposes an affirmative duty upon federal agencies to ensure equal access to employment opportunities to disabled individuals, reasonable accommodation was not possible without changing essential job duties. In this case, the applicant's reading ability was only at the first grade level. While the **employee bears the burden of making a prima facie showing that accommodation is possible, the agency has the ultimate burden of showing its inability to accommodate the disabled person**, which it was able to do, because reading skills were required to perform essential job duties.

Doe v. Garrett, 903 F.2d 1455 (11th Cir.1990),*cert. den.*, 499 U.S. 904, 111 S.Ct. 1102, 113 L.Ed.2d 213 (1991). Aggrieved individuals wishing to file suit under the Rehabilitation Act must first exhaust their **administrative remedies** as set forth in Title VII of the Civil Rights Act of 1964.

Dopico v. Goldschmidt, 687 F.2d 644 (2d Cir.1982). In a case filed by wheelchair users against a local public transit provider, the court held that the Rehabilitation Act requires recipients of federal funds to make special efforts to deliver mass transit services to disabled persons.

Dowden v. Tisch, 729 F.Supp. 1137 (E.D.Tex.1989), *aff'd,* 902 F.2d 957 (1990). An employee must notify his supervisors of disabilities in order to receive the protections of the Rehabilitation Act. A postal service worker who did not identify the extent of his disabling conditions and never sought accommodation was not **otherwise qualified** under the act.

Florence v. Frank, 774 F.Supp. 1054 (N.D.Tex.1991). The court granted the postal service's summary judgment motion because of the employee's failure to show that he was a qualified handicapped person under § 501. Ability to walk the postal route was an **essential job function**.

Fong v. U.S. Dept. of Treasury, 705 F.Supp. 41 (D.D.C.1989). An alcoholic employee who failed to notify his federal agency employer of his **alcoholism** and lied about his alcohol induced absences was not entitled to Rehabilitation Act protection.

Gallagher v. Catto, 778 F.Supp. 570 (D.D.C.1991). A federal agency was required by § 501 (29 U.S.C. § 791) to **reasonably accommodate** an alcoholic employee by offering the employee a choice between counseling and disciplinary action. Courts must consider **undue hardship** imposed on employers which retain such employees.

Gardener v. Morris, 752 F.2d 1271 (8th Cir. 1985). A civilian employee of the Army Corps of Engineers failed to exhaust his **administrative remedies** and could not show that the Army had failed to reasonably accommodate him, where his health was adversely affected in Saudi Arabia.

Gilbert v. Frank, 949 F.2d 637 (2d Cir.1991). A postal service applicant was rejected for employment because he could not lift loads of up to 70 pounds as required. The U.S. Court of Appeals, Second Circuit, affirmed the district court's decision that the applicant was a handicapped person who was not **otherwise qualified** for the job. The lifting requirement was an essential function of the job and the elimination of the requirement would have been an undue hardship. Reasonable accommodation does not require elimination of essential job functions.

Guice-Mills v. Derwinski, 778 F.Supp. 188 (S.D.N.Y.1991), *aff'd,* 967 F.2d 794 (2d Cir.1992). The head nurse at a VA hospital suffered from depression and job-related stress. She alleged that her condition caused her to be consistently late for work. She refused reassignment by her employer and quit working. The U.S. District Court for the Southern District of New York determined that although the nurse might be considered a person with handicaps, she was not entitled to Rehabilitation Act relief because the administrative problems created by the nurse's lateness created an **undue hardship** for the hospital.

Guillot v. Garrett, 970 F.2d 1320 (4th Cir.1992). Federal agency (Navy) which denied security clearance to civilian computer specialist was not required by § 501 regulations to reassign the employee to accommodate him because he was not a **qualified handicapped individual** under the Rehabilitation Act.

Hall v. U.S. Postal Serv., 857 F.2d 1073 (6th Cir.1988). Courts must apply an individualized inquiry in Rehabilitation Act cases to determine whether disabled employees may be **reasonably accommodated**.

Harris v. Adams, 873 F.2d 929 (6th Cir.1989). The U.S. Court of Appeals, Second Circuit, affirmed the district court's decision that a postal service applicant was not a handicapped person who was **otherwise qualified** for the job, because he failed to show that his condition limited any of his **major life activities**.

Harrison v. Marsh, 691 F.Supp. 1233 (W.D.Mo.1988). The Rehabilitation Act [29 U.S.C. § 791] is the **exclusive remedy** for federal employees in employment discrimination cases.

James v. Frank, 772 F.Supp. 984 (S.D.Ohio 1991). An **otherwise qualified** person is one who can perform essential job functions. Federal district courts are required to perform an individualized analysis of whether reasonable accommodations by the employer enable a handicapped individual to perform **essential job functions**.

Lucero v. Hart, 915 F.2d 1367 (9th Cir.1990). Reasonable accommodation case involving typing test.

Mackay v. U.S. Post Office, 752 F.Supp. 213 (N.D.Tex.1990). **Exhaustion of administrative remedies** case involving time limits for filing administrative action.

Mantolete v. Bolger, 767 F.2d 1416 (9th Cir.1985). A federal appeals court remanded an epileptic job applicant's case to the district court for a determination of whether she was a qualified handicapped person under the Rehabilitation Act. On remand, the district court was advised to consider evidence of the cost of accommodations and to determine whether the applicant's employment presented a reasonable probability of **substantial harm** to herself or coworkers. Section 501 imposed a duty on federal employers to consider **reasonable accommodations**.

McElrath v. Kemp, 714 F.Supp. 23 (D.D.C.1989). **Exhaustion of administrative remedies** case involving time limits for filing and **burden of proof**. An alcoholic HUD employee was reinstated to her job by a federal district court order in lieu of her treatment in an aftercare program and satisfactory work performance.

Nisperos v. Buck, 720 F.Supp. 1424 (N.D.Cal.1989), *aff'd*, 936 F.2d 579 (1991). A federal agency employee who abused cocaine was a **handicapped individual** under the Rehabilitation Act.

Norcross v. Sneed, 573 F.Supp. 533 (W.D.Ark.1983), *aff'd*, 755 F.2d 113 (8th Cir.1983). A blind applicant for a school librarian position was otherwise qualified under the Rehabilitation Act where evidence indicated that many of the **"required" job duties** had never actually been performed by librarians and they could be changed to accommodate the applicant.

Prewitt v. US Postal Service, 662 F.2d 292 (5th Cir.1981). The district court erroneously granted the postal service summary judgment under § 501 of the Rehabilitation Act of 1973 (29 U.S.C. § 791) because the applicant presented evidence that he could be **reasonably accommodated** if the service simply lowered work shelves so that he could reach them.

Reynolds v. Brock, 815 F.2d 571 (9th Cir.1987). The district court improperly granted summary judgment against an epileptic Department of Labor employee who was handicapped under the Rehabilitation Act, where the evidence indicated that her condition did not impair her job performance. An **otherwise qualified handicapped individual** is able to meet all program requirements, in spite of the handicap.

Rose v. US Postal Service, 774 F.2d 1355 (9th Cir. 1984). The Ninth Circuit Court of Appeals reversed a district court grant of summary judgment to the postal service, in a case brought by disabled persons who claimed that the Rehabilitation Act and Architectural Barriers Act required the service to make all its buildings **accessible**.

Sedor v. Frank, 756 F.Supp. 684 (D.C.Conn.1991). The court refused to grant the postal service summary judgment in a Rehabilitation Act complaint filed by a learning disabled employee who was fired for a long, unexcused absence. A fact issue existed concerning the employee's ability to understand **attendance** rules.

Smith v. US Postal Service, 742 F.2d 257 (6th Cir.1984). A retired postal service employee's case was dismissed for failure to exhaust **administrative remedies**.

Strathie v. Department of Transportation, 716 F.2d 227 (3d Cir.1983). The U.S. Court of Appeals, Third Circuit, reversed a district court summary judgment award for the State of Pennsylvania, because the lower court had failed to consider whether **reasonable accommodations** would enable hearing impaired school bus drivers to work without presenting a safety risk.

Thorne v. Cavazos, 744 F.Supp. 348 (D.D.C.1990). Exhaustion of **administrative remedies** case.

Wilber v. Brady, 780 F.Supp. 837 (D.D.C.1990). An alcoholic employee fired by a federal agency for criminal misconduct resulting from a vehicular homicide and driving while intoxicated charge was lawfully discharged despite the employee's claim that his disability was **alcoholism**.

Part 1613 Regulations—Equal Employment
Opportunity in the Federal Government
(29 CFR Part 1613)

The following regulations have been published over the course of almost 30 years by the U.S. Equal Employment Opportunity Commission (EEOC) as the implementing regulations for the Civil Rights Act of 1964 (29 U.S.C. 2000e-16), § 501 of the Rehabilitation Act of 1973 (29 U.S.C. § 791) and other civil rights legislation. Although government agencies are required to reasonably accommodate qualified handicapped persons under 29 CFR Part 1613.704(a), the complaining party must show an ability to perform essential job duties to gain relief under the Rehabilitation Act.

Section 501 of the Rehabilitation Act is enforced by the EEOC, which has published regulations at 29 CFR Part 1613.701 *et seq*. Under the Act, the Federal government is mandated to become a model employer of handicapped individuals (29 CFR Part 1613.703). EEOC definitions at 29 CFR Part 1613.702 are frequently cited by the courts and are also the model language for the employment sections of the ADA. In particular, see the definition of "qualified handicapped person" found at 29 CFR Part 1613.702(f).

* * *

Subpart A—[Reserved]

Subpart B—Equal Opportunity Without Regard to Race, Color, Religion, Sex, or National Origin

GENERAL PROVISIONS

AGENCY REGULATIONS FOR PROCESSING COMPLAINTS OF DISCRIMINATION

APPEAL TO THE COMMISSION

REPORTS TO THE COMMISSION

CONSOLIDATION OF COMPLAINTS

FREEDOM FROM REPRISAL OR INTERFERENCE

REMEDIAL ACTIONS

RIGHT TO FILE A CIVIL ACTION

Subpart C—Minority Group Statistics System

Subpart D—Processing Mixed Case Complaints

Subpart E—Nondiscrimination on Account of Age

GENERAL PROVISIONS

AGENCY REGULATIONS FOR PROCESSING COMPLAINTS OF
DISCRIMINATION

Subpart F—Class Complaints of Discrimination

AGENCY REGULATIONS FOR PROCESSING CLASS COMPLAINTS OF
DISCRIMINATION

APPEAL TO THE COMMISSION

CIVIL ACTIONS

Subpart G—Prohibition Against Discrimination Because of a Physical or Mental Handicap

GENERAL PROVISIONS

AGENCY REGULATIONS FOR PROCESSING COMPLAINTS OF DISCRIMINATION

Subpart H—Regulations for Processing Appealable Actions, Alleging Prohibited Discrimination, Pending on or Before January 10, 1979

APPENDIX A TO PART 1613—POLICY STATEMENT ON REMEDIES AND RELIEF FOR INDIVIDUAL CASES OF UNLAWFUL DISCRIMINATION

AUTHORITY: 42 U.S.C. 2000e-16; 29 U.S.C. 633a; 29 U.S.C. 791 and 794a; 29 U.S.C. 206(d); E.O. 10577, 3 CFR 218 (1954-1958 Comp.); E.O. 11222, 3 CFR 306 (1964-1965 Comp.); E.O. 11478, 3 CFR 133 (1969 Comp.); E.O. 12106, 44 FR 1053 (1978); Reorg. Plan No. 1 of 1978, 43 FR 19807 (1978), unless otherwise noted.

Subpart A—[Reserved]

Subpart B—Equal Opportunity Without Regard to Race, Color, Religion, Sex, or National Origin

SOURCE: 37 FR 22717, Oct. 21, 1972, unless otherwise noted. Redesignated at 43 FR 60901, Dec. 29, 1978.

GENERAL PROVISIONS

§ 1613.201 Purpose and applicability.

(a) *Purpose.* This subpart sets forth the regulations under which an agency shall establish a continuing affirmative program for equal opportunity in employment and personnel operations without regard to race, color, religion, sex, or national origin and under which the Commission will review an agency's program and entertain an appeal from a person dissatisfied with an agency's decision or other final action on his complaint of discrimination on grounds of race, color, religion, sex, or national origin.

(b) *Applicability.* (1) This subpart applies: (i) To military department[s] as defined in section 102 of title 5, United States Code, executive agencies (other than the General Accounting Office) as defined in section 105 of title 5, United States Code, the U.S. Postal Service, and the Postal Rate Commission, and to the employees thereof, including employees paid from nonappropriated funds, and (ii) to those portions of the legislative and judicial branches of the Federal Government and the government of the District of Columbia having positions in the competitive service and to the employees in those positions.

(2) This subpart does not apply to aliens employed outside the limits of the United States.

§ 1613.202 General policy.

It is the policy of the Government of the United States and of the government of the District of Columbia to provide equal opportunity in employment for all persons, to prohibit discrimination in employment because of race, color, religion, sex, or national origin, and to promote the full realization of equal employment opportunity through a continuing affirmative program in each agency.

§ 1613.203 Agency program.

The head of each agency shall exercise personal leadership in establishing, maintaining, and carrying out a continuing affirmative program designed to promote equal opportunity in every aspect of agency personnel policy and practice in the employment, development, advancement, and treatment of employees. Under the terms of its program, an agency shall:

(a) Provide sufficient resources to administer its equal employment opportunity program in a positive and effective manner and assure that the Principal and operating officials responsible for carrying out the equal employment opportunity program meet established qualifications requirements;

(b) Conduct a continuing campaign to eradicate every form of prejudice or discrimination based upon race, color, religion, sex, or national origin, from the agency's personnel policies and practices and working conditions, including disciplinary action against employees who engage in discriminatory practices;

(c) Utilize to the fullest extent the present skills of employees by all means, including the redesigning of jobs where feasible so that tasks not requiring the full utilization of skills of incumbents are concentrated in jobs with lower skill requirements;

(d) Provide the maximum feasible opportunity to employees to enhance their skills through on-the-job training, work-study programs, and other training measures so that they may perform at their highest potential and advance in accordance with their abilities;

(e) Communicate the agency's equal employment opportunity policy and program and its employment needs to all sources of job candidates without regard to race, color, religion, sex, or national origin, and solicit their recruitment assistance on a continuing basis;

(f) Participate at the community level with other employers, with schools and universities, and with other public and private groups in cooperative action to improve employment opportunities and community conditions that affect employability;

(g) Review, evaluate, and control managerial and supervisory performance in such a manner as to insure a continuing affirmative application and vigorous enforcement of the policy of equal opportunity, and provide orientation, training, and advice to managers and supervisors to assure their understanding and implementation of the equal employment opportunity policy and program;

(h) Provide recognition to employees, supervisors, managers, and units demonstrating superior accomplishment in equal employment opportunity;

(i) Inform its employees and recognized labor organizations of the affirmative equal employment opportunity policy and program and enlist their cooperation;

(j) Provide for counseling employees and applicants who believe they have been discriminated against because of race, color, religion, sex, or national origin and for resolving informally the matters raised by them;

(k) Provide for the prompt, fair, and impartial consideration and disposition of complaints involving issues of discrimination on grounds of race, color, religion, sex, or national origin; and

(l) Establish a system for periodically evaluating the effectiveness of the agency's overall equal employment opportunity effort.

§ 1613.204 Implementation of agency program.

To implement the program established under this subpart, an agency shall:

(a) Develop the plans, procedures, and regulations necessary to carry out its program established under this subpart;

(b) Appraise its personnel operations at regular intervals to assure their conformity with the policy in § 1613.202 and its program established in accordance with § 1613.203;

(c) Designate a Director of Equal Employment Opportunity and as many Equal Employment Opportunity Officers, Equal Employment Opportunity Counselors, Federal Women's Program Coordinators, and other persons as may be necessary, to assist the head of the agency to carry out the functions described in this subpart in all organizational units and locations of the agency. The functioning and the qualifications of the persons so designated shall be subject to review by the Commission. The Director of Equal Employment Opportunity shall be under the immediate supervision of the head of his agency, and shall be given the authority necessary to enable him to carry out his responsibilities under the regulations in this subpart;

(d) Assign to the Director of Equal Employment Opportunity the functions of:

(1) Advising the head of his agency with respect to the preparation of national and regional equal employment opportunity plans, procedures, regulations, reports, and other matters pertaining to the policy in § 1613.202 and the agency program required to be established under § 1613.203;

(2) Evaluating from time to time the sufficiency of the total agency program for equal employment opportunity and reporting thereon to the head of the agency with recommendations as to any improvement or correction needed, including remedial or disciplinary action with respect to managerial or supervisory employees who have failed in their responsibilities;

(3) When authorized by the head of the agency, making changes in programs and procedures designed to eliminate discriminatory practices and improve the agency's program for equal employment opportunity;

(4) Providing for counseling by an Equal Employment Opportunity Counselor, of any aggrieved employee or applicant for employment who believes that he has been discriminated against because of race, color, religion, sex, or national origin and for attempting to resolve on an informal basis the matter raised by the employee or applicant before a complaint of discrimination may be filed under § 1613.214;

(5) Providing for the receipt and investigation of individual complaints of discrimination in personnel matters within the agency, subject to §§ 1613.211 through 1613.222;

(6) Providing for the acceptance and processing and/or rejection of class complaints in accordance with subpart F of this part;

(7) When authorized by the head of the agency, making the decision under § 1613.221 for the head of the agency on complaints of discrimination and ordering such corrective measures as he may consider necessary, including the recommendation for such disciplinary action as is warranted by the circumstances when an employee has been found to have engaged in a discriminatory practice; and

(8) When not authorized to make the decision for the head of the agency on complaints of discrimination, reviewing, at his discretion, the record on any complaint before the decision is made under § 1613.221 and making such recommendations to the head of the agency or his designee as he considers desirable, including the recommendation for such disciplinary action as is warranted by the circumstances when an employee is found to have engaged in a discriminatory practice;

(e) Insure that equal opportunity for women is an integral part of the agency's overall program by assigning to the Federal Women's Program Coordinators the function of advising the Director of Equal Employment Opportunity on matters affecting the employment and advancement of women;

(f) Publicize to its employees and post permanently on official bulletin boards:

(1) The names and addresses of the Director of Equal Employment Opportunity and the Federal Women's Program Coordinators;

(2) The name and address of the appropriate Equal Employment Opportunity Officer;

(3) The name and address of the Equal Employment Opportunity Counselor and the organizational units he serves; his availability to counsel an employee or applicant for employment who believes that he has been discriminated against because of race, color, religion, sex, or national origin; and the requirement that an employee or applicant for employment must consult the Counselor as provided by § 1613.213 about his allegation of discrimination because of race, color, religion, sex, or national origin before a complaint as provided by § 1613.214 may be filed; and

(4) Time limits for contacting an Equal Employment Opportunity Counselor;

(g) Make reasonable accommodations to the religious needs of applicants and employees, including the needs of those who observe the Sabbath on other than Sunday, when those accommodations can be made (by substitution of another qualified employee, by a grant of leave, a change of a tour of duty, or other means) without undue hardship on the business of the agency. If an agency cannot accommodate an employee or applicant, it has a duty in a complaint arising under this subpart to demonstrate its inability to do so;

(h) Make readily available to its employees a copy of its regulations issued to carry out its program of equal employment opportunity; and

(i) Submit annually for the review and approval of the Commission written national and regional equal employment opportunity plans of action. Plans shall be submitted in a format prescribed by the Commission and shall include, but not be limited to:

(1) Provision for the establishment of training and education programs designed to provide maximum opportunity for employees to advance so as to perform at their highest potential;

(2) Description of the qualifications, in terms of training and experience relating to equal employment opportunity, of the principal and operating officials concerned with administration of the agency's equal employment opportunity program; and

(3) Description of the allocation of personnel and resources proposed by the agency to carry out its equal employment opportunity program.

[37 FR 22717, Oct. 21, 1972, as amended at 37 FR 25699, Dec. 2, 1972; 42 FR 11808, Mar. 1, 1977. Redesignated at 43 FR 60901, Dec. 29, 1978]

§ 1613.205 Commission review and evaluation of agency program operations.

The Commission shall review and evaluate agency program operations periodically, obtain such reports as it deems necessary, and report to the President as appropriate on overall progress. When it finds that an agency's program operations are not in conformity with the policy set forth in § 1613.202 and the regulations in this subpart, the Commission shall require improvement or corrective action to bring the agency's program operations into conformity with this policy and the regulations in this subpart. The head of each department and agency shall comply with the rules, regulations, orders, and instructions issued by the Commission.

AGENCY REGULATIONS FOR PROCESSING
COMPLAINTS OF DISCRIMINATION

§ 1613.211 General.

An agency shall insure that its regulations governing the processing of complaints of discrimination on grounds of race, color, religion, sex, national origin, age or handicapping condition comply with the principles and requirements in § § 1613.212 through 1613.222, except where excluded in § 1613.514.

[52 FR 41922, Oct. 30, 1987]

§ 1613.212 Coverage.

(a) The agency shall provide in its regulations for the acceptance of a complaint from any aggrieved employee or applicant for employment who believes that he or she has been discriminated against by that agency because of race, color, religion, sex, national origin, age or handicapping condition. A complaint may also be filed by an organization for the aggrieved person with that person's consent.

(b) The agency shall provide in its regulations for the acceptance of class complaints in accordance with Subpart F.

[37 FR 22717, Oct. 21, 1972, as amended at 42 FR 11808, Mar. 14, 1977. Redesignated at 43 FR 60901, Dec. 29, 1978, and amended at 52 FR 41922, Oct. 30, 1987]

§ 1613.213 Precomplaint processing.

(a) The agency shall require that an aggrieved person who believes that he or she was discriminated against because of race, color, religion, sex, national origin, age or handicapping condition consult with an Equal Employment Opportunity Counselor to try to resolve the matter. The agency shall require the Equal Employment Opportunity Counselor to make whatever inquiry he or she believes necessary into the matter; to seek a solution of the matter on an informal basis; to counsel the aggrieved person concerning the issues in the matter; to keep a record of the counseling activities so as to brief, periodically, the Equal Employment Opportunity Officer on those activities; and, when advised that a complaint of discrimination has been accepted from an aggrieved person, to submit a written report to the Equal Employment Opportunity Officer, with a copy to the aggrieved person, summarizing the counselor's actions and advice both to the agency and the aggrieved person concerning the issues in the matter. The Equal Employment Opportunity Counselor shall, insofar as is practicable, conduct the final interview with the aggrieved person not later than 21 calendar days after the date on which the matter was called to the counselor's attention by the aggrieved person. If, within 21 days, the matter has not been resolved to the satisfaction of the aggrieved person, that person shall be immediately informed in writing, at the time of the final interview, of his or her right to file a complaint of discrimination. The notice shall inform the complainant of his or her right to file a discrimination complaint at any time up to 15 calendar days after receipt of the notice of the appropriate official with whom to file a complaint and of complainant's duty to assure that the agency is immediately informed if the complainant retains counsel, or any other representative. The Counselor shall not attempt in any way to restrain the aggrieved person from filing a complaint. The Equal Employment Opportunity Counselor shall not reveal the identity of an aggrieved person who consulted the counselor, except when authorized to do so by the aggrieved person, until the agency has accepted a complaint of discrimination from that person.

(b) Upon initial contact or as soon thereafter as possible, the Equal Employment Opportunity Counselor shall inform each aggrieved person of the possible applicability of 5 U.S.C. 7121(d) to the alleged discriminatory action. The Equal Employment Opportunity Counselor shall communicate the substance of § 1613.219 concerning the election of remedies to each aggrieved person.

(c) The agency shall assure that full cooperation is provided by all employees to the Equal Employment Opportunity Counselor in the performance of his duties under this section.

(d) The Equal Employment Opportunity Counselor shall be free from restraint, interference, coercion, discrimination, or reprisal in connection with the performance of his duties under this section.

[37 FR 22717, Oct. 21, 1972, as amended at 37 FR 25699, Dec. 2, 1972. Redesignated at 43 FR 60901, Dec. 29, 1978, and amended at 45 FR 24131, Apr. 9, 1980; 52 FR 41922, Oct. 30, 1987]

§ 1613.214 Filing and processing of complaint.

(a) *Time limits.* (1) An agency shall require that a complaint be submitted in writing by the complainant or representative and be signed by the complainant. The complaint may be delivered in person or submitted by mail. The agency may accept the complaint for processing in accordance with this subpart only if:

(i) The complainant brought to the attention of the Equal Employment Opportunity Counselor the matter causing him/her to believe he/she had been discriminated against within 30 calendar days of the date of the alleged discriminatory event, the effective date of an alleged discriminatory personnel action, or the date that the aggrieved person knew or reasonably should have known of the discriminatory event or personnel action; and

(ii) The complainant or representative submitted the written complaint to an appropriate official within 15 calendar days after the date of receipt of the notice of the right to file a complaint.

(2) The appropriate officials to receive complaints are the head of the agency, the agency's Director of Equal Employment Opportunity, the head of a field installation, and such other officials as the agency may designate for that purpose. Upon receipt of the complaint, the agency official shall transmit it to the Director of Equal Employment Opportunity or appropriate Equal Employment Opportunity Officer who shall acknowledge its receipt in accordance with paragraph (a)(3) of this section.

(3) A complaint shall be deemed filed on the date it is received, if delivered to an appropriate official, or on the date postmarked if addressed to an appropriate official designated to receive complaints. The agency shall acknowledge, in writing, to the complainant or representative receipt of the complaint and advise the complainant in writing of all administrative rights and of the right to file a civil action as set forth in § 1613.281, including the time limits imposed on the exercise of these rights.

(4) The agency shall extend the time limits in this section when the complainant shows that he/she was not notified of the time limits and was not otherwise aware of them, was prevented by circumstances beyond the complainant's control from submitting the matter within the time limits; or for other reasons considered sufficient by the agency.

(b) *Representation and official time.*

(1) At the stage in the processing of a complaint, including the counseling stage under § 1613.213, the complainant shall have the right to be accompanied, represented, and advised by a representative of [the] complainant's choice.

(2) If the complainant is an employee of the agency, he/she shall have a reasonable amount of official time to prepare the complaint if otherwise on duty. If the complainant is an employee of the agency and he designates another employee of the agency as his/her representative, the representative shall have a reasonable amount of official time, if otherwise on duty, to prepare the complaint. The agency is not obligated to change work schedules, incur overtime wages, or pay travel expenses to facilitate the choice of a specific representative or to allow the complainant and representative to confer. However, the complainant and representative, if employed by the agency and otherwise in a pay status, shall be on official time, regardless of their tour of duty, when their presence is authorized or required by the agency or the Commission during the investigation, informal adjustment, or hearing on the complaint.

(3) In cases where the representation of a complainant or agency would conflict with the official or collateral duties of the representative, the Commission (or the agency prior to a hearing on the complaint) may, after giving the representative an opportunity to respond, disqualify the representative.

[52 FR 41922, Oct. 30, 1987]

§ 1613.215 Rejection or cancellation of complaint.

(a) The agency head or designee shall reject or cancel a complaint:

(1) That fails to state a claim under 1613.212 or that states the same claim that is pending before or has been decided previously by the agency;

(2) That alleges that an agency is proposing to take action that may be discriminatory;

(3) That is the basis of a pending civil action in a United States District Court in which the complainant is a party:

(4) That is filed untimely, unless the agency extended the time limits in accordance with § 1613.214(a)(4);

(5) That the complainant elected to pursue under a negotiated grievance procedure as identified in § 1613.219;

(6) That the complainant has failed to prosecute. The agency may cancel an allegation or a complaint for failure to prosecute only after it has provided the complainant with a written request, that includes a notice of the proposed cancellation, to provide certain information or otherwise proceed with the complaint, and the complainant has failed to satisfy the request within 15 calendar days of its receipt. However, instead of canceling for failure to prosecute, the complaint may be adjudicated if sufficient information for that purpose is available; or

(7) If the complainant refuses within 15 calendar days of receipt of an offer of settlement to accept an agency offer of full relief in adjustment of the complaint, provided that the agency's Director of Equal Employment Opportunity, or a designee reporting directly to the Director, has certified in writing that the agency's written offer of relief constitutes full relief. An offer of full relief under this subsection is the appropriate relief in § 1613.271. The offer need not contain the decision whether disciplinary action is necessary, but the basis for the decision shall be recorded separately from the complaint file.

(b) The agency head or designee shall transmit the decision to reject or cancel a complaint by letter to the complainant and the complainant's representative. The decision letter shall inform the complainant of the right to appeal the decision to the Commission, the time limit for filing an appeal with the Commission, and the complainant's right to file a civil action as described in § 1613.281.

[52 FR 41923, Oct. 30, 1987]

§ 1613.216 Investigation.

(a) The Equal Employment Opportunity Officer shall advise the Director of Equal Employment Opportunity of the acceptance of a complaint. The Director of Equal Employment Opportunity shall provide for the prompt investigation of the complaint. The person assigned to investigate the complaint shall not occupy a position in the agency that is directly or indirectly under the jurisdiction of the head of that part of the agency in which the complaint arose. The agency shall authorize the investigator to administer oaths and require that statements of witnesses shall be under oath or affirmation, without a pledge of confidence. The investigation shall include a thorough review of the circumstances under which the alleged discrimination occurred, the treatment of members of the complainant's group identified by his complaint as compared with the treatment of other employees in the organizational segment in which the alleged discrimination occurred, and any policies and practices related to the work situation which may constitute, or appear to constitute, discrimination even though they have not been expressly cited by the complainant. Information needed for an appraisal of the utilization of members of the complainant's group as compared to the utilization of persons outside the complainant's group shall be recorded in statistical form in the investigative file, but specific information as to a person's membership or nonmembership in the complainant's group needed to facilitate an adjustment of the complaint or to make an informed decision on the complaint shall, if available, be recorded by name in the investigative file. (As used in this subpart, the term "investigative file" shall mean the various documents and information acquired during the investigation under this section—including affidavits of the complainant and witnesses, and copies of, or extracts from records, policy statements, or regulations of the agency—organized to show their relevance to the complaint or the general environment out of which the complaint arose.) If necessary, the investigator may obtain information regarding the membership or nonmembership of a person in the complainant's group by asking each person concerned to provide the information voluntarily; he shall not require or coerce an employee to provide this information.

(b) The Director of Equal Employment Opportunity shall arrange to furnish to the person conducting the investigation a written authorization:

(1) To investigate all aspects of complaints of discrimination,

(2) To require all employees of the agency to cooperate with him in the conduct of the investigation, and

(3) To require employees of the agency having any knowledge of the matter complained of to furnish testimony under oath or affirmation without a pledge of confidence.

(c) The Commission may assume responsibility for the investigation of any portion or all of an agency's complaints upon the execution of a memorandum of understanding to this effect with the agency. The agency shall reimburse the Commission for all expenses incurred in connection with the investigation. The Commission shall forward to the agency upon completion of the investigation the investigative file and the recommended proposed disposition. The agency shall adopt as its proposed disposition of the complaint the Commission's recommended disposition unless within 30 days after the agency receives the investigative file and recommended disposition the complaint has been informally adjusted in accordance with § 1613.217(a), or the agency has notified the complainant of its own proposed disposition in accordance with § 1613.217(c).

[52 FR 41923, Oct. 30, 1987]

§ 1613.217 Adjustment of complaint and offer of hearing.

(a) The agency shall provide an opportunity for adjustment of the complaint on an informal basis after the complainant has reviewed the investigative file. For this purpose, the agency shall furnish the complainant, or the complainant's representative if there is one, a copy of the investigative file promptly after receiving [it] from the investigator, and provide opportunity for the complainant to discuss the investigative file with appropriate officials. If an adjustment of the complaint is arrived at, the terms of the adjustment shall be reduced to writing and made part of the complaint file, with a copy of the terms of the adjustment provided the complainant. An informal adjustment of a complaint may include an award of back pay, attorney's fees or other appropriate relief. Where the parties agree on an adjustment of the complaint, but cannot agree on whether attorney's fees or costs should be awarded or on the amount of attorney's fees or costs, the issue of the award of attorney's fees or costs or the amount which should be awarded may be severed and shall be the subject of a final decision under § 1613.221(d). The decision of whether to award attorney's fees or costs or of the amount to be awarded may be the subject of an appeal to the Commission under the provisions of §§ 1613.231 through 1613.240.

(b) Any settlement agreement knowingly and voluntarily agreed to by the parties, reached at any stage of the complaint process, shall be binding on both parties. If the complainant believes that the agency has failed to comply with the terms of a settlement agreement, the complainant shall notify the Director of Equal Employment Opportunity, in writing, of the alleged noncompliance with the settlement agreement, within 30 days of when the complainant knew or should have known of the alleged noncompliance. The complainant may request that the terms of the settlement agreement be specifically implemented or, alternatively, that the complaint be reinstated for further processing from the point processing ceased under the terms of the settlement agreement. Upon receipt of the complainant's written allegation of noncompliance with the settlement agreement, the agency shall have thirty (30) calendar days in which to resolve the matter and to respond to the complainant, in writing, concerning the matter. If, after thirty (30) calendar days from the date of the agency's receipt of the complainant's written allegations of noncompliance with the settlement agreement, the agency has not responded to the complainant, in writing, or if the complainant is not satisfied with the agency's attempt to resolve the matter, the complainant may appeal to the Commission for a determination as to whether the agency has complied with the terms of the settlement agreement. The complainant may file such an appeal 35 days after service of the allegations of noncompliance, but must file an appeal within 20 days of receipt of an agency's determination. Prior to rendering its determination, the Commission may request that the parties submit whatever additional information or documentation it may deem necessary or it may direct that an investigation or hearing on the matter be conducted, as may be appropriate. If the Commission determines that agreement has not been complied with and the noncompliance is not attributable to acts or conduct of the complainant, it may order such compliance or it may order that the complaint be reinstated for further processing from the point processing ceased under the terms of the settlement agreement. Complaints that alleged reprisal or further discrimination violate a settlement agreement shall be processed as individual complaints under § 1613.214 rather than under this section.

(c) If an adjustment of the complaint is not arrived at, the complainant shall be notified in writing:

(1) Of the proposed disposition of the complaint,

(2) Of the right to a hearing, unless a recommended decision is issued under § 1613.218(g), and decision by the agency head or designee if he/she notifies the agency in writing within 15 calendar days of the receipt of the notice that he/she desires a hearing, and

(3) Of the right to a decision by the head of the agency or designee without a hearing.

(d) If the complainant fails to notify the agency of his/her wishes within the 15-day period prescribed in paragraph (c) of this section, the appropriate Equal Employment Opportunity Officer may adopt the disposition of the complaint proposed in the notice sent to the complainant under paragraph (c) of this section as the decision of the agency on the complaint when delegated the authority to make a decision for the head of the agency under those circumstances. When this is done, the Equal Employment Opportunity Officer shall transmit the decision by letter to the complainant and the representative which shall inform the complainant of the right of appeal to the Commission and the time limit applicable to such an appeal and of the right to file a civil action as described in § 1613.281. If the Equal Employment Opportunity Officer does not issue a decision under this paragraph, the complaint, together with the complaint file, shall be forwarded to the head of the agency or designee for decision under § 1613.221.

[52 FR 41924, Oct. 30, 1987]

§ 1613.218 Hearing.

(a) *Administrative Judge.* The hearing shall be conducted by a Commission Administrative Judge with an appropriate security clearance, except in instances where the Commission finds it is practical to delegate this responsibility to a complaints examiner or Administrative Judge from another agency who shall not be an employee of the agency in which the complaint arose. (For purposes of this paragraph, the Department of Defense is considered to be a single agency.) When the Commission does not provide the Administrative Judge, it will supply the agency with the name of an Administrative Judge from another agency with an appropriate security clearance who has been certified by the Commission as qualified to conduct a hearing under this section.

(b) *Arrangement for hearing.* The agency in which the complaint arose shall transmit the complaint file containing all the documents described in § 1613.222 which have been acquired up to that point in the processing of the complaint, including the original copy of the investigative file (which shall be considered by the Administrative Judge in making a recommended decision on the complaint), to the Administrative Judge who shall review the complaint file to determine whether further investigation is needed before scheduling the hearing. When the Administrative Judge determines that further investigation is needed, the Administrative Judge shall remand the complaint to the Director of Equal Employment Opportunity for further investigation or arrange for the appearance of witnesses necessary to supply the needed information at the hearing. The requirements of § 1613.216 apply to any further investigation by the agency on the complaint. The Administrative Judge shall schedule the hearing for a convenient time and place.

(c) *Conduct of hearing.* (1) Attendance at the hearing is limited to persons determined by the Administrative Judge to have a direct connection with the complaint. Hearings are part of the investigative process and are thus closed to the public.

(2) The Administrative Judge shall conduct the hearing so as to bring out pertinent facts, including the production of pertinent documents. Rules of evidence shall not be applied strictly, but the Administrative Judge shall exclude irrelevant or unduly repetitious evidence. Information having a bearing on the complaint or employment policies or practices relevant to the complaint shall be received in evidence. The complainant and the agency, or the representative of either shall be given the opportunity at the hearing to cross-examine witnesses who appear and testify. Testimony shall be under oath or affirmation.

(d) *Powers of Administrative Judge.* In addition to the other powers vested in the Administrative Judge in accordance with this subpart, the Administrative Judge is authorized to:

(1) Administer oaths or affirmations;

(2) Regulate the course of the hearing;

(3) Rule on offers of proof and receive relevant evidence;

(4) Order the production of documents, records, comparative data, statistics, affidavits or the attendance of witnesses;

(5) Limit the number of witnesses whose testimony would be unduly repetitious; and

(6) Exclude any person from the hearing for contumacious conduct or misbehavior that obstructs the hearing. In cases of repeated or flagrant contumacious conduct or misbehavior by a representative, the Administrative Judge may refer the matter to the Commission, and the Commission may, after giving the representative an

opportunity to respond to the allegations of misconduct, suspend or disqualify the representative from further representational activity and report the misconduct to other appropriate authorities.

(e) If the complainant or agency in bad faith refuses or fails without adequate explanation to respond fully and in timely fashion to requests made or approved by the Administrative Judge for documents, records, comparative data, statistics, affidavits, or the attendance of witnesses, and the information is solely in the control of one party, such failure may, in appropriate circumstances, cause the Administrative Judge:

(1) To draw an adverse inference that the requested information would have reflected unfavorably on the party refusing to provide the requested information;

(2) To consider the matters to which the requested information pertains to be established in favor of the opposing party;

(3) To exclude other evidence offered by the party failing to produce the requested information;

(4) To take such other actions as deemed appropriate.

(f) *Witnesses at hearing.* The Administrative Judge shall request any agency subject to this subpart to make available as a witness at the hearing an employee requested by the complainant when the Administrative Judge determines that the appearance of an employee is necessary. The Administrative Judge may also request the appearance of an employee of any federal agency whose testimony he determines is necessary to furnish information pertinent to the complaint under consideration. The Administrative Judge shall give the complainant his reasons for the denial of a request for the appearance of employees as witnesses and shall insert those reasons in the record of the hearing. An agency to whom a request is made shall make its employees available as witnesses at a hearing on a complaint when requested to do so by the Administrative Judge and it is not administratively impracticable to comply with the request. When it is administratively impracticable to comply with the request for a witness, the agency to whom request is made shall provide an explanation to the Administrative Judge. If the explanation is inadequate, the Administrative Judge shall so advise the agency and it shall make the employee available as a witness at the hearing. If the explanation is adequate, the Administrative Judge shall insert it in the record of the hearing, provide a copy to the complainant, and make arrangements to secure testimony from the employee at another time or through written interrogatory. An employee of an agency shall be in a duty status during the time he/she is made available as a witness.

(g) If the Administrative Judge determines that there are no issues of material fact, the Administrative Judge may, after giving notice to the parties and providing them an opportunity to respond in writing within 15 calendar days, issue a recommended decision without holding a hearing. The recommended decision will conform to § 1613.218(i) in all other aspects.

(h) *Record of hearing.* The hearing shall be recorded and transcribed verbatim. All documents submitted to, and accepted by, the Administrative Judge at the hearing shall be made part of the record of the hearing. If the agency submits a document that is accepted, it shall furnish a copy of the document to the complainant. If the complainant submits a document that is accepted, the Administrative Judge shall make the document available to the agency representative for reproduction.

(i) Findings, analysis, and recommendations. The Administrative Judge shall transmit to the head of the agency or designee:

(1) The complaint file (including the record of the hearing),

(2) The findings and analysis of the Administrative Judge with regard to the matter which gave rise to the complaint and the general environment out of which the complaint arose, and

(3) The recommended decision of the Administrative Judge on the merits of the complaint, including recommended remedial action, where appropriate, with regard to the matter which gave rise to the complaint and the general environment out of which the complaint arose.

The Administrative Judge shall notify the complainant of the date on which this was done. In addition, the Administrative Judge shall transmit, by separate letter to the Director of Equal Employment Opportunity, whatever findings and recommendations he considers appropriate with respect to conditions in the agency which do not bear directly on the matter which gave rise to the complaint or which bear on the general environment out of which the complaint arose.

[52 FR 41925, Oct. 30, 1987]

§ 1613.219 Relationship to grievance procedures.

(a) Allegations of discrimination on grounds of race, color, religion, sex, national origin, age or handicapping condition may be raised under a grievance procedure by employees in agencies that are subject to the provisions of 5 U.S.C. 7121(d) and who are covered by a collective bargaining agreement that provides for allegations of discrimination to be raised in the negotiated grievance procedure. Allegations of discrimination by employees not covered by such a negotiated grievance procedure or by employees of agencies not subject to 5 U.S.C. 7121(d) shall be processed as complaints under § 1613.214 *et seq.*

(b) In cases where a person is covered by a negotiated grievance procedure permitting allegations of discrimination, a person wishing to file a complaint or a grievance on a matter of alleged employment discrimination must elect the forum in which to pursue the matter: either the process described in this part or a negotiated grievance procedure. An aggrieved employee who files a grievance in writing with an agency whose negotiated agreement with an employee organization permits the acceptance of grievance[s] which allege discrimination prohibited by this subpart, may not thereafter file a complaint on the same matter under the provisions of this subpart irrespective of whether the grievance has raised an allegation of discrimination within the negotiated grievance procedure. Any such complaints filed after a grievance has been filed on the same matter shall be rejected without prejudice to the complainant's rights to proceed through the negotiated grievance process, including the complainant's right to request the Commission to review a final decision as provided in 5 U.S.C. 7121(d) and at § 1613.231(b). The agency decision letter rejecting such a complaint shall advise the complainant of the right to appeal the agency decision to the Commission. An election, pursuant to this paragraph, to proceed under this part is indicated only by the filing of a formal complaint, in writing. Use of the pre-complaint process as described in § 1613.213 does not constitute an election for the purposes of this section.

[52 FR 41925, Oct. 30, 1987]

§ 1613.220 Avoidance of delay.

(a) The complaint shall be resolved promptly. To this end, both the complainant and the agency shall proceed with the complaint without undue delay so that the complaint is resolved within 180 calendar days after it was filed, including time spent in the processing of the complaint by the Administrative Judge under § 1613.218.

(b) The head of the agency or designee shall cancel a complaint if the complainant fails to prosecute the complaint without undue delay by following the procedures for cancelling a complaint under § 1613.215.

(c) The agency shall furnish the Commission reports on all complaints pending within the agency in a form specified by the Commission. If an agency has not issued a final decision, and has not requested the Commission to supply an Administrative Judge or complaints examiner, within 75 calendar days from the date a complaint was filed, the Commission may require the agency to take special measures to insure prompt processing of the complaint or may assume responsibility for processing the complaint, including supplying an investigator to conduct any necessary investigation on behalf of the agency. When the Commission supplies an investigator, the agency shall reimburse the Commission for all expenses incurred in connection with the investigation and shall notify the complainant in writing of the proposed disposition of the complaint no later than 15 calendar days after its receipt of the investigative report.

(d) When the Administrative Judge has submitted a recommended decision it shall become a final decision binding on the agency 60 calendar days after the receipt of the complete complaint file and the recommended decision by the agency unless the agency has already issued a final decision. In such event, the agency shall so notify the complainant of the decision and furnish to him a copy of the findings, analysis, and recommended decision of the Administrative Judge under § 1613.218(i) and a copy of the hearing record and also shall notify him in writing of the right to appeal to the Commission and the time limits applicable to such an appeal and of the right to file a civil action as described in § 1613.281. The agency shall provide the Administrative Judge with a copy of its final decision on each complaint on which a recommended decision has been issued.

[37 FR 22717, Oct. 21, 1972. Redesignated at 43 FR 60901, Dec. 29, 1978, and amended at 52 FR 10085, Mar. 30, 1987; 52 FR 41926, Oct. 30, 1987]

§ 1613.221 Decision by head of agency or designee.

(a) The head of the agency or designee shall make the decision of the agency on a complaint based on the preponderance of evidence in the complaint file. A person designated to make the decision for the head of the agency shall be one who is fair, impartial, and objective.

(b)(1) The decision of the agency shall be in writing, shall reflect the date of its issuance, and shall be transmitted to the complainant and his or her representative either by certified mail, return receipt requested, or by any other method which enables the agency to show the date of receipt.

(2) When the Administrative Judge has issued a recommended decision on the complaint under § 1613.218(g) or (i)(3), the decision letter shall transmit a copy of such recommended decision and a copy of the hearing record if a hearing was held. The decision of the agency shall adopt, reject, or modify the decision recommended by the Administrative Judge. If the decision is to reject or modify the recommended decision, the decision letter shall set forth the specific reasons in detail for rejecting or modifying the findings of fact or conclusions of law made by the Administrative Judge.

(3) When there has been no hearing and no recommended decision under § 1613.218(g), the decision letter shall set forth the findings, analysis, and decision of the head of the agency or his designee.

(c) The decision of the agency shall require any remedial action authorized by law determined to be necessary or desirable to resolve the issue of discrimination and to promote the policy of equal opportunity, whether or not there is a finding of discrimination. When discrimination is found, the agency shall:

(1) Advise the complainant and his or her representative that any request for attorney's fees or costs must be documented and submitted within 20 calendar days of receipt,

(2) Require remedial action to be taken in accordance with § 1613.271,

(3) Review the matter giving rise to the complaint to determine whether disciplinary action is appropriate and

(4) Record the basis for its decision to take, or not to take, disciplinary action but this decision shall not be recorded in the complaint file.

(d) When the final agency decision provides for an award of attorney's fees or costs, the amount of these awards shall be determined under § 1613.271(c). In the unusual situation in which the agency determines not to award attorney's fees or costs to a prevailing complainant, the agency shall set forth in its decision the specific reasons for denying the award.

(e) The decision letter shall inform the complainant of his or her right to appeal the decision of the agency to the Commission, and shall include the text of § 1613.233 (a) or (b), as appropriate. The decision letter shall also inform the complainant of his or her right to file a civil action in accordance with § 1613.281, and of the time limits applicable to such an appeal.

[52 FR 41926, Oct. 30, 1987]

§ 1613.222 Complaint file.

The agency shall establish a complaint file. Except as provided in § 1613.221(c), this file shall contain all documents pertinent to the complaint.

(a) The complaint file shall include copies of:

(1) The notice of the Equal Employment Opportunity Counselor to the aggrieved person under § 1613.213(a);

(2) The written report of the Equal Employment Opportunity Counselor on whatever precomplaint counseling efforts were made with regard to the complainant's case;

(3) The complaint;

(4) The investigative file,

(5) If the complaint is withdrawn by the complainant, a written statement of the complainant or representative to that effect;

(6) If adjustment of the complaint is arrived at under § 1613.217, the written record of the terms of adjustment;

(7) If no adjustment of the complaint is arrived at under § 1613.217, a copy of the letter notifying the complainant of the proposed disposition of the complaint and of the right to a hearing and documentation of the attempt to adjust the complaint;

(8) If decision is made under § 1613.217(d), a copy of the letter to the complainant transmitting that decision,

(9) If a hearing was held, the record of the hearing, together with the Administrative Judge's findings, analysis and recommendations, if any, made to the head of the agency or designee,

(10) If the Director of Equal Employment Opportunity is not the designee, the recommendations, if any, made by the Director to the head of the agency or designee,

(11) If decision is made under § 1613.221, a copy of the letter transmitting the decision of the head of the agency or designee, and

(12) Proof of the date of receipt of final agency decision, as required under § 1613.221(b)(1).

(b) The complaint file shall not contain any document that has not been made available to the complainant or the complainant's designated physician under 5 CFR 294.401.

[52 FR 41927, Oct. 30, 1987]

APPEAL TO THE COMMISSION

§ 1613.231 Right to appeal to the Commission.

(a) A complainant may appeal to the Commission the decision of the head of the agency or designee:

(1) To reject or cancel the complaint or any portion for reasons covered by § 1613.215; or

(2) Under the circumstances set forth in § 1613.217(b); or

(3) On the merits of the complaint, under § 1613.217(d), § 1613.220(d) or § 1613.221, or on the award of attorney's fees or costs.

(b) A complainant may appeal to the Commission on issues of employment discrimination raised in a negotiated grievance procedure covered by § 1613.219(a), where the agency's negotiated labor-management agreement permits such issues to be raised. A complainant may appeal the decision:

(1) Of the agency head or designee on the grievance;

(2) Of the arbitrator on the grievance; or

(3) Of the Federal Labor Relations Authority (FLRA) on exceptions to the arbitrator's award.

A complainant may not appeal under this subsection, however, when the matter initially raised in the negotiated grievance procedure is still ongoing in that process, is in arbitration or is before the FLRA. Any appeal prematurely filed in such circumstances shall be dismissed without prejudice.

[52 FR 41927, Oct. 30, 1987]

§ 1613.232 Where to appeal.

The complainant shall file his appeal in writing, either personally or by mail, with the Director, Office of Federal Operations, Equal Employment Opportunity Commission, 1801 L Street, NW., Washington, DC 20507.

[51 FR 22519, June 20, 1986, as amended at 56 FR 6983, Feb. 21, 1991; 57 FR 11431, Apr. 3, 1992]

§ 1613.233 Time limit.

(a) Except as provided in paragraph (c) of this section, a complainant may file a notice of appeal at any time up to 20 calendar days after receipt of the agency's notice of final decision on his or her complaint. An appeal shall be deemed filed on the date it is postmarked, or, in the absence of a postmark, on the date it is received by the Commission. Any statement or brief in support of the appeal must be submitted to the Commission and to the defendant agency within 30 calendar days of filing the notice of appeal. For purposes of this part, the decision of an agency shall be final only when the agency makes a determination on all of the issues in the complaint, including whether or not to award attorney's fees or costs. If a decision to award attorney's fees or costs is made, the decision will not be final until the procedure is followed for determining the amount of the award as set forth in § 1613.271(c).

(b) When issues of discrimination have been raised in a negotiated grievance process, a complainant may file a Notice of Appeal of such issues up to 20 days after: (1) Receipt of an agency decision on the grievance and expiration of the time during which the union and the agency may move the matter to the next [stage] of the grievance process; (2) receipt of an arbitrator's award; or (3) receipt of the decision of the FLRA on exceptions to the arbitrator's award.

(c) The 20-day time limit within which a notice of appeal must be filed will not be extended by the Commission unless, based upon a written statement by the complainant showing that he or she was not notified of the prescribed time limit and was not otherwise aware of it or that circumstances beyond his or her control prevented the filing of a Notice of Appeal within the prescribed time limit, the Commission exercises its discretion to extend the time limit and accept the Appeal.

[44 FR 34495, June 15, 1979, as amended at 48 FR 19707, May 2, 1983]

§ 1613.234 Appellate procedures and finality.

(a) *Procedures.* On behalf of the Commission, the Office of Federal Operations shall review the complaint file and all relevant written representations submitted by either party. The Office may remand a complaint to the agency for further investigation or a rehearing if it considers that action necessary or have additional investigation conducted by Commission personnel. There is no right to a hearing before the Office or the Commission upon appeal. The Office or the Commission shall issue a written decision setting forth its reasons for the decision and shall send copies to the complainant, the complainant's designated representative, and the agency. When corrective action is ordered, the agency shall report within the time specified to the Office that the corrective action has been taken.

(b) *Finality.* A decision issued under this section is final within the meaning of §§ 1613.281 and 1613.641 unless:

(1) Within 30 days of receipt [of] a decision issued under paragraph (a) of this section, either party files a timely request to reopen pursuant to § 1613.235, or

(2) The Commission on its own motion reopens the case.

[52 FR 41927, Oct. 30, 1987, as amended at 56 FR 6983, Feb. 21, 1991]

§ 1613.235 Reopening and reconsideration.

(a) The Commission may, in its discretion, reopen and reconsider any decision of the Commission notwithstanding any other provisions of this part.

(b) Parties may request reopening or reconsideration provided that such request is made within 30 days of receipt of a decision issued pursuant to § 1613.234 or within 20 days of receipt of another party's timely request to reopen. Such requests shall be submitted to the Office of Federal Operations. The request shall contain arguments or evidence which tend to establish that:

(1) New and material evidence is available that was not readily available when the previous decision was issued; or

(2) The previous decision involved an erroneous interpretation of law or regulation or misapplication of established policy; or

(3) The decision is of such exceptional nature as to have effects beyond the actual case at hand.

(c)(1) The party requesting reopening or reconsideration shall submit copies of the request and supporting documents to all other parties and their representatives at the time of the request along with proof of such submission.

(2) Any argument in opposition to the request to reopen or cross request to reopen shall be submitted to the Office of Federal Operations and to the requesting party within 20 days of receipt of the request to reopen along with proof of such submission.

(d) A decision on a request to reopen by either party is final and there is no further right by either party to request reopening.

[52 FR 41927, Oct. 30, 1987, as amended at 56 FR 6983, Feb. 21, 1991]

§ 1613.236 [Reserved]

§ 1613.237 Corrective action.

(a) Corrective action ordered by the Office of Federal Operations or the Commission is mandatory and binding on the agency except as provided in § 1613.234(b). Failure to implement ordered relief shall be subject to judicial enforcement as specified in § 1613.239(c).

(b) When the agency requests reopening and when the case involves removal, separation, or suspension continuing beyond the date of the request to reopen, and when the decision recommends retroactive restoration, the agency shall comply with the decision only to the extent of the temporary or conditional restoration of the employee to duty status in the position recommended by the Commission, pending the outcome of the agency request for reopening.

(1) Service under the temporary or conditional restoration provisions of this paragraph shall be credited toward the completion of a probationary or trial period, eligibility for a within-grade increase, or the completion of the service requirement for career tenure, provided the Commission—

(i) Upholds its decision after reopening the case, or

(ii) Refuses to reopen.

(2) The agency shall notify the Commission and the employee in writing, at the same time it requests reopening, that the remedial action it takes is temporary or conditional.

(c) When no request for reopening is filed within 30 days of receipt of the decision, or when a request to reopen is denied, the agency shall execute the action ordered and there is no further right to delay implementation of the ordered relief. The corrective action shall be completed not later than sixty (60) days after the decision becomes final.

[52 FR 41928, Oct. 30, 1987, as amended at 56 FR 6983, Feb. 21, 1991]

§ 1613.238 Enforcement of final decisions.

(a) *Petition for enforcement.* A complainant may petition the Commission for enforcement of a decision issued under the Commission's appellate jurisdiction. The petition shall be submitted to the Office of Federal Operations. The petition shall specifically set forth the reasons that lead the complainant to believe that the agency is not complying with the decision.

(b) *Compliance.* On behalf of the Commission, the Office of Federal Operations shall take all necessary action to ascertain whether the agency is implementing the decision of the Commission. If the agency is found not to be in compliance with the decision, efforts shall be undertaken to obtain compliance.

(c) *Clarification.* On behalf of the Commission, the Office of Federal Operations may, on its own motion or in response to a petition for enforcement or in connection with a timely request to reopen, issue a clarification of a prior decision. A clarification cannot change the result of a prior decision or enlarge or diminish the relief ordered but may further explain the meaning or intent of the prior decision.

(d) *Referral to the Commission.* Where the Director, Office of Federal Operations, is unable to obtain satisfactory compliance with the final decision, the Director shall submit appropriate findings and recommendations for enforcement to the Commission, or, as directed by the Commission, refer the matter to another appropriate agency.

[52 FR 41928, Oct. 30, 1987, as amended at 56 FR 6983, Feb. 21, 1991]

§ 1613.239 Enforcement action by the Commission.

(a) *Notice to show cause.* The Commission may issue a notice to the Head of any federal agency that has failed to comply with a decision to show cause why there is noncompliance. Such notice may request the Head of the agency or representative to appear before the Commission or to respond to the notice in writing with adequate evidence of compliance or with compelling reasons why compliance has not been effectuated.

(b) *Certification to the Office of Special Counsel.* Where appropriate and pursuant to the terms of a memorandum of agreement, the Commission may refer the matter to the Office of Special Counsel for enforcement action.

(c) *Notification to complainant of completion of administrative efforts.* Where the Commission has determined that an agency is not complying with a prior decision, or where an agency has failed or refused to submit its report of corrective action, the Commission shall notify the complainant of the right to file a civil action for enforcement of the decision pursuant to section 717 of title VII, section 15 of the Age Discrimination in Employment Act, or section 505 of the Rehabilitation Act, and to seek judicial review of the agency's refusal to implement corrective action pursuant to the Administrative Procedure Act, 5 U.S.C. 701 *et seq.,* and the Mandamus Statute, 28 U.S.C. 1361, or commence de novo proceedings pursuant to the appropriate statutes.

[52 FR 41928, Oct. 30, 1987]

§ 1613.240 Computation of time.

With respect to time periods specified in this subpart:

(a) The first day counted shall be the day after the event from which the time period begins to run and the last day of the period shall be included, unless it falls on a Saturday, Sunday, or Federal holiday, in which case the period shall be extended to include the next business day; and

(b) A document shall be deemed timely if it is delivered in person or postmarked before the expiration of the applicable filing period, or if, in the absence of a legible postmark, it is received by mail within five days from the expiration of the applicable filing period.

[52 FR 41928, Oct. 30, 1987]

REPORTS TO THE COMMISSION

§ 1613.241 Reports to the Commission on complaints.

Each agency shall report to the Commission information concerning precomplaint counseling and the status and disposition of complaints under this subpart at such times and in such manner as the Commission prescribes.

CONSOLIDATION OF COMPLAINTS

§ 1613.251 Joint processing and consolidation of complaints.

(a) Two or more complaints of discrimination filed by employees or applicants for employment with the agency consisting of substantially similar allegations of discrimination may, with the written permission of the complainants, be consolidated by the agency or Commission.

(b) Two or more individual complaints of discrimination from the same employee or applicant for employment may, at the discretion of the agency or the Commission, be joined for processing after notifying the individual that the complaints will be processed jointly.

[42 FR 11808, Mar. 1, 1977. Redesignated at 43 FR 60901, Dec. 29, 1978]

FREEDOM FROM REPRISAL OR INTERFERENCES

§ 1613.261 Freedom from restraint, interference, coercion and reprisal.

It is unlawful to restrain, interfere, coerce or discriminate against complainants, their representatives, witnesses, Directors of Equal Employment Opportunity, Equal Employment Opportunity Officers, Investigators, Counselors and other agency officials with responsibility for processing discrimination complaints because of involvement with a discrimination charge during any stage in the presentation and processing of a complaint, including the counseling stage under § 1613.213, or because an individual filed a charge of discrimination, testified, assisted or participated in any manner with an investigation, proceeding or hearing or because of any opposition to an unlawful employment practice under this part.

[52 FR 41928, Oct. 30, 1987]

§ 1613.262 Review of allegations of reprisal.

(a) An individual who alleges a violation of § 1613.261 may have the allegation reviewed as an individual complaint of discrimination under §§ 1613.211 through 1613.283.

(b) When a complainant alleges a violation of § 1613.261 in connection with the filing of a prior discrimination complaint and the prior complaint is in process at the agency when the allegation is made, the complainant may request the agency to consolidate the reprisal allegation with the prior complaint. If the prior complaint is at the hearing stage of the complaint process under § 1613.218, the complainant may request the Administrative Judge to consolidate the allegation with the complaint at the hearing. The agency or Administrative Judge may grant the request. *Provided,* That the request is made within 30 calendar days of:

(1) The act that forms the basis of the allegation,

(2) The effective date of the alleged discriminatory personnel action, or

(3) The date the complainant knew or should reasonably have known that § 1613.261 has been violated.

The agency or the Administrative Judge may exercise discretion and deny the request and require the allegation to be processed under § 1613.262(a).

[52 FR 41928, Oct. 30, 1987]

REMEDIAL ACTIONS

§ 1613.271 Remedial actions.

(a) When an agency, or the Commission, finds that an applicant or an employee has been discriminated against, the agency shall provide full relief, as explained in Appendix A of this part, which shall include the following elements in appropriate circumstances:

(1) Notification to all employees of the agency in the affected facility of their right to be free of unlawful discrimination and be assured that the particular types of discrimination found will not recur;

(2) Commitment that corrective, curative or preventive action will be taken, or measures adopted, to ensure that similar found violations of the law will not recur;

(3) An unconditional offer to each identified victim of discrimination of placement in the position the person would have occupied but for the discrimination suffered by that person, or a substantially equivalent position;

(4) Payment to each identified victim of discrimination on a make whole basis for any loss of earnings the person may have suffered as a result of the discrimination; and

(5) Commitment that the agency shall cease from engaging in the specific unlawful employment practice found in the case.

(b) *Remedial action involving an applicant.* (1) When an agency, or the Commission, finds that an applicant for employment has been discriminated against, the agency shall offer the applicant the position the applicant would have occupied absent discrimination or, if justified by the circumstances, a substantially equivalent position. The offer shall be made in writing. The individual shall have 15 calendar days from receipt of the offer within which to accept or decline the offer. Failure to notify the agency of his decision within the 15-day period will be considered a declination of the offer, unless the individual can show that circumstances beyond his control prevented him from responding within the time limit. If the offer is accepted, appointment shall be retroactive to the date the applicant would have been hired. Backpay, computed in the same manner prescribed by 5 CFR 550.805, shall be awarded from the date the individual would have entered on duty until the date the individual actually enters on duty. The individual shall be deemed to have performed service for the agency during this period of retroactivity for all purposes except for meeting service requirements for completion of a probationary or trial period that is required. If the offer of employment is declined, the agency shall award the individual a sum equal to the backpay he would have received, computed in the same manner prescribed by 5 CFR 550.805, from the date he would have been appointed until the date the offer was made, subject to the limitation of paragraph (b)(4) of this section. The agency shall inform the applicant, in its offer of employment, of his right to this award in the event the offer is declined.

(2) When an agency, or the Commission, finds that discrimination existed at the time the applicant was considered for employment but also finds clear and convincing evidence that the applicant would not have been hired even absent discrimination, the agency nevertheless shall take all steps necessary to eliminate the discriminatory practice and ensure it does not recur.

(3) This paragraph shall be cited as the authority under which the above-described appointments or awards of backpay shall be made.

(4) Backpay under this paragraph for complaints under title VII or the Rehabilitation Act may not extend from a date earlier than 2 years prior to the date on which the complaint was initially filed by the applicant.

(c) *Remedial action involving an employee.* When an agency, or the Commission, finds that an employee of the agency was discriminated against, the agency shall take remedial actions which shall include one or more of the following, but need not be limited to these actions:

(1) Retroactive promotion, with backpay computed in the same manner prescribed by 5 CFR 550.805, unless the record contains clear and convincing evidence that the employee would not have been promoted or employed at a higher grade, even absent discrimination. The backpay liability under title VII or the Rehabilitation Act may not accrue from a date earlier than 2 years prior to the date the discrimination complaint was filed, but, in any event, not to exceed the date the employee would have been promoted.

(2) If the record contains clear and convincing evidence that, although discrimination existed at the time selection for promotion was made, the employee would not have been promoted even absent discrimination, the agency shall eliminate any discriminatory practice and ensure it does not recur.

(3) Cancellation of an unwarranted personnel action and restoration of the employee.

(4) Expunction from the agency's records of any reference to or any record of an unwarranted disciplinary action that is not a personnel action.

(5) Full opportunity to participate in the employee benefit denied (e.g., training, preferential work assignments, overtime scheduling).

(d) Attorney's fees or costs—(1) Awards of attorney's fees or costs. The provisions of this subpart relating to the award of attorney's fees or costs shall apply to allegations of discrimination or retaliation prohibited by section 717 of title VII of the Civil Rights Act of 1964, as amended, 42 U.S.C. 2000e-16, and sections 501 and 505 of the Rehabilitation Act, 29 U.S.C. 791 and 794a. In a decision by an agency, under §§ 1613.217, 1613.220(d), 1613.221 or 1613.612 or by the Commission, under §§ 1613.234, 1613.235, 1613.262, 1613.631 or 1613.632, the agency or Commission may award the applicant or employee reasonable attorney's fees or costs incurred in the processing of the complaint or charge.

(i) A finding of discrimination raises a presumption of entitlement to an award of attorney's fees.

(ii) Any award of attorney's fees or costs shall be paid by the agency.

(iii) Attorney's fees are allowable only for the services of members of the Bar and law clerks, paralegals or law students under the supervision of members of the Bar, except that no award is allowable for the services of any employee of the Federal Government.

(iv) Attorney's fees shall be paid only for services performed after the filing of the complaint required in § 1613.214 and after the complainant has notified the agency that he/she is represented by an attorney, except that fees are allowable for a reasonable period of time prior to the notification of representation for any services performed in reaching a determination to represent the complainant. Written submissions to the agency which are signed by the representative shall be deemed to constitute notice of representation.

(2) Amount of awards. When a decision of the agency, under §§ 1613.217(c), 1613.220(d), 1613.221 or 1613.612 or of the Commission, under §§ 1613.234, 1613.235, 1613.262, 1613.631 or 1613.632 provides for an award of attorney's fees

or costs, the complainant's attorney shall submit a verified statement of costs and attorney's fees, as appropriate, to the agency within 20 days of receipt of the decision. A statement of attorney's fees shall be accompanied by an affidavit executed by the attorney of record itemizing the attorney's charges for legal services and both the verified statement and the accompanying affidavit shall be made a part of the complaint file. The amount of attorney's fees or costs to be awarded the complainant shall be determined by agreement between the complainant, the complainant's representative and the agency. Such agreement shall immediately be reduced to writing. If the complainant, the representative and the agency cannot reach an agreement on the amount of attorney's fees or costs within 20 calendar days of receipt of the verified statement and accompanying affidavit, the agency shall issue a decision determining the amount of attorney's fees or costs within 30 calendar days of receipt of the statement and affidavit. Such decision shall include the specific reasons for determining the amount of the award.

(i) The amount of attorney's fees shall be calculated in accordance with the existing caselaw using following standards:

(A) The starting point shall be the number of hours reasonably expended multiplied by a reasonable hourly rate.

(B) This amount may be reduced or increased in considering the following factors, although ordinarily many of these factors are subsumed within the calculation set forth above: The time and labor required, the novelty and difficulty of the questions, the skill requisite to perform the legal service properly, the preclusion of other employment by the attorney due to acceptance of the case, the customary fee, whether the fee is fixed or contingent, time limitations imposed by the client or the circumstances, the amount involved and the results obtained, the experience, reputation, and ability of the attorney, the undesirability of the case, the nature and length of the professional relationship with the client, and the awards in similar cases. Only in some cases of exceptional success shall any of these factors be used to enhance an award computed by the formula set forth in paragraph (d)(2)(i)(A).

(ii) The costs which may be awarded are those authorized by 28 U.S.C. 1920 to include—

(A) Fees of the reporter for all or any of the stenographic transcript necessarily obtained for use in the case;

(B) Fees and disbursements for printing and witnesses; and

(C) Fees for exemplification and copies of papers necessarily obtained for use in the case.

Witness fees shall be awarded in accordance with the provisions of 28 U.S.C. 1821, except that no award shall be made for a federal employee who is in a duty status when made available as a witness.

[52 FR 41929, Oct. 30, 1987]

RIGHT TO FILE A CIVIL ACTION

§ 1613.281 Statutory right.

An employee or applicant is authorized by section 717(c) of the Civil Rights Act, as amended, 84 Stat. 112, to file a civil action in an appropriate United States district court:

(a) Within thirty (30) calendar days of receipt of notice of final action taken by the agency on a complaint,

(b) After one hundred and eighty (180) calendar days from the date of filing a complaint with the agency if there has been no decision,

(c) Within thirty (30) calendar days after receipt of final action taken by the Commission on the complaint, or

(d) After one hundred and eighty (180) calendar days from the date of filing an appeal with the Commission, if there has been no Commission decision.

For purposes of this part, the decision of an agency shall be final only when the agency makes a determination on all of the issues in the complaint, including whether or not to award attorney's fees or costs. If a determination to award attorneys fees is made the decision will not be final until the procedure is followed for determining the amount of the award as set forth in § 1613.271(c).

[45 FR 24133, Apr. 9, 1980]

§ 1613.282 Notice of right.

An agency shall notify an employee or applicant of his right to file a civil action, and of the 30-day time limit for filing, in any final action on a complaint under §§ 1613.215, 1613.217, 1613.220, or § 1613.221. The Commission shall notify an employee or applicant of his right to file a civil action, and of the 30-day time limit for filing, in any decision under § 1613.234.

[37 FR 22717, Oct. 21, 1972, as amended at 37 FR 25699, Dec. 2, 1972. Redesignated at 43 FR 60901, Dec. 29, 1978]

§ 1613.283 Effect on administrative processing.

The filing of a civil action by an employee or applicant involving a complaint filed under this subpart terminates processing of that complaint.

[52 FR 41930, Oct. 30, 1987]

Subpart C—Minority Group Statistics System

§ 1613.301 Applicability.

(a) This subpart applies (1) to military departments as defined in section 102 of title 5, United States Code, Executive agencies (other than the General Accounting Office) as defined in section 105 of title 5, United States Code, the U.S. Postal Service, and the Postal Rate Commission, and to the employees thereof, including employees paid from nonappropriated funds, and (2) to those portions of the legislative and judicial branches of the Federal Government and the government of the District of Columbia having positions in the competitive service and to the employee[s] in those positions.

(b) This subpart does not apply to aliens employed outside the limits of the United States.

[34 FR 5371, Mar. 19, 1969, as amended at 34 FR 14024, Sept. 4, 1969; 36 FR 11999, June 24, 1971. Redesignated at 43 FR 60901, Dec. 29, 1978]

§ 1613.302 Agency systems.

(a) Each agency shall establish a system which provides statistical employment information by race or national origin.

(b) Data shall be collected only by visual identification and shall be disclosed only in the form of gross statistics. An agency shall not collect or maintain any information of the race or national origin of individual employees except when an automated data processing system is used in accordance with standards and requirements prescribed by the Commission to insure individual privacy and the separation of that information from personnel records.

(c) Each system is subject to the following controls:

(1) Only those categories of race and national origin prescribed by the Commission may be used;

(2) Only the specific procedures for the collection and maintenance of data that are prescribed or approved by the Commission may be used;

(3) The Commission shall review the operation of the agency system to insure adherence to Commission procedures and requirements. An agency may make an exception to the prescribed procedures and requirements only with the advance written approval of the Commission.

(d) The agency may use the data only in studies and analyses which contribute affirmatively to achieving the objectives of the equal employment opportunity program. An agency shall not establish a quota for the employment of persons on the basis of race, color, religion, sex, or national origin.

(e) An agency shall report to the Commission on employment by race and national origin in the form and at such times as the Commission may require.

[34 FR 5371, Mar. 19, 1969, as amended at 34 FR 14024, Sept. 4, 1969. Redesignated at 43 FR 60901, Dec. 29, 1978]

Subpart D—Processing Mixed Case Complaints

AUTHORITY: Sec. 717 of Title VII of the Civil Rights Act of 1964, as amended, 42 U.S.C. 2000e-16, secs. 501 and 505 of the Rehabilitation Act of 1973, as amended, 29 U.S.C. 791 and 794a, sec. 15 of the Age Discrimination in Employment Act of 1967, as amended, 29 U.S.C. 633a, sec. 6(d) of the Fair Labor Standards Act of 1938, as amended, 29 U.S.C. 206(d), Reorg. Plan No. 1 of 1978 (43 FR 19807) and E.O. 12106 (44 FR 1053).

SOURCE: 48 FR 19708, May 2, 1983, unless otherwise noted.

§ 1613.401 Purpose, scope and applicability.

(a) *Purpose.* This subpart sets forth the regulations under which the Equal Employment Opportunity Commission will carry out its [responsibilities] for the administration and enforcement of section 205 of the Civil Service Reform Act of 1978, 5 U.S.C. 7702, with respect to matters of alleged employment discrimination prohibited by section 717 of the Civil Rights Act of 1964, as amended, 42 U.S.C. 2000e-16, section 501 of the Rehabilitation Act of 1973, as amended, 29 U.S.C. 794a, section 15 of the Age Discrimination in Employment Act of 1967, as amended, 29 U.S.C. 633a, and section 6(d) of the Fair Labor Standards Act of 1938, as amended, 29 U.S.C. 206(d).

(b) *Scope.* This subpart shall govern the treatment of complaints in which allegations of discrimination are raised, in connection with an action appealable to the Merit Systems Protection Board (MSPB), provided that the action which forms the basis of the complaint was initiated on or after January 11, 1979 (the effective date of the Civil Service Reform Act). This subpart governs the procedures applicable: (1) When a complainant elects to bring the matter which forms the basis of the complaint before his/her agency, by filing a complaint of discrimination, pursuant to this part; (2) when an appealable action, pending before the MSPB, is remanded for agency processing, pursuant to 5 CFR 1201.155(c); and (3) when a petition to review the decision of the MSPB on the issues of discrimination is filed with the Commission, pursuant to 5 U.S.C. 7702(b).

(c) *Applicability.* This subpart applies to all persons who have a right of appeal to the MSPB.

§ 1613.402 Definitions.

(a) *Mixed case complaint.* A mixed case complaint is: (1) A complaint of employment discrimination filed with a federal agency, based on race, color, religion, sex, national origin, handicap, age, and/or reprisal, related to, or stemming from an action taken by an agency against the complainant, which action may be appealed to the MSPB, pursuant to any law, rule or regulation; or (2) a complaint of sex-based wage discrimination, filed with the Commission, related to or stemming from an action taken by an agency against a complainant, which action may be appealed to the MSPB, pursuant to any law, rule or regulation. The complaint may contain only an allegation of employment discrimination or it may contain additional allegations which the MSPB has jurisdiction to address.

(b) *Mixed case appeals.* A mixed case appeal is an appeal filed with the MSPB, which jurisdiction to entertain, and which alleges that the agency action which forms the basis for the appeal was effected, in whole or in part, because of discrimination on the basis of race, color, religion, sex, national origin, handicap, age and/or reprisal, or alleges that such appealable action resulted in sex-based wage discrimination.

(c) *Complaint.* A complaint is a formal complaint of discrimination, filed with the appropriate person designated to receive complaints at the agency, pursuant to § 1613.214 of subpart B of this part.

(d) *Proposal.* A proposal, as used in this subpart, means any document issued by an agency to an employee, pursuant to any requirements contained in regulations issued by the Office of Personnel Management (OPM), which proposes to take an action against that employee which, if effected, could be appealed by that employee to the MSPB.

(e) *Handicap definitions.* The definitions set forth at § 1613.702 of subpart G of this part are hereby incorporated by reference into this subpart and are applicable to any mixed case complaint which contains issues of handicap discrimination.

§ 1613.403 Election.

An aggrieved person may initially file a mixed case complaint with an agency, pursuant to this part, or (s)he may file a mixed case appeal directly with the MSPB, pursuant to 5 CFR 1201.151, but not both. An agency shall inform every employee who is the subject of an action which is appealable to the MSPB and who has raised the issue of discrimination either orally or in writing, during the processing of the action, of his/her right to file a mixed case complaint, if the employee believes the action to be based, in whole or in part, on discrimination, or to file a mixed case appeal with the MSPB. The person shall be advised that (s)he may not initially file both and that whichever is filed first (the mixed case complaint or the appeal) shall be considered an election to proceed in that forum. For the purposes of this subsection, filing of a mixed case complaint occurs when the complaint is filed with an [appropriate] agency official, in accordance with § 1613.214(a)(3) of subpart B of this part.

§ 1613.404 Retroactivity.

The following shall apply, with respect to mixed case complaints filed prior to the effective date of these regulations, where any issues in such mixed case complaints were also appealed to the MSPB:

(a) *Discrimination allegations considered.* If the MSPB considered, or is considering, the allegations of discrimination raised in the mixed case complaint, in connection with any appeal, the mixed case complaint before the agency shall be cancelled, pursuant to § 1613.405(b).

(b) *Discrimination allegations not considered.* If the MSPB was not presented with or did not consider the allegations of discrimination raised in the mixed case complaint in connection with any appeal, the agency shall process such mixed case complaint in accordance with § 1613.405(e). The final agency decision on such complaint shall advise the complainant of his/her right to file a civil action, pursuant to § 1613.417, and that (s)he may petition the MSPB to review his/her previous appellate decision, to include the allegations of discrimination raised with the agency which were not previously decided on appeal by the MSPB. The decision shall further advise the complainant that, whether or not the MSPB chooses to review its previous decision, the complainant may thereafter petition the EEOC to review the matter, pursuant to § 1613.414, provided that the complainant has fullfilled the procedural prerequisite of first petitioning the MSPB.

§ 1613.405 Procedures for agency processing of mixed case complaints.

(a) *Rejections.* Whenever an agency is presented with a mixed case complaint concerning an action that has previously been appealed by the complainant to the MSPB, the agency shall reject the complaint (in writing), citing this subsection as the authority therefor, regardless of whether the allegations of discrimination raised in the mixed case complaint were raised in the previous appeal to the MSPB. The agency shall advise the aggrieved person, as part of the decision rejecting such a complaint, that (s)he must bring the allegations of discrimination contained in the rejected complaint to the attention of the MSPB, pursuant to 5 CFR 1201.155.

(b) *Cancellation.* Whenever the agency learns that a mixed case complaint, which has been filed with and accepted by the agency, contains issues which also form the basis of an appeal which has been filed with the MSPB, the agency shall determine which was filed first (i.e., the mixed case complaint or the appeal). If the appeal to the MSPB was filed first, the agency shall cancel (in writing) that portion of the mixed case complaint related to the action appealed to the MSPB and advise the complainant, as part of the decision which cancels the complaint (in whole or in part), that (s)he must bring the allegations of discrimination to the attention of the MSPB, pursuant to 5 CFR 1201.155. If the mixed case complaint was filed first, the agency shall so advise the MSPB and request that the MSPB dismiss the appeal without prejudice and, thereafter, the agency shall process the complaint, pursuant to § 1613.405(e), and issue an agency decision within 120 calendar days. An agency may also cancel a mixed case complaint when it learns that the complainant has chosen to appeal the matter to the MSPB upon expiration of 120 calendar days from the date that the mixed case complaint was filed with the agency.

(c) *Effect of rejection or cancellation.* An agency decision to reject or cancel a mixed case complaint pursuant to § 1613.405(a) or (b) is not subject to appeal to the

EEOC, except where § 1613.405(a) or (b) has been misapplied to a nonmixed case matter (in which case an appeal may be filed pursuant to § 1613.231 of subpart B).

(d) *MSPB Remands.* The MSPB may remand allegations of discrimination to an agency or, in Equal Pay Act matters, to the EEOC, pursuant to 5 CFR 1201.155(a) or (c). In such cases, the agency or the EEOC shall investigate those allegations, as required by the MSPB or by applicable EEOC regulation.

(e) *Procedures.* When a complainant, pursuant to § 1613.403, elects to proceed initially through the agency, rather than with the MSPB, the procedures set forth in § § 1613.211 through 1613.221(d) of subpart B of this part shall govern the processing of the mixed case complaint, with the following exceptions:

(1) There shall be no hearing, as provided in § 1613.218 and as referenced in §§ 1613.217(b)(2) and 1613.221(b)(2) and (3);

(2) At the time that an agency advises a complainant of the acceptance of a mixed case complaint, pursuant to § 1613.214, the agency shall also advise the complainant of the following:

(i) The complaint shall be processed in accordance with this subpart;

(ii) If no agency decision is issued within 120 calendar days of the date of filing of the mixed case complaint, the complainant may appeal the matter to the MSPB at any time thereafter, up to, but not later than, one year from the filing of the complaint, or may file a civil action, as specified at § 1613.417(g); and

(iii) If the complainant is dissatisfied with the agency's decision on the mixed case complaint, (s)he may appeal the matter to the MSPB (not EEOC), within 20 calendar days of receipt of the agency's decision;

(3) At the time that an agency issues to the complainant its notice of proposed disposition, pursuant to § 1613.217(b), the agency shall advise the complainant that the complainant:

(i) May request a decision (pursuant to § 1613.221 of subpart B of this part) from the agency, without a hearing and, thereafter, appeal that decision to the MSPB (and, in connection therewith, request a hearing), within 20 calendar days of receipt of that agency decision, or

(ii) If no decision is received within 120 calendar days of filing the mixed case complaint, may appeal the matter directly to the MSPB (not EEOC) at any time after expiration of 120 calendar days, up to, but no later than, one year after filing the mixed case complaint and of his/her right to file a civil action, as described at § 1613.417(g);

(4) At the time that the agency issues its decision on a mixed case complaint (pursuant to § 1613.221) the agency shall advise the complainant of his/her right to appeal the matter to the MSPB (not EEOC), within 20 calendar days of receipt, and of his/her right to file a civil action, as described at § 1613.417(a).

§ 1613.406 Processing of complaints on proposals.

(a) *Where the agency decision is appealable to the MSPB.* (1) Any complaint which is filed, pursuant to this part, in connection with an agency proposal to take an action that is appealable to the MSPB, shall be consolidated, pursuant to § 1613.251 of subpart B of this part, with any subsequent mixed case complaint filed in connection with that agency decision to take such an action, either as proposed or as modified during the processing of the proposal, and shall be processed in accordance with this subpart.

(2) If, following a complaint on a proposal, the complainant subsequently files an appeal with the MSPB on the subsequent agency decision resulting from that proposal, the agency shall cancel the complaint on the proposal. The complainant

shall be advised by the agency that any allegations of discrimination contained in that complaint should be raised with the MSPB, in connection with the pending appeal.

(3) If a complaint is filed on a proposal, and no appeal is filed with the MSPB on the subsequent appealable agency decision resulting from that proposal, and no complaint is filed with the agency on that appealable decision, the complaint on the proposal shall be deemed to include the final decision as an issue (as of the effective date of such final decision) and shall be processed as a mixed case complaint, in accordance with § 1613.405.

(b) *Where the agency decision is not appealable to the MSPB.* Where a proposal does not result in an agency decision which is appealable to the MSPB (e.g., a proposal to remove which is modified by the agency decision to a 5 day suspension), such a complaint shall be processed pursuant to subparts B, E, F and/or G of this part, as appropriate.

§ 1613.407 Timely processing.

A mixed case complaint shall be processed in a timely manner by the agency, so that the agency's decision (pursuant to § 1613.221 of subpart B of this part) on such a complaint is issued within 120 calendar days from the date the complaint was filed. When a complaint concerning a proposal to take an action that is appealable to the MSPB is consolidated, pursuant to § 1613.406, with a mixed case complaint concerning an agency decision to take the action as proposed or as modified, and that agency decision is appealable to the MSPB, the 120 calendar day time frame for processing the consolidated mixed case complaint begins to run as of the date the complaint concerning that agency decision is filed. For the purposes of § 1613.406(a)(3), the 120 calendar day time frame for processing the complaint shall begin to run as of the effective date of the final decision.

§ 1613.414 Filing requirements.

(a) *Who may file.* Petitions to consider issues of prohibited discrimination may be filed by individuals (and/or their representatives) who have been before the Merit Systems Protection Board with a matter involving allegations of discrimination and have received a final decision pursuant to the Merit Systems Protection Board's regulations at 5 CFR 1201.151 *et seq.* and under 5 U.S.C. 7702.

(b) *Method of filing.* Filing should be made by certified or registered mail return receipt requested to the Office of Federal Operations, Equal Employment Opportunity Commission, 1801 L Street, NW., Washington, DC 20507.

(c) *Time to file.* In order to be timely any petition must be filed with the Commission either within thirty (30) days after receipt of notice of the final decision of the Merit Systems Protection Board, or within thirty (30) days after the initial decision of a Merit Systems Protection Board field office becomes final. The date of filing shall be determined by the date of mailing indicated on the certified or registered mail.

(Civil Service Reform Act of 1978, (5 U.S.C. 7702))

[45 FR 50327, July 29, 1980, as amended at 51 FR 22519, June 20, 1986; 56 FR 6983, Feb. 21, 1991; 57 FR 11431, Apr. 3, 1992]

§ 1613.415 Contents of petition.

(a) *Form.* Petitions must be written or typed, but may use any format including a simple letter format.

(b) *Contents.* Petitions must contain the following:

(1) The name and address of the individual;

(2) The name and address of the individual's representative, if any;

(3) A statement of the reasons why the individual and/or representative believes the decision of the Merit Systems Protection Board is incorrect, in whole or in part, with regard to issues of discrimination based on race, color, religion, sex, national origin, age, handicap and/or violations of the Equal Pay Act;

(4) A copy of the decision issued by the Merit Systems Protection Board; and

(5) The signature of the individual and/or representative, if any.

(Civil Service Reform Act of 1978, (5 U.S.C. 7702))

[45 FR 50327, July 29, 1980]

§ 1613.416 Consideration procedures.

(a) Once a petition is filed, the Commission will examine it and determine whether the Commission should consider the decision of the Merit Systems Protection Board and issue its own decision. The Commission's decision in such a case may differ from or concur with the Merit Systems Protection Board's decision.

(b) The Commission shall determine whether to consider the decision of the Merit Systems Protection Board within thirty (30) days after the date of the petition. For the purpose of this section the date of the petition shall be the date on which the Commission's Office of Federal Operations receives the petition. A determination of the Commission not to consider the decision shall not be used as evidence with respect to any issue of discrimination in any judicial proceeding concerning that issue.

(c) If the Commission makes a determination to consider the decision, the Commission shall within sixty (60) calendar days after the date of its determination, consider the entire record of the proceedings of the Merit Systems Protection Board and on the basis of the evidentiary record before the Board as supplemented in accordance with paragraph (d) of this section, either:

(1) Concur in the decision of the Merit Systems Protection Board, or

(2) Issue in writing a decision which differs from the decision of the Merit Systems Protection Board to the extent that the Commission finds that, as a matter of law:

(i) The decision of the Merit Systems Protection Board constitutes an incorrect interpretation of any provision of any law, rule, regulation, or policy directive referred to in 5 U.S.C. 7702(a)(1)(B), or (ii) the decision involving such provision is not supported by the evidence in the record as a whole.

(d) In considering any decision of the Merit Systems Protection Board, the Commission pursuant to 5 U.S.C. 7702(b)(4), may refer the case to the Merit Systems Protection Board for the taking (within such period as permits the Commission to make a decision within the 60-day period prescribed) of additional evidence or provide on its own for the taking of additional evidence to the extent the Commission considers it necessary to supplement the record.

(Civil Service Reform Act of 1978, (5 U.S.C. 7702))

[45 FR 50327, July 29, 1980, as amended at 56 FR 6983, Feb. 21, 1991]

§ 1613.417 Referral of case to Special Panel.

If the Merit Systems Protection Board (Board) reaffirms its decision under 5 CFR 1201.162(a)(2) with or without modification, the matter shall be immediately certified to the Special Panel established pursuant to 5 U.S.C. 7702(d). Upon certification, the Board shall, within five days (excluding Saturdays, Sundays, and Federal holidays), transmit to the Chairman of the Special Panel and to the Equal

Employment Opportunity Commission (EEOC) the administrative record in the proceeding including—

(a) The factual record compiled under this section which shall include a transcript of any hearing(s);

(b) The decisions issued by the Board and the Commission under 5 U.S.C. 7702; and

(c) A transcript of oral arguments made, or legal brief(s) filed, before the Board and/or the Commission.

[50 FR 52898, Dec. 27, 1985]

§ 1613.418 Organization of Special Panel.

(a) The Special Panel is composed of—

(1) A Chairman appointed by the President with the advice and consent of the Senate, and whose term is six (6) years;

(2) One member of the MSPB, designated by the Chairman of the Board each time a panel is convened;

(3) One member of the EEOC designated by the Chairman of the Commission each time a panel is convened.

(b) *Designation of Special Panel member*—(1) Time of designation. Within five days of certification of the case to the Special Panel, the Chairman of the MSPB and the Chairman of the EEOC shall each designate one member from their respective agencies to serve on the Special Panel.

(2) *Manner of designation.* Letters of designation shall be served on the Chairman of the Special Panel and the parties to the appeal.

[50 FR 52898, Dec. 27, 1985]

§ 1613.419 Practices and procedures of the Special Panel.

(a) *Scope.* The rules in this subpart apply to proceedings before the Special Panel.

(b) *Suspension of rules.* In the interest of expediting a decision, or for good cause shown, the Chairman of the Special Panel may, except where the rule is required by statute, suspend these rules on application of a party, or on his or her own motion, and may order proceedings in accordance with his or her direction.

(c) *Time limit for proceedings.* Pursuant to 5 U.S.C. 7702(d)(2)(A), the Special Panel shall issue a decision within 45 days after a matter has been certified to it.

(d) *Administrative assistance to Special Panel.* (1) The MSPB and the EEOC shall provide the Panel with such reasonable and necessary administrative resources as determined by the Chairman of the Special Panel.

(2) Assistance shall include, but is not limited to, processing vouchers for pay and travel expenses.

(3) The Board and the EEOC shall be responsible for all administrative costs incurred by the Special Panel and, to the extent practicable, shall equally divide the costs of providing such administrative assistance. The Chairman of the Special Panel shall resolve the manner in which costs are divided in the event of a disagreement between the Board and the EEOC.

(e) *Maintenance of the official record.* The Board shall maintain the official record. The Board shall transmit two copies of each submission filed to each member of the Special Panel in an expeditious manner.

(f) *Filing and service of pleadings.* (1) The parties shall file the original and six copies of all submissions with the Clerk, Merit Systems Protection Board, 1120

Vermont Avenue, NW., Washington, DC 20419. One copy of each submission shall be served on the other parties.

(2) A certificate of service specifying how and when service was made must accompany all submissions of the parties.

(3) Service may be by mail or by personal delivery during normal business hours (8:30 a.m.—5:00 p.m.). Due to the short statutory time limit, parties are required to file their submissions by overnight Express Mail, provided by the U.S. Postal Service, should they file by mail.

(4) The date of filing shall be determined by the date of mailing as indicated by the order date for Express Mail. If the filing is by personal delivery, it shall be considered filed on the date it is received in the office of the Clerk, Merit Systems Protection Board.

(g) *Briefs and responsive pleadings.* If the parties wish to submit written argument, briefs shall be filed with the Special Panel within fifteen (15) days from the date of the Board's Certification order. Due to the short statutory time limit responsive pleadings will not ordinarily be permitted.

(h) *Oral argument.* The parties have the right to oral argument if desired. Parties wishing to exercise this right shall so indicate at the time of filing their brief, or if no brief is filed, within fifteen (15) days from the date of the Board's certification order. Upon receipt of a request for argument the Chairman of the Special Panel shall determine the time and place for argument and the time to be allowed each side, and shall so notify the parties.

(i) *Postargument submissions.* Due to the short statutory time limit, no postargument submissions will be permitted, except by order of the Chairman of the Special Panel.

(j) *Procedural matters.* Any procedural matters not addressed in these regulations shall be resolved by written order of the Chairman of the Special Panel.

[50 FR 52898, Dec. 27, 1985]

§ 1613.420 Enforcement of Special Panel decision.

The Board shall, upon receipt of the decision of the Special Panel, order the agency concerned to take any action appropriate to carry out the decision of the Panel. The Board's regulations regarding enforcement of a final order of the Board shall apply. These regulations are set out at 5 CFR part 1201, subpart E.

[50 FR 52898, Dec. 27, 1985]

§ 1613.421 Right to file a civil action.

An individual who has a complaint processed pursuant to 5 CFR 1201.151 *et seq.* and these regulations is authorized by 5 U.S.C. 7702, to file a civil action based on the decision of the Merit Systems Protection Board in an appropriate U.S. District Court:

(a) Within thirty (30) calendar days of receipt of notice of the final action taken by an agency on a complaint unless an appeal is filed with the Merit Systems Protection Board; or

(b) Within thirty (30) calendar days of receipt of notice of the final decision or action taken by the Merit Systems Protection Board if the individual does not file a petition for consideration with the EEOC; or

(c) Within thirty (30) calendar days of receipt of notice that the Commission has determined not to consider the decision of the Merit Systems Protection Board; or

(d) Within thirty (30) calendar days of receipt of notice that the Commission concurs with the decision of the Merit Systems Protection Board; or

(e) If the Commission issues a decision different from the decision of the Merit Systems Protection Board, within thirty (30) calendar days of receipt of notice that the Merit Systems Protection Board concurs in and adopts in whole the decision of the Commission; or

(f) If the Merit Systems Protection Board does not concur with the decision of the Commission and reaffirms its initial decision or reaffirms its initial decision with a revision, within thirty (30) calendar days of the receipt of notice of the decision of the Special Panel; or

(g) After one-hundred and twenty (120) calendar days from the date of filing a formal complaint if there is no agency action or appeal to the Merit Systems Protection Board; or

(h) After one-hundred and twenty (120) calendar days from the date of filing an appeal with the Merit Systems Protection Board if the Merit Systems Protection Board has not yet made a decision; or

(i) After one hundred and eighty (180) calendar days from the date of filing a petition for consideration with the Commission if there is no decision by the Commission, reconsideration decision by the Merit Systems Protection Board or decision by the Special Panel.

(Civil Service Reform Act of 1978, (5 U.S.C. 7702))

[45 FR 50327, July 29, 1980. Redesignated at 50 FR 52897, Dec. 27, 1985]

Subpart E—Nondiscrimination on Account of Age

GENERAL PROVISIONS

§ 1613.501 Purpose and applicability.

(a) *Purpose.* This subpart sets forth the policy under which an agency shall establish a continuing program to assure nondiscrimination on account of age and the regulations under which an agency will process complaints of discrimination on account of age.

(b) *Applicability.* (1) This subpart applies (i) to military departments as defined in section 102 of title 5, United States Code, and Executive agencies as defined in section 105 of title 5, United States Code, the United States Postal Service and the Postal Rate Commission, and to the employees thereof, including employees paid from non-appropriated funds, and (ii) to those units of the legislative and judicial branches of the Federal Government and the Government of the District of Columbia having positions in the competitive service and to the employees of those positions.

(2) This subpart does not apply to aliens employed outside the limits of the United States.

(3) Except as provided by paragraph (b)(2) of this section, this subpart applies to applicants for positions to which paragraph (b)(1) of this section applies.

(4) This subpart applies to employees and applicants for employment who are at least 40 years of age.

(c) *Exceptions.* Reasonable exemptions to the provisions of this subpart may be established by the Commission for each position for which the Commission establishes a maximum age requirement on the basis of a determination that age is a bona fide occupational qualification necessary to the performance of the duties of the position.

[39 FR 24351, July 2, 1974, as amended at 42 FR 37530, July 22, 1977. Redesignated and amended at 43 FR 60901, Dec. 29, 1978]

§ 1613.502 General Policy.

It is [the] policy of the Government of the United States (and of the government of the District of Columbia) to prohibit discrimination in employment on account of age to assure that all personnel actions affecting employees or applicants for employment are free from discrimination on account of age.

[39 FR 24351, July 2, 1974. Redesignated at 43 FR 60901, Dec. 29, 1978]

AGENCY REGULATIONS FOR PROCESSING COMPLAINTS OF DISCRIMINATION

§ 1613.511 General.

An Agency shall provide regulations governing the acceptance and processing of complaints of discrimination on account of age which, subject to § 1613.514, comply with the principles and requirements in §§ 1613.213 through 1613.222, 1613.241 and 1613.261 through 1613.271 of this part.

[39 FR 24351, July 2, 1974. Redesignated at 43 FR 60901, Dec. 29, 1978]

§ 1613.512 Coverage.

The agency shall provide in its regulations for the acceptance of a complaint from any aggrieved employee or applicant for employment with the agency who believes that he or she has been discriminated against on account of age and who, at the time of the action complained of, was an employee or applicant for employment at least 40 years of age. A complaint may also be filed by an organization for the person with his or her consent.

[43 FR 60901, Dec. 29, 1978]

§ 1613.513 Effect on Administrative Processing.

The filing of a civil action by an employee or applicant involving a complaint filed under this subpart terminates processing of that complaint.

[52 FR 41930, Oct. 30, 1987]

§ 1613.514 Exclusions.

Sections 1613.281 and 1613.282 shall not apply to the processing of discrimination complaints on account of age. The reference to § 1613.281 in §§ 1613.215, 1613.217, 1613.220, and 1613.221 may not be included in agency regulations required by this subpart.

[42 FR 19147, Apr. 12, 1977. Redesignated at 43 FR 60901, Dec. 29, 1978]

§ 1613.521 Appeal to the Commission.

Except for the requirements in § 1613.234 that the decision of the Office of Review and Appeals contain a notice of the right to file a civil action in accordance with § 1613.282, §§ 1613.231 through 1613.240 of this part shall apply to this subpart.

[52 FR 41930, Oct. 30, 1987]

Subpart F—Class Complaints of Discrimination

AUTHORITY: 42 U.S.C. 2000e-16(b).

SOURCE; 42 FR 11808, Mar. 1, 1977, unless otherwise noted. Redesignated at 43 FR 60901, Dec. 29, 1978.

AGENCY REGULATIONS FOR PROCESSING CLASS COMPLAINTS OF DISCRIMINATION

§ 1613.601 Definitions.

(a) *A class* is a group of employees, former employees, or applicants for employment who, it is alleged, have been, are being, or may be, adversely affected by an agency personnel management policy or practice which discriminates against the group on the basis of their common race, color, religion, sex, national origin, age or handicapping condition.

(b) *A class complaint* is a written complaint of discrimination filed on behalf of a class by the agent of the class alleging that:

(1) The class is so numerous that a consolidated complaint of the members of the class is impractical;

(2) There are questions of fact common to the class;

(3) The claims of the agent of the class are typical of the claims of the class;

(4) The agent of the class, or his/her representative, if any, will fairly and [adequately] protect the interests of the class.

(c) *An agent of the class* is a class member who acts for the class during the processing of the class complaint.

(d) *Age* is an inclusive term which means the age of at least 40 years.

[42 FR 11808, Mar. 1, 1977, as amended at 42 FR 37530, July 22, 1977. Redesignated and amended at 43 FR 60901, Dec. 29, 1978; 52 FR 41930, Oct. 30, 1987]

§ 1613.602 Precomplaint processing.

(a) An employee or applicant who wishes to be an agent and who believes he/she has been discriminated against shall consult with an Equal Employment Opportunity Counselor within 30 calendar days of the matter giving rise to the allegation of individual discrimination, the effective date of a personnel action, or the date the aggrieved person knew or reasonably should have known of the discriminatory event or personnel action.

(b) The Counselor shall (1) advise the aggrieved person of the discrimination complaint procedures, of his/ her right to representation throughout the precomplaint and complaint processes, and of the right to anonymity only during the precomplaint process; (2) make whatever inquiry is believed necessary; (3) make an attempt at informal resolution through discussion with appropriate officials; (4) counsel the aggrieved person concerning the issues involved; (5) inform the Equal Employment Opportunity Officer and other appropriate officials when corrective action is believed necessary; (6) keep a record of all counseling activities; and (7) summarize actions and advice in writing both to the Equal Employment Opportunity Officer and the aggrieved person concerning the issues in the personnel management policy or practice.

(c) The Counselor shall conduct a final interview and terminate counseling with the aggrieved person not later than 30 calendar days after the date on which the allegation of discrimination was called to the attention of the Counselor. During the final interview, the Counselor shall inform the aggrieved person in writing that counseling is terminated, that he/she has the right to file a class complaint of discrimination with appropriate officials of the agency, and that he/she has a duty to assure that the agency is immediately informed if legal representation is obtained.

(d) The Counselor shall not attempt in any way to restrain the aggrieved person from filing a complaint nor to encourage the person to file a complaint.

(e) The Counselor shall not reveal the identity of an aggrieved person during the period of consultation, except, when authorized to do so by the aggrieved person.

(f) The agency shall ensure that full cooperation is provided by all employees to Counselors in the performance of their duties under this section. Counselors shall have routine access to personnel records of the agency without unwarranted invasion of privacy.

(g) Corrective action taken as a result of counseling shall be consistent with law, Executive order, and Civil Service regulations, rules, and instructions.

[37 FR 22717, Oct. 21, 1972. Redesignated at 43 FR 60901, Dec. 29, 1978, and amended at 45 FR 24133, Apr. 9. 1980; 52 FR 41930, Oct. 30, 1987]

§ 1613.603 Filing and presentation of a class complaint.

(a) The complaint must be [submitted] in writing by the agent or his/her representative and be signed by the agent.

(b) The complaint shall set forth specifically and in detail: (1) A description of the personnel management policy or practice giving rise to the complaint; and (2) a description of the resultant personnel action or matter adversely affecting the agent.

(c) The complaint must be filed not later than 15 calendar days after the agent's receipt of the notice of the right to file a complaint.

(d) The officials with whom complaints may be filed are the head of the agency, a designee of the head of the agency, and the Director of Equal Employment Opportunity.

(e) A complaint shall be deemed filed on the date it is postmarked, or, in the absence of a postmark, on the date it is received by an official with whom complaints may be filed.

(f) At all stages, including counseling, in the preparation and presentation of a complaint, or claim and appeal from a decision on a complaint, or claim, the agent or claimant shall have the right to be accompanied, represented, and advised by a representative of his/her own choosing, provided the choice of a representative does not involve a conflict of interest or conflict of position. The representative shall be designated in writing and the designation made a part of the class complaint file.

(g) If the agent is an employee in pay status, the agent shall have a reasonable amount of official time to prepare the complaint. If the agent is an employee of the agency and designates another employee of the agency as the agent's representative, the representative shall have a reasonable amount of official time, if otherwise on duty, to prepare the complaint. The agency is not obligated to change work schedules, incur overtime wages, or pay travel expenses to facilitate the choice of a specific representative or to allow the agent and representative to confer. However, the complainant and representative, if employed by the agency and otherwise in a pay status, shall be on official time, regardless of their tour of duty, when their presence is authorized or required by the agency or the Commission during the investigation, informal adjustment, or hearing on the complaint.

[42 FR 11808, Mar. 1, 1977. Redesignated at 43 FR 60901, Dec. 29, 1978, and amended at 52 FR 41930, Oct. 30, 1987]

§ 1613.604 Acceptance, Rejection or Cancellation.

(a) Within 10 calendar days of an agency's receipt of a complaint, the agency shall forward the complaint, along with a copy of the Counselor's report and any other information pertaining to timeliness or other relevant circumstances related to the complaint, to the Commission. The Commission shall assign the complaint to a Commission Administrative Judge except in instances where the Commission finds it more practical to delegate this responsibility to an Administrative Judge from another agency who is not an employee of the agency in which the complaint arose.

(b) The Administrative Judge may recommend that the agency reject the complaint, or a portion thereof, for any of the following reasons:

(1) It was not timely filed;

(2) It consists of an allegation identical to an allegation contained in a previous complaint filed on behalf of the same class which is pending in the agency or which has been resolved or decided by the agency;

(3) Failure to state a claim under this subpart;

(4) The agent failed to consult a Counselor in a timely manner;

(5) It lacks specificity and detail;

(6) It was not submitted in writing or was not signed by the agent;

(7) It does not meet the prerequisites of a class complaint under § 1613.601(b).

(c) If an allegation is not included in the Counselor's report, the Administrative Judge shall afford the agent 15 calendar days to explain whether the matter was discussed and if not, why he/she did not discuss the allegation with the Counselor. If the explanation is not satisfactory, the Administrative Judge may recommend that the agency reject the allegation. If the explanation is satisfactory, the Administrative Judge may refer the allegation to the agency for further counseling of the agent.

(d) If an allegation lacks specificity and detail, the Administrative Judge shall afford the agent 15 calendar days to provide specific and detailed information. The Administrative Judge may recommend that the agency reject the complaint if the agent fails to provide such information within the specified time period. If the information provided contains new allegations outside the scope of the complaint, the Administrative Judge must advise the agent how to proceed on an individual or class basis concerning these allegations.

(e) The Administrative Judge may recommend that the agency extend the time limits for filing a complaint and for consulting with a Counselor when the agent, or his/her representative, shows that he/she was not notified of the prescribed time limits and was not otherwise aware of them or that he/she was prevented by circumstances beyond his/her control from acting within the time limit.

(f) When appropriate the Administrative Judge may recommend that a class be divided into subclasses and that each subclass be treated as a class, and the provisions of this section then shall be construed and applied accordingly.

(g) The Administrative Judge may recommend that the agency cancel a complaint after it has been accepted because of failure of the agent to prosecute the complaint. This action may be taken only after the Administrative Judge has provided the agent a written request, including notice of proposed cancellation, that he/she provide certain information or otherwise proceed with the complaint, and the agent has failed to satisfy this request within 15 calendar days of receipt of the request.

(h) An agent must be informed by the Administrative Judge in a request under paragraph (c) or (d) of this section that his/her complaint may be rejected if the information is not provided.

(i) The head of the agency or designee shall terminate processing a class complaint of discrimination when the agent files a civil action in U.S. district court based on the same allegation of discrimination.

(j) The Administrative Judge's recommendation to the agency on whether to accept, reject, or cancel a complaint shall be transmitted in writing to the agency, the agent, and the agent's representative. The Administrative Judge's recommendation to accept, reject or cancel shall become the agency decision unless the agency rejects or modifies the decision within 30 calendar days of the receipt of the decision and complete complaint file. The agency shall notify the agent, the agent's representative, and the Administrative Judge of its decision to accept, reject, modify or cancel a complaint. Notice of a decision to reject or cancel shall inform the agent of the right to proceed with an individual complaint of discrimination, and to appeal the final agency decision on the matter to the Office of Review and Appeals and of his/her right to file a civil action.

[52 FR 41930, Oct. 30, 1987]

§ 1613.605 Notification and opting out.

(a) After acceptance of a class complaint, the agency, within 15 calendar days, shall use reasonable means, such as delivery, mailing, distribution, or posting, to notify all class members of the existence of the class complaint.

(b) A notice shall contain: (1) The name of the agency or organizational segment thereof, its location, and the date of acceptance of the complaint; (2) a description of the issues accepted as part of the class complaint; (3) an explanation that class members may remove themselves from the class by notifying the agency within 30 calendar days after issuance of the notice; and (4) an explanation of the binding nature of the final decision on or resolution of the complaint.

§ 1613.606 Avoidance of delay.

The complaint shall be processed promptly after it has been accepted. To this end, the parties shall proceed with the complaint so that the complaint is processed without undue delay.

[52 FR 41931, Oct. 30, 1987]

§ 1613.607 Freedom from restraint, interference, coercion, and reprisal.

(a) It is unlawful to restrain, interfere, coerce or discriminate against agents, complainants, their representatives, witnesses, Directors of Equal Employment Opportunity, Equal Employment Opportunity Officers, Investigators, Counselors and other agency officials with responsibility for processing discrimination complaints because of involvement with a discrimination charge during any stage in the presentation and processing of a complaint, including the counseling stage under § 1613.602, or because an individual testified, assisted or participated in any manner with an investigation, proceeding or hearing or because the individual opposed an unlawful employment practice under this part.

(b) A person identified in paragraph (a) of this section, if a Federal employee or applicant, may file a complaint of restraint, interference, coercion, or reprisal in connection with the presentation and processing of a complaint of discrimination. The complaint shall be filed and processed in accordance with provisions of subpart B.

[42 FR 11808, Mar. 1, 1977. Redesignated at 43 FR 60901, Dec. 29, 1978, and amended at 52 FR 41931, Oct. 30, 1987]

§ 1613.608 Obtaining evidence concerning the complaint.

(a) *General.* (1) Upon the acceptance of a complaint, the agency head or his/her designee shall designate an agency representative. The agency representative shall not be any individual designated under § 1613.204(c) of this part.

(2) In representing the agency, the agency representative shall consult with officials, if any, named or identified as responsible for the alleged discrimination, and other officials of the agency as necessary. In such consultation, the agency representative will be subject to the provisions of Civil Service regulations, rules, and instructions concerning privacy and access to individual personnel records and reports.

(b) *Development of evidence.* (1) The Administrative Judge shall notify the agent, or his/her representative and the agency representative that a period of not more than 60 calendar days will be allowed both parties to prepare their cases. This time period may be extended by the Administrative Judge upon the request of either party. Both parties are entitled to reasonable development of evidence on matters relevant to the issues raised in the complaint. Evidence may be developed through interrogatories, depositions, and requests for production of documents. It shall be grounds for objection to producing evidence that the information sought by either party is irrelevant, overburdensome, repetitious, or privileged.

(2) If mutual cooperation fails, either party may request the Administrative Judge to rule on a request to develop evidence. If the agent or agency in bad faith refuses or fails without adequate explanation to respond fully and in timely fashion to a request made or approved by the Administrative Judge for documents, records, comparative data, statistics, affidavits, or the attendance of witnesses, and the information is solely in the control of one party, such failure may, in appropriate circumstances, cause the Administrative Judge:

(i) To draw an adverse inference that the requested information would have reflected unfavorably on the party refusing to provide the requested information;

(ii) To consider the matters to which the requested information pertains to be established in favor of the opposing party;

(iii) To exclude other evidence offered by the party failing to produce the requested information;

(iv) To take such other actions as the Administrative Judge deems appropriate.

(3) During the time period for development of evidence, the Administrative Judge may, in his/her discretion, direct that an investigation of facts relevant to the complaint, or any portion thereof, be conducted by an Investigator trained and/or certified by the Commission.

(4) Both parties shall furnish the Administrative Judge all materials which they wish him/her to examine and such other material as he/she may request.

[42 FR 11808, Mar. 1, 1977. Redesignated at 43 FR 60901, Dec. 29, 1978, and amended at 52 FR 10086, Mar. 30, 1987; 52 FR 41931, Oct. 30, 1987]

§ 1613.609 Opportunities for resolution of the complaint.

(a) The Administrative Judge shall furnish the agent or his/her representative and the representative of the agency a copy of all materials obtained concerning the complaint and provide opportunity for the agent to discuss materials with the agency representative and attempt resolution of the complaint.

(b) At any time after acceptance of a complaint, the complaint may be resolved by agreement of the agency and the agent as long as the agreement is fair and reasonable.

(c) If resolution of the complaint is arrived at, the terms of the resolution shall be reduced to writing, and signed by the agent and the agency head or designee. A resolution may include a finding on the issue of discrimination, an award of attorney's fees or costs, and must include any corrective action agreed upon. Corrective action in the resolution must be consistent with law, Executive order, and Civil Service regulations, rules, and instructions. A copy of the resolution shall be provided to the agent.

(d) Notice of the resolution shall be given to all class members in the same manner as notification of the acceptance of the class complaint and shall state the terms of corrective action, if any, to be granted by the agency. A resolution shall bind all members of the class except in cases where the resolution benefits only the class agent or is otherwise alleged to be unfair or unreasonable, in which case any member of the class may petition the Director of Equal Employment Opportunity within 30 calendar days of the date of the notice of resolution to replace the class agent. Such a petition will be processed according to § 1613.604, and if it is found that the resolution did not comply with § 1613.609(b) and that the petitioner satisfied the requirements of § 1613.601(b), the Administrative Judge will recommend that the petitioner will replace the original class agent and act for the class during processing of the class complaint. Acceptance of a petition under this subsection vacates any agreement between the former class agent and the agency. An agency decision on such a petition shall inform the agent and the petitioner of the right to appeal the decision to the Office of Federal Operations.

(e) Any settlement agreement reached at any stage of the complaint process shall be binding on both parties. If the agent believes that the agency has failed to comply with the terms of a settlement agreement for reasons not attributable to acts or conduct of the agent, his/her representative or class members, the agent shall notify the Director of Equal Employment Opportunity, in writing, within 30 days of when the agent knew or should have known of the alleged noncompliance, or the alleged noncompliance with the settlement agreement. The agent may request that the terms of the settlement agreement be specifically implemented or, alternatively, that the complaint be reinstated for further processing from the point processing ceased under the terms of the settlement agreement. Upon receipt of the agent's written allegation of noncompliance with the settlement agreement, the agency shall have thirty (30) calendar days in which to resolve the matter and to respond to the agent, in writing, concerning the matter. If, after thirty (30) calendar days from the date of the agency's receipt of the agent's written allegations of noncompliance with the settlement agreement, the agency has not responded to the agent, in writing, or if the agent is not satisfied with the agency's attempt to resolve the matter, the agent may petition the Commission's Office of Federal Operations for a determination as to whether the agency has complied with the terms of the settlement agreement. The agent may file such an appeal 35 days after service of the allegations of noncompliance, but must file an appeal within 20 days of receipt of an agency's determination. Prior to rendering its determination, the Commission may request that the parties submit whatever additional information or documentation it may deem necessary and may direct that an investigation or hearing on the matter be conducted, as may be appropriate.

If the Commission determines that the agreement has not been complied with, it may order such compliance or it may order that the complaint be reinstated for further processing from the point processing ceased under the terms of the settlement agreement.

[52 FR 41932, Oct. 30, 1987, as amended at 56 FR 6983, Feb. 21, 1991]

§ 1613.610 Hearing.

On the expiration of the period allowed for preparation of the case, the Administrative Judge shall set a date for a hearing. The hearing shall be conducted in accordance with § 1613.218.

[52 FR 41932, Oct. 30, 1987]

§ 1613.611 Report of findings and recommendations.

(a) The Administrative Judge shall transmit to the agency head or his/her designee: (1) The record of the hearing; (2) his/her findings and analysis with regard to the complaint; and (3) his/her report of findings and recommended decision on the complaint, including corrective action pertaining to systemic relief for the class and any individual corrective action, where appropriate, with regard to the personnel action or matter which gave rise to the complaint.

(b) The Administrative Judge shall notify the agent of the date on which the report of findings and recommendations was forwarded to the agency head or his/her designee.

[42 FR 11808, Mar. 1, 1977. Redesignated at 43 FR 60901, Dec. 29, 1978, and amended at 52 FR 10086, Mar. 30, 1987]

§ 1613.612 Agency decision.

(a)(1) Within 60 calendar days of receipt of the report of findings and recommendations issued under § 1613.611, the agency head or his/her designee shall issue a decision to accept, reject, or modify the findings and recommendations of the Administrative Judge.

(2) The decision of the agency shall be in writing and shall be transmitted to the agent [or] his/her representative, along with a copy of the record of the hearing and a copy of the findings and recommendations of the Administrative Judge.

(3) When the agency's decision is to reject or modify the findings and recommendations of the Administrative Judge the decision shall contain the specific reasons in detail for the agency's action.

(b) If the agency has not issued a decision within 30 calendar days of its receipt of the Administrative Judge's report of findings and recommendations, the findings and recommendations shall become the final agency decision. The agency shall transmit the final agency decision and the record of the hearing to the agent or his/her representative within 5 calendar days of the expiration of the 30-day period.

(c) The decision of the agency shall require any remedial action authorized by law determined to be necessary or desirable to resolve the issue of discrimination and to promote the policy of equal opportunity, whether or not there is a finding of discrimination. When discrimination is found, the agency shall (1) advise the agent and his or her representative that any request for attorney's fees must be documented and submitted within 20 calendar days of receipt, (2) review the matter giving rise to the complaint to determine whether disciplinary action against alleged discriminatory officials is appropriate, and (3) record the basis for its decision to take, or not to take disciplinary action but this decision shall not be recorded in the complaint file.

(d) When the final agency decision provides for an award of attorney's fees and/or costs, the amount of these awards shall be determined under § 1613.271(c). When the agency determines not to award attorney's fees or costs, the agency shall set forth in its decision the specific reasons for denying the award.

(e) The agency shall inform the agent or his/her representative of the right to appeal the final agency decision to the Commission's Office of Federal Operations and his/her right to file a civil action in accordance with § 1613.641 of the regulations, and of the time limits applicable thereto.

(f) A final agency decision on a class complaint shall be binding on all members of the class and the agency.

[37 FR 22717, Oct. 21, 1972. Redesignated at 43 FR 60901, Dec. 29, 1978, and amended at 45 FR 24133, Apr. 9, 1980; 52 FR 10086, Mar. 30, 1987; 52 FR 41932, Oct. 30, 1987; 56 FR 6983, Feb. 21, 1991]

§ 1613.613 Notification of class members of decision.

Class members shall be notified by the agency, through the same media employed to give notice of the existence of the class complaint, of the agency decision and corrective action, if any. The notice, where appropriate, shall include information concerning the rights of class members to seek individual relief, and of the procedures to be followed. Notice shall be given by the agency within 10 calendar days of the transmittal of its decision to the agent.

§ 1613.614 Corrective action.

(a) When discrimination is found, an agency must eliminate or modify the personnel policy or practice out of which the complaint arose, and provide individual corrective action, including an award of attorney's fees and costs, to the agent in accordance with § 1613.271 of this part. Corrective action in all cases must be consistent with law, Executive order, and Civil Service regulations, rules and instructions.

(b) When discrimination is found and a class member believes that but for that discrimination he/she would have received employment or an employment benefit, the class member may file a written claim with the head of the agency or the Director of Equal Employment Opportunity of the agency within 30 calendar days of notification by the agency of the decision of the agency.

(c) The claim must include a specific, detailed showing that the claimant is a class member who was affected by a Personnel action or matter resulting from the discriminatory policy or practice within not more than 135 calendar days preceding the filing of the class complaint.

(d) The agency shall attempt to resolve the claim for relief within 60 calendar days after the date the claim was postmarked or, in the absence of a postmark, within 60 calendar days after the date it was received by an official with whom claims may be filed. If the agency and claimant do not agree that the claimant is a member of the class or upon the relief to which the claimant is entitled, the agency shall refer the claim, with recommendations concerning it, to the Administrative Judge.

(e) The Administrative Judge shall notify the claimant of the right to a hearing on the claim and shall allow the parties to the claim an opportunity to submit evidence and representations concerning the claim. If a hearing is requested, it shall be conducted in accordance with § 1613.218. If no hearing is requested, the Administrative Judge, in his/her discretion, may hold a hearing to obtain necessary evidence concerning the claim.

(f) The Administrative Judge shall issue a report of findings and recommendations on the claim which shall be treated the same as a report of findings and recommendations under §§ 1613.611 and 1613.612.

(g) If the Administrative Judge determines that the claimant is not a member of the class or that the claim was not timely filed he/she shall recommend rejection of the claim and give notice of his/her action to the agency, the claimant, and his/her representative. Such notice shall include advice as to the complainant's right to appeal to the Office of Federal Operations or to file a civil action in accordance with the provisions of this part.

[37 FR 22717, Oct. 21, 1972. Redesignated at 43 FR 60901, Dec. 29, 1978, and amended at 45 FR 24133, Apr. 9, 1980; 52 FR 10086, Mar. 30, 1987; 52 FR 41932, Oct. 30, 1987; 56 FR 6983, Feb. 21, 1991]

APPEAL TO THE COMMISSION

§ 1613.631 Appeal to the Office of Federal Operations.

(a) An agent may appeal to the Office of Federal Operations the decision of the head of the agency or designee:

(1) To reject or cancel a complaint, or a portion thereof, for reasons covered by § 1613.604;

(2) Under the circumstances set forth in § 1613.609 (d) or (e);

(3) On the merits of the complaint;

(4) On the issue of attorney's fees and costs and corrective action; or

(5) The failure of an agency to implement its final agency decision.

(b) A claimant may appeal to the Office of Federal Operations from a decision of the head of the agency or designee:

(1) To cancel or reject a claim for individual relief in accordance with § 1613.614 (f) and (g); and

(2) On the merits of the claim for individual relief including attorney's fees or costs.

(c) An appeal may be filed at any time after receipt of the agency's final decision, but not later than 20 calendar days after receipt of that decision except when the appellant shows that neither the appellant nor the appellant's representative was notified of the prescribed time limit and was not otherwise aware of it, or that the appellant or the appellant's representative was prevented by circumstances beyond the appellant's or representative's control from appealing within the prescribed time limit.

(d) An appeal shall be deemed timely if it is delivered in person or post-marked before the expiration of the filing period, or if, in the absence of a legible postmark, it is received by the Commission by mail within five days of the expiration of the filing period. The Office of Federal Operations' review will be made upon the existing record to determine if the agency decision is in accord with applicable law, Executive order, or Civil Service regulations, rules, and instructions and is supported by substantial evidence.

[52 FR 41932, Oct. 30, 1987, as amended at 56 FR 6983, Feb. 21, 1991]

§ 1613.632 Reopening and reconsideration by the Commissioners.

The Commissioners may reopen and reconsider any previous decision of a Commission office on their own motion or at the request of either party in accordance with provisions of § 1613.235.

[52 FR 41932, Oct. 30, 1987]

CIVIL ACTIONS

§ 1613.641 Statutory right.

(a) An agent who has filed a complaint or a claimant who has filed a claim for relief based on race, color, religion, sex, and/or national origin discrimination is authorized to file a civil action in an appropriate U.S. district court:

(1) Within 30 calendar days of his/her receipt of notice of final action taken by his/her agency on a complaint or claim;

(2) After 180 calendar days from the date he/she filed a complaint or claim with his/her agency if there has been no decision on the complaint or claim;

(3) Within 30 calendar days of his/her receipt of the decision of the Office of Federal Operations on his/her appeal; or

(4) After 180 calendar days from the date he/she filed an appeal with the Office of Federal Operations, if there has been no Office of Federal Operations decision.

For purposes of this part, the decision of an agency shall be final only when the agency makes a determination on all of the issues in the complaint, including whether or not to award attorney's fees and costs. If a determination to award attorneys fees is made the decision will not be final until the procedure is followed for determining the amount of the award as set forth in § 1613.271(c).

(b) An agent who filed a complaint or a claimant who has filed for relief based on age discrimination, is authorized to file a civil action in an appropriate U.S. district court.

[37 FR 22717, Oct. 21, 1972. Redesignated at 43 FR 60901, Dec. 29, 1978, and amended at 45 FR 24133, Apr. 9, 1980; 56 FR 6983, Feb. 21, 1991]

§ 1613.642 Notice of right.

When the agent alleges that the agency discriminated against a class on the basis of race, color, religion, sex, national origin, and/or age, or a claimant files for relief, the agency or the Commission shall notify him/her of his/her right to file a civil action in any final action on a complaint, or claim, under §§ 1613.604, 1613.612, 1613.614, or 1613.631.

§ 1613.643 Effect on administrative processing.

The filing of a civil action by an agent involving a complaint filed under this subpart terminates processing of that complaint. The filing of a civil action by a claimant involving a claim filed under this subpart, terminates processing of that claim.

[52 FR 41933, Oct. 30. 1987]

Subpart G—Prohibition Against Discrimination Because of a Physical or Mental Handicap

Authority: 5 U.S.C. 7153; § 5.1 Of the Civil Service Rules; 29 U.S.C. 791.

Source: 43 FR 12295, Mar. 24, 1978, unless otherwise noted. Redesignated at 43 FR 60901, Dec. 29, 1978.

GENERAL PROVISIONS

§ 1613.701 Purpose and applicability.

(a) *Purpose.* This subpart sets forth the policy under which an agency shall establish a continuing program to assure nondiscrimination on account of physical or mental handicap and the regulations under which an agency will process complaints of discrimination based on a physical or mental handicap.

(b) *Applicability.* (1) This subpart applies to executive agencies as defined in section 105 of title 5 of the United States Code and to those positions in the legislative and judicial branches of the Federal Government and the government of the District of Columbia which are in the competitive service.

(2) This subpart applies to the U.S. Postal Service and Postal Rate Commission.

(3) This subpart applies only to applicants and employees who have a handicap as defined in § 1613.702(a).

§ 1613.702 Definitions.

(a) *Handicapped person* is defined for this subpart as one who: (1) Has a physical or mental impairment which substantially limits one or more of such person's major life activities, (2) has a record of such an impairment, or (3) is regarded as having such an impairment.

(b) *Physical or mental impairment* means (1) any physiological disorder or condition, cosmetic disfigurement, or anatomical loss affecting one or more of the following body systems: Neurological; musculoskeletal; special sense organs; cardiovascular; reproductive; digestive; genito-urinary; hemic and lymphatic; skin; and endocrine; or (2) any mental or psychological disorder, such as mental retardation, organic brain syndrome, emotional or mental illness, and specific learning disabilities.

(c) *Major life activities* means functions, such as caring for one's self, performing manual tasks, walking, seeing, hearing, speaking, breathing, learning, and working.

(d) *Has a record of such an impairment* means has a history of, or has been classified (or misclassified) as having a mental or physical impairment that substantially limits one or more major life activities.

(e) *Is regarded as having such an impairment* means (1) has a physical or mental impairment that does not substantially limit major life activities but is treated by an employer as constituting such a limitation; (2) has a physical or mental impairment that substantially limits major life activities only as a result of the attitude of an employer toward such impairment; (3) or has none of the impairments defined in paragraph (b) of this section but is treated by an employer as having such an impairment.

(f) *Qualified handicapped person* means with respect to employment, a handicapped person who, with or without reasonable accommodation, can perform the essential functions of the position in question without endangering the health and safety of the individual or others and who, depending upon the type of appointing authority being used:

(1) Meets the experience and/or education requirements (which may include passing a written test) of the position in question, or

(2) Meets the criteria for appointment under one of the special appointing authorities for handicapped persons.

§ 1613.703 General policy.

Agencies shall give full consideration to the hiring, placement, and advancement of qualified mentally and physically handicapped persons. The Federal Government shall become a model employer of handicapped individuals. An agency shall not discriminate against a qualified physically or mentally handicapped person.

§ 1613.704 Reasonable accommodation.

(a) An agency shall make reasonable accommodation to the known physical or mental limitations of a qualified handicapped applicant or employee unless the agency can demonstrate that the accommodation would impose an undue hardship on the operation of its program.

(b) Reasonable accommodation may include, but shall not be limited to: (1) Making facilities readily accessible to and usable by handicapped persons, and (2) job restructuring, part-time or modified work schedules, acquisition or modification of equipment or devices, appropriate adjustment or modification of examinations, the provision of readers and interpreters, and other similar actions.

(c) In determining pursuant to paragraph (a) of this section whether an accommodation would impose an undue hardship on the operation of the agency in question, factors to be considered include: (1) The overall size of the agency's program with respect to the number of employees, number and type of facilities and size of budget; (2) the type of agency operation, including the composition and structure of the agency's work force; and (3) the nature and the cost of the accommodation.

§ 1613.705 Employment criteria.

(a) An agency may not make use of any employment test or other selection criterion that screens out or tends to screen out qualified handicapped persons or any class of handicapped persons unless: (1) The test score or other selection criterion, as used by the agency, is shown to be job-related for the position in question, and (2) alternative job-related tests or criteria that do not screen out or tend to screen out as many handicapped persons are not shown by the Civil Service Commission's Director of Personnel Research and Development Center to be available.

(b) An agency shall select and administer tests concerning employment so as to insure that, when administered to an applicant or employee who has a handicap that impairs sensory, manual, or speaking skills, the test results accurately reflect the applicant's or employee's ability to perform the position or type of positions in question rather than reflecting the applicant's or employee's impaired sensory, manual, or speaking skills (except where those skills are the factors that the test purports to measure).

§ 1613.706 Preemployment inquiries.

(a) Except as provided in paragraphs (b) and (c) of this section, an agency may not conduct a preemployment medical examination and may not make preemployment inquiry of an applicant as to whether the applicant is a handicapped person or as to the nature or severity of a handicap. An agency may, however, make preemployment inquiry into an applicant's ability to meet the medical qualification requirements, with or without reasonable accommodation, of the position in question, i.e., the minimum abilities necessary for safe and efficient performance of the duties of the position in question. The Civil Service Commission may also make an inquiry as to the nature and extent of a handicap for the purpose of special testing.

(b) Nothing in this section shall prohibit an agency from conditioning an offer of employment on the results of a medical examination conducted prior to the employee's entrance on duty, *Provided,* That: (1) All entering employees are subjected to such an examination regardless of handicap or when the preemployment medical questionnaire used for positions which do not routinely require medical examination indicates a condition for which further examination is required because of the job-related nature of the condition, and (2) the results of such an examination are used only in accordance with the requirements of this part. Nothing in this section shall be construed to prohibit the gathering of preemployment medical information for the purposes of special appointing authorities for handicapped persons.

(c) To enable and evaluate affirmative action to hire, place, or advance handicapped individuals, the agency may invite applicants for employment to indicate whether and to what extent they are handicapped, if: (1) The agency states clearly on any written questionnaire used for this purpose or makes clear orally, if no written questionnaire is used, that the information requested is intended for use solely in conjunction with affirmative action and (2) the agency states clearly that the information is being requested on a voluntary basis, that refusal to provide it will not subject the applicant or employee to any adverse treatment, and that it will be used only in accordance with this part.

(d) Information obtained in accordance with this section as to the medical condition or history of the applicant shall be kept confidential except that: (1) Managers, selecting officials, and others involved in the selection process or responsible for affirmative action may be informed that the applicant is a handicapped individual eligible for affirmative action; (2) supervisors and managers may be informed regarding necessary accommodations; (3) first aid and safety personnel may be informed, where appropriate, if the condition might require emergency treatment: (4) government officials investigating compliance with laws, regulations, and instructions relevant to equal employment opportunity and affirmative action for handicapped individuals shall be provided information upon request; and (5) statistics generated from information obtained may be used to manage, evaluate, and report on equal employment opportunity and affirmative action programs.

[43 FR 12295, Mar. 24, 1978. Redesignated at 43 FR 60901, Dec. 29, 1978, and amended at 46 FR 11285, Feb. 6, 1981]

§ 1613.707 Physical access to buildings.

(a) An agency shall not discriminate against qualified handicapped applicants or employees due to the inaccessibility of its facility.

(b) For the purpose of this subpart, a facility shall be deemed accessible if it is in compliance with the Architectural Barriers Act of 1968.

AGENCY REGULATIONS FOR PROCESSING COMPLAINTS OF
DISCRIMINATION

§ 1613.708 General.

An agency shall provide regulations governing the acceptance and processing of complaints of discrimination based on a physical or mental handicap which comply with the principles and requirements in §§ 1613.213 through 1613.283 and §§ 1613.601 through 1613.643. Nothing in the foregoing shall be construed to postpone the effective date of this rule.

[46 FR 51384, Oct. 20, 1981]

§ 1613.709 Coverage.

(a) An agency shall provide in its regulations for the acceptance of a complaint from any aggrieved employee or applicant for employment who believes that he or she has been discriminated against because of a handicap as defined in § 1613.702.

(b) An agency must process complaints of discrimination based on acts or actions that occurred 1 year prior to the effective date of these regulations *Provided:* (1) The complaint of discrimination was brought to the attention of the agency within 30 calendar days of the alleged discriminatory act, or, if a personnel action, within 30 calendar days of its effective date, (2) the complaint of discrimination was not adjudicated under some other grievance or appeals procedure, and (3) the complaint of discrimination is filed within 180 calendar days of the effective date of these regulations. Complaints of discrimination based on alleged discriminatory acts or personnel actions that occurred on or after the effective date of these regulations are subject to the time restraints set forth in § 1613.214(a).

(c) Notwithstanding the provision of subsection (b), a complainant may request an agency to process allegations of handicap discrimination which had been filed as a discrimination complaint or as a grievance, and were pending with the agency, the Civil Service Commission or in a Federal Court on April 10, 1978. Such requests for processing of allegations of handicap discrimination must be brought to the attention of the agency EEO counselor not later than 180 days from the publication of this subsection in final form in the FEDERAL REGISTER.

[43 FR 12295, Mar. 24, 1978. Redesignated at 43 FR 60901, Dec. 29, 1978, and amended at 45 FR 41634, June 20, 1980]

Subpart H—Regulations for Processing Appealable Actions, Alleging Prohibited Discrimination, Pending on or Before January 10, 1979

Authority: 42 U.S.C. 2000e-16; 29 U.S.C. 633a; 29 U.S.C. 791; Reorganization Plan No. 1 of 1978.

Source: 44 FR 50541, Aug. 28, 1979, unless otherwise noted.

§ 1613.801 Scope.

This subpart establishes regulations for the processing of an allegation that an action otherwise appealable to the Merit Systems Protection Board (the Board) was based in whole or in part on discrimination because of race, color, religion, sex, national origin, age, or handicap. This subpart applies only to administrative procedures pending before January 11, 1979, to which Section 205 of the Civil Service Reform Act of 1978, 5 U.S.C. 7702, is inapplicable.

§ 1613.802 Definitions.

(a) As used in this section, the term *prohibited discrimination* means discrimination prohibited by section 717 of the Civil Rights Act of 1964, as amended (42 U.S.C. 2000e-16); section 501 of the Rehabilitation Act of 1973, as amended (29 U.S.C. 791); and sections 12 and 15 of the Age Discrimination in Employment Act of 1967, as amended (29 U.S.C. 631 and 633a).

(b) As used in this section, the term *initial decision* means a decision on an appeal, rendered by a presiding official of the Board pursuant to 29 CFR part 1613 or 5 CFR part 772 (as in effect prior to January 11, 1979), in which issues of prohibited discrimination have been raised.

(c) As used in this section, the term *preliminary decision* means (1) an initial decision within the meaning of § 1613.802(b), which has not been reopened by a Board member or as to which no petition to reopen was filed by a party within 35 days after issuance of the decision; or (2) a decision by the Board itself pursuant to 29 CFR part 1613 or 5 CFR part 772 (as in effect prior to January 11, 1979), in which issues of prohibited discrimination are addressed, or a decision by the Board denying all petitions to reopen.

§ 1613.803 Election.

An appellant who alleges that an action otherwise appealable to the Board was based in whole or in part on prohibited discrimination shall elect to proceed under 29 CFR part 1613 (43 FR 60901, formerly 5 CFR part 713) or under 5 CFR part 772 (as in effect prior to January 11, 1979). This section is applicable only to persons who had not previously made an election under regulations of the former Civil Service Commission.

§ 1613.804 Election of Part 1613.

(a) When an appellant elects or has elected to proceed under 29 CFR part 1613 (43 FR 60901, formerly 5 CFR part 713) the provisions of part 1613 are applicable to that proceeding.

(b) The Commission hereby delegates to the Merit Systems Protection Board the authority to make initial and preliminary decisions on issues of prohibited discrimination in appeals from final agency decisions under 29 CFR part 1613 (43 FR 60901, formerly 5 CFR part 713).

§ 1613.805 Election of part 772.

(a) When a complainant elects or has elected to proceed under 5 CFR part 772, the allegations of discrimination shall be referred to the EEO Officer of the agency for investigation in accordance with 29 CFR 1613.216 (43 FR 60901, formerly 5 CFR 713.216).

(b) The Commission hereby delegates to the Merit Systems Protection Board the authority to make initial and preliminary decisions on issues of prohibited discrimination in appeals from final agency decisions under 5 CFR part 772.

§ 1613.806 Petition to EEOC; finality of decisions.

(a) A petition to review the preliminary decision of the Board shall be filed in writing with the Office of Federal Operations, Equal Employment Opportunity Commission, 1801 L Street, NW., Washington, DC 20507 (1) within 35 days after the initial decision of the Board becomes a preliminary decision (as contemplated in § 1613.802(c)(1)) or (2) within 35 days after the issuance of a preliminary decision by the Board.

(b) A decision of the EEOC on a petition to review the preliminary decision of the Board shall be final when issued.

(c) If a petition to review is not timely filed with the EEOC, the preliminary decision of the Board shall become final on all issues on the day after the expiration of the 35-day period for filing with EEOC, unless the EEOC chooses to exercise its discretion under the standards of 29 CFR 1613.233(b) and accept the late petition.

[44 FR 50541, Aug. 28, 1979, as amended at 51 FR 22519, June 20, 1986; 56 FR 6983, Feb. 21, 1991; 57 FR 11431, Apr. 3, 1992]

APPENDIX A TO PART 1613—POLICY STATEMENT ON REMEDIES AND RELIEF FOR INDIVIDUAL CASES OF UNLAWFUL DISCRIMINATION

On September 11, 1984, the Equal Employment Opportunity Commission announced its intent to achieve certainty and predictability of enforcement in those situations where the agency has reason to believe that a law it enforces has been violated. In keeping with this goal, the Commission recognizes that the basic effectiveness of the agency's law enforcement program is dependent upon securing prompt, comprehensive and complete relief for all individuals directly affected by violations of the statutes which the agency enforces. The Commission also recognizes that, in appropriate circumstances, remedial measures need to be designed to prevent the recurrence of similar unlawful employment practices. Predictable enforcement and full, corrective, remedial and preventive relief are the principal components of the method with which the Commission intends to pursue this agency's mission of eradicating discrimination in the workplace. Henceforth, in negotiating settlements, in drafting prayers for relief in litigation, pleadings or in issuing Commission Decisions or Orders, obtaining full remedial, corrective and preventive relief is the standard by which the agency is to be guided.

The Commission believes that a full remedy must be sought in each case where a District Director concludes the case has merit and has, or is prepared to, issue a letter of violation or a letter finding reasonable cause to believe that one of the statutes the agency enforces has been violated.

The remedy must be fashioned from the wide range of remedial measures available to this law enforcement agency which has broad authority under the statutes it enforces to seek appropriate forms of legal and equitable relief. The remedy must also be tailored, where possible, to cure the specific situation which gave rise to the violation of the statute involved.

Accordingly, all remedies and relief sought in court, agreed upon in conciliation, or ordered in Federal sector decisions should contain the following elements in appropriate circumstances:

(1) A requirement that all employees of respondent in the affected facility be notified of their right to be free of unlawful discrimination and be assured that the particular type of discrimination found or conciliated will not recur;

(2) A requirement that corrective, curative or preventive action be taken, or measures adopted, to ensure that similar found or conciliated violations of the law will not recur;

(3) A requirement that each identified victim of discrimination be unconditionally offered placement in the position the person would have occupied but for the discrimination suffered by that person;

(4) A requirement that each identified victim of discrimination be made whole for any loss of earnings the person may have suffered as a result of the discrimination; and

(5) A requirement that the respondent cease from engaging in the specific unlawful employment practice found or conciliated in the case.

The components of these remedial elements are as follows:

(1) *Notice Requirement.*

All respondents should be required to sign and conspicuously post, for a period of time, a notice to all employees in the affected facility (or to union members if respondent is a labor organization), prepared by the agency on E.E.O.C. forms, specifically advising respondent's employees or members of the following:

(a) That the notice is being posted as part of the remedy agreed to pursuant to a conciliation agreement with the agency or pursuant to an order of a particular Federal court or pursuant to a decision and order in a Federal sector case.

(b) That Federal law requires that there be no discrimination against any employee or applicant for employment because of the employee's race, color, religion, sex, national origin or age (between 40 and 70) with respect to hiring, firing, compensation, or other terms, conditions or privileges of employment (Federal sector notices will include handicap as an unlawful basis of discrimination).

(c) That respondent supports and will comply with such Federal law in all respects and will not take any action against employees because they have exercised their rights under the law.

(d) That respondent will not engage in the specific unlawful conduct which the District Director believes has occurred or is conciliating, or which the Commission or a court has found to have occurred.

(e) That respondent will, or has, taken the remedial action required by the conciliation agreement or the order of the Commission or Court.

(2) *Corrective, Curative or Preventive Provisions.*

In appropriate circumstances, a remedy must provide that the respondent take corrective, curative or preventive action designed to ensure that similar violations of the law will not recur. Similarly, corrective, curative or preventive measures may also be adopted in those situations where those measures are likely to prevent future similar violations.

Thus, where a policy or practice is discriminatory, the policy or practice must be changed. Similarly, if a particular supervisor or other agent of the respondent is identified as knowingly or intentionally being responsible for the discrimination that occurred, the respondent must be required to take corrective action so that the discriminatee or similarly situated employees not be subjected to similar discriminatory conduct. This corrective action may be accomplished, for example, by insulating employees from that individual for a period of time, or by requiring the respondent to discipline or remove the offending individual from personnel authority, or by requiring the respondent to educate the offender and other supervisors so that they may overcome their unlawful prejudices.

These and any other appropriate [measures], or any combination thereof, designed to meet this goal should be considered when negotiating settlements or drafting prayers for relief. This type of relief is not to be designed for punitive purposes. Rather, this relief is to be tailored to cure or correct the particular source of the identified discrimination and to minimize the chance of its recurrence.

In addition, the respondent must be required to take all other appropriate steps to eradicate the discrimination and its effects, such as the expunging of adverse materials relating to the unlawful employment practice from the discriminatee's personnel files.

(3) *Nondiscriminatory Placement.*

Each identified victim of discrimination is entitled to an immediate and unconditional offer of placement in the respondent's workforce, to the position the discriminatee would have occupied absent discrimination, or to a substantially equivalent position, even if the placement of the discriminatee results in the displacement of another of respondent's employees ("Nondiscriminatory Placement"). The Nondiscriminatory Placement may take place by initial employment, reinstatement, promotion, transfer or reassignment and must occur without any prejudice to, or loss of, any employment-related rights or privileges the discriminatee would have otherwise acquired had the discrimination not occurred.

If a Nondiscriminatory Placement position that the discriminatee should occupy no longer exists, then employment for which the discriminatee is qualified must be offered to the discriminatee in other areas of the respondent's operation. Finally, if none of the foregoing positions exist in which the discriminatee may be placed, then the respondent must make whole the discriminatee until a Nondiscriminatory Placement can be accomplished.

It is essential that victims of discrimination not suffer further and that respondents not gain by their misconduct. Accordingly, the contention by a respondent that a discriminatee is no longer suitable for Nondiscriminatory Placement due to a loss of skills, a change in job content or some other reason is not an acceptable excuse for a respondent's failure to accomplish a Nondiscriminatory Placement of a discriminatee.

The burden is upon the respondent to demonstrate that the inability of the discriminatee to accept Nondiscriminatory Placement unrelated to the respondent's discrimination such that the victim, rather than the respondent, should bear the loss. Similarly, the burden is also on the respondent to demonstrate a contention that postdiscrimination conduct by a discriminatee renders the discriminatee unworthy of Nondiscriminatory Placement.

In certain circumstances, the Nondiscriminatory Placement of a victim of discrimination may require the job placement of another of the respondent's employees. If displacement of an incumbent employee in order to accomplish Nondiscriminatory Placement on behalf of a discriminatee is clearly inappropriate in a particular setting or is unavailable as a remedy in a particular jurisdiction, then the respondent must make whole the discriminatee until a Nondiscriminatory Placement can be accomplished.

(4) *Backpay.*

Each identified victim of discrimination is entitled to be made whole for any loss of earnings the discriminatee may have suffered by reason of the discrimination. Each individual discriminatee must receive a sum of money equal to what would have been earned by the discriminatee in the employment lost through discrimination ("Gross Backpay") less what was actually earned from other employment during the period, after normal expenses incurred in seeking and holding the interim employment have been deducted ("Net Interim Earnings"). The difference between Gross Backpay and Net Interim Earnings is Net Backpay Due. Interest should be computed on all Net Backpay Due. Net Backpay accrues from the date of discrimination, except where the statutes limit the recovery, until the discrimination against the individual has been remedied.

Gross Backpay includes all forms of compensation such as wages, bonuses, vacation pay, and all other elements of reimbursement and fringe benefits such as pension and health insurance. Gross Backpay must also reflect fluctuations in working time, overtime rates, changing rates of pay, transfers, promotions, and other perquisites of employment that the discriminatee would have enjoyed but for the discrimination. In appropriate circumstances under the Equal Pay Act and the Age Discrimination in Employment Act liquidated damages based on backpay will also be available.

(5) *Cessation Provisions.*

All respondents must agree or be ordered to cease from engaging in the specific unlawful employment practices involved in the case. For example, a respondent should agree to cease discriminating on the unlawful basis and in the specific manner alleged or a respondent might be required to cease giving effect to certain specific discriminatory policies, practices or rules. In circumstances where a particular respondent has committed or has conciliated several unlawful employment practices, consideration must be given to including broad cessation language in an agreement or order which is designed to order the cessation of any further unlawful employment practices.

The Commission does not believe that the statutory requirement of conciliation requires the agency to abdicate its principal law enforcement responsibility. Thus, conciliation should not result in inadequate remedies. The possibility of pre-litigation conciliation does not constitute cause for unwarranted or undeserved concessions by a law enforcement agency when one of the laws it enforces has been violated. Rather, the concept of settlement constitutes recognition of the fact that there may be reasonable differences as to a suitable remedy between the maximum which may be reasonably demanded by the agency and the minimum which in good faith may be fairly argued for the respondent. Within this scope, conciliation must be actively pursued by the agency. In this regard, in all cases in which the District Director believes that one of the statutes the agency enforces has been violated or in which litigation has been authorized, full remedies containing the appropriate elements as set forth in this memorandum should be sought. In conciliation efforts, reasonable compromises or counterproposals to the full range of remedies described in this policy may be considered if those compromises or counterproposals address fully the remedial concepts described in this policy. Conciliation should be pursued with the goal of obtaining substantially complete relief through the conciliation process. Any divergence from this goal must be justified by the relevant facts and the law.

[52 FR 41933, Oct. 30, 1987]

Cases Interpreting EEOC Rehabilitation Act
Regulations

Boyd v. U.S. Postal Service, 752 F.2d 410 (9th Cir.1985). A postal employee suffering from post traumatic stress disorder did not bring his grievance to an EEO counselor, thereby failing to exhaust his administrative remedies under 29 CFR Part **1613.214(a)(i)**.

Bruegging v. Burke, 696 F.Supp. 674 (D.D.C.1987). A job applicant failed to show that he was denied a promotion because of his disability where he could not show an ability to perform essential job tasks. **29 CFR Part 1613.702(f)**.

Daubert v. U.S. Postal Service, 732 F.2d 1367 (10th Cir.1984). A postal service employee failed to disclose the full extent of a back injury which caused her to be reassigned to light duty within a few months of her hire date. Applying EEOC regulations at **29 CFR Part 1613.702(f)** and **1613.703**, the U.S. Court of Appeals, Tenth Circuit, affirmed the district court's decision that the employee failed to show discrimination on the basis of handicap, because she was not "otherwise qualified" for the job. The employee was unable to work for long periods of time without severe back pain.

Dexler v. Tisch, 660 F.Supp. 1418 (D.Conn.1987). An achondroplastic dwarf failed to show that the postal service could reasonably accommodate him because his short stature made him unable to perform many essential tasks. Reasonable accommodation is not defined in EEOC regulations but the regulation gives factors to guide courts. A reasonable accommodation is one that would not interfere unduly with postal service operations. **29 CFR Part 1613.704 (b)**.

Fields v. Lyng, 705 F.Supp.1134 (D.C.Md.1988). A labor relations specialist formerly employed by a federal agency was not an otherwise qualified handicapped individual and the agency had reasonably accommodated his behavior disorder. Continued employment would have imposed an undue hardship upon the employer under **29 CFR Part 1613.704 (a)**.

Forrisi v. U.S. Bowen, 794 F.2d 931 (4th Cir.1986). The U.S. Court of Appeals, Fourth Circuit, affirmed a district court decision finding that there had been no employment discrimination by the U.S. Department of Health and Human Services under § 501 when the department dismissed an acrophobic employee whose fear of heights made him unable to perform the essential job function of climbing ladders. The employee failed to alllege that his condition substantially limited him in the performance of major life activities under **29 CFR Part 1613.702(c)**, and failed to show that he was impaired under **29 CFR Part 1613.702(e)**.

Frye v. Aspin, 997 F.2d 526 (8th Cir.1993). The court dismissed a lawsuit filed by a disabled veteran employed by the Army and Air Force Exchange Service who was placed on leave without pay because of inability to perform job duties such as lifting. By rejecting a settlement offer (which included job reinstatement) under **29 CFR Part 1613.215(a)(7)**, he disqualified himself from Rehabilitation Act relief.

Fuller v. Frank, 916 F.2d 558 (9th Cir.1990). The postal service reasonably accommodated an alcoholic employee by providing numerous treatment opportunities for alcoholism, which is a covered handicap under **29 CFR Part 1613.704(a)**.

Guillot v. Garrett, 970 F.2d 1320 (4th Cir.1992). Federal agency (Navy) which denied security clearance to civilian computer specialist was not required by § 501 regulations to reassign the employee to accommodate him because he was not a qualified handicapped individual under the Rehabilitation Act.

Jasany v. U.S. Postal Service, 755 F.2d 1244 (6th Cir.1985). A postal worker's inability to perform a particular essential job task because of strabismus (crossed eyes) did not make him a handicapped individual under the Rehabilitation Act. The U.S. Court of Appeals, Sixth Circuit, held that the applicant was not a person who "has a physical or mental impairment which *substantially* limits one or more of such person's major life activities" under **29 CFR Part 1613.702(c)**, and affirmed the district court's decision in favor of the employer. The employer was not required to accommodate the applicant by eliminating an essential function of the job under **29 CFR Part 1613.702(f)**.

Langon v. U.S. Dept. of Health and Human Services, 749 F.Supp. 1 (D.D.C.1990). A federal employee with multiple sclerosis received poor work evaluations after she requested permission to work at home to avoid commuting to work. She claimed that the commute caused her great stress. The agency terminated her employment, a result which was affirmed by a federal district court, which ruled that she was not an **otherwise qualified** handicapped individual.

Lemere v. Burnley, 683 F.Supp. 275 (D.D.C.1988). An employee lost her status as a "qualified handicapped individual" under Rehabilitation Act regulations published by the EEOC at **29 CFR Part 1613.704(a)** because her unscheduled absences undermined her ability to perform the essential functions of her position.

McGuiness v. U.S. Postal Service, 744 F.2d 1318 (7th Cir.1984). A postal service employee's sole remedy was under the Rehabilitation Act § 505 (allowing a § 501 claim) and therefore no extension of the 30-day statute of limitation of **29 CFR Part 1613.214(a)(4)** could be had by filing a § 504 complaint.

Taylor v. U.S. Postal Service, 946 F.2d 1214 (6th Cir.1991). A federal district court held that a postal service applicant's inability to perform a single task because of his bad back did not establish a handicap under the Rehabilitation Act. The U.S. Court of Appeals, Sixth Circuit, held that the applicant was "regarded as handicapped" by the employer under **29 CFR Part 1613.702(b)(1)** and remanded the case for a determination of what reasonable accommodation might be possible by the employer. [Reversing 771 F.Supp. 882 (S.D.Ohio 1990]

Treadwell v. Alexander, 707 F.2d 473 (11th Cir.1983). The Army Corps of Engineers did not discriminate against an applicant for a park technician position because the physical criteria for employment were job-related, and reasonable accommodation of the applicant was impossible. Rehabilitation Act regulations at **29 CFR Part 1613.704** impose the ultimate burden of proof upon the employer to show inability to accommodate the alleged handicap, after the employee or applicant carries the initial burden of showing that the handicap can be accommodated.

Walders v. Garrett, 765 F.Supp. 303 (E.D.Va.1991). A qualified handicapped person under **29 CFR Part 1613.702(f)** is "one who is able to meet all of a program's requirements in spite of his handicaps."

Part 84 [Part 104] Regulations—Nondiscrimination on the Basis of Handicap in Programs and Activities Receiving or Benefiting from Federal Financial Assistance (45 CFR Part 84) (34 CFR Part 104)

The following regulations, found at both 45 CFR Part 84 and 34 CFR Part 104, were first published in 1978 by the U.S. Department of Health, Education and Welfare (HEW) as the original implementing regulations for § 504 of the Rehabilitation Act of 1973 (29 U.S.C. § 794). The 1978 amendment to the Act designated the HEW Secretary as the coordinating official to implement regulations under § 504 for all federal departments and agencies which furnished financial assistance in any program or activity. Hence, there is overlap among the original HEW regulations and other federal agency regulations.

In 1980, the Department of Education was established as a separate agency with a cabinet-level head, and the HEW became the Department of Health and Human Services (HHS). The regulations have remained essentially the same since then. Accordingly, to prevent duplication in this book, U.S. Department of Education regulatory subparts have been designated here within the HHS's regulations, with Department of Education CFR part sections and textual discrepancies designated by brackets. If no bracket appears (as in 45 CFR Part 84.55 and the notices which follow that regulation) there is no corresponding Department of Education Regulation. Readers should also note that 45 CFR Part 84.55 was declared invalid by the U.S. Supreme Court in *Bowen v. American Hospital Ass'n*, 476 U.S. 610, 106 S.Ct. 2101, 90 L.Ed.2d 584 (1986). See the notices which follow 45 CFR Part 84.55.

* * *

Title 45—Public Welfare
[Title 34—Education]

SUBTITLE A—DEPARTMENT OF HEALTH AND HUMAN SERVICES
[SUBTITLE A—DEPARTMENT OF EDUCATION]

Subpart A—General Provisions

Sec.

84.1 [104.1]	Purpose.
84.2 [104.2]	Application.
84.3 [104.3]	Definitions.
84.4 [104.4]	Discrimination prohibited.
84.5 [104.5]	Assurances required.
84.6 [104.6]	Remedial action, voluntary action, and self-evaluation.
84.7 [104.7]	Designation of responsible employee and adoption of grievance procedures.
84.8 [104.8]	Notice.
84.9 [104.9]	Administrative requirements for small recipients.
84.10 [104.10]	Effect of state or local law or other requirements and effect of employment opportunities.

Subpart B—Employment Practices

Subpart C—Program Accessibility

Subpart D—Preschool, Elementary, and Secondary Education

Subpart E—Postsecondary Education

Subpart F—Health, Welfare, and Social Services

Subpart G—Procedures

APPENDIX A—ANALYSIS OF FINAL REGULATION

AUTHORITY: Sec. 504, Rehabilitation Act of 1973, Pub. L. 93-112, 87 Stat. 394 (29 U.S.C. 794); sec. 111(a), Rehabilitation Act Amendments of 1974, Pub. L 93-516, 88 Stat. 1619 (29 U.S.C. 706); sec. 606, Education of the Handicapped Act (20 U.S.C. 1405), as amended by Pub. L. 94-142, 89 Stat. 795; sec. 321, Comprehensive Alcohol Abuse and Alcoholism Prevention, Treatment, and Rehabilitation Act of 1970, 84 Stat. 182 (42 U.S.C. 4581), as amended; sec. 407, Drug Abuse Office and Treatment Act of 1972, 86 Stat. 78 (21 U.S.C. 1174), as amended.

Subpart A—General Provisions

§ 84.1 [104.1] Purpose.

The purpose of this part is to effectuate section 504 of the Rehabilitation Act of 1973, which is designed to eliminate discrimination on the basis of handicap in any program or activity receiving Federal financial assistance.

§ 84.2 [104.2] Application.

This part applies to each recipient of Federal financial assistance from the Department of Health, Education, and Welfare [Department of Education] and to each program or activity that receives or benefits from such assistance.

§ 84.3 [104.3] Definitions.

As used in this part, the term:

(a) "The Act" means the Rehabilitation Act of 1973, Pub. L. 93-112, as amended by the Rehabilitation Act Amendments of 1974, Public Law 93-516, 29 U.S.C. 794.

(b) "Section 504" means section 504 of the Act.

(c) "Education of the Handicapped Act" means that statute as amended by the Education for all Handicapped Children Act of 1975, Pub. L. 94-142, 20 U.S.C. 1401 et seq.

(d) "Department" means the Department of Health, Education, and Welfare [Department of Education].

(e) "Director" means the Director of the Office for Civil Rights of the Department. ["Assistant Secretary" means the Assistant Secretary for Civil Rights of the Department of Education].

(f) "Recipient" means any state or its political subdivision, any instrumentality of a state or its political subdivision, any public or private agency, institution, organization, or other entity, or any person to which Federal financial assistance is extended directly or through another recipient, including any successor, assignee, or transferee of a recipient, but excluding the ultimate beneficiary of the assistance.

(g) "Applicant for assistance" means one who submits an application, request, or plan required to be approved by a Department official or by a recipient as a condition to becoming a recipient.

(h) "Federal financial assistance" means any grant, loan, contract (other than a procurement contract or a contract of insurance or guaranty), or any other arrangement by which the Department provides or otherwise makes available assistance in the form of:

(1) Funds;

(2) Services of Federal personnel; or

(3) Real and personal property or any interest in or use of such property, including:

(i) Transfers or leases of such property for less than fair market value or for reduced consideration; and

(ii) Proceeds from a subsequent transfer or lease of such property if the Federal share of its fair market value is not returned to the Federal Government.

(i) "Facility" means all or any portion of buildings, structures, equipment, roads, walks, parking lots, or other real or personal property or interest in such property.

(j) "Handicapped person." (1) "Handicapped persons" means any person who (i) has a physical or mental impairment which substantially limits one or more major life activities, (ii) has a record of such an impairment, or (iii) is regarded as having such an impairment.

(2) As used in paragraph (j)(1) of this section, the phrase:

(i) "Physical or mental impairment" means (A) any physiological disorder or condition, cosmetic disfigurement, or anatomical loss affecting one or more of the following body systems: neurological; musculoskeletal; special sense organs; respiratory, including speech organs; cardiovascular; reproductive; digestive; genitourinary; hemic and lymphatic; skin; and endocrine; or (B) any mental or psychological disorder, such as mental retardation, organic brain syndrome, emotional or mental illness, and specific learning disabilities.

(ii) "Major life activities" means functions such as caring for one's self, performing manual tasks, walking, seeing, hearing, speaking, breathing, learning, and working.

(iii) "Has a record of such an impairment" means has a history of, or has been misclassified as having, a mental or physical impairment that substantially limits one or more major life activities.

(iv) "Is regarded as having an impairment" means (A) has a physical or mental impairment that does not substantially limit major life activities but that is treated by a recipient as constituting such a limitation; (B) has a physical or mental impairment that substantially limits major life activities only as a result of the attitudes of others toward such impairment; or (C) has none of the impairments defined in paragraph (j)(2)(i) of this section but is treated by a recipient as having such an impairment.

(k) "Qualified handicapped person" means:

(1) With respect to employment, a handicapped person who, with reasonable accommodation, can perform the essential functions of the job in question;

(2) With respect to public preschool, elementary, secondary, or adult educational services, a handicapped person (i) of an age during which nonhandicapped persons are provided such services, (ii) of any age during which it is mandatory under state law to provide such services to handicapped persons, or (iii) to whom a state is required to provide a free appropriate public education under § 612 of the Education of the Handicapped Act; and

(3) With respect to postsecondary and vocational education services, a handicapped person who meets the academic and technical standards requisite to admission or participation in the recipient's education program or activity;

(4) With respect to other services, a handicapped person who meets the essential eligibility requirements for the receipt of such services.

(1) "Handicap" means any condition or characteristic that renders a person a handicapped person as defined in paragraph (j) of this section.

§ 84.4 [104.4] Discrimination prohibited.

(a) *General.* No qualified handicapped person shall, on the basis of handicap, be excluded from participation in, be denied the benefits of, or otherwise be subjected to discrimination under any program or activity which receives or benefits from Federal financial assistance.

(b) *Discriminatory actions prohibited.* (1) A recipient, in providing any aid, benefit, or service, may not, directly or through contractual, licensing, or other arrangements, on the basis of handicap:

(i) Deny a qualified handicapped person an opportunity to participate in or benefit from the aid, benefit, or service;

(ii) Afford a qualified handicapped person an opportunity to participate in or benefit from the aid, benefit, or service that is not equal to that afforded others;

(iii) Provide a qualified handicapped person with an aid, benefit, or service that is not as effective as that provided to others;

(iv) Provide different or separate aid, benefits, or services to handicapped persons or to any class of handicapped persons unless such action is necessary to provide qualified handicapped persons with aid, benefits, or services that are as effective as those provided to others;

(v) Aid or perpetuate discrimination against a qualified handicapped person by providing significant assistance to an agency, organization, or person that discriminates on the basis of handicap in providing any aid, benefit, or service to beneficiaries of the recipients program;

(vi) Deny a qualified handicapped person the opportunity to participate as a member of planning or advisory boards; or

(vii) Otherwise limit a qualified handicapped person in the enjoyment of any right, privilege, advantage, or opportunity enjoyed by others receiving an aid, benefit, or service.

(2) For purposes of this part, aids, benefits, and services, to be equally effective, are not required to produce the identical result or level of achievement for handicapped and nonhandicapped persons, but must afford handicapped persons equal opportunity to obtain the same result, to gain the same benefit, or to reach the same level of achievement, in the most integrated setting appropriate to the person's needs.

(3) Despite the existence of separate or different programs or activities provided in accordance with this part, a recipient may not deny a qualified handicapped person the opportunity to participate in such programs or activities that are not separate or different.

(4) A recipient may not, directly or through contractual or other arrangements, utilize criteria or methods of administration (i) that have the effect of subjecting qualified handicapped persons to discrimination on the basis of handicap, (ii) that have the purpose or effect of defeating or substantially impairing accomplishment of the objectives of the recipient's program with respect to handicapped persons, or (iii) that perpetuate the discrimination of another recipient if both recipients are subject to common administrative control or are agencies of the same State.

(5) In determining the site or location of a facility, an applicant for assistance or a recipient may not make selections (i) that have the effect of excluding handicapped persons from, denying them the benefits of, or otherwise subjecting them to discrimination under any program or activity that receives or benefits from Federal financial assistance or (ii) that have the purpose or effect of defeating or substantially impairing the accomplishment of the objectives of the program or activity with respect to handicapped persons.

(6) As used in this section, the aid, benefit, or service provided under a program or activity receiving or benefiting from Federal financial assistance includes any aid, benefit, or service provided in or through a facility that has been constructed, expanded, altered, leased or rented, or otherwise acquired, in whole or in part, with Federal financial assistance.

(c) *Programs limited by Federal law.* The exclusion of nonhandicapped persons from the benefits of a program limited by Federal statute or executive order to handicapped persons or the exclusion of a specific class of handicapped persons from a program limited by Federal statute or executive order to a different class of handicapped persons is not prohibited by this part.

§ 84.5 [104.5] Assurances required.

(a) *Assurances.* An applicant for Federal financial assistance for a program or activity to which this part applies shall submit an assurance, on a form specified by the Director [Assistant Secretary], that the program will be operated in compliance with this part. An applicant may incorporate these assurances by reference in subsequent applications to the Department.

(b) *Duration of obligation.* (1) In the case of Federal financial assistance extended in the form of real property or to provide real property or structures on the property, the assurance will obligate the recipient or, in the case of a subsequent transfer, the transferee, for the period during which the real property or structures are used for the purpose for which Federal financial assistance is extended or for another purpose involving the provision of similar services or benefits.

(2) In the case of Federal financial assistance extended to provide personal property, the assurance will obligate the recipient for the period during which it retains ownership or possession of the property.

(3) In all other cases the assurance will obligate the recipient for the period during which Federal financial assistance is extended.

(c) *Covenants.* (1) Where Federal financial assistance is provided in the form of real property or interest in the property from the Department, the instrument effecting or recording this transfer shall contain a covenant running with the land to assure nondiscrimination for the period during which the real property is used for a purpose for which the Federal financial assistance is extended or for another purpose involving the provision of similar services or benefits.

(2) Where no transfer of property is involved but property is purchased or improved with Federal financial assistance, the recipient shall agree to include the covenant described in paragraph (b)(2) of this section in the instrument effecting or recording any subsequent transfer of the property.

(3) Where Federal financial assistance is provided in the form of real property or interest in the property from the Department, the covenant shall also include a condition coupled with a right to be reserved by the Department to revert title to the property in the event of a breach of the covenant. If a transferee of real property proposes to mortgage or otherwise encumber the real property as security for financing construction of new, or improvement of existing, facilities on the property for the purposes for which the property was transferred, the Director [Assistant Secretary] may, upon request of the transferee and if necessary to accomplish such financing and upon such conditions as he or she deems appropriate, agree to forbear the exercise of such right to revert title for so long as the lien of such mortgage or other encumbrance remains effective.

§ 84.6 [104.6] Remedial action, voluntary action, and self-evaluation.

(a) *Remedial action.* (1) If the Director [Assistant Secretary] finds that a recipient has discriminated against persons on the basis of handicap in violation of section 504 or this part, the recipient shall take such remedial action as the Director [Assistant Secretary] deems necessary to overcome the effects of the discrimination.

(2) Where a recipient is found to have discriminated against persons on the basis of handicap in violation of section 504 or this part and where another recipient exercises control over the recipient that has discriminated, the Director [Assistant Secretary], where appropriate, may require either or both recipients to take remedial action.

(3) The Director [Assistant Secretary] may, where necessary to overcome the effects of discrimination in violation of section 504 or this part, require a recipient to take remedial action (i) with respect to handicapped persons who are no longer participants in the recipient's program but who were participants in the program when such discrimination occurred or (ii) with respect to handicapped persons who would have been participants in the program had the discrimination not occurred.

(b) *Voluntary action.* A recipient may take steps, in addition to any action that is required by this part, to overcome the effects of conditions that resulted in limited participation in the recipient's program or activity by qualified handicapped persons.

(c) *Self-evaluation.* (1) A recipient shall, within one year of the effective date of this part:

(i) Evaluate, with the assistance of interested persons, including handicapped persons or organizations representing handicapped persons, its current policies and practices and the effects thereof that do not or may not meet the requirements of this part;

(ii) Modify, after consultation with interested persons, including handicapped persons or organizations representing handicapped persons, any policies and practices that do not meet the requirements of this part; and

(iii) Take after consultation with interested persons, including handicapped persons or organizations representing handicapped persons, appropriate remedial steps to eliminate the effects of any discrimination that resulted from adherence to these policies and practices.

(2) A recipient that employs fifteen or more persons shall, for at least three years following completion of the evaluation required under paragraph (c)(1) of this section, maintain on file, make available for public inspection, and provide to the Director [Assistant Secretary] upon request: (i) a list of the interested persons consulted, (ii) a description of areas examined and any problems identified, and (iii) a description of any modifications made and of any remedial steps taken.

§ 84.7 [104.7] Designation of responsible employee and adoption of grievance procedures.

(a) *Designation of responsible employee.* A recipient that employs fifteen or more persons shall designate at least one person to coordinate its efforts to comply with this part.

(b) *Adoption of grievance procedures.* A recipient that employs fifteen or more persons shall adopt grievance procedures that incorporate appropriate due process standards and that provide for the prompt and equitable resolution of complaints alleging any action prohibited by this part. Such procedures need not be established with respect to complaints from applicants for employment or from applicants for admission to postsecondary educational institutions.

§ 84.8 [104.8] Notice

(a) A recipient that employs fifteen or more persons shall take appropriate initial and continuing steps to notify participants, beneficiaries, applicants, and employees, including those with impaired vision or hearing, and unions or professional organizations holding collective bargaining or professional agreements with the recipient that it does not discriminate on the basis of handicap in violation of section 504 and this part. The notification shall state, where appropriate, that the recipient does not discriminate in admission or access to, or treatment or employment in, its programs and activities. The notification shall also include an identification of the responsible employee designated pursuant to § 84.7(a) [§ 104.7(a)]. A recipient shall make the initial notification required by this paragraph within 90 days of the effective date of this part. Methods of initial and continuing notification may include the posting of notices, publication in newspapers and magazines, placement of notices in recipients' publication, and distribution of memoranda or other written communications.

(b) If a recipient publishes or uses recruitment materials or publications containing general information that it makes available to participants, beneficiaries, applicants, or employees, it shall include in those materials or publications a statement of the policy described in paragraph (a) of this section. A recipient may meet the requirement of this paragraph either by including appropriate inserts in existing materials and publications or by revising and reprinting the materials and publications.

§ 84.9 [104.9] Administrative requirements for small recipients.

The Director [Assistant Secretary] may require any recipient with fewer than fifteen employees, or any class of such recipients, to comply with §§ 84.7 [§ 104.7] and 84.8 [§ 104.8], in whole or in part, when the Director [Assistant Secretary] finds a violation of this part or finds that such compliance will not significantly impair the ability of the recipient or class of recipients to provide benefits or services.

§ 84.10 [104.10] Effect of state or local law or other requirements and effect of employment opportunities.

(a) The obligation to comply with this part is not obviated or alleviated by the existence of any state or local law or other requirement that, on the basis of handicap, imposes prohibitions or limits upon the eligibility of qualified handicapped persons to receive services or to practice any occupation or profession.

(b) The obligation to comply with this part is not obviated or alleviated because employment opportunities in any occupation or profession are or may be more limited for handicapped persons than for nonhandicapped persons.

Subpart B—Employment Practices

§ 84.11 [104.11] Discrimination prohibited.

(a) *General.* (1) No qualified handicapped person shall, on the basis of handicap, be subjected to discrimination in employment under any program or activity to which this part applies.

(2) A recipient that receives assistance under the Education of the Handicapped Act shall take positive steps to employ and advance in employment qualified handicapped persons in programs assisted under that Act.

(3) A recipient shall make all decisions concerning employment under any program or activity to which this part applies in a manner which ensures that

discrimination on the basis of handicap does not occur and may not limit, segregate, or classify applicants or employees in any way that adversely affects their opportunities or status because of handicap.

(4) A recipient may not participate in a contractual or other relationship that has the effect of subjecting qualified handicapped applicants or employees to discrimination prohibited by this subpart. The relationships referred to in this subparagraph include relationships with employment and referral agencies, with labor unions, with organizations providing or administering fringe benefits to employees of the recipient, and with organizations providing training and apprenticeship programs.

(b) *Specific activities.* The provisions of this subpart apply to:

(1) Recruitment, advertising, and the processing of applications for employment;

(2) Hiring, upgrading, promotion, award of tenure, demotion, transfer, layoff, termination, right of return from layoff, and rehiring;

(3) Rates of pay or any other form of compensation and changes in compensation;

(4) Job assignments, job classifications, organizational structures, position descriptions, lines of progression, and seniority lists;

(5) Leaves of absence, sick leave, or any other leave;

(6) Fringe benefits available by virtue of employment, whether or not administered by the recipient;

(7) Selection and financial support for training, including apprenticeship, professional meetings, conferences, and other related activities, and selection for leaves of absence to pursue training;

(8) Employer sponsored activities, including social or recreational programs; and

(9) Any other term, condition, or privilege of employment.

(c) A recipient's obligation to comply with this subpart is not affected by any inconsistent term of any collective bargaining agreement to which it is a party.

§ 84.12 [104.12] Reasonable accommodation.

(a) A recipient shall make reasonable accommodation to the known physical or mental limitations of an otherwise qualified handicapped applicant or employee unless the recipient can demonstrate that the accommodation would impose an undue hardship on the operation of its program.

(b) Reasonable accommodation may include: (1) making facilities used by employees readily accessible to and usable by handicapped persons, and

(2) job restructuring, part-time or modified work schedules, acquisition or modification of equipment or devices, the provision of readers or interpreters, and other similar actions.

(c) In determining pursuant to paragraph (a) of this section whether an accommodation would impose an undue hardship on the operation of a recipient's program, factors to be considered include:

(1) The overall size of the recipient's program with respect to the number of employees, number and type of facilities, and size of budget;

(2) The type of the recipient's operation, including the composition and structure of the recipient's workforce; and

(3) The nature and cost of the accommodation needed.

(d) A recipient may not deny any employment opportunity to a qualified handicapped employee or applicant if the basis for the denial is the need to make reasonable accommodation to the physical or mental limitations of the employee or applicant.

§ 84.13 [104.13] Employment criteria.

(a) A recipient may not make use of any employment test or other selection criterion that screens out or tends to screen out handicapped persons or any class of handicapped persons unless: (1) the test score or other selection criterion, as used by the recipient, is shown to be job-related for the position in question, and (2) alternative job-related tests or criteria that do not screen out or tend to screen out as many handicapped persons are not shown by the Director [Assistant Secretary] to be available.

(b) A recipient shall select and administer tests concerning employment so as best to ensure that, when administered to an applicant or employee who has a handicap that impairs sensory, manual, or speaking skills, the test results accurately reflect the applicant's or employee's job skills, aptitude, or whatever other factor the test purports to measure, rather than reflecting the applicant's or employee's impaired sensory, manual, or speaking skills (except where those skills are the factors that the test purports to measure).

§ 84.14 [104.14] Preemployment inquiries.

(a) Except as provided in paragraphs (b) and (c) of this section, a recipient may not conduct a preemployment medical examination or may not make preemployment inquiry of an applicant as to whether the applicant is a handicapped person or as to the nature or severity of a handicap. A recipient may, however, make preemployment inquiry into an applicant's ability to perform job-related functions.

(b) When a recipient is taking remedial action to correct the effects of past discrimination pursuant to § 84.6(a) [§ 104.6(a)], when a recipient is taking voluntary action to overcome the effects of conditions that resulted in limited participation in its federally assisted program or activity pursuant to § 84.6(b) [§ 104.6(b)], or when a recipient is taking affirmative action pursuant to section 503 of the Act, the recipient may invite applicants for employment to indicate whether and to what extent they are handicapped, *Provided*, That:

(1) The recipient states clearly on any written questionnaire used for this purpose or makes clear orally if no written questionnaire is used that the information requested is intended for use solely in connection with its remedial action obligations or its voluntary or affirmative action efforts; and

(2) The recipient states clearly that the information is being requested on a voluntary basis, that it will be kept confidential as provided in paragraph (d) of this section, that refusal to provide it will not subject the applicant or employee to any adverse treatment, and that it will be used only in accordance with this part.

(c) Nothing in this section shall prohibit a recipient from conditioning an offer of employment on the results of a medical examination conducted prior to the employee's entrance on duty, *Provided*, That: (1) All entering employees are subjected to such an examination regardless of handicap, and (2) the results of such an examination are used only in accordance with the requirements of this part.

(d) Information obtained in accordance with this section as to the medical condition or history of the applicant shall be collected and maintained on separate forms that shall be accorded confidentiality as medical records, except that:

(1) Supervisors and managers may be informed regarding restrictions on the work or duties of handicapped persons and regarding necessary accommodations;

(2) First aid and safety personnel may be informed, where appropriate, if the condition might require emergency treatment; and

(3) Government officials investigating compliance with the Act shall be provided relevant information upon request.

§§ 84.15-84.20 [Reserved]

Subpart C—Program Accessibility

§ 84.21 [104.21] Discrimination prohibited.

No qualified handicapped person shall, because a recipient's facilities are inaccessible to or unusable by handicapped persons, be denied the benefits of, be excluded from participation in, or otherwise be subjected to discrimination under any program or activity to which this part applies.

§ 84.22 [104.22] Existing facilities.

(a) *Program accessibility.* A recipient shall operate each program or activity to which this part applies so that the program or activity, when viewed in its entirety, is readily accessible to handicapped persons. This paragraph does not require a recipient to make each of its existing facilities or every part of a facility accessible to and usable by handicapped persons.

(b) *Methods.* A recipient may comply with the requirement of paragraph (a) of this section through such means as redesign of equipment, reassignment of classes or other services to accessible buildings, assignment of aids to beneficiaries, home visits, delivery of health, welfare, or other social services at alternate accessible sites, alteration of existing facilities and construction of new facilities in conformance with the requirements of § 84.23 [§ 104.23], or any other methods that result in making its program or activity accessible to handicapped persons. A recipient is not required to make structural changes in existing facilities where other methods are effective in achieving compliance with paragraph (a) of this section. In choosing among available methods for meeting the requirement of paragraph (a) of this section, a recipient shall give priority to those methods that offer programs and activities to handicapped persons in the most integrated setting appropriate.

(c) *Small health, welfare, or other social service providers.* If a recipient with fewer than fifteen employees that provides health, welfare, or other social services finds, after consultation with a handicapped person seeking its services, that there is no method of complying with paragraph (a) of this section other than making a significant alteration in its existing facilities, the recipient may, as an alternative, refer the handicapped person to other providers of those services that are accessible.

(d) *Time period.* A recipient shall comply with the requirement of paragraph (a) of this section within sixty days of the effective date of this part except that where structural changes in facilities are necessary, such changes shall be made within three years of the effective date of this part, but in any event as expeditiously as possible.

(e) *Transition plan.* In the event that structural changes to facilities are necessary to meet the requirement of paragraph (a) of this section, a recipient shall develop, within six months of the effective date of this part, a transition plan setting forth the steps necessary to complete such changes. The plan shall be developed with the assistance of interested persons, including handicapped persons or organizations representing handicapped persons. A copy of the transition plan shall be made available for public inspection. The plan shall, at a minimum:

(1) Identify physical obstacles in the recipient's facilities that limit the accessibility of its program or activity to handicapped persons;

(2) Describe in detail the methods that will be used to make the facilities accessible;

(3) Specify the schedule for taking the steps necessary to achieve full program accessibility and, if the time period of the transition plan is longer than one year, identify steps that will be taken during each year of the transition period; and

(4) Indicate the person responsible for implementation of the plan.

(f) *Notice.* The recipient shall adopt and implement procedures to ensure that interested persons, including persons with impaired vision or hearing, can obtain information as to the existence and location of services, activities, and facilities that are accessible to and usable by handicapped persons.

§ 84.23 [104.23] New Construction.

(a) *Design and construction.* Each facility or part of a facility constructed by, on behalf of, or for the use of a recipient shall be designed and constructed in such manner that the facility or part of the facility is readily accessible to and usable by handicapped persons, if the construction was commenced after the effective date of this part.

(b) *Alteration.* Each facility or part of a facility which is altered by, on behalf of, or for the use of a recipient after the effective date of this part in a manner that affects or could affect the usability of the facility or part of the facility shall, to the maximum extent feasible, be altered in such manner that the altered portion of the facility is readily accessible to and usable by handicapped persons.

(c) *Conformance with Uniform Federal Accessibility Standards.* (1) Effective as of January 18, 1991, design, construction, or alteration of buildings in conformance with sections 3-8 of the Uniform Federal Accessibility Standards (UFAS) (appendix A to 41 CFR subpart 101-19.6) shall be deemed to comply with the requirements of this section with respect to those buildings. Departures from particular technical and scoping requirements of UFAS by the use of other methods are permitted where substantial equivalent or greater access to and usability of the building is provided.

(2) For purposes of this section, section 4.1.6(1)(g) of UFAS shall be interpreted to exempt from the requirements of UFAS only mechanical rooms and other spaces that, because of their intended use, will not require accessibility to the public or beneficiaries or result in the employment or residence therein of persons with physical handicaps.

(3) This section does not require recipients to make building alterations that have little likelihood of being accomplished without removing or altering a load-bearing structural member.

[34 Part 104.23(c) incorporates the *American National Standards Institute Accessibility Standards,* rather than the *Uniform Federal Accessibility Standards,* which appear in 45 CFR Part 84.23(c), above].

[34 CFR Part 104.23(c): *American National Standards Institute Accessibility Standards.* Design, construction, or alteration of facilities in conformance with the "American National Standard Specifications for Making Buildings and Facilities Accessible to, and Usable by, the Physically Handicapped," published by the American National Standards Institute, Inc. (ANSI A117.1-1961 (R1971)), which is incorporated by reference in this part, shall constitute compliance with paragraphs (a) and (b) of this section. Departures from particular requirements of those standards by the use of other methods shall be permitted when it is clearly evident that equivalent access to the facility or part of the facility is thereby provided. Incorporation by reference provisions approved by the Director of the Federal Register: May 27, 1975. Incorporation documents are on file at the Office of the Federal Register. Copies of the standards are obtainable from American National Standards Institute, Inc. 1430 Broadway, New York, N.Y. 10018. 45 FR 30936, May 9, 1980, 45 FR 37426, June 3, 1980.]

[42 FR 22677, May 4, 1977, as amended at 55 FR 52138, 52142, Dec. 19, 1990]

§§ 84.24-84.30 [Reserved]

Subpart D—Preschool, Elementary, and Secondary Education

§ 84.31 [104.31] Application of this subpart.

Subpart D applies to preschool, elementary, secondary, and adult education programs and activities that receive or benefit from federal financial assistance and to recipients that operate, or that receive or benefit from Federal financial assistance for the operation of, such programs or activities.

§ 84.32 [104.32] Location and notification.

A recipient that operates a public elementary or secondary education program shall annually:

(a) Undertake to identify and locate every qualified handicapped person residing in the recipient's jurisdiction who is not receiving a public education; and

(b) Take appropriate steps to notify handicapped persons and their parents or guardians of the recipient's duty under this subpart.

§ 84.33 [104.33] Free appropriate public education.

(a) *General.* A recipient that operates a public elementary or secondary education program shall provide a free appropriate public education to each qualified handicapped person who is in the recipient's jurisdiction, regardless of the nature or severity of the person's handicap.

(b) *Appropriate education.* (1) For the purpose of this subpart, the provision of an appropriate education is the provision of regular or special education and related aids and services that (i) are designed to meet individual educational needs of handicapped persons as adequately as the needs of nonhandicapped persons are met and (ii) are based upon adherence to procedures that satisfy the requirements of §§ 84.34, 84.35, and 84.36 [§§ 104.34, 104.35, and 104.36].

(2) Implementation of an individualized education program developed in accordance with the Education of the Handicapped Act is one means of meeting the standard established in paragraph (b)(1)(i) of this section.

(3) A recipient may place a handicapped person in or refer such person to a program other than the one that it operates as its means of carrying out the requirements of this subpart. If so, the recipient remains responsible for ensuring that the requirements of this subpart are met with respect to any handicapped person so placed or referred.

(c) *Free education*—(1) *General.* For the purpose of this section, the provision of a free education is the provision of educational and related services without cost to the handicapped person or to his or her parents or guardian, except for those fees that are imposed on nonhandicapped persons or their parents or guardian. It may consist either of the provision of free services or, if a recipient places a handicapped person in or refers such person to a program not operated by the recipient as its means of carrying out the requirements of this subpart, of payment for the costs of the program. Funds available from any public or private agency may be used to meet the requirements of this subpart. Nothing in this section shall be construed to relieve an insurer or similar third party from an otherwise valid obligation to provide or pay for services provided to a handicapped person.

(2) *Transportation.* If a recipient places a handicapped person in or refers such person to a program not operated by the recipient as its means of carrying out the requirements of this subpart, the recipient shall ensure that adequate transportation to and from the program is provided at no greater cost than would be incurred by the person or his or her parents or guardian if the person were placed in the program operated by the recipient.

(3) *Residential placement.* If placement in a public or private residential program is necessary to provide a free appropriate public education to a handicapped person because of his or her handicap, the program, including nonmedical care and room and board, shall be provided at no cost to the person or his or her parents or guardian.

(4) *Placement of handicapped persons by parents.* If a recipient has made available, in conformance with the requirements of this section and § 84.34 [104.34], a free appropriate public education to a handicapped person and the person's parents or guardian choose to place the person in a private school, the recipient is not required to pay for the person's education in the private school. Disagreements between a parent or guardian and a recipient regarding whether the recipient has made such a program available or otherwise regarding the question of financial responsibility are subject to the due process procedures of § 84.36 [104.36].

(d) *Compliance.* A recipient may not exclude any qualified handicapped person from a public elementary or secondary education after the effective date of this part. A recipient that is not, on the effective date of this regulation, in full compliance with the other requirements of the preceding paragraphs of this section shall meet such requirements at the earliest practicable time and in no event later than September 1, 1978.

§ 84.34 [104.34] Educational setting.

(a) *Academic setting.* A recipient to which this subpart applies shall educate, or shall provide for the education of, each qualified handicapped person in its jurisdiction with persons who are not handicapped to the maximum extent appropriate to the needs of the handicapped person. A recipient shall place a handicapped person in the regular educational environment operated by the recipient unless it is demonstrated by the recipient that the education of the person in the regular environment with the use of supplementary aids and services cannot be achieved satisfactorily. Whenever a recipient places a person in a setting other than the regular educational environment pursuant to this paragraph, it shall take into account the proximity of the alternate setting to the person's home.

(b) *Nonacademic settings.* In providing or arranging for the provision of nonacademic and extracurricular services and activities, including meals, recess periods, and the services and activities set forth in § 84.37(a)(2) [104.37(a)(2)], a recipient shall ensure that handicapped persons participate with nonhandicapped persons in such activities and services to the maximum extent appropriate to the needs of the handicapped person in question.

(c) *Comparable facilities.* If a recipient, in compliance with paragraph (a) of this section, operates a facility that is identifiable as being for handicapped persons, the recipient shall ensure that the facility and the services and activities provided therein are comparable to the other facilities, services, and activities of the recipient.

§ 84.35 [104.35] Evaluation and placement.

(a) *Preplacement evaluation.* A recipient that operates a public elementary or secondary education program shall conduct an evaluation in accordance with the requirements of paragraph (b) of this section of any person who, because of handicap, needs or is believed to need special education or related services before taking any action with respect to the initial placement of the person in a regular or special education program and any subsequent significant change in placement.

(b) *Evaluation procedures.* A recipient to which this subpart applies shall establish standards and procedures for the evaluation and placement of persons who, because of handicap, need or are believed to need special education or related services which ensure that:

(1) Tests and other evaluation materials have been validated for the specific purpose for which they are used and are administered by trained personnel in conformance with the instructions provided by their producer;

(2) Tests and other evaluation materials include those tailored to assess specific areas of educational need and not merely those which are designed to provide a single general intelligence quotient; and

(3) Tests are selected and administered so as best to ensure that, when a test is administered to a student with impaired sensory, manual, or speaking skills, the test results accurately reflect the student's aptitude or achievement level or whatever other factor the test purports to measure, rather than reflecting the student's impaired sensory, manual, or speaking skills (except where those skills are the factors that the test purports to measure).

(c) *Placement procedures.* In interpreting evaluation data and in making placement decisions, a recipient shall (1) draw upon information from a variety of sources, including aptitude and achievement tests, teacher recommendations, physical condition, social or cultural background, and adaptive behavior, (2) establish procedures to ensure that information obtained from all such sources is documented and carefully considered, (3) ensure that the placement decision is made by a group of persons, including persons knowledgeable about the child, the meaning of the evaluation data, and the placement options, and (4) ensure that the placement decision is made in conformity with § 84.34 [104.34].

(d) *Reevaluation.* A recipient to which this section applies shall establish procedures, in accordance with paragraph (b) of this section, for periodic reevaluation of students who have been provided special education and related services. A reevaluation procedure consistent with the Education [of] the Handicapped Act is one means of meeting this requirement.

§ 84.36 [104.36] Procedural safeguards.

A recipient that operates a public elementary or secondary education program shall establish and implement, with respect to actions regarding the identification, evaluation, or educational placement of persons who, because of handicap, need or are believed to need special instruction or related services, a system of procedural safeguards that includes notice, an opportunity for the parents or guardian of the person to examine relevant records, an impartial hearing with opportunity for participation by the person's parents or guardian and representation by counsel, and a review procedure. Compliance with the procedural safeguards of section 615 of the Education of the Handicapped Act is one means of meeting this requirement.

§ 84.37 [104.37] Nonacademic services.

(a) *General.* (1) A recipient to which this subpart applies shall provide nonacademic and extracurricular services and activities in such manner as is necessary to afford handicapped students an equal opportunity for participation in such services and activities.

(2) Nonacademic and extracurricular services and activities may include counseling services, physical recreational athletics, transportation, health services, recreational activities, special interest groups or clubs sponsored by the recipient, referrals to agencies which provide assistance to handicapped persons, and employment of students, including both employment by the recipient and assistance in making available outside employment.

(b) *Counseling services.* A recipient to which this subpart applies that provides personal, academic, or vocational counseling, guidance, or placement services to its students shall provide these services without discrimination on the basis of handicap. The recipient shall ensure that qualified handicapped students are not counseled toward more restrictive career objectives than are nonhandicapped students with similar interests and abilities.

(c) *Physical education and athletics.* (1) In providing physical education courses and athletics and similar programs and activities to any of its students, a recipient to which this subpart applies may not discriminate on the basis of handicap. A recipient that offers physical education courses or that operates or sponsors interscholastic, club, or intramural athletics shall provide to qualified handicapped students an equal opportunity for participation in these activities.

(2) A recipient may offer to handicapped students physical education and athletic activities that are separate or different from those offered to nonhandicapped students only if separation or differentiation is consistent with the requirements of § 84.34 [104.34] and only if no qualified handicapped student is denied the opportunity to compete for teams or to participate in courses that are not separate or different.

§ 84.38 [104.38] Preschool and adult education programs.

A recipient to which this subpart applies that operates a preschool education or day care program or activity or an adult education program or activity may not, on the basis of handicap, exclude qualified handicapped persons from the program or activity and shall take into account the needs of such persons in determining the aid, benefits, or services to be provided under the program or activity.

§ 84.39 [104.39] Private education programs.

(a) A recipient that operates a private elementary or secondary education program may not, on the basis of handicap, exclude a qualified handicapped person from such program if the person can, with minor adjustments, be provided an appropriate education, as defined in § 84.33(b)(1) [104.33(b)(1)], within the recipient's program.

(b) A recipient to which this section applies may not charge more for the provision of an appropriate education to handicapped persons than to nonhandicapped persons except to the extent that any additional charge is justified by a substantial increase in cost to the recipient.

(c) A recipient to which this section applies that operates special education programs shall operate such programs in accordance with the provisions of §§ 84.35 [104.35] and 84.36 [104.36]. Each recipient to which this section applies is subject to the provisions of §§ 84.34, 84.37, and 84.38 [104.34, 104.37, and 104.38].

§ 84.40 [Reserved]

Subpart E—Postsecondary Education

§ 84.41 [104.41] Application of this subpart.

Subpart E applies to postsecondary education programs and activities, including postsecondary vocational education programs and activities, that receive or benefit from federal financial assistance and to recipients that operate, or that receive or benefit from federal financial assistance for the operation of, such programs or activities.

§ 84.42 [104.42] Admissions and recruitment.

(a) *General.* Qualified handicapped persons may not, on the basis of handicap, be denied admission or be subjected to discrimination in admission or recruitment by a recipient to which this subpart applies.

(b) *Admissions.* In administering its admission policies, a recipient to which this subpart applies:

(1) May not apply limitations upon the number or proportion of handicapped persons who may be admitted;

(2) May not make use of any test or criterion for admission that has a disproportionate, adverse effect on handicapped persons or any class of handicapped persons unless (i) the test or criterion, as used by the recipient, has been validated as a predictor of success in the education program or activity in question and (ii) alternate tests or criteria that have a less disproportionate, adverse effect are not shown by the Director [Assistant Secretary] to be available;

(3) Shall assure itself that (i) admissions tests are selected and administered so as best to ensure that, when a test is administered to an applicant who has a handicap that impairs sensory, manual, or speaking skills, the test results accurately reflect the applicant's aptitude or achievement level or whatever other factor the test purports to measure, rather than reflecting the applicant's impaired sensory, manual, or speaking skills (except where those skills are the factors that the test purports to measure); (ii) admissions tests that are designed for persons with impaired sensory, manual, or speaking skills are offered as often and in as timely a manner as are other admissions tests; and (iii) admissions tests are administered in facilities that, on the whole, are accessible to handicapped persons; and

(4) Except as provided in paragraph (c) of this section, may not make preadmission inquiry as to whether an applicant for admission is a handicapped person but, after admission, may make inquiries on a confidential basis as to handicaps that may require accommodation.

(c) *Preadmission inquiry exception.* When a recipient is taking remedial action to correct the effects of past discrimination pursuant to § 84.6(a) [104.6(a)] or when a recipient is taking voluntary action to overcome the effects of conditions that resulted in limited participation in its federally assisted program or activity pursuant to § 84.6(b) [104.6(b)], the recipient may invite applicants for admission to indicate whether and to what extent they are handicapped, *Provided,* That:

(1) The recipient states clearly on any written questionnaire used for his purpose or makes clear orally if no written questionnaire is used that the information requested is intended for use solely in connection with its remedial action obligations or its voluntary action efforts; and

(2) The recipient states clearly that the information is being requested on a voluntary basis, that it will be kept confidential, that refusal to provide it will not subject the applicant to any adverse treatment, and that it will be used only in accordance with this part.

(d) *Validity studies.* For the purpose of paragraph (b)(2) of this section, a recipient may base prediction equations on first year grades, but shall conduct periodic validity studies against the criterion of overall success in the education program or activity in question in order to monitor the general validity of the test scores.

§ 84.43 [104.43] Treatment of students; general.

(a) No qualified handicapped student shall, on the basis of handicap, be excluded from participation in, be denied the benefits of, or otherwise be subjected to discrimination under any academic, research, occupational training, housing, health, insurance, counseling, financial aid, physical education, athletics, recreation, transportation, other extracurricular, or other postsecondary education program or activity to which this subpart applies.

(b) A recipient to which this subpart applies that considers participation by students in education programs or activities not operated wholly by the recipient, as part of, or equivalent to, an education program or activity operated by the recipient shall assure itself that the other education program or activity, as a whole provides an equal opportunity for the participation of qualified handicapped persons.

(c) A recipient to which this subpart applies may not, on the basis of handicap, exclude any qualified handicapped student from any course, course of study, or other part of its education program or activity.

(d) A recipient to which this subpart applies shall operate its programs and activities in the most integrated setting appropriate.

§ 84.44 [104.44] Academic adjustments.

(a) *Academic requirements.* A recipient to which this subpart applies shall make such modifications to its academic requirements as are necessary to ensure that such requirements do not discriminate or have the effect of discriminating, on the basis of handicap, against a qualified handicapped applicant or student. Academic requirements that the recipient can demonstrate are essential to the program of instruction being pursued by such student or to any directly related licensing requirement will not be regarded as discriminatory within the meaning of this section. Modifications may include changes in the length of time permitted for the completion of degree requirements, substitution of specific courses required for the completion of degree requirements, and adaptation of the manner in which specific courses are conducted.

(b) *Other rules.* A recipient to which this subpart applies may not impose upon handicapped students other rules, such as the prohibition of tape recorders in classrooms or of dog guides in campus buildings, that have the effect of limiting the participation of handicapped students in the recipient's education program or activity.

(c) *Course examinations.* In its course examinations or other procedures for evaluating students' academic achievement in its program, a recipient to which this subpart applies shall provide such methods for evaluating the achievement of students who have a handicap that impairs sensory, manual, or speaking skills as will best ensure that the results of the evaluation [represent] the student's achievement in the course, rather than reflecting the student's impaired sensory, manual, or speaking skills (except where such skills are the factors that the test purports to measure).

(d) *Auxiliary aids.* (1) A recipient to which this subpart applies shall take such steps as are necessary to ensure that no handicapped student is denied the benefits of, excluded from participation in, or otherwise subjected to discrimination under the education program or activity operated by the recipient because of the absence of educational auxiliary aids for students with impaired sensory, manual, or speaking skills.

(2) Auxiliary aids may include taped texts, interpreters or other effective methods of making orally delivered materials available to students with hearing impairments, readers in libraries for students with visual impairments, classroom equipment adapted for use by students with manual impairments, and other similar services and actions. Recipients need not provide attendants, individually prescribed devices, readers for personal use or study, or other devices or services of a personal nature.

§ 84.45 [104.45] Housing.

(a) *Housing provided by the recipient.* A recipient that provides housing to its nonhandicapped students shall provide comparable, convenient, and accessible housing to handicapped students at the same cost as to others. At the end of the transition period provided for in Subpart C, such housing shall be available in sufficient quantity and variety so that the scope of handicapped students' choice of living accommodations is, as a whole, comparable to that of nonhandicapped students.

(b) *Other housing.* A recipient that assists any agency, organization, or person in making housing available to any of its students shall take such action as may be necessary to assure itself that such housing is, as a whole, made available in a manner that does not result in discrimination on the basis of handicap.

§ 84.46 [104.46] Financial and employment assistance to students.

(a) *Provision of financial assistance.* (1) In providing financial assistance to qualified handicapped persons, a recipient to which this subpart applies may not (i), on the basis of handicap, provide less assistance than is provided to nonhandicapped persons, limit eligibility for assistance, or otherwise discriminate or (ii) assist any entity or person that provides assistance to any of the recipient's students in a manner that discriminates against qualified handicapped persons on the basis of handicap.

(2) A recipient may administer or assist in the administration of scholarships, fellowships, or other forms of financial assistance established under wills, trusts, bequests, or similar legal instruments that require awards to be made on the basis of factors that discriminate or have the effect of discriminating on the basis of handicap only if the overall effect of the award of scholarships, fellowships, and other forms of financial assistance is not discriminatory on the basis of handicap.

(b) *Assistance in making available outside employment.* A recipient that assists any agency, organization, or person in providing employment opportunities to any of its students shall assure itself that such employment opportunities, as a whole, are made available in a manner that would not violate Subpart B if they were provided by the recipient.

(c) *Employment of students by recipients.* A recipient that employs any of its students may not do so in a manner that violates Subpart B.

§ 84.47 [104.47] Nonacademic services.

(a) *Physical education and athletics.* (1) In providing physical education courses and athletics and similar programs and activities to any of its students, a recipient to which this subpart applies may not discriminate on the basis of handicap. A recipient that offers physical education courses or that operates or sponsors intercollegiate, club, or intramural athletics shall provide to qualified handicapped students an equal opportunity for participation in these activities.

(2) A recipient may offer to handicapped students physical education and athletic activities that are separate or different only if separation or differentiation is consistent with the requirements of § 84.43(d) [104.43(d)] and only if no qualified handicapped

student is denied the opportunity to compete for teams or to participate in courses that are not separate or different.

(b) *Counseling and placement services.* A recipient to which this subpart applies that provides personal, academic, or vocational counseling, guidance, or placement services to its students shall provide these services without discrimination on the basis of handicap. The recipient shall ensure that qualified handicapped students are not counseled toward more restrictive career objectives than are nonhandicapped students with similar interests and abilities. This requirement does not preclude a recipient from providing factual information about licensing and certification requirements that may present obstacles to handicapped persons in their pursuit of particular careers.

(c) *Social organizations.* A recipient that provides significant assistance to fraternities, sororities, or similar organizations shall assure itself that the membership practices of such organizations do not permit discrimination otherwise prohibited by this subpart.

§§ 84.48-84.50 [Reserved]

Subpart F—Health, Welfare, and Social Services

§ 84.51 [104.51] Application of this subpart.

Subpart F applies to health, welfare, and other social service programs and activities that receive or benefit from federal financial assistance and to recipients that operate, or that receive benefit from federal financial assistance for the operation of, such programs or activities.

§ 84.52 [104.52] Health, welfare, and other social services.

(a) *General.* In providing health, welfare, or other social services or benefits, a recipient may not, on the basis of handicap:

(1) Deny a qualified handicapped person these benefits or services;

(2) Afford a qualified handicapped person an opportunity to receive benefits or services that is not equal to that offered nonhandicapped persons;

(3) Provide a qualified handicapped person with benefits or services that are not as effective (as defined in § 84.4(b) [104.4(b)]) as the benefits or services provided to others;

(4) Provide benefits or services in a manner that limits or has the effect of limiting the participation of qualified handicapped persons; or

(5) Provide different or separate benefits or services to handicapped persons except where necessary to provide qualified handicapped persons with benefits and services that are as effective as those provided to others.

(b) *Notice.* A recipient that provides notice concerning benefits or services or written material concerning waivers of rights or consent to treatment shall take such steps as are necessary to ensure that qualified handicapped persons, including those with impaired sensory or speaking skills, are not denied effective notice because of their handicap.

(c) *Emergency treatment for the hearing impaired.* A recipient hospital that provides health services or benefits shall establish a procedure for effective communication with persons with impaired hearing for the purpose of providing emergency health care.

(d) *Auxiliary aids.* (1) A recipient to which this subpart applies that employs fifteen or more persons shall provide appropriate auxiliary aids to persons with impaired sensory, manual, or speaking skills, where necessary to afford such persons an equal opportunity to benefit from the service in question.

(2) The Director [Assistant Secretary] may require recipients with fewer than fifteen employees to provide auxiliary aids where the provision of aids would not significantly impair the ability of the recipient to provide its benefits or services.

(3) For the purposes of this paragraph, auxiliary aids may include brailled and taped material, interpreters, and other aids for persons with impaired hearing or vision.

§ 84.53 [104.53] Drug and alcohol addicts.

A recipient to which this subpart applies that operates a general hospital or outpatient facility may not discriminate in admission or treatment against a drug or alcohol abuser or alcoholic who is suffering from a medical condition, because of the person's drug or alcohol abuse or alcoholism.

§ 84.54 [104.54] Education of institutionalized persons.

A recipient to which this subpart applies and that operates or supervises a program or activity for persons who are institutionalized because of handicap shall ensure that each qualified handicapped person, as defined in § 84.3(k)(2) [104.3(k)(2)], in its program or activity is provided an appropriate education, as defined in § 84.33(b) [104.33(b)]. Nothing in this section shall be interpreted as altering in any way the obligations of recipients under Subpart D.

§ 84.55 [no corresponding Education Department regulation]
Procedures relating to health care for handicapped infants.

(a) *Infant Care Review Committees.* The Department encourages each recipient health care provider that provides health care services to infants in programs receiving Federal financial assistance to establish an Infant Care Review Committee (ICRC) to assist the provider in delivering health care and related services to infants and in complying with this part. The purpose of the committee is to assist the health care provider in the development of standards, policies and procedures for providing treatment to handicapped infants and in making decisions concerning medically beneficial treatment in specific cases. While the Department recognizes the value of ICRC's in assuring appropriate medical care to infants, such committees are not required by this section. An ICRC should be composed of individuals representing a broad range of perspectives, and should include a practicing physician, a representative of a disability organization, a practicing nurse, and other individuals. A suggested model ICRC is set forth in paragraph (f) of this section.

(b) *Posting of informational notice.* (1) Each recipient health care provider that provides health care services to infants in programs or activities receiving Federal financial assistance shall post and keep posted in appropriate places an informational notice.

(2) The notice must be posted at location(s) where nurses and other medical professionals who are engaged in providing health care and related services to infants will see it. To the extent it does not impair accomplishment of the requirement that copies of the notice be posted where such personnel will see it, the notice need not be posted in area(s) where parents of infant patients will see it.

(3) Each health care provider for which the content of the following notice (identified as Notice A) is truthful may use Notice A. For the content of the notice to be truthful: (i) The provider must have a policy consistent with that stated in the notice;

(ii) the provider must have a procedure for review of treatment deliberations and decisions to which the notice applies, such as (but not limited to) an Infant Care Review Committee; and (iii) the statements concerning the identity of callers and retaliation are truthful.

Notice A:

PRINCIPLES OF TREATMENT OF DISABLED INFANTS

It is the policy of this hospital, consistent with Federal law, that, nourishment and medically beneficial treatment (as determined with respect for reasonable medical judgments) should not be withheld from handicapped infants solely on the basis of their present or anticipated mental or physical impairments.

This Federal law, section 504 of the Rehabilitation Act of 1973, prohibits discrimination on the basis of handicap in programs or activities receiving Federal financial assistance. For further information, or to report suspected noncompliance, call:

[Identify designated hospital contact point and telephone number] or

[Identify appropriate child protective services agency and telephone number] or

U.S. Department of Health and Human Services (HHS): 800-368-1019 (Toll-free; available 24 hours a day; TDD capability).

The identity of callers will be held confidential. Retaliation by this hospital against any person for providing information about possible noncompliance is prohibited by this hospital and Federal regulations.

(4) Health care providers other than those described in paragraph (b)(3) of this section must post the following notice (identified as Notice B):

Notice B

PRINCIPLES OF TREATMENT OF DISABLED INFANTS

Federal law prohibits discrimination on the basis of handicap. Under this law, nourishment and medically beneficial treatment (as determined with respect for reasonable medical judgments) should not be withheld from handicapped infants solely on the basis of their present or anticipated mental or physical impairments.

This Federal law, section 504 of the Rehabilitation Act of 1973, applies to programs or activities receiving Federal financial assistance. For further information, or to report suspected noncompliance, call:

[Identify appropriate child protective services agency and telephone number] or

U.S. Department of Health and Human Services (HHS): 800-368-1019 (Toll-free; available 24 hours a day: TDD capability).

The identity of callers will be held confidential. Federal regulations prohibit retaliation by this hospital against any person who provides information about possible violations.

(5) The notice must be no smaller than 5 by 7 inches, and the type size no smaller than that generally used for similar internal communications to staff. The recipient must insert the specified information on the notice it selects. Recipient hospitals in Washington, D.C. must list 863-0100 as the telephone number for HHS. No other

alterations may be made to the notice. Copies of the notices may be obtained from the Department of Health and Human Services upon request, or the recipient may produce its own notices in conformance with the specified wording.

(c) *Responsibilities of recipient state child protective services agencies.* (1) Within 60 days of the effective date of this section, each recipient state child protective services agency shall establish and maintain in written form methods of administration and procedures to assure that the agency utilizes its full authority pursuant to state law to prevent instances of unlawful medical neglect of handicapped infants. These methods of administration and procedures shall include:

(i) A requirement that health care providers report on a timely basis to the state agency circumstances which they determine to constitute known or suspected instances of unlawful medical neglect of handicapped infants;

(ii) A method by which the state agency can receive reports of suspected unlawful medical neglect of handicapped infants from health care providers, other individuals, and the Department on a timely basis;

(iii) Immediate review of reports of suspected unlawful medical neglect of handicapped infants and, where appropriate, on-site investigation of such reports;

(iv) Provision of child protective services to such medically neglected handicapped infants, including, where appropriate, seeking a timely court order to compel the provision of necessary nourishment and medical treatment; and

(v) Timely notification to the responsible Department official of each report of suspected unlawful medical neglect involving the withholding, solely on the basis of present or anticipated physical or mental impairments, of treatment or nourishment from a handicapped infant who, in spite of such impairments, will medically benefit from the treatment or nourishment, the steps taken by the state agency to investigate such report, and the state agency's final disposition of such report.

(2) Whenever a hospital at which an infant who is the subject of a report of suspected unlawful medical neglect is being treated has an Infant Care Review Committee (ICRC) the Department encourages the state child protective services agency to consult with the ICRC in carrying out the state agency's authorities under its state law and methods of administration. In developing its methods of administration and procedures, the Department encourages child protective services agencies to adopt guidelines for investigations similar to those of the Department regarding the involvement of ICRC's.

(d) *Expedited access to records.* Access to pertinent records and facilities of a recipient pursuant to 45 CFR 80.6(c) (made applicable to this part by 45 CFR 84.61) shall not be limited to normal business hours when, in the judgment of the responsible Department official, immediate access is necessary to protect the life or health of a handicapped individual.

(e) *Expedited action to effect compliance.* The requirement of 45 CFR 80.8(d)(3) pertaining to notice to recipients prior to the initiation of action to effect compliance (made applicable to this part by 45 CFR 84.61) shall not apply when, in the judgment of the responsible Department official, immediate action to effect compliance is necessary to protect the life or health of a handicapped individual. In such cases the recipient will, as soon as practicable, be given oral or written notice of its failure to comply, of the action to be taken to effect compliance, and its continuing opportunity to comply voluntarily.

(f) *Model Infant Care Review Committee.* Recipient health care providers wishing to establish Infant Care Review Committees should consider adoption of the following model. This model is advisory. Recipient health care providers are not required to establish a review committee or, if one is established, to adhere to this model. In seeking to determine compliance with this part, as it relates to health care for handicapped infants, by health care providers that have an ICRC established and operated substantially in accordance with this model, the Department will, to the extent possible, consult with the ICRC.

(1) *Establishment and purpose.* (i) The hospital establishes an Infant Care Review Committee (ICRC) or joins with one or more other hospitals to create a joint ICRC. The establishing document will state that the ICRC is for the purpose of facilitating the development and implementation of standards, policies and procedures designed to assure that, while respecting reasonable medical judgments, treatment and nourishment not be withheld, solely on the basis of present or anticipated physical or mental impairments, from handicapped infants who, in spite of such impairments, will benefit medically from the treatment or nourishment.

(ii) The activities of the ICRC will be guided by the following principles:

(A) The interpretative guidelines of the Department relating to the applicability of this part to health care for handicapped infants.

(B) As stated in the "Principles of Treatment of Disabled Infants" of the coalition of major medical and disability organizations, including the American Academy of Pediatrics, National Association of Children's Hospitals and Related Institutions, Association for Retarded Citizens, Down's Syndrome Congress, Spina Bifida Association, and others:

When medical care is clearly beneficial, it should always be provided. When appropriate medical care is not available, arrangements should be made to transfer the infant to an appropriate medical facility. Consideration such as anticipated or actual limited potential of an individual and present or future lack of available community resources are irrelevant and must not determine the decisions concerning medical care. The individual's medical condition should be the sole focus of the decision. These are very strict standards.

It is ethically and legally justified to withhold medical or surgical procedures which are clearly futile and will only prolong the act of dying. However, supportive care should be provided, including sustenance as medically indicated and relief of pain and suffering. The needs of the dying person should be respected. The family also should be supported in its grieving.

In cases where it is uncertain whether medical treatment will be beneficial, a person's disability must not be the basis for a decision to withhold treatment. At all times during the process when decisions are being made about the benefit or futility of medical treatment, the person should be cared for in the medically most appropriate ways. When doubt exists at any time about whether to treat, a presumption always should be in favor of treatment.

(C) As stated by the President's Commission for the Study of Ethical Problems in Medicine and Biomedical and Behavioral Research:

This [standard for providing medically beneficial treatment] is a very strict standard in that it excludes consideration of the negative effects of an impaired child's life on other persons, including parents, siblings, and society. Although abiding by this standard may be difficult in specific cases, it is all too easy to undervalue the lives of handicapped infants; the Commission finds it imperative to counteract this by treating them no less vigorously than their healthy peers or than older children with similar handicaps would be treated.

(iii) The ICRC will carry out its purposes by:

(A) Recommending institutional policies concerning the withholding or withdrawal of medical or surgical treatments to infants, including guidelines for ICRC action for specific categories of life-threatening conditions affecting infants;

(B) Providing advice in specific cases when decisions are being considered to withhold or withdraw from infant life-sustaining medical or surgical treatment; and

(C) Reviewing retrospectively on a regular basis infant medical records in situations in which life-sustaining medical or surgical treatment has been withheld or withdrawn.

(2) *Organization and staffing.* The ICRC will consist of at least 7 members and include the following:

(i) A practicing physician (e.g., a pediatrician, a neonatologist, or a pediatric surgeon),

(ii) A practicing nurse,

(iii) A hospital administrator,

(iv) A representative of the legal profession,

(v) A representative of a disability group, or a developmental disability expert,

(vi) A lay community member, and

(vii) A member of a facility's organized medical staff, who shall serve as chairperson.

In connection with review of specific cases, one member of the ICRC shall be designated to act as "special advocate" for the infant, as provided in paragraph (f)(3)(ii)(E) of the section. The hospital will provide staff support for the ICRC, including legal counsel. The ICRC will meet on a regular basis, or as required below in connection with review of specific cases. It shall adopt or recommend to the appropriate hospital official or body such administrative policies as terms of office and quorum requirements. The ICRC will recommend procedures to ensure that both hospital personnel and patient families are fully informed of the existence and function of the ICRC and its availability on a 24-hour basis.

(3) *Operation of ICRC*—(i) *Prospective policy development.* (A) The ICRC will develop and recommend for adoption by the hospital institutional policies concerning the withholding or withdrawal of medical treatment for infants with life-threatening conditions. These will include guidelines for management of specific types of cases or diagnoses, for example, Down's Syndrome and spina bifida, and procedures to be followed in such recurring circumstances as, for example, brain death and parental refusal to consent to life-saving treatment. The hospital, upon recommendation of the ICRC, may require attending physicians to notify the ICRC of the presence in the facility of an infant with a diagnosis specified by the ICRC, e.g., Down's Syndrome and spina bifida.

(B) In recommending these policies and guidelines, the ICRC will consult with medical and other authorities on issues involving disabled individuals, e.g., neonatologists, pediatric surgeons, county and city agencies which provide services for the disabled, and disability advocacy organizations. It will also consult with appropriate committees of the medical staff, to ensure that the ICRC policies and guidelines build on existing staff by-laws, rules and regulations concerning consultations and staff membership requirements. The ICRC will also inform and educate hospital staff on the policies and guidelines it develops.

(ii) Review of specific cases. In addition to regularly scheduled meetings, interim ICRC meetings will take place under specified circumstances to permit review of individual cases. The hospital will, to the extent possible, require in each case that life-sustaining treatment be continued until the ICRC can review the case and provide advice.

(A) Interim ICRC meetings will be convened within 24 hours (or less if indicated) when there is disagreement between the family of an infant and the infant's physician as to the withholding or withdrawal of treatment, when a preliminary decision to withhold or withdraw life-sustaining treatment has been made in certain categories of cases identified by the ICRC, when there is disagreement between members of the hospital's medical and/or nursing staffs, or when otherwise appropriate.

(B) Such interim ICRC meetings will take place upon the request of any member of the ICRC or hospital staff or parent or guardian of the infant. The ICRC will have procedures to preserve the confidentiality of the identity of persons making such requests, and such persons shall be protected from reprisal. When appropriate, the ICRC or a designated member will inform the requesting individual of the ICRC's recommendation.

(C) The ICRC may provide for telephone and other forms of review when the timing and nature of the case, as identified in policies developed by the ICRC, make the convening of an interim meeting impracticable.

(D) Interim meetings will be open to the affected parties. The ICRC will ensure that the interests of the parents, the physician, and the child are fully considered; that family members have been fully informed of the patient's condition and prognosis; that they have been provided with a listing which describes the services furnished by parent support groups and public and private agencies in the geographic vicinity to infants with conditions such as that before the ICRC; and that the ICRC will facilitate their access to such services and groups.

(E) To ensure a comprehensive evaluation of all options and factors pertinent to the committee's deliberations, the chairperson will designate one member of the ICRC to act, in connection with that specific case, as special advocate for the infant. The special advocate will seek to ensure that all considerations in favor of the provision of life-sustaining treatment are fully evaluated and considered by the ICRC.

(F) In cases in which there is disagreement on treatment between a physician and an infant's family, and the family wishes to continue life-sustaining treatment, the family's wishes will be carried out, for as long as the family wishes, unless such treatment is medically contraindicated. When there is physician/family disagreement and the family refuses consent to life-sustaining treatment, and the ICRC, after due deliberation, agrees with the family, the ICRC will recommend that the treatment be withheld. When there is physician/family disagreement and the family refuses consent, but the ICRC disagrees with the family, the ICRC will recommend to the hospital board or appropriate official that the case be referred immediately to an appropriate court or child protective agency, and every effort shall be made to continue treatment, preserve the status quo, and prevent worsening of the infant's condition until such time as the court or agency renders a decision or takes other appropriate action. The ICRC will also follow this procedure in cases in which the family and physician agree that life-sustaining treatment should be withheld or withdrawn, but the ICRC disagrees.

(iii) *Retrospective record review.* The ICRC, at its regularly-scheduled meeting, will review all records involving withholding or termination of medical or surgical treatment to infants consistent with hospital policies developed by the ICRC, unless the case was previously before the ICRC pursuant to paragraph (f)(3)(ii) of this section. If the ICRC finds that a deviation was made from the institutional policies in a given case, it shall conduct a review and report the findings to appropriate hospital personnel for appropriate action.

(4) *Records.* The ICRC will maintain records of all of its deliberations and summary descriptions of specific cases considered and the disposition of those cases. Such records will be kept in accordance with institutional policies on confidentiality of medical information. They will be made available to appropriate government agencies, or upon court order, or as otherwise required by law.

Note: The mandatory provisions set forth in paragraphs (b)-(e) inclusive of this section are subject to an injunction prohibiting their enforcement. In *Bowen v. American Hospital Association*, 476 U.S. 610, 106 S.Ct. 2101 90 L.Ed.2d 584 (1986), the Supreme Court upheld the action of a United States District Court, 585 F.Supp. 541 (S.D.N.Y. 1984), declaring invalid and enjoining enforcement of provision under this section, promulgated January 12, 1984.
(Information collection requirements contained in paragraph (c) have been approved by the Office of Management and Budget under control number 0990-0114)
[49 FR 1651, Jan. 12, 1984, as amended at 52 FR 3012, Jan. 30, 1987]

§§ 84.56-84.60 [Reserved]

Subpart G—Procedures

§ 84.61 [104.61] Procedures.

The procedural provisions applicable to title VI of the Civil Rights Act of 1964 apply to this part. These procedures are found in §§ 80.6 through 80.10 [100.6 through 100.10] and Part 81 [101] of this Title.

§§ 84.62-84.99 [Reserved]

Note: Incorporation by reference provisions approved by the Director of the Federal Register, May 27, 1975. Incorporated documents are on file at the office of the Federal Register.

APPENDIX A [TO 45 CFR PART 84 AND 34 CFR PART 104]— ANALYSIS OF FINAL REGULATION

Subpart A—General Provisions

Definitions—1. *"Recipient."* Section 84.23 [104.23] contains definitions used throughout the regulation.

Most of the comments concerning § 84.3(f), which contains the definition of "recipient," commended the inclusion of recipients whose sole source of federal financial assistance is Medicaid. The Secretary believes that such Medicaid providers should be regarded as recipients under the statute and the regulation and should be held individually responsible for administering services in a nondiscriminatory fashion. Accordingly, § 84.3(f) has not been changed. Small Medicaid providers, however, are exempt from some of the regulation's administrative provisions (those that apply to recipients with fifteen or more employees). And such recipients will be permitted to refer patients to accessible facilities in certain limited circumstances under revised § 84.22(b). The Secretary recognizes the difficulties involved in federal enforcement of this regulation with respect to thousands of individual Medicaid providers. As in the case of title VI of the Civil Rights Act of 1964, the Office for Civil Rights will concentrate its compliance efforts on the state Medicaid agencies and will look primarily to them to ensure compliance by individual providers. [This paragraph is not included in the analysis following 34 CFR Part 104].

One other comment requested that the regulation specify that nonpublic elementary and secondary schools that are not otherwise recipients do not become recipients by virtue of the fact their students participate in certain federally funded programs. The Secretary believes it unnecessary to amend the regulation in this regard, because almost identical language in the Department's regulations implementing title VI and title IX of the Education Amendments of 1972 has consistently been interpreted so as not to render such schools recipients. These schools, however, are indirectly subject to the substantive requirements of this regulation through the application of § 84.4(b)(iv) [§ 104.4(b)(iv)], which prohibits recipients from assisting agencies that discriminate on the basis of handicap in providing services to beneficiaries of the recipients' programs.

2. *"Federal financial assistance."* In § 84.3(h) [§ 104.3(h)], defining federal financial assistance, a clarifying change has been made: procurement contracts are specifically excluded. They are covered, however, by the Department of Labor's regulation under section 503. The Department has never considered such contracts to be contracts of assistance; the explicit exemption has been added only to avoid possible confusion.

The proposed regulation's exemption of contracts of insurance or guaranty has been retained. A number of comments argued for its deletion on the ground that section 504, unlike title VI and title IX, contains no statutory exemption for such contracts. There is no indication, however, in the legislative history of the Rehabilitation Act of 1973 or of the amendments to that Act in 1974, that Congress intended section 504 to have a broader application, in terms of federal financial assistance, than other civil rights statutes. Indeed, Congress directed that section 504 be implemented in the same manner as titles VI and IX. In view of the long established exemption of contracts of insurance or guaranty under title VI, we think it unlikely that Congress intended section 504 to apply to such contracts.

In its May 1976 Notice of Intent, the Department suggested that the arrangement under which individual practitioners, hospitals, and other facilities receive reimbursement for providing services to beneficiaries under Part B of title XVIII of the Social Security Act (Medicare) constitutes a contract of insurance or guaranty and thus falls within the exemption from the regulation. This explanation oversimplified the Department's view of whether Medicare Part B constitutes Federal financial assistance. The Department's position has consistently been that, whether or not Medicare Part B arrangements involve a contract of insurance or guaranty, no Federal financial assistance flows from the Department to the doctor or other practitioner under the program, since Medicare Part B—like other social security programs—is basically a program of payments to direct beneficiaries. [This paragraph is not included in the analysis following 34 CFR Part 104].

3. *"Handicapped person."* Section 84.3(j) [§ 104.3(j)], which defines the class of persons protected under the regulation, has not been substantially changed. The definition of handicapped person in paragraph (j)(1) conforms to the statutory definition of handicapped person that is applicable to section 504, as set forth in section 111(a) of the Rehabilitation Act Amendments of 1974, Pub. L. 93-516.

The first of the three parts of the statutory and regulatory definition includes any person who has a physical or mental impairment that substantially limits one or more major life activities. Paragraph (j)(2)(i) further defines physical or mental impairments. The definition does not set forth a list of specific diseases and conditions that constitute physical or mental impairments because of the difficulty of ensuring the comprehensiveness of any such list. The term includes, however, such diseases and conditions as orthopedic, visual, speech, and hearing impairments, cerebral palsy, epilepsy, muscular dystrophy, multiple sclerosis, cancer, heart disease, diabetes, mental retardation, emotional illness, and, as discussed below, drug addiction and alcoholism.

It should be emphasized that a physical or mental impairment does not constitute a handicap for purposes of section 504 unless its severity is such that it results in a substantial limitation of one or more major life activities. Several comments observed the lack of any definition in the proposed regulation of the phrase "substantially limits." The Department does not believe that a definition of this term is possible at this time.

A related issue raised by several comments is whether the definition of handicapped person is unreasonably broad. Comments suggested narrowing the definition in various ways. The most common recommendation was that only "traditional" handicaps be covered. The Department continues to believe, however, that it has no flexibility within the statutory definition to limit the term to persons who have those severe, permanent, or progressive conditions that are most commonly regarded as handicaps. The Department intends, however, to give particular attention in its enforcement of section 504 to eliminating discrimination against persons with the severe handicaps that were the focus of concern in the Rehabilitation Act of 1973.

The definition of handicapped person also includes specific limitations on what persons are classified as handicapped under the regulation. The first of the three parts of the definition specifies that only physical and mental handicaps are included. Thus, environmental, cultural, and economic disadvantage are not in themselves covered; nor are prison records, age, or homosexuality. Of course, if a person who has any of these characteristics also has a physical or mental handicap, the person is included within the definition of handicapped person.

In paragraph (j)(2)(i), physical or mental impairment is defined to include, among other impairments, specific learning disabilities. The Department will interpret the term as it is used in section 602 of the Education of the Handicapped Act, as amended. Paragraph (15) of section 602 uses the term "specific learning disabilities" to describe such conditions as perceptual handicaps, brain injury, minimal brain dysfunction, dyslexia, and developmental aphasia.

Paragraph (j)(2)(i) has been shortened, but not substantively changed, by the deletion of clause (C), which made explicit the inclusion of any condition which is mental or physical but whose precise nature is not at present known. Clauses (A) and (B) clearly comprehend such conditions.

The second part of the statutory and regulatory definition of handicapped person includes any person who has a record of a physical or mental impairment that substantially limits a major life activity. Under the definition of "record" in paragraph (j)(2)(iii), persons who have a history of a handicapping condition but no longer have the condition, as well as persons who have been incorrectly classified as having such a condition, are protected from discrimination under section 504. Frequently occurring examples of the first group are persons with histories of mental or emotional illness, heart disease, or cancer; of the second group, persons who have been misclassified as mentally retarded.

The third part of the statutory and regulatory definition of handicapped person includes any person who is regarded as having a physical or mental impairment that substantially limits one or more major life activities. It includes many persons who are ordinarily considered to be handicapped but who do not technically fall within the first two parts of the statutory definition, such as persons with a limp. This part of the definition also includes some persons who might not ordinarily be considered handicapped, such as persons with disfiguring scars, as well as persons who have no physical or mental impairment but are treated by a recipient as if they were handicapped.

4. *Drug addicts and alcoholics.* As was the case during the first comment period, the issue of whether to include drug addicts and alcoholics within the definition of handicapped person was of major concern to many commenters. The arguments presented on each side of the issue were similar during the two comment periods, as was the preference of commenters for exclusion of this group of persons. While some comments reflected misconceptions about the implications of including alcoholics and drug addicts within the scope of the regulation, the Secretary understands the concerns that underlie the comments on this question and recognizes that application of section 504 to active alcoholics and drug addicts presents sensitive and difficult questions that must be taken into account in interpretation and enforcement.

The Secretary has carefully examined the issue and has obtained a legal opinion from the Attorney General. That opinion concludes that drug addiction and alcoholism are "physical or mental impairments" within the meaning of section 7(6) of the Rehabilitation Act of 1973, as amended, and that drug addicts and alcoholics are therefore handicapped for purposes of section 504 if their impairment substantially limits one of their major life activities. The Secretary therefore believes that he is without authority to exclude these conditions from the definition. There is a medical and legal consensus that alcoholism and drug addiction are diseases, although there is disagreement as to whether they are primarily mental or physical. In addition, while Congress did not focus specifically on the problems of drug addiction and alcoholism in enacting section 504, the committees that considered the Rehabilitation Act of 1973 were made aware of the Department's long-standing practice of treating addicts and alcoholics as handicapped individuals eligible for rehabilitation services under the Vocational Rehabilitation Act.

The Secretary wishes to reassure recipients that inclusion of addicts and alcoholics within the scope of the regulation will not lead to the consequences feared by many commenters. It cannot be emphasized too strongly that the statute and the regulation apply only to discrimination against qualified handicapped persons solely by reason of their handicap. The fact that drug addiction and alcoholism may be handicaps does not mean that these conditions must be ignored in determining whether an individual is qualified for services or employment opportunities. On the contrary, a recipient may hold a drug addict or alcoholic to the same standard of performance and behavior to which it holds others, even if any unsatisfactory performance or behavior is related to the person's drug addiction or alcoholism. In other words, while an alcoholic or drug addict may not be denied services or disqualified from employment solely because of his or her condition, the behavioral manifestations of the condition may be taken into account in determining whether he or she is qualified.

With respect to the employment of a drug addict or alcoholic, if it can be shown that the addiction or alcoholism prevents successful performance of the job, the person need not be provided the employment opportunity in question. For example, in making employment decisions, a recipient may judge addicts and alcoholics on the same basis it judges all other applicants and employees. Thus, a recipient may consider—for all applicants including drug addicts and alcoholics—past personnel records, absenteeism, disruptive, abusive or dangerous behavior, violations of rules and unsatisfactory work performance. Moreover, employers may enforce rules prohibiting the possession or use of alcohol or drugs in the work-place, provided that such rules are enforced against all employees.

With respect to services, there is evidence that drug addicts and alcoholics are often denied treatment at hospitals for conditions unrelated to their addiction or alcoholism. In addition, some addicts and alcoholics have been denied emergency treatment. These practices have been specifically prohibited by section 407 of the Drug Abuse Office and Treatment Act of 1972 (21 U.S.C. 1174) and section 321 of the Comprehensive Alcohol Abuse and Alcoholism Prevention, Treatment, and Rehabilitation Act of 1979 (42 U.S.C. 4581), as amended. These statutory provisions are also administered by the Department's Office for Civil Rights and are implemented in § 84.53 of this regulation. [This paragraph is not included in the analysis following 34 Part 104.]

With respect to other services, the implications of coverage of alcoholics and drug addicts are two-fold: first, no person may be excluded from services solely by reason of the presence or history of these conditions; second, to the extent that the manifestations of the condition prevent the person from meeting the basic eligibility requirements of the program or cause substantial interference with the operation of the program, the condition may be taken into consideration. Thus, a college may not exclude an addict or alcoholic as a student, on the basis of addiction or alcoholism, if the person can successfully participate in the education program and complies with the rules of the college and if his or her behavior does not impede the performance of other students.

Of great concern to many commenters was the question of what effect the inclusion of drug addicts and alcoholics as handicapped persons would have on school disciplinary rules prohibiting the use or possession of drugs or alcohol by students. Neither such rules nor their application to drug addicts or alcoholics is prohibited by this regulation, provided that the rules are enforced evenly with respect to all students.

5. *"Qualified handicapped person."* Paragraph (k) of § 84.3 [§ 104.3] defines the term "qualified handicapped person." Throughout the regulation, this term is used instead of the statutory term "otherwise qualified handicapped person." The Department believes that the omission of the word "otherwise" is necessary in order to comport with the intent of the statute because, read literally, "otherwise" qualified handicapped persons include persons who are qualified except for their handicap, rather than in spite of their handicap. Under such a literal reading, a blind person possessing all the qualifications for driving a bus except sight could be said to be "otherwise qualified" for the job of driving. Clearly, such a result was not intended by Congress. In all other respects, the terms "qualified" and "otherwise qualified" are intended to be interchangeable.

Section 84.3(k)(1) [§ 104.3(k)(1)] defines a qualified handicapped person with respect to employment as a handicapped person who can, with reasonable accommodation, perform the essential functions of the job in question. The term "essential functions" does not appear in the corresponding provision of the Department of Labor's section 503 regulation, and a few commenters objected to its inclusion on the ground that a handicapped person should be able to perform all job tasks. However, the Department believes that inclusion of the phrase is useful in emphasizing that handicapped persons should not be disqualified simply because they may have difficulty in performing tasks that bear only a marginal relationship to a particular job. Further, we are convinced that inclusion of the phrase is not inconsistent with the Department of Labor's application of its definition.

Certain commenters urged that the definition of qualified handicapped person be amended so as explicitly to place upon the employer the burden of showing that a particular mental or physical characteristic is essential. Because the same result is achieved by the requirement contained in paragraph (a) of § 84.13 [§ 104.13], which requires an employer to establish that any selection criterion that tends to screen out handicapped persons is job-related, that recommendation has not been followed.

Section 84.3(k)(2) [§ 104.3(k)(2)] (formerly § 84.3(k)(3)) defines qualified handicapped person, with respect to preschool, elementary, and secondary programs, in terms of age. Several commenters recommended that eligibility for the services be based upon the standard of substantial benefit, rather than age, because of the need of many handicapped children for early or extended services if they are to have an equal opportunity to benefit from education programs. No change has been made in this provision, again because of the extreme difficulties in administration that would result from the choice of the former standard. Under the remedial action provisions of § 84.6(a)(3) [§ 104.6(a)(3)], however, persons beyond the age limits prescribed in § 84.3(k)(2) [§ 104.3(k)(2)] may in appropriate cases be required to be provided services that they were formerly denied because of a recipient's violation of section 504.

Section 84.3(k)(2) [§ 104.3(k)(2)] states that a handicapped person is qualified for preschool, elementary, or secondary services if the person is of an age at which nonhandicapped persons are eligible for such services or at which state law mandates the provision of educational services to handicapped persons. In addition, the extended age ranges for which recipients must provide full educational opportunity to all handicapped persons in order to be eligible for assistance under the Education of the Handicapped Act—generally, 3-18 as of September 1978, and 3-21 as of September 1980 are incorporated by reference in this paragraph.

Section 84.3(k)(3) [§ 104.3(k)(3)] (formerly § 84.3(k)(2)) defines qualified handicapped person with respect to postsecondary educational programs. As revised, the paragraph means that both academic and technical standards must be met by applicants to these programs. The term "technical standards" refers to all nonacademic admissions criteria that are essential to participation in the program in question.

6. *General prohibitions against discrimination.* Section 84.4 [§ 104.4] contains general prohibitions against discrimination applicable to all recipients of assistance from this Department.

Paragraph (b)(1)(i) prohibits the exclusion of qualified handicapped persons from aids, benefits, or services, and paragraph (ii) requires that equal opportunity to participate or benefit be provided. Paragraph (iii) requires that services provided to handicapped persons be as effective as those provided to the nonhandicapped. In paragraph (iv), different or separate services are prohibited except when necessary to provide equally effective benefits.

In this context, the term "equally effective," defined in paragraph (b)(2), is intended to encompass the concept of equivalent, as opposed to identical, services and to acknowledge the fact that, in order to meet the individual needs of handicapped persons to the same extent that the corresponding needs of nonhandicapped persons are met, adjustments to regular programs or the provision of different programs may sometimes be necessary. [The following sentence is excluded from the analysis following 34 CFR Part 104.] For example, a welfare office that uses the telephone for communicating with its clients must provide alternative modes of communicating with its deaf clients. This standard parallels the one established under title VI of the Civil Rights Act of 1964 with respect to the provision of educational services to students whose primary language is not English. See *Lau v. Nichols*, 414 U.S. 563 (1974). To be equally effective, however, an aid, benefit or service need not produce equal results; it merely must afford an equal opportunity to achieve equal results.

It must be emphasized that, although separate services must be required in some instances, the provision of unnecessarily separate or different services is discriminatory. The addition to paragraph (b)(2) of the phrase "in the most integrated setting appropriate to the person's needs" is intended to reinforce this general concept. A new paragraph (b)(3) has also been added to § 84.4 [§ 104.4], requiring recipients to give qualified handicapped persons the option of participating in regular programs despite the existence of permissibly separate or different programs. The requirement has been reiterated in §§ 84.38 [§ 104.38] and 84.47 [§ 104.47] in connection with physical education and athletics programs.

Section 84.4(b)(1)(v) [§ 104.4(b)(1)(v)] prohibits a recipient from supporting another entity or person that subjects participants or employees in the recipient's program to discrimination on the basis of handicap. This section would, for example, prohibit financial support by a recipient to a community recreational group or to a professional or social organization that discriminates against handicapped persons. Among the criteria to be considered in each case are the substantiality of the relationship between the recipient and the other entity, including financial support by the recipient, and whether the other entity's activities relate so closely to the recipient's program or activity that they fairly should be considered activities of the recipient itself. Paragraph (b)(1)(vi) was added in response to comment in order to make explicit the prohibition against denying qualified handicapped persons the opportunity to serve on planning and advisory boards responsible for guiding federally assisted programs or activities.

Several comments appeared to interpret § 84.4(b)(5) [§ 104.4(b)(5)], which proscribes discriminatory site selection, to prohibit a recipient that is located on hilly terrain from erecting any new buildings at its present site. That, of course, is not the case. This paragraph is not intended to apply to construction of additional buildings at an existing site. Of course, any such facilities must be made accessible in accordance with the requirements of § 84.23 [§ 104.23].

7. *Assurances of compliance.* Section 84.5(a) [§ 104.5(a)] requires a recipient to submit to the Director [Assistant Secretary] an assurance that each of its programs and activities receiving or benefiting from federal financial assistance from this Department will be conducted in compliance with this regulation. [The following sentence is excluded from the analysis following 34 CFR Part 104.] To facilitate the submission of assurances by thousands of Medicaid providers, the Department will follow the title VI procedures of accepting, in lieu of assurances, certification on Medicaid vouchers. Many commenters also sought relief from the paperwork requirements imposed by the Department's enforcement of its various civil rights responsibilities by requesting the Department to issue one form incorporating title VI, title IX, and section 504 assurances. The Secretary is sympathetic to this request. While it is not feasible to adopt a single civil rights assurance form at this time, the Office for Civil Rights will work toward that goal.

8. *Private rights of action.* Several comments urged that the regulation incorporate [a] provision granting beneficiaries a private right of action against recipients under section 504. To confer such a right is beyond the authority of the executive branch of government. There is, however, case law holding that such a right exists. *Lloyd v. Regional Transportation Authority,* 548 F.2d 1277 (7th Cir.1977); see *Hairston v. Drosick,* Civil No. 75-0691 (S.D.W.Va., Jan. 14, 1976); *Gurmankin v. Castanzo,* 411 F.Supp. 982 (E.D.Pa.1976); cf. *Lau v. Nichols, supra.*

9. *Remedial action.* Where there has been a finding of discrimination, § 84.6 [§ 104.6] requires a recipient to take remedial action to overcome the effects of the discrimination. Actions that might be required under paragraph (a)(1) include provision of services to persons previously discriminated against, reinstatement of employees, and development of a remedial action plan. Should a recipient fail to take required remedial action, the ultimate sanctions of court action or termination of federal financial assistance may be imposed.

Paragraph (a)(2) extends the responsibility for taking remedial action to a recipient that exercises control over a noncomplying recipient. Paragraph (a)(3) also makes clear that handicapped persons who are not in the program at the time that remedial action is required to be taken may also be the subject of such remedial action. This paragraph has been revised in response to comments in order to include persons who would have been in the program if discriminatory practices had not existed. Paragraphs (a)(1), (2), and (3) have also been amended in response to comments to make plain that, in appropriate cases, remedial action might be required to redress clear violations of the statute itself that occurred before the effective date of this regulation.

10. *Voluntary action.* In § 84.6(b) [§ 104.6(b)], the term "voluntary action" has been substituted for the term "affirmative action" because the use of the latter term led to some confusion. We believe the term "voluntary action" more accurately reflects the purpose of the paragraph. This provision allows action, beyond that required by the regulation, to overcome conditions that led to limited participation by handi-

capped persons, whether or not the limited participation was caused by any discriminatory actions on the part of the recipient. Several commenters urged that paragraphs (a) and (b) be revised to require remedial action to overcome effects of prior discriminatory practices regardless of whether there has been an express finding of discrimination. The self-evaluation requirement in paragraph (c) accomplishes much the same purpose.

11. *Self-evaluation.* Paragraph (c) requires recipients to conduct a self-evaluation in order to determine whether their policies or practices may discriminate against handicapped persons and to take steps to modify any discriminatory policies and practices and their effects. The Department received many comments approving of the addition to paragraph (c) of a requirement that recipients seek the assistance of handicapped persons in the self-evaluation process. This paragraph has been further amended to require consultation with handicapped persons or organizations representing them before recipients undertake the policy modifications and remedial steps prescribed in paragraphs (c)(ii) and (iii).

Paragraph (c)(2), which sets forth the recordkeeping requirements concerning self-evaluation, now applies only to recipients with fifteen or more employees. This change was made as part of an effort to reduce unnecessary or counterproductive administrative obligations on small recipients. For those recipients required to keep records, the requirements have been made more specific; records must include a list of persons consulted and a description of areas examined, problems identified, and corrective steps taken. Moreover, the records must be made available for public inspection.

12. *Grievance procedure.* Section 84.7 [§ 104.7] (formerly § 84.8) requires recipients with fifteen or more employees to designate an individual responsible for coordinating its compliance efforts and to adopt a grievance procedure. Two changes were made in the section in response to comment. A general requirement that appropriate due process procedures be followed has been added. It was decided that the details of such procedures could not at this time be specified because of the varied nature of the persons and entities who must establish the procedures and of the programs to which they apply. A sentence was also added to make clear that grievance procedures are not required to be made available to unsuccessful applicants for employment or to applicants for admission to colleges and universities.

The regulation does not require that grievance procedures be exhausted before recourse is sought from the Department. However, the Secretary believes that it is desirable and efficient in many cases for complainants to seek resolution of their complaints and disputes at the local level and therefore encourages them to use available grievance procedures.

A number of comments asked whether compliance with this section or the notice requirements of § 84.8 could be coordinated with comparable action required by the title IX regulation. The Department encourages such efforts.

13. *Notice.* Section 84.8 [§ 104.8] (formerly § 84.9) sets forth requirements for dissemination of statements of nondiscrimination policy by recipients.

It is important that both handicapped persons and the public at large be aware of the obligations of recipients under section 504. Both the Department and recipients have responsibilities in this regard. Indeed the Department intends to undertake a major public information effort to inform persons of their rights under section 504 and this regulation. In § 84.8 [§ 104.8] the Department has sought to impose a clear obligation on major recipients to notify beneficiaries and employees of the requirements of section 504, without dictating the precise way in which this notice must be given. At the same time, we have avoided imposing requirements on small recipients (those with fewer than fifteen employees) that would create unnecessary and counter-productive paperwork burdens on them and unduly stretch the enforcement resources of the Department.

Section 84.8(a) [§ 104.8(a)], as simplified, requires recipients with fifteen or more employees to take appropriate steps to notify beneficiaries and employees of the recipient's obligations under section 504. The last sentence of § 84.8(a) [§ 104.8(a)] has been revised to list possible, rather than required, means of notification. Section 84.8(b) [§ 104.8(b)] requires recipients to include a notification of their policy of nondiscrimination in recruitment and other general information materials.

In response to a number of comments, § 84.8 [§ 104.8] has been revised to delete the requirements of publication in local newspapers, which has proved to be both troublesome and ineffective. Several commenters suggested that notification on separate forms be allowed until present stocks of publications and forms are depleted. This final regulation explicitly allows this method of compliance. The separate form should, however, be included with each significant publication or form that is distributed.

Former § 84.9(b)(2), [Section 104] which prohibited the use of materials that might give the impression that a recipient excludes qualified handicapped persons from its program, has been deleted. The Department is convinced by the comments that this provision is unnecessary and difficult to apply. The Department encourages recipients, however, to include in their recruitment and other general information materials photographs of handicapped persons and ramps and other features of accessible buildings.

Under new § 84.9 [§ 104.9] the Director [Assistant Secretary] may, under certain circumstances, require recipients with fewer than fifteen employees to comply with one or more of these requirements. Thus, if experience shows a need for imposing notice or other requirements on particular recipients or classes of small recipients, the Department is prepared to expand the coverage of these sections.

14. *Inconsistent state laws.* Section 84.10(a) [§ 104.10(a)] states that compliance with the regulation is not excused by state or local laws limiting the eligibility of qualified handicapped persons to receive services or to practice an occupation. The provision thus applies only with respect to state or local laws that justifiably differentiate on the basis of handicap.

Paragraph (b) further points out that the presence of limited employment opportunities in a particular profession, does not excuse a recipient from complying with the regulation. Thus, a law school could not deny admission to a blind applicant because blind lawyers may find it more difficult to find jobs than do nonhandicapped lawyers.

Subpart B—Employment Practices

Subpart B prescribes requirements for nondiscrimination in the employment practices of recipients of federal financial assistance administered by the Department. This subpart is consistent with the employment provisions of the Department's regulation implementing title IX of the Education Amendments of 1972 (45 CFR Part 86) [(34 CFR Part 106)] and the regulation of the Department of Labor under section 503 of the Rehabilitation Act, which requires certain Federal contractors to take affirmative action in the employment and advancement of qualified handicapped persons. All recipients subject to title IX are also subject to this regulation. In addition, many recipients subject to this regulation receive federal procurement contracts in excess of $2500 and are therefore also subject to section 503.

15. *Discriminatory practices.* Section 84.11 [§ 104.11] sets forth general provisions with respect to discrimination in employment. A new paragraph (a)(2) has been added to clarify the employment obligations of recipients that receive federal funds under Part B of the Education of the Handicapped Act, as amended (EHA). Section 606 of the EHA obligates elementary or secondary school systems that receive EHA funds to take positive steps to employ and advance in employment qualified handicapped persons. This obligation is similar to the nondiscrimination requirement of section 504 but requires recipients to take additional steps to hire and promote handicapped persons. In enacting section 606 Congress chose the words "positive steps" instead of "affirmative action" advisedly and did not intend section 606 to incorporate the types of activities required under Executive Order 11246 (affirmative action on the basis of race, color, sex, or national origin) or under sections 501 and 503 of the Rehabilitation Act of 1973.

Paragraph (b) of § 84.11 [§ 104.11] sets forth the specific aspects of employment covered by the regulation. Paragraph (c) provides that inconsistent provisions of collective bargaining agreements do not excuse noncompliance.

16. *Reasonable accommodation.* The reasonable accommodation requirement of § 84.12 [§ 104.12] generated a substantial number of comments. The Department remains convinced that its approach is both fair and effective. Moreover, the Department of Labor reports that it has experienced little difficulty in administering the requirement of reasonable accommodation. The provision therefore remains basically unchanged from the proposed regulation.

Section 84.12 [§ 104.12] requires a recipient to make reasonable accommodation to the known physical or mental limitations of a handicapped applicant or employee unless the recipient can demonstrate that the accommodation would impose an undue hardship on the operation of its program. Where a handicapped person is not qualified to perform a particular job, where reasonable accommodation does not overcome the effects of a person's handicap, or where reasonable accommodation causes undue hardship to the employer, failure to hire or promote the handicapped person will not be considered discrimination.

Section 84.12(b) [§ 104.12(b)] lists some of the actions that constitute reasonable accommodation. The list is neither all-inclusive not meant to suggest that employers must follow all of the actions listed.

Reasonable accommodation includes modification of work schedules, including parttime employment, and job restructuring. Job restructuring may entail shifting nonessential duties to other employees. In other cases, reasonable accommodation may include physical modifications or relocation of particular offices or jobs so that they are in facilities or parts of facilities that are accessible to and usable by handicapped persons. If such accommodations would cause undue hardship to the employer, they need not be made.

Paragraph (c) of this section sets forth the factors that the Office for Civil Rights will consider in determining whether an accommodation necessary to enable an applicant or employee to perform the duties of a job would impose an undue hardship. The weight given to each of these factors in making the determination as to whether an accommodation constitutes undue hardship will vary depending on the facts of a particular situation. Thus, a small day-care center might not be required to expend more than a nominal sum, such as that necessary to equip a telephone for use by a secretary with impaired hearing, but a large school district might be required to make available a teacher's aide to a blind applicant for a teaching job. Further, it might be considered reasonable to require a state welfare agency to accommodate a deaf employee by providing an interpreter, while it would constitute an undue hardship to impose that requirement on a provider of foster home care services.

The reasonable accommodation standard in § 84.12 [§ 104.12] is similar to the obligation imposed upon federal contractors in the regulation implementing section 503 of the Rehabilitation Act of 1973, administered by the Department of Labor. Although the wording of the reasonable accommodation provisions of the two regulations is not identical, the obligation that the two regulations impose is the same, and the federal government's policy in implementing the two sections will be uniform. The Department adopted the factors listed in paragraph (c) instead of the "business necessity" standard of the Labor regulation because that term seemed inappropriate to the nature of the programs operated by the majority of institutions subject to this regulation, e.g., public school systems, hospitals, colleges and universities, nursing homes, day-care centers, and welfare offices. The factors listed in paragraph (c) are intended to make the rationale underlying the business necessity standard applicable to and understandable by recipients of HEW funds.

17. *Tests and selection criteria.* Revised § 84.13(a) [§ 104.13(a)] prohibits employers from using test or other selection criteria that screen out or tend to screen out handicapped persons unless the test or criterion is shown to be job-related and alternative tests or criteria that do not screen out or tend to screen out as many handicapped persons are not shown by the Director to be available. This paragraph is an application of the principle established under title VII of the Civil Rights Act of 1964 in *Griggs v. Duke Power Company,* 401 U.S. 494 (1971).

Under the proposed section, a statistical showing of adverse impact on handicapped persons was required to trigger an employer's obligation to show that employment criteria and qualifications relating to handicap were necessary. This requirement was changed because the small number of handicapped persons taking tests would make statistical showings of "disproportionate, adverse effect" difficult and burdensome. Under the altered, more workable provision, once it is shown that an employment test substantially limits the opportunities of handicapped persons, the employer must show the test to be job-related. A recipient is no longer limited to using predictive validity studies as the method for demonstrating that a test or other selection criterion is in fact job-related. Nor, in all cases, are predictive validity studies sufficient to demonstrate that a test or criterion is job-related. In addition, § 84.13(a) [§ 104.13(a)] has been revised to place the burden on the Director, rather than the recipient, to identify alternate tests.

Section 84.13(b) [§ 104.13(b)] requires that a recipient take into account that some tests and criteria depend upon sensory, manual, or speaking skills that may not themselves be necessary to the job in question but that may make the handicapped person unable to pass the test. The recipient must select and administer tests so as best to ensure that the test will measure the handicapped person's ability to perform on the job rather than the person's ability to see, hear, speak, or perform manual tasks, except, of course, where such skills are the factors that the test purports to measure. For example, a person with a speech impediment may be perfectly qualified for jobs that do not or need not, with reasonable accommodation, require ability to speak clearly. Yet, if given an oral test, the person will be unable to perform in a satisfactory manner. The test results will not, therefore, predict job performance but instead will reflect impaired speech.

18. *Preemployment inquiries.* Section 84.14 [§ 104.14], concerning preemployment inquiries, generated a large number of comments. Commenters representing

handicapped persons strongly favored a ban on preemployment inquiries on the ground that such inquiries are often used to discriminate against handicapped persons and are not necessary to serve any legitimate interests of employers. Some recipients, on the other hand, argued that preemployment inquiries are necessary to determine qualifications of the applicant, safety hazards caused by a particular handicapping condition, and accommodations that might be required.

The Secretary has concluded that a general prohibition of preemployment inquiries is appropriate. However, a sentence has been added to paragraph (a) to make clear that an employer may inquire into an applicant's ability to perform job-related tasks but may not ask if the person has a handicap. For example, an employer may not ask on an employment form if an applicant is visually impaired but may ask if the person has a current driver's license (if that is a necessary qualification for the position in question). Similarly, employers may make inquiries about an applicant's ability to perform a job safely. Thus, an employer may not ask if an applicant is an epileptic but may ask whether the person can perform a particular job without endangering other employees.

Section 84.14(b) [§ 104.14(b)] allows preemployment inquiries only if they are made in conjunction with required remedial action to correct past discrimination, with voluntary action to overcome past conditions that have limited the participation of handicapped persons, or with obligations under section 503 of the Rehabilitation Act of 1973. In these instances, paragraph (b) specifies certain safeguards that must be followed by the employer.

Finally, the revised provision allows an employer to condition offers of employment to handicapped persons on the results of medical examinations, so long as the examinations are administered to all employees in a nondiscriminatory manner and the results are treated on a confidential basis.

19. *Specific acts of discrimination.* Sections 84.15 [§ 104.15] (recruitment), 84.16 [§ 104.16] (compensation), 84.17 [§ 104.17] (job classification and structure) and 84.18 [§ 104.18] (fringe benefits) have been deleted from the regulation as unnecessarily duplicative of § 84.11 [§ 104.11] (discrimination prohibited). The deletion of these sections in no way changes the substantive obligations of employers subject to this regulation from those set forth in the July 16 proposed regulation. These deletions bring the regulation closer in form to the Department of Labor's section 503 regulation.

Proposed § 84.18 [§ 104.18], concerning fringe benefits, had allowed for differences in benefits or contributions between handicapped and nonhandicapped persons in situations only where such differences could be justified on an actuarial basis. Section 84.11 [§ 104.11] simply bars discrimination in providing fringe benefits and does not address the issue of actuarial differences. The Department believes that currently available data and experience do not demonstrate a basis for promulgating a regulation specifically allowing for differences in benefits or contributions.

Subpart C—Program Accessibility

In general, subpart C prohibits the exclusion of qualified handicapped persons from federally assisted programs or activities because a recipient's facilities are inaccessible or unusable.

20. *Existing facilities.* Section 84.22 [§ 104.22] maintains the same standard for nondiscrimination in regard to existing facilities as was included in the proposed

regulation. The section states that a recipient's program or activity, when viewed in its entirety, must be readily accessible to and usable by handicapped persons. Paragraphs (a) and (b) make clear that a recipient is not required to make each of its existing facilities accessible to handicapped persons if its program as a whole is accessible. Accessibility to the recipient's program or activity may be achieved by a number of means, including redesign of equipment, reassignment of classes or other services to accessible buildings, and making aides available to beneficiaries. In choosing among methods of compliance, recipients are required to give priority consideration to methods that will be consistent with provision of services in the most appropriate integrated setting. Structural changes in existing facilities are required only where there is no other feasible way to make the recipient's program accessible.

Under § 84.22 [§ 104.22], a university does not have to make all of its existing classroom buildings accessible to handicapped students if some of its buildings are already accessible and if it is possible to reschedule or relocate enough classes so as to offer all required courses and a reasonable selection of elective courses in accessible facilities. If sufficient relocation of classes is not possible using existing facilities, enough alterations to ensure program accessibility are required. A university may not exclude a handicapped student from a specifically requested course offering because it is not offered in an accessible location, but it need not make every section of that course accessible.

Commenters representing several institutions of higher education have suggested that it would be appropriate for one postsecondary institution in a geographical area to be made accessible to handicapped persons and for other colleges and universities in that area to participate in that school's program, thereby developing an educational consortium for the postsecondary education of handicapped students. The Department believes that such a consortium, when developed and applied only to handicapped persons, would not constitute compliance with § 84.22 [§ 104.22], but would discriminate against qualified handicapped persons by restricting their choice in selecting institutions of higher education and would, therefore, be inconsistent with the basic objectives of the statute.

Nothing in this regulation, however, should be read as prohibiting institutions from forming consortia for the benefit of all students. Thus, if three colleges decide that it would be cost-efficient for one college to offer biology, the second physics, and the third chemistry to all students at the three colleges, the arrangement would not violate section 504. On the other hand, it would violate the regulation if the same institutions set up a consortium under which one college undertook to make its biology lab accessible, another its physics lab, and a third its chemistry lab, and under which mobility-impaired handicapped students (but not other students) were required to attend the particular college that is accessible for the desired courses.

Similarly, while a public school district need not make each of its buildings completely accessible, it may not make only one facility or part of a facility accessible if the result is to segregate handicapped students in a single setting.

All recipients that provide health, welfare, or other social services may also comply with § 84.22 [§ 104.22] by delivering services at alternate accessible sites or making home visits. Thus, for example, a pharmacist might arrange to make home deliveries of drugs. Under revised § 84.22(c) [§ 104.22(c)], small providers of health, welfare, and social services (those with fewer than fifteen employees) may refer a beneficiary to an accessible provider of the desired service, but only if no means of meeting the program accessibility requirement other than a significant alteration in existing facilities is available. The referring recipient has the responsibility of determining that the other provider is in fact accessible and willing to provide the service. The Secretary believes this "last resort" referral provision is appropriate to avoid imposition of additional costs in the health care area, to encourage providers to remain in the Medicaid program and to avoid imposing significant costs on small, low-budget providers such as day-care centers or foster homes.

A recent change in the tax law may assist some recipients in meeting their obligations under this section. Under section 2122 of the Tax Reform Act of 1976, recipients that pay federal income tax are eligible to claim a tax deduction of up to $25,000 for architectural and transportation modifications made to improve accessibility for handicapped persons. Many physicians and dentists, among others, may be eligible for this tax deduction. See 42 FR 17870 (April 4, 1977), adopting 26 CFR 7.190.

Several commenters expressed concern about the feasibility of compliance with the program accessibility standard. The Secretary believes that the standard is flexible enough to permit recipients to devise ways to make their programs accessible short of extremely expensive or impractical physical changes in facilities. Accordingly, the section does not allow for waivers. The Department is ready at all times to provide technical assistance to recipients in meeting their program accessibility responsibilities. For this purpose, the Department is establishing a special technical assistance unit. Recipients are encouraged to call upon the unit staff for advice and guidance both on structural modifications and on other ways of meeting the program accessibility requirement.

Paragraph (d) has been amended to require recipients to make all nonstructural adjustments necessary for meeting the program accessibility standard within sixty days. Only where structural changes in facilities are necessary will a recipient be permitted up to three years to accomplish program accessibility. It should be emphasized that the three-year time period is not a waiting period and that all changes must be accomplished as expeditiously as possible. Further, it is the Department's belief, after consultation with experts in the field, that outside ramps to buildings can be constructed quickly and at relatively low cost. Therefore, it will be expected that such structural additions will be made promptly to comply with § 84.22(d) [§ 104.22(d)].

The regulation continues to provide, as did the proposed version, that a recipient planning to achieve program accessibility by making structural changes must develop a transition plan for such changes within six months of the effective date of the regulation. A number of commenters suggested extending that period to one year. The Secretary believes that such an extension is unnecessary and unwise. Planning for any necessary structural changes should be undertaken promptly to ensure that they can be completed within the three-year period. The elements of the transition plan as required by the regulation remain virtually unchanged from the proposal but § 84.22(d) [§ 104.22(d)] now includes a requirement that the recipient make the plan available for public inspection.

Several commenters expressed concern that the program accessibility standard would result in the segregation of handicapped persons in educational institutions. The regulation will not be applied to permit such a result. See § 84.4(c)(2)(iv) [§ 104.4(c)(2)(iv)], prohibiting unnecessarily separate treatment; § 84.35 [§ 104.35], requiring that students in elementary and secondary schools be educated in the most integrated setting appropriate to their needs; and new § 84.43(d) [§ 104.43(d)], applying the same standard to postsecondary education.

We have received some comments from organizations of handicapped persons on the subject of requiring, over an extended period of time, a barrier-free environment—that is, requiring the removal of all architectural barriers in existing facilities. The Department has considered these comments but has decided to take no further action at this time concerning these suggestions, believing that such action should only be considered in light of experience in implementing the program accessibility standard.

21. *New construction.* Section 84.23 [§ 104.23] requires that all new facilities, as well as alterations that could affect access to and use of existing facilities, be designed and constructed in a manner so as to make the facility accessible to and usable by handicapped persons. Section 84.23(a) [§ 104.23(a)] has been amended so that it applies to each newly constructed facility if the construction was commenced after the effective date of the regulation. The words "if construction has commenced" will be considered to mean "if goundbreaking has taken place." Thus, a recipient will not be required to alter the design of a facility that has progressed beyond groundbreaking prior to the effective date of the regulation.

Paragraph (b) requires certain alterations to conform to the requirement of physical accessibility in paragraph (a). If an alteration is undertaken to a portion of a building the accessibility of which could be improved by the manner in which the alteration is carried out, the alteration must be made in that manner. Thus, if a doorway or wall is being altered, the door or other wall opening must be made wide enough to accommodate wheelchairs. On the other hand, if the alteration consists of altering ceilings, the provisions of this section are not applicable because this alteration cannot be done in a way that affects the accessibility of that portion of the building. The phrase "to the maximum extent feasible" has been added to allow for the occasional case in which the nature of an existing facility is such as to make it impractical or prohibitively expensive to renovate the building in a manner that results in its being entirely barrier-free. In all such cases, however, the alteration should provide the maximum amount of physical accessibility feasible.

As proposed, § 84.23(c) [§ 104.23(c)] required compliance with the American National Standards Institute (ANSI) standard on building accessibility as the minimum necessary for compliance with the accessibility requirement of §§ 84.23 (a) and (b) [§§ 104.23 (a) and (b)]. The reference to the ANSI standard created some ambiguity, since the standard itself provides for waivers where other methods are equally effective in providing accessibility to the facility. Moreover, the Secretary does not wish to discourage innovation in barrier-free construction by requiring absolute adherence to a rigid design standard. Accordingly, § 84.23(c) [§ 104.23(c)] has been revised to permit departures from particular requirements of the ANSI standard where the recipient can demonstrate that equivalent access to the facility is provided.

Section 84.23(d) [§ 104.23(d)] of the proposed regulation, providing for a limited deferral of action concerning facilities that are subject to section 502 as well as section 504 of the Act, has been deleted. The Secretary believes that the provision is unnecessary and inappropriate to this regulation. The Department will, however, seek to coordinate enforcement activities under this regulation with those of the Architectural and Transportation Barriers Compliance Board.

Subpart D—Preschool, Elementary, and Secondary Education

Subpart D sets forth requirements for nondiscrimination in preschool, elementary, secondary, and adult education programs and activities, including secondary vocational education programs. In this context, the term "adult education" refers only to those educational programs and activities for adults that are operated by elementary and secondary schools.

The provisions of Subpart D apply to state and local educational agencies. Although the subpart applies, in general, to both public and private education programs and activities that are federally assisted, §§ 84.32 and 84.33 [§§ 104.32 and 104.33] apply only to public programs and § 84.39 [§ 104.39] applies only to private programs; §§ 84.35 and 84.36 [§§ 104.35 and 84.36] apply both to public programs and to those private programs that include special services for handicapped students.

Subpart B generally conforms to the standards established for the education of handicapped persons in *Mills v. Board of Education of the District of Columbia,* 348 F.Supp. 866 (D.D.C.1972), *Pennsylvania Association for Retarded Children v. Commonwealth of Pennsylvania,* 334 F.Supp. 1257 (E.D.Pa.1971), 343 F.Supp. 279 (E.D.Pa.1972), and *Lebanks v. Spears,* 60 F.R.D. 135, (E.D.La.1973), as well as in the Education of the Handicapped Act, as amended by Public Law 94-142 (the EHA).

The basic requirements common to those cases, to the EHA, and to this regulation are (1) that handicapped persons, regardless of the nature or severity of their handicap, be provided a free appropriate public education, (2) that handicapped students be educated with nonhandicapped students to the maximum extent appropriate to their needs, (3) that educational agencies undertake to identify and locate all unserved handicapped children, (4) that evaluation procedures be improved in order to avoid the inappropriate education that results from the misclassification of students, and (5) that procedural safeguards be established to enable parents and guardians to influence decisions regarding the evaluation and placement of their children. These requirements are designed to ensure that no handicapped child is excluded from school on the basis of handicap and, if a recipient demonstrates that placement in a regular educational setting cannot be achieved satisfactorily, that the student is provided with adequate alternative services suited to the student's needs without additional cost to the student's parents or guardian. Thus, a recipient that operates a public school system must either educate handicapped children in its regular program or provide such children with an appropriate alternative education at public expense.

It is not the intention of the Department, except in extraordinary circumstances, to review the result of individual placement and other educational decisions, so long as the school district complies with the "process" requirements of this subpart (concerning identification and location, evaluation, and due process procedures). However, the Department will place a high priority on investigating cases which may involve exclusion of a child from the education system or a pattern or practice of discriminatory placements or education.

22. *Location and notification.* Section 84.32 [§ 104.32] requires public schools to take steps annually to identify and locate handicapped children who are not receiving an education and to publicize to handicapped children and their parents the rights and duties established by section 504 and this regulation. This section has been shortened without substantive change.

23. *Free appropriate public education.* Former §§ 84.34 [104.34] ("Free education") and 84.36(a) [104.36(a)] ("Suitable education") have been consolidated and revised in new § 84.33 [§ 104.33]. Under § 84.34(a) [§ 104.34(a)], a recipient is responsible for providing a free appropriate public education to each qualified handicapped person who is in the recipient's jurisdiction. The word "in" encompasses the concepts of both domicile and actual residence. If a recipient places a child in a

program other than its own, it remains financially responsible for the child, whether or not the other program is operated by another recipient or educational agency. Moreover, a recipient may not place a child in a program that is inappropriate or that otherwise violates the requirements of Subpart D. And in no case may a recipient refuse to provide services to a handicapped child in its jurisdiction because of another person's or entity's failure to assume financial responsibility.

Section 84.33(b) [§ 104.33(b)] concerns the provision of appropriate educational services to handicapped children. To be appropriate, such services must be designed to meet handicapped children's individual educational needs to the same extent that those of nonhandicapped children are met. An appropriate education could consist of education in regular classes, education in regular classes with the use of supplementary services, or special education and related services. Special education may include specially designed instruction in classrooms, at home, or in private or public institutions and may be accompanied by such related services as developmental, corrective, and other supportive services (including psychological, counseling, and medical diagnostic services). The placement of the child must however, be consistent with the requirements of § 84.34 [§ 104.34] and be suited to his or her educational needs.

The quality of the educational services provided to handicapped students must equal that of the services provided to nonhandicapped students; thus, handicapped students' teachers must be trained in the instruction of persons with the handicap in question and appropriate materials and equipment must be available. The Department is aware that the supply of adequately trained teachers may, at least at the outset of the imposition of this requirement, be insufficient to meet the demand of all recipients. This factor will be considered in determining the appropriateness of the remedy for noncompliance with this section. A new § 84.33(b)(2) [§ 104.33(b)(2)] has been added, which allows this requirement to be met through the full implementation of an individualized education program developed in accordance with the standards of the EHA.

Paragraph (c) of § 84.33 [§ 104.33] sets forth the specific financial obligations of a recipient. If a recipient does not itself provide handicapped persons with the requisite services, it must assume the cost of any alternate placement. If, however, a recipient offers adequate services and if alternate placement is chosen by a student's parent or guardian, the recipient need not assume the cost of the outside services. (If the parent or guardian believes that his or her child cannot be suitably educated in the recipient's program, he or she may make use of the procedures established in § 84.36 [§ 104.36]). Under this paragraph, a recipient's obligation extends beyond the provision of tuition payments in the case of placement outside the regular program. Adequate transportation must also be provided. Recipients must also pay for psychological services and those medical services necessary for diagnostic and evaluative purposes.

If the recipient places a student, because of his or her handicap, in a program that necessitates his or her being away from home, the payments must also cover room and board and nonmedical care (including custodial and supervisory care). When residential care is necessitated not by the student's handicap but by factors such as the student's home conditions, the recipient is not required to pay the cost of room and board.

Two new sentences have been added to paragraph (c)(1) to make clear that a recipient's financial obligations need not be met solely through its own funds. Recipients may rely on funds from any public or private source including insurers and similar third parties.

The EHA requires a free appropriate education to be provided to handicapped children "no later than September 1, 1978," but section 504 contains no authority for delaying enforcement. To resolve this problem, a new paragraph (d) has been added to § 84.33 [§ 104.33]. Section 84.33(d) [§ 104.33(d)] requires recipients to achieve full compliance with the free appropriate public education requirements of § 84.33 [§ 104.33] as expeditiously as possible, but in no event later than September 1, 1978. The provision also makes clear that, as of the effective date of this regulation, no recipient may exclude a qualified handicapped child from its educational program. This provision against exclusion is consistent with the order of providing services set forth in section 612(3) of the EHA, which places the highest priority on providing services to handicapped children who are not receiving an education.

24. *Educational setting.* Section 84.34 [§ 104.34] prescribes standards for educating handicapped persons with nonhandicapped persons to the maximum extent appropriate to the needs of the handicapped person in question. A handicapped student may be removed from the regular educational setting only where the recipient can show that the needs of the student would, on balance, be served by placement in another setting.

Although under § 84.34 [§ 104.34], the needs of the handicapped person are determinative as to proper placement, it should be stressed that, where a handicapped student is so disruptive in a regular classroom that the education of other students is significantly impaired, the needs of the handicapped child cannot be met in that environment. Therefore, regular placement would not be appropriate to his or her needs and would not be required by § 84.34 [§ 104.34].

Among the factors to be considered in placing a child is the need to place the child as close to home as possible. A new sentence has been added to paragraph (a) requiring recipients to take this factor into account. As pointed out in several comments, the parents' right under § 84.36 [§ 104.36] to challenge the placement of their child extends not only to placement in special classes or separate schools but also to placement in a distant school and, in particular, to residential placement. An equally appropriate educational program may exist closer to home; this issue may be raised by the parent or guardian under §§ 84.34 and 84.36 [§§ 104.34 and 104.36].

New paragraph (b) specifies that handicapped children must also be provided nonacademic services in as integrated a setting as possible. This requirement is especially important for children whose educational needs necessitate their being solely with other handicapped children during most of each day. To the maximum extent appropriate, children in residential settings are also to be provided opportunities for participation with other children.

Section 84.34(c) (formerly § 84.38) [§ 104.34(c)] requires that any facilities that are identifiable as being for handicapped students be comparable in quality to other facilities of the recipient. A number of comments objected to this section on the basis that it encourages the creation and maintenance of such facilities. This is not the intent of the provision. A separate facility violates section 504 unless it is indeed necessary to the provision of an appropriate education to certain handicapped students. In those instances in which such facilities are necessary (as might be the case, for example, for severely retarded persons), this provision requires that the educational services provided be comparable to those provided in the facilities of the recipient that are not identifiable as being for handicapped persons.

25. *Evaluation and placement.* Because the failure to provide handicapped persons with an appropriate education is so frequently the result of misclassification or misplacement, section 84.33(b)(1) [§ 104.33(b)(1)] makes compliance with its

provisions contingent upon adherence to certain procedures designed to ensure appropriate classification and placement. These procedures, delineated in §§ 84.35 and 84.36 [§§ 104.35 and 104.36], are concerned with testing and other evaluation methods and with procedural due process rights.

Section 84.35(a) [§ 104.35(a)] [require] that an individual evaluation be conducted before any action is taken with respect either to the initial placement of a handicapped child in a regular or special education program or to any subsequent significant change in that placement. Thus, a full reevaluation is not required every time an adjustment in placement is made. "Any action" includes denials of placement.

Paragraphs (b) and (c) of § 84.35 [§ 104.35] [establish] procedures designed to ensure that children are not misclassified, unnecessarily labeled as being handicapped, or incorrectly placed because of inappropriate selection, administration, or interpretation of evaluation materials. This problem has been extensively documented in "Issues in the Classification of Children," a report by the Project on Classification of Exceptional Children, in which the HEW Interagency Task Force participated. The provisions of these paragraphs are aimed primarily at abuses in the placement process that result from misuse of, or undue or misplaced reliance on, standardized scholastic aptitude tests.

Paragraph (b) has been shortened but not substantively changed. The requirement in former subparagraph (1) that recipients provide and administer evaluation materials in the native language of the student has been deleted as unnecessary, since the same requirement already exists under title VI and is more appropriately covered under that statute. Subparagraphs (1) and (2) are, in general, intended to prevent misinterpretation and similar misuse of test scores and, in particular, to avoid undue reliance on general intelligence tests. Subparagraph (3) requires a recipient to administer tests to a student with impaired sensory, manual, or speaking skills in whatever manner is necessary to avoid distortion of the test results by the impairment. Former subparagraph (4) has been deleted as unnecessarily repetitive of the other provisions of this paragraph.

Paragraph (c) requires a recipient to draw upon a variety of sources in the evaluation process so that the possibility of error in classification is minimized. In particular, it requires that all significant factors relating to the learning process, including adaptive behavior, be considered. (Adaptive behavior is the effectiveness with which the individual meets the standards of personal independence and social responsibility expected of his or her age and cultural group). Information from all sources must be documented and considered by a group of persons, and the procedure must ensure that the child is placed in the most integrated setting appropriate.

The proposed regulation would have required a complete individual reevaluation of the student each year. The Department has concluded that it is inappropriate in the section 504 regulation to require full reevaluations on such a rigid schedule. Accordingly, § 84.35(c) [§ 104.35(c)] requires periodic reevaluations and specifies that reevaluations in accordance with the EHA will constitute compliance. The proposed regulation implementing the EHA allows reevaluation at three-year intervals except under certain specified circumstances.

Under § 84.36 [§ 104.36], a recipient must establish a system of due process procedures to be afforded to parents or guardians before the recipient takes any action regarding the identification, evaluation, or educational placement of a person who, because of handicap, needs or is believed to need special education or related services. This section has been revised. Because the due process procedures of the EHA, incorporated by reference in the proposed section 504 regulation, are inappropriate for some recipients not subject to that Act, the section now specifies minimum necessary procedures: notice, a right to inspect records, an impartial hearing with a right to representation by counsel, and a review procedure. The EHA procedures remain one means of meeting the regulation's due process requirements, however, and are recommended to recipients as a model.

26. *Nonacademic services.* Section 84.37 [§ 104.37] requires a recipient to provide nonacademic and extracurricular services and activities in such manner as is necessary to afford handicapped students an equal opportunity for participation. Because these services and activities are part of a recipient's education program, they must, in accordance with the provisions of § 84.34 [§ 104.34], be provided in the most integrated setting appropriate.

Revised paragraph (c)(2) does permit separation or differentiation with respect to the provision of physical education and athletics activities, but only if qualified handicapped students are also allowed the opportunity to compete for regular teams or participate in regular activities. Most handicapped students are able to participate in one or more regular physical education and athletics activities. For example, a student in a wheelchair can participate in [a] regular archery course, as can a deaf student in a wrestling course.

Finally, the one-year transition period provided in former § 84.37(a)(3) [in a proposed section] was deleted in response to the almost unanimous objection of commenters to that provision.

27. *Preschool and adult education.* Section 84.38 [§ 104.38] prohibits discrimination on the basis of handicap in preschool and adult education programs. Former paragraph (b), which emphasized that compensatory programs for disadvantaged children are subject to section 504, has been deleted as unnecessary, since it is comprehended by paragraph (a).

28. *Private education.* Section 84.39 [§ 104.39] sets forth the requirements applicable to recipients that operate private education programs and activities. The obligations of these recipients have been changed in two significant respects: first, private schools are subject to the evaluation and due process provisions of the subpart only if they operate special education programs; second, under § 84.39(b) [§ 104.39(b)], they may charge more for providing services to handicapped students than to nonhandicapped students to the extent that additional charges can be justified by increased costs.

Paragraph (a) of § 84.39 [§ 104.39] is intended to make clear that recipients that operate private education programs and activities are not required to provide an appropriate education to handicapped students with special educational needs if the recipient does not offer programs designed to meet those needs. Thus, a private school that has no program for mentally retarded persons is neither required to admit such a person into its program nor to arrange or pay for the provision of the person's education in another program. A private recipient without a special program for blind students, however, would not be permitted to exclude, on the basis of blindness, a blind applicant who is able to participate in the regular program with minor adjustments in the manner in which the program is normally offered.

Subpart E—Postsecondary Education

Subpart E prescribes requirements for nondiscrimination in recruitment, admission, and treatment of students in postsecondary education programs and activities, including vocational education.

29. *Admission and recruitment.* In addition to a general prohibition of discrimination on the basis of handicap in § 84.42(a) [§ 104.42(a)], the regulation delineates, in § 84.42(b) [§ 104.42(b)], specific prohibitions concerning the establishment of limitations on admission of handicapped students, the use of tests or selection criteria, and preadmission inquiry. Several changes have been made in this provision.

Section 84.42(b) [§ 104.42(b)] provides that postsecondary educational institutions may not use any test or criterion for admission that has a disproportionate, adverse effect on handicapped persons unless it has been validated as a predictor of academic success and alternate tests or criteria with a less disproportionate, adverse effect are shown by the Department to be available. There are two significant changes in this approach from the July 16 proposed regulation.

First, many commenters expressed concern that § 84.42(b)(2)(ii) [§ 104.42(b)(2)(ii)] could be interpreted to require a "global search" for alternate tests that do not have a disproportionate, adverse impact on handicapped persons. This was not the intent of the provision, and, therefore, it has been amended to place the burden on the Director of the Office for Civil Rights [Assistant Secretary for Civil Rights], rather than on the recipient, to identify alternate tests.

Second, a new paragraph (d), concerning validity studies, has been added. Under the proposed regulation, overall success in an education program, not just first-year grades, was the criterion against which admissions tests were to be validated. This approach has been changed to reflect the comment of professional testing services that use of first-year grades would be less disruptive of present practice and that periodic validity studies against overall success in the education program would be [a] sufficient check on the reliability of first-year grades.

Section 84.42(b)(3) [§ 104.42(b)(3)] also requires a recipient to assure itself that admissions tests are selected and administered to applicants with impaired sensory, manual, or speaking skills in such manner as is necessary to avoid unfair distortion of test results. Methods have been developed for testing the aptitude and achievement of persons who are not able to take written tests or even to make the marks required for mechanically scored objective tests; in addition, methods for testing persons with visual or hearing impairments are available. A recipient, under this paragraph, must assure itself that such methods are used with respect to the selection and administration of any admissions tests that it uses.

Section 84.42(b)(3)(iii) [§ 104.42(b)(3)(iii)] has been amended to require that admissions tests be administered in facilities that, on the whole, are accessible. In this context, "on the whole" means that not all of the facilities need be accessible so long as a sufficient number of facilities are available to handicapped persons.

Revised § 84.42(b)(4) [§ 104.42(b)(4)] generally prohibits preadmission inquiries as to whether an applicant has a handicap. The considerations that led to this revision are similar to those underlying the comparable revision of § 84.14 [§ 104.14] on preemployment inquiries. The regulation does, however, allow inquiries to be made, after admission but before enrollment, as to handicaps that may require accommodation.

New paragraph (c) parallels the section on preemployment inquiries and allows postsecondary institutions to inquire about applicants' handicaps before admission, subject to certain safeguards, if the purpose of the inquiry is to take remedial action to correct past discrimination or to take voluntary action to overcome the limited participation of handicapped persons in postsecondary educational institutions.

Proposed § 84.42(c) [§ 104.42(c)], which would have allowed different admissions criteria in certain cases for handicapped persons, was widely misinterpreted in comments from both handicapped persons and recipients. We have concluded that the section is unnecessary, and it has been deleted.

30. *Treatment of students.* Section 84.43 [§ 104.43] contains general provisions prohibiting the discriminatory treatment of qualified handicapped applicants. Paragraph (b) requires recipients to ensure that equal opportunities are provided to its handicapped students in education programs and activities that are not operated by the recipient. The recipient must be satisfied that the outside education program or activity as a whole is nondiscriminatory. For example, a college must ensure that discrimination on the basis of handicap does not occur in connection with teaching assignments of student teachers in elementary or secondary schools not operated by the college. Under the "as a whole" wording, the college could continue to use elementary or secondary school systems that discriminate if, and only if, the college's student teaching program, when viewed in its entirety, offered handicapped student teachers the same range and quality of choice in student teaching assignments afforded nonhandicapped students.

Paragraph (c) of this section prohibits a recipient from excluding qualified handicapped students from any course, course of study, or other part of its education program or activity. This paragraph is designed to eliminate the practice of excluding handicapped persons from specific courses and from areas of concentration because of factors such as ambulatory difficulties of the student or assumptions by the recipient that no job would be available in the area in question for a person with that handicap.

New paragraph (d) requires postsecondary institutions to operate their programs and activities so that handicapped students are provided services in the most integrated setting appropriate. Thus, if a college had several elementary physics classes and had moved one such class to the first floor of the science building to accommodate students in wheelchairs, it would be a violation of this paragraph for the college to concentrate handicapped students with no mobility impairments in the same class.

31. *Academic adjustments.* Paragraph (a) of § 84.44 [§ 104.44] requires that a recipient make certain adjustments to academic requirements and practices that discriminate or have the effect of discriminating on the basis of handicap. This requirement, like its predecessor in the proposed regulation, does not obligate an institution to waive course or other academic requirements. But such institutions must accommodate those requirements to the needs of individual handicapped students. For example, an institution might permit an otherwise qualified handicapped student who is deaf to substitute an art appreciation or music history course for a required course in music appreciation or could modify the manner in which the music appreciation course is conducted for the deaf student. It should be stressed that academic requirements that can be demonstrated by the recipient to be essential to its program of instruction or to particular degrees need not be changed.

Paragraph (b) provides that postsecondary institutions may not impose rules that have the effect of limiting the participation of handicapped students in the education program. Such rules include prohibition of tape recorders or braillers in classrooms and dog guides in campus buildings. Several recipients expressed concern about allowing students to tape record lectures because the professor may later want to copyright the lectures. This problem may be solved by requiring students to sign agreements that they will not release the tape recording or transcription or otherwise hinder the professor's ability to obtain a copyright.

Paragraph (c) of this section, concerning the administration of course examinations to students with impaired sensory, manual, or speaking skills, parallels the regulation's provisions on admissions testing (§ 84.42(b) [§ 104.42(b)]) and will be similarly interpreted.

Under § 84.44(d) [§ 104.44(d)], a recipient must ensure that no handicapped student is subject to discrimination in the recipient's program because of the absence of necessary auxiliary educational aids. Colleges and universities expressed concern about the costs of compliance with this provision.

The Department emphasizes that recipients can usually meet this obligation by assisting students in using existing resources for auxiliary aids such as state vocational rehabilitation agencies and private charitable organizations. Indeed, the Department anticipates that the bulk of auxiliary aids will be paid for by state and private agencies, not by colleges or universities. In those circumstances where the recipient institution must provide the educational auxiliary aid, the institution has flexibility in choosing the methods by which the aids will be supplied. For example, some universities have used students to work with the institution's handicapped students. Other institutions have used existing private agencies that tape texts for handicapped students free of charge in order to reduce the number of readers needed for visually impaired students.

As long as no handicapped person is excluded from a program because of the lack of an appropriate aid, the recipient need not have all such aids on hand at all times. Thus, readers need not be available in the recipient's library at all times so long as the schedule of times when a reader is available is established, is adhered to, and is sufficient. Of course, recipients are not required to maintain a complete braille library.

32. *Housing.* Section 84.45(a) [§ 104.45(a)] requires postsecondary institutions to provide housing to handicapped students at the same cost as they provide it to other students and in a convenient, accessible, and comparable manner. Commenters, particularly blind persons, pointed out that some handicapped persons can live in any college housing and need not wait to the end of the transition period in Subpart C to be offered the same variety and scope of housing accommodations given to nonhandicapped persons. The Department concurs with this position and will interpret this section accordingly.

A number of colleges and universities reacted negatively to paragraph (b) of this section. It provides that, if a recipient assists in making off-campus housing available to its students, it should develop and implement procedures to assure itself that off-campus housing, as a whole, is available to handicapped students. Since postsecondary institutions are presently required to assure themselves that off-campus housing is provided in a manner that does not discriminate on the basis of sex (§ 86.32 [§ 106.32] of the title IX regulation), they may use the procedures developed under title IX in order to comply with § 84.45(b) [§ 104.45(b)]. It should be emphasized that not every off-campus living accommodation need be made accessible to handicapped persons.

33. *Health and insurance.* Section 84.46 of the proposed regulation [A proposed section], providing that recipients may not discriminate on the basis of handicap in the provision of health and related services, has been deleted as duplicative of the general provisions of section 84.43 [§ 104.43]. This deletion represents no change in the obligation of recipients to provide nondiscriminatory health and insurance plans. The Department will continue to require that nondiscriminatory health services be provided to handicapped students. Recipients are not required, however, to provide specialized services and aids to handicapped persons in health programs. If, for example, a college infirmary treats only simple disorders such as cuts, bruises, and colds, its obligation to handicapped persons is to treat such disorders for them.

34. *Financial assistance.* Section 84.46(a) [§ 104.46(a)] (formerly § 84.47), prohibiting discrimination in providing financial assistance, remains substantively the same. It provides that recipients may not provide less assistance to or limit the eligibility of qualified handicapped persons for such assistance, whether the assistance is provided directly by the recipient or by another entity through the recipient's sponsorship. Awards that are made under wills, trusts, or similar legal instruments in a discriminatory manner are permissible, but only if the overall effect of the recipient's provision of financial assistance is not discriminatory on the basis of handicap.

It will not be considered discriminatory to deny, on the basis of handicap, an athletic scholarship to a handicapped person if the handicap renders the person unable to qualify for the award. For example, a student who has a neurological disorder might be denied a varsity football scholarship on the basis of his inability to play football, but a deaf person could not, on the basis of handicap, be denied a scholarship for the school's diving team. The deaf person could, however, be denied a scholarship on the basis of comparative diving ability.

Commenters on § 84.46(b) [§ 104.46(b)], which applies to assistance in obtaining outside employment for students, expressed similar concerns to those raised under § 84.43(b) [§ 104.43(b)], concerning cooperative programs. This paragraph has been changed in the same manner as § 84.43(b) [§ 104.43(b)] to include the "as a whole" concept and will be interpreted in the same manner as § 84.43(b) [§ 104.43(b)].

35. *Nonacademic services.* Section 84.47 [§ 104.47] (formerly § 84.48) establishes nondiscrimination standards for physical education and athletics counseling and placement services, and social organizations. This section sets the same standards as does § 84.38 [§ 104.38] of Subpart D, discussed above, and will be interpreted in a similar fashion.

Subpart F—Health, Welfare, and Social Services

Subpart F applies to recipients that operate health, welfare, and social services programs. The Department received fewer comments on this subpart than on others.

Although many commented that Subpart F lacked specificity, these commenters provided neither concrete suggestions nor additions. Nevertheless, some changes have been made, pursuant to comment, to clarify the obligations of recipients in specific areas. In addition, in an effort to reduce duplication in the regulation, the section governing recipients providing health services (proposed § 84.52) has been consolidated with the section regulating providers of welfare and social services (proposed § 84.53). Since the separate provisions that appeared in the proposed regulation were almost identical, no substantive change should be inferred from their consolidation.

Several commenters asked whether Subpart F applies to vocational rehabilitation agencies whose purpose is to assist in the rehabilitation of handicapped persons. To the extent that such agencies receive financial assistance from the Department, they are covered by Subpart F and all other relevant subparts of the regulation. Nothing in this regulation, however, precludes such agencies from servicing only handicapped persons. Indeed, § 84.4(c) [§ 104.4(c)] permits recipients to offer services or benefits that are limited by federal law to handicapped persons or classes of handicapped persons.

Many comments suggested requiring state health, welfare, and social service agencies to take an active role in the enforcement of section 504 with regard to local health and social service providers. The Department believes that the possibility for federal-state cooperation in the administration and enforcement of section 504 warrants further consideration. Moreover, the Department will rely largely on state Medicaid agencies, as it has under title VI, for monitoring compliance by individual Medicaid providers. [The last sentence in this paragraph is omitted in the analysis following 34 CFR Part 104, as are the words "health, welfare, and" in the first sentence in this paragraph.]

A number of comments also discussed whether section 504 should be read to require payment of compensation to institutionalized handicapped patients who perform services for the institution in which they reside. The Department of Labor has recently issued a proposed regulation under the Fair Labor Standards Act (FLSA) that covers the question of compensation for institutionalized persons, 42 FR 15224 (March 18, 1977). This Department will seek information and comment from the Department of Labor concerning that agency's experience administering the FLSA regulation.

36. *Health, welfare, and other social service providers.* As already noted, § 84.53 has been combined with proposed § 84.53 into a single section covering health, welfare, and other social services. [The preceding sentence is omitted in the analysis following 34 CFR Part 104.] Section 84.52(a) [§ 104.52(a)] has been expanded in several respects. The addition of new paragraph (a)(2) is intended to make clear the basic requirement of equal opportunity to receive benefits or services in the health, welfare, and social services areas. The paragraph parallels §§ 84.4(b)(ii) [§ 104.4(b)(ii)] and 84.43(b) [§ 104.43(b)]. New paragraph (a)(3) requires the provision of effective benefits or services, as defined in §84.4(b)(2) [§ 104.4(b)(2)] (i.e., benefits or services which "afford handicapped persons equal opportunity to obtain the same result (or) to gain the same benefit * * *").

Section 84.52(a) [§ 104.52(a)] also includes provisions concerning the limitation of benefits or services to handicapped persons and the subjection of handicapped persons to different eligibility standards. (These provisions were previously included in the welfare recipient section (§84.53(a)).) [The parenthetical sentence is omitted from 34 CFR Part 104.] One common misconception about the regulation is that it would require specialized hospitals and other health care providers to treat all handicapped persons. The regulation makes no such requirement. Thus, a burn treatment center need not provide other types of medical treatment to handicapped persons unless it provides such medical services to nonhandicapped persons. It could not, however, refuse to treat the burns of a deaf person because of his or her deafness.

Commenters had raised the question of whether the prohibition against different standards of eligibility might preclude recipients from providing special services to handicapped persons or classes of handicapped persons. The regulation will not be so interpreted, and the specific section in question has been eliminated. Section 84.4(c) [§ 104.4(c)] makes clear that special programs for handicapped persons are permitted.

A new paragraph (a)(5) concerning the provision of different or separate services or benefits has been added. This provision prohibits such treatment unless necessary to provide qualified handicapped persons with benefits and services that are as effective as those provided to others.

[The next three paragraphs do not appear in the analysis following 34 CFR Part 104.]

Section 84.52(a)(2) of the proposed regulation has been omitted as duplicative of revised § 84.22(b) and (c) in Subpart C. As discussed above, these sections permit health care providers to arrange to meet patients in accessible facilities and to make referrals in carefully limited circumstances.

Section 84.52(a)(3) of the proposed regulation has been redesignated § 84.52(b) and has been amended to cover written material concerning waivers of rights or consent to treatment as well as general notices concerning health benefits or services. The section requires the recipient to ensure that qualified handicapped persons are not denied effective notice because of their handicap. For example, recipients could use several different types of notice in order to reach persons with impaired vision or hearing, such as brailled messages, radio spots, and tactile devices on cards or envelopes to inform blind persons of the need to call the recipient for further information.

Sections 84.52(a)(4), 84.52(a)(5), and 84.52(b) have been omitted from the regulation as unnecessary. They are clearly comprehended by the more general sections banning discrimination.

[The following paragraph appears in the analysis following 34 CFR Part 104, but is not included in the analysis following 45 CFR Part 84]:

[Section 104.52(b) has been amended to cover written materials concerning waivers of rights or consent to treatment as well as general notices concerning health benefits or services. The section requires the recipient to ensure that qualified handicapped persons are not denied effective notice because of their handicap. For example, recipients could use several different types of notice in order to reach persons with impaired vision or hearing, such as brailled messages, radio spots, and [tactile] devices on cards or envelopes to inform blind persons of the need to call the recipient for further information.]

Section 84.52(c) [104.52(c)] is a new section requiring recipient hospitals to establish a procedure for effective communication with persons with impaired hearing for the purpose of providing emergency health care. Although it would be appropriate for a hospital to fulfill its responsibilities under this section by having a full-time interpreter for the deaf on staff, there may be other means of accomplishing the desired result of assuring that some means of communication is immediately available for deaf persons needing emergency treatment.

Section 84.52(d) [104.52(d)], also a new provision, requires recipients with fifteen or more employees to provide appropriate auxiliary aids for persons with impaired sensory, manual, or speaking skills. Further, the Director [Assistant Secretary] may require a small provider to furnish auxiliary aids where the provision of aids would not adversely affect the ability of the recipient to provide its health benefits or services. [The next sentence does not appear in the analysis following 34 CFR Part 104.] Thus, although a small nonprofit neighborhood clinic might not be obligated to have available an interpreter for deaf persons, the Director may require provision of such aids as may be reasonably available to ensure that qualified handicapped persons are not denied appropriate benefits or services because of their handicaps.

37. *Treatment of Drug Addicts and Alcoholics.* Section 84.53 [104.53] is a new section that prohibits discrimination in the treatment and admission of drug and alcohol addicts to hospitals and outpatient facilities. [The following two sentences are not included in the analysis following 34 CFR Part 104.] This section is included pursuant to section 407, Public Law 92-255, The Drug Abuse Office and Treatment Act of 1972 (21 U.S.C. 1174), as amended, and section 321, Public Law 91-616, the Comprehensive Alcohol Abuse and Alcoholism Prevention, Treatment, and Rehabilitation Act of 1970 (42 U.S.C. 4581), as amended, and section 821, Public Law 93-282. Section 504 itself also prohibits such discriminatory treatment and, in addition, prohibits similar discriminatory treatment by other types of health providers. Section 84.53 [104.53] prohibits discrimination against drug abusers by operators of outpa-

tient facilities, despite the fact that section 407 pertains only to hospitals, because of the broader application of section 504. This provision does not mean that all hospitals and outpatient facilities must treat drug addiction and alcoholism. It simply means, for example, that a cancer clinic may not refuse to treat cancer patients simply because they are also alcoholics.

38. *Education of institutionalized persons.* The regulation retains § 84.54 [104.54] of the proposed regulation that requires that an appropriate education be provided to qualified handicapped persons who are confined to residential institutions or day care centers.

Subpart G—Procedures

In § 84.61 [104.61], the Secretary has adopted the title VI complaint and enforcement procedures for use in implementing section 504 until such time as they are superseded by the issuance of a consolidated procedural regulation applicable to all of the civil rights statutes and executive orders administered by the Department.

APPENDIX B TO PART 84 [PART 104]—GUIDELINES FOR ELIMINATING DISCRIMINATION AND DENIAL OF SERVICES ON THE BASIS OF RACE, COLOR, NATIONAL ORIGIN, SEX, AND HANDICAP IN VOCATIONAL EDUCATION PROGRAMS

EDITORIAL NOTE: For the text of these guidelines, see 45 CFR Part 80 [34 CFR Part 100], Appendix B. [**Appendix B to 34 CFR Part 100 is reproduced in full, below**].

[44 FR 17168, Mar. 21, 1979]

APPENDIX C TO PART 84—GUIDELINES RELATING TO HEALTH CARE FOR HANDICAPPED INFANTS

[This appendix is omitted from 34 CFR Part 104].

(a) *Interpretative guidelines relating to the applicability of this part to health care for handicapped infants.* The following are interpretative guidelines of the Department set forth here to assist recipients and the public in understanding the Department's interpretation of section 504 and the regulations contained in this part as applied to matters concerning health care for handicapped infants. These interpretative guidelines are illustrative; they do not independently establish rules of conduct.

(1) With respect to programs and activities receiving Federal financial assistance, health care providers may not, solely on the basis of present or anticipated physical or mental impairments of an infant, withhold treatment or nourishment from the infant who, in spite of such impairments, will medically benefit from the treatment or nourishment.

(2) Futile treatment or treatment that will do no more than temporarily prolong the act of dying of a terminally ill infant is not considered treatment that will medically benefit the infant.

(3) In determining whether certain possible treatments will be medically beneficial to an infant, reasonable medical judgments in selecting among alternative courses of treatment will be respected.

(4) Section 504 and the provisions of this part are not applicable to parents (who are not recipients of Federal financial assistance). However, each recipient health care provider must in all aspects of its health care programs receiving Federal financial assistance provide health care and related services in a manner consistent with the requirements of section 504 and this part. Such aspects include decisions on whether to report, as required by State law or otherwise, to the appropriate child protective services agency a suspected instance of medical neglect of a child, or to take other action to seek review or parental decisions to withhold consent for medically indicated treatment. Whenever parents make a decision to withhold consent for medically beneficial treatment or nourishment, such recipient providers may not, solely on the basis of the infant's present or anticipated future mental or physical impairments, fail to follow applicable procedures on reporting such incidents to the child protective services agency or to seek judicial review.

(5) The following are examples of applying these interpretative guidelines. These examples are stated in the context of decisions made by recipient health care providers. Were these decisions made by parents, the guideline stated in section (a)(4) would apply. These examples assume no facts or complications other than those stated. Because every case must be examined on its individual facts, these are merely illustrative examples to assist in understanding the framework for applying the nondiscrimination requirements of section 504 and this part.

(i) Withholding of medically beneficial surgery to correct an intestinal obstruction in an infant with Down's Syndrome when the withholding is based upon the anticipated future mental retardation of the infant and there are no medical contraindications to the surgery that would otherwise justify withholding the surgery would constitute a discriminatory act, violative of section 504.

(ii) Withholding of treatment for medically correctable physical anomalies in children born with spina bifida when such denial is based on anticipated mental impairment[,] paralysis or incontinence of the infant, rather than on reasonable medical judgments that treatment would be futile, too unlikely of success given complications in the particular case, or otherwise not of medical benefit to the infant, would constitute a discriminatory act, violative of section 504.

(iii) Withholding of medical treatment for an infant born with anencephaly, who will inevitably die within a short period of time, would not constitute a discriminatory act because the treatment would be futile and so no more than temporarily prolong the act of dying.

(iv) Withholding of certain potential treatments from a severely premature and low birth weight infant on the grounds of reasonable medical judgments concerning the improbability of success or risks of potential harm to the infant would not violate section 504.

(b) *Guidelines for HHS investigations relating to health care for handicapped infants.* The following are guidelines of the Department in conducting investigations relating to health care for handicapped infants. They are set forth here to assist recipients and the public in understanding applicable investigative procedures. These guidelines do not establish rules of conduct, create or affect legally enforceable rights of any person, or modify existing rights, authorities or responsibilities pursuant to this part. These guidelines reflect the Department's recognition of the special circumstances presented in connection with complaints of suspected life-threatening noncompliance with this part involving health care for handicapped infants. These guidelines do not apply to other investigations pursuant to this part, or other civil rights statutes and rules. Deviations from these guidelines may occur when, in the judgment of the responsible Department official, other action is necessary to protect the life or health of a handicapped infant.

(1) Unless impracticable, whenever the Department receives a complaint of suspected life-threatening noncompliance with this part in connection with health care for a handicapped infant in a program or activity receiving Federal financial assistance, HHS will immediately conduct a preliminary inquiry into the matter by initiating telephone contact with the recipient hospital to obtain information relating to the condition and treatment of the infant who is the subject of the complaint. The preliminary inquiry, which may include additional contact with the complainant and a requirement that pertinent records be provided to the Department, will generally be completed within 24 hours (or sooner if indicated) after receipt of the complaint.

(2) Unless impracticable, whenever a recipient hospital has an Infant Care Review Committee, established and operated substantially in accordance with the provisions of 45 CFR 84.55(f), the Department will, as part of its preliminary inquiry, solicit the information available to, and the analysis and recommendations of, the ICRC. Unless, in the judgment of the responsible Department official, other action is necessary to protect the life or health of a handicapped infant, prior to initiating an on-site investigation, the Department will await receipt of this information from the ICRC for 24 hours (or less if indicated) after receipt of the complaint. The Department may require a subsequent written report of the ICRC's findings, accompanied by pertinent records and documentation.

(3) On the basis of the information obtained during preliminary inquiry, including information provided by the hospital (including the hospital's ICRC, if any), information provided by the complainant, and all other information obtained, the Department will determine whether there is a need for an on-site investigation of the complaint. Whenever the Department determines that doubt remains that the recipient hospital or some other recipient is in compliance with this part or additional documentation is desired to substantiate a conclusion, the Department will initiate an

on-site investigation or take some other appropriate action. Unless impracticable, prior to initiating an on-site investigation, the Department's medical consultant (referred to in paragraph 6) will contact the hospital's ICRC or appropriate medical personnel of the recipient's hospital.

(4) In conducting on-site investigations, when a recipient hospital has an ICRC established and operated substantially in accordance with the provisions of 45 CFR 84.55(f), the investigation will begin with, or include at the earliest practicable time, a meeting with the ICRC or its designees. In all on-site investigations, the Department will make every effort to minimize any potential inconvenience or disruption, accommodate the schedules of health care professionals and avoid making medical records unavailable. The Department will also seek to coordinate its investigation with any related investigations by the state child protective services agency so as to minimize potential disruption.

(5) It is the policy of the Department to make no comment to the public or media regarding the substance of a pending preliminary inquiry or investigation.

(6) The Department will obtain the assistance of a qualified medical consultant to evaluate the medical information (including medical records) obtained in the course of a preliminary inquiry or investigation. The name, title and telephone number of the Department's medical consultant will be made available to the recipient hospital. The Department's medical consultant will, if appropriate, contact medical personnel of the recipient hospital in connection with the preliminary inquiry, investigation or medical consultant's evaluation. To the extent practicable, the medical consultant will be a specialist with respect to the condition of the infant who is the subject of the preliminary inquiry or investigation. The medical consultant may be an employee of the Department or another person who has agreed to serve, with or without compensation, in that capacity.

(7) The Department will advise the recipient hospital of its conclusions as soon as possible following the completion of a preliminary inquiry or investigation. Whenever final administrative findings following an investigation of a complaint of suspected life-threatening noncompliance cannot be made promptly, the Department will seek to notify the recipient and the complainant of the Department's decision on whether the matter will be immediately referred to the Department of Justice pursuant to 45 CFR 80.8.

(8) Except as necessary to determine or effect compliance, the Department will (i) in conducting preliminary inquiries and investigations, permit information provided by the recipient hospital to the Department to be furnished without names or other identifying information relating to the infant and the infant's family; and (ii) to the extent permitted by law, safeguard the confidentiality of information obtained.

[49 FR 1653, Jan. 12, 1984]

Part 80 [Part 100] Regulations—Nondiscrimination under programs receiving Federal assistance through the Department of Health and Human Services [Education] effectuation of Title VI of the Civil Rights Act of 1964

***

§ 80.6 [100.6] Compliance information.

(a) *Cooperation and assistance.* The responsible Department official shall to the fullest extent practicable seek the cooperation of recipients in obtaining compliance with this part and shall provide assistance and guidance to recipients to help them comply voluntarily with this part.

(b) *Compliance reports.* Each recipient shall keep such records and submit to the responsible Department official or his designee timely, complete and accurate compliance reports at such times, and in such form and containing such information, as the responsible Department official or his designee may determine to be necessary to enable him to ascertain whether the recipient has complied or is complying with this part. For example, recipients should have available for the Department racial and ethnic data showing the extent to which members of minority groups are beneficiaries of and participants in federally assisted programs. In the case of any program under which a primary recipient extends Federal financial assistance to any other recipient, such other recipient shall also submit such compliance reports to the primary recipient as may be necessary to enable the primary recipient to carry out its obligations under this part.

(c) *Access to sources of information.* Each recipient shall permit access by the responsible Department official or his designee during normal business hours to such of its books, records, accounts, and other sources of information, and its facilities as may be pertinent to ascertain compliance with this part. Where any information required of a recipient is in the exclusive possession of any other agency, institution or person and this agency, institution or person shall fail or refuse to furnish this information the recipient shall so certify in its report and shall set forth what efforts it has made to obtain the information. Asserted considerations of privacy or confidentiality may not operate to bar the Department from evaluating or seeking to enforce compliance with this part. Information of a confidential nature obtained in connection with compliance evaluation or enforcement shall not be disclosed except where necessary in formal enforcement proceedings or where otherwise required by law.

(d) *Information to beneficiaries and participants.* Each recipient shall make available to participants, beneficiaries, and other interested persons such information regarding the provisions of this regulation and its applicability to the program for which the recipient receives Federal financial assistance, and make such information available to them in such manner, as the responsible Department official finds necessary to apprise such persons of the protections against discrimination assured them by the Act and this regulation.

(Sec. 601, 602 Civil Rights Act of 1964; 78 Stat. 252; 42 U.S.C. 2000d, 2000d-1) [29 FR 16298, Dec. 4, 1964, as amended at 32 FR 14555, Oct. 19, 1967; 38 FR 17981, 17982, July 5, 1973]

§ 80.7 [100.7] Conduct of investigations.

(a) *Periodic compliance reviews.* The responsible Department official or his designee shall from time to time review the practices of recipients to determine whether they are complying with this part.

(b) *Complaints.* Any person who believes himself or any specific class of individuals to be subjected to discrimination prohibited by this part may by himself or by a representative file with the responsible Department official or his designee a written complaint. A complaint must be filed not later than 180 days from the date of the alleged discrimination, unless the time for filing is extended by the responsible Department official or his designee.

(c) *Investigations.* The responsible Department official or his designee will make a prompt investigation whenever a compliance review, report, complaint, or any other information indicates a possible failure to comply with this part. The investigation should include, where appropriate, a review of the pertinent practices and policies of the recipient, the circumstances under which the possible noncompliance with this part occurred, and other factors relevant to a determination as to whether the recipient has failed to comply with this part.

(d) *Resolution of matters.* (1) If an investigation pursuant to paragraph (c) of this section indicates a failure to comply with this part, the responsible Department official or his designee will so inform the recipient and the matter will be resolved by informal means whenever possible. If it has been determined that the matter cannot be resolved by informal means, action will be taken as provided for in § 80.8 [§ 100.8].

(2) If an investigation does not warrant action pursuant to subparagraph (1) of this paragraph [(d)] the responsible Department official or his designee will so inform the recipient and the complainant, if any, in writing.

(e) *Intimidatory or retaliatory acts prohibited.* No recipient or other person shall intimidate, threaten, coerce, or discriminate against any individual for the purpose of interfering with any right or privilege secured by section 601 of the Act or this part, or because he has made a complaint, testified, assisted, or participated in any manner in an investigation, proceeding or hearing under this part. The identity of complainants shall be kept confidential except to the extent necessary to carry out the purposes of this part, including the conduct of any investigation, hearing, or judicial proceeding arising thereunder.

§ 80.8 [100.8] Procedure for effecting compliance.

(a) *General.* If there appears to be a failure or threatened failure to comply with this regulation, and if the noncompliance or threatened noncompliance cannot be corrected by informal means, compliance with this part may be effected by the suspension or termination of or refusal to grant or to continue Federal financial assistance or by any other means authorized by law. Such other means may include, but are not limited to, (1) a reference to the Department of Justice with a recommendation that appropriate proceedings be brought to enforce any rights of the United States under any law of the United States (including other titles of the Act), or any assurance or other contractual undertaking, and (2) any applicable proceeding under State or local law.

(b) *Noncompliance with § 80.4 [§ 100.4].* If an applicant fails or refuses to furnish an assurance required under § 80.4 [§ 100.4] or otherwise fails or refuses to comply with a requirement imposed by or pursuant to that section Federal financial assistance may be refused in accordance with the procedures of paragraph (c) of this section. The Department shall not be required to provide assistance in such a case during the pendency of the administrative proceedings under such paragraph except that the Department shall continue assistance during the pendency of such proceedings where such assistance is due and payable pursuant to an application therefor approved prior to the effective date of this part.

(c) *Termination of or refusal to grant or to continue Federal financial assistance.* No order suspending, terminating or refusing to grant or continue Federal financial assistance shall become effective until (1) the responsible Department official has advised the applicant or recipient of his failure to comply and has determined that compliance cannot be secured by voluntary means, (2) there has been an express finding on the record, after opportunity for hearing, of a failure by the applicant or recipient to comply with a requirement imposed by or pursuant to this part, (3) the expiration of 30 days after the Secretary has filed with the committee of the House and the committee of the Senate having legislative jurisdiction over the program involved, a full written report of the circumstances and the grounds for such action. Any action to suspend or terminate or to refuse to grant or to continue Federal financial assistance shall be limited to the particular political entity, or part thereof, or other applicant or recipient as to whom such a finding has been made and shall be limited in its effect to the particular program, or part thereof, in which such noncompliance has been so found.

(d) *Other means authorized by law.* No action to effect compliance by any other means authorized by law shall be taken until (1) the responsible Department official has determined that compliance cannot be secured by voluntary means, (2) the recipient or other person has been notified of its failure to comply and of the action to be taken to effect compliance, and (3) the expiration of at least 10 days from the mailing of such notice to the recipient or other person. During this period of at least 10 days additional efforts shall be made to persuade the recipient or other person to comply with the regulation and to take such corrective action as may be appropriate. (Sec. 601, 602, Civil Rights Act of 1964; 78 Stat. 252; 42 U.S.C. 2000d-5) [29 FR 16298, Dec. 4, 1964, as amended at 32 FR 14556, Oct. 19, 1967; 38 FR 17982, July 5, 1973]

§ 80.9 [100.9] Hearings.

(a) *Opportunity for hearing.* Whenever an opportunity for a hearing is required by § 80.8(c) [§ 100.8(c)], reasonable notice shall be given by registered or certified mail, return receipt requested, to the affected applicant or recipient. This notice shall advise the applicant or recipient of the action proposed to be taken, the specific provision under which the proposed action against it is to be taken, and the matters of fact or law asserted as the basis for this action, and either (1) fix a date not less than 20 days after the date of such notice within which the applicant or recipient may request of the responsible Department official that the matter be scheduled for hearing or (2) advise the applicant or recipient that the matter in question has been set down for hearing at a stated place and time. The time and place so fixed shall be reasonable and shall be subject to change for cause. The complainant, if any, shall be advised of the time and place of the hearing. An applicant or recipient may waive a hearing and submit written information and argument for the record. The failure of an applicant or recipient to request a hearing for which a date has been set shall be deemed to be a waiver of the right to a hearing under section 602 of the Act and § 80.8(c) [§ 100.8(c)] of this regulation and consent to the making of a decision on the basis of such information as may be filed as the record.

(b) *Time and place of hearing.* Hearings shall be held at the offices of the Department in Washington, D.C., at a time fixed by the responsible Department official unless he determines that the convenience of the applicant or recipient or of the Department requires that another place be selected. Hearings shall be held before a hearing examiner designated in accordance with 5 U.S.C. 3105 and 3344 (section 11 of the Administrative Procedure Act).

(c) *Right to counsel.* In all proceedings under this section, the applicant or recipient and the Department shall have the right to be represented by counsel.

(d) *Procedures, evidence, and record.* (1) The hearing, decision, and any administrative review thereof shall be conducted in conformity with sections 5-8 of the Administrative Procedure Act, and in accordance with such rules of procedure as are proper (and not inconsistent with this section) relating to the conduct of the hearing, giving of notices subsequent to those provided for in paragraph (a) of this section, taking of testimony, exhibits, arguments and briefs, requests for findings, and other related matters. Both the Department and the applicant or recipient shall be entitled to introduce all relevant evidence on the issues as stated in the notice for hearing or as determined by the officer conducting the hearing at the outset of or during the hearing. Any person (other than a Government employee considered to be on official business) who, having been invited or requested to appear and testify as a witness on the Government's behalf, attends at a time and place scheduled for a hearing provided for by this part, may be reimbursed for his travel and actual expenses of attendance in an amount not to exceed the amount payable under the standardized travel regulations to a Government employee traveling on official business.

(2) Technical rules of evidence shall not apply to hearings conducted pursuant to this part, but rules or principles designed to assure production of the most credible evidence available and to subject testimony to test by cross-examination shall be applied where reasonably necessary by the officer conducting the hearing. The hearing officer may exclude irrelevant, immaterial, or unduly repetitious evidence. All documents and other evidence offered or taken for the record shall be open to examination by the parties and opportunity shall be given to refute facts and arguments advanced on either side of the issues. A transcript shall be made of the oral evidence except to the extent the substance thereof is stipulated for the record. All decisions shall be based upon the hearing record and written findings shall be made.

(e) *Consolidated or Joint Hearings.* In cases in which the same or related facts are asserted to constitute noncompliance with this regulation with respect to two or more programs to which this part applies, or noncompliance with this part and the regulations of one or more other Federal departments or agencies issued under Title VI of the Act, the responsible Department official may, by agreement with such other departments or agencies where applicable, provide for the conduct of consolidated or joint hearings, and for the application to such hearings of rules of procedures not inconsistent with this part. Final decisions in such cases, insofar as this regulation is concerned, shall be made in accordance with § 80.10 [§ 100.10].

(Sec. 602, Civil Rights Act of 1964; 78 Stat. 252; 42 U.S.C. 2000d-1)

[29 FR 16298, Dec. 4, 1964, as amended at 32 FR 14555, Oct. 19, 1967; 38 FR 17981, 17982, July 5, 1973]

§ 80.10 [100.10] Decisions and notices.

(a)*Decisions by hearing examiners.* After a hearing is held by a hearing examiner such hearing examiner shall either make an initial decision, if so authorized, or certify the entire record including his recommended findings and proposed decision to the reviewing authority for a final decision, and a copy of such initial decision or certification shall be mailed to the applicant or recipient and to the complainant, if any. Where the initial decision referred to in this paragraph or in paragraph (c) of this section is made by the hearing examiner, the applicant or recipient or the counsel for the Department may, within the period provided for in the rules of procedure issued by the responsible Department official, file with the reviewing authority exceptions to the initial decision, with his reasons therefor. Upon the filing of such exceptions the reviewing authority shall review the initial decision and issue its own decision thereof including the reasons therefor. In the absence of exceptions the initial decision shall constitute the final decision, subject to the provisions of paragraph (e) of this section.

(b) *Decisions on record or review by the reviewing authority.* Whenever a record is certified to the reviewing authority for decision or it reviews the decision of a hearing examiner pursuant to paragraph (a) or (c) of this section, the applicant or recipient shall be given reasonable opportunity to file with it briefs or other written statements of its contentions, and a copy of the final decision of the reviewing authority shall be given in writing to the applicant or recipient and to the complainant, if any.

(c) *Decisions on record where a hearing is waived.* Whenever a hearing is waived pursuant to § 80.9(a) [§ 100.9(a)] the reviewing authority shall make its final decision on the record or refer the matter to a hearing examiner for an initial decision to be made on the record. A copy of such decision shall be given in writing to the applicant or recipient, and to the complainant, if any.

(d) *Rulings required.* Each decision of a hearing examiner or reviewing authority shall set forth a ruling on each finding, conclusion, or exception presented, and shall identify the requirement or requirements imposed by or pursuant to this part with which it is found that the applicant or recipient has failed to comply.

(e) *Review in certain cases by the Secretary.* If the Secretary has not personally made the final decision referred to in paragraphs (a), (b), or (c) of this section, a recipient or applicant or the counsel for the Department may request the Secretary to review a decision of the Reviewing Authority in accordance with rules of procedure issued by the responsible Department official. Such review is not a matter of right and shall be granted only where the Secretary determines there are special and important reasons therefor. The Secretary may grant or deny such request, in whole or in part. He may also review such a decision upon his own motion in accordance with rules of procedure issued by the responsible Department official. In the absence of a review under this paragraph, a final decision referred to in paragraphs (a), (b), (c) of this section shall become the final decision of the Department when the Secretary transmits it as such to Congressional committees with the report required under section 602 of the Act. Failure of an applicant or recipient to file an exception with the Reviewing Authority or to request review under this paragraph shall not be deemed a failure to exhaust administrative remedies for the purpose of obtaining judicial review.

(f) *Content of orders.* The final decision may provide for suspension or termination of, or refusal to grant or continue Federal financial assistance, in whole or in part, to which this regulation applies, and may contain such terms, conditions, and other provisions as are consistent with and will effectuate the purposes of the Act and this regulation, including provisions designed to assure that no Federal financial assistance to which this regulation applies will thereafter be extended under such law or laws to the applicant or recipient determined by such decision to be in default in its performance of an assurance given by it pursuant to this regulation, or to have otherwise failed to comply with this regulation unless and until it corrects its noncompliance and satisfies the responsible Department official that it will fully comply with this regulation.

(g) *Post-termination proceedings.* (1) An applicant or recipient adversely affected by an order issued under paragraph (f) of this section shall be restored to full eligibility to receive Federal financial assistance if it satisfies the terms and conditions of that order for such eligibility or if it brings itself into compliance with this part and provides reasonable assurance that it will fully comply with this part. An elementary or secondary school or school system which is unable to file an assurance of compliance with § 80.3 [§ 100.3] shall be restored to full eligibility to receive Federal financial assistance, if it files a court order or a plan for desegregation which meets the requirements of § 80.4(c) [§ 100.4(c)], and provides reasonable assurance that it will comply with the court order or plan.

(2) Any applicant or recipient adversely affected by an order entered pursuant to paragraph (f) of this section may at any time request the responsible Department official to restore fully its eligibility to receive Federal financial assistance. Any such request shall be supported by information showing that the applicant or recipient has met the requirements of paragraph (g)(1) of this section. If the responsible Department official determines that those requirements have been satisfied, he shall restore such eligibility.

(3) If the responsible Department official denies any such request, the applicant or recipient may submit a request for a hearing in writing, specifying why it believes such official to have been in error. It shall thereupon be given an expeditious hearing, with a decision on the record, in accordance with rules of procedure issued by the responsible Department official. The applicant or recipient will be restored to such eligibility if it proves at such hearing that it satisfied the requirements of paragraph (g)(1) of this section. While proceedings under this paragraph are pending, the sanctions imposed by the order issued under paragraph (f) of this section shall remain in effect.

(Sec. 602, Civil Rights Act of 1964; 78 Stat. 252; 42 U.S.C. 2000d-1)

[29 FR 16298, Dec. 4, 1964, as amended at 32 FR 14555, Oct. 19, 1967; 38 FR 17981, 17982, July 5, 1973]

APPENDIX B TO PART 100—GUIDELINES FOR ELIMINATING DISCRIMINATION AND DENIAL OF SERVICES ON THE BASIS OF RACE, COLOR, NATIONAL ORIGIN, SEX, AND HANDICAP IN VOCATIONAL EDUCATION PROGRAMS

I. SCOPE AND COVERAGE

A. APPLICATION OF GUIDELINES

These Guidelines apply to recipients of any Federal financial assistance from the Department of Education that offer or administer programs of vocational education or training. This includes State agency recipients.

B. DEFINITION OF RECIPIENT

The definition of *recipient* of Federal financial assistance is established by Department regulations implementing Title VI, Title IX, and Section 504 (34 CFR 100.13(i), 106.2(h), 104.3(f)).

For the purposes of Title VI:

The term *recipient* means any State, political subdivision of any State, or instrumentality of any State or political subdivision, any public or private agency, institution, or organization, or other entity, or any individual, in any State, to whom Federal financial assistance is extended, directly or through another recipient, for any program, including any successor, assignee, or transferee thereof, but such [term] does not include any ultimate beneficiary [e.g., students] under any such program. (34 CFR 100.13(i)).

For the purposes of Title IX:

Recipient means any State or political subdivision thereof, or any instrumentality of a State or political subdivision thereof, any public or private agency, institution, or organization, or other entity, or any person to whom Federal financial assistance is extended, directly or through another recipient and which operates an education program or activity which receives or benefits from such assistance, including any subunit, successor, assignee, or transferee thereof. (34 CFR 106.2(h)).

For the purposes of Section 504:

Recipient means any State or its political subdivision, any instrumentality of a State or its political subdivision, any public or private agency, institution, or organization, or other entity, or any person to which Federal financial assistance is extended, directly or through another recipient, including any successor, assignee, or transferee of a recipient, but excluding the ultimate beneficiary of the assistance. (34 CFR 104.3(f)).

C. EXAMPLES OF RECIPIENTS COVERED BY THESE GUIDELINES

The following education agencies, when they provide vocational education, are examples of recipients covered by these Guidelines:

1. The board of education of a public school district and its administrative agency.

2. The administrative board of a specialized vocational high school serving students from more than one school district.

3. The administrative board of a technical or vocational school that is used exclusively or principally for the provision of *vocational* education to persons who have completed or left high school (including persons seeking a certificate or an associate degree through a vocational program offered by the school) and who are available for study in preparation for entering the labor market.

4. The administrative board of a postsecondary institution, such as a technical institute, skill center, junior college, community college, or four year college that has a department or division that provides vocational education to students seeking immediate employment, a certificate or an associate degree.

5. The administrative board of a proprietary (private) vocational education school.

6. A State agency recipient itself operating a vocational education facility.

D. EXAMPLES OF SCHOOLS TO WHICH THESE GUIDELINES APPLY

The following are examples of the types of schools to which these Guidelines apply.

1. A junior high school, middle school, or those grades of a comprehensive high school that offers instruction to inform, orient, or prepare students for vocational education at the secondary level.

2. A vocational education facility operated by a State agency.

3. A comprehensive high school that has a department exclusively or principally used for providing vocational education; or that offers at least one vocational program to secondary level students who are available for study in preparation for entering the labor market; or that offers adult vocational education to persons who have completed or left high school and who are available for study in preparation for entering the labor market.

4. A comprehensive high school, offering the activities described above, that receives students on a contract basis from other school districts for the purpose of providing vocational education.

5. A specialized high school used exclusively or principally for the provision of vocational education, that enrolls students [from] one or more school districts for the purpose of providing vocational education.

6. A technical or vocational school that primarily provides vocational education to persons who have completed or left high school and who are available for study in preparation for entering the labor market, including students seeking an associate degree or certificate through a course of vocational instruction offered by the school.

7. A junior college, a community college, or four-year college that has a department or division that provides vocational education to students seeking immediate employment, an associate degree or a certificate through a course of vocational instruction offered by the school.

8. A proprietary school, licensed by the State that offers vocational education.

NOTE: Subsequent sections of these Guidelines may use the term *secondary vocational education center* in referring to the institutions described in paragraphs 3, 4 and 5 above or the term *postsecondary vocational education center* in referring to institutions described in paragraphs 6 and 7 above or the term *vocational education center* in referring to any or all institutions described above.

II. RESPONSIBILITIES ASSIGNED ONLY TO STATE
AGENCY RECIPIENTS

A. RESPONSIBILITIES OF ALL STATE AGENCY RECIPIENTS

State agency recipients, in addition to complying with all other provisions of the Guidelines relevant to them, may not require, approve of, or engage in any discrimination or denial of services on the basis of race, color, national origin, sex, or handicap in performing any of the following activities:

1. Establishment of criteria or formulas for distribution of Federal or State funds to vocational education programs in the State;

2. Establishment of requirements for admission to or requirements for the administration of vocational education programs;

3. Approval of action by local entities providing vocational education. (For example, a State agency must ensure compliance with Section IV of these Guidelines if and when it reviews a vocational education agency decision to create or change a geographic service area.);

4. Conducting its own programs. (For example, in employing its staff it may not discriminate on the basis of sex or handicap.)

B. STATE AGENCIES PERFORMING OVERSIGHT RESPONSIBILITIES

The State agency responsible for the administration of vocational education programs must adopt a compliance program to prevent, identify and remedy discrimination on the basis of race, color, national origin, sex or handicap by its subrecipients. (A "subrecipient," in this context, is a local agency or vocational education center that receives financial assistance through a State agency.) This compliance program must include:

1. Collecting and analyzing civil rights related data and information that subrecipients compile for their own purposes or that are submitted to State and Federal officials under existing authorities;

2. Conducting periodic compliance reviews of selected subrecipients (i.e., an investigation of a subrecipient to determine whether it engages in unlawful discrimination in any aspect of its program); upon finding unlawful discrimination, notifying the subrecipient of steps it must take to attain compliance and attempting to obtain voluntary compliance;

3. Providing technical assistance upon request to subrecipients. This will include assisting subrecipients to identify unlawful discrimination and instructing them in remedies for and prevention of such discrimination;

4. Periodically reporting its activities and findings under the foregoing paragraphs, including findings of unlawful discrimination under paragraph 2, immediately above, to the Office for Civil Rights.

State agencies are not required to terminate or defer assistance to any subrecipient. Nor are they required to conduct hearings. The responsibilities of the Office for Civil Rights to collect and analyze data, to conduct compliance reviews, to investigate complaints and to provide technical assistance are not diminished or attenuated by the requirements of Section II of the Guidelines.

C. STATEMENT OF PROCEDURES AND PRACTICES

Within one year from the publication of these Guidelines in final form, each State agency recipient performing oversight responsibilities must submit to the Office for Civil Rights the methods of administration and related procedures it will follow to comply with the requirements described in paragraphs A and B immediately above. The Department will review each submission and will promptly either approve it, or return it to State officials for revision.

III. DISTRIBUTION OF FEDERAL FINANCIAL ASSISTANCE AND OTHER FUNDS FOR VOCATIONAL EDUCATION

A. AGENCY RESPONSIBILITIES

Recipients that administer grants for vocational education must distribute Federal, State, or local vocational education funds so that no student or group of students is unlawfully denied an equal opportunity to benefit from vocational education on the basis of race, color, national origin, sex, or handicap.

B. DISTRIBUTION OF FUNDS

Recipients may not adopt a formula or other method for the allocation of Federal, State, or local vocational education funds that has the effect of discriminating on the basis of race, color, national origin, sex, or handicap. However, a recipient may adopt a formula or other method of allocation that uses as a factor race, color, national origin, sex, or handicap [or an index or proxy for race, color, national origin, sex, or handicap e.g., number of persons receiving Aid to Families with Dependent Children or with limited English speaking ability] if the factor is included to compensate for past discrimination or to comply with those provisions of the Vocational Education Amendments of 1976 designed to assist specified protected groups.

C. EXAMPLE OF A PATTERN SUGGESTING UNLAWFUL DISCRIMINATION

In each State it is likely that some local recipients will enroll greater proportions of minority students in vocational education than the State-wide proportion of minority students in vocational education. A funding formula or other method of allocation that results in such local recipients receiving per-pupil allocations of Federal or State vocational education funds lower than the Statewide average per-pupil allocation will be presumed unlawfully discriminatory.

D. DISTRIBUTION THROUGH COMPETITIVE GRANTS OR CONTRACTS

Each State agency that establishes criteria for awarding competitive vocational education grants or contracts must establish and apply the criteria without regard to the race, color, national origin, sex, or handicap of any or all of a recipient's students, except to compensate for past discrimination.

E. APPLICATION PROCESSES FOR COMPETITIVE OR DISCRETIONARY GRANTS

State agencies must disseminate information needed to satisfy the requirements of any application process for competitive or discretionary grants so that all recipients, including those having a high percentage of minority or handicapped students, are informed of and able to seek funds. State agencies that provide technical assistance for the completion of the application process must provide such assistance without discrimination against any one recipient or class of recipients.

F. ALTERATION OF FUND DISTRIBUTION TO PROVIDE EQUAL OPPORTUNITY

If the Office for Civil Rights finds that a recipient's system for distributing vocational education funds unlawfully discriminates on the basis of race, color, national origin, sex, or handicap, it will require the recipient to adopt an alternative nondiscriminatory method of distribution. The Office for Civil Rights may also require the recipient to compensate for the effects of its past unlawful discrimination in the distribution of funds.

IV. ACCESS AND ADMISSION OF STUDENTS TO VOCATIONAL EDUCATION PROGRAMS

A. RECIPIENT RESPONSIBILITIES

Criteria controlling student eligibility for admission to vocational education schools, facilities and programs may not unlawfully discriminate on the basis of race, color, national origin, sex, or handicap. A recipient may not develop, impose, maintain, approve, or implement such discriminatory admissions criteria.

B. SITE SELECTION FOR VOCATIONAL SCHOOLS

State and local recipients may not select or approve a site for a vocational education facility for the purpose or with the effect of excluding, segregating, or otherwise discriminating against students on the basis of race, color, or national origin. Recipients must locate vocational education facilities at sites that are readily accessible to both nonminority and minority communities, and that do not tend to identify the facility or program as intended for nonminority or minority students.

C. ELIGIBILITY FOR ADMISSION TO VOCATIONAL EDUCATION CENTERS BASED ON RESIDENCE

Recipients may not establish, approve or maintain geographic boundaries for a vocational education center service area or attendance zone, (hereinafter "service area"), that unlawfully exclude students on the basis of race, color, or national origin. The Office for Civil Rights will presume, subject to rebuttal, that any one or combination of the following circumstances indicates that the boundaries of a given service area are unlawfully constituted:

1. A school system or service area contiguous to the given service area, contains minority or nonminority students in substantially greater proportion than the given service area;

2. A substantial number of minority students who reside outside the given vocational education center service area, and who are not eligible for the center reside, nonetheless, as close to the center as a substantial number of non-minority students who are eligible for the center;

3. The over-all vocational education program of the given service area in comparison to the over-all vocational education program of a contiguous school system or service area enrolling a substantially greater proportion of minority students:

(a) Provides its students with a broader range of curricular offerings, facilities and equipment; or (b) provides its graduates greater opportunity for employment in jobs:

(i) For which there is a demonstrated need in the community or region; (ii) that pay higher entry level salaries or wages; or (iii) that are generally acknowledged to offer greater prestige or status.

D. ADDITIONS AND RENOVATIONS TO EXISTING VOCATIONAL EDUCATION FACILITIES

A recipient may not add to, modify, or renovate the physical plant of a vocational education facility in a manner that creates, maintains, or increases student segregation on the basis of race, color, national origin, sex, or handicap.

E. REMEDIES FOR VIOLATIONS OF SITE SELECTION AND GEOGRAPHIC SERVICE AREA REQUIREMENTS

If the conditions specified in paragraphs IV, A, B, C, or D, immediately above, are found and not rebutted by proof of nondiscrimination, the Office for Civil Rights will require the recipient(s) to submit a plan to remedy the discrimination. The following are examples of steps that may be included in the plan, where necessary to overcome the discrimination:

(1) Redrawing of the boundaries of the vocational education center's service area to include areas unlawfully excluded and/or to exclude areas unlawfully included; (2) provision of transportation to students residing in areas unlawfully excluded; (3) provision of additional programs and services to students who would have been eligible for attendance at the vocational education center but for the discriminatory service area or site selection; (4) reassignment of students; and (5) construction of new facilities or expansion of existing facilities.

F. ELIGIBILITY FOR ADMISSION TO SECONDARY VOCATIONAL EDUCATION CENTERS BASED ON NUMERICAL LIMITS IMPOSED ON SENDING SCHOOLS

A recipient may not adopt or maintain a system for admission to a secondary vocational education center or program that limits admission to a fixed number of students from each sending school included in the center's service area if such a system disproportionately excludes students from the center on the basis of race, sex, national origin or handicap. (Example: Assume 25 percent of a school district's high school students are black and that most of those black students are enrolled in one high school; the white students, 75 percent of the district's total enrollment, are generally enrolled in the five remaining high schools. This paragraph prohibits a system of admission to the secondary vocational education center that limits eligibility to a fixed and equal number of students from each of the district's six high schools.)

G. REMEDIES FOR VIOLATION OF ELIGIBILITY BASED ON NUMERICAL LIMITS REQUIREMENTS

If the Office for Civil Rights finds a violation of paragraph F, above, the recipient must implement an alternative system of admissions that does not disproportionately exclude students on the basis of race, color, national origin, sex, or handicap.

H. ELIGIBILITY FOR ADMISSION TO VOCATIONAL EDUCATION CENTERS, BRANCHES OR ANNEXES BASED UPON STUDENT OPTION

A vocational education center, branch or annex, open to all students in a service area and predominantly enrolling minority students or students of one race, national origin or sex, will be presumed unlawfully segregated if:

(1) It was established by a recipient for members of one race, national origin or sex; or (2) it has since its construction been attended primarily by members of one race, national origin or sex; or (3) most of its program offerings have traditionally been selected predominantly by members of one race, national origin or sex.

I. REMEDIES FOR FACILITY SEGREGATION UNDER STUDENT OPTION PLANS

If the conditions specified in paragraph IV-H are found and not rebutted by proof of nondiscrimination, the Office for Civil Rights will require the recipient(s) to submit a plan to remedy the segregation. The following are examples of steps that may be included in the plan, where necessary to overcome the discrimination:

(1) Elimination of program duplication in the segregated facility and other proximate vocational facilities; (2) relocation or "clustering" of programs or courses; (3) adding programs and courses that traditionally have been identified as intended for members of a particular race, national origin or sex to schools that have traditionally served members of the other sex or traditionally served persons of a different race or national origin; (4) merger of programs into one facility through school closings or new construction; (5) intensive outreach recruitment and counseling; (6) providing free transportation to students whose enrollment would promote desegregation.

J. [RESERVED]

K. ELIGIBILITY BASED ON EVALUATION OF EACH APPLICANT UNDER ADMISSIONS CRITERIA

Recipients may not judge candidates for admission to vocational education programs on the basis of criteria that have the effect of disproportionately excluding persons of a particular race, color, national origin, sex, or handicap. However, if a recipient can demonstrate that such criteria have been validated as essential to participation in a given program and that alternative equally valid criteria that do not have such a disproportionate adverse effect are unavailable, the criteria will be judged nondiscriminatory. Examples of admissions criteria that must meet this test are past academic performance, record of disciplinary infractions, counselors' approval, teachers' recommendations, interest inventories, high school diplomas and standardized tests, such as the Test of Adult Basic Education (TABE).

An introductory, preliminary, or exploratory course may not be established as a prerequisite for admission to a program unless the course has been and is available without regard to race, color, national origin, sex, and handicap. However, a course that was formerly only available on a discriminatory basis may be made a prerequisite for admission to a program if the recipient can demonstrate that:

(a) The course is essential to participation in the program; *and* (b) the course is presently available to those seeking enrollment for the first time and to those formerly excluded.

L. ELIGIBILITY OF NATIONAL ORIGIN MINORITY PERSONS WITH LIMITED ENGLISH LANGUAGE SKILLS

Recipients may not restrict an applicant's admission to vocational education programs because the applicant, as a member of a national origin minority with limited English language skills, cannot participate in and benefit from vocational instruction to the same extent as a student whose primary language is English. It is the responsibility of the recipient to identify such applicants and assess their ability to participate in vocational instruction.

Acceptable methods of identification include: (1) Identification by administrative staff, teachers, or parents of secondary level students; (2) identification by the student in postsecondary or adult programs; and (3) appropriate diagnostic procedures, if necessary.

Recipients must take steps to open all vocational programs to these national origin minority students. A recipient must demonstrate that a concentration of students with limited English language skills in one or a few programs is not the result of discriminatory limitations upon the opportunities available to such students.

M. REMEDIAL ACTION IN BEHALF OF PERSONS WITH LIMITED ENGLISH LANGUAGE SKILLS

If the Office for Civil Rights finds that a recipient has denied national origin minority persons admission to a vocational school or program because of their limited English language skills or has assigned students to vocational programs solely on the basis of their limited English language skills, the recipient will be required to submit a remedial plan that insures national origin minority students equal access to vocational education programs.

N. EQUAL ACCESS FOR HANDICAPPED STUDENTS

Recipients may not deny handicapped students access to vocational education programs or courses because of architectural or equipment barriers, or because of the need for related aids and services or auxiliary aids. If necessary, recipients must:

(1) Modify instructional equipment; (2) modify or adapt the manner in which the courses are offered; (3) house the program in facilities that are readily accessible to mobility impaired students or alter facilities to make them readily accessible to mobility impaired students; and (4) provide auxiliary aids that effectively make lectures and necessary materials available to postsecondary handicapped students; (5)

provide related aids or services that assure secondary students an appropriate education.

Academic requirements that the recipient can demonstrate are essential to a program of instruction or to any directly related licensing requirement will not be regarded as discriminatory. However, where possible, a recipient must adjust those requirements to the needs of individual handicapped students.

Access to vocational programs or courses may not be denied handicapped students on the ground that employment opportunities in any occupation or profession may be more limited for handicapped persons than for non-handicapped persons.

O. PUBLIC NOTIFICATION

Prior to the beginning of each school year, recipients must advise students, parents, employees and the general public that all vocational opportunities will be offered without regard to race, color, national origin, sex, or handicap. Announcement of this policy of non-discrimination may be made, for example, in local newspapers, recipient publications and/or other media that reach the general public, program beneficiaries, minorities (including national origin minorities with limited English language skills), women, and handicapped persons. A brief summary of program offerings and admission criteria should be included in the announcement; also the name, address and telephone number of the person designated to coordinate Title IX and Section 504 compliance activity.

If a recipient's service area contains a community of national origin minority persons with limited English language skills, public notification materials must be disseminated to that community in its language and must state that recipients will take steps to assure that the lack of English language skills will not be a barrier to admission and participation in vocational education programs.

V. COUNSELING AND PREVOCATIONAL PROGRAMS

A. RECIPIENT RESPONSIBILITIES

Recipients must insure that their counseling materials and activities (including student program selection and career/employment selection), promotional, and recruitment efforts do not discriminate on the basis of race, color, national origin, sex, or handicap.

B. COUNSELING AND PROSPECTS FOR SUCCESS

Recipients that operate vocational education programs must insure that counselors do not direct or urge any student to enroll in a particular career or program, or measure or predict a student's prospects for success in any career or program based upon the student's race, color, national origin, sex, or handicap. Recipients may not counsel handicapped students toward more restrictive career objectives than nonhandicapped students with similar abilities and interests. If a vocational program disproportionately enrolls male or female students, minority or nonminority students, or handicapped students, recipients must take steps to insure that the disproportion does not result from unlawful discrimination in counseling activities.

C. STUDENT RECRUITMENT ACTIVITIES

Recipients must conduct their student recruitment activities so as not to exclude or limit opportunities on the basis of race, color, national origin, sex, or handicap. Where recruitment activities involve the presentation or portrayal of vocational and career opportunities, the curricula and programs described should cover a broad range of occupational opportunities and not be limited on the basis of the race, color, national origin, sex, or handicap of the students or potential students to whom the presentation is made. Also, to the extent possible, recruiting teams should include persons of different races, national origins, sexes, and handicaps.

D. COUNSELING OF STUDENTS WITH LIMITED ENGLISH-SPEAKING ABILITY OR HEARING IMPAIRMENTS

Recipients must insure that counselors can effectively communicate with national origin minority students with limited English language skills and with students who have hearing impairments. This requirement may be satisfied by having interpreters available.

E. PROMOTIONAL ACTIVITIES

Recipients may not undertake promotional efforts (including activities of school officials, counselors, and vocational staff) in a manner that creates or perpetuates stereotypes or limitations based on race, color, national origin, sex or handicap. Examples of promotional efforts are career days, parents' night, shop demonstrations, visitations by groups of prospective students and by representatives from business and industry. Materials that are part of promotional efforts may not create or perpetuate stereotypes through text or illustration. To the extent possible they should portray males or females, minorities or handicapped persons in programs and occupations in which these groups traditionally have not been represented. If a recipient's service area contains a community of national origin minority persons with limited English language skills, promotional literature must be distributed to that community in its language.

VI. EQUAL OPPORTUNITY IN THE VOCATIONAL EDUCATION INSTRUCTIONAL SETTING

A. ACCOMMODATIONS FOR HANDICAPPED STUDENTS

Recipients must place secondary level handicapped students in the regular educational environment of any vocational education program to the maximum extent appropriate to the needs of the student unless it can be demonstrated that the education of the handicapped person in the regular environment with the use of supplementary aids and services cannot be achieved satisfactorily. Handicapped students may be placed in a program only after the recipient satisfies the provisions of the Department's Regulation, 34 CFR part 104, relating to evaluation, placement, and procedural safeguards. If a separate class or facility is identifiable as being for handicapped persons, the facility, the programs, and the services must be comparable to the facilities, programs, and services offered to nonhandicapped students.

B. STUDENT FINANCIAL ASSISTANCE

Recipients may not award financial assistance in the form of loans, grants, scholarships, special funds, subsidies, compensation for work, or prizes to vocational education students on the basis of race, color, national origin, sex, or handicap, except to overcome the effects of past discrimination. Recipients may administer sex restricted financial assistance where the assistance and restriction are established by will, trust, bequest, or any similar legal instrument, if the overall effect of all financial assistance awarded does not discriminate on the basis of sex. Materials and information used to notify students of opportunities for financial assistance may not contain language or examples that would lead applicants to believe the assistance is provided on a discriminatory basis. If a recipient's service area contains a community of national origin minority persons with limited English language skills, such information must be disseminated to that community in its language.

C. HOUSING IN RESIDENTIAL POSTSECONDARY VOCATIONAL EDUCATION CENTERS

Recipients must extend housing opportunities without discrimination based on race, color, national origin, sex, or handicap. This obligation extends to recipients that provide on-campus housing and/or that have agreements with providers of off-campus housing. In particular, a recipient postsecondary vocational education program that provides on-campus or off-campus housing to its nonhandicapped students must provide, at the same cost and under the same conditions, comparable convenient and accessible housing to handicapped students.

D. COMPARABLE FACILITIES

Recipients must provide changing rooms, showers, and other facilities for students of one sex that are comparable to those provided to students of the other sex. This may be accomplished by alternating use of the same facilities or by providing separate, comparable facilities.

Such facilities must be adapted or modified to the extent necessary to make the vocational education program readily accessible to handicapped persons.

VII. WORK STUDY, COOPERATIVE VOCATIONAL EDUCATION, JOB PLACEMENT, AND APPRENTICE TRAINING

A. RESPONSIBILITIES IN COOPERATIVE VOCATIONAL EDUCATION PROGRAMS, WORK STUDY PROGRAMS, AND JOB PLACEMENT PROGRAMS

A recipient must insure that: (a) It does not discriminate against its students on the basis of race, color, national origin, sex, or handicap in making available opportunities in cooperative education, work study and job placement programs; and (b) students participating in cooperative education, work study and job placement programs are not discriminated against by employers or prospective employers on the basis of race, color, national origin, sex, or handicap in recruitment, hiring, placement, assignment to work tasks, hours of employment, levels of responsibility, and in pay.

If a recipient enters into a written agreement for the referral or assignment of students to an employer, the agreement must contain an assurance from the employer that students will be accepted and assigned to jobs and otherwise treated without regard to race, color, national origin, sex, or handicap.

Recipients may not honor any employer's request for students who are free of handicaps or for students of a particular race, color, national origin, or sex. In the event an employer or prospective employer is or has been subject to court action involving discrimination in employment, school officials should rely on the court's findings if the decision resolves the issue of whether the employer has engaged in unlawful discrimination.

B. APPENTICE TRAINING PROGRAMS

A recipient may not enter into any agreement for the provision or support of apprentice training for students or union members with any labor union or other sponsor that discriminates against its members or applicants for membership on the basis of race, color, national origin, sex, or handicap. If a recipient enters into a written agreement with a labor union or other sponsor providing for apprentice training, the agreement must contain an assurance from the union or other sponsor:

(1) That it does not engage in such discrimination against its membership or applicants for membership; and (2) that apprentice training will be offered and conducted for its membership free of such discrimination.

VIII. EMPLOYMENT OF FACULTY AND STAFF

A. EMPLOYMENT GENERALLY

Recipients may not engage in any employment practice that discriminates against any employee or applicant for employment on the basis of sex or handicap. Recipients may not engage in any employment practice that discriminates on the basis of race, color, or national origin if such discrimination tends to result in segregation, exclusion or other discrimination against students.

B. RECRUITMENT

Recipients may not limit their recruitment for employees to schools, communities, or companies disproportionately composed of persons of a particular race, color, national origin, sex, or handicap except for the purpose of overcoming the effects of past discrimination. Every source of faculty must be notified that the recipient does not discriminate in employment on the basis of race, color, national origin, sex, or handicap.

C. PATTERNS OF DISCRIMINATION

Whenever the Office for Civil Rights finds that in light of the representation of protected groups in the relevant labor market there is a significant underrepresentation or overrepresentation of protected group persons on the staff of a vocational education school or program, it will presume that the disproportion results from unlawful discrimination. This presumption can be overcome by proof that qualified persons of the particular race, color, national origin, or sex, or that qualified handicapped persons are not in fact available in the relevant labor market.

D. SALARY POLICIES

Recipients must establish and maintain faculty salary scales and policy based upon the conditions and responsibilities of employment, without regard to race, color, national origin, sex or handicap.

E. EMPLOYMENT OPPORTUNITIES FOR HANDICAPPED APPLICANTS

Recipients must provide equal employment opportunities for teaching and administrative positions to handicapped applicants who can perform the essential functions of the position in question. Recipients must make reasonable accommodation for the physical or mental limitations of handicapped applicants who are otherwise qualified unless recipients can demonstrate that the accommodation would impose an undue hardship.

F. THE EFFECTS OF PAST DISCRIMINATION

Recipients must take steps to overcome the effects of past discrimination in the recruitment, hiring, and assignment of faculty. Such steps may include the recruitment or reassignment of qualified persons of a particular race, national origin, or sex, or who are handicapped.

G. STAFF OF STATE ADVISORY COUNCILS OF VOCATIONAL EDUCATION

State Advisory Councils of Vocational Education are recipients of Federal financial assistance and therefore must comply with Section VIII of the Guidelines.

H. EMPLOYMENT AT STATE OPERATED VOCATIONAL EDUCATION CENTERS THROUGH STATE CIVIL-SERVICE AUTHORITIES

Where recruitment and hiring of staff for State operated vocational education centers is conducted by a State civil service employment authority, the State education agency operating the program must insure that recruitment and hiring of staff for the vocational education center is conducted in accordance with the requirements of these Guidelines.

IX. PROPRIETARY VOCATIONAL EDUCATION SCHOOLS

A. RECIPIENT RESPONSIBILITIES

Proprietary vocational education schools that are recipients of Federal financial assistance through Federal student assistance programs or otherwise are subject to all of the requirements of the Department's regulations and these Guidelines.

B. ENFORCEMENT AUTHORITY

Enforcement of the provisions of Title IX of the Education Amendments of 1972 and Section 504 of the Rehabilitation Act of 1973 is the responsibility of the Department of Education. However, authority to enforce Title VI of the Civil rights

Act of 1964 for proprietary vocational education schools has been delegated to the Veterans Administration.

When the Office for Civil Rights receives a Title VI complaint alleging discrimination by a proprietary vocational education school it will forward the complaint to the Veterans Administration and cite the applicable requirements of the Department's regulations and these Guidelines. The complainant will be notified of such action.

[45 FR 30918, May 9, 1980; 45 FR 37426, June 3, 1980]

Part 81 [101] Regulations—Practice and Procedure for Hearings Under Part 80 [100] of this Title

Subpart L—Posttermination Proceedings

81.121 [§ 101.121]   Posttermination proceedings.

Subpart M—Definitions

81.131 [§ 101.131]   Definitions.

AUTHORITY: 5 U.S.C. 301 and 45 CFR 80.9(d) [34 CFR 100.9(d)].

SOURCE: 32 FR 151596, Nov. 2, 1967, unless otherwise noted. [45 FR 30931, May 9, 1980, unless otherwise noted].

Subpart A—General Information

§ 81.1 [101.1] Scope of rules.
The rules of procedure in this part supplement §§ 80.9 and 80.10 [§§ 100.9 and 100.10] of this subtitle and govern the practice for hearings, decisions, and administrative review conducted by the Department of Health and Human Services [Department of Education], pursuant to Title VI of the Civil Rights Act of 1964 (sec. 602, 78 Stat. 252) and Part 80 [100] of this subtitle.

§ 81.2 [101.2] Records to be public.
All pleadings, correspondence, exhibits, transcripts of testimony, exceptions, briefs, decisions, and other documents filed in the docket in any proceeding may be inspected and copied in the office of the Civil Rights hearing clerk. Inquiries may be made at the Central Information Center, Department of Health and Human Services, 330 Independence Ave SW., Washington, D.C. 20201 [Department of Education, 400 Maryland Avenue SW., Washington, D.C 20202].

§ 81.3 [101.3] Use of gender and number.
As used in this part, words importing the singular number may extend and be applied to several persons or things, and vice versa. Words importing the masculine gender may be applied to females or organizations.

§ 81.4 [101.4] Suspension of rules.
Upon notice to all parties, the reviewing authority or the presiding officer, with respect to matters pending before them, may modify or waive any rule in this part upon determination that no party will be unduly prejudiced and the ends of justice will thereby be served.

Subpart B—Appearance and Practice

§ 81.11 [101.11] Appearance.
A party may appear in person or by counsel and participate fully in any proceeding. A State agency or a corporation may appear by any of its officers or by any employee it authorizes to appear on its behalf. Counsel must be members in good standing of the bar of a State, Territory, or possession of the United States or of the District of Columbia or the Commonwealth of Puerto Rico.

§ 81.12 [101.12] Authority for representation.

Any individual acting in a representative capacity in any proceeding may be required to show his authority to act in such capacity.

§ 81.13 [101.13] Exclusion from hearing for misconduct.

Disrespectful, disorderly, or contumacious language or contemptuous conduct, refusal to comply with directions, or continued use of dilatory tactics by any person at any hearing before a presiding officer shall constitute grounds for immediate exclusion of such person from the hearing by the presiding officer.

Subpart C—Parties

§ 81.21 [101.21] Parties [General Counsel deemed a party.]

(a) The term party shall include an applicant or recipient or other person to whom a notice of hearing or opportunity for hearing has been mailed naming him a respondent.

(b) The General Counsel of the Department of Health and Human Services [Assistant Secretary for Civil Rights of the Department of Education,] shall be deemed a party to all proceedings.

§ 81.22 [101.22] Amici curiae.

(a) Any interested person or organization may file a petition to participate in a proceeding as an amicus curiae. Such petition shall be filed prior to the prehearing conference, or if none is held, before the commencement of the hearing, unless the petitioner shows good cause for filing the petition later. The presiding officer may grant the petition if he finds that the petitioner has a legitimate interest in the proceedings, that such participation will not unduly delay the outcome, and may contribute materially to the proper disposition thereof. An amicus curiae is not a party and may not introduce evidence at a hearing.

(b) An amicus curiae may submit a statement of position to the presiding officer prior to the beginning of a hearing, and shall serve a copy on each party. The amicus curiae may submit a brief on each occasion a decision is to be made or a prior decision is subject to review. His brief shall be filed and served on each party within the time limits applicable to the party whose position he deems himself to support; or if he does not deem himself to support the position of any party, within the longest time limit applicable to any party at that particular stage of the proceedings.

(c) When all parties have completed their initial examination of a witness, any amicus curiae may request the presiding officer to propound specific questions to the witness. The presiding officer, in his discretion, may grant any such request if he believes the proposed additional testimony may assist materially in elucidating factual matters at issue between the parties and will not expand the issues.

§ 81.23 [101.23] Complainants not parties.

A person submitting a complaint pursuant to § 80.7(b) [§ 100.7(b)] of this title is not a party to the proceedings governed by this part, but may petition, after proceedings are initiated, to become an amicus curiae.

Subpart D—Form, Execution, Service and Filing of Documents

§ 81.31 [101.31] Form of documents to be filed.

Documents to be filed under the rules in this part shall be dated, the original signed in ink, shall show the docket description and title of the proceeding, and shall show the title, if any, and address of the signatory. Copies need not be signed but the name of the person signing the original shall be reproduced. Documents shall be legible and shall not be more than 8 1/2 inches wide and 12 inches long.

§ 81.32 [101.32] Signature of documents.

The signature of a party, authorized officer, employee or attorney constitutes a certificate that he has read the document, that to the best of his knowledge, information, and belief there is good ground to support it, and that it is not interposed for delay. If a document is not signed or is signed with intent to defeat the purpose of this section, it may be stricken as sham and false and the proceeding may proceed as though the document had not been filed. Similar action may be taken if scandalous or indecent matter is inserted.

§ 81.33 [101.33] Filing and service.

All notices by a Department official, and all written motions, requests, petitions, memoranda, pleadings, exceptions, briefs, decisions, and correspondence to a Department official from a party, or vice versa, relating to a proceeding after its commencement shall be filed and served on all parties. Parties shall supply the original and two copies of documents submitted for filing. Filings shall be made with the Civil Rights hearing clerk at the address stated in the notice of hearing or notice of opportunity for hearing, during regular business hours. Regular business hours are every Monday through Friday (legal holidays in the District of Columbia excepted) from 9 a.m. to 5:30 p.m., eastern standard or daylight saving time, whichever is effective in the District of Columbia at the time. Originals only on exhibits and transcripts of testimony need be filed. For requirements of service on amici curiae, see § 81.107 [§ 101.107].

§ 81.34 [101.34] Service—how made.

Service shall be made by personal delivery of one copy to each person to be served or by mailing by first-class mail, properly addressed with postage prepaid. When a party or amicus has appeared by attorney or other representative, service upon such attorney or representative will be deemed service upon the party or amicus. Documents served by mail preferably should be mailed in sufficient time to reach the addressee by the date on which the original is due to be filed, and should be air mailed if the addressee is more than 300 miles distant.

§ 81.35 [101.35] Date of service.

The date of service shall be the day when the matter is deposited in the U.S. mail or is delivered in person, except that the date of service of the initial notice of hearing or opportunity for hearing shall be the date of its delivery, or of its attempted delivery if refused.

§ 81.36 [101.36] Certificate of service.

The original of every document filed and required to be served upon parties to a proceeding shall be endorsed with a certificate of service signed by the party making service or by his attorney or representative, stating that such service has been made, the date of service, and the manner of service, whether by mail or personal delivery.

Subpart E—Time

§ 81.41 [101.41] Computation.

In computing any period of time under the rules in this part or in an order issued hereunder, the time begins with the day following the act, event, or default, and includes the last day of the period, unless it is a Saturday, Sunday, or legal holiday observed in the District of Columbia, in which event it includes the next following business day. When the period of time prescribed or allowed is less than 7 days, intermediate Saturdays, Sundays, and legal holidays shall be excluded from the computation.

§ 81.42 [101.42] Extension of time or postponement.

Requests for extension of time should be served on all parties and should set forth the reasons for the application. Applications may be granted upon a showing of good cause by the applicant. From the designation of a presiding officer until the issuance of his decision such requests should be addressed to him. Answers to such requests are permitted, if made promptly.

§ 81.43 [101.43] Reduction of time to file documents.

For good cause, the reviewing authority or the presiding officer, with respect to matters pending before them, may reduce any time limit prescribed by the rules in this part, except as provided by law or in Part 80 of this title.

Subpart F—Proceedings Prior to Hearing

§ 81.51 [101.51] Notice of hearing or opportunity for hearing.

Proceedings are commenced by mailing a notice of hearing or opportunity for hearing to an affected applicant or recipient, pursuant to § 80.9 [§ 100.9] of this title.

§ 81.52 [101.52] Answer to notice.

The respondent, applicant or recipient may file an answer to the notice within 20 days after service thereof. Answers shall admit or deny specifically and in detail each allegation of the notice, unless the respondent party is without knowledge, in which case his answer should so state, and the statement will be deemed a denial. Allegations of fact in the notice not denied or controverted by answer shall be deemed admitted. Matters alleged as affirmative defenses shall be separately stated and numbered. Failure of the respondent to file an answer within the 20-day period following service of the notice may be deemed an admission of all matters of fact recited in the notice.

§ 81.53 [101.53] Amendment of notice or answer.

The General Counsel [Assistant Secretary for Civil Rights] may amend the notice of hearing or opportunity for hearing once as a matter of course before an answer thereto is served, and each respondent may amend his answer once as a matter of course not later than 10 days before the date fixed for hearing but in no event later than 20 days from the date of service of his original answer. Otherwise a notice or answer may be amended only by leave of the presiding officer. A respondent shall file his answer to an amended notice within the time remaining for filing the answer to the original notice or within 10 days after service of the amended notice, whichever period may be the longer, unless the presiding officer otherwise orders.

§ 81.54 [101.54] Request for hearing.

Within 20 days after service of a notice of opportunity for hearing which does not fix a date for hearing the respondent, either in his answer or in a separate document, may request a hearing. Failure of the respondent to request a hearing shall be deemed a waiver of the right to a hearing and to constitute his consent to the making of a decision on the basis of such information as is available.

§ 81.55 [101.55] Consolidation.

The responsible Department official may provide for proceedings in the Department to be joined or consolidated for hearing with proceedings in other Federal departments or agencies, by agreement with such other departments or agencies. All parties to any proceeding consolidated subsequently to service of the notice of hearing or opportunity for hearing shall be promptly served with notice of such consolidation.

§ 81.56 [101.56] Motions.

Motions and petitions shall state the relief sought, the authority relied upon, and the facts alleged. If made before or after the hearing, these matters shall be in writing. If made at the hearing, they may be stated orally; but the presiding officer may require that they be reduced to writing and filed and served on all parties in the same manner as a formal motion. Motions, answers, and replies shall be addressed to the presiding officer, if the case is pending before him. A repetitious motion will not be entertained.

§ 81.57 [101.57] Responses to motions and petitions.

Within 8 days after written motion or petition is served, or such other period as the reviewing authority or the presiding officer may fix, any party may file a response thereto. An immediate oral response may be made to an oral motion.

§ 81.58 [101.58] Disposition of motions and petitions.

The reviewing authority or the presiding officer may not sustain or grant a written motion or petition prior to expiration of the time for filing responses thereto, but may overrule or deny such motion or petition without awaiting response: *Provided, however,* That prehearing conferences, hearings and decisions need not be delayed pending disposition of motions or petitions. Oral motions and petitions may be ruled on immediately. Motions and petitions submitted to the reviewing authority or the presiding officer, respectively, and not disposed of in separate rulings or in their respective decisions will be deemed denied. Oral arguments shall not be held on written motions or petitions unless the presiding officer in his discretion expressly so orders.

Subpart G—Responsibilities and Duties of Presiding Officer

§ 81.61 [101.61] Who presides.

A hearing examiner assigned under 5 U.S.C. 3105 or 3344 (formerly section 11 of the Administrative Procedure Act) shall preside over the taking of evidence in any hearing to which these rules of procedure apply.

§ 81.62 [101.62] Designation of hearing examiner.

The designation of the hearing examiner as presiding officer shall be in writing, and shall specify whether the examiner is to make an initial decision or to certify the entire record including his recommended findings and proposed decision to the reviewing authority, and may also fix the time and place of hearing. A copy of such order shall be served on all parties. After service of an order designating a hearing examiner to preside, and until such examiner makes his decision, motions and petitions shall be submitted to him. In the case of the death, illness, disqualification or unavailability of the designated hearing examiner, another hearing examiner may be designated to take his place.

§ 81.63 [101.63] Authority of presiding officer.

The presiding officer shall have the duty to conduct a fair hearing, to take all necessary action to avoid delay, and to maintain order. He shall have all powers necessary to these ends, including (but not limited to) the power to:

(a) Arrange and issue notice of the date, time, and place of hearings, or, upon due notice to the parties, to change the date, time, and place of hearings previously set.

(b) Hold conferences to settle, simplify, or fix the issues in a proceeding, or to consider other matters that may aid in the expeditious disposition of the proceeding.

(c) Require parties and amici curiae to state their position with respect to the various issues in the proceeding.

(d) Administer oaths and affirmations.

(e) Rules on motions and other procedural items on matters pending before him.

(f) Regulate the course of the hearing and conduct of counsel therein.

(g) Examine witnesses and direct witnesses to testify.

(h) Receive, rule on, exclude or limit evidence.

(i) Fix the time for filing motions, petitions, briefs, or other items in matters pending before him.

(j) Issue initial or recommended decisions.

(k) Take any action authorized by the rules in this part or in conformance with the provisions of 5 U.S.C. 551-559 (the Administrative Procedure Act).

Subpart H—Hearing Procedures

§ 81.71 [101.71] Statement of position and trial briefs.

The presiding officer may require parties and amici curiae to file written statements of position prior to the beginning of a hearing. The presiding officer may also require the parties to submit trial briefs.

§ 81.72 [101.72] Evidentiary purpose.

(a) The hearing is directed to receiving factual evidence and expert opinion testimony related to the issues in the proceeding. Argument will not be received in evidence; rather it should be presented in statements, memoranda, or briefs, as determined by the presiding officer. Brief opening statements, which shall be limited to statement of the party's position and what he intends to prove, may be made at hearings.

(b) Hearings for the reception of evidence will be held only in cases where issues of fact must be resolved in order to determine whether the respondent has failed to comply with one or more applicable requirements of Part 80 [100] of this title. In any case where it appears from the respondent's answer to the notice of hearing or opportunity for hearing, from his failure timely to answer, or from his admissions or stipulations in the record, that there are no matters of material fact in dispute, the reviewing authority or presiding officer may enter an order so finding, vacating the hearing date if one has been set, and fixing the time for filing briefs under § 81.101 [§ 101.101]. Thereafter the proceedings shall go to conclusion in accordance with Subpart J of this part. The presiding officer may allow an appeal from such order in accordance with § 81.86 [§ 101.86].

§ 81.73 [101.73] Testimony.

Testimony shall be given orally under oath or affirmation by witnesses at the hearing; but the presiding officer, in his discretion, may require or permit that the direct testimony of any witness be prepared in writing and served on all parties in advance of the hearing. Such testimony may be adopted by the witness at the hearing, and filed as part of the record thereof. Unless authorized by the presiding officer, witnesses will not be permitted to read prepared testimony into the record. Except as provided in §§ 81.75 and 81.76 [§§ 101.75 and 101.76], witnesses shall be available at the hearing for cross-examination.

§ 81.74 [101.74] Exhibits.

Proposed exhibits shall be exchanged at the prehearing conference, or otherwise prior to the hearing if the presiding officer so requires. Proposed exhibits not so exchanged may be denied admission as evidence. The authenticity of all proposed exhibits exchanged prior to hearing will be deemed admitted unless written objection thereto is filed prior to the hearing or unless good cause is shown at the hearing for failure to file such written objection.

§ 81.75 [101.75] Affidavits.

An affidavit is not inadmissible as such. Unless the presiding officer fixes other time periods affidavits shall be filed and served on the parties not later than 15 days prior to the hearing, and not less than 7 days prior to hearing a party may file and serve written objection to any affidavit on the ground that he believes it necessary to test the truth of assertions therein at hearing. In such event the assertions objected to will not be received in evidence unless the affiant is made available for cross-examination, or the presiding officer determines that cross-examination is not necessary for the full and true disclosure of facts referred to in such assertions. Notwithstanding any objection, however, affidavits may be considered in the case of any respondent who waives a hearing.

§ 81.76 [101.76] Depositions.

Upon such terms as may be just, for the convenience of the parties or of the Department, the presiding officer may authorize or direct the testimony of any witness to be taken by deposition.

§ 81.77 [101.77] Admissions as to facts and documents.

Not later than 15 days prior to the scheduled date of the hearing except for good cause shown, or prior to such earlier date as the presiding officer may order, any party may serve upon an opposing party a written request for the admission of the genuineness and authenticity of any relevant documents described in and exhibited with the request, or for the admission of the truth of any relevant matters of fact stated in the request. Each of the matters of which an admission is requested shall be deemed admitted, unless within a period designated in the request (not less than 10 days after service thereof, or within such further time as the presiding officer or the reviewing authority if no presiding officer has yet been designated may allow upon motion and notice) the party to whom the request is directed serves upon the requesting party a sworn statement either denying specifically the matters of which an admission is requested or setting forth in detail the reasons why he cannot truthfully either admit or deny such matters. Copies of requests for admission and answers thereto shall be served on all parties. Any admission made by a party to such request is only for the purposes of the pending proceeding, or any proceeding or action instituted for the enforcement of any order entered therein, and shall not constitute an admission by him for any other purpose or be used against him in any other proceeding or action.

§ 81.78 [101.78] Evidence.

Irrelevant, immaterial, unreliable, and unduly repetitious evidence will be excluded.

§ 81.79 [101.79] Cross-examination.

A witness may be cross-examined on any matter material to the proceeding without regard to the scope of his direct examination.

§ 81.80 [101.80] Unsponsored written material.

Letters expressing views or urging action and other unsponsored written material regarding matters in issue in a hearing will be placed in the correspondence section of the docket of the proceeding. These data are not deemed part of the evidence or record in the hearing.

§ 81.81 [101.81] Objections.

Objections to evidence shall be timely and briefly state the ground relied upon.

§ 81.82 [101.82] Exceptions to rulings of presiding officer unnecessary.

Exceptions to rulings of the presiding officer are unnecessary. It is sufficient that a party, at the time the ruling of the presiding officer is sought, makes known the action which he desires the presiding officer to take, or his objection to an action taken, and his grounds therefor.

§ 81.83 [101.83] Official notice.

Where official notice is taken or is to be taken of a material fact not appearing in the evidence of record, any party, on timely request, shall be afforded an opportunity to show the contrary.

§ 81.84 [101.84] Public document items.

Whenever there is offered (in whole or in part) a public document, such as an official report, decision, opinion, or published scientific or economic statistical data issued by any of the executive departments (or their subdivisions), legislative agencies or committees, or administrative agencies of the Federal Government (including Government-owned corporations), or similar document issued by a State or its agencies, and such document (or part thereof) has been shown by the offeror to be reasonably available to the public, such document need not be produced or marked for identification, but may be offered for official notice, as a public document item by specifying the document or relevant part thereof.

§ 81.85 [101.85] Offer of proof.

An offer of proof made in connection with an objection taken to any ruling of the presiding officer rejecting or excluding proffered oral testimony shall consist of a statement of the substance of the evidence which counsel contends would be adduced by such testimony; and, if the excluded evidence consists of evidence in documentary or written form or of reference to documents or records, a copy of such evidence shall be marked for identification and shall accompany the record as the offer of proof.

§ 81.86 [101.86] Appeals from ruling of presiding officer.

Rulings of the presiding officer may not be appealed to the reviewing authority prior to his consideration of the entire proceeding except with the consent of the presiding officer and where he certifies on the record or in writing that the allowance of an interlocutory appeal is clearly necessary to prevent exceptional delay, expense, or prejudice to any party, or substantial detriment to the public interest. If an appeal is allowed, any party may file a brief with the reviewing authority within such period as the presiding officer directs. No oral argument will be heard unless the reviewing authority directs otherwise. At any time prior to submission of the proceeding to it for decision, the reviewing authority may direct the presiding officer to certify any question or the entire record to it for decision. Where the entire record is so certified, the presiding officer shall recommend a decision.

Subpart I—The Record

§ 81.91 [101.91] Official transcript.

The Department will designate the official reporter for all hearings. The official transcripts of testimony taken, together with any exhibits, briefs, or memoranda of law filed therewith shall be filed with the Department. Transcripts of testimony in hearings may be obtained from the official reporter by the parties and the public at rates not to exceed the maximum rates fixed by the contract between the Department and the reporter. Upon notice to all parties, the presiding officer may authorize corrections to the transcript which involve matters of substance.

§ 81.92 [101.92] Record for decision.

The transcript of testimony, exhibits, and all papers and requests filed in the proceedings, except the correspondence section of the docket, including rulings and any recommended or initial decision shall constitute the exclusive record for decision.

Subpart J—Posthearing Procedures, Decisions

§ 81.101 [101.101] Posthearing briefs: proposed findings and conclusions.

(a) The presiding officer shall fix the time for filing Posthearing briefs, which may contain proposed findings of fact and conclusions of law, and, if permitted, reply briefs.

(b) Briefs should include a summary of the evidence relied upon together with references to exhibit numbers and pages of the transcript, with citations of the authorities relied upon.

§ 81.102 [101.102] Decisions following hearing.

When the time for submission of Posthearing briefs has expired, the presiding officer shall certify the entire record, including his recommended findings and proposed decision, to the responsible Department official; or if so authorized he shall make an initial decision. A copy of the recommended findings and proposed decision, or of the initial decision, shall be served upon all parties, and amici, if any.

§ 81.103 [101.103] Exceptions to initial or recommended decisions.

Within 20 days after the mailing of an initial or recommended decision, any party may file exceptions to the decision, stating reasons therefor, with the reviewing authority. Any other party may file a response thereto within 30 days after the mailing of the decision. Upon the filing of such exceptions, the reviewing authority shall review the decision and issue its own decision thereon.

§ 81.104 [101.104] Final decisions.

(a) Where the hearing is conducted by a hearing examiner who makes an initial decision, if no exceptions thereto are filed within the 20-day period specified in § 81.103 [§ 101.103], such decision shall become the final decision of the Department, and shall constitute "final agency action" within the meaning of 5 U.S.C. 704 (formerly section 10(c) of the Administrative Procedure Act), subject to the provisions of § 81.106 [§ 101.106].

(b) Where the hearing is conducted by a hearing examiner who makes a recommended decision, or upon the filing of exceptions to a hearing examiner's initial decision, the reviewing authority shall review the recommended or initial decision and shall issue its own decision thereon, which shall become the final decision of the Department, and shall constitute "final agency action" within the meaning of 5 U.S.C. 704 (formerly section 10(c) of the Administrative Procedure Act), subject to the provisions of § 81.106 [§ 101.106].

(c) All final decisions shall be promptly served on all parties, and amici, if any.

§ 81.105 [101.105] Oral argument to the reviewing authority.

(a) If any party desires to argue a case orally on exceptions or replies to exceptions to an initial or recommended decision, he shall make such request in writing. The reviewing authority may grant or deny such requests in its discretion. If granted, it will serve notice of oral argument on all parties. The notice will set forth the order of presentation, the amount of time allotted, and the time and place for argument. The names of persons who will argue should be filed with the Department hearing clerk not later than 7 days before the date set for oral argument.

(b) The purpose of oral argument is to emphasize and clarify the written argument in the briefs. Reading at length from the brief or other texts is not favored. Participants should confine their arguments to points of controlling importance and to points upon which exceptions have been filed. Consolidations of appearances at oral argument by parties taking the same side will permit the parties' interests to be presented more effectively in the time allotted.

(c) Pamphlets, charts, and other written material may be presented at oral argument only if such material is limited to facts already in the record and is served on all parties and filed with the Department hearing clerk at least 7 days before the argument.

§ 81.106 [101.106] Review by the Secretary.

Within 20 days after an initial decision becomes a final decision pursuant to § 81.104(a) [§ 101.104(a)], or within 20 days of the mailing of a final decision referred to in § 81.104(b) [§ 101.104(b)], as the case may be, a party may request the Secretary to review the final decision. The Secretary may grant or deny such request, in whole or in part, or serve notice of his intent to review the decision in whole or in part upon his own motion. If the Secretary grants the requested review, or if he serves notice of intent to review upon his own motion, each party to the decision shall have 20 days following notice of the Secretary's proposed action within which to file exceptions to the decision and supporting briefs and memoranda, or briefs and memoranda in support of the decision. Failure of a party to request review under this paragraph shall not be deemed a failure to exhaust administrative remedies for the purpose of obtaining judicial review.

§ 81.107 [101.107] Service on amici curiae.

All briefs, exceptions, memoranda, requests, and decisions referred to in this Subpart J shall be served upon amici curiae at the same times and in the same manner required for service on parties. Any written statements of position and trial briefs required of parties under §81.71 [§ 101.71] shall be served on amici.

Subpart K—Judicial Standards of Practice

§ 81.111 [101.111] Conduct.

Parties and their representatives are expected to conduct themselves with honor and dignity and observe judicial standards of practice and ethics in all proceedings. They should not indulge in offensive personalities, unseemly wrangling, or intemperate accusations or characterizations. A representative of any party whether or not a lawyer shall observe the traditional responsibilities of lawyers as officers of the court and use his best efforts to restrain his client from improprieties in connection with a proceeding.

§ 81.112 [101.112] Improper conduct.

With respect to any proceeding it is improper for any interested person to attempt to sway the judgment of the reviewing authority by undertaking to bring pressure or influence to bear upon any officer having a responsibility for a decision in the proceeding, or his decisional staff. It is improper that such interested persons or any members of the Department's staff or the presiding officer give statements to communications media, by paid advertisement or otherwise, designed to influence the judgment of any officer having a responsibility for a decision in the proceeding, or his decisional staff. It is improper for any person to solicit communications to any such officer, or his decisional staff, other than proper communications by parties or amici curiae.

§ 81.113 [101.113] Ex parte communications.

Only persons employed by or assigned to work with the reviewing authority who perform no investigative or prosecuting function in connection with a proceeding shall communicate ex parte with the reviewing authority, or the presiding officer, or any employee or person involved in the decisional process in such proceedings with respect to the merits of that or a factually related proceeding. The reviewing authority, the presiding officer, or any employee or person involved in the decisional process of a proceeding shall communicate ex parte with respect to the merits of that or a factually related proceeding only with persons employed by or assigned to work with them and who perform no investigative or prosecuting function in connection with the proceeding.

§ 81.114 [101.114] Expeditious treatment.

Requests for expeditious treatment of matters pending before the responsible Department official or the presiding officer are deemed communications on the merits, and are improper except when forwarded from parties to a proceeding and served upon all other parties thereto. Such communications should be in the form of a motion.

§ 81.115 [101.115] Matters not prohibited.

A request for information which merely inquires about the status of a proceeding without discussing issues or expressing points of view is not deemed an ex parte communication. Such requests should be directed to the Civil Rights hearing clerk. Communications with respect to minor procedural matters or inquiries or emergency requests for extensions of time are not deemed ex parte communications prohibited by § 81.113 [§ 101.113]. Where feasible, however, such communications should be by letter with copies to all parties. Ex parte communications between a respondent and the responsible Department official or the Secretary with respect to securing such respondent's voluntary compliance with any requirement of Part 80 [100] of this title are not prohibited.

§ 81.116 [101.116] Filing of ex parte communications.

A prohibited communication in writing received by the Secretary, the reviewing authority, or by the presiding officer, shall be made public by placing it in the correspondence file of the docket in the case and will not be considered as part of the record for decision. If the prohibited communication is received orally, a memorandum setting forth its substance shall be made and filed in the correspondence section of the docket in the case. A person referred to in such memorandum may file a comment for inclusion in the docket if he considers the memorandum to be incorrect.

Subpart L—Posttermination Proceedings

§ 81.121 [101.121] Posttermination proceedings.

(a) An applicant or recipient adversely affected by the order terminating, discontinuing, or refusing Federal financial assistance in consequence of proceedings pursuant to this title may request the responsible Department official for an order authorizing payment, or permitting resumption, of Federal financial assistance. Such request shall be in writing and shall affirmatively show that since entry of the order, it has brought its program or activity into compliance with the requirements of the Act, and with the Regulation thereunder, and shall set forth specifically, and in detail, the steps which it has taken to achieve such compliance. If the responsible Department official denies such request the applicant or recipient shall be given an expeditious hearing if it so requests in writing and specifies why it believes the responsible Department official to have been in error. The request for such a hearing shall be addressed to the responsible Department official and shall be made within 30 days after the applicant or recipient is informed that the responsible Department official has refused to authorize payment or permit resumption of Federal financial assistance.

(b) In the event that a hearing shall be requested pursuant to paragraph (a) of this section, the hearing procedures established by this part shall be applicable to the proceedings, except as otherwise provided in this section.

Subpart M—Definitions

§ 81.131 [101.131] Definitions.

The definitions contained in § 80.13 [§ 100.13] of this subtitle apply to this part, unless the context otherwise requires, and the term "reviewing authority" as used herein includes the Secretary of Health and Human Services [Secretary of Education], with respect to action by that official under § 81.106 [§ 101.106].

Transition provisions: (a) The amendments herein shall become effective upon publication in the FEDERAL REGISTER.

(b) These rules shall apply to any proceeding or part thereof to which Part 80 of this title as amended effective October 19, 1967 (published in the FEDERAL REGISTER for Oct. 19, 1967), and as the same may be hereafter amended, applies. In the case of any proceeding or part thereof governed by the provisions of Part 80 as that part existed prior to such amendment, the rules in this Part 81 shall apply as if these amendments were not in effect.

[34 CFR Part 101.131(b) reads as follows]:

(b) These rules shall apply to any proceeding or part thereof to which part 100 of this title applies. In the case of any proceeding or part thereof governed by the provisions of 34 CFR, part 100 (Title VI regulations of the Department of Education) as that part existed prior to the amendments published in the FEDERAL REGISTER on Oct. 19, 1967 (effective on that date), the rules in this part 101 shall apply as if those amendments were not in effect.

Cases Interpreting Rehabilitation Act Regulations
45 CFR § 84 and 34 CFR § 104

Carter v. Orleans Parish Pub. Schools, 725 F.2d 261 (5th Cir.1984). Section 504 protections extend to individuals improperly classified as handicapped (under definitions found in § 706(7)(B) and **45 CFR Part 85.3(j)(2)(iv)(C)**. Section 504 damages are not recoverable in the absence of proof of intentional discrimination.

Chiari v. City of League City, 920 F.2d 311 (5th Cir.1991). A handicapped individual who cannot perform essential job duties is not entitled to Rehabilitation Act protection under **45 CFR Part 84.3(k)(1)**.

Coleman v. Darden, 595 F.2d 533 (10th Cir.1979). The U.S. Court of Appeals, 10th Circuit, affirmed the summary judgment order of a federal district court which ruled that the EEOC did not discriminate against an applicant with blindness who was not selected for a legal research analyst job. The applicant had failed to gain admission to the Colorado state bar within 14 months as required and also failed to show that the EEOC had eliminated him from consideration due to his lack of sight. Summary judgment was appropriate because federal agencies are covered under Rehabilitation Act § 501, rather than § 504, as the applicant had claimed. See **45 CFR Part 84.3**.

Council for the Hearing Impaired Long Island, Inc. v. Ambach, 610 F.Supp. 1051 (E.D.N.Y.1985). Special education teachers at private schools presented a fact issue which precluded summary judgment against them in their Rehabilitation Act complaint for higher pay. There was an issue under **34 CFR Part 104.33(b)(i)** concerning the ability of special education students to receive a free appropriate public education by lower-paid teachers.

Dept. of Educ. v. Katherine D., 531 F.Supp. 517 (D.Hawaii 1982), *aff'd in part, rev'd in part,* 727 F.2d 809 (9th Cir.1983), *cert. den.,* 471 U.S. 1117, 105 S.Ct. 2360, 86 L.Ed.2d 260 (1985). The Hawaii state department of education could be responsible for private child care center expenses of a child with cystic fibrosis under the EHA, but not under the Rehabilitation Act. **45 CFR Part 84.33(c)(4), 34 CFR Part 104.33(c)(4)**.

Doe by Lavery v. Attorney General of the U.S., 814 F.Supp. 844 (N.D.Cal.1992). An otherwise qualified person is one who can perform "the essential functions" of the job in question. **45 CFR Part 84.3(k)**.

Doe v. Syracuse School Dist., 508 F.Supp. 333 (N.D.N.Y.1981). The court granted an applicant's summary judgment motion in a case interpreting Rehabilitation Act regulations found at **45 CFR Part 84.14**. The regulation prohibits certain preemployment inquiries by employers receiving federal funds.

Georgia Ass'n. of Retarded Citizens v. McDaniel, 716 F.2d 1565 (11th Cir.1983), *vacated on other grounds,* 468 U.S. 1213, 104 S.Ct. 3581, 82 L.Ed.2d 880 (1984), *remanded,* 740 F.2d 902, *cert. den.* 469 U.S. 1228, 105 S.Ct. 1228, 84 L.Ed.2d 365 (1985). *Later proceeding,* 855 F.2d 794, 866 F.2d 1420, *cert. den.,* 490 U.S. 1090, 109 S.Ct. 2431, 104 L.Ed.2d 988 (1988). An association of handicapped individuals filed a Rehabilitation Act lawsuit against the state of Georgia for its policy of limiting public education to 180 days per year because the policy amounted to denial of access to educational benefits to disabled students.

Halasz v. Univ. of New England, 816 F.Supp. 43 (D.Me.1993). Section 504 regulations at **34 CFR Part 104.42(b)(4)** (which prohibit federal funding recipients from making preadmission inquiries concerning impairments) did not prohibit the recipient university from receiving information volunteered by the applicant and using the information to place a student in its special programs.

Hessler v. State Bd. of Educ., 700 F.2d 134 (4th Cir.1983). A private school placement case was properly dismissed under the Rehabilitation Act and IDEA because the educational agency was not required to consider private placement unless appropriate public school services were unavailable.

Jones v. Illinois Dept. of Rehabilitation Serv., 689 F.2d 724 (7th Cir.1982). The Illinois state rehabilitation services department was required to provide a sign language interpreter to a hearing impaired student as a reasonable accommodation which would allow the student to derive educational benefits from college courses. The student was a "qualified handicapped person" under **34 CFR Part 104.3(k)(3)**.

Joyner v. Dumpson, 712 F.2d 770 (2d Cir.1983). Under **34 CFR Part 104.51** and **45 CFR Part 84.52**, summary judgment for special residential care applicants was improper without a showing of whether the city agency discriminated against them or denied benefits solely on the basis of handicap by requiring parents to temporarily transfer custody of children to the program.

New Mexico Ass'n. for Retarded Citizens v. New Mexico, 678 F.2d 847 (10th Cir.1982). Disabled students were entitled to trial under § 504 regulations at **34 CFR Part 104.33(a)**, which require school districts to provide a free appropriate public education, because of evidence of state's failure to adequately fund services, failure to adequately diagnose and identify disabled students and accommodate and integrate them into programs.

Santiago v. Temple Univ., 739 F.Supp. 974 (E.D.Pa.1990). A university was granted summary judgment against an employee who was unable to come to work on a regular basis. The case interprets federal regulations at **34 CFR Part 104.3 (j)(2)(ii)** defining **major life activities** as things such as "caring for one's self, performing manual tasks, walking, seeing, hearing, speaking, breathing, learning, and working."

Stutts v. Freeman, 694 F.2d 666 (11th Cir.1983). The Tennessee Valley Authority impermissibly relied on a standardized test which had the effect of screening out a dyslexic job applicant. The authority failed to provide reasonable accommodation as required by **45 CFR Part 84.12**.

U.S. v. Bd. of Trustees for Univ. of Ala., 908 F.2d 740 (11th Cir.1990). The court upheld Rehabilitation Act regulations at **34 CFR Part 104.44** concerning auxiliary aids in a case brought by students seeking to force a university to provide equal transportation to handicapped students and to provide auxiliary aids without regard to finances.

PART TWO

AMERICANS WITH DISABILITIES ACT

Americans with Disabilities Act (ADA) Overview

The ADA is a federal civil rights (antidiscrimination) statute which protects the rights of disabled Americans in specified subject areas, including employment, public accommodation, transit, and telecommunications. It was passed with the express Congressional finding that "some 43,000,000 Americans have one or more physical or mental disabilities, and this number is increasing . . ." [42 U.S.C. 12101]. Its fundamental goals are to eliminate discrimination against persons with disabilities by removing social and architectural barriers which exist and tend to segregate them from full participation in society. The primary method of achieving full integration of disabled persons into society is by accommodation of their impairments. The ADA and its regulations require covered entities such as employers, state and local government agencies, public accommodations, public transit systems, and other entities to refrain from discrimination against individuals with disabilities and to considers ways of reasonably accommodating their disabilities. Although this book includes the full text of ADA Titles I, II, III and V, the editors have not included regulations for Titles III and IV, because they do not focus on areas of litigation in employment and education law. Also excluded from this book is the text of ADA Title IV, concerning telecommunications relay services.

The ADA employs different standards for accessibility in the separate Titles of the Act. For instance, private employers are not held to the same accessibility standards under Title I as are places of public accommodation under Title III. Whereas Title I protections are directed at the relationship between individual employers and their job applicants and employees, Title III broadly requires places of public accommodation to make goods and services accessible to all persons. Existing buildings must be made accessible by removing architectural and communications barriers if this is readily achievable. State and local government entities are similarly held to different standards under Title II. Such entities are required to provide "program accessibility" by operating services in a readily accessible and usable format to persons with disabilities, unless this would cause a fundamental alteration in the program or service, or would unduly burden the program's finances or administration. The act takes into account the varying interests of public and private employers and individuals with disabilities.

Exempt agencies include executive agencies of the U.S. Government which are covered by similar requirements of § 501 of the Rehabilitation Act of 1973, and other corporations which are exempt from Title VII of the Civil Rights Act of 1964 including U.S. government-owned corporations, Indian tribes, bona fide private clubs (but not labor organizations), and IRS exempt organizations. Federal contractors and subcontractors working on federal projects which are covered by § 503 of the Rehabilitation Act of 1973 may invite individuals with disabilities to self-identify their status on job applications to comply with affirmative action requirements. Self-disclosure is also permitted if required by other federal laws and regulations.

Some key ADA concepts used in these Titles are discussed below to introduce readers to the terminology of ADA Titles I and II. For further descriptions of ADA terms, see the Glossary section of this book, 42 U.S.C. § 12111 (the primary definitional section of the ADA), EEOC Interpretive Guidance following Title I regulations, and the Department of Justice Analysis following Title II regulations.

ADA Title I - General Rule

Title I of the ADA (42 U.S.C. §§ 12101-12111) promotes equal opportunity in employment by prohibiting discrimination against persons with disabilities and by requiring the removal of societal and architectural barriers to persons with disabilities. It is enforced by the U.S. Equal Employment Opportunity Commission (EEOC). Its operative section is 42 U.S.C. § 12112, which states:

(a) **General rule.** No covered entity shall discriminate against a qualified individual with a disability because of the disability of such individual in regard to job application procedures, the hiring, advancement, or discharge of employees, employee compensation, job training, and other terms, conditions, and privileges of employment.

Employers are further required to make individualized determinations on a case-by-case basis in deciding whether and how to reasonably accommodate persons with disabilities. Failure to reasonably accommodate the disabilities of employees and employment applicants constitutes employment discrimination under the ADA.

The ADA prohibits employers from making pre-employment screening inquiries concerning applicant disabilities, even if the applicant has a visible impairment or volunteers information about his or her disability to the employer. This applies to questions on application forms, in job interviews and during background and reference checks. Prior to making an employment offer, the employer may ask the applicant if she or he has the ability to perform a specific job duty. The employer may even ask the applicant to describe or even demonstrate how he or she intends to perform a specific job. However, the employer cannot phrase these inquiries in terms of a disability. The employer may also make a conditional job offer based upon the applicant's successful completion of a post-offer medical examination, but all job candidates must take the same examination. As a practical matter, employers must review their job application forms to eliminate questions such as "have you ever been treated for any of the following conditions or diseases . . .," "have you ever been treated for drug addiction or alcoholism," "have you ever filed a workers' compensation claim," and "is there any health-related reason you may not be able to perform any of the job duties for this position?" Employers may not inquire into medical history, use of prescription drugs, treatment for mental health, consultation with psychiatrists or physicians, hospitalization, prior employment absences and physical defects. Instead of focusing on the applicant's physical and mental history, the employer must ask questions relating to the ability of the applicant to perform specific job duties in a manner which is not likely to reveal that the applicant has a disability.

Reasonable accommodation

The ADA term "reasonable accommodation" is a concept which includes any adjustment or modification of a program, activity, employment, practice, service, or building which creates an equal opportunity for a person with a disability. Reasonable accommodation is the ADA method of integrating individuals with a disability into society. Employers must reasonably accommodate qualified applicants and employees unless the employer can demonstrate that the accommodation imposes an undue hardship on the business. Schools must not discriminate against students and applicants by requiring them to take examinations which are unrelated to educational purposes. It is the obligation of the individual with a disability to request a reasonable accommodation, but a qualified individual with a disability may refuse the accommodation in some circumstances. However, this may disqualify the individual if the lack of accommodation prevents the individual from performing essential job functions. It is the individual's fundamental obligation to advise the employer or prospective employer of the accommodation needed, because employers are only required to accommodate known disabilities. However, employers are required to notify job applicants of their obligation to reasonably accommodate qualified individuals with disabilities. The ADA states (at 42 U.S.C. § 12111(9)) that **reasonable accommodation** may include:

> (A) making existing facilities used by employees readily accessible to and usable by individuals with disabilities; and
> (B) job restructuring, part-time or modified work schedules, reassignment to a vacant position, acquisition or modification of equipment or devices, appropriate adjustment or modifications of examinations, training materials or policies, the provision of qualified readers or interpreters, and other similar accommodations for individuals with disabilities.

Reasonable accommodation is a means of overcoming unnecessary barriers to the employment of qualified individuals with disabilities. It is not necessary for an employer to eliminate or transfer to other employees "essential" job functions. An individual with a disability who cannot perform essential job duties is not a qualified individual with a disability and is not entitled to relief under the ADA. An individual is entitled to reasonable accommodation if the person meets the ADA definition of a qualified individual with a disability, by meeting all prerequisites for performing the essential functions of the job, except those which cannot be met because of the disability. Unless the employer can show undue hardship, the employer is required to provide reasonable accommodation if it will enable a qualified individual with a disability to perform the essential functions of the job.

Ideally, employers, service providers and individuals with disabilities will work together to develop reasonable accommodations in the workplace. An informal, interactive process is the first step in achieving reasonable accommodation. Employers should first evaluate what job functions are "essential." The individual with a disability then identifies how any barriers to performing essential job functions could be overcome with the use of reasonable accommodations. The parties may then implement the most appropriate accommodation.

Qualified individual with a disability

Under Title I of the ADA (at 42 U.S.C. § 12111(8)), a **qualified individual with a disability** is "an individual with a disability who, with or without reasonable accommodation, can perform the essential functions of the employment position that such individual holds or desires." A primary issue under this section is the definition of "essential functions" of a job. The same section requires that "consideration shall be given to the employer's judgment as to what functions of a job are essential." EEOC regulations at 29 CFR Part 1630.2(m) state only that essential functions are those job duties which are "fundamental and not marginal." Essential tasks are also identified in the regulation as those which require a degree of specialization or expertise. If the job position exists to perform the function, it is essential, and it may also be considered essential if other employees are available to perform it. Employers may rely upon written job descriptions prepared before advertising or interviewing applicants for the job as evidence of what functions are essential. Important Rehabilitation Act precedents which define "otherwise qualified" under the Rehabilitation Act (and hence by law applicable to the ADA) include *Southeastern Community College v. Davis,* 442 U.S. 397, 99 S.Ct. 2361, 60 L.Ed.2d 980 (1979), *School Board of Nassau County v. Arline,* 480 U.S. 273, 107 S.Ct. 1123, 94 L.Ed.2d 307 (1987), and *Chiari v. City of League City,* 920 F.2d 311 (5th Cir.1991).

The Undue Hardship defense

The undue hardship defense relieves employers from making accommodations on behalf of individuals with disabilities which are unduly burdensome. The brief statutory section is more thoroughly discussed in EEOC regulations at 29 CFR Part 1630.2(p); see also Department of Education regulations under the Rehabilitation Act of 1973 at 34 CFR Parts 104.12(c) and 104.3(k). According to the EEOC regulations, consideration of undue hardship includes analysis of the nature and cost of the accommodation requested, the employer's size, number and type of facilities, size of budget, and the composition and structure of the workforce.

ADA Title II - General Rule

ADA Title II is based on § 504 of the Rehabilitation Act of 1973. It prohibits discrimination on the basis of disability in all federally assisted programs and activities. See 42 U.S.C. § 12133, Enforcement. Also see *Galloway v. Sup. Court of Dist. of Columbia,* 816 F.Supp. 12 (D.D.C.1993). The general rule of ADA Title II is found at 42 U.S.C. § 12132:

Discrimination. Subject to the provisions of this subchapter, no qualified individual with a disability shall, by reason of such disability, be excluded from participation in or be denied the benefits of the services, programs, or activities of a public entity, or be subjected to discrimination by any such entity.

Title II of the ADA (42 U.S.C. §§ 12131-12161) is divided into two subtitles. Subtitle A protects qualified individuals with disabilities from discrimination in state and local government services, programs and activities. It is enforced by the U.S. Department of Justice (DOJ). Subtitle A extends the protections of § 504 of the Rehabilitation Act of 1973 to all state and local programs, services and activities, including those that do not receive the assistance of the federal government. Significantly, all governmental activities of public entities are covered, even those carried out by private contractors. DOJ Title II regulations under Subtitle A incorporate specific ADA language and are based on the general provisions of § 504. According to the analysis for 28 CFR Part 35.103, "[b]ecause title II of the ADA essentially extends the antidiscrimination prohibition embodied in section 504 to all actions of State and local governments, the standards adopted in this part are generally the same as those required under section 504 for federally assisted programs." Title II Subtitle B, which covers public transportation, applies § 504 requirements to public transit entities, including those that do not receive the assistance of the federal government. Subtitle B regulations are published by the U.S. Department of Transportation (DOT). Title II permits employee drug testing designed to ensure that individuals who formerly illegally used drugs are no longer currently using drugs illegally. Temporary mental and physical impairments may be covered under ADA Title II, if a major life activity is substantially limited. This matter is to be determined on a case-by-case basis.

A public entity must not offer its programs or services at disparate rates to reflect the cost of making the programs or services accessible. The costs of removing architectural barriers or providing free interpreting services may be passed along to the entire public. For instance, a college may raise tuition to help defray the costs of removing architectural barriers, but it may not charge wheelchair users a higher rate of tuition. Public entities must similarly refrain from making unnecessary inquiries into a participant's disabled status. Medical examinations performed in compliance with the ADA must be kept confidential and maintained in separate files.

In many areas, the ADA incorporates Section 504 concepts, and the laws complement each other and may provide cumulative remedies for disabled persons. To the extent that the ADA does not incorporate other laws, the ADA does not preclude disabled persons from obtaining the maximum possible benefit from available statutes. According to Department of Justice analysis following 28 CFR Part 35.103, "a plaintiff may choose to pursue claims under a State law that does not confer greater substantive rights, or even confers lower substantive rights, if the alleged violation is protected under the alternative law and the remedies are greater." ... "A plaintiff may join a State tort claim to a case brought under the ADA. In such a case, the plaintiff must, of course, prove all the elements of the State tort claim in order to prevail under that cause of action."

ADA Titles III - V

ADA Title III prohibits discrimination on the basis of disability by places of public accommodation, including hotels, restaurants, theaters, auditoriums, laundromats, museums, parks, zoos, private schools, and many other entities which are not religiously-affiliated. See 42 U.S.C. §§ 12181-12189. It is enforced by the U.S. Attorney General's office, and adopts the procedures and remedies of Title II of the Civil Rights Act of 1964. The general rule of ADA Title III is found at 42 U.S.C. § 12182:

(a) **General rule**. No individual shall be discriminated against on the basis of disability in the full and equal enjoyment of the goods, services, facilities, privileges, advantages, or accommodations of any place of public accommodation by any person who owns, leases (or leases to), or operates a place of public accommodation.

ADA Title IV amends Title II of the Communications Act of 1934. It is enforced by the Federal Communications Commission to "ensure the availability of interstate and intrastate telecommunications relay services to hearing and speech-impaired individuals to the extent possible and in the most efficient manner." See 47 U.S.C. § 201, et seq. The text of ADA Title IV, which is not included in this book, is found at 47 U.S.C. § 225.

ADA Title V contains miscellaneous provisions, including the judicial standards to be applied in analyzing ADA cases (42 U.S.C. § 12201), the ADA's relationship to other laws, and more definitions. It includes an anti-retaliation and anti-coercion section (42 U.S.C. § 12203), and a section abrogating Eleventh Amendment immunity (42 U.S.C. § 12202). One Title V clause (at 42 U.S.C. § 12201) limits the applicability of ADA coverage to the insurance industry by stating that Titles I through IV of the ADA "shall not be construed to prohibit or restrict" insurers, hospitals, medical service companies, health maintenance organizations, agents and plan benefit administrators from underwriting and classifying risks consistent with state laws. It also prohibits employers from denying benefits and coverage to qualified individuals with disabilities because the employer's current insurance plan fails to cover the disabled individual's disability or would cause the employer's insurance costs to increase.

Statutory Text—Chapter 126—Equal Opportunity for Individuals with Disabilities

SUBPART I—PUBLIC TRANSPORTATION OTHER THAN BY AIRCRAFT OR CERTAIN RAIL OPERATIONS

SUBPART II—PUBLIC TRANSPORTATION BY INTERCITY COMMUTER RAIL

CHAPTER REFERRED TO IN OTHER SECTIONS

This chapter is referred to in title 26 section 44; title 38 section 2027; title 49 App. sections 1607a, 1608, 1622, 1623.

§ 12101. Findings and purpose

(a) Findings

The Congress finds that—

(1) some 43,000,000 Americans have one or more physical or mental disabilities, and this number is increasing as the population as a whole is growing older;

(2) historically, society has tended to isolate and segregate individuals with disabilities, and, despite some improvements, such forms of discrimination against individuals with disabilities continue to be a serious and pervasive social problem;

(3) discrimination against individuals with disabilities persists in such critical areas as employment, housing, public accommodations, education, transportation, communication, recreation, institutionalization, health services, voting, and access to public services;

(4) unlike individuals who have experienced discrimination on the basis of race, color, sex, national origin, religion, or age, individuals who have experienced discrimination on the basis of disability have often had no legal recourse to redress such discrimination;

(5) individuals with disabilities continually encounter various forms of discrimination, including outright intentional exclusion, the discriminatory effects of architectural, transportation, and communication barriers, overprotective rules and policies, failure to make modifications to existing facilities and practices, exclusionary qualification standards and criteria, segregation, and relegation to lesser services, programs, activities, benefits, jobs, or other opportunities;

(6) census data, national polls, and other studies have documented that people with disabilities, as a group, occupy an inferior status in our society, and are severely disadvantaged socially, vocationally, economically, and educationally;

(7) individuals with disabilities are a discrete and insular minority who have been faced with restrictions and limitations, subjected to a history of purposeful unequal treatment, and relegated to a position of political powerlessness in our society, based on characteristics that are beyond the control of such individuals and resulting from stereotypic assumptions not truly indicative of the individual ability of such individuals to participate in, and contribute to, society;

(8) the Nation's proper goals regarding individuals with disabilities are to assure equality of opportunity, full participation, independent living, and economic self-sufficiency for such individuals; and

(9) the continuing existence of unfair and unnecessary discrimination and prejudice denies people with disabilities the opportunities to compete on an equal basis and to pursue those opportunities for which our free society is justifiably famous, and costs the United States billions of dollars in unnecessary expenses resulting from dependency and nonproductivity.

(b) Purpose

It is the purpose of this chapter—

(1) to provide a clear and comprehensive national mandate for the elimination of discrimination against individuals with disabilities;

(2) to provide clear, strong, consistent, enforceable standards addressing discrimination against individuals with disabilities;

(3) to ensure that the Federal Government plays a central role in enforcing the standards established in this chapter on behalf of individuals with disabilities; and

(4) to invoke the sweep of congressional authority, including the power to enforce the fourteenth amendment and to regulate commerce, in order to address the major areas of discrimination faced day-to-day by people with disabilities.

(Pub. L. 101-336, § 2, July 26, 1990, 104 Stat. 328.)

REFERENCES IN TEXT

This chapter, referred to in subsec. (b), was in the original "this Act", meaning Pub. L. 101-336, July 26, 1990, 104 Stat. 327, which is classified principally to this chapter. For complete classification of this Act to the Code, see Short Title note set out below and Tables.

SHORT TITLE

Section l(a) of Pub. L. 101-336 provided that: "This Act [enacting this chapter and section 225 of Title 47, Telegraphs, Telephones, and Radiotelegraphs, amending section 706 of Title 29, Labor, and sections 152, 221, and 611 of Title 47, and enacting provisions set out as notes under sections 12111, 12131, 12141, 12161, and 12181 of this title] may be cited as the 'Americans with Disabilities Act of 1990'."

§ 12102. Definitions

As used in this chapter:

(1) Auxiliary aids and services

The term "auxiliary aids and services" includes—
(A) qualified interpreters or other effective methods of making aurally delivered materials available to individuals with hearing impairments;
(B) qualified readers, taped texts, or other effective methods of making visually delivered materials available to individuals with visual impairments;
(C) acquisition or modification of equipment or devices; and
(D) other similar services and actions.

(2) Disability

The term "disability" means, with respect to an individual—
(A) a physical or mental impairment that substantially limits one or more of the major life activities of such individual;
(B) a record of such an impairment; or
(C) being regarded as having such an impairment.

(3) State

The term "State" means each of the several States, the District of Columbia, the Commonwealth of Puerto Rico, Guam, American Samoa, the Virgin Islands, the Trust Territory of the Pacific Islands, and the Commonwealth of the Northern Mariana Islands.

(Pub. L. 101-336, § 3, July 26, 1990, 104 Stat. 329.)

SECTION REFERRED TO IN OTHER SECTIONS
This section is referred to in section 12211 of this title; title 20 section 2471.

SUBCHAPTER I—EMPLOYMENT

SUBCHAPTER REFERRED TO IN OTHER SECTIONS
This subchapter is referred to in sections 1981a, 12201, 12203, 12206 of this title.

§ 12111. Definitions

As used in this subchapter:

(1) Commission
The term "Commission" means the Equal Employment Opportunity Commission established by section 2000e-4 of this title.

(2) Covered entity

The term "covered entity" means an employer, employment agency, labor organization, or joint labor-management committee.

(3) Direct threat

The term "direct threat" means a significant risk to the health or safety of others that cannot be eliminated by reasonable accommodation.

(4) Employee

The term "employee" means an individual employed by an employer. With respect to employment in a foreign country, such term includes an individual who is a citizen of the United States.

(5) Employer

(A) In general

The term "employer" means a person engaged in an industry affecting commerce who has 15 or more employees for each working day in each of 20 or more calendar weeks in the current or preceding calendar year, and any agent of such person, except that, for two years following the effective date of this subchapter, an employer means a person engaged in an industry affecting commerce who has 25 or more employees for each working day in each of 20 or more calendar weeks in the current or preceding year, and any agent of such person.

(B) Exceptions

The term "employer"; does not include—
(i) the United States, a corporation wholly owned by the government of the United States, or an Indian tribe; or
(ii) a bona fide private membership club (other than a labor organization) that is exempt from taxation under section 501(c) of title 26.

(6) Illegal use of drugs

(A) In general

The term "illegal use of drugs" means the use of drugs, the possession or distribution of which is unlawful under the Controlled Substances Act [21 U.S.C. 801 et seq.]. Such term does not include the use of a drug taken under supervision by a licensed health care professional, or other uses authorized by the Controlled Substances Act or other provisions of Federal law.

(B) Drugs

The term "drug" means a controlled substance, as defined in schedules I through V of section 202 of the Controlled Substances Act [21 U.S.C. 812].

(7) Person, etc.

The terms "person", "labor organization", "employment agency", "commerce", and "industry affecting commerce", shall have the same meaning given such terms in section 2000e of this title.

(8) Qualified individual with a disability

The term "qualified individual with a disability" means an individual with a disability who, with or without reasonable accommodation, can perform the essential functions of the employment position that such individual holds or desires. For the purposes of this subchapter, consideration shall be given to the employer's judgment as to what functions of a job are essential, and if an employer has prepared a written description before advertising or interviewing applicants for the job, this description shall be considered evidence of the essential functions of the job.

(9) Reasonable accommodation

The term "reasonable accommodation" may include—
(A) making existing facilities used by employees readily accessible to and usable by individuals with disabilities; and
(B) job restructuring, part-time or modified work schedules, reassignment to a vacant position, acquisition or modification of equipment or devices, appropriate adjustment or modifications of examinations, training materials or policies, the provision of qualified readers or interpreters, and other similar accommodations for individuals with disabilities.

(10) Undue hardship

(A) In general

The term "undue hardship" means an action requiring significant difficulty or expense, when considered in light of the factors set forth in subparagraph (B).

(B) Factors to be considered

In determining whether an accommodation would impose an undue hardship on a covered entity, factors to be considered include—
(i) the nature and cost of the accommodation needed under this chapter;
(ii) the overall financial resources of the facility or facilities involved in the provision of the reasonable accommodation; the number of persons employed at such facility; the effect on expenses and resources, or the impact otherwise of such accommodation upon the operation of the facility;
(iii) the overall financial resources of the covered entity; the overall size of the business of a covered entity with respect to the number of its employees; the number, type, and location of its facilities; and
(iv) the type of operation or operations of the covered entity, including the composition, structure, and functions of the workforce of such entity; the geographic separateness, administrative, or fiscal relationship of the facility or facilities in question to the covered entity.

(Pub. L. 101-336, title I, § 101, July 26, 1990, 104 Stat. 330; Pub. L. 102-166, title I, § 109(a), Nov. 21, 1991, 105 Stat. 1077.)

REFERENCES IN TEXT

The effective date of this subchapter, referred to in par. (5)(A), is 24 months after July 26, 1990, see section 108 of Pub. L. 101-336, set out as an Effective Date note below.

The Controlled Substances Act, referred to in par. (6)(A), is title II of Pub. L. 91-513, Oct. 27, 1970, 84 Stat. 1242, as amended, which is classified principally to subchapter I (§ 801 et seq.) of chapter 13 of Title 21, Food and Drugs. For complete classification of this Act to the Code, see Short Title note set out under section 801 of Title 21 and Tables.

This chapter, referred to in par. (10)(B)(i), was in the original "this Act", meaning Pub. L. 101-336, July 26, 1990, 104 Stat. 327, which is classified principally to this chapter. For complete classification of this Act to the Code, see Short Title note set out under section 12101 of this title and Tables.

AMENDMENTS

1991—Par. (4), Pub. L. 102-166 inserted at end "With respect to employment in a foreign country, such term includes an individual who is a citizen of the United States."

EFFECTIVE DATE OF 1991 AMENDMENT

Amendment by Pub. L. 102-166 inapplicable to conduct occurring before Nov. 21, 1991, see section 109(c) of Pub. L. 102-166, set out as a note under section 2000e of this title.

EFFECTIVE DATE

Section 108 of title I of Pub. L. 101-336 provided that: "This title [enacting this subchapter] shall become effective 24 months after the date of enactment [July 26, 1990]."

SECTION REFERRED TO IN OTHER SECTIONS

This section is referred to in title 38 section 2027.

§ 12112. Discrimination

(a) General rule

No covered entity shall discriminate against a qualified individual with a disability because of the disability of such individual in regard to job application procedures, the hiring, advancement, or discharge of employees, employee compensation, job training, and other terms, conditions, and privileges of employment.

(b) Construction

As used in subsection (a) of this section, the term "discriminate" includes—

(1) limiting, segregating, or classifying a job applicant or employee in a way that adversely affects the opportunities or status of such applicant or employee because of the disability of such applicant or employee;

(2) participating in a contractual or other arrangement or relationship that has the effect of subjecting a covered entity's qualified applicant or employee with a disability to the discrimination prohibited by this subchapter (such relationship includes a relationship with an employment or referral agency, labor union, an organization providing fringe benefits to an employee of the covered entity, or an organization providing training and apprenticeship programs);

(3) utilizing standards, criteria, or methods of administration—

(A) that have the effect of discrimination on the basis of disability; or

(B) that perpetuate the discrimination of others who are subject to common administrative control;

(4) excluding or otherwise denying equal jobs or benefits to a qualified individual because of the known disability of an individual with whom the qualified individual is known to have a relationship or association;

(5)(A) not making reasonable accommodations to the known physical or mental limitations of an otherwise qualified individual with a disability who is an applicant or employee, unless such covered entity can demonstrate that the accommodation would impose an undue hardship on the operation of the business of such covered entity; or

(B) denying employment opportunities to a job applicant or employee who is an otherwise qualified individual with a disability, if such denial is based on the need of such covered entity to make reasonable accommodation to the physical or mental impairments of the employee or applicant;

(6) using qualification standards, employment tests or other selection criteria that screen out or tend to screen out an individual with a disability or a class of individuals with disabilities unless the standard, test or other selection criteria, as used by the covered entity, is shown to be job-related for the position in question and is consistent with business necessity; and

(7) failing to select and administer tests concerning employment in the most effective manner to ensure that, when such test is administered to a job applicant or employee who has a disability that impairs sensory, manual, or speaking skills, such test results accurately reflect the skills, aptitude, or whatever other factor of such applicant or employee that such test purports to measure, rather than reflecting the impaired sensory, manual, or speaking skills of such employee or applicant (except where such skills are the factors that the test purports to measure).

(c) Covered entities in foreign countries

(1) In general
It shall not be unlawful under this section for a covered entity to take any action that constitutes discrimination under this section with respect to an employee in a workplace in a foreign country if compliance with this section would cause such covered entity to violate the law of the foreign country in which such workplace is located.

(2) Control of corporation

(A) Presumption

If an employer controls a corporation whose place of incorporation is a foreign country, any practice that constitutes discrimination under this section and is engaged in by such corporation shall be presumed to be engaged in by such employer.

(B) Exception

This section shall not apply with respect to the foreign operations of an employer that is a foreign person not controlled by an American employer.

(C) Determination

For purposes of this paragraph, the determination of whether an employer controls a corporation shall be based on—
(i) the interrelation of operations;
(ii) the common management;
(iii) the centralized control of labor relations; and
(iv) the common ownership or financial control,
of the employer and the corporation.

(d) Medical examinations and inquiries

(1) In general

The prohibition against discrimination as referred to in subsection (a) of this section shall include medical examinations and inquiries.

(2) Preemployment

(A) Prohibited examination or inquiry

Except as provided in paragraph (3), a covered entity shall not conduct a medical examination or make inquiries of a job applicant as to whether such applicant is an individual with a disability or as to the nature or severity of such disability.

(B) Acceptable inquiry

A covered entity may make preemployment inquiries into the ability of an applicant to perform job-related functions.

(3) Employment entrance examination

A covered entity may require a medical examination after an offer of employment has been made to a job applicant and prior to the commencement of the employment duties of such applicant, and may condition an offer of employment on the results of such examination, if—
(A) all entering employees are subjected to such an examination regardless of disability;

(B) information obtained regarding the medical condition or history of the applicant is collected and maintained on separate forms and in separate medical files and is treated as a confidential medical record, except that—

(i) supervisors and managers may be informed regarding necessary restrictions on the work or duties of the employee and necessary accommodations;

(ii) first aid and safety personnel may be informed, when appropriate, if the disability might require emergency treatment; and

(iii) government officials investigating compliance with this chapter shall be provided relevant information on request; and

(C) the results of such examination are used only in accordance with this subchapter.

(4) Examination and inquiry

(A) Prohibited examinations and inquiries

A covered entity shall not require a medical examination and shall not make inquiries of an employee as to whether such employee is an individual with a disability or as to the nature or severity of the disability, unless such examination or inquiry is shown to be job-related and consistent with business necessity.

(B) Acceptable examinations and inquiries

A covered entity may conduct voluntary medical examinations, including voluntary medical histories, which are part of an employee health program available to employees at that work site. A covered entity may make inquiries into the ability of an employee to perform job-related functions.

(C) Requirement

Information obtained under subparagraph (B) regarding the medical condition or history of any employee are subject to the requirements of subparagraphs (B) and (C) of paragraph (3).

(Pub. L. 101-336, title I, § 102, July 26, 1990, 104 Stat. 331; Pub. L. 102-166, title I, § 109(b)(2), Nov. 21, 1991, 105 Stat. 1077.)

AMENDMENTS

1991—Subsecs. (c), (d). Pub. L. 102-166 added subsec. (c) and redesignated former subsec. (c) as (d).

EFFECTIVE DATE OF 1991 AMENDMENT

Amendment by Pub. L. 102-166 inapplicable to conduct occurring before Nov. 21, 1991, see section 109(c) of Pub. L. 102-166, set out as a note under section 2000e of this title.

SECTION REFERRED TO IN OTHER SECTIONS

This section is referred to in section 1981a of this title; title 2 section 1202.

§ 12113. Defenses

(a) In general

It may be a defense to a charge of discrimination under this chapter that an alleged application of qualification standards, tests, or selection criteria that screen out or tend to screen out or otherwise deny a job or benefit to an individual with a disability has been shown to be job-related and consistent with business necessity, and such performance cannot be accomplished by reasonable accommodation, as required under this subchapter.

(b) Qualification standards

The term "qualification standards" may include a requirement that an individual shall not pose a direct threat to the health or safety of other individuals in the workplace.

(c) Religious entities

(1) In general

This subchapter shall not prohibit a religious corporation, association, educational institution, or society from giving preference in employment to individuals of a particular religion to perform work connected with the carrying on by such corporation, association, educational institution, or society of its activities.

(2) Religious tenets requirement

Under this subchapter, a religious organization may require that all applicants and employees conform to the religious tenets of such organization.

(d) List of infectious and communicable diseases

(1) In general

The Secretary of Health and Human Services, not later than 6 months after July 26, 1990, shall—
(A) review all infectious and communicable diseases which may be transmitted through handling the food supply;
(B) publish a list of infectious and communicable diseases which are transmitted through handling the food supply;
(C) publish the methods by which such diseases are transmitted; and
(D) widely disseminate such information regarding the list of diseases and their modes of transmissability to the general public.
Such list shall be updated annually.

(2) Applications

In any case in which an individual has an infectious or communicable disease that is transmitted to others through the handling of food, that is included on the list developed by the Secretary of Health and Human Services under paragraph (1), and which cannot be eliminated by reasonable accommodation, a covered entity may refuse to assign or continue to assign such individual to a job involving food handling.

(3) Construction

Nothing in this chapter shall be construed to preempt, modify, or amend any State, county, or local law, ordinance, or regulation applicable to food handling which is designed to protect the public health from individuals who pose a significant risk to the health or safety of others, which cannot be eliminated by reasonable accommodation, pursuant to the list of infectious or communicable diseases and the modes of transmissability published by the Secretary of Health and Human Services.

(Pub. L. 101-336, title I, § 103, July 26, 1990, 104 Stat. 333.)

SECTION REFERRED TO IN OTHER SECTIONS

This section is referred to in title 2 section 1202.

§ 12114. Illegal use of drugs and alcohol

(a) Qualified individual with a disability

For purposes of this subchapter, the term "qualified individual with a disability" shall not include any employee or applicant who is currently engaging in the illegal use of drugs, when the covered entity acts on the basis of such use.

(b) Rules of construction

Nothing in subsection (a) of this section shall be construed to exclude as a qualified individual with a disability an individual who—
(1) has successfully completed a supervised drug rehabilitation program and is no longer engaging in the illegal use of drugs, or has otherwise been rehabilitated successfully and is no longer engaging in such use;
(2) is participating in a supervised rehabilitation program and is no longer engaging in such use; or
(3) is erroneously regarded as engaging in such use, but is not engaging in such use;
except that it shall not be a violation of this chapter for a covered entity to adopt or administer reasonable policies or procedures, including but not limited to drug testing, designed to ensure that an individual described in paragraph (1) or (2) is no longer engaging in the illegal use of drugs.

(c) Authority of covered entity

A covered entity—

(1) may prohibit the illegal use of drugs and the use of alcohol at the workplace by all employees;

(2) may require that employees shall not be under the influence of alcohol or be engaging in the illegal use of drugs at the workplace;

(3) may require that employees behave in conformance with the requirements established under the Drug-Free Workplace Act of 1988 (41 U.S.C. 701 et seq.);

(4) may hold an employee who engages in the illegal use of drugs or who is an alcoholic to the same qualification standards for employment or job performance and behavior that such entity holds other employees, even if any unsatisfactory performance or behavior is related to the drug use or alcoholism of such employee; and

(5) may, with respect to Federal regulations regarding alcohol and the illegal use of drugs, require that—

(A) employees comply with the standards established in such regulations of the Department of Defense, if the employees of the covered entity are employed in an industry subject to such regulations, including complying with regulations (if any) that apply to employment in sensitive positions in such an industry, in the case of employees of the covered entity who are employed in such positions (as defined in the regulations of the Department of Defense);

(B) employees comply with the standards established in such regulations of the Nuclear Regulatory Commission, if the employees of the covered entity are employed in an industry subject to such regulations, including complying with regulations (if any) that apply to employment in sensitive positions in such an industry, in the case of employees of the covered entity who are employed in such positions (as defined in the regulations of the Nuclear Regulatory Commission); and

(C) employees comply with the standards established in such regulations of the Department of Transportation, if the employees of the covered entity are employed in a transportation industry subject to such regulations, including complying with such regulations (if any) that apply to employment in sensitive positions in such an industry, in the case of employees of the covered entity who are employed in such positions (as defined in the regulations of the Department of Transportation).

(d) Drug testing

(1) In general

For purposes of this subchapter, a test to determine the illegal use of drugs shall not be considered a medical examination.

(2) Construction

Nothing in this subchapter shall be construed to encourage, prohibit, or authorize the conducting of drug testing for the illegal use of drugs by job applicants or employees or making employment decisions based on such test results.

(e) Transportation employees

Nothing in this subchapter shall be construed to encourage, prohibit, restrict, or authorize the otherwise lawful exercise by entities subject to the jurisdiction of the Department of Transportation of authority to—

(1) test employees of such entities in, and applicants for, positions involving safety-sensitive duties for the illegal use of drugs and for on-duty impairment by alcohol; and

(2) remove such persons who test positive for illegal use of drugs and on-duty impairment by alcohol pursuant to paragraph (1) from safety-sensitive duties in implementing subsection (c) of this section.

(Pub. L. 101-336, title I, § 104, July 26, 1990, 104 Stat. 334.)

REFERENCES IN TEXT

The Drug-Free Workplace Act of 1988, referred to in subsec. (c)(3), is subtitle D (§ § 5151-5160) of title V of Pub. L. 100-690, Nov. 18, 1988, 102 Stat. 4304, which is classified generally to chapter 10 (§ 701 et seq.) of Title 41, Public Contracts. For complete classification of this Act to the Code, see Short Title note set out under section 701 of Title 41 and Tables.

SECTION REFERRED TO IN OTHER SECTIONS

This section is referred to in title 2 section 1202.

§ 12115. Posting notices

Every employer, employment agency, labor organization, or joint labor-management committee covered under this subchapter shall post notices in an accessible format to applicants, employees, and members describing the applicable provisions of this chapter, in the manner prescribed by section 2000e-10 of this title.

(Pub. L. 101-336, title I, § 105, July 26, 1990, 104 Stat. 336.)

§ 12116. Regulations

Not later than 1 year after July 26, 1990, the Commission shall issue regulations in an accessible format to carry out this subchapter in accordance with subchapter II of chapter 5 of title 5.

(Pub. L. 101-336, title I, § 106, July 26, 1990, 104 Stat. 336.)

SECTION REFERRED TO IN OTHER SECTIONS

This section is referred to in section 12117 of this title.

§ 12117. Enforcement

(a) Powers, remedies, and procedures

The powers, remedies, and procedures set forth in sections 2000e-4, 2000e-5, 2000e-6, 2000e-8, and 2000e-9 of this title shall be the powers, remedies, and procedures this subchapter provides to the Commission, to the Attorney General, or to any person alleging discrimination on the basis of disability in violation of any provision of this chapter, or regulations promulgated under section 12116 of this title, concerning employment.

(b) Coordination

The agencies with enforcement authority for actions which allege employment discrimination under this subchapter and under the Rehabilitation Act of 1973 [29 U.S.C. 701 et seq.] shall develop procedures to ensure that administrative complaints filed under this subchapter and under the Rehabilitation Act of 1973 are dealt with in a manner that avoids duplication of effort and prevents imposition of inconsistent or conflicting standards for the same requirements under this subchapter and the Rehabilitation Act of 1973. The Commission, the Attorney General, and the Office of Federal Contract Compliance Programs shall establish such coordinating mechanisms (similar to provisions contained in the joint regulations promulgated by the Commission and the Attorney General at part 42 of title 28 and part 1691 of title 29, Code of Federal Regulations, and the Memorandum of Understanding between the Commission and the Office of Federal Contract Compliance Programs dated January 16, 1981 (46 Fed. Reg. 7435, January 23, 1981)) in regulations implementing this subchapter and Rehabilitation Act of 1973 not later than 18 months after July 26, 1990.

(Pub. L. 101-336, title I, § 107, July 26, 1990, 104 Stat. 336.)

REFERENCES IN TEXT

The Rehabilitation Act of 1973, referred to in subsec. (b), is Pub. L. 93-112, Sept. 26, 1973, 87 Stat. 355, as amended, which is classified principally to chapter 16 (§ 701 et seq.) of Title 29, Labor. For complete classification of this Act to the Code, see Short Title note set out under section 701 of Title 29 and Tables.

SECTION REFERRED TO IN OTHER SECTIONS

This section is referred to in sections 1981a, 12203 of this title.

SUBCHAPTER II—PUBLIC SERVICES

SUBCHAPTER REFERRED TO IN OTHER SECTIONS

This subchapter is referred to in sections 12201, 12203, 12204, 12206 of this title.

PART A—PROHIBITION AGAINST DISCRIMINATION AND OTHER GENERALLY APPLICABLE PROVISIONS

PART REFERRED TO IN OTHER SECTIONS

This part is referred to in section 12206 of this title.

§ 12131. Definitions

As used in this subchapter:

(1) Public entity
The term "public entity" means—
(A) any State or local government;
(B) any department, agency, special purpose district, or other instrumentality of a State or States or local government; and
(C) the National Railroad Passenger Corporation, and any commuter authority (as defined in section 502(8) of title 45).

(2) Qualified individual with a disability
The term "qualified individual with a disability" means an individual with a disability who, with or without reasonable modifications to rules, policies, or practices, the removal of architectural, communication, or transportation barriers, or the provision of auxiliary aids and services, meets the essential eligibility requirements for the receipt of services or the participation in programs or activities provided by a public entity.

(Pub. L. 101-336, title II, § 201, July 26, 1990, 104 Stat.)

EFFECTIVE DATE

Section 205 of Pub. L. 101-336 provided that:
"(a) GENERAL RULE.—Except as provided in subsection (b), this subtitle [subtitle A (§ § 201-205) of title II of Pub. L. 101-336, enacting this part] shall become effective 18 months after the date of enactment of this Act [July 26, 1990].
"(b) EXCEPTION.—Section 204 [section 12134 of this title] shall become effective on the date of enactment of this Act."

SECTION REFERRED TO IN OTHER SECTIONS

This section is referred to in section 12181 of this title.

§ 12132. Discrimination

Subject to the provisions of this subchapter, no qualified individual with a disability shall, by reason of such disability, be excluded from participation in or be denied the benefits of the services, programs, or activities of a public entity, or be subjected to discrimination by any such entity.

(Pub. L. 101-336, title II, § 202, July 26, 1990, 104 Stat. 337.)

SECTION REFERRED TO IN OTHER SECTIONS

This section is referred to in sections 12133, 12142, 12143, 12144, 12146, 12147, 12148, 12162 of this title.

§ 12133. Enforcement

The remedies, procedures, and rights set forth in section 794a of title 29 shall be the remedies, procedures, and rights this subchapter provides to any person alleging discrimination on the basis of disability in violation of section 12132 of this title.

(Pub. L. 101-336, title II, § 203, July 26, 1990, 104 Stat. 337.)

SECTION REFERRED TO IN OTHER SECTIONS

This section is referred to in section 12203 of this title.

§ 12134. Regulations

(a) In general

Not later than 1 year after July 26, 1990, the Attorney General shall promulgate regulations in an accessible format that implement this part. Such regulations shall not include any matter within the scope of the authority of the Secretary of Transportation under section 12143, 12149, or 12164 of this title.

(b) Relationship to other regulations

Except for "program accessibility, existing facilities", and "communications", regulations under subsection (a) of this section shall be consistent with this chapter and with the coordination regulations under part 41 of title 28, Code of Federal Regulations (as promulgated by the Department of Health, Education, and Welfare on January 13, 1978), applicable to recipients of Federal financial assistance under section 794 of title 29. With respect to "program accessibility, existing facilities", and "communications", such regulations shall be consistent with regulations and analysis as in part 39 of title 28 of the Code of Federal Regulations, applicable to federally conducted activities under section 794 of title 29.

(c) Standards

Regulations under subsection (a) of this section shall include standards applicable to facilities and vehicles covered by this part, other than facilities, stations, rail passenger cars, and vehicles covered by part B of this subchapter. Such standards shall be consistent with the minimum guidelines and requirements issued by the Architectural and Transportation Barriers Compliance Board in accordance with section 12204(a) of this title.

(Pub. L. 101-336, title II, § 204, July 26, 1990, 104 Stat. 337.)

REFERENCES IN TEXT

This chapter, referred to in subsec. (b), was in the original "this Act", meaning Pub. L. 101-336, July 26, 1990, 104 Stat. 327, which is classified principally to this chapter. For complete classification of this Act to the Code, see Short Title note set out under section 12101 of this title and Tables.

EFFECTIVE DATE

Section effective July 26, 1990, see section 205(b) of Pub. L. 101-336, set out as a note under section 12131 of this title.

PART B—ACTIONS APPLICABLE TO PUBLIC TRANSPORTATION PROVIDED BY PUBLIC ENTITIES CONSIDERED DISCRIMINATORY

PART REFERRED TO IN OTHER SECTIONS

This part is referred to in sections 12134, 12206 of this title.

SUBPART I—PUBLIC TRANSPORTATION OTHER THAN BY AIR-CRAFT OR CERTAIN RAIL OPERATIONS

§ 12141. Definitions

As used in this subpart:

(1) Demand responsive system

The term "demand responsive system" means any system of providing designated public transportation which is not a fixed route system.

(2) Designated public transportation

The term "designated public transportation" means transportation (other than public school transportation) by bus, rail, or any other conveyance (other than transportation by aircraft or intercity or commuter rail transportation (as defined in section 12161 of this title)) that provides the general public with general or special service (including charter service) on a regular and continuing basis.

(3) Fixed route system

The term "fixed route system" means a system of providing designated public transportation on which a vehicle is operated along a prescribed route according to a fixed schedule.

(4) Operates

The term "operates", as used with respect to a fixed route system or demand responsive system, includes operation of such system by a person under a contractual or other arrangement or relationship with a public entity.

(5) Public school transportation

The term "public school transportation" means transportation by schoolbus vehicles of schoolchildren, personnel, and equipment to and from a public elementary or secondary school and school-related activities.

(6) Secretary

The term "Secretary" means the Secretary of Transportation.

(Pub. L. 101-336, title II, § 221, July 26, 1990, 104 Stat. 338.)

EFFECTIVE DATE

Section 231 of Pub. L. 101-336 provided that:
"(a) GENERAL RULE.—Except as provided in subsection (b), this part [part I (§§ 221-231) of subtitle B of title II of Pub. L. 101-336, enacting this subpart] shall become effective 18 months after the date of enactment of this Act [July 26, 1990].
"(b) EXCEPTION.—Sections 222, 223 (other than subsection (a)), 224, 225, 227(b), 228(b), and 229 [sections 12142, 12143(b) to (f), 12144, 12145, 12147(b), 12148(b), and 12149 of this title] shall become effective on the date of enactment of this Act."

§ 12142. Public entities operating fixed route systems

(a) Purchase and lease of new vehicles

It shall be considered discrimination for purposes of section 12132 of this title and section 794 of title 29 for a public entity which operates a fixed route system to purchase or lease a new bus, a new rapid rail vehicle, a new light rail vehicle, or any other new vehicle to be used on such system, if the solicitation for such purchase or lease is made after the 30th day following July 26, 1990, and if such bus, rail vehicle, or other vehicle is not readily accessible to and usable by individuals with disabilities, including individuals who use wheelchairs.

(b) Purchase and lease of used vehicles

Subject to subsection (c)(1) of this section, it shall be considered discrimination for purposes of section 12132 of this title and section 794 of title 29 for a public entity which operates a fixed route system to purchase or lease, after the 30th day following July 26, 1990, a used vehicle for use on such system unless such entity makes demonstrated good faith efforts to purchase or lease a used vehicle for use on such system that is readily accessible to and usable by individuals with disabilities, including individuals who use wheelchairs.

(c) Remanufactured vehicles

(1) General rule

Except as provided in paragraph (2), it shall be considered discrimination for purposes of section 12132 of this title and section 794 of title 29 for a public entity which operates a fixed route system—

(A) to remanufacture a vehicle for use on such system so as to extend its usable life for 5 years or more, which remanufacture begins (or for which the solicitation is made) after the 30th day following July 26, 1990; or

(B) to purchase or lease for use on such system a remanufactured vehicle which has been remanufactured so as to extend its usable life for 5 years or more, which purchase or lease occurs after such 30th day and during the period in which the usable life is extended;

unless, after remanufacture, the vehicle is, to the maximum extent feasible, readily accessible to and usable by individuals with disabilities, including individuals who use wheelchairs.

(2) Exception for historic vehicles

(A) General rule

If a public entity operates a fixed route system any segment of which is included on the National Register of Historic Places and if making a vehicle of historic character to be used solely on such segment readily accessible to and usable by individuals with disabilities would significantly alter the historic character of such vehicle, the public entity only has to make (or to purchase or lease a remanufactured vehicle with) those modifications which are necessary to meet the requirements of paragraph (1) and which do not significantly alter the historic character of such vehicle.

(B) Vehicles of historic character defined by regulations

For purposes of this paragraph and section 12148(b) of this title, a vehicle of historic character shall be defined by the regulations issued by the Secretary to carry out this subsection.

(Pub. L. 101-336, title II, § 222, July 26, 1990, 104 Stat. 339.)

EFFECTIVE DATE

Section effective July 26, 1990, see section 231(b) of Pub. L. 101-336, set out as a note under section 12141 of this title.

SECTION REFERRED TO IN OTHER SECTIONS

This section is referred to in sections 12145, 12148 of this title.

§ 12143. Paratransit as a complement to fixed route service

(a) General rule

It shall be considered discrimination for purposes of section 12132 of this title and section 794 of title 29 for a public entity which operates a fixed route system (other than a system which provides solely commuter bus service) to fail to provide with respect to the operations of its fixed route system, in accordance with this section, paratransit and other special transportation services to individuals with disabilities, including individuals who use wheelchairs, that are sufficient to provide to such individuals a level of service (1) which is comparable to the level of designated public transportation services provided to individuals without disabilities using such system; or (2) in the case of response time, which is comparable, to the extent practicable, to the level of designated public transportation services provided to individuals without disabilities using such system.

(b) Issuance of regulations

Not later than 1 year after July 26, 1990, the Secretary shall issue final regulations to carry out this section.

(c) Required contents of regulations

(1) Eligible recipients of service

The regulations issued under this section shall require each public entity which operates a fixed route system to provide the paratransit and other special transportation services required under this section—

(A)(i) to any individual with a disability who is unable, as a result of a physical or mental impairment (including a vision impairment) and without the assistance of another individual (except an operator of a wheelchair lift or other boarding assistance device), to board, ride, or disembark from any vehicle on the system which is readily accessible to and usable by individuals with disabilities;

(ii) to any individual with a disability who needs the assistance of a wheelchair lift or other boarding assistance device (and is able with such assistance) to board, ride, and disembark from any vehicle which is readily accessible to and usable by individuals with disabilities if the individual wants to travel on a route on the system during the hours of operation of the system at a time (or within a reasonable period of such time) when such a vehicle is not being used to provide designated public transportation on the route; and

(iii) to any individual with a disability who has a specific impairment-related condition which prevents such individual from traveling to a boarding location or from a disembarking location on such system;

(B) to one other individual accompanying the individual with the disability; and

(C) to other individuals, in addition to the one individual described in subparagraph (B), accompanying the individual with a disability provided that space for these additional individuals is available on the paratransit vehicle carrying the individual with a disability and that the transportation of such additional individuals will not result in a denial of service to individuals with disabilities.

For purposes of clauses (i) and (ii) of subparagraph (A), boarding or disembarking from a vehicle does not include travel to the boarding location or from the disembarking location.

(2) Service area

The regulations issued under this section shall require the provision of paratransit and special transportation services required under this section in the service area of each public entity which operates a fixed route system, other than any portion of the service area in which the public entity solely provides commuter bus service.

(3) Service criteria

Subject to paragraphs (1) and (2), the regulations issued under this section shall establish minimum service criteria for determining the level of services to be required under this section.

(4) Undue financial burden limitation

The regulations issued under this section shall provide that, if the public entity is able to demonstrate to the satisfaction of the Secretary that the provision of paratransit and other special transportation services otherwise required under this section would impose an undue financial burden on the public entity, the public entity, notwithstanding any other provision of this section (other than paragraph (5)), shall only be required to provide such services to the extent that providing such services would not impose such a burden.

(5) Additional services

The regulations issued under this section shall establish circumstances under which the Secretary may require a public entity to provide, notwithstanding paragraph (4), paratransit and other special transportation services under this section beyond the level of paratransit and other special transportation services which would otherwise be required under paragraph (4).

(6) Public participation

The regulations issued under this section shall require that each public entity which operates a fixed route system hold a public hearing, provide an opportunity for public comment, and consult with individuals with disabilities in preparing its plan under paragraph (7).

(7) Plans

The regulations issued under this section shall require that each public entity which operates a fixed route system—
(A) within 18 months after July 26, 1990, submit to the Secretary, and commence implementation of, a plan for providing paratransit and other special transportation services which meets the requirements of this section; and
(B) on an annual basis thereafter, submit to the Secretary, and commence implementation of, a plan for providing such services.

(8) Provision of services by others

The regulations issued under this section shall—
(A) require that a public entity submitting a plan to the Secretary under this section identify in the plan any person or other public entity which is providing a paratransit or other special transportation service for individuals with disabilities in the service area to which the plan applies; and
(B) provide that the public entity submitting the plan does not have to provide under the plan such service for individuals with disabilities.

(9) Other provisions

The regulations issued under this section shall include such other provisions and requirements as the Secretary determines are necessary to carry out the objectives of this section.

(d) Review of plan

(1) General rule

The Secretary shall review a plan submitted under this section for the purpose of determining whether or not such plan meets the requirements of this section, including the regulations issued under this section.

(2) Disapproval

If the Secretary determines that a plan reviewed under this subsection fails to meet the requirements of this section, the Secretary shall disapprove the plan and notify the public entity which submitted the plan of such disapproval and the reasons therefor.

(3) Modification of disapproved plan

Not later than 90 days after the date of disapproval of a plan under this subsection, the public entity which submitted the plan shall modify the plan to meet the requirements of this section and shall submit to the Secretary, and commence implementation of, such modified plan.

(e) "Discrimination" defined

As used in subsection (a) of this section, the term "discrimination" includes—
(1) a failure of a public entity to which the regulations issued under this section apply to submit, or commence implementation of, a plan in accordance with subsections (c)(6) and (c)(7) of this section;
(2) a failure of such entity to submit, or commence implementation of, a modified plan in accordance with subsection (d)(3) of this section;
(3) submission to the Secretary of a modified plan under subsection (d)(3) of this section which does not meet the requirements of this section; or

(4) a failure of such entity to provide paratransit or other special transportation services in accordance with the plan or modified plan the public entity submitted to the Secretary under this section.

(f) Statutory construction

Nothing in this section shall be construed as preventing a public entity—

(1) from providing paratransit or other special transportation services at a level which is greater than the level of such services which are required by this section,

(2) from providing paratransit or other special transportation services in addition to those paratransit and special transportation services required by this section, or

(3) from providing such services to individuals in addition to those individuals to whom such services are required to be provided by this section.

(Pub. L. 101-336, title II, § 223, July 26, 1990, 104 Stat. 340.)

EFFECTIVE DATE

Subsec. (a) of this section effective 18 months after July 26, 1990, and subsecs. (b) to (f) of this section effective July 26, 1990, see section 231 of Pub. L. 101-336, set out as a note under section 12141 of this title.

SECTION REFERRED TO IN OTHER SECTIONS

This section is referred to in sections 12134, 12149 of this title.

§ 12144. Public entity operating a demand responsive system

If a public entity operates a demand responsive system, it shall be considered discrimination, for purposes of section 12132 of this title and section 794 of title 29, for such entity to purchase or lease a new vehicle for use on such system, for which a solicitation is made after the 30th day following July 26, 1990, that is not readily accessible to and usable by individuals with disabilities, including individuals who use wheelchairs, unless such system, when viewed in its entirety, provides a level of service to such individuals equivalent to the level of service such system provides to individuals without disabilities.

(Pub. L. 101-336, title II, § 224, July 26, 1990, 104 Stat. 342.)

EFFECTIVE DATE

Section effective July 26, 1990, see section 231(b) of Pub. L. 101-336, set out as a note under section 12141 of this title.

SECTION REFERRED TO IN OTHER SECTIONS

This section is referred to in section 12145 of this title.

§ 12145. Temporary relief where lifts are unavailable

(a) Granting

With respect to the purchase of new buses, a public entity may apply for, and the Secretary may temporarily relieve such public entity from the obligation under section 12142(a) or 12144 of this title to purchase new buses that are readily accessible to and usable by individuals with disabilities if such public entity demonstrates to the satisfaction of the Secretary—

(1) that the initial solicitation for new buses made by the public entity specified that all new buses were to be lift-equipped and were to be otherwise accessible to and usable by individuals with disabilities;

(2) the unavailability from any qualified manufacturer of hydraulic, electromechanical, or other lifts for such new buses;

(3) that the public entity seeking temporary relief has made good faith efforts to locate a qualified manufacturer to supply the lifts to the manufacturer of such buses in sufficient time to comply with such solicitation; and

(4) that any further delay in purchasing new buses necessary to obtain such lifts would significantly impair transportation services in the community served by the public entity.

(b) Duration and notice to Congress

Any relief granted under subsection (a) of this section shall be limited in duration by a specified date, and the appropriate committees of Congress shall be notified of any such relief granted.

(c) Fraudulent application

If, at any time, the Secretary has reasonable cause to believe that any relief granted under subsection (a) of this section was fraudulently applied for, the Secretary shall—

(1) cancel such relief if such relief is still in effect; and

(2) take such other action as the Secretary considers appropriate.

(Pub. L. 101-336, title II, § 225, July 26, 1990, 104 Stat. 343.)

EFFECTIVE DATE

Section effective July 26, 1990, see section 231(b) of Pub. L. 101-336, set out as a note under section 12141 of this title.

§ 12146. New facilities

For purposes of section 12132 of this title and section 794 of title 29, it shall be considered discrimination for a public entity to construct a new facility to be used in the provision of designated public transportation services unless such facility is readily accessible to and usable by individuals with disabilities, including individuals who use wheelchairs.

(Pub. L. 101-336, title II, § 226, July 26, 1990, 104 Stat. 343.)

EFFECTIVE DATE

Section effective 18 months after July 26, 1990, see section 231(a) of Pub. L. 101-336, set out as a note under section 12141 of this title.

SECTION REFERRED TO IN OTHER SECTIONS

This section is referred to in section 12150 of this title.

§ 12147. Alterations of existing facilities

(a) General rule

With respect to alterations of an existing facility or part thereof used in the provision of designated public transportation services that affect or could affect the usability of the facility or part thereof, it shall be considered discrimination, for purposes of section 12132 of this title and section 794 of title 29, for a public entity to fail to make such alterations (or to ensure that the alterations are made) in such a manner that, to the maximum extent feasible, the altered portions of the facility are readily accessible to and usable by individuals with disabilities, including individuals who use wheelchairs, upon the completion of such alterations. Where the public entity is undertaking an alteration that affects or could affect usability of or access to an area of the facility containing a primary function, the entity shall also make the alterations in such a manner that, to the maximum extent feasible, the path of travel to the altered area and the bathrooms, telephones, and drinking fountains serving the altered area, are readily accessible to and usable by individuals with disabilities, including individuals who use wheelchairs, upon completion of such alterations, where such alterations to the path of travel or the bathrooms, telephones, and drinking fountains serving the altered area are not disproportionate to the overall alterations in terms of cost and scope (as determined under criteria established by the Attorney General).

(b) Special rule for stations

(1) General rule

For purposes of section 12132 of this title and section 794 of title 29, it shall be considered discrimination for a public entity that provides designated public transportation to fail, in accordance with the provisions of this subsection, to make key stations (as determined under criteria established by the Secretary by regulation) in rapid rail and light rail systems readily accessible to and usable by individuals with disabilities, including individuals who use wheelchairs.

(2) Rapid rail and light rail key stations

(A) Accessibility

Except as otherwise provided in this paragraph, all key stations (as determined under criteria established by the Secretary by regulation) in rapid rail and light rail systems shall be made readily accessible to and usable by individuals with disabilities, including individuals who use wheelchairs, as soon as practicable but in no event later than the last day of the 3-year period beginning on July 26, 1990.

(B) Extension for extraordinarily expensive structural changes

The Secretary may extend the 3-year period under subparagraph (A) up to a 30-year period for key stations in a rapid rail or light rail system which stations need extraordinarily expensive structural changes to, or replacement of, existing facilities; except that by the last day of the 20th year following July 26, 1990, at least 2/3 of such key stations must be readily accessible to and usable by individuals with disabilities.

(3) Plans and milestones

The Secretary shall require the appropriate public entity to develop and submit to the Secretary a plan for compliance with this subsection—
(A) that reflects consultation with individuals with disabilities affected by such plan and the results of a public hearing and public comments on such plan, and
(B) that establishes milestones for achievement of the requirements of this subsection.

(Pub. L. 101-336, title 11, § 227, July 26, 1990, 104 Stat. 343.)

EFFECTIVE DATE

Subsec. (a) of this section effective 18 months after July 26, 1990, and subsec. (b) of this section effective July 26, 1990, see section 231 of Pub. L. 101-336, set out as a note under section 12141 of this title.

SECTION REFERRED TO IN OTHER SECTIONS

This section is referred to in sections 12148, 12150 of this title.

§ 12148. Public transportation programs and activities in existing facilities and one car per train rule

(a) Public transportation programs and activities in existing facilities

(1) In general

With respect to existing facilities used in the provision of designated public transportation services, it shall be considered discrimination, for purposes of section 12132 of this title and section 794 of title 29, for a public entity to fail to operate a designated public transportation program or activity conducted in such facilities so that, when viewed in the entirety, the program or activity is readily accessible to and usable by individuals with disabilities.

(2) Exception

Paragraph (1) shall not require a public entity to make structural changes to existing facilities in order to make such facilities accessible to individuals who use wheelchairs, unless and to the extent required by section 12147(a) of this title (relating to alterations) or section 12147(b) of this title (relating to key stations).

(3) Utilization

Paragraph (1) shall not require a public entity to which paragraph (2) applies, to provide to individuals who use wheelchairs services made available to the general public at such facilities when such individuals could not utilize or benefit from such services provided at such facilities.

(b) One car per train rule

(1) General rule

Subject to paragraph (2), with respect to 2 or more vehicles operated as a train by a light or rapid rail system, for purposes of section 12132 of this title and section 794 of title 29, it shall be considered discrimination for a public entity to fail to have at least 1 vehicle per train that is accessible to individuals with disabilities, including individuals who use wheelchairs, as soon as practicable but in no event later than the last day of the 5-year period beginning on the effective date of this section.

(2) Historic trains

In order to comply with paragraph (1) with respect to the remanufacture of a vehicle of historic character which is to be used on a segment of a light or rapid rail system which is included on the National Register of Historic Places, if making such vehicle readily accessible to and usable by individuals with disabilities would significantly alter the historic character of such vehicle, the public entity which operates such system only has to make (or to purchase or lease a remanufactured vehicle with) those modifications which are necessary to meet the requirements of section 12142(c)(1) of this title and which do not significantly alter the historic character of such vehicle.

(Pub. L. 101-336, title II, § 228, July 26, 1990, 104 Stat. 344.)

REFERENCES IN TEXT

The effective date of this section, referred to in subsec. (b)(1), probably means the effective date of subsec. (b), which is effective on date of enactment of Pub. L. 101-336, which was approved July 26, 1990. The effective date of subsec. (a) is 18 months after July 26, 1990. See section 231 of Pub. L. 101-336, set out as an Effective Date note under section 12141 of this title.

EFFECTIVE DATE

Subsec. (a) of this section effective 18 months after July 26, 1990, and subsec. (b) of this section effective July 26, 1990, see section 231 of Pub. L. 101-336, set out as a note under section 12141 of this title.

SECTION REFERRED TO IN OTHER SECTIONS

This section is referred to in section 12142 of this title.

§ 12149. Regulations

(a) In general

Not later than 1 year after July 26, 1990, the Secretary of Transportation shall issue regulations, in an accessible format, necessary for carrying out this subpart (other than section 12143 of this title).

(b) Standards

The regulations issued under this section and section 12143 of this title shall include standards applicable to facilities and vehicles covered by this part. The standards shall be consistent with the minimum guidelines and requirements issued by the Architectural and Transportation Barriers Compliance Board in accordance with section 12204 of this title.

(Pub. L. 101-336, title II, § 229, July 26, 1990, 104 Stat. 345.)

EFFECTIVE DATE

Section effective July 26, 1990, see section 231(b) of Pub. L. 101-336, set out as a note under section 12141 of this title.

SECTION REFERRED TO IN OTHER SECTIONS

This section is referred to in sections 12134, 12150 of this title.

§ 12150. Interim accessibility requirements

If final regulations have not been issued pursuant to section 12149 of this title, for new construction or alterations for which a valid and appropriate State or local building permit is obtained prior to the issuance of final regulations under such section, and for which the construction or alteration authorized by such permit begins within one year of the receipt of such permit and is completed under the terms of such permit, compliance with the Uniform Federal Accessibility Standards in effect at the time the building permit is issued shall suffice to satisfy the requirement that facilities be readily accessible to and usable by persons with disabilities as required under sections 12146 and 12147 of this title, except that, if such final regulations have not been issued one year after the Architectural and Transportation Barriers Compliance Board has issued the supplemental minimum guidelines required under section 12204(a) of this title, compliance with such supplemental minimum guidelines shall be necessary to satisfy the requirement that facilities be readily accessible to and usable by persons with disabilities prior to issuance of the final regulations.

(Pub. L. 101-336, title II, § 230, July 26, 1990, 104 Stat. 345.)

EFFECTIVE DATE

Section effective 18 months after July 26, 1990, see section 231(a) of Pub. L. 101-336, set out as a note under section 12141 of this title.

SUBPART II—PUBLIC TRANSPORTATION BY INTERCITY AND COMMUTER RAIL

§ 12161. Definitions

As used in this subpart:

(1) Commuter authority

The term "commuter authority" has the meaning given such term in section 502(8) of title 45.

(2) Commuter rail transportation

The term "commuter rail transportation" has the meaning given the term "commuter service" in section 502(9) of title 45.

(3) Intercity rail transportation

The term "intercity rail transportation" means transportation provided by the National Railroad Passenger Corporation.

(4) Rail passenger car

The term "rail passenger car" means, with respect to intercity rail transportation, single-level and bi-level coach cars, single-level and bi-level dining cars, single-level and bi-level sleeping cars, single-level and bi-level lounge cars, and food service cars.

(5) Responsible person

The term "responsible person" means—
(A) in the case of a station more than 50 percent of which is owned by a public entity, such public entity;
(B) in the case of a station more than 50 percent of which is owned by a private party, the persons providing intercity or commuter rail transportation to such station, as allocated on an equitable basis by regulation by the Secretary of Transportation; and
(C) in a case where no party owns more than 50 percent of a station, the persons providing intercity or commuter rail transportation to such station and the owners of the station, other than private party owners, as allocated on an equitable basis by regulation by the Secretary of Transportation.

(6) Station

The term "station" means the portion of a property located appurtenant to a right-of-way on which intercity or commuter rail transportation is operated, where such portion is used by the general public and is related to the provision of such transportation, including passenger platforms, designated waiting areas, ticketing areas, restrooms, and, where a public entity providing rail transportation owns the property, concession areas, to the extent that such public entity exercises control over the selection, design, construction, or alteration of the property, but such term does not include flag stops.

(Pub. L. 101-336, title II, § 241, July 26, 1990, 104 Stat. 346.)

EFFECTIVE DATE

Section 246 of Pub. L. 101-336 provided that:
"(a) GENERAL RULE.—Except as provided in subsection (b), this part [part II (§§ 241-246) of subtitle B of title II of Pub. L. 101-336, enacting this subpart] shall become effective 18 months after the date of enactment of this Act [July 26, 1990].
"(b) Exception.—Sections 242 and 244 [sections 12162 and 12164 of this title] shall become effective on the date of enactment of this Act."

SECTION REFERRED TO IN OTHER SECTIONS

This section is referred to in section 12141 of this title.

§ 12162. Intercity and commuter rail actions considered discriminatory

(a) Intercity rail transportation

(1) One car per train rule

It shall be considered discrimination for purposes of section 12132 of this title and section 794 of title 29 for a person who provides intercity rail transportation to fail to have at least one passenger car per train that is readily accessible to and usable by individuals with disabilities, including individuals who use wheelchairs, in accordance with regulations issued under section 12164 of this title, as soon as practicable, but in no event later than 5 years after July 26, 1990.

(2) New intercity cars

(A) General rule

Except as otherwise provided in this subsection with respect to individuals who use wheelchairs, it shall be considered discrimination for purposes of section 12132 of this title and section 794 of title 29 for a person to purchase or lease any new rail passenger cars for use in intercity rail transportation, and for which a solicitation is made later than 30 days after July 26, 1990, unless all such rail cars are readily accessible to and usable by individuals with disabilities, including individuals who use wheelchairs, as prescribed by the Secretary of Transportation in regulations issued under section 12164 of this title.

(B) Special rule for single-level passenger coaches for individuals who use wheelchairs

Single-level passenger coaches shall be required to—
(i) be able to be entered by an individual who uses a wheelchair;
(ii) have space to park and secure a wheelchair;

(iii) have a seat to which a passenger in a wheelchair can transfer; and a space to fold and store such passenger's wheelchair; and

(iv) have a restroom usable by an individual who uses a wheelchair,

only to the extent provided in paragraph (3).

(C) Special rule for single-level dining cars for individuals who use wheelchairs

Single-level dining cars shall not be required to—

(i) be able to be entered from the station platform by an individual who uses a wheelchair; or

(ii) have a restroom usable by an individual who uses a wheelchair if no restroom is provided in such car for any passenger.

(D) Special rule for bi-level dining cars for individuals who use wheelchairs

Bi-level dining cars shall not be required to—

(i) be able to be entered by an individual who uses a wheelchair;

(ii) have space to park and secure a wheelchair;

(iii) have a seat to which a passenger in a wheelchair can transfer, or a space to fold and store such passenger's wheelchair; or

(iv) have a restroom usable by an individual who uses a wheelchair.

(3) Accessibility of single-level coaches

(A) General rule

It shall be considered discrimination for purposes of section 12132 of this title and section 794 of title 29 for a person who provides intercity rail transportation to fail to have on each train which includes one or more single-level rail passenger coaches—

(i) a number of spaces—

(I) to park and secure wheelchairs (to accommodate individuals who wish to remain in their wheelchairs) equal to not less than one-half of the number of single-level rail passenger coaches in such train; and

(II) to fold and store wheelchairs (to accommodate individuals who wish to transfer to coach seats) equal to not less than one-half of the number of single-level rail passenger coaches in such train,

as soon as practicable, but in no event later than 5 years after July 26, 1990; and

(ii) a number of spaces—

(I) to park and secure wheelchairs (to accommodate individuals who wish to remain in their wheelchairs) equal to not less than the total number of single-level rail passenger coaches in such train; and

(II) to fold and store wheelchairs (to accommodate individuals who wish to transfer to coach seats) equal to not less than the total number of single-level rail passenger coaches in such train,

as soon as practicable, but in no event later than 10 years after July 26, 1990.

(B) Location

Spaces required by subparagraph (A) shall be located in single-level rail passenger coaches or food service cars.

(C) Limitation

Of the number of spaces required on a train by subparagraph (A), not more than two spaces to park and secure wheelchairs nor more than two spaces to fold and store wheelchairs shall be located in any one coach or food service car.

(D) Other accessibility features

Single-level rail passenger coaches and food service cars on which the spaces required by subparagraph (A) are located shall have a restroom usable by an individual who uses a wheelchair and shall be able to be entered from the station platform by an individual who uses a wheelchair.

(4) Food service

(A) Single-level dining cars

On any train in which a single-level dining car is used to provide food service—
(i) if such single-level dining car was purchased after July 26, 1990, table service in such car shall be provided to a passenger who uses a wheelchair if—
(I) the car adjacent to the end of the dining car through which a wheelchair may enter is itself accessible to a wheelchair;
(II) such passenger can exit to the platform from the car such passenger occupies, move down the platform, and enter the adjacent accessible car described in subclause (I) without the necessity of the train being moved within the station; and
(III) space to park and secure a wheelchair is available in the dining car at the time such passenger wishes to eat (if such passenger wishes to remain in a wheelchair), or space to store and fold a wheelchair is available in the dining car at the time such passenger wishes to eat (if such passenger wishes to transfer to a dining car seat); and
(ii) appropriate auxiliary aids and services, including a hard surface on which to eat, shall be provided to ensure that other equivalent food service is available to individuals with disabilities, including individuals who use wheelchairs, and to passengers traveling with such individuals.
Unless not practicable, a person providing intercity rail transportation shall place an accessible car adjacent to the end of a dining car described in clause (i) through which an individual who uses a wheelchair may enter.

(B) Bi-level dining cars

On any train in which a bi-level dining car is used to provide food service—
(i) if such train includes a bi-level lounge car purchased after July 26, 1990, table service in such lounge car shall be provided to individuals who use wheelchairs and to other passengers; and
(ii) appropriate auxiliary aids and services, including a hard surface on which to eat, shall be provided to ensure that other equivalent food service is available to

individuals with disabilities, including individuals who use wheelchairs, and to passengers traveling with such individuals.

(b) Commuter rail transportation

(1) One car per train rule

It shall be considered discrimination for purposes of section 12132 of this title and section 794 of title 29 for a person who provides commuter rail transportation to fail to have at least one passenger car per train that is readily accessible to and usable by individuals with disabilities, including individuals who use wheelchairs, in accordance with regulations issued under section 12164 of this title, as soon as practicable, but in no event later than 5 years after July 26, 1990.

(2) New commuter rail cars

(A) General rule

It shall be considered discrimination for purposes of section 12132 of this title and section 794 of title 29 for a person to purchase or lease any new rail passenger cars for use in commuter rail transportation, and for which a solicitation is made later than 30 days after July 26, 1990, unless all such rail cars are readily accessible to and usable by individuals with disabilities, including individuals who use wheelchairs, as prescribed by the Secretary of Transportation in regulations issued under section 12164 of this title.

(B) Accessibility

For purposes of section 12132 of this title and section 794 of title 29, a requirement that a rail passenger car used in commuter rail transportation be accessible to or readily accessible to and usable by individuals with disabilities, including individuals who use wheelchairs, shall not be construed to require—
　(i) a restroom usable by an individual who uses a wheelchair if no restroom is provided in such car for any passenger;
　(ii) space to fold and store a wheelchair; or
　(iii) a seat to which a passenger who uses a wheelchair can transfer.

(c) Used rail cars

It shall be considered discrimination for purposes of section 12132 of this title and section 794 of title 29 for a person to purchase or lease a used rail passenger car for use in intercity or commuter rail transportation, unless such person makes demonstrated good faith efforts to purchase or lease a used rail car that is readily accessible to and usable by individuals with disabilities, including individuals who use wheelchairs, as prescribed by the Secretary of Transportation in regulations issued under section 12164 of this title.

(d) Remanufactured rail cars

(1) Remanufacturing

It shall be considered discrimination for purposes of section 12132 of this title and section 794 of title 29 for a person to remanufacture a rail passenger car for use in intercity or commuter rail transportation so as to extend its usable life for 10 years or more, unless the rail car, to the maximum extent feasible, is made readily accessible to and usable by individuals with disabilities, including individuals who use wheelchairs, as prescribed by the Secretary of Transportation in regulations issued under section 12164 of this title.

(2) Purchase or lease

It shall be considered discrimination for purposes of section 12132 of this title and section 794 of title 29 for a person to purchase or lease a remanufactured rail passenger car for use in intercity or commuter rail transportation unless such car was remanufactured in accordance with paragraph (1).

(e) Stations

(1) New stations

It shall be considered discrimination for purposes of section 12132 of this title and section 794 of title 29 for a person to build a new station for use in intercity or commuter rail transportation that is not readily accessible to and usable by individuals with disabilities, including individuals who use wheelchairs, as prescribed by the Secretary of Transportation in regulations issued under section 12164 of this title.

(2) Existing stations

(A) Failure to make readily accessible

(i) General rule

It shall be considered discrimination for purposes of section 12132 of this title and section 794 of title 29 for a responsible person to fail to make existing stations in the intercity rail transportation system, and existing key stations in commuter rail transportation systems, readily accessible to and usable by individuals with disabilities, including individuals who use wheelchairs, as prescribed by the Secretary of Transportation in regulations issued under section 12164 of this title.

(ii) Period for compliance

(I) Intercity rail

All stations in the intercity rail transportation system shall be made readily accessible to and usable by individuals with disabilities, including individuals who use wheelchairs, as soon as practicable, but in no event later than 20 years after July 26, 1990.

(II) Commuter rail

Key stations in commuter rail transportation systems shall be made readily accessible to and usable by individuals with disabilities, including individuals who use wheelchairs, as soon as practicable but in no event later than 3 years after July 26, 1990, except that the time limit may be extended by the Secretary of Transportation up to 20 years after July 26, 1990, in a case where the raising of the entire passenger platform is the only means available of attaining accessibility or where other extraordinarily expensive structural changes are necessary to attain accessibility.

(iii) Designation of key stations

Each commuter authority shall designate the key stations in its commuter rail transportation system, in consultation with individuals with disabilities and organizations representing such individuals, taking into consideration such factors as high ridership and whether such station serves as a transfer or feeder station. Before the final designation of key stations under this clause, a commuter authority shall hold a public hearing.

(iv) Plans and milestones

The Secretary of Transportation shall require the appropriate person to develop a plan for carrying out this subparagraph that reflects consultation with individuals with disabilities affected by such plan and that establishes milestones for achievement of the requirements of this subparagraph.

(B) Requirement when making alterations

(i) General rule

It shall be considered discrimination, for purposes of section 12132 of this title and section 794 of title 29, with respect to alterations of an existing station or part thereof in the intercity or commuter rail transportation systems that affect or could affect the usability of the station or part thereof, for the responsible person, owner, or person in control of the station to fail to make the alterations in such a manner that, to the maximum extent feasible, the altered portions of the station are readily accessible to and usable by individuals with disabilities, including individuals who use wheelchairs, upon completion of such alterations.

(ii) Alterations to a primary function area

It shall be considered discrimination, for purposes of section 12132 of this title and section 794 of title 29, with respect to alterations that affect or could affect the usability of or access to an area of the station containing a primary function, for the responsible person, owner, or person in control of the station to fail to make the alterations in such a manner that, to the maximum extent feasible, the path of travel to the altered area, and the bathrooms, telephones, and drinking fountains serving the altered area, are readily accessible to and usable by individuals with disabilities, including individuals who use wheelchairs, upon completion of such alterations, where such alterations to the path of travel or the bathrooms, telephones, and drinking fountains serving the altered area are not disproportionate to the overall alterations in terms of cost and scope (as determined under criteria established by the Attorney General).

(C) Required cooperation

It shall be considered discrimination for purposes of section 12132 of this title and section 794 of title 29 for an owner, or person in control, of a station governed by subparagraph (A) or (B) to fail to provide reasonable cooperation to a responsible person with respect to such station in that responsible person's efforts to comply with such subparagraph. An owner, or person in control, of a station shall be liable to a responsible person for any failure to provide reasonable cooperation as required by this subparagraph. Failure to receive reasonable cooperation required by this subparagraph shall not be a defense to a claim of discrimination under this chapter.

(Pub. L. 101-336, title II, § 242, July 26, 1990, 104 Stat. 347.)

EFFECTIVE DATE

Section effective July 26, 1990, see section 246(b) of Pub. L. 101-336, set out as a note under section 12161 of this title.

SECTION REFERRED TO IN OTHER SECTIONS

This section is referred to in sections 12165, 12181 of this title.

§ 12163. Conformance of accessibility standards

Accessibility standards included in regulations issued under this subpart shall be consistent with the minimum guidelines issued by the Architectural and Transportation Barriers Compliance Board under section 12204(a) of this title.

(Pub. L. 101-336, title II, § 243, July 26, 1990, 104 Stat. 352.)

EFFECTIVE DATE

Section effective 18 months after July 26, 1990, see section 246(a) of Pub. L. 101-336, set out as a note under section 12161 of this title.

§ 12164. Regulations

Not later than 1 year after July 26, 1990, the Secretary of Transportation shall issue regulations, in an accessible format, necessary for carrying out this subpart.

(Pub. L. 101-336, title 11, § 244, July 26, 1990, 104 Stat. 352.)

EFFECTIVE DATE

Section effective July 26, 1990, see section 246(b) of Pub. L. 101-336, set out as a note under section 12161 of this title.

SECTION REFERRED TO IN OTHER SECTIONS

This section is referred to in sections 12134, 12162, 12165 of this title.

§ 12165. Interim accessibility requirements

(a) Stations

If final regulations have not been issued pursuant to section 12164 of this title, for new construction or alterations for which a valid and appropriate State or local building permit is obtained prior to the issuance of final regulations under such section, and for which the construction or alteration authorized by such permit begins within one year of the receipt of such permit and is completed under the terms of such permit, compliance with the Uniform Federal Accessibility Standards in effect at the time the building permit is issued shall suffice to satisfy the requirement that stations be readily accessible to and usable by persons with disabilities as required under section 12162(e) of this title, except that, if such final regulations have not been issued one year after the Architectural and Transportation Barriers Compliance Board has issued the supplemental minimum guidelines required under section 12204(a) of this title, compliance with such supplemental minimum guidelines shall be necessary to satisfy the requirement that stations be readily accessible to and usable by persons with disabilities prior to issuance of the final regulations.

(b) Rail passenger cars

If final regulations have not been issued pursuant to section 12164 of this title, a person shall be considered to have complied with the requirements of section 12162(a) through (d) of this title that a rail passenger car be readily accessible to and usable by individuals with disabilities, if the design for such car complies with the laws and regulations (including the Minimum Guidelines and Requirements for Accessible Design and such supplemental minimum guidelines as are issued under section 12204(a) of this title) governing accessibility of such cars, to the extent that such laws and regulations are not inconsistent with this subpart and are in effect at the time such design is substantially completed.

(Pub. L. 101-336, title II, § 245, July 26, 1990, 104 Stat. 352.)

EFFECTIVE DATE

Section effective 18 months after July 26, 1990, see section 246(a) of Pub. L. 101-336, set out as a note under section 12161 of this title.

SUBCHAPTER III—PUBLIC ACCOMMODATIONS AND SERVICES OPERATED BY PRIVATE ENTITIES

SUBCHAPTER REFERRED TO IN OTHER SECTIONS

This subchapter is referred to in sections 12201, 12203, 12204, 12206 of this title.

§ 12181. Definitions

As used in this subchapter:

(1) Commerce
The term "commerce" means travel, trade, traffic, commerce, transportation, or communication—
(A) among the several States;
(B) between any foreign country or any territory or possession and any State; or
(C) between points in the same State but through another State or foreign country.

(2) Commercial facilities
The term "commercial facilities" means facilities—
(A) that are intended for nonresidential use; and
(B) whose operations will affect commerce.

Such term shall not include railroad locomotives, railroad freight cars, railroad cabooses, railroad cars described in section 12162 of this title or covered under this subchapter, railroad rights-of-way, or facilities that are covered or expressly exempted from coverage under the Fair Housing Act of 1968 (42 U.S.C. 3601 et seq.).

(3) Demand responsive system
The term "demand responsive system" means any system of providing transportation of individuals by a vehicle, other than a system which is a fixed route system.

(4) Fixed route system
The term "fixed route system" means a system of providing transportation of individuals (other than by aircraft) on which a vehicle is operated along a prescribed route according to a fixed schedule.

(5) Over-the-road bus
The term "over-the-road bus" means a bus characterized by an elevated passenger deck located over a baggage compartment.

(6) Private entity
The term "private entity" means any entity other than a public entity (as defined in section 12131(1) of this title).

(7) Public accommodation
The following private entities are considered public accommodations for purposes of this subchapter, if the operations of such entities affect commerce—

(A) an inn, hotel, motel, or other place of lodging, except for an establishment located within a building that contains not more than five rooms for rent or hire and that is actually occupied by the proprietor of such establishment as the residence of such proprietor;

(B) a restaurant, bar, or other establishment serving food or drink;

(C) a motion picture house, theater, concert hall, stadium, or other place of exhibition or entertainment;

(D) an auditorium, convention center, lecture hall, or other place of public gathering;

(E) a bakery, grocery store, clothing store, hardware store, shopping center, or other sales or rental establishment;

(F) a laundromat, dry-cleaner, bank, barber shop, beauty shop, travel service, shoe repair service, funeral parlor, gas station, office of an accountant or lawyer, pharmacy, insurance office, professional office of a health care provider, hospital, or other service establishment;

(G) a terminal, depot, or other station used for specified public transportation;

(H) a museum, library, gallery, or other place of public display or collection;

(I) a park, zoo, amusement park, or other place of recreation;

(J) a nursery, elementary, secondary, undergraduate, or postgraduate private school, or other place of education;

(K) a day care center, senior citizen center, homeless shelter, food bank, adoption agency, or other social service center establishment; and

(L) a gymnasium, health spa, bowling alley, golf course, or other place of exercise or recreation.

(8) Rail and railroad

The terms "rail" and "railroad" have the meaning given the term "railroad" in section 431(e) of title 45.

(9) Readily achievable

The term "readily achievable" means easily accomplishable and able to be carried out without much difficulty or expense. In determining whether an action is readily achievable, factors to be considered include—

(A) the nature and cost of the action needed under this chapter;

(B) the overall financial resources of the facility or facilities involved in the action; the number of persons employed at such facility; the effect on expenses and resources, or the impact otherwise of such action upon the operation of the facility;

(C) the overall financial resources of the covered entity; the overall size of the business of a covered entity with respect to the number of its employees; the number, type, and location of its facilities; and

(D) the type of operation or operations of the covered entity, including the composition, structure, and functions of the workforce of such entity; the geographic separateness, administrative or fiscal relationship of the facility or facilities in question to the covered entity.

(10) Specified public transportation

The term "specified public transportation" means transportation by bus, rail, or any other conveyance (other than by aircraft) that provides the general public with general or special service (including charter service) on a regular and continuing basis.

(11) Vehicle
The term "vehicle" does not include a rail passenger car, railroad locomotive, railroad freight car, railroad caboose, or a railroad car described in section 12162 of this title or covered under this subchapter.

(Pub. L. 101-336, title III, § 301, July 26, 1990, 104 Stat. 353.)

REFERENCES IN TEXT

The Fair Housing Act of 1968, referred to in par. (2), probably means the Fair Housing Act, title VIII of Pub. L. 90-284, Apr. 11, 1968, 82 Stat. 81, as amended, which is classified principally to subchapter I of chapter 45 (§ 3601 et seq.) of this title. For complete classification of this Act to the Code, see Short Title note set out under section 3601 of this title and Tables.

This chapter, referred to in par. (9)(A), was in the original "this Act", meaning Pub. L. 101-336, July 26, 1990, 104 Stat. 327, which is classified principally to this chapter. For complete classification of this Act to the Code, see Short Title note set out under section 12101 of this title and Tables.

EFFECTIVE DATE

Section 310 of title III of Pub. L. 101-336 provided that:
"(a) GENERAL RULE.—Except as provided in subsections (b) and (c), this title [enacting this subchapter] shall become effective 18 months after the date of the enactment of this Act [July 26, 1990].

"(b) CIVIL ACTIONS.—Except for any civil action brought for a violation of section 303 [section 12183 of this title], no civil action shall be brought for any act or omission described in section 302 [section 12182 of this title] which occurs—

"(1) during the first 6 months after the effective date, against businesses that employ 25 or fewer employees and have gross receipts of $1,000,000 or less; and

"(2) during the first year after the effective date, against businesses that employ 10 or fewer employees and have gross receipts of $500,000 or less.

"(c) EXCEPTION.—Sections 302(a) [section 12182(a) of this title] for purposes of section 302(b)(2)(B) and (C) only, 304(a) [section 12184(a) of this title] for purposes of section 304(b)(3) only, 304(b)(3), 305 [section 12185 of this title], and 306 [section 12186 of this title] shall take effect on the date of the enactment of this Act [July 26, 1990]."

§ 12182. Prohibition of discrimination by public accommodations

(a) General rule

No individual shall be discriminated against on the basis of disability in the full and equal enjoyment of the goods, services, facilities, privileges, advantages, or accommodations of any place of public accommodation by any person who owns, leases (or leases to), or operates a place of public accommodation.

(b) Construction

(1) General prohibition
(A) Activities
(i) Denial of participation

It shall be discriminatory to subject an individual or class of individuals on the basis of a disability or disabilities of such individual or class, directly, or through contractual, licensing, or other arrangements, to a denial of the opportunity of the individual or class to participate in or benefit from the goods, services, facilities, privileges, advantages, or accommodations of an entity.

(ii) Participation in unequal benefit

It shall be discriminatory to afford an individual or class of individuals, on the basis of a disability or disabilities of such individual or class, directly, or through contractual, licensing, or other arrangements with the opportunity to participate in or benefit from a good, service, facility, privilege, advantage, or accommodation that is not equal to that afforded to other individuals.

(iii) Separate benefit

It shall be discriminatory to provide an individual or class of individuals, on the basis of a disability or disabilities of such individual or class, directly, or through contractual, licensing, or other arrangements with a good, service, facility, privilege, advantage, or accommodation that is different or separate from that provided to other individuals, unless such action is necessary to provide the individual or class of individuals with a good, service, facility, privilege, advantage, or accommodation, or other opportunity that is as effective as that provided to others.

(iv) Individual or class of individuals

For purposes of clauses (i) through (iii) of this subparagraph, the term "individual or class of individuals" refers to the clients or customers of the covered public accommodation that enters into the contractual, licensing or other arrangement.

(B) Integrated settings

Goods, services, facilities, privileges, advantages, and accommodations shall be afforded to an individual with a disability in the most integrated setting appropriate to the needs of the individual.

(C) Opportunity to participate

Notwithstanding the existence of separate or different programs or activities provided in accordance with this section, an individual with a disability shall not be denied the opportunity to participate in such programs or activities that are not separate or different.

(D) Administrative methods

An individual or entity shall not, directly or through contractual or other arrangements, utilize standards or criteria or methods of administration—
(i) that have the effect of discriminating on the basis of disability; or
(ii) that perpetuate the discrimination of others who are subject to common administrative control.

(E) Association

It shall be discriminatory to exclude or otherwise deny equal goods, services, facilities, privileges, advantages, accommodations, or other opportunities to an individual or entity because of the known disability of an individual with whom the individual or entity is known to have a relationship or association.

(2) Specific prohibitions

(A) Discrimination

For purposes of subsection (a) of this section, discrimination includes—
(i) the imposition or application of eligibility criteria that screen out or tend to screen out an individual with a disability or any class of individuals with disabilities from fully and equally enjoying any goods, services, facilities, privileges, advantages, or accommodations, unless such criteria can be shown to be necessary for the provision of the goods, services, facilities, privileges, advantages, or accommodations being offered;
(ii) a failure to make reasonable modifications in policies, practices, or procedures, when such modifications are necessary to afford such goods, services, facilities, privileges, advantages, or accommodations to individuals with disabilities, unless the entity can demonstrate that making such modifications would fundamentally alter the nature of such goods, services, facilities, privileges, advantages, or accommodations;
(iii) a failure to take such steps as may be necessary to ensure that no individual with a disability is excluded, denied services, segregated or otherwise treated differently than other individuals because of the absence of auxiliary aids and services, unless the entity can demonstrate that taking such steps would fundamentally alter the nature of the good, service, facility, privilege, advantage, or accommodation being offered or would result in an undue burden;
(iv) a failure to remove architectural barriers, and communication barriers that are structural in nature, in existing facilities, and transportation barriers in existing vehicles and rail passenger cars used by an establishment for transporting individuals (not including barriers that can only be removed through the retrofitting of vehicles or rail passenger cars by the installation of a hydraulic or other lift), where such removal is readily achievable; and
(v) where an entity can demonstrate that the removal of a barrier under clause (iv) is not readily achievable, a failure to make such goods, services, facilities, privileges, advantages, or accommodations available through alternative methods if such methods are readily achievable.

(B) Fixed route system

(i) Accessibility

It shall be considered discrimination for a private entity which operates a fixed route system and which is not subject to section 12184 of this title to purchase or lease a vehicle with a seating capacity in excess of 16 passengers (including the driver) for use on such system, for which a solicitation is made after the 30th day following the effective date of this subparagraph, that is not readily accessible to and usable by individuals with disabilities, including individuals who use wheelchairs.

(ii) Equivalent service

If a private entity which operates a fixed route system and which is not subject to section 12184 of this title purchases or leases a vehicle with a seating capacity of 16 passengers or less (including the driver) for use on such system after the effective date of this subparagraph that is not readily accessible to or usable by individuals with disabilities, it shall be considered discrimination for such entity to fail to operate such system so that, when viewed in its entirety, such system ensures a level of service to individuals with disabilities, including individuals who use wheelchairs, equivalent to the level of service provided to individuals without disabilities.

(C) Demand responsive system

For purposes of subsection (a) of this section, discrimination includes—
(i) a failure of a private entity which operates a demand responsive system and which is not subject to section 12184 of this title to operate such system so that, when viewed in its entirety, such system ensures a level of service to individuals with disabilities, including individuals who use wheelchairs, equivalent to the level of service provided to individuals without disabilities; and
(ii) the purchase or lease by such entity for use on such system of a vehicle with a seating capacity in excess of 16 passengers (including the driver), for which solicitations are made after the 30th day following the effective date of this subparagraph, that is not readily accessible to and usable by individuals with disabilities (including individuals who use wheelchairs) unless such entity can demonstrate that such system, when viewed in its entirety, provides a level of service to individuals with disabilities equivalent to that provided to individuals without disabilities.

(D) Over-the-road buses

(i) Limitation on applicability

Subparagraphs (B) and (C) do not apply to over-the-road buses.

(ii) Accessibility requirements

For purposes of subsection (a) of this section, discrimination includes (I) the purchase or lease of an over-the-road bus which does not comply with the regulations issued under section 12186(a)(2) of this title by a private entity which provides transportation of individuals and which is not primarily engaged in the business of transporting people, and (II) any other failure of such entity to comply with such regulations.

(3) Specific construction

Nothing in this subchapter shall require an entity to permit an individual to participate in or benefit from the goods, services, facilities, privileges, advantages and accommodations of such entity where such individual poses a direct threat to the health or safety of others. The term "direct threat" means a significant risk to the health or safety of others that cannot be eliminated by a modification of policies, practices, or procedures or by the provision of auxiliary aids or services.

(Pub. L. 101-336, title III, § 302, July 26, 1990, 104 Stat. 355.)

REFERENCES IN TEXT

For the effective date of this subparagraph, referred to in subsec. (b)(2)(B), (C)(ii), see section 310 of Pub. L. 101-336, set out as an Effective Date note under section 12181 of this title.

EFFECTIVE DATE

Section effective 18 months after July 26, 1990, but with subsec. (a) of this section (for purposes of subsec. (b)(2)(B), (C) only) effective July 26, 1990, and with certain qualifications with respect to bringing of civil actions, see section 310 of Pub. L. 101-336, set out as a note under section 12181 of this title.

SECTION REFERRED TO IN OTHER SECTIONS

This section is referred to in sections 12183, 12184, 12186, 12188 of this title.

§ 12183. New construction and alterations in public accommodations and commercial facilities

(a) Application of term

Except as provided in subsection (b) of this section, as applied to public accommodations and commercial facilities, discrimination for purposes of section 12182(a) of this title includes—

(1) a failure to design and construct facilities for first occupancy later than 30 months after July 26, 1990, that are readily accessible to and usable by individuals with disabilities, except where an entity can demonstrate that it is structurally impracticable to meet the requirements of such subsection in accordance with standards set forth or incorporated by reference in regulations issued under this subchapter; and

(2) with respect to a facility or part thereof that is altered by, on behalf of, or for the use of an establishment in a manner that affects or could affect the usability of the facility or part thereof, a failure to make alterations in such a manner that, to the maximum extent feasible, the altered portions of the facility are readily accessible to and usable by individuals with disabilities, including individuals who use wheel-

chairs. Where the entity is undertaking an alteration that affects or could affect usability of or access to an area of the facility containing a primary function, the entity shall also make the alterations in such a manner that, to the maximum extent feasible, the path of travel to the altered area and the bathrooms, telephones, and drinking fountains serving the altered area, are readily accessible to and usable by individuals with disabilities where such alterations to the path of travel or the bathrooms, telephones, and drinking fountains serving the altered area are not disproportionate to the overall alterations in terms of cost and scope (as determined under criteria established by the Attorney General).

(b) Elevator

Subsection (a) of this section shall not be construed to require the installation of an elevator for facilities that are less than three stories or have less than 3,000 square feet per story unless the building is a shopping center, a shopping mall, or the professional office of a health care provider or unless the Attorney General determines that a particular category of such facilities requires the installation of elevators based on the usage of such facilities.

(Pub. L. 101-336, title III, § 303, July 26, 1990, 104 Stat. 358.)

EFFECTIVE DATE

Section effective 18 months after July 26, 1990, see section 310(a), (b) of Pub. L. 101-336, set out as a note under section 12181 of this title.

SECTION REFERRED TO IN OTHER SECTIONS

This section is referred to in sections 12184, 12186, 12188 of this title.

§ 12184. Prohibition of discrimination in specified public transportation services provided by private entities

(a) General rule

No individual shall be discriminated against on the basis of disability in the full and equal enjoyment of specified public transportation services provided by a private entity that is primarily engaged in the business of transporting people and whose operations affect commerce.

(b) Construction

For purposes of subsection (a) of this section, discrimination includes—
(1) the imposition or application by [an] entity described in subsection (a) of this section of eligibility criteria that screen out or tend to screen out an individual with a disability or any class of individuals with disabilities from fully enjoying the specified public transportation services provided by the entity, unless such criteria can be shown to be necessary for the provision of the services being offered;
(2) the failure of such entity to—

(A) make reasonable modifications consistent with those required under section 12182(b)(2)(A)(ii) of this title;

(B) provide auxiliary aids and services consistent with the requirements of section 12182(b)(2)(A)(iii) of this title; and

(C) remove barriers consistent with the requirements of section 12182(b)(2)(A) of this title and with the requirements of section 12183(a)(2) of this title;

(3) the purchase or lease by such entity of a new vehicle (other than an automobile, a van with a seating capacity of less than 8 passengers, including the driver, or an over-the-road bus) which is to be used to provide specified public transportation and for which a solicitation is made after the 30th day following the effective date of this section, that is not readily accessible to and usable by individuals with disabilities, including individuals who use wheelchairs; except that the new vehicle need not be readily accessible to and usable by such individuals if the new vehicle is to be used solely in a demand responsive system and if the entity can demonstrate that such system, when viewed in its entirety, provides a level of service to such individuals equivalent to the level of service provided to the general public;

(4)(A) the purchase or lease by such entity of an over-the-road bus which does not comply with the regulations issued under section 12186(a)(2) of this title; and

(B) any other failure of such entity to comply with such regulations; and

(5) the purchase or lease by such entity of a new van with a seating capacity of less than 8 passengers, including the driver, which is to be used to provide specified public transportation and for which a solicitation is made after the 30th day following the effective date of this section that is not readily accessible to or usable by individuals with disabilities, including individuals who use wheelchairs; except that the new van need not be readily accessible to and usable by such individuals if the entity can demonstrate that the system for which the van is being purchased or leased, when viewed in its entirety, provides a level of service to such individuals equivalent to the level of service provided to the general public;

(6) the purchase or lease by such entity of a new rail passenger car that is to be used to provide specified public transportation, and for which a solicitation is made later than 30 days after the effective date of this paragraph, that is not readily accessible to and usable by individuals with disabilities, including individuals who use wheelchairs; and

(7) the remanufacture by such entity of a rail passenger car that is to be used to provide specified public transportation so as to extend its usable life for 10 years or more, or the purchase or lease by such entity of such a rail car, unless the rail car, to the maximum extent feasible, is made readily accessible to and usable by individuals with disabilities, including individuals who use wheelchairs.

(c) Historical or antiquated cars

(1) Exception

To the extent that compliance with subsection (b)(2)(C) or (b)(7) of this section would significantly alter the historic or antiquated character of a historical or antiquated rail passenger car, or a rail station served exclusively by such cars, or would result in violation of any rule, regulation, standard, or order issued by the Secretary of Transportation under the Federal Railroad Safety Act of 1970 [45 U.S.C. 431 et seq.], such compliance shall not be required.

(2) Definition

As used in this subsection, the term "historical or antiquated rail passenger car" means a rail passenger car—

(A) which is not less than 30 years old at the time of its use for transporting individuals;

(B) the manufacturer of which is no longer in the business of manufacturing rail passenger cars; and

(C) which—

(i) has a consequential association with events or persons significant to the past; or

(ii) embodies, or is being restored to embody, the distinctive characteristics of a type of rail passenger car used in the past, or to represent a time period which has passed.

(Pub. L. 101-336, title III, § 304, July 26, 1990, 104 Stat. 359.)

REFERENCES IN TEXT

For the effective date of this section, referred to in subsec. (b)(3), (5), see section 310 of Pub. L. 101-336, set out as an Effective Date note under section 12181 of this title.

The effective date of this paragraph, referred to in subsec. (b)(6), is 18 months after July 26, 1990, see section 310(a) of Pub. L. 101-336, set out as an Effective Date note under section 12181 of this title.

The Federal Railroad Safety Act of 1970, referred to in subsec. (c)(1), is title II of Pub. L. 91-458, Oct. 16, 1970, 84 Stat. 971, as amended, which is classified generally to subchapter II (§ 431 et seq.) of chapter 13 of Title 45, Railroads. For complete classification of this Act to the Code, see Short Title note set out under section 421 of Title 45 and Tables.

EFFECTIVE DATE

Section effective 18 months after July 26, 1990, but with subsec. (a) of this section (for purposes of subsec. (b)(3) only) and subsec. (b)(3) of this section effective July 26, 1990, see section 310(a), (c) of Pub. L. 101-336, set out as a note under section 12181 of this title.

SECTION REFERRED TO IN OTHER SECTIONS

This section is referred to in sections 12182, 12185, 12186, 12206 of this title.

§ 12185. Study

(a) Purposes

The Office of Technology Assessment shall undertake a study to determine—

(1) the access needs of individuals with disabilities to over-the-road buses and over-the-road bus service; and

(2) the most cost-effective methods for providing access to over-the-road buses and over-the-road bus service to individuals with disabilities, particularly individuals who use wheelchairs, through all forms of boarding options.

(b) Contents

The study shall include, at a minimum, an analysis of the following:

(1) The anticipated demand by individuals with disabilities for accessible over-the-road buses and over-the-road bus service.

(2) The degree to which such buses and service, including any service required under sections 12184(b)(4) and 12186(a)(2) of this title, are readily accessible to and usable by individuals with disabilities.

(3) The effectiveness of various methods of providing accessibility to such buses and service to individuals with disabilities.

(4) The cost of providing accessible over-the-road buses and bus service to individuals with disabilities, including consideration of recent technological and cost saving developments in equipment and devices.

(5) Possible design changes in over-the-road buses that could enhance accessibility, including the installation of accessible restrooms which do not result in a loss of seating capacity.

(6) The impact of accessibility requirements on the continuation of over-the-road bus service, with particular consideration of the impact of such requirements on such service to rural communities.

(c) Advisory committee

In conducting the study required by subsection (a) of this section, the Office of Technology Assessment shall establish an advisory committee, which shall consist of—

(1) members selected from among private operators and manufacturers of over-the-road buses;

(2) members selected from among individuals with disabilities, particularly individuals who use wheelchairs, who are potential riders of such buses; and

(3) members selected for their technical expertise on issues included in the study, including manufacturers of boarding assistance equipment and devices.

The number of members selected under each of paragraphs (1) and (2) shall be equal, and the total number of members selected under paragraphs (1) and (2) shall exceed the number of members selected under paragraph (3).

(d) Deadline

The study required by subsection (a) of this section, along with recommendations by the Office of Technology Assessment, including any policy options for legislative action, shall be submitted to the President and Congress within 36 months after July 26, 1990. If the President determines that compliance with the regulations issued pursuant to section 12186(a)(2)(B) of this title on or before the applicable deadlines specified in section 12186(a)(2)(B) of this title will result in a significant reduction in intercity over-the-road bus service, the President shall extend each such deadline by 1 year.

(e) Review

In developing the study required by subsection (a) of this section, the Office of Technology Assessment shall provide a preliminary draft of such study to the Architectural and Transportation Barriers Compliance Board established under section 792 of title 29. The Board shall have an opportunity to comment on such draft study, and any such comments by the Board made in writing within 120 days after the Board's receipt of the draft study shall be incorporated as part of the final study required to be submitted under subsection (d) of this section.

(Pub. L. 101-336, title III, § 305, July 26, 1990, 104 Stat. 360.)

EFFECTIVE DATE

Section effective July 26, 1990, see section 310(c) of Pub. L 101-336, set out as a note under section 12181 of this title.

TERMINATION OF ADVISORY COMMITTEES

Advisory committees established after Jan. 5, 1973, to terminate not later than the expiration of the 2-year period beginning on the date of their establishment, unless, in the case of a committee established by the President or an officer of the Federal Government, such committee is renewed by appropriate action prior to the expiration of such 2-year period, or in the case of a committee established by Congress, its duration is otherwise provided for by law. See section 14 of Pub. L. 92-463, Oct. 6, 1972, 86 Stat. 770, 776, set out in the Appendix to Title 5, Government Organization and Employees.

SECTION REFERRED TO IN OTHER SECTIONS

This section is referred to in section 12186 of this title.

§ 12186. Regulations

(a) Transportation provisions

(1) General rule

Not later than 1 year after July 26, 1990, the Secretary of Transportation shall issue regulations in an accessible format to carry out [section] 12182(b)(2)(B) and (C) of this title and to carry out section 12184 of this title (other than subsection (b)(4)).

(2) Special rules for providing access to over-the-road buses

(A) Interim requirements

(i) Issuance

Not later than 1 year after July 26, 1990, the Secretary of Transportation shall issue regulations in an accessible format to carry out sections 12184(b)(4) and

12182(b)(2)(D)(ii) of this title that require each private entity which uses an over-the-road bus to provide transportation of individuals to provide accessibility to such bus; except that such regulations shall not require any structural changes in over-the-road buses in order to provide access to individuals who use wheelchairs during the effective period of such regulations and shall not require the purchase of boarding assistance devices to provide access to such individuals.

(ii) Effective period

The regulations issued pursuant to this subparagraph shall be effective until the effective date of the regulations issued under subparagraph (B).

(B) Final requirement

(i) Review of study and interim requirements

The Secretary shall review the study submitted under section 12185 of this title and the regulations issued pursuant to subparagraph (A).

(ii) Issuance

Not later than 1 year after the date of the submission of the study under section 12185 of this title, the Secretary shall issue in an accessible format new regulations to carry out sections 12184(b)(4) and 12182(b)(2)(D)(ii) of this title that require, taking into account the purposes of the study under section 12185 of this title and any recommendations resulting from such study, each private entity which uses an over-the-road bus to provide transportation to individuals to provide accessibility to such bus to individuals with disabilities, including individuals who use wheelchairs.

(iii) Effective period

Subject to section 12185(d) of this title, the regulations issued pursuant to this subparagraph shall take effect—
(I) with respect to small providers of transportation (as defined by the Secretary), 7 years after July 26, 1990; and
(II) with respect to other providers of transportation, 6 years after July 26, 1990.

(C) Limitation on requiring installation of accessible restrooms

The regulations issued pursuant to this paragraph shall not require the installation of accessible restrooms in over-the-road buses if such installation would result in a loss of seating capacity.

(3) Standards

The regulations issued pursuant to this subsection shall include standards applicable to facilities and vehicles covered by sections 12182(b)(2) and 12184 of this title.

(b) Other provisions

Not later than 1 year after July 26, 1990, the Attorney General shall issue regulations in an accessible format to carry out the provisions of this subchapter not referred to in subsection (a) of this section that include standards applicable to facilities and vehicles covered under section 12182 of this title.

(c) Consistency with ATBCB guidelines

Standards included in regulations issued under subsections (a) and (b) of this section shall be consistent with the minimum guidelines and requirements issued by the Architectural and Transportation Barriers Compliance Board in accordance with section 12204 of this title.

(d) Interim accessibility standards

(1) Facilities

If final regulations have not been issued pursuant to this section, for new construction or alterations for which a valid and appropriate State or local building permit is obtained prior to the issuance of final regulations under this section, and for which the construction or alteration authorized by such permit begins within one year of the receipt of such permit and is completed under the terms of such permit, compliance with the Uniform Federal Accessibility Standards in effect at the time the building permit is issued shall suffice to satisfy the requirement that facilities be readily accessible to and usable by persons with disabilities as required under section 12183 of this title, except that, if such final regulations have not been issued one year after the Architectural and Transportation Barriers Compliance Board has issued the supplemental minimum guidelines required under section 12204(a) of this title, compliance with such supplemental minimum guidelines shall be necessary to satisfy the requirement that facilities be readily accessible to and usable by persons with disabilities prior to issuance of the final regulations.

(2) Vehicles and rail passenger cars

If final regulations have not been issued pursuant to this section, a private entity shall be considered to have complied with the requirements of this subchapter, if any, that a vehicle or rail passenger car be readily accessible to and usable by individuals with disabilities, if the design for such vehicle or car complies with the laws and regulations (including the Minimum Guidelines and Requirements for Accessible Design and such supplemental minimum guidelines as are issued under section 12204(a) of this title) governing accessibility of such vehicles or cars, to the extent that such laws and regulations are not inconsistent with this subchapter and are in effect at the time such design is substantially completed.

(Pub. L. 101-336, title III, § 306, July 26, 1990, 104 Stat. 361.)

EFFECTIVE DATE

Section effective July 26, 1990, see section 310(c) of Pub. L. 101-336, set out as a note under section 12181 of this title.

SECTION REFERRED TO IN OTHER SECTIONS

This section is referred to in sections 12182, 12184, 12185 of this title.

§ 12187. Exemptions for private clubs and religious organizations

The provisions of this subchapter shall not apply to private clubs or establishments exempted from coverage under title II of the Civil Rights Act of 1964 (42 U.S.C. 2000-a(e)) [42 U.S.C. 2000a et seq.] or to religious organizations or entities controlled by religious organizations, including places of worship.

(Pub. L. 101-336, title III, § 307, July 26, 1990, 104 Stat. 363.)

REFERENCES IN TEXT

The Civil Rights Act of 1964, referred to in text, is Pub. L 88-352, July 2, 1964, 78 Stat. 241, as amended. Title II of the Act is classified generally to subchapter II (§ 2000a et seq.) of chapter 21 of this title. For complete classification of this Act to the Code, see Short Title note set out under section 2000a of this title and Tables.

EFFECTIVE DATE

Section effective 18 months after July 26, 1990, see section 310(a) of Pub. L. 101-336, set out as a note under section 12181 of this title.

§ 12188. Enforcement

(a) In general

(1) Availability of remedies and procedures

The remedies and procedures set forth in section 2000a-3(a) of this title are the remedies and procedures this subchapter provides to any person who is being subjected to discrimination on the basis of disability in violation of this subchapter or who has reasonable grounds for believing that such person is about to be subjected to discrimination in violation of section 12183 of this title. Nothing in this section shall require a person with a disability to engage in a futile gesture if such person has actual notice that a person or organization covered by this subchapter does not intend to comply with its provisions.

(2) Injunctive relief

In the case of violations of sections 12182(b)(2)(A)(iv) and [. . .] 12183(a) of this title, injunctive relief shall include an order to alter facilities to make such facilities readily accessible to and usable by individuals with disabilities to the extent required by this subchapter. Where appropriate, injunctive relief shall also include requiring the provision of an auxiliary aid or service, modification of a policy, or provision of alternative methods, to the extent required by this subchapter.

(b) Enforcement by Attorney General

(1) Denial of rights
(A) Duty to investigate
(i) In general

The Attorney General shall investigate alleged violations of this subchapter, and shall undertake periodic reviews of compliance of covered entities under this subchapter.

(ii) Attorney General certification

On the application of a State or local government, the Attorney General may, in consultation with the Architectural and Transportation Barriers Compliance Board, and after prior notice and a public hearing at which persons, including individuals with disabilities, are provided an opportunity to testify against such certification, certify that a State law or local building code or similar ordinance that establishes accessibility requirements meets or exceeds the minimum requirements of this chapter for the accessibility and usability of covered facilities under this subchapter. At any enforcement proceeding under this section, such certification by the Attorney General shall be rebuttable evidence that such State law or local ordinance does meet or exceed the minimum requirements of this chapter.

(B) Potential violation

If the Attorney General has reasonable cause to believe that—
(i) any person or group of persons is engaged in a pattern or practice of discrimination under this subchapter; or
(ii) any person or group of persons has been discriminated against under this subchapter and such discrimination raises an issue of general public importance.
the Attorney General may commence a civil action in any appropriate United States district court.

(2) Authority of court

In a civil action under paragraph (1)(B), the court—
(A) may grant any equitable relief that such court considers to be appropriate, including, to the extent required by this subchapter—
(i) granting temporary, preliminary, or permanent relief;
(ii) providing an auxiliary aid or service, modification of policy, practice, or procedure, or alternative method; and
(iii) making facilities readily accessible to and usable by individuals with disabilities;
(B) may award such other relief as the court considers to be appropriate, including monetary damages to persons aggrieved when requested by the Attorney General; and
(C) may, to vindicate the public interest, assess a civil penalty against the entity in an amount—
(i) not exceeding $50,000 for a first violation; and
(ii) not exceeding $100,000 for any subsequent violation.

(3) Single violation

For purposes of paragraph (2)(C), in determining whether a first or subsequent violation has occurred, a determination in a single action, by judgment or settlement, that the covered entity has engaged in more than one discriminatory act shall be counted as a single violation.

(4) Punitive damages

For purposes of subsection (b)(2)(B) of this section, the term "monetary damages" and "such other relief" does not include punitive damages.

(5) Judicial consideration

In a civil action under paragraph (1)(B), the court, when considering what amount of civil penalty, if any, is appropriate, shall give consideration to any good faith effort or attempt to comply with this chapter by the entity. In evaluating good faith, the court shall consider, among other factors it deems relevant, whether the entity could have reasonably anticipated the need for an appropriate type of auxiliary aid needed to accommodate the unique needs of a particular individual with a disability.

(Pub. L. 101-336, title III, § 308, July 26, 1990, 104 Stat. 363.)

EFFECTIVE DATE

Section effective 18 months after July 26, 1990, see section 310(a) of Pub. L. 101-336, set out as a note under section 12181 of this title.

CIVIL ACTIONS FOR VIOLATIONS BY PUBLIC ACCOMMODATIONS

For provisions directing that, except for any civil action brought for a violation of section 12183 of this title, no civil action shall be brought for any act or omission described in section 12182 of this title which occurs (1) during the first six months after the effective date of this subchapter, against businesses that employ 25 or fewer employees and have gross receipts of $1,000,000 or less, and (2) during the first year after the effective date, against businesses that employ 10 or fewer employees and have gross receipts of $500,000 or less, see section 310(b) of Pub. L. 101-336, set out as an Effective Date note under section 12181 of this title.

SECTION REFERRED TO IN OTHER SECTIONS

This section is referred to in section 12203 of this title.

§ 12189. Examinations and courses

Any person that offers examinations or courses related to applications, licensing, certification, or credentialing for secondary or postsecondary education, professional, or trade purposes shall offer such examinations or courses in a place and manner accessible to persons with disabilities or offer alternative accessible arrangements for such individuals.

(Pub. L. 101-336, title III, § 309, July 26, 1990, 104 Stat. 365.)

EFFECTIVE DATE

Section effective 18 months after July 26, 1990, see section 310(a) of Pub. L. 101-336, set out as a note under section 12181 of this title.

SUBCHAPTER V—MISCELLANEOUS PROVISIONS

§ 12201. Construction

(a) In general

Except as otherwise provided in this chapter, nothing in this chapter shall be construed to apply a lesser standard than the standards applied under title V of the Rehabilitation Act of 1973 (29 U.S.C. 790 et seq.) or the regulations issued by Federal agencies pursuant to such title.

(b) Relationship to other laws

Nothing in this chapter shall be construed to invalidate or limit the remedies, rights, and procedures of any Federal law or law of any State or political subdivision of any State or jurisdiction that provides greater or equal protection for the rights of individuals with disabilities than are afforded by this chapter. Nothing in this chapter shall be construed to preclude the prohibition of, or the imposition of restrictions on, smoking in places of employment covered by subchapter I of this chapter, in transportation covered by subchapter II or III of this chapter, or in places of public accommodation covered by subchapter III of this chapter.

(c) Insurance

Subchapters I through III of this chapter and title IV of this Act shall not be construed to prohibit or restrict—
(1) an insurer, hospital or medical service company, health maintenance organization, or any agent, or entity that administers benefit plans, or similar organizations from underwriting risks, classifying risks, or administering such risks that are based on or not inconsistent with State law; or
(2) a person or organization covered by this chapter from establishing, sponsoring, observing or administering the terms of a bona fide benefit plan that are based on underwriting risks, classifying risks, or administering such risks that are based on or not inconsistent with State law; or
(3) a person or organization covered by this chapter from establishing, sponsoring, observing or administering the terms of a bona fide benefit plan that is not subject to State laws that regulate insurance.
Paragraphs (1), (2), and (3) shall not be used as a subterfuge to evade the purposes of subchapter[s] I and III of this chapter.

(d) Accommodations and services

Nothing in this chapter shall be construed to require an individual with a disability to accept an accommodation, aid, service, opportunity, or benefit which such individual chooses not to accept.

(Pub. L. 101-336, title V, § 501, July 26, 1990, 104 Stat. 369.)

REFERENCES IN TEXT

This chapter, referred to in text, was in the original "this Act", meaning Pub. L. 101-336, July 26, 1990, 104 Stat. 327, which is classified principally to this chapter. For complete classification of this Act to the Code, see Short Title note set out under section 12101 of this title and Tables.

The Rehabilitation Act of 1973, referred to in subsec. (a), is Pub. L. 93-112, Sept. 26, 1973, 87 Stat. 355, as amended. Title V of the Rehabilitation Act of 1973 is classified generally to subchapter V (§ 790 et seq.) of chapter 16 of Title 29, Labor. For complete classification of this Act to the Code, see Short Title note set out under section 701 of Title 29 and Tables.

Title IV of this Act, referred to in subsec. (c), means title IV of Pub. L. 101-336, July 26, 1990, 104 Stat. 366,which enacted section 225 of Title 47. Telegraphs, Telephones, and Radiotelegraphs, and amended sections 152, 221, and 611 of Title 47.

§ 12202. State immunity

A State shall not be immune under the eleventh amendment to the Constitution of the United States from an action in a Federal or State court of competent jurisdiction for a violation of this chapter. In any action against a State for a violation of the requirements of this chapter, remedies (including remedies both at law and in equity) are available for such a violation to the same extent as such remedies are available for such a violation in an action against any public or private entity other than a State.

(Pub. L. 101-336, title V, § 502, July 26, 1990, 104 Stat. 370.)

§ 12203. Prohibition against retaliation and coercion

(a) Retaliation

No person shall discriminate against any individual because such individual has opposed any act or practice made unlawful by this chapter or because such individual made a charge, testified, assisted, or participated in any manner in an investigation, proceeding, or hearing under this chapter.

(b) Interference, coercion, or intimidation

It shall be unlawful to coerce, intimidate, threaten, or interfere with any individual in the exercise or enjoyment of, or on account of his or her having exercised or enjoyed, or on account of his or her having aided or encouraged any other individual in the exercise or enjoyment of, any right granted or protected by this chapter.

(c) Remedies and procedures

The remedies and procedures available under sections 12117, 12133, and 12188 of this title shall be available to aggrieved persons for violations of subsections (a) and (b) of this section, with respect to subchapter I, subchapter II and subchapter III of this chapter, respectively.

(Pub. L. 101-336, title V, § 503, July 26, 1990, 104 Stat. 370.)

§ 12204. Regulations by Architectural and Transportation Barriers Compliance Board

(a) Issuance of guidelines

Not later than 9 months after July 26, 1990, the Architectural and Transportation Barriers Compliance Board shall issue minimum guidelines that shall supplement the existing Minimum Guidelines and Requirements for Accessible Design for purposes of subchapters II and III of this chapter.

(b) Contents of guidelines

The supplemental guidelines issued under subsection (a) of this section shall establish additional requirements, consistent with this chapter, to ensure that buildings, facilities, rail passenger cars, and vehicles are accessible, in terms of architecture and design, transportation, and communication, to individuals with disabilities.

(c) Qualified historic properties

(1) In general

The supplemental guidelines issued under subsection (a) of this section shall include procedures and requirements for alterations that will threaten or destroy the historic significance of qualified historic buildings and facilities as defined in 4.1.7(1)(a) of the Uniform Federal Accessibility Standards.

(2) Sites eligible for listing in National Register

With respect to alterations of buildings or facilities that are eligible for listing in the National Register of Historic Places under the National Historic Preservation Act (16 U.S.C. 470 et seq.), the guidelines described in paragraph (1) shall, at a minimum, maintain the procedures and requirements established in 4.1.7(1) and (2) of the Uniform Federal Accessibility Standards.

(3) Other sites

With respect to alterations of buildings or facilities designated as historic under State or local law, the guidelines described in paragraph (1) shall establish procedures equivalent to those established by 4.1.7(1)(b) and (c) of the Uniform Federal Accessibility Standards, and shall require, at a minimum, compliance with the requirements established in 4.1.7(2) of such standards.

(Pub. L. 101-336, title V, § 504, July 26, 1990, 104 Stat. 370.)

REFERENCES IN TEXT

The National Historic Preservation Act, referred to in subsec. (c)(2), is Pub. L. 89-665, Oct. 15, 1966, 80 Stat. 915, as amended, which is classified generally to subchapter II (§ 470 et seq.) of chapter IA of Title 16, Conservation. For complete classification of this Act to the Code, see section 470(a) of Title 16 and Tables.

SECTION REFERRED TO IN OTHER SECTIONS

This section is referred to in sections 12134, 12149, 12150, 12163, 12165, 12186 of this title.

§ 12205. Attorney's fees

In any action or administrative proceeding commenced pursuant to this chapter, the court or agency, in its discretion, may allow the prevailing party, other than the United States, a reasonable attorney's fee, including litigation expenses, and costs, and the United States shall be liable for the foregoing the same as a private individual.

(Pub. L. 101-336, title V, § 505, July 26, 1990, 104 Stat. 371.)

§ 12206. Technical assistance

(a) Plan for assistance

(1) In general

Not later than 180 days after July 26, 1990, the Attorney General, in consultation with the Chair of the Equal Employment Opportunity Commission, the Secretary of Transportation, the Chair of the Architectural and Transportation Barriers Compliance Board, and the Chairman of the Federal Communications Commission, shall develop a plan to assist entities covered under this chapter, and other Federal agencies, in understanding the responsibility of such entities and agencies under this chapter.

(2) Publication of plan

The Attorney General shall publish the plan referred to in paragraph (1) for public comment in accordance with subchapter II of chapter 5 of title 5 (commonly known as the Administrative Procedure Act).

(b) Agency and public assistance

The Attorney General may obtain the assistance of other Federal agencies in carrying out subsection (a) of this section, including the National Council on Disability, the President's Committee on Employment of People with Disabilities, the Small Business Administration, and the Department of Commerce.

(c) Implementation

(1) Rendering assistance

Each Federal agency that has responsibility under paragraph (2) for implementing this chapter may render technical assistance to individuals and institutions that have rights or duties under the respective subchapter or subchapters of this chapter for which such agency has responsibility.

(2) Implementation of subchapters

(A) Subchapter I

The Equal Employment Opportunity Commission and the Attorney General shall implement the plan for assistance developed under subsection (a) of this section, for subchapter I of this chapter.

(B) Subchapter II

(i) Part A

The Attorney General shall implement such plan for assistance for part A of subchapter II of this chapter.

(ii) Part B

The Secretary of Transportation shall implement such plan for assistance for part B of subchapter II of this chapter.

(C) Subchapter III

The Attorney General, in coordination with the Secretary of Transportation and the Chair of the Architectural Transportation Barriers Compliance Board, shall implement such plan for assistance for subchapter III of this chapter, except for section 12184 of this title, the plan for assistance for which shall be implemented by the Secretary of Transportation.

(D) Title IV

The Chairman of the Federal Communications Commission, in coordination with the Attorney General, shall implement such plan for assistance for title IV.

(3) Technical assistance manuals

Each Federal agency that has responsibility under paragraph (2) for implementing this chapter shall, as part of its implementation responsibilities, ensure the availability and provision of appropriate technical assistance manuals to individuals or entities with rights or duties under this chapter no later than six months after applicable final regulations are published under subchapters I, II, and III of this chapter and title IV.

(d) Grants and contracts

(1) In general

Each Federal agency that has responsibility under subsection (c)(2) of this section for implementing this chapter may make grants or award contracts to effectuate the purposes of this section, subject to the availability of appropriations. Such grants and contracts may be awarded to individuals, institutions not organized for profit and no part of the net earnings of which inures to the benefit of any private shareholder or individual (including educational institutions), and associations representing individuals who have rights or duties under this chapter. Contracts may be awarded to entities organized for profit, but such entities may not be the recipients [of] grants described in this paragraph.

(2) Dissemination of information

Such grants and contracts, among other uses, may be designed to ensure wide dissemination of information about the rights and duties established by this chapter and to provide information and technical assistance about techniques for effective compliance with this chapter.

(e) Failure to receive assistance

An employer, public accommodation, or other entity covered under this chapter shall not be excused from compliance with the requirements of this chapter because of any failure to receive technical assistance under this section, including any failure in the development or dissemination of any technical assistance manual authorized by this section.

(Pub. L. 101-336, title V, § 506, July 26, 1990, 104 Stat. 371.)

REFERENCES IN TEXT

Title IV, referred to in subsec. (c)(2)(D), (3), means title IV of Pub. L. 101-336, July 26, 1990, 104 Stat. 366, which enacted section 225 of Title 47, Telegraphs, Telephones, and Radiotelegraphs, and amended sections 152, 221, and 611 of Title 47.

§ 12207. Federal wilderness areas

(a) Study

The National Council on Disability shall conduct a study and report on the effect that wilderness designations and wilderness land management practices have on the ability of individuals with disabilities to use and enjoy the National Wilderness Preservation System as established under the Wilderness Act (16 U.S.C. 1131 et seq.).

(b) Submission of report

Not later than 1 year after July 26, 1990, the National Council on Disability shall submit the report required under subsection (a) of this section to Congress.

(c) Specific wilderness access

(1) In general

Congress reaffirms that nothing in the Wilderness Act [16 U.S.C. 1131 et seq.] is to be construed as prohibiting the use of a wheelchair in a wilderness area by an individual whose disability requires use of a wheelchair, and consistent with the Wilderness Act no agency is required to provide any form of special treatment or accommodation, or to construct any facilities or modify any conditions of lands within a wilderness area in order to facilitate such use.

(2) "Wheelchair" defined

For purposes of paragraph (1), the term "wheelchair" means a device designed solely for use by a mobility-impaired person for locomotion, that is suitable for use in an indoor pedestrian area.

(Pub. L. 101-336, title V, § 507, July 26, 1990, 104 Stat. 372.)

REFERENCES IN TEXT

The Wilderness Act, referred to in subsecs. (a) and (c)(1), is Pub. L. 88-577, Sept. 3, 1964, 78 Stat. 890, as amended, which is classified generally to chapter 23 (§ 1131 et seq.) of Title 16, Conservation. For complete classification of this Act to the Code, see Short Title note set out under section 1131 of Title 16 and Tables.

§ 12208. Transvestites

For the purposes of this chapter, the term "disabled" or "disability" shall not apply to an individual solely because that individual is a transvestite.

(Pub. L. 101-336, title V, § 508, July 26, 1990, 104 Stat. 373.)

§ 12209. Coverage of Congress and agencies of legislative branch

(a) Coverage of Senate

(1) Commitment to Rule XLII

The Senate reaffirms its commitment to Rule XLII of the Standing Rules of the Senate which provides as follows:
"No member, officer, or employee of the Senate shall, with respect to employment by the Senate or any office thereof—
"(a) fail or refuse to hire an individual;
"(b) discharge an individual; or
"(c) otherwise discriminate against an individual with respect to promotion, compensation, or terms, conditions, or privileges of employment
on the basis of such individual's race, color, religion, sex, national origin, age, or state of physical handicap."

(2) Matters other than employment

(A) In general

The rights and protections under this chapter shall, subject to subparagraph (B), apply with respect to the conduct of the Senate regarding matters other than employment.

(B) Remedies

The Architect of the Capitol shall establish remedies and procedures to be utilized with respect to the rights and protections provided pursuant to subparagraph (A). Such remedies and procedures shall apply exclusively, after approval in accordance with subparagraph (C).

(C) Proposed remedies and procedures

For purposes of subparagraph (B), the Architect of the Capitol shall submit proposed remedies and procedures to the Senate Committee on Rules and Administration. The remedies and procedures shall be effective upon the approval of the Committee on Rules and Administration.

(3) Exercise of rulemaking power

Notwithstanding any other provision of law, enforcement and adjudication of the rights and protections referred to in paragraph (2)(A) shall be within the exclusive jurisdiction of the United States Senate. The provisions of paragraph (1), (2) are enacted by the Senate as an exercise of the rulemaking power of the Senate, with full recognition of the right of the Senate to change its rules, in the same manner, and to the same extent, as in the case of any other rule of the Senate.

(b) Coverage of House of Representatives

(1) In general

Notwithstanding any other provision of this chapter or of law, the purposes of this chapter shall, subject to paragraphs (2) and (3), apply in their entirety to the House of Representatives.

(2) Employment in the House

(A) Application

The rights and protections under this chapter shall, subject to subparagraph (B), apply with respect to any employee in an employment position in the House of Representatives and any employing authority of the House of Representatives.

(B) Administration

(i) In general

In the administration of this paragraph, the remedies and procedures made applicable pursuant to the resolution described in clause (ii) shall apply exclusively.

(ii) Resolution

The resolution referred to in clause (i) is House Resolution 15 of the One Hundred First Congress, as agreed to January 3, 1989, or any other provision that continues in effect the provisions of, or is a successor to, the Fair Employment Practices Resolution (House Resolution 558 of the One Hundredth Congress, as agreed to October 4, 1988).

(C) Exercise of rulemaking power

The provisions of subparagraph (B) are enacted by the House of Representatives as an exercise of the rulemaking power of the House of Representatives, with full recognition of the right of the House to change its rules, in the same manner, and to the same extent as in the case of any other rule of the House.

(3) Matters other than employment

(A) In general

The rights and protections under this chapter shall, subject to subparagraph (B), apply with respect to the conduct of the House of Representatives regarding matters other than employment.

(B) Remedies

The Architect of the Capitol shall establish remedies and procedures to be utilized with respect to the rights and protections provided pursuant to subparagraph (A). Such remedies and procedures shall apply exclusively, after approval in accordance with subparagraph (C).

(C) Approval

For purposes of subparagraph (B), the Architect of the Capitol shall submit proposed remedies and procedures to the Speaker of the House of Representatives. The remedies and procedures shall be effective upon the approval of the Speaker, after consultation with the House Office Building Commission.

(c) Instrumentalities of Congress

(1) In general

The rights and protections under this chapter shall, subject to paragraph (2), apply with respect to the conduct of each instrumentality of the Congress.

(2) Establishment of remedies and procedures by instrumentalities

The chief official of each instrumentality of the Congress shall establish remedies and procedures to be utilized with respect to the rights and protections provided pursuant to paragraph (1). Such remedies and procedures shall apply exclusively, except for the employees who are defined as Senate employees, in section 1201(c)(1) of title 2.

(3) Report to Congress

The chief official of each instrumentality of the Congress shall, after establishing remedies and procedures for purposes of paragraph (2), submit to the Congress a report describing the remedies and procedures.

(4) Definition of instrumentalities

For purposes of this section, instrumentalities of the Congress include the following: the Architect of the Capitol, the Congressional Budget Office, the General Accounting Office, the Government Printing Office, the Library of Congress, the Office of Technology Assessment, and the United States Botanic Garden.

(5) Construction

Nothing in this section shall alter the enforcement procedures for individuals with disabilities provided in the General Accounting Office Personnel Act of 1980 and regulations promulgated pursuant to that Act.

(Pub. L. 101-336, title V, § 509, July 26, 1990, 104 Stat. 373; Pub. L. 102-166, title 111, § 315, Nov. 21, 1991, 105 Stat. 1095.)

REFERENCES IN TEXT

House Resolution No. 558, One Hundredth Congress, Oct. 4, 1988, as continued in effect by House Resolution No. 15, One Hundred First Congress, Jan. 3, 1989, referred to in subsec. (b)(2)(B)(ii), is set out as a note under section 60k of Title 2, The Congress.

The General Accounting Office Personnel Act of 1980, referred to in subsec. (c)(5), is Pub. L. 96-191, Feb. 15, 1980, 94 Stat. 27, which was classified principally to section 52-1 et seq. of former Title 31, and which was substantially repealed by Pub. L. 97-258, § 5(b), Sept. 13, 1982, 96 Stat. 1068, and reenacted by the first section thereof principally in subchapters III (§ 731 et seq.) and IV (§ 751 et seq.) of chapter 7 of Title 31, Money and Finance.

AMENDMENTS

1991—Subsec. (a)(2). Pub. L. 102-166, § 315(1), redesignated par. (6) as (2) and struck out former par. (2) which read as follows: "APPLICATION TO SENATE EMPLOYMENT.—The rights and protections provided pursuant to this chapter, the Civil Rights Act of 1990 (S. 2104, 101st Congress), the Civil Rights Act of 1964 [42 U.S.C. 2000a et seq.], the Age Discrimination in Employment Act of 1967[29 U.S.C.

621 et seq.], and the Rehabilitation Act of 1973 [29 U.S.C. 701 et seq.] shall apply with respect to employment by the United States Senate."

Subsec. (a)(3). Pub. L. 102-166, § 315(1), redesignated par. (7) as (3), substituted "(2)(A)" for "(2) and (6)(A)" and "(2)" for "(3), (4), (5), (6)(B), and (6)(C)", and struck out former par. (3) which read as follows: "INVESTIGATION AND ADJUDICA-TION OF CLAIMS.—All claims raised by any individual with respect to Senate employment, pursuant to the Acts referred to in paragraph (2), shall be investigated and adjudicated by the Select Committee on Ethics, pursuant to S. Res. 338, 88th Congress, as amended, or such other entity as the Senate may designate."

Subsec. (a)(4), (5). Pub. L. 102-166, § 315(1), struck out pars. (4) and (5) which read as follows:

"(4) RIGHTS OF EMPLOYEES.—The Committee on Rules and Administration shall ensure that Senate employees are informed of their rights under the Acts referred to in paragraph (2).

"(5) APPLICABLE REMEDIES.—When assigning remedies to individuals found to have a valid claim under the Acts referred to in paragraph (2), the Select Committee on Ethics, or such other entity as the Senate may designate, should to the extent practicable apply the same remedies applicable to all other employees covered by the Acts referred to in paragraph (2). Such remedies shall apply exclusively."

Subsec. (a)(6), (7). Pub. L. 102-166, § 315(1), redesignated pars. (6) and (7) as (2) and (3), respectively.

Subsec. (c)(2). Pub. L. 102-166, § 315(2), inserted ", except for the employees who are defined as Senate employees, in section 1201(c)(1) of title 2" after "shall apply exclusively".

EFFECTIVE DATE OF 1991 AMENDMENT

Amendment by Pub. L. 102-166 effective Nov. 21, 1991, except as otherwise provided, see section 402 of Pub. L. 102-166, set out as a note under section 1981 of this title.

§ 12210. Illegal use of drugs

(a) In general

For purposes of this chapter, the term "individual with a disability" does not include an individual who is currently engaging in the illegal use of drugs, when the covered entity acts on the basis of such use.

(b) Rules of construction

Nothing in subsection (a) of this section shall be construed to exclude as an individual with a disability an individual who—

(1) has successfully completed a supervised drug rehabilitation program and is no longer engaging in the illegal use of drugs, or has otherwise been rehabilitated successfully and is no longer engaging in such use;

(2) is participating in a supervised rehabilitation program and is no longer engaging in such use; or

(3) is erroneously regarded as engaging in such use, but is not engaging in such use;

except that it shall not be a violation of this chapter for a covered entity to adopt or administer reasonable policies or procedures, including but not limited to drug testing, designed to ensure that an individual described in paragraph (1) or (2) is no longer engaging in the illegal use of drugs; however, nothing in this section shall be construed to encourage, prohibit, restrict, or authorize the conducting of testing for the illegal use of drugs.

(c) Health and other services

Notwithstanding subsection (a) of this section and section 12211(b)(3) of this title, an individual shall not be denied health services, or services provided in connection with drug rehabilitation, on the basis of the current illegal use of drugs if the individual is otherwise entitled to such services.

(d) "Illegal use of drugs" defined

(1) In general

The term "illegal use of drugs" means the use of drugs, the possession or distribution of which is unlawful under the Controlled Substances Act [21 U.S.C. 801 et seq.]. Such term does not include the use of a drug taken under supervision by a licensed health care professional, or other uses authorized by the Controlled Substances Act or other provisions of Federal law.

(2) Drugs

The term "drug" means a controlled substance, as defined in schedules I through V of section 202 of the Controlled Substances Act [21 U.S.C. 812].

(Pub. L. 101-336, title V, § 510, July 26, 1990, 104 Stat. 375.)

REFERENCES IN TEXT

The Controlled Substances Act, referred to in subsec. (d)(1), is title II of Pub. L. 91-513, Oct. 27, 1970, 84 Stat. 1242, as amended, which is classified principally to subchapter I (§ 801 et seq.) of chapter 13 of Title 21, Food and Drugs. For complete classification of this Act to the Code, see Short Title note set out under section 801 of Title 21 and Tables.

§ 12211. Definitions

(a) Homosexuality and bisexuality

For purposes of the definition of "disability" in section 12102(2) of this title, homosexuality and bisexuality are not impairments and as such are not disabilities under this chapter.

(b) Certain conditions

Under this chapter, the term "disability" shall not include—
(1) transvestism, transsexualism, pedophilia, exhibitionism, voyeurism, gender identity disorders not resulting from physical impairments, or other sexual behavior disorders;
(2) compulsive gambling, kleptomania, or pyromania; or
(3) psychoactive substance use disorders resulting from current illegal use of drugs.

(Pub. L. 101-336, title V, § 511, July 26, 1990, 104 Stat. 376.)

§ 12212. Alternative means of dispute resolution

Where appropriate and to the extent authorized by law, the use of alternative means of dispute resolution, including settlement negotiations, conciliation, facilitation, mediation, factfinding, minitrials, and arbitration, is encouraged to resolve disputes arising under this chapter.

(Pub. L. 101-336, title V, § 513, July 26, 1990, 104 Stat. 377.)

§ 12213. Severability

Should any provision in this chapter be found to be unconstitutional by a court of law, such provision shall be severed from the remainder of the chapter, and such action shall not affect the enforceability of the remaining provisions of the chapter.

(Pub. L. 101-336, title V, § 514, July 26, 1990, 104 Stat. 378.)

Cases Interpreting the Americans with
Disabilities Act of 1990 (42 U.S.C. § 12101 *et seq.*)

Because the ADA was passed into law in 1990, took effect in 1991, and did not apply to employers with 15 or fewer employees until July 1992, there were only a handful of reported cases as this volume reached its publication date. The most important of these are summarized below. Because the ADA expressly states that case law developed by the courts in interpreting § 504 of the Rehabilitation Act of 1973 are to be used as guidance, readers are strongly urged to review the Rehabilitation Act section of this book. The ADA itself, as noted in the Preface/User's Guide, was built upon the language of § 504 and its regulations. See 42 U.S.C. § 12117(b). In addition, the courts are mandated to apply the same legal analysis in ADA cases as that used in § 504 cases. It should be noted that the ADA and Rehabilitation Act are also primarily enforced by the same federal agencies, the Department of Justice and the Equal Employment Opportunity Commission. Until more ADA cases are reported by the courts, attorneys and their clients should rely upon Rehabilitation Act precedents.

Anderson v. Little League Baseball, Inc., 794 F.Supp. 342 (D.Ariz.1992). A little league baseball organization adopted an official policy which permitted coaches in wheelchairs to sit in dugout areas, but excluded them from being in coaching boxes near the field. The policy cited safety considerations, alleging the possibility of player collisions with wheelchairs. A coach with spinal injuries (who had coached from his wheelchair for three previous years without incident) sued the league in the U.S. District Court for the District of Arizona for a temporary restraining order enjoining enforcement of the policy. The court held that the league's **failure to conduct any individualized assessment** of the threat to player safety, and no determination of whether **reasonable modifications of the policy might mitigate the risk** under 28 CFR Part 36.208(c) fell short of the requirements set forth in the ADA. It held that the policy discriminated against the coach on the basis of his disability and enjoined the league from enforcing the policy pending a further hearing.

Barraclough v. ADP Automotive Claims Services, Inc., 818 F.Supp. 1310 (N.D.Cal.1993). A California employer hired an applicant with a speech impairment and physical disability as a temporary employee. When the temporary employment ended after five months, the employee alleged employment discrimination on the basis of disability and sued the employer in a state court under the California Fair Employment and Housing Act. The employee's attorney served the employer with requests for admissions, which included a request for the employer to admit that it had violated the ADA, even though the incident had occurred in September 1991, months before the effective date of the ADA. When it learned that the employee intended to advance an ADA claim, the employer promptly removed the matter to a federal district court. The employee filed a motion to remand the case to state court.

The U.S. District Court for the Northern District of California observed that the alleged discrimination occurred prior to the effective date of the ADA, July 26, 1992. Although the employee was correct that the **federal court had no basis for jurisdiction because the only federal claim advanced was without merit**, she could not be allowed a remand by pointing out her own error. The court therefore dismissed the ADA complaint as meritless and awarded the employer all its attorney's fees and costs in the consideration of the case before remanding the state portion of the claim to state court.

Breece v. Alliance Tractor-Trailer Training II, Inc., 824 F.Supp. 576 (E.D.Va.1993). A man with a severe hearing impairment applied for enrollment in a Virginia truck driving school. He visited the school and met with a recruiter and the school president. The applicant suggested that his hearing impairment could be accommodated by having a sign language interpreter ride along in the vehicle during the school's extensive road training. The applicant was invited back to the school to meet with a teacher to suggest possible accommodations, but did not do so. The school then determined that it could not safely accommodate the applicant and rejected his application.

The applicant then filed a lawsuit in the U.S. District Court for the Eastern District of Virginia, and the matter proceeded to trial without a jury. The evidence introduced at trial included demonstrations of the applicant's severe hearing impairment and his difficulty understanding an interpreter. His expert witness testified that an earphone amplification device could be used and that a driving simulator and more in-class instruction were **reasonable accommodations which the school had refused to consider**. School employees testified that the proposed accommodations were unsafe and fundamentally altered the nature of the school's road-oriented training program. The court ruled that **the ADA and Rehabilitation Act "forbid courts from requiring a fundamental alteration** in a defendant's program to accommodate a handicapped individual." It agreed with the school that the proposed accommodations would fundamentally alter the school's program and that the applicant's impairment created a safety risk to himself and others. The school had relied upon the best available objective evidence in reaching its decision (see 28 CFR Part 36.208(c)), and it had not violated the ADA.

Buhl v. Hannigan, 20 Cal.Rptr.2d 740 (Cal.App.4th Dist.1993). A California appellate court affirmed the trial court's dismissal of a lawsuit filed by a group of motorcyclists who claimed that a state law requiring cyclists to wear helmets violated their rights. A motorcyclist with a hearing impairment alleged that the law violated the ADA. He stated that he could not ride his motorcycle while wearing a helmet because it produced hearing aid feedback. The court found **no ADA coverage for the private operation of motor vehicles** or motorcycles.

Carparts Dist. Center, Inc. v. Automotive Wholesaler's Ass'n of New England, 826 F.Supp. 583 (D.N.H.1993). A self-employed automotive parts distributor participated in a member-funded group health care benefit plan under which he insured himself and his employees. Lifetime plan benefits were provided up to $1 million per person. After the distributor was diagnosed HIV-positive, the plan limited benefits payable for HIV-related illnesses to $25,000. The distributor died of HIV-related causes and his estate filed a lawsuit against the plan and plan sponsor in the U.S. District Court for the District of New Hampshire. The estate claimed that the limitation on plan benefits violated the Americans with Disabilities Act (ADA), 42 U.S.C. § 12101 *et seq.*, as a discriminatory employment practice under ADA Title I, and a violation of ADA Title III, which prohibits discrimination against individuals with disabilities in the provision of goods, services, facilities, privileges, and public accommodations.

The court determined that the **plan was not a "covered entity"** under ADA Title I, because neither the plan nor the sponsor were employers of the distributor. **Title I applied only to employers, employment agencies, labor organizations and joint labor-management committees**. Title III was also inapplicable to the estate's case, because the plan and sponsor were **not "public accommodations"** under the language of that Title. According to the court, the ADA definition of public accommodation was limited to actual physical structures with physical boundaries for use by the public. Although the plan limitation had the effect of preventing HIV sufferers from obtaining medical treatment, there was no available remedy to the estate under the ADA. **Title V of the ADA expressly excludes the insurance industry from coverage**, except in the event of a subterfuge to evade application of ADA Titles I and III. The court dismissed the estate's ADA complaint, as well as a complaint it had advanced under 42 U.S.C. § 1983.

Coleman v. Zatechka, 824 F.Supp. 1360 (D.Neb.1993). The University of Nebraska, Lincoln (UNL) established a blanket policy of excluding students with disabilities from participating in the roommate candidate pool for dormitory rooms. It set aside a block of rooms for students with disabilities who required attendants, with the alleged intention of accommodating student privacy and avoiding antici-pated room change requests. A UNL student with cerebral palsy required an attendant for assistance in dressing, showering and toileting. UNL refused to place her name in the pool of roommate candidates for random assignment in two consecutive years. It did, however, attempt to locate a roommate for the student, without success. The student filed a lawsuit against UNL in the U.S. District Court for the District of Nebraska, alleging that UNL's policy violated the ADA and § 504 of the Rehabilita-tion Act.

According to the court, the only requirements for participating in the roommate candidate pool were admission to the university and completion of a residence hall contract without specifying a particular roommate. Although UNL argued that it was necessary to impose additional requirements upon students with disabilities because the use of personal attendants might intrude upon nondisabled roommates' space and privacy, the court disagreed. It noted that the **policy made no individualized inquiry** into the actual intrusiveness alleged by UNL in cases of personal care attendants, **and the policy was neither necessary for the provision of services, nor an "essential eligibility requirement"** under 28 CFR Part 35.130(b)(8).

The court condemned UNL for its policy, which "however well intentioned it may have been, sanctions the attitude that students with disabilities are less desirable and suggests that others should not be required to live with them. Such standoffishness places less value on the human worth of individuals with disabilities—because of their disabilities. As implemented, the policy unnecessarily separates students with disabilities from those without disabilities and thus strikes at the essence of the ADA and specifically violates the statute's stated purpose...." The court granted the relief requested by the student, including an order requiring UNL to assign a roommate to the student in the event that she reapplied the following year. It also awarded her attorney's fees and $1,000 in compensatory damages under § 504 of the Rehabilita-tion Act.

D'Amico v. New York State Board of Law Examiners, 813 F.Supp. 217 (W.D.N.Y.1993). A New York student graduated from a New York law school despite several visual disabilities which could not be corrected by using lenses. Her myopia and bilateral partial amblyopia made reading extremely difficult, and her vision became blurred when she read for extended time periods. By taking frequent breaks from her reading, the student was able to graduate from law school and she registered for the state bar examination. The state board of law examiners assented to some of the accommodations she requested. It extended her time allotment on the first day of the examination to nine and one half hours, and allowed her nine hours on the second day, three hours more than the usual limit. She was also allowed to use a large print examination, and other accommodations, but she failed to pass. When the applicant reregistered for a second bar examination, her physician advised that the test should be taken over a period of four days instead of two. Although the board agreed to a number of accommodations, such as the granting of unlimited time over a two day period, it would not permit the applicant to take the recommended four days. The student sued the board in the U.S. District Court for the Western District of New York, alleging that it had **failed to reasonably accommodate** her under the ADA.

The court observed that ADA § 12189 required that courses and examinations be **offered in a place and manner which is accessible to persons with disabilities,** unless alternative accessible arrangements are available. Under the ADA, the applicant was required to show that she was disabled, that her request for accommodation was reasonable, and that the request was denied. In this case, the applicant had satisfied all these requirements, with the help of the uncontested expert testimony of her physician that she needed four days to take the examination. The physician's uncontested opinion was deserving of great evidentiary weight, and the board of law examiners did not have the medical expertise to determine what testing conditions reasonably accommodated the applicant. The board's action was contrary to the letter and spirit of the ADA and the court granted the applicant's motion for a preliminary injunction which would allow her to take the test over four days.

Galloway v. Sup. Court of Dist. of Columbia, 816 F.Supp. 12 (D.D.C.1993). A Washington, D.C. resident with blindness received notice of his selection for jury duty. When he reported for duty, court personnel told him that the court's policy excluded persons with blindness from serving as jurors. The resident filed a lawsuit in the U.S. District Court for the District of Columbia under the ADA and § 504 of the Rehabilitation Act, claiming that the policy violated both acts.

The court first determined that the court system was within Rehabilitation Act coverage because it was a program receiving federal financial assistance, and the resident was a "handicapped individual" under the Act. He was **otherwise qualified** to serve as a juror, because the court system could not show that visual observation was an essential function of a juror and there were several active judges with blindness who successfully presided over cases in state and federal courts. The court system **failed to offer any form of accommodation** to the resident. The exclusion of persons with blindness also violated Title II of the ADA, because the lack of vision alone could not alone make a person unfit to serve as a juror. The court also ruled that the policy violated 42 U.S.C. § 1983, granted the resident's summary judgment motion, denied the court system's summary judgment motion, declared the policy of categorically excluding individuals with blindness from jury service unlawful, and enjoined the court system from enforcing the policy.

Kent v. Director, Missouri Department of Elementary and Secondary Education and Division of Vocational Rehabilitation, 792 F.Supp. 59 (E.D.Mo.1992). A Missouri resident filed numerous applications for employment training services and vocational rehabilitation with the Missouri Department of Elementary and Secondary Education and Division of Vocational Rehabilitation over a period of 20 years. The resident refused to be examined by a psychiatrist or psychologist for religious reasons. Consequently, the department offered no rehabilitative services and placed him on "extended evaluation status." He sued the department in the U.S. District Court for the Eastern District of Missouri under Title I of the ADA, seeking $10 million in damages.

The department filed a motion to dismiss the matter and the resident filed a motion for a trial date.

The court referred the case to a federal magistrate, who ruled that the resident **must obtain a right-to-sue letter from the EEOC in order to commence a Title I lawsuit in federal court**. Accordingly, the case was dismissed without prejudice in order to allow the resident to comply. The resident's motion for a trial date was dismissed as moot. The editors urge readers to compare this case with *Petersen v. University of Wisconsin Board of Regents,* 818 F.Supp. 1276 (W.D.Wis.1993), below, in which another federal district court observed that an aggrieved party may file a Title II lawsuit directly in a federal court without first exhausting administrative remedies by the filing of an EEOC complaint.

Kinney v. Yerusalim, 812 F.Supp. 547 (E.D.Pa.1993). Disabled individuals who either lived or worked in Philadelphia filed a class action suit against the city commissioner of streets and the Secretary of the Pennsylvania Department of Transportation under Title II of the Americans with Disabilities Act, seeking an order to compel the secretary and city to install curb ramps on all streets which the city had resurfaced since the effective date of the ADA. The disabled individuals contended that resurfacing of streets constituted an "alteration" under ADA regulations found at 28 CFR Part 35.151(a), (b) and (e). The city argued that it intended to install ramps when it performed work on curbs, but that street resurfacing did not constitute an alteration under the ADA and its regulations. It noted the language of 28 CFR Part 35.151(b), which requires only that **the altered part of the facility be readily accessible and usable by individuals with disabilities.**

The U.S. District Court for the District of Pennsylvania held that ADA Title II regulations apply whenever an alteration "affects or could affect the usability of the facility." According to U.S. Department of Justice interpretations of the regulations, "usability" is a term which is broadly interpreted. Because the **resurfacing of a street** affected the usability of streets and curbs, it **constituted an alteration under the ADA**. Accordingly, the city was obligated to install curb ramps or slopes. The city was not entitled to the **"undue burden" defense** of 28 CFR Part 35.150(3), because the defense was available only in limited circumstances not present in this case. Because new construction and alterations "present an immediate opportunity to provide for accessibility," the undue hardship and undue burden defenses were inapplicable. The removal of architectural barriers to the disabled is a major congressional concern in passing the ADA, and the court granted the order requested by the disabled individuals.

Matter of Ultraflex Enterprises' Appeal From Decertification In the Minnesota Small Business Procurement Program, 497 N.W.2d 641 (Minn.App.1993). A mentally disabled Minnesota individual founded a word processing business. He attempted to participate in a state small business procurement program, created by the state Small Business Procurement Act, which targeted groups including businesses owned by women, minorities and persons with substantial physical disabilities. However, an amendment to the act redefined targeted individuals and excluded persons with only mental disabilities from the benefits of the act. The state Department of Administration notified the individual with a mental disability that because of the amendment, he was no longer qualified for the small business procurement program. When the department's decision was upheld in an administrative appeal, the individual appealed to the Minnesota Court of Appeals.

The court rejected the individual's argument that the amended Small Business Procurement Act discriminated against persons with mental disabilities. It also ruled that the state had not denied him his right to equal protection under the state and federal constitutions. The legislation had a rational basis which did not violate the constitutional rights of persons with mental disabilities, because there was no evidence of discrimination against businesses owned and operated by persons with mental disabilities. The amended legislation did not violate the ADA or the Minnesota Human Rights Act and it was **permissible for the legislature to target persons with physical disabilities and not persons with mental disabilities**. The administrative decision was affirmed.

Petersen v. University of Wisconsin Board of Regents, 818 F.Supp. 1276 (W.D.Wis.1993). A University of Wisconsin employee who worked in the small business development center of the School of Business was not rehired by the university. The university failed to renew the employee's contract because of the employee's "personal needs" resulting from his disability. He sued the university under ADA Title II, which does not focus on employment discrimination but instead broadly prohibits recipients of federal funding from discriminating on the basis of disability. The university claimed that the lawsuit should be dismissed because the employee had failed to file an administrative complaint with the EEOC, which constituted a failure to exhaust administrative remedies.

The court ruled that a **person suing under the ADA may avoid the requirement of exhausting administrative remedies under ADA Title I** (the employment chapter enforced by the EEOC) by filing a federal court action under the ADA's more general Title II, which contains no requirement for exhausting administrative remedies. The court stated that, according to the U.S. Department of Justice, which enforces Title II, **administrative remedies under Title II are optional** and a party bringing suit under Title II may proceed directly to federal court. Department of Justice regulations (at 28 CFR Part 35.140) expressly contemplate the filing of employment complaints under Title II and cross-reference Title I employment standards without imposing any obligation upon complaining parties to make any administrative filing. The court denied the university's motion to dismiss the lawsuit.

Robinson v. Eichler, 795 F.Supp. 1253 (D.Conn.1992). A nonprofit organization purchased a building which was formerly used as a college dormitory in New Haven, Connecticut. It intended to house a family consisting of a single woman, her adult son and his wife, and ten minor children, six of whom were adopted, and four of whom were foster children awaiting adoption. All of the children were disabled and members of minority groups. A neighbor sued the organization in a Connecticut trial court, seeking to prevent the family from occupying the property, citing a zoning ordinance as legal authority for a restraining order. At the court hearing for injunctive relief, the judge demanded to know in what respect the children were disabled. The organization's attorney claimed that for privacy reasons, he could not divulge the information. Following an abrupt recess in the hearing, the attorney attempted to remove the case to the U.S. District Court for the District of Connecticut, arguing that the ADA, the Fair Housing Act (FHA) and other federal civil rights acts required removal to a federal court. The district court granted the neighbor's motion to remand the case to state court and it dismissed the federal court action, ruling that the **FHA did not preempt local zoning ordinances** so that removal was required.

U.S. Equal Employment Opportunity Commission v. AIC Security Investigation, Ltd., et al., 820 F.Supp. 1060 (N.D.Ill.1993). An executive director of a security company was diagnosed as having an inoperable brain tumor. He continued to work, and although his treatment caused him to miss substantial amounts of time from the office, he was able to handle many job duties at home. When the company discharged the director, he filed a lawsuit against it in the U.S. District Court for the Northern District of Illinois under the ADA. The company sought to dismiss the case without a trial, and filed a motion for summary judgment.

The court summarized the applicability of § 504 of the Rehabilitation Act legal precedents to ADA cases under 42 U.S.C. § 12117(b). **"[T]he ADA expressly contemplates that the voluminous precedent arising out of Section 504 of the Rehabilitation Act may serve as guidance or determinations involving the ADA."** 820 F.Supp. at 1064. The Rehabilitation Act also helps define **"qualified individual with a disability"** under the ADA, 42 U.S.C. § 12111(8). "Accordingly, only those persons who are qualified — that is, **able, with or without reasonable accommodation, to perform the essential functions of a particular job** — may state a claim under the ADA." 820 F.Supp. at 1064. "What is material is that the job gets done." 820 F.Supp. at 1064. Even though the employer had alleged that the employee's memory loss had led to some serious problems, and some transfer of job duties was required, substantial factual issues required that the matter proceed to a trial and the employer was not entitled to summary judgment.

U.S. Equal Employment Opportunity Commission v. AIC Security Investigation, Ltd., et al., 823 F.Supp. 571 (N.D.Ill.1993). [See the case summary, above.] The case summarized above went to trial, where a jury determined that the company had **terminated the director's employment solely because of his disability, despite his ability to perform essential job functions.** It awarded the director $572,000 in backpay, compensatory damages and punitive damages against the company, its president and owner. The company brought a motion to reduce the damage award. The court determined that the compensatory award of $50,000 was not excessive in view of the evidence. However, the jury had improperly awarded punitive damages by failing to aggregate the awards as required by statute. Accordingly, the court reduced the punitive damage award from $500,000 to $150,000, resulting in a net award of $222,000 to the director.

Williams v. Secretary of the Executive Office of Human Services, 414 Mass. 551, 609 N.E.2d 447 (Mass.1993). Massachusetts residents claiming to represent the interests of homeless and mentally disabled persons in that state sued the Massachusetts Department of Mental Health (DMH) for an order which would require the DMH to modify its services and care. They also sought an order requiring the DMH to change its method of discharging patients. A Massachusetts trial court granted several dismissal motions brought by the DMH but refused to grant the DMH summary judgment under the ADA. All parties appealed to the Supreme Judicial Court of Massachusetts.

The court held that the disabled persons were unable to show that the DMH policies had inappropriately segregated them under ADA regulations at **28 CFR Part 35.130(d), which requires public entities to administer services "in the most integrated setting** to the needs of qualified individuals with disabilities." The ADA did not require the DMH to provide specific services, such as setting aside placements for integrated housing. It cited a Rehabilitation Act case, *Alexander v. Choate,* 469

U.S. 287, 105 S.Ct. 712, 83 L.Ed.2d 661 (1985), which held that states are not restricted in allocating their resources in the most effective manner, so long as the allocation is nondiscriminatory.

The supreme judicial court further held that the DMH had not violated the Fair Housing Amendments Act of 1988 (42 U.S.C. § 3604(f)) by its practice of refusing to refer dual-diagnosed individuals to independent living situations. The court affirmed the trial court grant of summary judgment to the DMH for violation of the individuals' equal protection rights, citing *City of Cleburne, Texas v. Cleburne Living Center, Inc.*, 473 U.S. 432, 105 S.Ct. 3249, 87 L.Ed.2d 313 (1985), a case which held that mental disability does not constitute a suspect class requiring strict judicial scrutiny. It also affirmed the summary judgment rulings of the trial court in favor of the DMH on claims of federal and state due process violations and tort claims.

29 CFR Part 1630—Regulations to Implement the Equal Employment Provisions of the Americans with Disabilities Act

The following regulations were published on July 26, 1991 by the U.S. Equal Employment Opportunity Commission (EEOC) under ADA Title I. The regulations describe procedural processes available through the EEOC and broadly prohibit discrimination on the basis of disability in all state and local government programs and activities. As required by Congress in the ADA, these regulations are based on Department of Education regulations implementing § 504 of the Rehabilitation Act of 1973 (29 U.S.C. § 794), found at 45 CFR Part 84 and 34 CFR Part 104 (which appear in this volume).

Because of the lack of legal precedent under these regulations, users of this book are urged to review the cases cited in the Appendix to Part 1630 following the regulations. Many of the cases are summarized in the **Case Law Guide to § 504 of the Rehabilitation Act of 1973** section of this book.

* * *

AUTHORITY: 42 U.S.C. 12116.

SOURCE: 56 FR 35734, July 26, 1991, unless otherwise noted.

EFFECTIVE DATE NOTE: At 56 FR 35734, July 26, 1991, part 1630 was added, effective July 26, 1992.

§ 1630.1 Purpose, applicability, and construction.

(a) *Purpose.* The purpose of this part is to implement title I of the Americans with Disabilities Act (42 U.S.C. 12101, *et seq.*) (ADA), requiring equal employment opportunities for qualified individuals with disabilities, and sections 3(2), 3(3), 501,

503, 506(e), 508, 510, and 511 of the ADA as those sections pertain to the employment of qualified individuals with disabilities.

(b) *Applicability.* This part applies to "covered entities" as defined at 1630.2(b).

(c) *Construction*—(1) *In general.* Except as otherwise provided in this part, this part does not apply a lesser standard than the standards applied under title V of the Rehabilitation Act of 1973 (29 U.S.C. 790-794a), or the regulations issued by Federal agencies pursuant to that title.

(2) *Relationship to other laws.* This part does not invalidate or limit the remedies, rights, and procedures of any Federal law or law of any State or political subdivision of any State or jurisdiction that provides greater or equal protection for the rights of individuals with disabilities than are afforded by this part.

§ 1630.2 Definitions.

(a) *Commission* means the Equal Employment Opportunity Commission established by section 705 of the Civil Rights Act of 1964 (42 U.S.C. 2000e-4).

(b) *Covered Entity* means an employer, employment agency, labor organization, or joint labor management committee.

(c) *Person, labor organization, employment agency, commerce and industry affecting commerce* shall have the same meaning given those terms in section 701 of the Civil Rights Act of 1964 (42 U.S.C. 2000e).

(d) *State* means each of the several States, the District of Columbia, the Commonwealth of Puerto Rico, Guam, American Samoa, the Virgin Islands, the Trust Territory of the Pacific Islands, and the Commonwealth of the Northern Mariana Islands.

(e) *Employer*—(1) *In general.* The term employer means a person engaged in an industry affecting commerce who has 15 or more employees for each working day in each of 20 or more calendar weeks in the current or preceding calendar year, and any agent of such person, except that, from July 26, 1992 through July 25, 1994, an employer means a person engaged in an industry affecting commerce who has 25 or more employees for each working day in each of 20 or more calendar weeks in the current or preceding year and any agent of such person.

(2) *Exceptions.* The term employer does not include—

(i) The United States, a corporation wholly owned by the government of the United States, or an Indian tribe; or

(ii) A bona fide private membership club (other than a labor organization) that is exempt from taxation under section 501(c) of the Internal Revenue Code of 1986.

(f) *Employee* means an individual employed by an employer.

(g) *Disability* means, with respect to an individual—

(1) A physical or mental impairment that substantially limits one or more of the major life activities of such individual;

(2) A record of such an impairment; or

(3) being regarded as having such an impairment.

(See § 1630.3 for exceptions to this definition).

(h) *Physical or mental impairment* means:

(1) Any physiological disorder, or condition, cosmetic disfigurement, or anatomical loss affecting one or more of the following body systems: neurological, musculoskeletal, special sense organs, respiratory (including speech organs), cardiovascular, reproductive, digestive, genito-urinary, hemic and lymphatic, skin, and endocrine; or

(2) Any mental or psychological disorder, such as mental retardation, organic brain syndrome, emotional or mental illness, and specific learning disabilities.

(i) *Major Life Activities* means functions such as caring for oneself, performing manual tasks, walking, seeing, hearing, speaking, breathing, learning, and working.

(j) *Substantially limits*—(1) The term *substantially limits* means:

(i) Unable to perform a major life activity that the average person in the general population can perform; or

(ii) Significantly restricted as to the condition, manner or duration under which an individual can perform a particular major life activity as compared to the condition, manner, or duration under which the average person in the general population can perform that same major life activity.

(2) The following factors should be considered in determining whether an individual is substantially limited in a major life activity:

(i) The nature and severity of the impairment;

(ii) The duration or expected duration of the impairment; and

(iii) The permanent or long term impact, or the expected permanent or long term impact of or resulting from the impairment.

(3) With respect to the major life activity of *working*—

(i) The term *substantially limits* means significantly restricted in the ability to perform either a class of jobs or a broad range of jobs in various classes as compared to the average person having comparable training, skills and abilities. The inability to perform a single, particular job does not constitute a substantial limitation in the major life activity of working.

(ii) In addition to the factors listed in paragraph (j)(2) of this section, the following factors may be considered in determining whether an individual is substantially limited in the major life activity of "working":

(A) The geographical area to which the individual has reasonable access;

(B) The job from which the individual has been disqualified because of an impairment, and the number and types of jobs utilizing similar training, knowledge, skills or abilities, within that geographical area, from which the individual is also disqualified because of the impairment (class of jobs); and/or

(C) The job from which the individual has been disqualified because of an impairment, and the number and types of other jobs not utilizing similar training, knowledge, skills or abilities, within that geographical area, from which the individual is also disqualified because of the impairment (broad range of jobs in various classes).

(k) *Has a record of such impairment* means has a history of, or has been misclassified as having, a mental or physical impairment that substantially limits one or more major life activities.

(1) *Is regarded as having such an impairment* means:

(1) Has a physical or mental impairment that does not substantially limit major life activities but is treated by a covered entity as constituting such limitation;

(2) Has a physical or mental impairment that substantially limits major life activities only as a result of the attitudes of others toward such impairment; or

(3) Has none of the impairments defined in paragraph (h) (1) or (2) of this section but is treated by a covered entity as having a substantially limiting impairment.

(m) *Qualified individual with a disability* means an individual with a disability who satisfies the requisite skill, experience, education and other job-related requirements of the employment position such individual holds or desires, and who, with or without reasonable accommodation, can perform the essential functions of such position. (See § 1630.3 for exceptions to this definition).

(n) *Essential functions*—(1) *In general.* The term *essential functions* means the fundamental job duties of the employment position the individual with a disability holds or desires. The term "essential functions" does not include the marginal functions of the position.

(2) A job function may be considered essential for any of several reasons, including but not limited to the following:

(i) The function may be essential because the reason the position exists is to perform that function;

(ii) The function may be essential because of the limited number of employees available among whom the performance of that job function can be distributed; and/or

(iii) The function may be highly specialized so that the incumbent in the position is hired for his or her expertise or ability to perform the particular function.

(3) Evidence of whether a particular function is essential includes, but is not limited to:

(i) The employer's judgment as to which functions are essential;

(ii) Written job descriptions prepared before advertising or interviewing applicants for the job;

(iii) The amount of time spent on the job performing the function;

(iv) The consequences of not requiring the incumbent to perform the function;

(v) The terms of a collective bargaining agreement;

(vi) The work experience of past incumbents in the job; and/or

(vii) The current work experience of incumbents in similar jobs.

(o) *Reasonable accommodation.* (1) The term *reasonable accommodation* means:

(i) Modifications or adjustments to a job application process that enable a qualified applicant with a disability to be considered for the position such qualified applicant desires; or

(ii) Modifications or adjustments to the work environment, or to the manner or circumstances under which the position held or desired is customarily performed, that enable a qualified individual with a disability to perform the essential functions of that position; or

(iii) Modifications or adjustments that enable a covered entity's employee with a disability to enjoy equal benefits and privileges of employment as are enjoyed by its other similarly situated employees without disabilities.

(2) *Reasonable accommodation* may include but is not limited to:

(i) Making existing facilities used by employees readily accessible to and usable by individuals with disabilities; and

(ii) Job restructuring; part-time or modified work schedules; reassignment to a vacant position; acquisition or modifications of equipment or devices; appropriate adjustment or modifications of examinations, training materials, or policies; the provision of qualified readers or interpreters; and other similar accommodations for individuals with disabilities.

(3) To determine the appropriate reasonable accommodation it may be necessary for the covered entity to initiate an informal, interactive process with the qualified individual with a disability in need of the accommodation. This process should identify the precise limitations resulting from the disability and potential reasonable accommodations that could overcome those limitations.

(p) *Undue hardship*—(1) *In general. Undue hardship* means, with respect to the provision of an accommodation, significant difficulty or expense incurred by a covered entity, when considered in light of the factors set forth in paragraph (p)(2) of this section.

(2) *Factors to be considered.* In determining whether an accommodation would impose an undue hardship on a covered entity, factors to be considered include:

(i) The nature and net cost of the accommodation needed under this part, taking into consideration the availability of tax credits and deductions, and/ or outside funding;

(ii) The overall financial resources of the facility or facilities involved in the provision of the reasonable accommodation, the number of persons employed at such facility, and the effect on expenses and resources;

(iii) The overall financial resources of the covered entity, the overall size of the business of the covered entity with respect to the number of its employees, and the number, type and location of its facilities;

(iv) The type of operation or operations of the covered entity, including the composition, structure and functions of the workforce of such entity, and the geographic separateness and administrative or fiscal relationship of the facility or facilities in question to the covered entity; and

(v) The impact of the accommodation upon the operation of the facility, including the impact on the ability of other employees to perform their duties and the impact on the facility's ability to conduct business.

(q) *Qualification standards* means the personal and professional attributes including the skill, experience, education, physical, medical, safety and other require-ments established by a covered entity as requirements which an individual must meet in order to be eligible for the position held or desired.

(r) *Direct Threat* means a significant risk of substantial harm to the health or safety of the individual or others that cannot be eliminated or reduced by reasonable accommodation. The determination that an individual poses a "direct threat" shall be based on an individualized assessment of the individual's present ability to safely perform the essential functions of the job. This assessment shall be based on a reasonable medical judgment that relies on the most current medical knowledge and/ or on the best available objective evidence. In determining whether an individual would pose a direct threat, the factors to be considered include:

(1) The duration of the risk;

(2) The nature and severity of the potential harm;

(3) The likelihood that the potential harm will occur; and

(4) The imminence of the potential harm.

§ 1630.3 Exceptions to the definitions of "Disability" and "Qualified Individual with a Disability."

(a) The terms *disability* and *qualified individual with a disability* do not include individuals currently engaging in the illegal use of drugs, when the covered entity acts on the basis of such use.

(1) *Drug* means a controlled substance, as defined in schedules I through V of Section 202 of the Controlled Substances Act (21 U.S.C. 812)

(2) *Illegal use of drugs* means the use of drugs the possession or distribution of which is unlawful under the Controlled Substances Act, as periodically updated by the Food and Drug Administration. This term does not include the use of a drug taken

under the supervision of a licensed health care professional, or other uses authorized by the Controlled Substances Act or other provisions of Federal law.

(b) However, the terms *disability* and *qualified* individual with a disability may not exclude an individual who:

(1) Has successfully completed a supervised drug rehabilitation program and is no longer engaging in the illegal use of drugs, or has otherwise been rehabilitated successfully and is no longer engaging in the illegal use of drugs; or

(2) Is participating in a supervised rehabilitation program and is no longer engaging in such use; or

(3) Is erroneously regarded as engaging in such use, but is not engaging in such use.

(c) It shall not be a violation of this part for a covered entity to adopt or administer reasonable policies or procedures, including but not limited to drug testing, designed to ensure that an individual described in paragraph (b) (1) or (2) of this section is no longer engaging in the illegal use of drugs. (See § 1630.16(c) Drug testing).

(d) *Disability* does not include:

(1) Transvestism, transsexualism, pedophilia, exhibitionism, voyeurism, gender identity disorders not resulting from physical impairments, or other sexual behavior disorders;

(2) Compulsive gambling, kleptomania, or pyromania; or

(3) Psychoactive substance use disorders resulting from current illegal use of drugs.

(e) *Homosexuality and bisexuality* are not impairments and so are not disabilities as defined in this part.

§ 1630.4 Discrimination prohibited.

It is unlawful for a covered entity to discriminate on the basis of disability against a qualified individual with a disability in regard to:

(a) Recruitment, advertising, and job application procedures;

(b) Hiring, upgrading, promotion, award of tenure, demotion, transfer, layoff, termination, right of return from layoff, and rehiring;

(c) Rates of pay or any other form of compensation and changes in compensation;

(d) Job assignments, job classifications, organizational structures, position descriptions, lines of progression, and seniority lists;

(e) Leaves of absence, sick leave, or any other leave;

(f) Fringe benefits available by virtue of employment, whether or not administered by the covered entity;

(g) Selection and financial support for training, including: apprenticeships, Professional meetings, conferences and other related activities, and selection for leaves of absence to pursue training;

(h) Activities sponsored by a covered entity including social and recreational programs; and

(i) Any other term, condition, or privilege of employment.

The term *discrimination* includes, but is not limited to, the acts described in §§ 1630.5 through 1630.13 of this part.

§ 1630.5 Limiting segregating, and classifying.

It is unlawful for a covered entity to limit, segregate, or classify a job applicant or employee in a way that adversely affects his or her employment opportunities or status on the basis of disability.

§ 1630.6 Contractual or other arrangements.

(a) *In general.* It is unlawful for a covered entity to participate in a contractual or other arrangement or relationship that has the effect of subjecting the covered entity's own qualified applicant or employee with a disability to the discrimination prohibited by this part.

(b) *Contractual or other arrangement defined.* The phrase *contractual or other arrangement or relationship* includes, but is not limited to, a relationship with an employment or referral agency; labor union, including collective bargaining agreements; an organization providing fringe benefits to an employee of the covered entity; or an organization providing training and apprenticeship programs.

(c) *Application.* This section applies to a covered entity, with respect to its own applicants or employees, whether the entity offered the contract or initiated the relationship, or whether the entity accepted the contract or acceded to the relationship. A covered entity is not liable for the actions of the other party or parties to the contract which only affect that other party's employees or applicants.

§ 1630.7 Standards, criteria, or methods of administration.

It is unlawful for a covered entity to use standards, criteria, or methods of administration, which are not job-related and consistent with business necessity, and:

(a) That have the effect of discriminating on the basis of disability; or

(b) That perpetuate the discrimination of others who are subject to common administrative control.

§ 1630.8 Relationship or association with an individual with a disability.

It is unlawful for a covered entity to exclude or deny equal jobs or benefits to, or otherwise discriminate against, a qualified individual because of the known disability of an individual with whom the qualified individual is known to have a family, business, social or other relationship or association.

§ 1630.9 Not making reasonable accommodation.

(a) It is unlawful for a covered entity not to make reasonable accommodation to the known physical or mental limitations of an otherwise qualified applicant or employee with a disability, unless such covered entity can demonstrate that the accommodation would impose an undue hardship on the operation of its business.

(b) It is unlawful for a covered entity to deny employment opportunities to an otherwise qualified job applicant or employee with a disability based on the need of such covered entity to make reasonable accommodation to such individual's physical or mental impairments.

(c) A covered entity shall not be excused from the requirements of this part because of any failure to receive technical assistance authorized by section 506 of the ADA, including any failure in the development or dissemination of any technical assistance manual authorized by that Act.

(d) A qualified individual with a disability is not required to accept an accommodation, aid, service, opportunity or benefit which such qualified individual chooses not to accept. However, if such individual rejects a reasonable accommodation, aid, service, opportunity or benefit that is necessary to enable the individual to perform the essential functions of the position held or desired, and cannot, as a result of that rejection, perform the essential functions of the position, the individual will not be considered a qualified individual with a disability.

§ 1630.10 Qualification standards, tests, and other selection criteria.

It is unlawful for a covered entity to use qualification standards, employment tests or other selection criteria that screen out or tend to screen out an individual with a disability or a class of individuals with disabilities, on the basis of disability, unless the standard, test or other selection criteria, as used by the covered entity, is shown to be job-related for the position in question and is consistent with business necessity.

§ 1630.11 Administration of tests.

It is unlawful for a covered entity to fail to select and administer tests concerning employment in the most effective manner to ensure that, when a test is administered to a job applicant or employee who has a disability that impairs sensory, manual or speaking skills, the test results accurately reflect the skills, aptitude, or whatever other factor of the applicant or employee that the test purports to measure, rather than reflecting the impaired sensory, manual, or speaking skills of such employee or applicant (except where such skills are the factors that the test purports to measure).

§ 1630.12 Retaliation and coercion.

(a) *Retaliation.* It is unlawful to discriminate against any individual because that individual has opposed any act or practice made unlawful by this part or because that individual made a charge, testified, assisted, or participated in any manner in an investigation, proceeding, or hearing to enforce any provision contained in this part.

(b) *Coercion, interference or intimidation.* It is unlawful to coerce, intimidate, threaten, harass or interfere with any individual in the exercise or enjoyment of, or because that individual aided or encouraged any other individual in the exercise of, any right granted or protected by this part.

§ 1630.13 Prohibited medical examinations and inquiries.

(a) *Pre-employment examination or inquiry.* Except as permitted by § 1630.14, it is unlawful for a covered entity to conduct a medical examination of an applicant or to make inquiries as to whether an applicant is an individual with a disability or as to the nature or severity of such disability.

(b) *Examination or inquiry of employees.* Except as permitted by § 1630.14, it is unlawful for a covered entity to require a medical examination of an employee or to make inquiries as to whether an employee is an individual with a disability or as to the nature or severity of such disability.

§ 1630.14 Medical examinations and inquiries specifically permitted.

(a) *Acceptable Pre-employment inquiry.* A covered entity may make pre-employment inquiries into the ability of an applicant to perform job-related functions, and/or may ask an applicant to describe or to demonstrate how, with or without reasonable accommodation, the applicant will be able to perform job-related functions.

(b) *Employment entrance examination.* A covered entity may require a medical examination (and/or inquiry) after making an offer of employment to a job applicant and before the applicant begins his or her employment duties, and may condition an offer of employment on the results of such examination (and/or inquiry), if all entering employees in the same job category are subjected to such an examination (and/or inquiry) regardless of disability.

(1) Information obtained under paragraph (b) of this section regarding the medical condition or history of the applicant shall be collected and maintained on

separate forms and in separate medical files and be treated as a confidential medical record, except that:

(i) Supervisors and managers may be informed regarding necessary restrictions on the work or duties of the employee and necessary accommodations;

(ii) First aid and safety personnel may be informed, when appropriate, if the disability might require emergency treatment; and

(iii) Government officials investigating compliance with this part shall be provided relevant information on request.

(2) The results of such examination shall not be used for any purpose inconsistent with this part.

(3) Medical examinations conducted in accordance with this section do not have to be job-related and consistent with business necessity. However, if certain criteria are used to screen out an employee or employees with disabilities as a result of such an examination or inquiry, the exclusionary criteria must be job-related and consistent with business necessity, and performance of the essential job functions cannot be accomplished with reasonable accommodation as required in this part. (See § 1630.15(b) Defenses to charges of discriminatory application of selection criteria.)

(c) *Examination of employees.* A covered entity may require a medical examination (and/or inquiry) of an employee that is job-related and consistent with business necessity. A covered entity may make inquiries into the ability of an employee to perform job-related functions.

(1) Information obtained under paragraph (c) of this section regarding the medical condition or history of any employee shall be collected and maintained on separate forms and in separate medical files and be treated as a confidential medical record, except that:

(i) Supervisors and managers may be informed regarding necessary restrictions on the work or duties of the employee and necessary accommodations;

(ii) First aid and safety personnel may be informed, when appropriate, if the disability might require emergency treatment; and

(iii) Government officials investigating compliance with this part shall be provided relevant information on request.

(2) Information obtained under paragraph (c) of this section regarding the medical condition or history of any employee shall not be used for any purpose inconsistent with this part.

(d) *Other acceptable examinations and inquiries.* A covered entity may conduct voluntary medical examinations and activities, including voluntary medical histories, which are part of an employee health program available to employees at the work site.

(1) Information obtained under paragraph (d) of this section regarding the medical condition or history of any employee shall be collected and maintained on separate forms and in separate medical files and be treated as a confidential medical record, except that:

(i) Supervisors and managers may be informed regarding necessary restrictions on the work or duties of the employee and necessary accommodations;

(ii) First aid and safety personnel may be informed, when appropriate, if the disability might require emergency treatment; and

(iii) Government officials investigating compliance with this part shall be provided relevant information on request.

(2) Information obtained under paragraph (d) of this section regarding the medical condition or history of any employee shall not be used for any purpose inconsistent with this part.

§ 1630.15 Defenses.

Defenses to an allegation of discrimination under this part may include, but are not limited to, the following:

(a) *Disparate treatment charges.* It may be a defense to a charge of disparate treatment brought under §§ 1630.4 through 1630.8 and 1630.11 through 1630.12 that the challenged action is justified by a legitimate, nondiscriminatory reason.

(b) *Charges of discriminatory application of selection criteria*—(1) *In general.* It may be a defense to a charge of discrimination, as described in § 1630.10, that an alleged application of qualification standards, tests, or selection criteria that screens out or tends to screen out or otherwise denies a job or benefit to an individual with a disability has been shown to be job-related and consistent with business necessity, and such performance cannot be accomplished with reasonable accommodation, as required in this part.

(2) *Direct threat as a qualification standard.* The term "qualification standard" may include a requirement that an individual shall not pose a direct threat to the health or safety of the individual or others in the workplace. (See § 1630.2(r) defining direct threat.)

(c) *Other disparate impact charges.* It may be a defense to a charge of discrimination brought under this part that a uniformly applied standard, criterion, or policy has a disparate impact on an individual with a disability or a class of individuals with disabilities that the challenged standard, criterion or policy has been shown to be job-related and consistent with business necessity, and such performance cannot be accomplished with reasonable accommodation, as required in this part.

(d) *Charges of not making reasonable accommodation.* It may be a defense to a charge of discrimination, as described in § 1630.9, that a requested or necessary accommodation would impose an undue hardship on the operation of the covered entity's business.

(e) *Conflict with other federal laws.* It may be a defense to a charge of discrimination under this part that a challenged action is required or necessitated by another Federal law or regulation, or that another Federal law or regulation prohibits an action (including the provision of a particular reasonable accommodation) that would otherwise be required by this part.

(f) *Additional defenses.* It may be a defense to a charge of discrimination under this part that the alleged discriminatory action is specifically permitted by § 1630.14 or § 1630.16.

§ 1630.16 Specific activities permitted.

(a) *Religious entities.* A religious corporation, association, educational institution, or society is permitted to give preference in employment to individuals of a particular religion to perform work connected with the carrying on by that corporation, association, educational institution, or society of its activities. A religious entity may require that all applicants and employees conform to the religious tenets of such organization. However, a religious entity may not discriminate against a qualified individual, who satisfies the permitted religious criteria, because of his or her disability.

(b) *Regulation of alcohol and drugs.* A covered entity:

(1) May prohibit the illegal use of drugs and the use of alcohol at the workplace by all employees;

(2) May require that employees not be under the influence of alcohol or be engaging in the illegal use of drugs at the workplace;

(3) May require that all employees behave in conformance with the requirements established under the Drug-Free Workplace Act of 1988 (41 U.S.C. 701 *et seq.*);

(4) May hold an employee who engages in the illegal use of drugs or who is an alcoholic to the same qualification standards for employment or job performance and behavior to which the entity holds its other employees, even if any unsatisfactory performance or behavior is related to the employee's drug use or alcoholism;

(5) May require that its employees employed in an industry subject to such regulations comply with the standards established in the regulations (if any) of the Departments of Defense and Transportation, and of the Nuclear Regulatory Commission, regarding alcohol and the illegal use of drugs; and

(6) May require that employees employed in sensitive positions comply with the regulations (if any) of the Departments of Defense and Transportation and of the Nuclear Regulatory Commission that apply to employment in sensitive positions subject to such regulations.

(c) *Drug testing*—(1) *General policy.* For purposes of this part, a test to determine the illegal use of drugs is not considered a medical examination. Thus, the administration of such drug tests by a covered entity to its job applicants or employees is not a violation of § 1630.13 of this part. However, this part does not encourage, prohibit, or authorize a covered entity to conduct drug tests of job applicants or employees to determine the illegal use of drugs or to make employment decisions based on such test results.

(2) *Transportation Employees.* This part does not encourage, prohibit, or authorize the otherwise lawful exercise by entities subject to the jurisdiction of the Department of Transportation of authority to:

(i) Test employees of entities in, and applicants for, positions involving safety sensitive duties for the illegal use of drugs or for on-duty impairment by alcohol; and

(ii) Remove from safety-sensitive positions persons who test positive for illegal use of drugs or on-duty impairment by alcohol pursuant to paragraph (c)(2)(i) of this section.

(3) *Confidentiality.* Any information regarding the medical condition or history of any employee or applicant obtained from a test to determine the illegal use of drugs, except information regarding the illegal use of drugs, is subject to the requirements of § 1630.14(b)(2) and (3) of this part.

(d) *Regulation of smoking.* A covered entity may prohibit or impose restrictions on smoking in places of employment. Such restrictions do not violate any provision of this part.

(e) *Infectious and communicable diseases; food handling jobs*—(1) *In general.* Under title I of the ADA, section 103(d)(1), the Secretary of Health and Human Services is to prepare a list, to be updated annually, of infectious and communicable diseases which are transmitted through the handling of food. (Copies may be obtained from Center for Infectious Diseases, Centers for Disease Control, 1600 Clifton Road, NE., Mailstop C09, Atlanta, GA 30333.) If an individual with a disability is disabled by one of the infectious or communicable diseases included on this list, and if the risk of transmitting the disease associated with the handling of food cannot be eliminated by reasonable accommodation, a covered entity may refuse to assign or continue to assign such individual to a job involving food handling. However, if the individual with a disability is a current employee, the employer must consider whether he or she can be accommodated by reassignment to a vacant position not involving food handling.

(2) *Effect on state or other laws.* This part does not preempt, modify, or amend any State, county, or local law, ordinance or regulation applicable to food handling which:

(i) Is in accordance with the list, referred to in paragraph (e)(1) of this section, of infectious or communicable diseases and the modes of transmissibility published by the Secretary of Health and Human Services; and

(ii) Is designed to protect the public health from individuals who pose a significant risk to the health or safety of others, where that risk cannot be eliminated by reasonable accommodation.

(f) *Health insurance, life insurance, and other benefit plans*—(1) An insurer, hospital, or medical service company, health maintenance organization, or any agent or entity that administers benefit plans, or similar organizations may underwrite risks, classify risks, or administer such risks that are based on or not inconsistent with State law.

(2) A covered entity may establish, sponsor, observe or administer the terms of a bona fide benefit plan that are based on underwriting risks, classifying risks, or administering such risks that are based on or not inconsistent with State law.

(3) A covered entity may establish, sponsor, observe, or administer the terms of a bona fide benefit plan that is not subject to State laws that regulate insurance.

(4) The activities described in paragraphs (f) (1), (2), and (3) of this section are permitted unless these activities are being used as a subterfuge to evade the purposes of this part.

APPENDIX TO PART 1630—INTERPRETIVE GUIDANCE ON TITLE I OF THE AMERICANS WITH DISABILITIES ACT

BACKGROUND

The ADA is a federal antidiscrimination statute designed to remove barriers which prevent qualified individuals with disabilities from enjoying the same employment opportunities that are available to persons without disabilities.

Like the Civil Rights Act of 1964 that prohibits discrimination on the bases of race, color, religion, national origin, and sex, the ADA seeks to ensure access to equal employment opportunities based on merit. It does not guarantee equal results, establish quotas, or require preferences favoring individuals with disabilities over those without disabilities.

However, while the Civil Rights Act of 1964 prohibits any consideration of personal characteristics such as race or national origin, the ADA necessarily takes a different approach. When an individual's disability creates a barrier to employment opportunities, the ADA requires employers to consider whether reasonable accommodation could remove the barrier.

The ADA thus establishes a process in which the employer must assess a disabled individual's ability to perform the essential functions of the specific job held or desired. While the ADA focuses on eradicating barriers, the ADA does not relieve a disabled employee or applicant from the obligation to perform the essential functions of the job. To the contrary, the ADA is intended to enable disabled persons to compete in the workplace based on the same performance standards and requirements that employers expect of persons who are not disabled.

However, where that individual's functional limitation impedes such job performance, an employer must take steps to reasonably accommodate, and thus help overcome the particular impediment, unless to do so would impose an undue hardship. Such accommodations usually take the form of adjustments to the way a job customarily is performed, or to the work environment itself.

This process of identifying whether, and to what extent, a reasonable accommodation is required should be flexible and involve both the employer and the individual with a disability. Of course, the determination of whether an individual is qualified for a particular position must necessarily be made on a case-by-case basis. No specific form of accommodation is guaranteed for all individuals with a particular disability. Rather, an accommodation must be tailored to match the needs of the disabled individual with the needs of the job's essential functions.

This case-by-case approach is essential if qualified individuals of varying abilities are to receive equal opportunities to compete for an infinitely diverse range of jobs. For this reason, neither the ADA nor this part can supply the "correct" answer in advance for each employment decision concerning an individual with a disability. Instead, the ADA simply establishes parameters to guide employers in how to consider, and take into account, the disabling condition involved.

INTRODUCTION

The Equal Employment Opportunity Commission (the Commission or EEOC) is responsible for enforcement of title I of the Americans with Disabilities Act (ADA), 42 U.S.C. 12101 *et seq.* (1990), which prohibits employment discrimination on the basis of disability. The Commission believes that it is essential to issue interpretive guidance concurrently with the issuance of this part in order to ensure that qualified individuals with disabilities understand their rights under this part and to facilitate and encourage compliance by covered entities. This appendix represents the Commission's interpretation of the issues discussed, and the Commission will be guided by it when resolving charges of employment discrimination. The appendix addresses the major provisions of this part and explains the major concepts of disability rights.

The terms "employer" or "employer or other covered entity" are used interchangeably throughout the appendix to refer to all covered entities subject to the employment provisions of the ADA.

Section 1630.1 Purpose, Applicability and Construction

Section 1630.1(a) Purpose

The Americans with Disabilities Act was signed into law on July 26, 1990. It is an antidiscrimination statute that requires that individuals with disabilities be given the same consideration for employment that individuals without disabilities are given. An individual who is qualified for an employment opportunity cannot be denied that opportunity because of the fact that the individual is disabled. The purpose of title I and this part is to ensure that qualified individuals with disabilities are protected from discrimination on the basis of disability.

The ADA uses the term "disabilities" rather than the term "handicaps" used in the Rehabilitation Act of 1973, 29 U.S.C. 701-796. Substantively, these terms are equivalent. As noted by the House Committee on the Judiciary, "[t]he use of the term 'disabilities' instead of the term 'handicaps' reflects the desire of the Committee to use the most current terminology. It reflects the preference of persons with disabilities to use that term rather than 'handicapped' as used in previous laws, such as the Rehabilitation Act of 1973 * * *." H.R. Rep. No. 485 part 3, 101st Cong., 2d Sess. 26-27 (1990) (hereinafter House Judiciary Report); see also S. Rep. No. 116, 101st Cong., 1st Sess. 21 (1989) (hereinafter Senate Report); H.R. Rep. No. 485 part 2, 101st Cong., 2d Sess. 50-51 (1990) [hereinafter House Labor Report].

The use of the term "Americans" in the title of the ADA is not intended to imply that the Act only applies to United States citizens. Rather, the ADA protects all qualified individuals with disabilities, regardless of their citizenship status or nationality.

Section 1630.1(b) and (c) Applicability and Construction

Unless expressly stated otherwise, the standards applied in the ADA are not intended to be lesser than the standards applied under the Rehabilitation Act of 1973.

The ADA does not preempt any Federal law, or any state or local law, that grants to individuals with disabilities protection greater than or equivalent to that provided by the ADA. This means that the existence of a lesser standard of protection to individuals with disabilities under the ADA will not provide a defense to failing to meet a higher standard under another law. Thus, for example, title I of the ADA would not be a defense to failing to collect information required to satisfy the affirmative action requirements of section 503 of the Rehabilitation Act. On the other hand, the existence of a lesser standard under another law will not provide a defense to failing to meet a higher standard under the ADA. See House Labor Report at 135; House Judiciary Report at 69-70.

This also means that an individual with a disability could choose to pursue claims under a state discrimination or tort law that does not confer greater substantive rights, or even confers fewer substantive rights, if the potential available remedies would be greater than those available under the ADA and this part. The ADA does not restrict an individual with a disability from pursuing such claims in addition to charges brought under this part. House Judiciary at 69-70.

The ADA does not automatically preempt medical standards or safety requirements established by Federal law or regulations. It does not preempt State, county, or local laws, ordinances or regulations that are consistent with this part, and are designed to protect the public health from individuals who pose a direct threat, that cannot be eliminated or reduced by reasonable accommodation, to the health or safety of others. However, the ADA does preempt inconsistent requirements established by state or local law for safety or security sensitive positions. See Senate Report at 27; House Labor Report at 57.

An employer allegedly in violation of this part cannot successfully defend its actions by relying on the obligation to comply with the requirements of any state or local law that imposes prohibitions or limitations on the eligibility of qualified individuals with disabilities to practice any occupation or profession. For example, suppose a municipality has an ordinance that prohibits individuals with tuberculosis from teaching school children. If an individual with dormant tuberculosis challenges a private school's refusal to hire him or her because of the tuberculosis, the private school would not be able to rely on the city ordinance as a defense under the ADA.

Sections 1630.2(a)-(f) Commission,
Covered Entity, etc.

The definitions section of part 1630 includes several terms that are identical, or almost identical, to the terms found in title VII of the Civil Rights Act of 1964. Among these terms are "Commission," "Person," "State," and "Employer." These terms are to be given the same meaning under the ADA that they are given under title VII

In general, the term "employee" has the same meaning that it is given under title VII. However, the ADA's definition of "employee" does not contain an exception, as does title VII, for elected officials and their personal staffs. It should be further noted that all state and local governments are covered by title II of the ADA whether or not they are also covered by this part. Title II, which is enforced by the Department of Justice, becomes effective on January 26, 1992. See 28 CFR part 35.

The term "covered entity" is not found in title VII. However, the title VII definitions of the entities included in the term "covered entity" (e.g., employer, employment agency, etc.) are applicable to the ADA.

Section 1630.2(g) Disability

In addition to the term "covered entity," there are several other terms that are unique to the ADA. The first of these is the term "disability." Congress adopted the definition of this term from the Rehabilitation Act definition of the term "individual with handicaps." By so doing, Congress intended that the relevant caselaw developed under the Rehabilitation Act be generally applicable to the term "disability" as used in the ADA. Senate Report at 21; House Labor Report at 50; House Judiciary Report at 27.

The definition of the term "disability" is divided into three parts. An individual must satisfy at least one of these parts in order to be considered an individual with a disability for purposes of this part. An individual is considered to have a "disability" if that individual either (1) has a physical or mental impairment which substantially limits one or more of that person's major life activities, (2) has a record of such an impairment, or, (3) is regarded by the covered entity as having such an impairment. To understand the meaning of the term "disability," it is necessary to understand, as a preliminary matter, what is meant by the terms "physical or mental impairment," "major life activity," and "substantially limits." Each of these terms is discussed below.

Section 1630.2(h) Physical or Mental Impairment

This term adopts the definition of the term "physical or mental impairment" found in the regulations implementing section 504 of the Rehabilitation Act at 34 CFR part 104. It defines physical or mental impairment as any physiological disorder or condition, cosmetic disfigurement, or anatomical loss affecting one or more of several body systems, or any mental or psychological disorder.

The existence of an impairment is to be determined without regard to mitigating measures such as medicines, or assistive or prosthetic devices. See Senate Report at 23, House Labor Report at 52, House Judiciary Report at 28. For example, an individual with epilepsy would be considered to have an impairment even if the symptoms of the disorder were completely controlled by medicine. Similarly, an individual with hearing loss would be considered to have an impairment even if the condition were correctable through the use of a hearing aid.

It is important to distinguish between conditions that are impairments and physical, psychological, environmental, cultural and economic characteristics that are not impairments. The definition of the term "impairment" does not include physical characteristics such as eye color, hair color, lefthandedness, or height, weight or muscle tone that are within "normal" range and are not the result of a physiological disorder. The definition, likewise, does not include characteristic predisposition to illness or disease. Other conditions, such as pregnancy, that are not the result of a physiological disorder are also not impairments. Similarly, the definition does not include common personality traits such as poor judgment or a quick temper where these are not symptoms of a mental or psychological disorder. Environmental, cultural, or economic disadvantages such as poverty, lack of education or a prison record are not impairments. Advanced age, in and of itself, is also not an impairment. However, various medical conditions commonly associated with age, such as hearing loss, osteoporosis, or arthritis would constitute impairments within the meaning of this part. See Senate Report at 22-23; House Labor Report at 51-52; House Judiciary Report at 28-29.

Section 1630.2(i) Major Life Activities

This term adopts the definition of the term "major life activities" found in the regulations implementing section 504 of the Rehabilitation Act at 34 CFR part 104. "Major life activities" are those basic activities that the average person in the general population can perform with little or no difficulty. Major life activities include caring for oneself, performing manual tasks, walking, seeing, hearing, speaking, breathing, learning, and working. This list is not exhaustive. For example, other major life activities include, but are not limited to, sitting, standing, lifting, reaching. See Senate Report at 22; House Labor Report at 52; House Judiciary Report at 28.

Section 1630.2(j) Substantially Limits

Determining whether a physical or mental impairment exists is only the first step in determining whether or not an individual is disabled. Many impairments do not impact an individual's life to the degree that they constitute disabling impairments. An impairment rises to the level of disability if the impairment substantially limits one or more of the individual's major life activities. Multiple impairments that combine to substantially limit one or more of an individual's major life activities also constitute a disability.

The ADA and this part, like the Rehabilitation Act of 1973, do not attempt a "laundry list" of impairments that are "disabilities." The determination of whether an individual has a disability is not necessarily based on the name or diagnosis of the impairment the person has, but rather on the effect of that impairment on the life of the individual. Some impairments may be disabling for particular individuals but not for others, depending on the stage of the disease or disorder, the presence of other impairments that combine to make the impairment disabling or any number of other factors.

Other impairments, however, such as HIV infection, are inherently substantially limiting.

On the other hand, temporary, non-chronic impairments of short duration, with little or no long term or permanent impact, are usually not disabilities. Such impairments may include, but are not limited to, broken limbs, sprained joints, concussions, appendicitis, and influenza. Similarly, except in rare circumstances, obesity is not considered a disabling impairment.

An impairment that prevents an individual from performing a major life activity substantially limits that major life activity. For example, an individual whose legs are paralyzed is substantially limited in the major life activity of walking because he or she is unable, due to the impairment, to perform that major life activity.

Alternatively, an impairment is substantially limiting if it significantly restricts the duration, manner or condition under which an individual can perform a particular major life activity as compared to the average person in the general population's ability to perform that same major life activity. Thus, for example, an individual who, because of an impairment, can only walk for very brief periods of time would be substantially limited in the major life activity of walking. An individual who uses artificial legs would likewise be substantially limited in the major life activity of walking because the individual is unable to walk without the aid of prosthetic devices. Similarly, a diabetic who without insulin would lapse into a coma would be substantially limited because the individual cannot perform major life activities without the aid of medication. See Senate Report at 23; House Labor Report at 52. It should be noted that the term "average person" is not intended to imply a precise mathematical "average."

Part 1630 notes several factors that should be considered in making the determination of whether an impairment is substantially limiting. These factors are (1) the nature and severity of the impairment, (2) the duration or expected duration of the impairment, and (3) the permanent or long term impact, or the expected permanent or long term impact of, or resulting from, the impairment. The term "duration," as used in this context, refers to the length of time an impairment persists, while the term "impact" refers to the residual effects of an impairment. Thus, for example, a broken leg that takes eight weeks to heal is an impairment of fairly brief duration. However, if the broken leg heals improperly, the "impact" of the impairment would be the resulting permanent limp. Likewise, the effect on cognitive functions resulting from traumatic head injury would be the "impact" of that impairment.

The determination of whether an individual is substantially limited in a major life activity must be made on a case by case basis, without regard to mitigating measures such as medicines, or assistive or prosthetic devices. An individual is not substantially limited in a major life activity if the limitation, when viewed in light of the factors noted above, does not amount to a significant restriction when compared with the abilities of the average person. For example, an individual who had once been able to walk at an extraordinary speed would not be substantially limited in the major life activity of walking if, as a result of a physical impairment, he or she were only able to walk at an average speed, or even at moderately below average speed.

It is important to remember that the restriction on the performance of the major life activity must be the result of a condition that is an impairment. As noted earlier, advanced age, physical or personality characteristics, and environmental, cultural, and economic disadvantages are not impairments. Consequently, even if such factors substantially limit an individual's ability to perform a major life activity, this limitation will not constitute a disability. For example, an individual who is unable to read because he or she was never taught to read would not be an individual with a disability because lack of education is not an impairment. However, an individual who is unable to read because of dyslexia would be an individual with a disability because dyslexia, a learning disability, is an impairment.

If an individual is not substantially limited with respect to any other major life activity, the individual's ability to perform the major life activity of working should be considered. If an individual is substantially limited in any other major life activity, no determination should be made as to whether the individual is substantially limited in working. For example, if an individual is blind, *i.e.,* substantially limited in the major life activity of seeing, there is no need to determine whether the individual is also substantially limited in the major life activity of working. The determination of whether an individual is substantially limited in working must also be made on a case by case basis.

This part lists specific factors that may be used in making the determination of whether the limitation in working is "substantial." These factors are:

(1) The geographical area to which the individual has reasonable access;

(2) The job from which the individual has been disqualified because of an impairment, and the number and types of jobs utilizing similar training, knowledge, skills or abilities, within that geographical area, from which the individual is also disqualified because of the impairment (class of jobs); and/or

(3) The job from which the individual has been disqualified because of an impairment, and the number and types of other jobs not utilizing similar training, knowledge, skills or abilities, within that geographical area, from which the individual is also disqualified because of the impairment (broad range of jobs in various classes).

Thus, an individual is not substantially limited in working just because he or she is unable to perform a particular job for one employer, or because he or she is unable to perform a specialized job or profession requiring extraordinary skill, prowess or talent. For example, an individual who cannot be a commercial airline pilot because of a minor vision impairment, but who can be a commercial airline co-pilot or a pilot for a courier service, would not be substantially limited in the major life activity of working. Nor would a professional baseball pitcher who develops a bad elbow and can no longer throw a baseball be considered substantially limited in the major life activity of working. In both of these examples, the individuals are not substantially limited in the ability to perform any other major life activity and, with regard to the major life activity of working, are only unable to perform either a particular specialized job or a narrow range of jobs. See *Forrisi v. Bowen,* 794 F.2d 931 (4th Cir. 1986); *Jasany v. U.S. Postal Service,* 755 F.2d 1244 (6th Cir. 1985); *E.E. Black, Ltd. v. Marshall,* 497 F.Supp. 1088 (D. Hawaii 1980). [Editorial Note: See the **Cases interpreting EEOC Rehabilitation Act Regulations** section of this book for summaries of the *Forrisi and Jasany* cases.]

On the other hand, an individual does not have to be totally unable to work in order to be considered substantially limited in the major life activity of working. An individual is substantially limited in working if the individual is significantly restricted in the ability to perform a class of jobs or a broad range of jobs in various classes, when compared with the ability of the average person with comparable qualifications to perform those same jobs. For example, an individual who has a back condition that prevents the individual from performing any heavy labor job would be substantially limited in the major life activity of working because the individual's impairment eliminates his or her ability to perform a class of jobs. This would be so even if the individual were able to perform jobs in another class, *e.g.,* the class of semi-skilled jobs. Similarly, suppose an individual has an allergy to a substance found in most high rise office buildings, but seldom found elsewhere, that makes breathing extremely difficult. Since this individual would be substantially limited in the ability to perform the broad range of jobs in various classes that are conducted in high rise office buildings within the geographical area to which he or she has reasonable access, he or she would be substantially limited in working.

The terms "number and types of jobs" and "number and types of other jobs," as used in the factors discussed above, are not intended to require an onerous evidentiary showing. Rather, the terms only require the presentation of evidence of general employment demographics and/or of recognized occupational classifications that indicate the approximate number of jobs *(e.g.,* "few," "many," "most") from which an individual would be excluded because of an impairment.

If an individual has a "mental or physical impairment" that "substantially limits" his or her ability to perform one or more "major life activities," that individual will satisfy the first part of the regulatory definition of "disability" and will be considered an individual with a disability. An individual who satisfies this first part of the definition of the term "disability" is not required to demonstrate that he or she satisfies either of the other parts of the definition. However, if an individual is unable to satisfy this part of the definition, he or she may be able to satisfy one of the other parts of the definition.

Section 1630.2(k) Record of a Substantially Limiting Condition

The second part of the definition provides that an individual with a record of an impairment that substantially limits a major life activity is an individual with a disability. The intent of this provision, in part, is to ensure that people are not discriminated against because of a history of disability. For example, this provision protects former cancer patients from discrimination based on their prior medical history. This provision also ensures that individuals are not discriminated against because they have been misclassified as disabled. For example, individuals misclassified as learning disabled are protected from discrimination on the basis of that erroneous classification. Senate Report at 23; House Labor Report at 52-53; House Judiciary Report at 29.

This part of the definition is satisfied if a record relied on by an employer indicates that the individual has or has had a substantially limiting impairment. The impairment indicated in the record must be an impairment that would substantially limit one or more of the individual's major life activities. There are many types of records that could potentially contain this information, including but not limited to, education, medical, or employment records.

The fact that an individual has a record of being a disabled veteran, or of disability retirement, or is classified as disabled for other purposes does not guarantee that the individual will satisfy the definition of "disability" under part 1630. Other statutes, regulations and programs may have a definition of "disability" that is not the same as the definition set forth in the ADA and contained in part 1630. Accordingly, in order for an individual who has been classified in a record as "disabled" for some other purpose to be considered disabled for purposes of part 1630, the impairment indicated in the record must be a physical or mental impairment that substantially limits one or more of the individual's major life activities.

Section 1630.2(1) Regarded as Substantially Limited in a Major Life Activity

If an individual cannot satisfy either the first part of the definition of "disability" or the second "record of" part of the definition, he or she may be able to satisfy the third part of the definition. The third part of the definition provides that an individual who is regarded by an employer or other covered entity as having an impairment that substantially limits a major life activity is an individual with a disability.

There are three different ways in which an individual may satisfy the definition of "being regarded as having a disability":

(1) The individual may have an impairment which is not substantially limiting but is perceived by the employer or other covered entity as constituting a substantially limiting impairment;

(2) The individual may have an impairment which is only substantially limiting because of the attitudes of others toward the impairment; or

(3) The individual may have no impairment at all but is regarded by the employer or other covered entity as having a substantially limiting impairment.

Senate Report at 23; House Labor Report at 53; House Judiciary Report at 29.

An individual satisfies the first part of this definition if the individual has an impairment that is not substantially limiting, but the covered entity perceives the impairment as being substantially limiting. For example, suppose an employee has controlled high blood pressure that is not substantially limiting. If an employer reassigns the individual to less strenuous work because of unsubstantiated fears that the individual will suffer a heart attack if he or she continues to perform strenuous work, the employer would be regarding the individual as disabled.

An individual satisfies the second part of the "regarded as" definition if the individual has an impairment that is only substantially limiting because of the attitudes of others toward the condition. For example, an individual may have a prominent facial scar or disfigurement, or may have a condition that periodically causes an involuntary jerk of the head but does not limit the individual's major life activities. If an employer discriminates against such an individual because of the negative reactions of customers, the employer would be regarding the individual as disabled and acting on the basis of that perceived disability. See Senate Report at 24; House Labor Report at 53; House Judiciary Report at 30-31.

An individual satisfies the third part of the "regarded as" definition of "disability" if the employer or other covered entity erroneously believes the individual has a substantially limiting impairment that the individual actually does not have. This situation could occur, for example, if an employer discharged an employee in response to a rumor that the employee is infected with Human Immunodeficiency Virus (HIV). Even though the rumor is totally unfounded and the individual has no impairment at all, the individual is considered an individual with a disability because the employer perceived of this individual as being disabled. Thus, in this example, the employer, by discharging this employee, is discriminating on the basis of disability.

The rationale for the "regarded as" part of the definition of disability was articulated by the Supreme Court in the context of the Rehabilitation Act of 1973 in *School Board of Nassau County v. Arline,* 480 U.S. 273 (1987). [Editorial Note: For a summary of *Arline,* see the **Cases interpreting § 504 of the Rehabilitation Act of 1973** section of this book.] The Court noted that, although an individual may have an impairment that does not in fact substantially limit a major life activity, the reaction of others may prove just as disabling. "Such an impairment might not diminish a person's physical or mental capabilities, but could nevertheless substantially limit that person's ability to work as a result of the negative reactions of others to the impairment." 480 U.S. at 283. The Court concluded that by including "regarded as" in the Rehabilitation Act's definition, "Congress acknowledged that society's accumulated myths and fears about disability and diseases are as handicapping as are the physical limitations that flow from actual impairment." 480 U.S. at 284.

An individual rejected from a job because of the "myths, fears and stereotypes" associated with disabilities would be covered under this part of the definition of disability, whether or not the employer's or other covered entity's perception were shared by others in the field and whether or not the individual's actual physical or mental condition would be considered a disability under the first or second part of this definition. As the legislative history notes, sociologists have identified common attitudinal barriers that frequently result in employers excluding individuals with disabilities. These include concerns regarding productivity, safety, insurance, liability, attendance, cost of accommodation and accessibility, workers' compensation costs, and acceptance by coworkers and customers.

Therefore, if an individual can show that an employer or other covered entity made an employment decision because of a perception of disability based on "myth, fear or stereotype," the individual will satisfy the "regarded as" part of the definition of disability. If the employer cannot articulate a non-discriminatory reason for the employment action, an inference that the employer is acting on the basis of "myth, fear or stereotype" can be drawn.

Section 1630.2(m) Qualified Individual With a Disability

The ADA prohibits discrimination on the basis of disability against qualified individuals with disabilities. The determination of whether an individual with a disability is "qualified" should be made in two steps. The first step is to determine if the individual satisfies the prerequisites for the position, such as possessing the appropriate educational background, employment experience, skills, licenses, etc. For example, the first step in determining whether an accountant who is paraplegic is qualified for a certified public accountant (CPA) position is to examine the individual's credentials to determine whether the individual is a licensed CPA. This is sometimes referred to in the Rehabilitation Act caselaw as determining whether the individual is "otherwise qualified" for the position. See Senate Report at 33; House Labor Report at 64-65. (See § 1630.9 Not Making Reasonable Accommodation).

The second step is to determine whether or not the individual can perform the essential functions of the position held or desired, with or without reasonable accommodation. The purpose of this second step is to ensure that individuals with disabilities who can perform the essential functions of the position held or desired are not denied employment opportunities because they are not able to perform marginal functions of the position. House Labor Report at 55.

The determination of whether an individual with a disability is qualified is to be made at the time of the employment decision. This determination should be based on the capabilities of the individual with a disability at the time of the employment decision, and should not be based on speculation that the employee may become unable in the future or may cause increased health insurance premiums or workers compensation costs.

Section 1630.2(n) Essential Functions

The determination of which functions are essential may be critical to the determination of whether or not the individual with a disability is qualified. The essential functions are those functions that the individual who holds the position must be able to perform unaided or with the assistance of a reasonable accommodation.

The inquiry into whether a particular function is essential initially focuses on whether the employer actually requires employees in the position to perform the functions that the employer asserts are essential. For example, an employer may state that typing is an essential function of a position. If, in fact, the employer has never required any employee in that particular position to type, this will be evidence that typing is not actually an essential function of the position.

If the individual who holds the position is actually required to perform the function the employer asserts is an essential function, the inquiry will then center around whether removing the function would fundamentally alter that position. This determination of whether or not a particular function is essential will generally include one or more of the following factors listed in part 1630.

The first factor is whether the position exists to perform a particular function. For example, an individual may be hired to proofread documents. The ability to proofread the documents would then be an essential function, since this is the only reason the position exists.

The second factor in determining whether a function is essential is the number of other employees available to perform that job function or among whom the performance of that job function can be distributed. This may be a factor either because the total number of available employees is low, or because of the fluctuating demands of the business operation. For example, if an employer has a relatively small number of available employees for the volume of work to be performed, it may be necessary that each employee perform a multitude of different functions. Therefore, the performance of those functions by each employee becomes more critical and the options for reorganizing the work become more limited. In such a situation, functions that might not be essential if there were a larger staff may become essential because the staff size is small compared to the volume of work that has to be done. See *Treadwell v. Alexander,* 707 F.2d 473 (11th Cir. 1983). [Editorial Note: For a summary of *Treadwell,* see the **Cases interpreting EEOC Rehabilitation Act Regulations** section of this book.]

A similar situation might occur in a larger work force if the workflow follows a cycle of heavy demand for labor intensive work followed by low demand periods. This type of workflow might also make the performance of each function during the peak periods more critical and might limit the employer's flexibility in reorganizing operating procedures. See *Dexler v. Tisch,* 660 F.Supp. 1418 (D. Conn. 1987). [Editorial Note: For a summary of *Dexler,* see the **Cases interpreting EEOC Rehabilitation Act Regulations** section of this book.]

The third factor is the degree of expertise or skill required to perform the function. In certain professions and highly skilled positions the employee is hired for his or her expertise or ability to perform the particular function. In such a situation, the performance of that specialized task would be an essential function.

Whether a particular function is essential is a factual determination that must be made on a case by case basis. In determining whether or not a particular function is essential, all relevant evidence should be considered. Part 1630 lists various types of evidence, such as an established job description, that should be considered in determining whether a particular function is essential. Since the list is not exhaustive, other relevant evidence may also be presented. Greater weight will not be granted to the types of evidence included on the list than to the types of evidence not listed.

Although part 1630 does not require employers to develop or maintain job descriptions, written job descriptions prepared before advertising or interviewing applicants for the job, as well as the employer's judgment as to what functions are essential are among the relevant evidence to be considered in determining whether a particular function is essential. The terms of a collective bargaining agreement are also relevant to the determination of whether a particular function is essential. The work experience of past employees in the job or of current employees in similar jobs is likewise relevant to the determination of whether a particular function is essential. See H.R. Conf. Rep. No. 101-596, 101st Cong., 2d Sess. 58 (1990) [hereinafter Conference Report]; House Judiciary Report at 33-34. See also *Hall v. U.S. Postal Service,* 857 F.2d 1073 (6th Cir. 1988). [Editorial Note: For a summary of *Hall,* see the **Cases interpreting § 501 of the Rehabilitation Act of 1973** section of this book.]

The time spent performing the particular function may also be an indicator of whether that function is essential. For example, if an employee spends the vast majority of his or her time working at a cash register, this would be evidence that operating the cash register is an essential function. The consequences of failing to require the employee to perform the function may be another indicator of whether a particular function is essential. For example, although a firefighter may not regularly have to carry an unconscious adult out of a burning building, the consequence of failing to require the firefighter to be able to perform this function would be serious.

It is important to note that the inquiry into essential functions is not intended to second guess an employer's business judgment with regard to production standards, whether qualitative or quantitative, nor to require employers to lower such standards. (See § 1630.10 Qualification Standards, Tests and Other Selection Criteria). If an employer requires its typists to be able to accurately type 75 words per minute, it will not be called upon to explain why an inaccurate work product, or a typing speed of 65 words per minute, would not be adequate. Similarly, if a hotel requires its service workers to thoroughly clean 16 rooms per day, it will not have to explain why it requires thorough cleaning, or why it chose a 16 room rather than a 10 room requirement. However, if an employer does require accurate 75 word per minute typing or the thorough cleaning of 16 rooms, it will have to show that it actually imposes such requirements on its employees in fact, and not simply on paper. It should also be noted that, if it is alleged that the employer intentionally selected the particular level of production to exclude individuals with disabilities, the employer may have to offer a legitimate, nondiscriminatory reason for its selection.

Section 1630.2(o) Reasonable Accommodation

An individual is considered a "qualified individual with a disability" if the individual can perform the essential functions of the position held or desired with or without reasonable accommodation. In general, an accommodation is any change in the work environment or in the way things are customarily done that enables an individual with a disability to enjoy equal employment opportunities. There are three categories of reasonable accommodation. These are (1) accommodations that are required to ensure equal opportunity in the application process; (2) accommodations that enable the employer's employees with disabilities to perform the essential functions of the position held or desired; and (3) accommodations that enable the employer's employees with disabilities to enjoy equal benefits and privileges of employment as are enjoyed by employees without disabilities. It should be noted that nothing in this part prohibits employers or other covered entities from providing accommodations beyond those required by this part.

Part 1630 lists the examples, specified in title I of the ADA, of the most common types of accommodation that an employer or other covered entity may be required to provide. There are any number of other specific accommodations that may be appropriate for particular situations but are not specifically mentioned in this listing. This listing is not intended to be exhaustive of accommodation possibilities. For example, other accommodations could include permitting the use of accrued paid leave or providing additional unpaid leave for necessary treatment, making employer provided transportation accessible, and providing reserved parking spaces. Providing personal assistants, such as a page turner for an employee with no hands or a travel attendant to act as a sighted guide to assist a blind employee on occasional business trips, may also be a reasonable accommodation. Senate Report at 31; House Labor Report at 62; House Judiciary Report at 39.

It may also be a reasonable accommodation to permit an individual with a disability the opportunity to provide and utilize equipment, aids or services that an employer is not required to provide as a reasonable accommodation. For example, it would be a reasonable accommodation for an employer to permit an individual who is blind to use a guide dog at work, even though the employer would not be required to provide a guide dog for the employee.

The accommodations included on the list of reasonable accommodations are generally self explanatory. However, there are a few that require further explanation. One of these is the accommodation of making existing facilities used by employees readily accessible to, and usable by, individuals with disabilities. This accommodation includes both those areas that must be accessible for the employee to perform essential job functions, as well as non-work areas used by the employer's employees for other purposes. For example, accessible break rooms, lunch rooms, training rooms, restrooms etc., may be required as reasonable accommodations.

Another of the potential accommodations listed is "job restructuring." An employer or other covered entity may restructure a job by reallocating or redistributing nonessential, marginal job functions. For example, an employer may have two jobs, each of which entails the performance of a number of marginal functions. The employer hires a qualified individual with a disability who is able to perform some of the marginal functions of each job but not all of the marginal functions of either job. As an accommodation, the employer may redistribute the marginal functions so that all of the marginal functions that the qualified individual with a disability can perform are made a part of the position to be filled by the qualified individual with a disability. The remaining marginal functions that the individual with a disability cannot perform would then be transferred to the other position. See Senate Report at 31; House Labor Report at 62.

An employer or other covered entity is not required to reallocate essential functions. The essential functions are by definition those that the individual who holds the job would have to perform, with or without reasonable accommodation, in order to be considered qualified for the position. For example, suppose a security guard position requires the individual who holds the job to inspect identification cards. An employer would not have to provide an individual who is legally blind with an assistant to look at the identification cards for the legally blind employee. In this situation the assistant would be performing the job for the individual with a disability rather than assisting the individual to perform the job. See *Coleman v. Darden,* 595 F.2d 533 (10th Cir. 1979). [Editorial Note: For a summary of *Darden,* see the **Cases interpreting Rehabilitation Act Regulations** section of this book.]

An employer or other covered entity may also restructure a job by altering when and/ or how an essential function is performed. For example, an essential function customarily performed in the early morning hours may be rescheduled until later in the day as a reasonable accommodation to a disability that precludes performance of the function at the customary hour. Likewise, as a reasonable accommodation, an employee with a disability that inhibits the ability to write, may be permitted to computerize records that were customarily maintained manually.

Reassignment to a vacant position is also listed as a potential reasonable accommodation. In general, reassignment should be considered only when accommodation within the individual's current position would pose an undue hardship. Reassignment is not available to applicants. An applicant for a position must be qualified for, and be able to perform the essential functions of, the position sought with or without reasonable accommodation.

Reassignment may not be used to limit, segregate, or otherwise discriminate against employees with disabilities by forcing reassignments to undesirable positions or to designated offices or facilities. Employers should reassign the individual to an equivalent position, in terms of pay, status, etc., if the individual is qualified, and if the position is vacant within a reasonable amount of time. A "reasonable amount of time" should be determined in light of the totality of the circumstances. As an example, suppose there is no vacant position available at the time that an individual with a disability requests reassignment as a reasonable accommodation. The employer, however, knows that an equivalent position for which the individual is qualified, will become vacant next week. Under these circumstances, the employer should reassign the individual to the position when it becomes available.

An employer may reassign an individual to a lower graded position if there are no accommodations that would enable the employee to remain in the current position and there are no vacant equivalent positions for which the individual is qualified with or without reasonable accommodation. An employer, however, is not required to maintain the reassigned individual with a disability at the salary of the higher graded position if it does not so maintain reassigned employees who are not disabled. It should also be noted that an employer is not required to promote an individual with a disability as an accommodation. See Senate Report at 31-32; House Labor Report at 63.

The determination of which accommodation is appropriate in a particular situation involves a process in which the employer and employee identify the precise limitations imposed by the disability and explore potential accommodations that would overcome those limitations. This process is discussed more fully in § 1630.9 Not Making Reasonable Accommodation.

Section 1630.2(p) Undue Hardship

An employer or other covered entity is not required to provide an accommodation that will impose an undue hardship on the operation of the employer's or other covered entity's business. The term "undue hardship" means significant difficulty or expense in, or resulting from, the provision of the accommodation. The "undue hardship" provision takes into account the financial realities of the particular employer or other covered entity. However, the concept of undue hardship is not limited to financial difficulty. "Undue hardship" refers to any accommodation that would be unduly costly, extensive, substantial, or disruptive, or that would fundamentally alter the nature or operation of the business. See Senate Report at 35; House Labor Report at 67.

For example, suppose an individual with a disabling visual impairment that makes it extremely difficult to see in dim lighting applies for a position as a waiter in a nightclub and requests that the club be brightly lit as a reasonable accommodation. Although the individual may be able to perform the job in bright lighting, the nightclub will probably be able to demonstrate that that particular accommodation, though inexpensive, would impose an undue hardship if the bright lighting would destroy the ambience of the nightclub and/or make it difficult for the customers to see the stage show. The fact that that particular accommodation poses an undue hardship, however, only means that the employer is not required to provide that accommodation. If there is another accommodation that will not create an undue hardship, the employer would be required to provide the alternative accommodation.

An employer's claim that the cost of a particular accommodation will impose an undue hardship will be analyzed in light of the factors outlined in part 1630. In part, this analysis requires a determination of whose financial resources should be considered in deciding whether the accommodation is unduly costly. In some cases the financial resources of the employer or other covered entity in its entirety should be considered in determining whether the cost of an accommodation poses an undue hardship. In other cases, consideration of the financial resources of the employer or other covered entity as a whole may be inappropriate because it may not give an accurate picture of the financial resources available to the particular facility that will actually be required to provide the accommodation. See House Labor Report at 68-69; House Judiciary Report at 40-41; see also Conference Report at 56-57.

If the employer or other covered entity asserts that only the financial resources of the facility where the individual will be employed should be considered, part 1630 requires a factual determination of the relationship between the employer or other covered entity and the facility that will provide the accommodation. As an example, suppose that an independently owned fast food franchise that receives no money from the franchisor refuses to hire an individual with a hearing impairment because it asserts that it would be an undue hardship to provide an interpreter to enable the individual to participate in monthly staff meetings. Since the financial relationship between the franchisor and the franchise is limited to payment of an annual franchise fee, only the financial resources of the franchise would be considered in determining whether or not providing the accommodation would be an undue hardship. See House Labor Report at 68; House Judiciary Report at 40.

If the employer or other covered entity can show that the cost of the accommodation would impose an undue hardship, it would still be required to provide the accommodation if the funding is available from another source, *e.g.,* a State vocational rehabilitation agency, or if Federal, State or local tax deductions or tax credits are available to offset the cost of the accommodation. If the employer or other covered entity receives, or is eligible to receive, monies from an external source that would pay the entire cost of the accommodation, it cannot claim cost as an undue hardship. In the absence of such funding, the individual with a disability requesting the accommodation should be given the option of providing the accommodation or of paying that portion of the cost which constitutes the undue hardship on the operation of the business. To the extent that such monies pay or would pay for only part of the cost of the accommodation, only that portion of the cost of the accommodation that could not be recovered—the final net cost to the entity—may be considered in determining undue hardship. (See § 1630.9 Not Making Reasonable Accommodation). See Senate Report at 36; House Labor Report at 69.

Section 1630.2(r) Direct Threat

An employer may require, as a qualification standard, that an individual not pose a direct threat to the health or safety of himself/herself or others. Like any other qualification standard, such a standard must apply to all applicants or employees and not just to individuals with disabilities. If, however, an individual poses a direct threat as a result of a disability, the employer must determine whether a reasonable accommodation would either eliminate the risk or reduce it to an acceptable level. If no accommodation exists that would either eliminate or reduce the risk, the employer may refuse to hire an applicant or may discharge an employee who poses a direct threat.

An employer, however, is not permitted to deny an employment opportunity to an individual with a disability merely because of a slightly increased risk. The risk can only be considered when it poses a significant risk, *i.e.,* high probability, of substantial harm; a speculative or remote risk is insufficient. See Senate Report at 27; House Report Labor Report at 56-57; House Judiciary Report at 45.

Determining whether an individual poses a significant risk of substantial harm to others must be made on a case by case basis. The employer should identify the specific risk posed by the individual. For individuals with mental or emotional disabilities, the employer must identify the specific behavior on the part of the individual that would pose the direct threat. For individuals with physical disabilities, the employer must identify the aspect of the disability that would pose the direct threat. The employer should then consider the four factors listed in part 1630:

(1) The duration of the risk;

(2) The nature and severity of the potential harm;

(3) The likelihood that the potential harm will occur; and

(4) The imminence of the potential harm. Such consideration must rely on objective, factual evidence—not on subjective perceptions, irrational fears, patronizing attitudes, or stereotypes—about the nature or effect of a particular disability, or of disability generally. See Senate Report at 27; House Labor Report at 56-57; House Judiciary Report at 45-46. See also *Strathie v. Department of Transportation,* 716 F.2d 227 (3d Cir. 1983). Relevant evidence may include input from the individual with a disability, the experience of the individual with a disability in previous similar

positions, and opinions of medical doctors, rehabilitation counselors, or physical therapists who have expertise in the disability involved and/or direct knowledge of the individual with the disability.

An employer is also permitted to require that an individual not pose a direct threat of harm to his or her own safety or health. If performing the particular functions of a job would result in a high probability of substantial harm to the individual, the employer could reject or discharge the individual unless a reasonable accommodation that would not cause an undue hardship would avert the harm. For example, an employer would not be required to hire an individual, disabled by narcolepsy, who frequently and unexpectedly loses consciousness for a carpentry job the essential functions of which require the use of power saws and other dangerous equipment, where no accommodation exists that will reduce or eliminate the risk.

The assessment that there exists a high probability of substantial harm to the individual, like the assessment that there exists a high probability of substantial harm to others, must be strictly based on valid medical analyses and/or on other objective evidence. This determination must be based on individualized factual data, using the factors discussed above, rather than on stereotypic or patronizing assumptions and must consider potential reasonable accommodations. Generalized fears about risks from the employment environment, such as exacerbation of the disability caused by stress, cannot be used by an employer to disqualify an individual with a disability. For example, a law firm could not reject an applicant with a history of disabling mental illness based on a generalized fear that the stress of trying to make partner might trigger a relapse of the individual's mental illness. Nor can generalized fears about risks to individuals with disabilities in the event of an evacuation or other emergency be used by an employer to disqualify an individual with a disability. See Senate Report at 56; House Labor Report at 73-74; House Judiciary Report at 45. See also *Mantolete v. Bolger,* 767 F.2d 1416 (9th Cir. 1985); *Bentivegna v. U.S. Department of Labor,* 694 F.2d 619 (9th Cir. 1982). [Editorial Note: For a summary of *Mantolete,* see the **Cases interpreting § 501 of the Rehabilitation Act of 1973** section of this book. For a summary of *Bentivegna,* see the **Cases interpreting § 504 of the Rehabilitation Act of 1973.**]

Section 1630.3 Exceptions to the Definitions of "Disability" and "Qualified Individual with a Disability"

Section 1630.3 (a) through (c) Illegal Use of Drugs

Part 1630 provides that an individual currently engaging in the illegal use of drugs is not an individual with a disability for purposes of this part when the employer or other covered entity acts on the basis of such use. Illegal use of drugs refers both to the use of unlawful drugs, such as cocaine, and to the unlawful use of prescription drugs.

Employers, for example, may discharge or deny employment to persons who illegally use drugs, on the basis of such use, without fear of being held liable for discrimination. The term "currently engaging" is not intended to be limited to the use of drugs on the day of, or within a matter of days or weeks before, the employment action in question. Rather, the provision is intended to apply to the illegal use of drugs that has occurred recently enough to indicate that the individual is actively engaged in such conduct. See Conference Report at 64.

Individuals who are erroneously perceived as engaging in the illegal use of drugs, but are not in fact illegally using drugs are not excluded from the definitions of the terms "disability" and "qualified individual with a disability." Individuals who are no longer illegally using drugs and who have either been rehabilitated successfully or are in the process of completing a rehabilitation program are, likewise, not excluded from the definitions of those terms. The term "rehabilitation program" refers to both in-patient and out-patient programs, as well as to appropriate employee assistance programs, professionally recognized self-help programs, such as Narcotics Anonymous, or other programs that provide professional (not necessarily medical) assistance and counseling for individuals who illegally use drugs. See Conference Report at 64; see also House Labor Report at 77; House Judiciary Report at 47.

It should be noted that this provision simply provides that certain individuals are not excluded from the definitions of "disability" and "qualified individual with a disability." Consequently, such individuals are still required to establish that they satisfy the requirements of these definitions in order to be protected by the ADA and this part. An individual erroneously regarded as illegally using drugs, for example, would have to show that he or she was regarded as a drug addict in order to demonstrate that he or she meets the definition of "disability" as defined in this part.

Employers are entitled to seek reasonable assurances that no illegal use of drugs is occurring or has occurred recently enough so that continuing use is a real and ongoing problem. The reasonable assurances that employers may ask applicants or employees to provide include evidence that the individual is participating in a drug treatment program and/or evidence, such as drug test results, to show that the individual is not currently engaging in the illegal use of drugs. An employer, such as a law enforcement agency, may also be able to impose a qualification standard that excludes individuals with a history of illegal use of drugs if it can show that the standard is job-related and consistent with business necessity. (See § 1630.10 Qualification Standards, Tests and Other Selection Criteria) See Conference Report at 64.

Section 1630.4 Discrimination Prohibited

This provision prohibits discriminating against a qualified individual with a disability in all aspects of the employment relationship. The range of employment decisions covered by this nondiscrimination mandate is to be construed in a manner consistent with the regulations implementing section 504 of the Rehabilitation Act of 1973.

Part 1630 is not intended to limit the ability of covered entities to choose and maintain a qualified workforce. Employers can continue to use job-related criteria to select qualified employees, and can continue to hire employees who can perform the essential functions of the job.

Section 1630.5 Limiting, Segregating and Classifying

This provision and the several provisions that follow describe various specific forms of discrimination that are included within the general prohibition of § 1630.4. Covered entities are prohibited from restricting the employment opportunities of qualified individuals with disabilities on the basis of stereotypes and myths about the individual's disability. Rather, the capabilities of qualified individuals with disabilities must be determined on an individualized, case by case basis. Covered entities are also prohibited from segregating qualified employees with disabilities into separate work areas or into separate lines of advancement.

Thus, for example, it would be a violation of this part for an employer to limit the duties of an employee with a disability based on a presumption of what is best for an individual with such a disability, or on a presumption about the abilities of an individual with such a disability. It would be a violation of this part for an employer to adopt a separate track of job promotion or progression for employees with disabilities based on a presumption that employees with disabilities are uninterested in, or incapable of, performing particular jobs. Similarly, it would be a violation for an employer to assign or reassign (as a reasonable accommodation) employees with disabilities to one particular office or installation, or to require that employees with disabilities only use particular employer provided non-work facilities such as segregated break-rooms, lunch rooms, or lounges. It would also be a violation of this part to deny employment to an applicant or employee with a disability based on generalized fears about the safety of an individual with such a disability, or based on generalized assumptions about the absenteeism rate of an individual with such a disability.

In addition, it should also be noted that this part is intended to require that employees with disabilities be accorded equal access to whatever health insurance coverage the employer provides to other employees. This part does not, however, affect pre-existing condition clauses included in health insurance policies offered by employers. Consequently, employers may continue to offer policies that contain such clauses, even if they adversely affect individuals with disabilities, so long as the clauses are not used as a subterfuge to evade the purposes of this part.

So, for example, it would be permissible for an employer to offer an insurance policy that limits coverage for certain procedures or treatments to a specified number per year. Thus, if a health insurance plan provided coverage for five blood transfusions a year to all covered employees, it would not be discriminatory to offer this plan simply because a hemophiliac employee may require more than five blood transfusions annually. However, it would not be permissible to limit or deny the hemophiliac employee coverage for other procedures, such as heart surgery or the setting of a broken leg, even though the plan would not have to provide coverage for the additional blood transfusions that may be involved in these procedures. Likewise, limits may be placed on reimbursements for certain procedures or on the types of drugs or procedures covered (e.g. limits on the number of permitted X-rays or non-coverage of experimental drugs or procedures), but that limitation must be applied equally to individuals with and without disabilities. See Senate Report at 28-29; House Labor Report at 58-59; House Judiciary Report at 36.

Leave policies or benefit plans that are uniformly applied do not violate this part simply because they do not address the special needs of every individual with a disability. Thus, for example, an employer that reduces the number of paid sick leave days that it will provide to all employees, or reduces the amount of medical insurance coverage that it will provide to all employees, is not in violation of this part, even if the benefits reduction has an impact on employees with disabilities in need of greater sick leave and medical coverage. Benefits reductions adopted for discriminatory reasons are in violation of this part. See *Alexander v. Choate,* 469 U.S. 287 (1985). See Senate Report at 85; House Labor Report at 137. (See also, the discussion at § 1630.16(f) Health Insurance, Life Insurance, and Other Benefit Plans). [Editorial Note: For a summary of *Alexander,* see the **Cases interpreting § 504 of the Rehabilitation Act of 1973** section of this book.]

Section 1630.6 Contractual or Other Arrangements

An employer or other covered entity may not do through a contractual or other relationship what it is prohibited from doing directly. This provision does not affect the determination of whether or not one is a "covered entity" or "employer" as defined in § 1630.2.

This provision only applies to situations where an employer or other covered entity has entered into a contractual relationship that has the effect of discriminating against its own employees or applicants with disabilities. Accordingly, it would be a violation for an employer to participate in a contractual relationship that results in discrimination against the employer's employees with disabilities in hiring, training, promotion, or in any other aspect of the employment relationship. This provision applies whether or not the employer or other covered entity intended for the contractual relationship to have the discriminatory effect.

Part 1630 notes that this provision applies to parties on either side of the contractual or other relationship. This is intended to highlight that an employer whose employees provide services to others, like an employer whose employees receive services, must ensure that those employees are not discriminated against on the basis of disability. For example, a copier company whose service representative is a dwarf could be required to provide a stepstool, as a reasonable accommodation, to enable him to perform the necessary repairs. However, the employer would not be required, as a reasonable accommodation, to make structural changes to its customer's inaccessible premises.

The existence of the contractual relationship adds no new obligations under part 1630. The employer, therefore, is not liable through the contractual arrangement for any discrimination by the contractor against the contractor's own employees or applicants, although the contractor, as an employer, may be liable for such discrimination.

An employer or other covered entity, on the other hand, cannot evade the obligations imposed by this part by engaging in a contractual or other relationship. For example, an employer cannot avoid its responsibility to make reasonable accommodation subject to the undue hardship limitation through a contractual arrangement. See Conference Report at 59; House Labor Report at 59-61; House Judiciary Report at 36-37.

To illustrate, assume that an employer is seeking to contract with a company to provide training for its employees. Any responsibilities of reasonable accommodation applicable to the employer in providing the training remain with that employer even if it contracts with another company for this service. Thus, if the training company were planning to conduct the training at an inaccessible location, thereby making it impossible for an employee who uses a wheelchair to attend, the employer would have a duty to make reasonable accommodation unless to do so would impose an undue hardship. Under these circumstances, appropriate accommodations might include (1) having the training company identify accessible training sites and relocate the training program; (2) having the training company make the training site accessible; (3) directly making the training site accessible or providing the training company with the means by which to make the site accessible; (4) identifying and contracting with another training company that uses accessible sites; or (5) any other accommodation that would result in making the training available to the employee.

As another illustration, assume that instead of contracting with a training company, the employer contracts with a hotel to host a conference for its employees.

The employer will have a duty to ascertain and ensure the accessibility of the hotel and its conference facilities. To fulfill this obligation the employer could, for example, inspect the hotel first-hand or ask a local disability group to inspect the hotel. Alternatively, the employer could ensure that the contract with the hotel specifies it will provide accessible guest rooms for those who need them and that all rooms to be used for the conference, including exhibit and meeting rooms, are accessible. If the hotel breaches this accessibility provision, the hotel may be liable to the employer, under a non-ADA breach of contract theory, for the cost of any accommodation needed to provide access to the hotel and conference, and for any other costs accrued by the employer. (In addition, the hotel may also be independently liable under title III of the ADA). However, this would not relieve the employer of its responsibility under this part nor shield it from charges of discrimination by its own employees. See House Labor Report at 40; House Judiciary Report at 37.

Section 1630.8 Relationship or Association With an Individual With a Disability

This provision is intended to protect any qualified individual, whether or not that individual has a disability, from discrimination because that person is known to have an association or relationship with an individual who has a known disability. This protection is not limited to those who have a familial relationship with an individual with a disability.

To illustrate the scope of this provision, assume that a qualified applicant without a disability applies for a job and discloses to the employer that his or her spouse has a disability. The employer thereupon declines to hire the applicant because the employer believes that the applicant would have to miss work or frequently leave work early in order to care for the spouse. Such a refusal to hire would be prohibited by this provision. Similarly, this provision would prohibit an employer from discharging an employee because the employee does volunteer work with people who have AIDS, and the employer fears that the employee may contract the disease.

This provision also applies to other benefits and privileges of employment. For example, an employer that provides health insurance benefits to its employees for their dependents may not reduce the level of those benefits to an employee simply because that employee has a dependent with a disability. This is true even if the provision of such benefits would result in increased health insurance costs for the employer.

It should be noted, however, that an employer need not provide the applicant or employee without a disability with a reasonable accommodation because that duty only applies to qualified applicants or employees with disabilities. Thus, for example, an employee would not be entitled to a modified work schedule as an accommodation to enable the employee to care for a spouse with a disability. See Senate Report at 30; House Labor Report at 61-62; House Judiciary Report at 38-39.

Section 1630.9 Not Making Reasonable Accommodation

The obligation to make reasonable accommodation is a form of non-discrimination. It applies to all employment decisions and to the job application process. This obligation does not extend to the provision of adjustments or modifications that are primarily for the personal benefit of the individual with a disability. Thus, if an adjustment or modification is job-related, *e.g.*, specifically assists the individual in performing the duties of a particular job, it will be considered a type of reasonable accommodation. On the other hand, if an adjustment or modification assists the individual throughout his or her daily activities, on and off the job, it will be considered a personal item that the employer is not required to provide. Accordingly, an employer would generally not be required to provide an employee with a disability with a prosthetic limb, wheelchair, or eyeglasses. Nor would an employer have to provide as an accommodation any amenity or convenience that is not job-related, such as a private hot plate, hot pot or refrigerator that is not provided to employees without disabilities. See Senate Report at 31; House Labor Report at 62.

It should be noted, however, that the provision of such items may be required as a reasonable accommodation where such items are specifically designed or required to meet job-related rather than personal needs. An employer, for example, may have to provide an individual with a disabling visual impairment with eyeglasses specifically designed to enable the individual to use the office computer monitors, but that are not otherwise needed by the individual outside of the office.

The term "supported employment," which has been applied to a wide variety of programs to assist individuals with severe disabilities in both competitive and non-competitive employment, is not synonymous with reasonable accommodation. Examples of supported employment include modified training materials, restructuring essential functions to enable an individual to perform a job, or hiring an outside professional ("job coach") to assist in job training. Whether a particular form of assistance would be required as a reasonable accommodation must be determined on an individualized, case by case basis without regard to whether that assistance is referred to as "supported employment." For example, an employer, under certain circumstances, may be required to provide modified training materials or a temporary "job coach" to assist in the training of a qualified individual with a disability as a reasonable accommodation. However, an employer would not be required to restructure the essential functions of a position to fit the skills of an individual with a disability who is not otherwise qualified to perform the position, as is done in certain supported employment programs. See 34 CFR part 363. It should be noted that it would not be a violation of this part for an employer to provide any of these personal modifications or adjustments, or to engage in supported employment or similar rehabilitative programs.

The obligation to make reasonable accommodation applies to all services and programs provided in connection with employment, and to all non-work facilities provided or maintained by an employer for use by its employees. Accordingly, the obligation to accommodate is applicable to employer sponsored placement or counseling services, and to employer provided cafeterias, lounges, gymnasiums, auditoriums, transportation and the like.

The reasonable accommodation requirement is best understood as a means by which barriers to the equal employment opportunity of an individual with a disability are removed or alleviated. These barriers may, for example, be physical or structural obstacles that inhibit or prevent the access of an individual with a disability to job sites, facilities or equipment. Or they may be rigid work schedules that permit no flexibility as to when work is performed or when breaks may be taken, or inflexible job procedures that unduly limit the modes of communication that are used on the job, or the way in which particular tasks are accomplished.

The term "otherwise qualified" is intended to make clear that the obligation to make reasonable accommodation is owed only to an individual with a disability who is qualified within the meaning of § 1630.2(m) in that he or she satisfies all the skill, experience, education and other job-related selection criteria. An individual with a disability is "otherwise qualified," in other words, if he or she is qualified for a job, except that, because of the disability, he or she needs a reasonable accommodation to be able to perform the job's essential functions.

For example, if a law firm requires that all incoming lawyers have graduated from an accredited law school and have passed the bar examination, the law firm need not provide an accommodation to an individual with a visual impairment who has not met these selection criteria. That individual is not entitled to a reasonable accommodation because the individual is not "otherwise qualified" for the position.

On the other hand, if the individual has graduated from an accredited law school and passed the bar examination, the individual would be "otherwise qualified." The law firm would thus be required to provide a reasonable accommodation, such as a machine that magnifies print, to enable the individual to perform the essential functions of the attorney position, unless the necessary accommodation would impose an undue hardship on the law firm. See Senate Report at 33-34; House Labor Report at 64-65.

The reasonable accommodation that is required by this part should provide the qualified individual with a disability with an equal employment opportunity. Equal employment opportunity means an opportunity to attain the same level of performance, or to enjoy the same level of benefits and privileges of employment as are available to the average similarly situated employee without a disability. Thus, for example, an accommodation made to assist an employee with a disability in the performance of his or her job must be adequate to enable the individual to perform the essential functions of the relevant position. The accommodation, however, does not have to be the "best" accommodation possible, so long as it is sufficient to meet the job-related needs of the individual being accommodated. Accordingly, an employer would not have to provide an employee disabled by a back impairment with a state-of-the art mechanical lifting device if it provided the employee with a less expensive or more readily available device that enabled the employee to perform the essential functions of the job. See Senate Report at 35; House Labor Report at 66; see also *Carter v. Bennett,* 840 F.2d 63 (D.C. Cir. 1988). [Editorial Note: For a summary of *Carter,* see the **Cases interpreting § 501 of the Rehabilitation Act of 1973** section of this book.]

Employers are obligated to make reasonable accommodation only to the physical or mental limitations resulting from the disability of a qualified individual with a disability that is known to the employer. Thus, an employer would not be expected to accommodate disabilities of which it is unaware. If an employee with a known disability is having difficulty performing his or her job, an employer may inquire whether the employee is in need of a reasonable accommodation. In general, however, it is the responsibility of the individual with a disability to inform the employer that an accommodation is needed. When the need for an accommodation is not obvious, an employer, before providing a reasonable accommodation, may require that the individual with a disability provide documentation of the need for accommodation. See Senate Report at 34; House Labor Report at 65.

Process of Determining the Appropriate Reasonable Accommodation

Once a qualified individual with a disability has requested provision of a reasonable accommodation, the employer must make a reasonable effort to determine the appropriate accommodation. The appropriate reasonable accommodation is best determined through a flexible, interactive process that involves both the employer and the qualified individual with a disability. Although this process is described below in terms of accommodations that enable the individual with a disability to perform the essential functions of the position held or desired, it is equally applicable to accommodations involving the job application process, and to accommodations that enable the individual with a disability to enjoy equal benefits and privileges of employment. See Senate Report at 34-35; House Labor Report at 65-67.

When a qualified individual with a disability has requested a reasonable accommodation to assist in the performance of a job, the employer, using a problem solving approach, should:

(1) Analyze the particular job involved and determine its purpose and essential functions;

(2) Consult with the individual with a disability to ascertain the precise job-related limitations imposed by the individual's disability and how those limitations could be overcome with a reasonable accommodation;

(3) In consultation with the individual to be accommodated, identify potential accommodations and assess the effectiveness each would have in enabling the individual to perform the essential functions of the position; and

(4) Consider the preference of the individual to be accommodated and select and implement the accommodation that is most appropriate for both the employee and the employer.

In many instances, the appropriate reasonable accommodation may be so obvious to either or both the employer and the qualified individual with a disability that it may not be necessary to proceed in this step-by-step fashion. For example, if an employee who uses a wheelchair requests that his or her desk be placed on blocks to elevate the desktop above the arms of the wheelchair and the employer complies, an appropriate accommodation has been requested, identified, and provided without either the employee or employer being aware of having engaged in any sort of "reasonable accommodation process."

However, in some instances neither the individual requesting the accommodation nor the employer can readily identify the appropriate accommodation. For example, the individual needing the accommodation may not know enough about the equipment used by the employer or the exact nature of the work site to suggest an appropriate accommodation. Likewise, the employer may not know enough about the individual's disability or the limitations that disability would impose on the performance of the job to suggest an appropriate accommodation. Under such circumstances, it may be necessary for the employer to initiate a more defined problem solving process, such as the step-by-step process described above, as part of its reasonable effort to identify the appropriate reasonable accommodation.

This process requires the individual assessment of both the particular job at issue, and the specific physical or mental limitations of the particular individual in need of reasonable accommodation. With regard to assessment of the job, "individual assessment" means analyzing the actual job duties and determining the true purpose or object of the job. Such an assessment is necessary to ascertain which job functions are the essential functions that an accommodation must enable an individual with a disability to perform.

After assessing the relevant job, the employer, in consultation with the individual requesting the accommodation, should make an assessment of the specific limitations imposed by the disability on the individual's performance of the job's essential functions. This assessment will make it possible to ascertain the precise barrier to the employment opportunity which, in turn, will make it possible to determine the accommodation(s) that could alleviate or remove that barrier.

If consultation with the individual in need of the accommodation still does not reveal potential appropriate accommodations, then the employer, as part of this process, may find that technical assistance is helpful in determining how to accommodate the particular individual in the specific situation. Such assistance could be sought from the Commission, from state or local rehabilitation agencies, or from disability constituent organizations. It should be noted, however, that, as provided in § 1630.9(c) of this part, the failure to obtain or receive technical assistance from the federal agencies that administer the ADA will not excuse the employer from its reasonable accommodation obligation.

Once potential accommodations have been identified, the employer should assess the effectiveness of each potential accommodation in assisting the individual in need of the accommodation in the performance of the essential functions of the position. If more than one of these accommodations will enable the individual to perform the essential functions or if the individual would prefer to provide his or her own accommodation, the preference of the individual with a disability should be given primary consideration. However, the employer providing the accommodation has the ultimate discretion to choose between effective accommodations, and may choose the less expensive accommodation or the accommodation that is easier for it to provide. It should also be noted that the individual's willingness to provide his or her own accommodation does not relieve the employer of the duty to provide the accommodation should the individual for any reason be unable or unwilling to continue to provide the accommodation.

Reasonable Accommodation Process
Illustrated

The following example illustrates the informal reasonable accommodation process. Suppose a Sack Handler position requires that the employee pick up fifty pound sacks and carry them from the company loading dock to the storage room, and that a sack handler who is disabled by a back impairment requests a reasonable accommodation. Upon receiving the request, the employer analyzes the Sack Handler job and determines that the essential function and purpose of the job is not the requirement that the job holder physically lift and carry the sacks, but the requirement that the job holder cause the sack to move from the loading dock to the storage room.

The employer then meets with the sack handler to ascertain precisely the barrier posed by the individual's specific disability to the performance of the job's essential function of relocating the sacks. At this meeting the employer learns that the individual can, in fact, lift the sacks to waist level, but is prevented by his or her disability from carrying the sacks from the loading dock to the storage room. The employer and the individual agree that any of a number of potential accommodations, such as the provision of a dolly, hand truck, or cart, could enable the individual to transport the sacks that he or she has lifted.

Upon further consideration, however, it is determined that the provision of a cart is not a feasible effective option. No carts are currently available at the company, and those that can be purchased by the company are the wrong shape to hold many of the bulky and irregularly shaped sacks that must be moved. Both the dolly and the hand truck, on the other hand, appear to be effective options. Both are readily available to the company, and either will enable the individual to relocate the sacks that he or she has lifted. The sack handler indicates his or her preference for the dolly. In consideration of this expressed preference, and because the employer feels that the dolly will allow the individual to move more sacks at a time and so be more efficient than would a hand truck, the employer ultimately provides the sack handler with a dolly in fulfillment of the obligation to make reasonable accommodation.

Section 1630.9(b)

This provision states that an employer or other covered entity cannot prefer or select a qualified individual without a disability over an equally qualified individual with a disability merely because the individual with a disability will require a reasonable accommodation. In other words, an individual's need for an accommodation cannot enter into the employer's or other covered entity's decision regarding hiring, discharge, promotion, or other similar employment decisions, unless the accommodation would impose an undue hardship on the employer. See House Labor Report at 70.

Section 1630.9(d)

The purpose of this provision is to clarify that an employer or other covered entity may not compel a qualified individual with a disability to accept an accommodation, where that accommodation is neither requested nor needed by the individual. However, if a necessary reasonable accommodation is refused, the individual may not be considered qualified. For example, an individual with a visual impairment that restricts his or her field of vision but who is able to read unaided would not be required to accept a reader as an accommodation. However, if the individual were not able to read unaided and reading was an essential function of the job, the individual would not be qualified for the job if he or she refused a reasonable accommodation that would enable him or her to read. See Senate Report at 34; House Labor Report at 65; House Judiciary Report at 71-72.

Section 1630.10 Qualification Standards, Tests, and Other Selection Criteria

The purpose of this provision is to ensure that individuals with disabilities are not excluded from job opportunities unless they are actually unable to do the job. It is to ensure that there is a fit between job criteria and an applicant's (or employee's) actual ability to do the job. Accordingly, job criteria that even unintentionally screen out, or tend to screen out, an individual with a disability or a class of individuals with disabilities because of their disability may not be used unless the employer demonstrates that that criteria, as used by the employer, are job-related to the position to which they are being applied and are consistent with business necessity. The concept of "business necessity" has the same meaning as the concept of "business necessity" under section 504 of the Rehabilitation Act of 1973.

Selection criteria that exclude, or tend to exclude, an individual with a disability or a class of individuals with disabilities because of their disability but do not concern an essential function of the job would not be consistent with business necessity.

The use of selection criteria that are related to an essential function of the job may be consistent with business necessity. However, selection criteria that are related to an essential function of the job may not be used to exclude an individual with a disability if that individual could satisfy the criteria with the provision of a reasonable accommodation. Experience under a similar provision of the regulations implementing section 504 of the Rehabilitation Act indicates that challenges to selection criteria are, in fact, most often resolved by reasonable accommodation. It is therefore anticipated that challenges to selection criteria brought under this part will generally be resolved in a like manner.

This provision is applicable to all types of selection criteria, including safety requirements, vision or hearing requirements, walking requirements, lifting requirements, and employment tests. See Senate Report at 37-39; House Labor Report at 70-72; House Judiciary Report at 42. As previously noted, however, it is not the intent of this part to second guess an employer's business judgment with regard to production standards. (See section 1630.2(n) Essential Functions). Consequently, production standards will generally not be subject to a challenge under this provision.

The Uniform Guidelines on Employee Selection Procedures (UGESP) 29 CFR part 1607 do not apply to the Rehabilitation Act and are similarly inapplicable to this part.

Section 1630.11 Administration of Tests

The intent of this provision is to further emphasize that individuals with disabilities are not to be excluded from jobs that they can actually perform merely because a disability prevents them from taking a test, or negatively influences the results of a test, that is a prerequisite to the job. Read together with the reasonable accommodation requirement of section 1630.9, this provision requires that employment tests be administered to eligible applicants or employees with disabilities that impair sensory, manual, or speaking skills in formats that do not require the use of the impaired skill.

The employer or other covered entity is, generally, only required to provide such reasonable accommodation if it knows, prior to the administration of the test, that the individual is disabled and that the disability impairs sensory, manual or speaking skills. Thus, for example, it would be unlawful to administer a written employment test to an individual who has informed the employer, prior to the administration of the test, that he is disabled with dyslexia and unable to read. In such a case, as a reasonable accommodation and in accordance with this provision, an alternative oral test should be administered to that individual. By the same token, a written test may need to be substituted for an oral test if the applicant taking the test is an individual with a disability that impairs speaking skills or impairs the processing of auditory information.

Occasionally, an individual with a disability may not realize, prior to the administration of a test, that he or she will need an accommodation to take that particular test. In such a situation, the individual with a disability, upon becoming aware of the need for an accommodation, must so inform the employer or other covered entity. For example, suppose an individual with a disabling visual impairment does not request an accommodation for a written examination because he or she is usually able to take written tests with the aid of his or her own specially designed lens. When the test is distributed, the individual with a disability discovers that the lens is insufficient to distinguish the words of the test because of the unusually low color contrast between the paper and the ink, the individual would be entitled, at that point, to request an accommodation. The employer or other covered entity would, thereupon, have to provide a test with higher contrast, schedule a retest, or provide any other effective accommodation unless to do so would impose an undue hardship.

Other alternative or accessible test modes or formats include the administration of tests in large print or braille, or via a reader or sign interpreter. Where it is not possible to test in an alternative format, the employer may be required, as a reasonable accommodation, to evaluate the skill to be tested in another manner (*e.g.,* through an interview, or through education license, or work experience requirements). An employer may also be required, as a reasonable accommodation, to allow more time to complete the test. In addition, the employer's obligation to make reasonable accommodation extends to ensuring that the test site is accessible. (See § 1630.9 Not Making Reasonable Accommodation) See Senate Report at 37-38; House Labor Report at 70-72; House Judiciary Report at 42; see also *Stutts v. Freeman,* 694 F.2d 666 (11th Cir. 1983); *Crane v. Dole,* 617 F.Supp. 156 (D.D.C. 1985). [Editorial Note: For a summary of *Stutts,* see the **Cases interpreting Rehabilitation Act Regulations** section of this book.]

This provision does not require that an employer offer every applicant his or her choice of test format. Rather, this provision only requires that an employer provide, upon advance request, alternative, accessible tests to individuals with disabilities that impair sensory, manual, or speaking skills needed to take the test.

This provision does not apply to employment tests that require the use of sensory, manual, or speaking skills where the tests are intended to measure those skills. Thus, an employer could require that an applicant with dyslexia take a written test for a particular position if the ability to read is the skill the test is designed to measure. Similarly, an employer could require that an applicant complete a test within established time frames if speed were one of the skills for which the applicant was being tested. However, the results of such a test could not be used to exclude an individual with a disability unless the skill was necessary to perform an essential function of the position and no reasonable accommodation was available to enable the individual to perform that function, or the necessary accommodation would impose an undue hardship.

Section 1630.13 Prohibited Medical Examinations and Inquiries

Section 1630.13(a) Pre-employment Examination or Inquiry

This provision makes clear that an employer cannot inquire as to whether an individual has a disability at the pre-offer stage of the selection process. Nor can an employer inquire at the pre-offer stage about an applicant's workers' compensation history.

Employers may ask questions that relate to the applicant's ability to perform job-related functions. However, these questions should not be phrased in terms of disability. An employer, for example, may ask whether the applicant has a driver's license, if driving is a job function, but may not ask whether the applicant has a visual disability. Employers may ask about an applicant's ability to perform both essential and marginal job functions. Employers, though, may not refuse to hire an applicant with a disability because the applicant's disability prevents him or her from performing marginal functions. See Senate Report at 39; House Labor Report at 72-73; House Judiciary Report at 42-43.

Section 1630.13(b) Examination or Inquiry of Employees

The purpose of this provision is to prevent the administration to employees of medical tests or inquiries that do not serve a legitimate business purpose. For example, if an employee suddenly starts to use increased amounts of sick leave or starts to appear sickly, an employer could not require that employee to be tested for AIDS, HIV infection, or cancer unless the employer can demonstrate that such testing is job-related and consistent with business necessity. See Senate Report at 39; House Labor Report at 75; House Judiciary Report at 44.

Section 1630.14 Medical Examinations and Inquiries Specifically Permitted

Section 1630.14(a) Pre-employment Inquiry

Employers are permitted to make pre-employment inquiries into the ability of an applicant to perform job-related functions. This inquiry must be narrowly tailored. The employer may describe or demonstrate the job function and inquire whether or not the applicant can perform that function with or without reasonable accommodation. For example, an employer may explain that the job requires assembling small parts and ask if the individual will be able to perform that function, with or without reasonable accommodation. See Senate Report at 39; House Labor Report at 73; House Judiciary Report at 43.

An employer may also ask an applicant to describe or to demonstrate how, with or without reasonable accommodation, the applicant will be able to perform job-related functions. Such a request may be made of all applicants in the same job category regardless of disability. Such a request may also be made of an applicant whose known disability may interfere with or prevent the performance of a job-related function, whether or not the employer routinely makes such a request of all applicants in the job category. For example, an employer may ask an individual with one leg who applies for a position as a home washing machine repairman to demonstrate or to explain how, with or without reasonable accommodation, he would be able to transport himself and his tools down basement stairs. However, the employer may not inquire as to the nature or severity of the disability. Therefore, for example, the employer cannot ask how the individual lost the leg or whether the loss of the leg is indicative of an underlying impairment.

On the other hand, if the known disability of an applicant will not interfere with or prevent the performance of a job-related function, the employer may only request a description or demonstration by the applicant if it routinely makes such a request of all applicants in the same job category. So, for example, it would not be permitted for an employer to request that an applicant with one leg demonstrate his ability to assemble small parts while seated at a table, if the employer does not routinely request that all applicants provide such a demonstration.

An employer that requires an applicant with a disability to demonstrate how he or she will perform a job-related function must either provide the reasonable accommodation the applicant needs to perform the function or permit the applicant to explain how, with the accommodation, he or she will perform the function. If the job-related function is not an essential function, the employer may not exclude the applicant with a disability because of the applicant's inability to perform that function. Rather, the employer must, as a reasonable accommodation, either provide an accommodation that will enable the individual to perform the function, transfer the function to another position, or exchange the function for one the applicant is able to perform.

An employer may not use an application form that lists a number of potentially disabling impairments and ask the applicant to check any of the impairments he or she may have. In addition, as noted above, an employer may not ask how a particular individual became disabled or the prognosis of the individual's disability. The employer is also prohibited from asking how often the individual will require leave for treatment or use leave as a result of incapacitation because of the disability. However, the employer may state the attendance requirements of the job and inquire whether the applicant can meet them.

An employer is permitted to ask, on a test announcement or application form, that individuals with disabilities who will require a reasonable accommodation in order to take the test [to] inform the employer within a reasonable established time period prior to the administration of the test. The employer may also request that documentation of the need for the accommodation accompany the request. Requested accommodations may include accessible testing sites, modified testing conditions and accessible test formats. (See § 1630.11 Administration of Tests).

Physical agility tests are not medical examinations and so may be given at any point in the application or employment process. Such tests must be given to all similarly situated applicants or employees regardless of disability. If such tests screen out or tend to screen out an individual with a disability or a class of individuals with disabilities, the employer would have to demonstrate that the test is job-related and consistent with business necessity and that performance cannot be achieved with reasonable accommodation. (See § 1630.9 Not Making Reasonable Accommodation: Process of Determining the Appropriate Reasonable Accommodation).

As previously noted, collecting information and inviting individuals to identify themselves as individuals with disabilities as required to satisfy the affirmative action requirements of section 503 of the Rehabilitation Act is not restricted by this part. (See § 1630.1 (b) and (c) Applicability and Construction).

Section 1630.14(b) Employment Entrance Examination

An employer is permitted to require postoffer medical examinations before the employee actually starts working. The employer may condition the offer of employment on the results of the examination, provided that all entering employees in the same job category are subjected to such an examination, regardless of disability, and that the confidentiality requirements specified in this part are met.

This provision recognizes that in many industries, such as air transportation or construction, applicants for certain positions are chosen on the basis of many factors including physical and psychological criteria, some of which may be identified as a result of post-offer medical examinations given prior to entry on duty. Only those employees who meet the employer's physical and psychological criteria for the job, with or without reasonable accommodation, will be qualified to receive confirmed offers of employment and begin working.

Medical examinations permitted by this section are not required to be job-related and consistent with business necessity. However, if an employer withdraws an offer of employment because the medical examination reveals that the employee does not satisfy certain employment criteria, either the exclusionary criteria must not screen out or tend to screen out an individual with a disability or a class of individuals with disabilities, or they must be job-related and consistent with business necessity. As part of the showing that an exclusionary criteria is job-related and consistent with business necessity, the employer must also demonstrate that there is no reasonable accommodation that will enable the individual with a disability to perform the essential functions of the job. See Conference Report at 59-60; Senate Report at 39; House Labor Report at 73-74; House Judiciary Report at 43.

As an example, suppose an employer makes a conditional offer of employment to an applicant, and it is an essential function of the job that the incumbent be available to work every day for the next three months. An employment entrance examination then reveals that the applicant has a disabling impairment that, according to reasonable medical judgment that relies on the most current medical knowledge, will require treatment that will render the applicant unable to work for a portion of the three month period. Under these circumstances, the employer would be able to withdraw the employment offer without violating this part.

The information obtained in the course of a permitted entrance examination or inquiry is to be treated as a confidential medical record and may only be used in a manner not inconsistent with this part. State workers' compensation laws are not preempted by the ADA or this part. These laws require the collection of information from individuals for state administrative purposes that do not conflict with the ADA or this part. Consequently, employers or other covered entities may submit information to state workers' compensation offices or second injury funds in accordance with state workers' compensation laws without violating this part.

Consistent with this section and with § 1630.16(f) of this part, information obtained in the course of a permitted entrance examination or inquiry may be used for insurance purposes described in § 1630.16(f).

Section 1630.14(c) Examination of Employees

This provision permits employers to make inquiries or require medical examinations (fitness for duty exams) when there is a need to determine whether an employee is still able to perform the essential functions of his or her job. The provision permits employers or other covered entities to make inquiries or require medical examinations necessary to the reasonable accommodation process described in this part. This provision also permits periodic physicals to determine fitness for duty or other medical monitoring if such physicals or monitoring are required by medical standards or requirements established by Federal, state, or local law that are consistent with the ADA and this part (or in the case of a federal standard, with section 504 of the Rehabilitation Act) in that they are job-related and consistent with business necessity.

Such standards may include federal safety regulations that regulate bus and truck driver qualifications, as well as laws establishing medical requirements for pilots or other air transportation personnel. These standards also include health standards promulgated pursuant to the Occupational Safety and Health Act of 1970, the Federal Coal Mine Health and Safety Act of 1969, or other similar statutes that require that employees exposed to certain toxic and hazardous substances be medically monitored at specific intervals. See House Labor Report at 74-75.

The information obtained in the course of such examination or inquiries is to be treated as a confidential medical record and may only be used in a manner not inconsistent with this part.

Section 1630.14(d) Other Acceptable Examinations and Inquiries

Part 1630 permits voluntary medical examinations, including voluntary medical histories, as part of employee health programs. These programs often include, for example, medical screening for high blood pressure, weight control counseling, and cancer detection. Voluntary activities, such as blood pressure monitoring and the administering of prescription drugs, such as insulin, are also permitted. It should be noted, however, that the medical records developed in the course of such activities must be maintained in the confidential manner required by this part and must not be used for any purpose in violation of this part, such as limiting health insurance eligibility. House Labor Report at 75; House Judiciary Report at 43-44.

Section 1630.15 Defenses

The section on defenses in part 1630 is not intended to be exhaustive. However, it is intended to inform employers of some of the potential defenses available to a charge of discrimination under the ADA and this part.

Section 1630.15(a) Disparate Treatment Defenses

The "traditional" defense to a charge of disparate treatment under title VII, as expressed in *McDonnell Douglas Corp. v. Green,* 411 U.S. 792 (1973), *Texas Department of Community Affairs v. Burdine,* 450 U.S. 248 (1981), and their progeny, may be applicable to charges of disparate treatment brought under the ADA. See *Prewitt v. U.S. Postal Service,* 662 F.2d 292 (5th Cir. 1981). [Editorial Note: For a summary of *Prewitt,* see the **Cases interpreting § 501 of the Rehabilitation Act of 1973** section of this book.] Disparate treatment means, with respect to title I of the ADA, that an individual was treated differently on the basis of his or her disability. For example, disparate treatment has occurred where an employer excludes an employee with a severe facial disfigurement from staff meetings because the employer does not like to look at the employee. The individual is being treated differently because of the employer's attitude towards his or her perceived disability. Disparate treatment has also occurred where an employer has a policy of not hiring individuals with AIDS regardless of the individuals' qualifications.

The crux of the defense to this type of charge is that the individual was treated differently not because of his or her disability but for a legitimate nondiscriminatory reason such as poor performance unrelated to the individual's disability. The fact that the individual's disability is not covered by the employer's current insurance plan or would cause the employer's insurance premiums or workers' compensation costs to increase, would not be a legitimate nondiscriminatory reason justifying disparate treatment of an individual with a disability. Senate Report at 85; House Labor Report at 136 and House Judiciary Report at 70. The defense of a legitimate nondiscriminatory reason is rebutted if the alleged nondiscriminatory reason is shown to be pretextual.

Section 1630.15 (b) and (c) Disparate Impact Defenses

Disparate impact means, with respect to title I of the ADA and this part, that uniformly applied criteria have an adverse impact on an individual with a disability or a disproportionately negative impact on a class of individuals with disabilities. Section 1630.15(b) clarifies that an employer may use selection criteria that have such a disparate impact, *i.e.,* that screen out or tend to screen out an individual with a disability or a class of individuals with disabilities only when they are job-related and consistent with business necessity.

For example, an employer interviews two candidates for a position, one of whom is blind. Both are equally qualified. The employer decides that while it is not essential to the job it would be convenient to have an employee who has a driver's license and so could occasionally be asked to run errands by car. The employer hires the individual who is sighted because this individual has a driver's license. This is an example of a uniformly applied criterion, having a driver's permit, that screens out an individual who has a disability that makes it impossible to obtain a driver's permit. The employer would, thus, have to show that this criterion is job-related and consistent with business necessity. See House Labor Report at 55.

However, even if the criterion is job-related and consistent with business necessity, an employer could not exclude an individual with a disability if the criterion could be met or job performance accomplished with a reasonable accommodation. For example, suppose an employer requires, as part of its application process, an interview that is job-related and consistent with business necessity. The employer would not be able to refuse to hire a hearing impaired applicant because he or she could not be interviewed. This is so because an interpreter could be provided as a reasonable accommodation that would allow the individual to be interviewed, and thus satisfy the selection criterion.

With regard to safety requirements that screen out or tend to screen out an individual with a disability or a class of individuals with disabilities, an employer must demonstrate that the requirement, as applied to the individual, satisfies the "direct threat" standard in § 1630.2(r) in order to show that the requirement is job-related and consistent with business necessity.

Section 1630.15(c) clarifies that there may be uniformly applied standards, criteria and policies not relating to selection that may also screen out or tend to screen out an individual with a disability or a class of individuals with disabilities. Like selection criteria that have a disparate impact, non-selection criteria having such an impact may also have to be job-related and consistent with business necessity, subject to consideration of reasonable accommodation.

It should be noted, however, that some uniformly applied employment policies or practices, such as leave policies, are not subject to challenge under the adverse impact theory. "No-leave" policies (*e.g.,* no leave during the first six months of employment) are likewise not subject to challenge under the adverse impact theory. However, an employer, in spite of its "no-leave" policy, may, in appropriate circumstances, have to consider the provision of leave to an employee with a disability as a reasonable accommodation, unless the provision of leave would impose an undue hardship. See discussion at § 1630.5 Limiting, Segregating and Classifying, and § 1630.10 Qualification Standards, Tests, and Other Selection Criteria.

Section 1630.15(d) Defense to Not Making Reasonable Accommodation

An employer or other covered entity alleged to have discriminated because it did not make a reasonable accommodation, as required by this part, may offer as a defense that it would have been an undue hardship to make the accommodation.

It should be noted, however, that an employer cannot simply assert that a needed accommodation will cause it undue hardship, as defined in § 1630.2(p), and thereupon be relieved of the duty to provide accommodation. Rather, an employer will have to present evidence and demonstrate that the accommodation will, in fact, cause it undue hardship. Whether a particular accommodation will impose an undue hardship for a particular employer is determined on a case by case basis. Consequently, an accommodation that poses an undue hardship for one employer at a particular time may not pose an undue hardship for another employer, or even for the same employer at another time. Likewise, an accommodation that poses an undue hardship for one employer in a particular job setting, such as a temporary construction worksite, may not pose an undue hardship for another employer, or even for the same employer at a permanent worksite. See House Judiciary Report at 42.

The concept of undue hardship that has evolved under section 504 of the Rehabilitation Act and is embodied in this part is unlike the "undue hardship" defense associated with the provision of religious accommodation under title VII of the Civil Rights Act of 1964. To demonstrate undue hardship pursuant to the ADA and this part, an employer must show substantially more difficulty or expense than would be needed to satisfy the "de minimis" title VII standard of undue hardship. For example, to demonstrate that the cost of an accommodation poses an undue hardship, an employer would have to show that the cost is undue as compared to the employer's budget. Simply comparing the cost of the accommodation to the salary of the individual with a disability in need of the accommodation will not suffice. Moreover, even if it is determined that the cost of an accommodation would unduly burden an employer, the employer cannot avoid making the accommodation if the individual with a disability can arrange to cover that portion of the cost that rises to the undue hardship level, or can otherwise arrange to provide the accommodation. Under such circumstances, the necessary accommodation would no longer pose an undue hardship. See Senate Report at 36; House Labor Report at 68-69; House Judiciary Report at 40-41.

Excessive cost is only one of several possible bases upon which an employer might be able to demonstrate undue hardship. Alternatively, for example, an employer could demonstrate that the provision of a particular accommodation would be unduly disruptive to its other employees or to the functioning of its business. The terms of a collective bargaining agreement may be relevant to this determination. By way of illustration, an employer would likely be able to show undue hardship if the employer could show that the requested accommodation of the upward adjustment of the business' thermostat would result in it becoming unduly hot for its other employees, or for its patrons or customers. The employer would thus not have to provide this accommodation. However, if there were an alternate accommodation that would not result in undue hardship, the employer would have to provide that accommodation.

It should be noted, moreover, that the employer would not be able to show undue hardship if the disruption to its employees were the result of those employees' fears or prejudices toward the individual's disability and not the result of the provision of the accommodation. Nor would the employer be able to demonstrate undue hardship by showing that the provision of the accommodation has a negative impact on the morale of its other employees but not on the ability of these employees to perform their jobs.

Section 1630.15(e) Defense—Conflicting Federal Laws and Regulations

There are several Federal laws and regulations that address medical standards and safety requirements. If the alleged discriminatory action was taken in compliance with another Federal law or regulation, the employer may offer its obligation to comply with the conflicting standard as a defense. The employer's defense of a conflicting Federal requirement or regulation may be rebutted by a showing of pretext, or by showing that the Federal standard did not require the discriminatory action, or that there was a nonexclusionary means to comply with the standard that would not conflict with this part. See House Labor Report at 74.

Section 1630.16 Specific Activities Permitted

Section 1630.16(a) Religious Entities

Religious organizations are not exempt from title I of the ADA or this part. A religious corporation, association, educational institution, or society may give a preference in employment to individuals of the particular religion, and may require that applicants and employees conform to the religious tenets of the organization. However, a religious organization may not discriminate against an individual who satisfies the permitted religious criteria because that individual is disabled. The religious entity, in other words, is required to consider qualified individuals with disabilities who satisfy the permitted religious criteria on an equal basis with qualified individuals without disabilities who similarly satisfy the religious criteria. See Senate Report at 42: House Labor Report at 76-77; House Judiciary Report at 46.

Section 1630.16(b) Regulation of Alcohol and Drugs

This provision permits employers to establish or comply with certain standards regulating the use of drugs and alcohol in the workplace. It also allows employers to hold alcoholics and persons who engage in the illegal use of drugs to the same performance and conduct standards to which it holds all of its other employees. Individuals disabled by alcoholism are entitled to the same protections accorded other individuals with disabilities under this part. As noted above, individuals currently engaging in the illegal use of drugs are not individuals with disabilities for purposes of part 1630 when the employer acts on the basis of such use.

Section 1630.16(c) Drug Testing

This provision reflects title I's neutrality toward testing for the illegal use of drugs. Such drug tests are neither encouraged, authorized nor prohibited. The results of such drug tests may be used as a basis for disciplinary action. Tests for the illegal use of drugs are not considered medical examinations for purposes of this part. If the results reveal information about an individual's medical condition beyond whether the individual is currently engaging in the illegal use of drugs, this additional information is to be treated as a confidential medical record. For example, if a test for the illegal use of drugs reveals the presence of a controlled substance that has been lawfully prescribed for a particular medical condition, this information is to be treated as a confidential medical record. See House Labor Report at 79; House Judiciary Report at 47.

Section 1630.16(e) Infectious and Communicable Diseases; Food Handling Jobs

This provision addressing food handling jobs applies the "direct threat" analysis to the particular situation of accommodating individuals with infectious or communicable diseases that are transmitted through the handling of food. The Department of Health and Human Services is to prepare a list of infectious and communicable diseases that are transmitted through the handling of food. If an individual with a disability has one of the listed diseases and works in or applies for a position in food handling, the employer must determine whether there is a reasonable accommodation that will eliminate the risk of transmitting the disease through the handling of food.

If there is an accommodation that will not pose an undue hardship, and that will prevent the transmission of the disease through the handling of food, the employer must provide the accommodation to the individual. The employer, under these circumstances, would not be permitted to discriminate against the individual because of the need to provide the reasonable accommodation and would be required to maintain the individual in the food handling job.

If no such reasonable accommodation is possible, the employer may refuse to assign, or to continue to assign the individual to a position involving food handling. This means that if such an individual is an applicant for a food handling position the employer is not required to hire the individual. However, if the individual is a current employee, the employer would be required to consider the accommodation of reassignment to a vacant position not involving food handling for which the individual is qualified. Conference Report at 61-63. (See 1630.2(r) Direct Threat).

Section 1630.16(f) Health Insurance, Life Insurance, and Other Benefit Plans

This provision is a limited exemption that is only applicable to those who establish, sponsor, observe or administer benefit plans, such as health and life insurance plans. It does not apply to those who establish, sponsor, observe or administer plans not involving benefits, such as liability insurance plans.

The purpose of this provision is to permit the development and administration of benefit plans in accordance with accepted principles of risk assessment. This provision is not intended to disrupt the current regulatory structure for self-insured employers. These employers may establish, sponsor, observe, or administer the terms of a bona fide benefit plan not subject to state laws that regulate insurance. This provision is also not intended to disrupt the current nature of insurance underwriting, or current insurance industry practices in sales, underwriting, pricing, administrative and other services, claims and similar insurance related activities based on classification of risks as regulated by the States.

The activities permitted by this provision do not violate part 1630 even if they result in limitations on individuals with disabilities, provided that these activities are not used as a subterfuge to evade the purposes of this part. Whether or not these activities are being used as a subterfuge is to be determined without regard to the date the insurance plan or employee benefit plan was adopted.

However, an employer or other covered entity cannot deny a qualified individual with a disability equal access to insurance or subject a qualified individual with a disability to different terms or conditions of insurance based on disability alone, if the disability does not pose increased risks. Part 1630 requires that decisions not based on risk classification be made in conformity with non-discrimination requirements. See Senate Report at 84-86; House Labor Report at 136-138; House Judiciary Report at 70-71. See the discussion of § 1630.5 Limiting, Segregating and Classifying.

28 CFR Part 35—Regulations to Implement the Nondiscrimination on the Basis of Disability in State And Local Government Services Provisions of the Americans with Disabilities Act

The following regulations were published on July 26, 1991 by the U.S. Department of Justice under ADA Title II. The regulations describe Title II procedural processes available through the U.S. Department of Justice and broadly prohibit discrimination on the basis of disability in all state and local government programs and activities.

* * *

APPENDIX A TO PART 35—PREAMBLE TO REGULATION ON NONDIS-CRIMINATION ON THE BASIS OF DISABILITY IN STATE AND LOCAL GOVERNMENT SERVICES (PUBLISHED July 26, 1991)

AUTHORITY: 5 U.S.C. 301; 28 U.S.C. 509, 510; Title II, Pub. L. 101-336 (42 U.S.C. 12134).

SOURCE: 56 FR 35716, July 26, 1991, unless otherwise noted.

Subpart A—General

§ 35.101 Purpose.

The purpose of this part is to effectuate subtitle A of title II of the Americans with Disabilities Act of 1990 (42 U.S.C. 12131), which prohibits discrimination on the basis of disability by public entities.

§ 35.102 Application.

(a) Except as provided in paragraph (b) of this section, this part applies to all services, programs, and activities provided or made available by public entities.

(b) To the extent that public transportation services, programs, and activities of public entities are covered by subtitle B of title II of the ADA (42 U.S.C. 12141), they are not subject to the requirements of this part.

§ 35.103 Relationship to other laws.

(a) *Rule of interpretation.* Except as otherwise provided in this part, this part shall not be construed to apply a lesser standard than the standards applied under title V of the Rehabilitation Act of 1973 (29 U.S.C. 791) or the regulations issued by Federal agencies pursuant to that title.

(b) *Other laws.* This part does not invalidate or limit the remedies, rights, and procedures of any other Federal laws, or State or local laws (including State common law) that provide greater or equal protection for the rights of individuals with disabilities or individuals associated with them.

§ 35.104 Definitions.

For purposes of this part, the term—

Act means the Americans with Disabilities Act (Pub. L. 101-336, 104 Stat. 327, 42 U.S.C. 12101-12213 and 47 U.S.C. 225 and 611).

Assistant Attorney General means the Assistant Attorney General, Civil Rights Division, United States Department of Justice.

Auxiliary aids and services includes—

(1) Qualified interpreters, notetakers, transcription services, written materials, telephone handset amplifiers, assistive listening devices, assistive listening systems, telephones compatible with hearing aids, closed caption decoders, open and closed captioning, telecommunications devices for deaf persons (TDD's), videotext displays, or other effective methods of making aurally delivered materials available to individuals with hearing impairments;

(2) Qualified readers, taped texts, audio recordings, Brailled materials, large print materials, or other effective methods of making visually delivered materials available to individuals with visual impairments;

(3) Acquisition or modification of equipment or devices; and

(4) Other similar services and actions.

Complete complaint means a written statement that contains the complainant's name and address and describes the public entity's alleged discriminatory action in sufficient detail to inform the agency of the nature and date of the alleged violation of this part. It shall be signed by the complainant or by someone authorized to do so on his or her behalf. Complaints filed on behalf of classes or third parties shall describe or identify (by name, if possible) the alleged victims of discrimination.

Current illegal use of drugs means illegal use of drugs that occurred recently enough to justify a reasonable belief that a person's drug use is current or that continuing use is a real and ongoing problem.

Designated agency means the Federal agency designated under subpart G of this part to oversee compliance activities under this part for particular components of State and local governments.

Disability means, with respect to an individual, a physical or mental impairment that substantially limits one or more of the major life activities of such individual; a record of such an impairment; or being regarded as having such an impairment.

(1)(i) The phrase *physical or mental impairment* means—

(A) Any physiological disorder or condition, cosmetic disfigurement, or anatomical loss affecting one or more of the following body systems: Neurological, musculoskeletal, special sense organs, respiratory (including speech organs), cardiovascular, reproductive, digestive, genitourinary, hemic and lymphatic, skin, and endocrine:

(B) Any mental or psychological disorder such as mental retardation, organic brain syndrome, emotional or mental illness, and specific learning disabilities.

(ii) The phrase *physical or mental impairment* includes, but is not limited to, such contagious and noncontagious diseases and conditions as orthopedic, visual, speech and hearing impairments, cerebral palsy, epilepsy, muscular dystrophy, multiple sclerosis, cancer, heart disease, diabetes, mental retardation, emotional illness, specific learning disabilities, HIV disease (whether symptomatic or asymptomatic), tuberculosis, drug addiction, and alcoholism.

(iii) The phrase *physical or mental impairment* does not include homosexuality or bisexuality.

(2) The phrase *major life activities* means functions such as caring for one's self, performing manual tasks, walking, seeing, hearing, speaking, breathing, learning, and working.

(3) The phrase *has a record of such an impairment* means has a history of, or has been misclassified as having, a mental or physical impairment that substantially limits one or more major life activities.

(4) The phrase *is regarded as having an impairment means—*

(i) Has a physical or mental impairment that does not substantially limit major life activities but that is treated by a public entity as constituting such a limitation;

(ii) Has a physical or mental impairment that substantially limits major life activities only as a result of the attitudes of others toward such impairment; or

(iii) Has none of the impairments defined in paragraph (1) of this definition but is treated by a public entity as having such an impairment.

(5) The term *disability* does not include—

(i) Transvestism, transsexualism, pedophilia, exhibitionism, voyeurism, gender identity disorders not resulting from physical impairments, or other sexual behavior disorders:

(ii) Compulsive gambling, kleptomania, or pyromania; or

(iii) Psychoactive substance use disorders resulting from current illegal use of drugs.

Drug means a controlled substance, as defined in schedules I through V of section 202 of the Controlled Substances Act (21 U.S.C. 812).

Facility means all or any portion of buildings, structures, sites, complexes, equipment, rolling stock or other conveyances, roads, walks, passageways, parking lots, or other real or personal property, including the site where the building, property, structure, or equipment is located.

Historic preservation programs means programs conducted by a public entity that have preservation of historic properties as a primary purpose.

Historic Properties means those properties that are listed or eligible for listing in the National Register of Historic Places or properties designated as historic under State or local law.

Illegal use of drugs means the use of one or more drugs, the possession or distribution of which is unlawful under the Controlled Substances Act (21 U.S.C. 812). The term *illegal use of drugs* does not include the use of a drug taken under supervision by a licensed health care professional, or other uses authorized by the Controlled Substances Act or other provisions of Federal law.

Individual with a disability means a person who has a disability. The term *individual with a disability* does not include an individual who is currently engaging in the illegal use of drugs, when the public entity acts on the basis of such use.

Public entity means—(1) Any State or local government;

(2) Any department, agency, special purpose district, or other instrumentality of a State or States or local government; and

(3) The National Railroad Passenger Corporation, and any commuter authority (as defined in section 103(8) of the Rail Passenger Service Act).

Qualified individual with a disability means an individual with a disability who, with or without reasonable modifications to rules, policies, or practices, the removal of architectural, communication, or transportation barriers, or the provision of auxiliary aids and services, meets the essential eligibility requirements for the receipt of services or the participation in programs or activities provided by a public entity.

Qualified interpreter means an interpreter who is able to interpret effectively, accurately, and impartially both receptively and expressively, using any necessary specialized vocabulary.

Section 504 means section 504 of the Rehabilitation Act of 1973 (Pub. L. 93-112, 87 Stat. 394 (29 U.S.C. 794)), as amended.

State means each of the several States, the District of Columbia, the Commonwealth of Puerto Rico, Guam, American Samoa, the Virgin Islands, the Trust Territory of the Pacific Islands, and the Commonwealth of the Northern Mariana Islands.

§ 35.105 Self-evaluation.

(a) A public entity shall, within one year of the effective date of this part, evaluate its current services, policies, and practices, and the effects thereof, that do not or may not meet the requirements of this part and, to the extent modification of any such services, policies, and practices is required, the public entity shall proceed to make the necessary modifications.

(b) A public entity shall provide an opportunity to interested persons, including individuals with disabilities or organizations representing individuals with disabilities, to participate in the self-evaluation process by submitting comments.

(c) A public entity that employs 50 or more persons shall, for at least three years following completion of the self-evaluation, maintain on file and make available for public inspection:

(1) A list of the interested persons consulted;

(2) A description of areas examined and any problems identified; and

(3) A description of any modifications made.

(d) If a public entity has already complied with the self-evaluation requirement of a regulation implementing section 504 of the Rehabilitation Act of 1973, then the requirements of this section shall apply only to those policies and practices that were not included in the previous self-evaluation.

§ 35.106 Notice.

A public entity shall make available to applicants, participants, beneficiaries, and other interested persons information regarding the provisions of this part and its applicability to the services, programs, or activities of the public entity, and make such information available to them in such manner as the head of the entity finds necessary to apprise such persons of the protections against discrimination assured them by the Act and this part.

§ 35.107 Designation of responsible employee and adoption of grievance procedures.

(a) *Designation of responsible employee.* A public entity that employs 50 or more persons shall designate at least one employee to coordinate its efforts to comply with and carry out its responsibilities under this part, including any investigation of any complaint communicated to it alleging its noncompliance with this part or alleging any actions that would be prohibited by this part. The public entity shall make available to all interested individuals the name, office address, and telephone number of the employee or employees designated pursuant to this paragraph.

(b) *Complaint procedure.* A public entity that employs 50 or more persons shall adopt and publish grievance procedures providing for prompt and equitable resolution of complaints alleging any action that would be prohibited by this part.

§§ 35.108—35.129 [Reserved]

Subpart B—General Requirements

§ 35.130 General prohibitions against discrimination.

(a) No qualified individual with a disability shall, on the basis of disability, be excluded from participation in or be denied the benefits of the services, programs, or activities of a public entity, or be subjected to discrimination by any public entity.

(b) (1) A public entity, in providing any aid, benefit, or service, may not, directly or through contractual, licensing, or other arrangements, on the basis of disability—

(i) Deny a qualified individual with a disability the opportunity to participate in or benefit from the aid, benefit, or service;

(ii) Afford a qualified individual with a disability an opportunity to participate in or benefit from the aid, benefit, or service that is not equal to that afforded others;

(iii) Provide a qualified individual with a disability with an aid, benefit, or service that is not as effective in affording equal opportunity to obtain the same result, to gain the same benefit, or to reach the same level of achievement as that provided to others;

(iv) Provide different or separate aids, benefits, or services to individuals with disabilities or to any class of individuals with disabilities than is provided to others unless such action is necessary to provide qualified individuals with disabilities with aids, benefits, or services that are as effective as those provided to others;

(v) Aid or perpetuate discrimination against a qualified individual with a disability by providing significant assistance to an agency, organization, or person that discriminates on the basis of disability in providing any aid, benefit, or service to beneficiaries of the public entity's program;

(vi) Deny a qualified individual with a disability the opportunity to participate as a member of planning or advisory boards;

(vii) Otherwise limit a qualified individual with a disability in the enjoyment of any right, privilege, advantage, or opportunity enjoyed by others receiving the aid, benefit, or service.

(2) A public entity may not deny a qualified individual with a disability the opportunity to participate in services, programs, or activities that are not separate or different, despite the existence of permissibly separate or different programs or activities.

(3) A public entity may not, directly or through contractual or other arrangements, utilize criteria or methods of administration:

(i) That have the effect of subjecting qualified individuals with disabilities to discrimination on the basis of disability;

(ii) That have the purpose or effect of defeating or substantially impairing accomplishment of the objectives of the public entity's program with respect to individuals with disabilities; or

(iii) That perpetuate the discrimination of another public entity if both public entities are subject to common administrative control or are agencies of the same State.

(4) A public entity may not, in determining the site or location of a facility, make selections—

(i) That have the effect of excluding individuals with disabilities from, denying them the benefits of, or otherwise subjecting them to discrimination; or

(ii) That have the purpose or effect of defeating or substantially impairing the accomplishment or the objectives of the service, program, or activity with respect to individuals with disabilities.

(5) A public entity, in the selection of procurement contractors, may not use criteria that subject qualified individuals with disabilities to discrimination on the basis of disability.

(6) A public entity may not administer a licensing or certification program in a manner that subjects qualified individuals with disabilities to discrimination on the basis of disability, nor may a public entity establish requirements for the programs or activities of licensees or certified entities that subject qualified individuals with disabilities to discrimination on the basis of disability. The programs or activities of entities that are licensed or certified by a public entity are not, themselves, covered by this part.

(7) A public entity shall make reasonable modifications in policies, practices, or procedures when the modifications are necessary to avoid discrimination on the basis of disability, unless the public entity can demonstrate that making the modifications would fundamentally alter the nature of the service, program, or activity.

(8) A public entity shall not impose or apply eligibility criteria that screen out or tend to screen out an individual with a disability or any class of individuals with disabilities from fully and equally enjoying any service, program, or activity, unless such criteria can be shown to be necessary for the provision of the service, program, or activity being offered.

(c) Nothing in this part prohibits a public entity from providing benefits, services, or advantages to individuals with disabilities, or to a particular class of individuals with disabilities beyond those required by this part.

(d) A public entity shall administer services, programs, and activities in the most integrated setting appropriate to the needs of qualified individuals with disabilities.

(e)(1) Nothing in this part shall be construed to require an individual with a disability to accept an accommodation, aid, service, opportunity, or benefit provided under the ADA or this part which such individual chooses not to accept.

(2) Nothing in the Act or this part authorizes the representative or guardian of an individual with a disability to decline food, water, medical treatment, or medical services for that individual.

(f) A public entity may not place a surcharge on a particular individual with a disability or any group of individuals with disabilities to cover the costs of measures, such as the provision of auxiliary aids or program accessibility, that are required to provide that individual or group with the nondiscriminatory treatment required by the Act or this part.

(g) A public entity shall not exclude or otherwise deny equal services, programs, or activities to an individual or entity because of the known disability of an individual with whom the individual or entity is known to have a relationship or association.

§ 35.131 Illegal use of drugs.

(a) *General.* (1) Except as provided in paragraph (b) of this section, this part does not prohibit discrimination against an individual based on that individual's current illegal use of drugs.

(2) A public entity shall not discriminate on the basis of illegal use of drugs against an individual who is not engaging in current illegal use of drugs and who—

(i) Has successfully completed a supervised drug rehabilitation program or has otherwise been rehabilitated successfully;

(ii) Is participating in a supervised rehabilitation program; or

(iii) Is erroneously regarded as engaging in such use.

(b) *Health and drug rehabilitation services.* (1) A public entity shall not deny health services, or services provided in connection with drug rehabilitation, to an individual on the basis of that individual's current illegal use of drugs, if the individual is otherwise entitled to such services.

(2) A drug rehabilitation or treatment program may deny participation to individuals who engage in illegal use of drugs while they are in the program.

(c) *Drug testing.* (1) This part does not prohibit a public entity from adopting or administering reasonable policies or procedures, including but not limited to drug testing, designed to ensure that an individual who formerly engaged in the illegal use of drugs is not now engaging in current illegal use of drugs.

(2) Nothing in paragraph (c) of this section shall be construed to encourage, prohibit, restrict, or authorize the conduct of testing for the illegal use of drugs.

§ 35.132 Smoking.

This part does not preclude the prohibition of, or the imposition of restrictions on, smoking in transportation covered by this part.

§ 35.133 Maintenance of accessible features.

(a) A public accommodation shall maintain in operable working condition those features of facilities and equipment that are required to be readily accessible to and usable by persons with disabilities by the Act or this part.

(b) This section does not prohibit isolated or temporary interruptions in service or access due to maintenance or repairs.

35.134 Retaliation or coercion.

(a) No private or public entity shall discriminate against any individual because that individual has opposed any act or practice made unlawful by this part, or because that individual made a charge, testified, assisted, or participated in any manner in an investigation, proceeding, or hearing under the Act or this part.

(b) No private or public entity shall coerce, intimidate, threaten, or interfere with any individual in the exercise or enjoyment of, or on account of his or her having exercised or enjoyed, or on account of his or her having aided or encouraged any other individual in the exercise or enjoyment of, any right granted or protected by the Act or this part.

§ 35.135 Personal devices and services.

This part does not require a public entity to provide to individuals with disabilities personal devices, such as wheelchairs; individually prescribed devices, such as prescription eyeglasses or hearing aids; readers for personal use or study; or services of a personal nature including assistance in eating, toileting, or dressing.

§§ 35.136—35.139 [Reserved]

Subpart C—Employment

§ 35.140 Employment discrimination prohibited.

(a) No qualified individual with a disability shall, on the basis of disability, be subjected to discrimination in employment under any service, program, or activity conducted by a public entity.

(b)(1) For purposes of this part, the requirements of title I of the Act, as established by the regulations of the Equal Employment Opportunity Commission in 29 CFR part 1630, apply to employment in any service, program, or activity conducted by a public entity if that public entity is also subject to the jurisdiction of title I.

(2) For the purposes of this part, the requirements of section 504 of the Rehabilitation Act of 1973, as established by the regulations of the Department of Justice in 28 CFR part 41, as those requirements pertain to employment, apply to employment in any service, program, or activity conducted by a public entity if that public entity is not also subject to the jurisdiction of title I.

§§ 35.141—35.148 [Reserved]

Subpart D—Program Accessibility

§ 35.149 Discrimination prohibited.

Except as otherwise provided in § 35.150, no qualified individual with a disability shall, because a public entity's facilities are inaccessible to or unusable by individuals with disabilities, be excluded from participation in, or be denied the benefits of the services, programs, or activities of a public entity, or be subjected to discrimination by any public entity.

§ 35.150 Existing facilities.

(a) *General.* A public entity shall operate each service, program, or activity so that the service, program, or activity, when viewed in its entirety, is readily accessible to and usable by individuals with disabilities. This paragraph does not—

(1) Necessarily require a public entity to make each of its existing facilities accessible to and usable by individuals with disabilities;

(2) Require a public entity to take any action that would threaten or destroy the historic significance of an historic property; or

(3) Require a public entity to take any action that it can demonstrate would result in a fundamental alteration in the nature of a service, program, or activity or in undue financial and administrative burdens. In those circumstances where personnel of the public entity believe that the proposed action would fundamentally alter the service, program, or activity or would result in undue financial and administrative burdens, a public entity has the burden of proving that compliance with § 35.150(a) of this part would result in such alteration or burdens. The decision that compliance would result in such alteration or burdens must be made by the head of a public entity or his or her designee after considering all resources available for use in the funding and operation of the service, program, or activity, and must be accompanied by a written statement of the reasons for reaching that conclusion. If an action would result in such an alteration or such burdens, a public entity shall take any other action that would not result in such an alteration or such burdens but would nevertheless ensure that individuals with disabilities receive the benefits or services provided by the public entity.

(b) *Methods*—(1) *General.* A public entity may comply with the requirements of this section through such means as redesign of equipment, reassignment of services to accessible buildings, assignment of aides to beneficiaries, home visits, delivery of services at alternate accessible sites, alteration of existing facilities and construction of new facilities, use of accessible rolling stock or other conveyances, or any other methods that result in making its services, programs, or activities readily accessible to and usable by individuals with disabilities. A public entity is not required to make structural changes in existing facilities where other methods are effective in achieving compliance with this section. A public entity, in making alterations to existing buildings, shall meet the accessibility requirements of 35.151. In choosing among available methods for meeting the requirements of this section, a public entity shall give priority to those methods that offer services, programs, and activities to qualified individuals with disabilities in the most integrated setting appropriate.

(2) *Historic preservation programs.* In meeting the requirements of 35.150(a) in historic preservation programs, a public entity shall give priority to methods that provide physical access to individuals with disabilities. In cases where a physical alteration to an historic property is not required because of paragraph (a)(2) or (a)(3) of this section, alternative methods of achieving program accessibility include—

(i) Using audio-visual materials and devices to depict those portions of an historic property that cannot otherwise be made accessible;

(ii) Assigning persons to guide individuals with handicaps into or through portions of historic properties that cannot otherwise be made accessible; or

(iii) Adopting other innovative methods.

(c) *Time period for compliance.* Where structural changes in facilities are undertaken to comply with the obligations established under this section, such changes shall be made within three years of January 26, 1992, but in any event as expeditiously as possible.

(d) *Transition plan.* (1) In the event that structural changes to facilities will be undertaken to achieve program accessibility, a public entity that employs 50 or more persons shall develop, within six months of January 26, 1992, a transition plan setting forth the steps necessary to complete such changes. A public entity shall provide an opportunity to interested persons, including individuals with disabilities or organizations representing individuals with disabilities, to participate in the development of the transition plan by submitting comments. A copy of the transition plan shall be made available for public inspection.

(2) If a public entity has responsibility or authority over streets, roads, or walkways, its transition plan shall include a schedule for providing curb ramps or other sloped areas where pedestrian walks cross curbs, giving priority to walkways serving entities covered by the Act, including State and local government offices and facilities, transportation, places of public accommodation, and employers, followed by walkways serving other areas.

(3) The plan shall, at a minimum—

(i) Identify physical obstacles in the public entity's facilities that limit the accessibility of its programs or activities to individuals with disabilities;

(ii) Describe in detail the methods that will be used to make the facilities accessible;

(iii) Specify the schedule for taking the steps necessary to achieve compliance with this section and, if the time period of the transition plan is longer than one year, identify steps that will be taken during each year of the transition period; and

(iv) Indicate the official responsible for implementation of the plan.

(4) If a public entity has already complied with the transition plan requirement of a Federal agency regulation implementing section 504 of the Rehabilitation Act of 1973, then the requirements of this paragraph (d) shall apply only to those policies and practices that were not included in the previous transition plan.

§ 35.151 New construction and alterations.

(a) *Design and construction.* Each facility or part of a facility constructed by, on behalf of, or for the use of a public entity shall be designed and constructed in such manner that the facility or part of the facility is readily accessible to and usable by individuals with disabilities, if the construction was commenced after January 26, 1992.

(b) *Alteration.* Each facility or part of a facility altered by, on behalf of, or for the use of a public entity in a manner that affects or could affect the usability of the facility or part of the facility shall, to the maximum extent feasible, be altered in such manner that the altered portion of the facility is readily accessible to and usable by individuals with disabilities, if the alteration was commenced after January 26, 1992.

(c) *Accessibility standards.* Design, construction, or alteration of facilities in conformance with the Uniform Federal Accessibility Standards (UFAS) (appendix A to 41 CFR part 101-19.6) or with the Americans with Disabilities Act Accessibility Guidelines for Buildings and Facilities (ADAAG) (appendix A to 28 CFR part 36) shall be deemed to comply with the requirements of this section with respect to those facilities, except that the elevator exemption contained at section 4.1.3(5) and section 4.1.6(1)(j) of ADAAG shall not apply. Departures from particular requirements of either standard by the use of other methods shall be permitted when it is clearly evident that equivalent access to the facility or part of the facility is thereby provided.

(d) *Alterations: Historic properties.* (1) Alterations to historic properties shall comply, to the maximum extent feasible, with section 4.1.7 of UFAS or section 4.1.7 of ADAAG.

(2) If it is not feasible to provide physical access to an historic property in a manner that will not threaten or destroy the historic significance of the building or facility, alternative methods of access shall be provided pursuant to the requirements of § 35.150.

(e) *Curb ramps.* (1) Newly constructed or altered streets, roads, and highways must contain curb ramps or other sloped areas at any intersection having curbs or other barriers to entry from a street level pedestrian walkway.

(2) Newly constructed or altered street level pedestrian walkways must contain curb ramps or other sloped areas at intersections to streets, roads, or highways.

§§ 35.152—35.159 [Reserved]

Subpart E—Communications

§ 35.160 General.

(a) A public entity shall take appropriate steps to ensure that communications with applicants, participants, and members of the public with disabilities are as effective as communications with others.

(b)(1) A public entity shall furnish appropriate auxiliary aids and services where necessary to afford an individual with a disability an equal opportunity to participate in, and enjoy the benefits of, a service, program, or activity conducted by a public entity.

(2) In determining what type of auxiliary aid and service is necessary, a public entity shall give primary consideration to the requests of the individual with disabilities.

§ 35.161 Telecommunication devices for the deaf (TDD's).

Where a public entity communicates by telephone with applicants and beneficiaries, TDD's or equally effective telecommunication systems shall be used to communicate with individuals with impaired hearing or speech.

§ 35.162 Telephone emergency services.

Telephone emergency services, including 911 services, shall provide direct access to individuals who use TDD's and computer modems.

§ 35.163 information and signage.

(a) A public entity shall ensure that interested persons, including persons with impaired vision or hearing, can obtain information as to the existence and location of accessible services, activities, and facilities.

(b) A public entity shall provide signage at all inaccessible entrances to each of its facilities, directing users to an accessible entrance or to a location at which they can obtain information about accessible facilities. The international symbol for accessibility shall be used at each accessible entrance of a facility.

§ 35.164 Duties.

This subpart does not require a public entity to take any action that it can demonstrate would result in a fundamental alteration in the nature of a service, program, or activity or in undue financial and administrative burdens. In those circumstances where personnel of the public entity believe that the proposed action would fundamentally alter the service, program, or activity or would result in undue financial and administrative burdens, a public entity has the burden of proving that compliance with this subpart would result in such alteration or burdens. The decision that compliance would result in such alteration or burdens must be made by the head of the public entity or his or her designee after considering all resources available for use in the funding and operation of the service, program, or activity and must be accompanied by a written statement of the reasons for reaching that conclusion. If an action required to comply with this subpart would result in such an alteration or such burdens, a public entity shall take any other action that would not result in such an alteration or such burdens but would nevertheless ensure that, to the maximum extent possible, individuals with disabilities receive the benefits or services provided by the public entity.

§§ 35.165—35.169 [Reserved]

Subpart F—Compliance Procedures

§ 35.170 Complaints.

(a) *Who may file.* An individual who believes that he or she or a specific class of individuals has been subjected to discrimination on the basis of disability by a public entity may, by himself or herself or by an authorized representative, file a complaint under this part.

(b) *Time for filing.* A complaint must be filed not later than 180 days from the date of the alleged discrimination, unless the time for filing is extended by the designated agency for good cause shown. A complaint is deemed to be filed under this section on the date it is first filed with any Federal agency.

(c) *Where to file.* An individual may file a complaint with any agency that he or she believes to be the appropriate agency designated under subpart G of this part, or with any agency that provides funding to the public entity that is the subject of the complaint, or with the Department of Justice for referral as provided in § 35.171(a)(2).

§ 35.171 Acceptance of complaints.

(a) *Receipt of complaints.* (1)(i) Any Federal agency that receives a complaint of discrimination on the basis of disability by a public entity shall promptly review the complaint to determine whether it has jurisdiction over the complaint under section 504.

(ii) If the agency does not have section 504 jurisdiction, it shall promptly determine whether it is the designated agency under subpart G of this part responsible for complaints filed against that public entity.

(2)(i) If an agency other than the Department of Justice determines that it does not have section 504 jurisdiction and is not the designated agency, it shall promptly refer the complaint, and notify the complainant that it is referring the complaint to the Department of Justice.

(ii) When the Department of Justice receives a complaint for which it does not have jurisdiction under section 504 and is not the designated agency, it shall refer the complaint to an agency that does have jurisdiction under section 504 or to the appropriate agency designated in subpart G of this part or, in the case of an employment complaint that is also subject to title I of the Act, to the Equal Employment Opportunity Commission.

(3)(i) If the agency that receives a complaint has section 504 jurisdiction, it shall process the complaint according to its procedures for enforcing section 504.

(ii) If the agency that receives a complaint does not have section 504 jurisdiction, but is the designated agency, it shall process the complaint according to the procedures established by this subpart.

(b) *Employment complaints.* (1) If a complaint alleges employment discrimination subject to title I of the Act, and the agency has section 504 jurisdiction, the agency shall follow the procedures issued by the Department of Justice and the Equal Employment Opportunity Commission under section 107(b) of the Act.

(2) If a complaint alleges employment discrimination subject to title I of the Act, and the designated agency does not have section 504 jurisdiction, the agency shall refer the complaint to the Equal Employment Opportunity Commission for processing under title I of the Act.

(3) Complaints alleging employment discrimination subject to this part, but not to title I of the Act shall be processed in accordance with the procedures established by this subpart.

(c) *Complete complaints.* (1) A designated agency shall accept all complete complaints under this section and shall promptly notify the complainant and the public entity of the receipt and acceptance of the complaint.

(2) If the designated agency receives a complaint that is not complete, it shall notify the complainant and specify the additional information that is needed to make the complaint a complete complaint. If the complainant fails to complete the complaint, the designated agency shall close the complaint without prejudice.

§ 35.172 Resolution of complaints.

(a) The designated agency shall investigate each complete complaint, attempt informal resolution, and, if resolution is not achieved, issue to the complainant and the public entity a Letter of Findings that shall include—

(1) Findings of fact and conclusions of law;

(2) A description of a remedy for each violation found; and

(3) Notice of the rights available under paragraph (b) of this section.

(b) If the designated agency finds noncompliance, the procedures in §§ 35.173 and 35.174 shall be followed. At any time, the complainant may file a private suit pursuant to section 203 of the Act, whether or not the designated agency finds a violation.

§ 35.173 Voluntary compliance agreements.

(a) When the designated agency issues a noncompliance Letter of Findings, the designated agency shall—

(1) Notify the Assistant Attorney General by forwarding a copy of the Letter of Findings to the Assistant Attorney General; and

(2) Initiate negotiations with the public entity to secure compliance by voluntary means.

(b) Where the designated agency is able to secure voluntary compliance, the voluntary compliance agreement shall—

(1) Be in writing and signed by the parties;

(2) Address each cited violation;

(3) Specify the corrective or remedial action to be taken, within a stated period of time, to come into compliance;

(4) Provide assurance that discrimination will not recur; and

(5) Provide for enforcement by the Attorney General.

§ 35.174 Referral.

If the public entity declines to enter into voluntary compliance negotiations or if negotiations are unsuccessful, the designated agency shall refer the matter to the Attorney General with a recommendation for appropriate action.

§ 35.175 Attorney's fees.

In any action or administrative proceeding commenced pursuant to the Act or this part, the court or agency, in its discretion, may allow the prevailing party, other than the United States, a reasonable attorney's fee, including litigation expenses, and costs, and the United States shall be liable for the foregoing the same as a private individual.

§ 35.176 Alternative means of dispute resolution.

Where appropriate and to the extent authorized by law, the use of alternative means of dispute resolution, including settlement negotiations, conciliation, facilitation, mediation, factfinding, minitrials, and arbitration, is encouraged to resolve disputes arising under the Act and this part.

§ 35.177 Effect of unavailability of technical assistance.

A public entity shall not be excused from compliance with the requirements of this part because of any failure to receive technical assistance, including any failure in the development or dissemination of any technical assistance manual authorized by the Act.

§ **35.178 State immunity.**

A State shall not be immune under the eleventh amendment to the Constitution of the United States from an action in [a] Federal or State court of competent jurisdiction for a violation of this Act. In any action against a State for a violation of the requirements of this Act, remedies (including remedies both at law and in equity) are available for such a violation to the same extent as such remedies are available for such a violation in an action against any public or private entity other than a State.

§§ **35.179—35.189 [Reserved]**

Subpart G—Designated Agencies

§ **35.190 Designated agencies.**

(a) The Assistant Attorney General shall coordinate the compliance activities of Federal agencies with respect to State and local government components, and shall provide policy guidance and interpretations to designated agencies to ensure the consistent and effective implementation of the requirements of this part.

(b) The Federal agencies listed in paragraph (b)(1) through (8) of this section shall have responsibility for the implementation of subpart F of this part for components of State and local governments that exercise responsibilities, regulate, or administer services, programs, or activities in the following functional areas.

(1) *Department of Agriculture:* All programs, services, and regulatory activities relating to farming and the raising of livestock, including extension services.

(2) *Department of Education:* All programs, services, and regulatory activities relating to the operation of elementary and secondary education systems and institutions, institutions of higher education and vocational education (other than schools of medicine, dentistry, nursing, and other health-related schools), and libraries.

(3) *Department of Health and Human Services:* All programs, services, and regulatory activities relating to the provision of health care and social services, including schools of medicine, dentistry, nursing, and other health-related schools, the operation of health care and social service providers and institutions, including "grass-roots" and community services organizations and programs, and preschool and daycare programs.

(4) *Department of Housing and Urban Development:* All programs, services, and regulatory activities relating to state and local public housing, and housing assistance and referral.

(5) *Department of Interior.* All programs, services, and regulatory activities relating to lands and natural resources, including parks and recreation, water and waste management, environmental protection, energy, historic and cultural preservation, and museums.

(6) *Department of Justice:* All programs, services, and regulatory activities relating to law enforcement, public safety, and the administration of justice, including courts and correctional institutions; commerce and industry, including general economic development, banking and finance, consumer protection, insurance, and small business; planning, development, and regulation (unless assigned to other designated agencies); state and local government support services (e.g., audit, personnel, comptroller, administrative services); all other government functions not assigned to other designated agencies.

(7) *Department of Labor:* All programs, services, and regulatory activities relating to labor and the work force.

(8) *Department of Transportation:* All programs, services, and regulatory activities relating to transportation, including highways, public transportation, traffic management (non-law enforcement), automobile licensing and inspection, and driver licensing.

(c) Responsibility for the implementation of subpart F of this part for components of State or local governments that exercise responsibilities, regulate, or administer services, programs, or activities relating to functions not assigned to specific designated agencies by paragraph (b) of this section may be assigned to other specific agencies by the Department of Justice.

(d) If two or more agencies have apparent responsibility over a complaint, the Assistant Attorney General shall determine which one of the agencies shall be the designated agency for purposes of that complaint.

§§ 35.191—35.999 [Reserved]

APPENDIX A TO PART 35—PREAMBLE TO REGULATION ON NONDISCRIMINATION ON THE BASIS OF DISABILITY IN STATE AND LOCAL GOVERNMENT SERVICES (PUBLISHED JULY 26, 1991)

NOTE: For the convenience of the reader, this appendix contains the text of the preamble to the final regulation on nondiscrimination on the basis of disability in State and local government services beginning at the heading "Section-by-Section Analysis" and ending before "List of Subjects in 28 CFR Part 35" (56 FR 35696, July 26, 1991).

SECTION-BY-SECTION ANALYSIS

Subpart A—General

Section 35.101 Purpose

Section 35.101 states the purpose of the rule, which is to effectuate subtitle A of title II of the Americans with Disabilities Act of 1990 (the Act), which prohibits discrimination on the basis of disability by public entities. This part does not, however, apply to matters within the scope of the authority of the Secretary of Transportation under subtitle B of title II of the Act.

Section 35.102 Application

This provision specifies that, except as provided in paragraph (b), the regulation applies to all services, programs, and activities provided or made available by public entities, as that term is defined in § 35.104. Section 504 of the Rehabilitation Act of 1973 (29 U.S.C. 794), which prohibits discrimination on the basis of handicap in federally assisted programs and activities, already covers those programs and activities of public entities that receive Federal financial assistance. Title II of the ADA extends this prohibition of discrimination to include all services, programs, and activities provided or made available by State and local governments or any of their instrumentalities or agencies, regardless of the receipt of Federal financial assistance. Except as provided in § 35.134, this part does not apply to private entities.

The scope of title II's coverage of public entities is comparable to the coverage of Federal Executive agencies under the 1978 amendment to section 504, which extended section 504's application to all programs and activities "conducted by" Federal Executive agencies, in that title II applies to anything a public entity does. Title II coverage, however, is not limited to "Executive" agencies, but includes activities of the legislative and judicial branches of State and local governments. All governmental activities of public entities are covered, even if they are carried out by contractors. For example, a State is obligated by title II to ensure that the services, programs, and activities of a State park inn operated under contract by a private entity are in compliance with title II's requirements. The private entity operating the inn would also be subject to the obligations of public accommodations under title III of the Act and the Department's title III regulations at 28 CFR part 36.

Aside from employment, which is also covered by title I of the Act, there are two major categories of programs or activities covered by this regulation: those involving general public contact as part of ongoing operations of the entity and those directly administered by the entities for program beneficiaries and participants. Activities in the first category include communication with the public (telephone contacts, office walkins, or interviews) and the public's use of the entity's facilities. Activities in the second category include programs that provide State or local government services or benefits.

Paragraph (b) of § 35.102 explains that to the extent that the public transportation services, programs, and activities of public entities are covered by subtitle B of title II of the Act, they are subject to the regulation of the Department of Transportation (DOT) at 49 CFR part 37, and are not covered by this part. The Department of Transportation's ADA regulation establishes specific requirements for construction of transportation facilities and acquisition of vehicles. Matters not covered by subtitle B, such as the provision of auxiliary aids, are covered by this rule. For example, activities that are covered by the Department of Transportation's regulation implementing subtitle B are not required to be included in the self-evaluation required by § 35.105. In addition, activities not specifically addressed by DOT's ADA regulation may be covered by DOT's regulation implementing section 504 for its federally assisted programs and activities at 49 CFR part 27. Like other programs of public entities that are also recipients of Federal financial assistance, those programs would be covered by both the section 504 regulation and this part. Although airports operated by public entities are not subject to DOT's ADA regulation, they are subject to subpart A of title II and to this rule.

Some commenters asked for clarification about the responsibilities of public school systems under section 504 and the ADA with respect to programs, services, and activities that are not covered by the Individuals with Disabilities Education Act (IDEA), including, for example, programs open to parents or to the public, graduation ceremonies, parent-teacher organization meetings, plays and other events open to the public, and adult education classes. Public school systems must comply with the ADA in all of their services, programs, or activities, including those that are open to parents or to the public. For instance, public school systems must provide program accessibility to parents and guardians with disabilities to these programs, activities, or services, and appropriate auxiliary aids and services whenever necessary to ensure effective communication, as long as the provision of the auxiliary aids results neither in an undue burden or in a fundamental alteration of the program.

Section 35.103 Relationship to Other Laws

Section 35.103 is derived from sections 501 (a) and (b) of the ADA. Paragraph (a) of this section provides that, except as otherwise specifically provided by this part, title II of the ADA is not intended to apply lesser standards than are required under title V of the Rehabilitation Act of 1973, as amended (29 U.S.C. 790-94), or the regulations implementing that title. The standards of title V of the Rehabilitation Act apply for purposes of the ADA to the extent that the ADA has not explicitly adopted a different standard than title V. Because title II of the ADA essentially extends the antidiscrimination prohibition embodied in section 504 to all actions of State and local governments, the standards adopted in this part are generally the same as those required under section 504 for federally assisted programs. Title II, however, also incorporates those provisions of titles I and III of the ADA that are not inconsistent with the regulations implementing section 504. Judiciary Committee report. H.R. Rep. No. 485, 101st Cong., 2d Sess., pt. 3, at 51 (1990) (hereinafter "Judiciary report"); Education and Labor Committee report, H.R. Rep. No. 485, 101st Cong., 2d Sess., pt. 2, at 84 (1990) (hereinafter "Education and Labor report"). Therefore, this part also includes appropriate provisions derived from the regulations implementing those titles. The inclusion of specific language in this part, however, should not be interpreted as an indication that a requirement is not included under a regulation implementing section 504.

Paragraph (b) makes clear that Congress did not intend to displace any of the rights or remedies provided by other Federal laws (including section 504) or other State laws (including State common law) that provide greater or equal protection to individuals with disabilities. As discussed above, the standards adopted by title II of the ADA for State and local government services are generally the same as those required under section 504 for federally assisted programs and activities. Subpart F of the regulation establishes compliance procedures for processing complaints covered by both this part and section 504.

With respect to State law, a plaintiff may choose to pursue claims under a State law that does not confer greater substantive rights, or even confers lower substantive rights, if the alleged violation is protected under the alternative law and the remedies are greater. For example, a person with a physical disability could seek damages under a State law that allows compensatory and punitive damages for discrimination on the basis of physical disability, but not on the basis of mental disability. In that situation, the State law would provide narrower coverage, by excluding mental disabilities, but broader remedies, and an individual covered by both laws could choose to bring an action under both laws. Moreover, State tort claims confer greater remedies and are not preempted by the ADA. A plaintiff may join a State tort claim to a case brought under the ADA. In such a case, the plaintiff must, of course, prove all the elements of the State tort claim in order to prevail under that cause of action.

Section 35.104 Definitions

"Act." The word "Act" is used in this part to refer to the Americans with Disabilities Act of 1990, Public Law 101-336, which is also referred to as the "ADA."

"Assistant Attorney General." The term "Assistant Attorney General" refers to the Assistant Attorney General of the Civil Rights Division of the Department of Justice.

"Auxiliary aids and services." Auxiliary aids and services include a wide range of services and devices for ensuring effective communication. The proposed definition in § 35.104 provided a list of examples of auxiliary aids and services that were taken from the definition of auxiliary aids and services in section 3(1) of the ADA and were supplemented by examples from regulations implementing section 504 in federally conducted programs (see 28 CFR 39.103).

A substantial number of commenters suggested that additional examples be added to this list. The Department has added several items to this list but wishes to clarify that the list is not an all-inclusive or exhaustive catalogue of possible or available auxiliary aids or services. It is not possible to provide an exhaustive list, and an attempt to do so would omit the new devices that will become available with emerging technology.

Subparagraph (1) lists several examples, which would be considered auxiliary aids and services to make aurally delivered materials available to individuals with hearing impairments. The Department has changed the phrase used in the proposed rules, "orally delivered materials," to the statutory phrase, "aurally delivered materials," to track section 3 of the ADA and to include non-verbal sounds and alarms, and computer generated speech.

The Department has added videotext displays, transcription services, and closed and open captioning to the list of examples. Videotext displays have become an important means of accessing auditory communications through a public address system. Transcription services are used to relay aurally delivered material almost simultaneously in written form to persons who are deaf or hearing-impaired. This technology is often used at conferences, conventions, and hearings. While the proposed rule expressly included television decoder equipment as an auxiliary aid or service, it did not mention captioning itself. The final rule rectifies this omission by mentioning both closed and open captioning.

Several persons and organizations requested that the Department replace the term "telecommunications devices for deaf persons" or "TDD's" with the term "text telephone." The Department has declined to do so. The Department is aware that the Architectural and Transportation Barriers Compliance Board (ATBCB) has used the phrase "text telephone" in lieu of the statutory term "TDD" in its final accessibility guidelines. Title IV of the ADA, however, uses the term "Telecommunications Device for the Deaf" and the Department believes it would be inappropriate to abandon this statutory term at this time.

Several commenters urged the Department to include in the definition of "auxiliary aids and services" devices that are now available or that may become available with emerging technology. The Department declines to do so in the rule. The Department, however, emphasizes that, although the definition would include "state of the art" devices, public entities are not required to use the newest or most advanced technologies as long as the auxiliary aid or service that is selected affords effective communication.

Subparagraph (2) lists examples of aids and services for making visually delivered materials accessible to persons with visual impairments. Many commenters proposed additional examples, such as signage or mapping, audio description services, secondary auditory programs, telebraillers, and reading machines. While the Department declines to add these items to the list, they are auxiliary aids and services and may be appropriate depending on the circumstances.

Subparagraph (3) refers to acquisition or modification of equipment or devices. Several commenters suggested the addition of current technological innovations in microelectronics and computerized control systems (e.g., voice recognition systems, automatic dialing telephones, and infrared elevator and light control systems) to the list of auxiliary aids. The Department interprets auxiliary aids and services as those aids and services designed to provide effective communications, i.e., making aurally and visually delivered information available to persons with hearing, speech, and vision impairments. Methods of making services, programs, or activities accessible to, or usable by, individuals with mobility or manual dexterity impairments are addressed by other sections of this part, including the provision for modifications in policies, practices, or procedures (§ 35.130 (b)(7)).

Paragraph (b)(4) deals with other similar services and actions. Several commenters asked for clarification that "similar services and actions" include retrieving items from shelves, assistance in reaching a marginally accessible seat, pushing a barrier aside in order to provide an accessible route, or assistance in removing a sweater or coat. While retrieving an item from a shelf might be an "auxiliary aid or service" for a blind person who could not locate the item without assistance, it might be a method of providing program access for a person using a wheelchair who could not reach the shelf, or a reasonable modification to a self-service policy for an individual who lacked the ability to grasp the item. As explained above, auxiliary aids and services are those aids and services required to provide effective communications. Other forms of assistance are more appropriately addressed by other provisions of the final rule.

"Complete complaint." "Complete complaint" is defined to include all the information necessary to enable the Federal agency designated under subpart G as responsible for investigation of a complaint to initiate its investigation.

"Current illegal use of drugs." The phrase "current illegal use of drugs" is used in § 35.131. Its meaning is discussed in the preamble for that section.

"Designated agency." The term "designated agency" is used to refer to the Federal agency designated under subpart G of this rule as responsible for carrying out the administrative enforcement responsibilities established by subpart F of the rule.

"Disability." The definition of the term "disability" is the same as the definition in the title III regulation codified at 28 CFR part 36. It is comparable to the definition of the term "individual with handicaps" in section 7(8) of the Rehabilitation Act and section 802(h) of the Fair Housing Act. The Education and Labor Committee report makes clear that the analysis of the term "individual with handicaps" by the Department of Health, Education, and Welfare (HEW) in its regulations implementing section 504 (42 FR 22685 (May 4, 1977)) [These regulations now appear at both 34 CFR Part 104 and 45 CFR Part 84, and are included in this book following the text of the Rehabilitation Act] and the analysis by the Department of Housing and Urban Development in its regulation implementing the Fair Housing Amendments Act of 1988 (54 FR 3232 (Jan. 23, 1989)) should also apply fully to the term "disability" (Education and Labor report at 50).

The use of the term "disability" instead of "handicap" and the term "individual with a disability" instead of "individual with handicaps" represents an effort by Congress to make use of up-to-date, currently accepted terminology. As with racial and ethnic epithets, the choice of terms to apply to a person with a disability is overlaid with stereotypes, patronizing attitudes, and other emotional connotations. Many individuals with disabilities, and organizations representing such individuals, object to the use of such terms as "handicapped person" or "the handicapped." In other recent legislation, Congress also recognized this shift in terminology, e.g., by changing the name of the National Council on the Handicapped to the National Council on Disability (Pub. L. 100-630).

In enacting the Americans with Disabilities Act, Congress concluded that it was important for the current legislation to use terminology most in line with the sensibilities of most Americans with disabilities. No change in definition or substance is intended nor should one be attributed to this change in phraseology.

The term "disability" means, with respect to an individual—

(A) A physical or mental impairment that substantially limits one or more of the major life activities of such individual;

(B) A record of such an impairment; or

(C) Being regarded as having such an impairment. If an individual meets any one of these three tests, he or she is considered to be an individual with a disability for purposes of coverage under the Americans with Disabilities Act.

Congress adopted this same basic definition of "disability," first used in the Rehabilitation Act of 1973 and in the Fair Housing Amendments Act of 1988, for a number of reasons. First, it has worked well since it was adopted in 1974. Second, it would not be possible to guarantee comprehensiveness by providing a list of specific disabilities, especially because new disorders may be recognized in the future, as they have since the definition was first established in 1974.

Test A—A physical or mental impairment that substantially limits one or more of the major life activities of such individual

Physical or mental impairment. Under the first test, an individual must have a physical or mental impairment. As explained in paragraph (1)(i) of the definition, "impairment" means any physiological disorder or condition, cosmetic disfigurement, or anatomical loss affecting one or more of the following body systems: neurological; musculoskeletal; special sense organs (which would include speech organs that are not respiratory such as vocal cords, soft palate, tongue, etc.); respiratory, including speech organs; cardiovascular; reproductive; digestive; genitourinary; hemic and lymphatic; skin; and endocrine. It also means any mental or psychological disorder, such as mental retardation, organic brain syndrome, emotional or mental illness, and specific learning disabilities. This list closely tracks the one used in the regulations for section 504 of the Rehabilitation Act of 1973 (see. *e.g.,* 45 CFR 84.3(j)(2)(i)).

Many commenters asked that "traumatic brain injury" be added to the list in paragraph (1)(i). Traumatic brain injury is already included because it is a physiological condition affecting one of the listed body systems, i.e., "neurological." Therefore, it was unnecessary to add the term to the regulation, which only provides representative examples of physiological disorders.

It is not possible to include a list of all the specific conditions, contagious and noncontagious diseases, or infections that would constitute physical or mental impairments because of the difficulty of ensuring the comprehensiveness of such a list, particularly in light of the fact that other conditions or disorders may be identified in the future. However, the list of examples in paragraph (1)(ii) of the definition includes: orthopedic, visual, speech and hearing impairments, cerebral palsy, epilepsy, muscular dystrophy, multiple sclerosis, cancer, heart disease, diabetes, mental retardation, emotional illness, specific learning disabilities, HIV disease (symptomatic or asymptomatic), tuberculosis, drug addiction, and alcoholism. The phrase "symptomatic or asymptomatic" was inserted in the final rule after "HIV disease" in response to commenters who suggested the clarification was necessary.

The examples of "physical or mental impairments'' in paragraph (1)(ii) are the same as those contained in many section 504 regulations, except for the addition of the phrase "contagious and noncontagious" to describe the types of diseases and conditions included, and the addition of "HIV disease (symptomatic or asymptomatic)" and "tuberculosis" to the list of examples. These additions are based on the committee reports, caselaw, and official legal opinions interpreting section 504. In *School Board of Nassau County v. Arline,* 480 U.S. 273 (1987), a case involving an individual with tuberculosis, the Supreme Court held that people with contagious diseases are entitled to the protections afforded by section 504. Following the *Arline* decision, this Department's Office of Legal Counsel issued a legal opinion that concluded that symptomatic HIV disease is an impairment that substantially limits a major life activity; therefore it has been included in the definition of disability under this part. The opinion also concluded that asymptomatic HIV disease is an impairment that substantially limits a major life activity, either because of its actual effect on the individual with HIV disease or because the reactions of other people to individuals with HIV disease cause such individuals to be treated as though they are disabled. See Memorandum from Douglas W. Kmiec, Acting Assistant Attorney General, Office of Legal Counsel, Department of Justice, to Arthur B. Culvahouse, Jr., Counsel to the President (Sept. 27, 1988), reprinted in Hearings on S. 933, the Americans with

Disabilities Act, Before the Subcomm. on the Handicapped of the Senate Comm. on Labor and Human Resources, 101st. Cong., 1st Sess. 346 (1989).

Paragraph (1)(iii) states that the phrase "physical or mental impairment" does not include homosexuality or bisexuality. These conditions were never considered impairments under other Federal disability laws. Section 511(a) of the statute makes clear that they are likewise not to be considered impairments under the Americans with Disabilities Act.

Physical or mental impairment does not include simple physical characteristics, such as blue eyes or black hair. Nor does it include environmental, cultural, economic, or other disadvantages, such as having a prison record, or being poor. Nor is age a disability. Similarly, the definition does not include common personality traits such as poor judgment or a quick temper where these are not symptoms of a mental or psychological disorder. However, a person who has these characteristics and also has a physical or mental impairment may be considered as having a disability for purposes of the Americans with Disabilities Act based on the impairment.

Substantial Limitation of a Major Life Activity. Under Test A, the impairment must be one that "substantially limits a major life activity." Major life activities include such things as caring for one's self, performing manual tasks, walking, seeing, hearing, speaking, breathing, learning, and working.

For example, a person who is paraplegic is substantially limited in the major life activity of walking, a person who is blind is substantially limited in the major life activity of seeing, and a person who is mentally retarded is substantially limited in the major life activity of learning. A person with traumatic brain injury is substantially limited in the major life activities of caring for one's self, learning, and working because of memory deficit, confusion, contextual difficulties, and inability to reason appropriately.

A person is considered an individual with a disability for purposes of Test A, the first prong of the definition, when the individual's important life activities are restricted as to the conditions, manner, or duration under which they can be performed in comparison to most people. A person with a minor, trivial impairment, such as a simple infected finger, is not impaired in a major life activity. A person who can walk for 10 miles continuously is not substantially limited in walking merely because, on the eleventh mile, he or she begins to experience pain, because most people would not be able to walk eleven miles without experiencing some discomfort.

The Department received many comments on the proposed rule's inclusion of the word "temporary" in the definition of "disability." The preamble indicated that impairments are not necessarily excluded from the definition of "disability" simply because they are temporary, but that the duration, or expected duration, of an impairment is one factor that may properly be considered in determining whether the impairment substantially limits a major life activity. The preamble recognized, however, that temporary impairments, such as a broken leg, are not commonly regarded as disabilities, and only in rare circumstances would the degree of the limitation and its expected duration be substantial. Nevertheless, many commenters objected to inclusion of the word "temporary" both because it is not in the statute and because it is not contained in the definition of "disability" set forth in the title I regulations of the Equal Employment Opportunity Commission (EEOC). The word "temporary" has been deleted from the final rule to conform with the statutory language.

The question of whether a temporary impairment is a disability must be resolved on a case-by-case basis, taking into consideration both the duration (or expected duration) of the impairment and the extent to which it actually limits a major life activity of the affected individual.

The question of whether a person has a disability should be assessed without regard to the availability of mitigating measures, such as reasonable modification or auxiliary aids and services. For example, a person with hearing loss is substantially limited in the major life activity of hearing, even though the loss may be improved through the use of a hearing aid. Likewise, persons with impairments, such as epilepsy or diabetes, that substantially limit a major life activity, are covered under the first prong of the definition of disability, even if the effects of the impairment are controlled by medication.

Many commenters asked that environmental illness (also known as multiple chemical sensitivity) as well as allergy to cigarette smoke be recognized as disabilities. The Department, however, declines to state categorically that these types of allergies or sensitivities are disabilities, because the determination as to whether an impairment is a disability depends on whether, given the particular circumstances at issue, the impairment substantially limits one or more major life activities (or has a history of, or is regarded as having such an effect).

Sometimes respiratory or neurological functioning is so severely affected that an individual will satisfy the requirements to be considered disabled under the regulation. Such an individual would be entitled to all of the protections afforded by the Act and this part. In other cases, individuals may be sensitive to environmental elements or to smoke but their sensitivity will not rise to the level needed to constitute a disability. For example, their major life activity of breathing may be somewhat, but not substantially, impaired. In such circumstances, the individuals are not disabled and are not entitled to the protections of the statute despite their sensitivity to environmental agents.

In sum, the determination as to whether allergies to cigarette smoke, or allergies or sensitivities characterized by the commenters as environmental illness are disabilities covered by the regulation must be made using the same case-by-case analysis that is applied to all other physical or mental impairments. Moreover, the addition of specific regulatory provisions relating to environmental illness in the final rule would be inappropriate at this time pending future consideration of the issue by the Architectural and Transportation Barriers Compliance Board, the Environmental Protection Agency, and the Occupational Safety and Health Administration of the Department of Labor.

Test B—A record of such an impairment

This test is intended to cover those who have a record of an impairment. As explained in paragraph (3) of the rule's definition of disability, this includes a person who has a history of an impairment that substantially limited a major life activity, such as someone who has recovered from an impairment. It also includes persons who have been misclassified as having an impairment.

This provision is included in the definition in part to protect individuals who have recovered from a physical or mental impairment that previously substantially limited them in a major life activity. Discrimination on the basis of such a past impairment is prohibited. Frequently occurring examples of the first group (those who have a history of an impairment) are persons with histories of mental or emotional illness, heart disease, or cancer; examples of the second group (those who have been misclassified as having an impairment) are persons who have been misclassified as having mental retardation or mental illness.

Test C—Being regarded as having such an impairment

This test, as contained in paragraph (4) of the definition, is intended to cover persons who are treated by a public entity as having a physical or mental impairment that substantially limits a major life activity. It applies when a person is treated as if he or she has an impairment that substantially limits a major life activity, regardless of whether that person has an impairment.

The Americans with Disabilities Act uses the same "regarded as" test set forth in the regulations implementing section 504 of the Rehabilitation Act. See, e.g., 28 CFR 42.540(k)(2)(iv), which provides:

(iv) "Is regarded as having an impairment" means (A) Has a physical or mental impairment that does not substantially limit major life activities but that is treated by a recipient as constituting such a limitation; (B) Has a physical or mental impairment that substantially limits major life activities only as a result of the attitudes of others toward such impairment; or (C) Has none of the impairments defined in paragraph (k)(2)(i) of this section but is treated by a recipient as having such an impairment.

The perception of the covered entity is a key element of this test. A person who perceives himself or herself to have an impairment, but does not have an impairment, and is not treated as if he or she has an impairment, is not protected under this test.

A person would be covered under this test if a public entity refused to serve the person because it perceived that the person had an impairment that limited his or her enjoyment of the goods or services being offered.

For example, persons with severe burns often encounter discrimination in community activities, resulting in substantial limitation of major life activities. These persons would be covered under this test based on the attitudes of others towards the impairment, even if they did not view themselves as "impaired."

The rationale for this third test, as used in the Rehabilitation Act of 1973, was articulated by the Supreme Court in *Arline,* 480 U.S. 273 (1987). The Court noted that although an individual may have an impairment that does not in fact substantially limit a major life activity, the reaction of others may prove just as disabling. "Such an impairment might not diminish a person's physical or mental capabilities, but could nevertheless substantially limit that person's ability to work as a result of the negative reactions of others to the impairment." *Id.* at 283. The Court concluded that, by including this test in the Rehabilitation Act's definition, "Congress acknowledged that society's accumulated myths and fears about disability and diseases are as handicapping as are the physical limitations that flow from actual impairment." *Id.* at 284.

Thus, a person who is denied services or benefits by a public entity because of myths, fears, and stereotypes associated with disabilities would be covered under this third test whether or not the person's physical or mental condition would be considered a disability under the first or second test in the definition.

If a person is refused admittance on the basis of an actual or perceived physical or mental condition, and the public entity can articulate no legitimate reason for the refusal (such as failure to meet eligibility criteria), a perceived concern about admitting persons with disabilities could be inferred and the individual would qualify for coverage under the "regarded as" test. A person who is covered because of being regarded as having an impairment is not required to show that the public entity's perception is inaccurate (e.g., that he will be accepted by others) in order to receive benefits from the public entity.

Paragraph (5) of the definition lists certain conditions that are not included within the definition of "disability." The excluded conditions are: Transvestism, transsexualism, pedophilia, exhibitionism, voyeurism, gender identity disorders not resulting from physical impairments, other sexual behavior disorders, compulsive gambling, kleptomania, pyromania, and psychoactive substance use disorders resulting from current illegal use of drugs. Unlike homosexuality and bisexuality, which are not considered impairments under either section 504 or the Americans with Disabilities Act (see the definition of "disability," paragraph (1)(iv)), the conditions listed in paragraph (5), except for transvestism, are not necessarily excluded as impairments under section 504. (Transvestism was excluded from the definition of disability for section 504, by the Fair Housing Amendments Act of 1988, Pub. L. 100-430, section 6(b)).

"Drug." The definition of the term "drug" is taken from section 510(d)(2) of the ADA.

"Facility." "Facility" means all or any portion of buildings, structures, sites, complexes, equipment, rolling stock or other conveyances, roads, walks, passageways, parking lots, or other real or personal property, including the site where the building, property, structure, or equipment is located. It includes both indoor and outdoor areas where human-constructed improvements, structures, equipment, or property have been added to the natural environment.

Commenters raised questions about the applicability of this part to activities operated in mobile facilities, such as bookmobiles or mobile health screening units. Such activities would be covered by the requirement for program accessibility in § 35.150, and would be included in the definition of "facility" as "other real or personal property," although standards for new construction and alterations of such facilities are not yet included in the accessibility standards adopted by § 35.151. Sections 35.150 and 35.151 specifically address the obligations of public entities to ensure accessibility by providing curb ramps at pedestrian walkways.

"Historic preservation programs" and "Historic properties" are defined in order to aid in the interpretation of § § 35.150 (a)(2) and (b)(2), which relate to accessibility of historic preservation programs, and § 35.151(d), which relates to the alteration of historic properties.

"Illegal use of drugs." The definition of "illegal use of drugs" is taken from section 510(d)(1) of the Act and clarifies that the term includes the illegal use of one or more drugs.

"Individual with a disability" means a person who has a disability but does not include an individual who is currently illegally using drugs, when the public entity acts on the basis of such use. The phrase "current illegal use of drugs" is explained in § 35.131.

"Public entity." The term "public entity" is defined in accordance with section 201(1) of the ADA as any State or local government; any department, agency, special purpose district, or other instrumentality of a State or States or local government; or the National Railroad Passenger Corporation, and any commuter authority (as defined in section 103(8) of the Rail Passenger Service Act).

"Qualified individual with a disability." The definition of "qualified individual with a disability" is taken from section 201(2) of the Act, which is derived from the definition of "qualified handicapped person" in the Department of Health and Human Services' regulation implementing section 504 (45 CFR § 84.3(k)). It combines the definition at 45 CFR 84.3(k)(1) for employment ("a handicapped person who, with reasonable accommodation, can perform the essential functions of the job in question") with the definition for other services at 45 CFR 84.3(k)(4) ("a handicapped person who meets the essential eligibility requirements for the receipt of such services").

Some commenters requested clarification of the term "essential eligibility requirements." Because of the variety of situations in which an individual's qualifications will be at issue, it is not possible to include more specific criteria in the definition. The "essential eligibility requirements" for participation in some activities covered under this part may be minimal. For example, most public entities provide information about their operations as a public service to anyone who requests it. In such situations, the only "eligibility requirement" for receipt of such information would be the request for it. Where such information is provided by telephone, even the ability to use a voice telephone is not an "essential eligibility requirement," because § 35.161 requires a public entity to provide equally effective telecommunication systems for individuals with impaired hearing or speech.

For other activities, identification of the "essential eligibility requirements" may be more complex. Where questions of safety are involved, the principles established in § 36.208 of the Department's regulation implementing title III of the ADA, to be codified at 28 CFR, part 36, will be applicable. That section implements section 302(b)(3) of the Act, which provides that a public accommodation is not required to permit an individual to participate in or benefit from the goods, services, facilities, privileges, advantages and accommodations of the public accommodation, if that individual poses a direct threat to the health or safety of others.

A "direct threat" is a significant risk to the health or safety of others that cannot be eliminated by a modification of policies, practices, or procedures, or by the provision of auxiliary aids or services. In *School Board of Nassau County v. Arline,* 480 U.S. 273 (1987), the Supreme Court recognized that there is a need to balance the interests of people with disabilities against legitimate concerns for public safety. Although persons with disabilities are generally entitled to the protection of this part, a person who poses a significant risk to others will not be "qualified," if reasonable modifications to the public entity's policies, practices, or procedures will not eliminate that risk.

The determination that a person poses a direct threat to the health or safety of others may not be based on generalizations or stereotypes about the effects of a particular disability. It must be based on an individualized assessment, based on reasonable judgment that relies on current medical evidence or on the best available objective evidence, to determine: the nature, duration, and severity of the risk; the probability that the potential injury will actually occur; and whether reasonable modifications of policies, practices, or procedures will mitigate the risk. This is the test established by the Supreme Court in *Arline.* Such an inquiry is essential if the law is to achieve its goal of protecting disabled individuals from discrimination based on prejudice, stereotypes, or unfounded fear, while giving appropriate weight to legitimate concerns, such as the need to avoid exposing others to significant health and safety risks. Making this assessment will not usually require the services of a physician. Sources for medical knowledge include guidance from public health authorities, such as the U.S. Public Health Service, the Centers for Disease Control, and the National Institutes of Health, including the National Institute of Mental Health.

"Qualified interpreter." The Department received substantial comment regarding the lack of a definition of "qualified interpreter." The proposed rule defined auxiliary aids and services to include the statutory term, "qualified interpreters" (§ 35.104), but did not define it. Section 35.160 requires the use of auxiliary aids including qualified interpreters and commenters stated that a lack of guidance on what the term means would create confusion among those trying to secure interpreting services and often result in less than effective communication.

Many commenters were concerned that, without clear guidance on the issue of "qualified" interpreter, the rule would be interpreted to mean "available, rather than qualified" interpreters. Some claimed that few public entities would understand the difference between a qualified interpreter and a person who simply knows a few signs or how to fingerspell.

In order to clarify what is meant by "qualified interpreter" the Department has added a definition of the term to the final rule. A qualified interpreter means an interpreter who is able to interpret effectively, accurately, and impartially both receptively and expressively, using any necessary specialized vocabulary. This definition focuses on the actual ability of the interpreter in a particular interpreting context to facilitate effective communication between the public entity and the individual with disabilities.

Public comment also revealed that public entities have at times asked persons who are deaf to provide family members or friends to interpret. In certain circumstances, notwithstanding that the family member or friend is able to interpret or is a certified interpreter, the family member or friend may not be qualified to render the necessary interpretation because of factors such as emotional or personal involvement or considerations of confidentiality that may adversely affect the ability to interpret "effectively, accurately, and impartially."

The definition of "qualified interpreter" in this rule does not invalidate or limit standards for interpreting services of any State or local law that are equal to or more stringent than those imposed by this definition. For instance, the definition would not supersede any requirement of State law for use of a certified interpreter in court proceedings.

"Section 504." The Department added a definition of "section 504" because the term is used extensively in subpart F of this part.

"State." The definition of "State" is identical to the statutory definition in section 3(3) of the ADA.

Section 35.105 Self-evaluation

Section 35.105 establishes a requirement, based on the section 504 regulations for federally assisted and federally conducted programs, that a public entity evaluate its current policies and practices to identify and correct any that are not consistent with the requirements of this part. As noted in the discussion of § 35.102, activities covered by the Department of Transportation's regulation implementing subtitle B of title II are not required to be included in the self-evaluation required by this section.

Experience has demonstrated the self evaluation process to be a valuable means of establishing a working relationship with individuals with disabilities, which has promoted both effective and efficient implementation of section 504. The Department expects that it will likewise be useful to public entities newly covered by the ADA.

All public entities are required to do a self-evaluation. However, only those that employ 50 or more persons are required to maintain the self-evaluation on file and make it available for public inspection for three years. The number 50 was derived from the Department of Justice's section 504 regulations for federally assisted programs, 28 CFR 42.505(c). The Department received comments critical of this limitation, some suggesting the requirement apply to all public entities and others suggesting that the number be changed from 50 to 15. The final rule has not been changed. Although many regulations implementing section 504 for federally assisted programs do use 15 employees as the cut-off for this record-keeping requirement, the Department believes that it would be inappropriate to extend it to those smaller public entities covered by this regulation that do not receive Federal financial assistance. This approach has the benefit of minimizing paperwork burdens on small entities.

Paragraph (d) provides that the self evaluation required by this section shall apply only to programs not subject to section 504 or those policies and practices, such as those involving communications access, that have not already been included in a self-evaluation required under an existing regulation implementing section 504. Because most self-evaluations were done from five to twelve years ago, however, the Department expects that a great many public entities will be reexamining all of their policies and programs. Programs and functions may have changed, and actions that were supposed to have been taken to comply with section 504 may not have been fully implemented or may no longer be effective. In addition, there have been statutory amendments to section 504 which have changed the coverage of section 504, particularly the Civil Rights Restoration Act of 1987, Public Law No. 100-259, 102 Stat. 28 (1988), which broadened the definition of a covered "program or activity."

Several commenters suggested that the Department clarify public entities' liability during the one-year period for compliance with the self-evaluation requirement. The self-evaluation requirement does not stay the effective date of the statute nor of this part. Public entities are, therefore, not shielded from discrimination claims during that time.

Other commenters suggested that the rule require that every self-evaluation include an examination of training efforts to assure that individuals with disabilities are not subjected to discrimination because of insensitivity, particularly in the law enforcement area. Although the Department has not added such a specific requirement to the rule, it would be appropriate for public entities to evaluate training efforts because, in many cases, lack of training leads to discriminatory practices, even when the policies in place are nondiscriminatory.

Section 35.106 Notice

Section 35.106 requires a public entity to disseminate sufficient information to applicants, participants, beneficiaries, and other interested persons to inform them of the rights and protections afforded by the ADA and this regulation. Methods of providing this information include, for example, the publication of information in handbooks, manuals, and pamphlets that are distributed to the public to describe a public entity's programs and activities; the display of informative posters in service centers and other public places; or the broadcast of information by television or radio. In providing the notice, a public entity must comply with the requirements for effective communication in § 35.160. The preamble to that section gives guidance on how to effectively communicate with individuals with disabilities.

Section 35.107 Designation of Responsible Employee and Adoption of Grievance Procedures

Consistent with § 35.105, self-evaluation, the final rule requires that public entities with 50 or more employees designate a responsible employee and adopt grievance procedures. Most of the commenters who suggested that the requirement that self evaluation be maintained on file for three years not be limited to those employing 50 or more persons made a similar suggestion concerning § 35.107. Commenters recommended either that all public entities be subject to § 35.107, or that "50 or more persons" be changed to "15 or more persons." As explained in the discussion of § 35.105, the Department has not adopted this suggestion.

The requirement for designation of an employee responsible for coordination of efforts to carry out responsibilities under this part is derived from the HEW regulation implementing section 504 in federally assisted programs. The requirement for designation of a particular employee and dissemination of information about how to locate that employee helps to ensure that individuals dealing with large agencies are able to easily find a responsible person who is familiar with the requirements of the Act and this part and can communicate those requirements to other individuals in the agency who may be unaware of their responsibilities. This paragraph in no way limits a public entity's obligation to ensure that all of its employees comply with the requirements of this part, but it ensures that any failure by individual employees can be promptly corrected by the designated employee.

Section 35.107(b) requires public entities with 50 or more employees to establish grievance procedures for resolving complaints of violations of this part. Similar requirements are found in the section 504 regulations for federally assisted programs (see, e.g., 45 CFR 84.7(b)). The rule, like the regulations for federally assisted programs, provides for investigation and resolution of complaints by a Federal enforcement agency. It is the view of the Department that public entities subject to this part should be required to establish a mechanism for resolution of complaints at the local level without requiring the complainant to resort to the Federal complaint procedures established under subpart F. Complainants would not, however, be required to exhaust the public entity's grievance procedures before filing a complaint under subpart F. Delay in filing the complaint at the Federal level caused by pursuit of the remedies available under the grievance procedure would generally be considered good cause for extending the time allowed for filing under § 35.170(b).

Subpart B—General Requirements

Section 35.130 General Prohibitions Against Discrimination

The general prohibitions against discrimination in the rule are generally based on the prohibitions in existing regulations implementing section 504 and, therefore, are already familiar to State and local entities covered by section 504. In addition, § 35.130 includes a number of provisions derived from title III of the Act that are implicit to a certain degree in the requirements of regulations implementing section 504.

Several commenters suggested that this part should include the section of the proposed title III regulation that implemented section 309 of the Act, which requires that courses and examinations related to applications, licensing, certification, or credentialing be provided in an accessible place and manner or that alternative accessible arrangements be made. The Department has not adopted this suggestion. The requirements of this part, including the general prohibitions of discrimination in this section, the program access requirements of subpart D, and the communications requirements of subpart E, apply to courses and examinations provided by public entities. The Department considers these requirements to be sufficient to ensure that courses and examinations administered by public entities meet the requirements of section 309. For example, a public entity offering an examination must ensure that modifications of policies, practices, or procedures or the provision of auxiliary aids and services furnish the individual with a disability an equal opportunity to demonstrate his or her knowledge or ability. Also, any examination specially designed for individuals with disabilities must be offered as often and in as timely a manner as are other examinations. Further, under this part, courses and examinations must be offered in the most integrated setting appropriate. The analysis of § 35.130(d) is relevant to this determination.

A number of commenters asked that the regulation be amended to require training of law enforcement personnel to recognize the difference between criminal activity and the effects of seizures or other disabilities such as mental retardation, cerebral palsy, traumatic brain injury, mental illness, or deafness. Several disabled commenters gave personal statements about the abuse they had received at the hands of law enforcement personnel. Two organizations that commented cited the Judiciary report at 50 as authority to require law enforcement training.

The Department has not added such a training requirement to the regulation. Discriminatory arrests and brutal treatment are already unlawful police activities. The general regulatory obligation to modify policies, practices, or procedures requires law enforcement to make changes in policies that result in discriminatory arrests or abuse of individuals with disabilities. Under this section law enforcement personnel would be required to make appropriate efforts to determine whether perceived strange or disruptive behavior or unconsciousness is the result of a disability. The Department notes that a number of States have attempted to address the problem of arresting disabled persons for noncriminal conduct resulting from their disability through adoption of the Uniform Duties to Disabled Persons Act, and encourages other jurisdictions to consider that approach.

Paragraph (a) restates the nondiscrimination mandate of section 202 of the ADA. The remaining paragraphs in § 35.130 establish the general principles for analyzing whether any particular action of the public entity violates this mandate.

Paragraph (b) prohibits overt denials of equal treatment of individuals with disabilities. A public entity may not refuse to provide an individual with a disability with an equal opportunity to participate in or benefit from its program simply because the person has a disability.

Paragraph (b)(1)(i) provides that it is discriminatory to deny a person with a disability the right to participate in or benefit from the aid, benefit, or service provided by a public entity. Paragraph (b)(1)(ii) provides that the aids, benefits, and services provided to persons with disabilities must be equal to those provided to others, and paragraph (b)(1)(iii) requires that the aids, benefits, or services provided to individuals with disabilities must be as effective in affording equal opportunity to obtain the same result, to gain the same benefit, or to reach the same level of achievement as those provided to others. These paragraphs are taken from the regulations implementing section 504 and simply restate principles long established under section 504.

Paragraph (b)(1)(iv) permits the public entity to develop separate or different aids, benefits, or services when necessary to provide individuals with disabilities with an equal opportunity to participate in or benefit from the public entity's programs or activities, but only when necessary to ensure that the aids, benefits, or services are as effective as those provided to others. Paragraph (b)(1)(iv) must be read in conjunction with paragraphs (b)(2), (d), and (e). Even when separate or different aids, benefits, or services would be more effective, paragraph (b)(2) provides that a qualified individual with a disability still has the right to choose to participate in the program that is not designed to accommodate individuals with disabilities. Paragraph (d) requires that a public entity administer services, programs, and activities in the most integrated setting appropriate to the needs of qualified individuals with disabilities.

Paragraph (b)(2) specifies that, notwithstanding the existence of separate or different programs or activities provided in accordance with this section, an individual with a disability shall not be denied the opportunity to participate in such programs or activities that are not separate or different. Paragraph (e), which is derived from section 501(d) of the Americans with Disabilities Act, states that nothing in this part shall be construed to require an individual with a disability to accept an accommodation, aid, service, opportunity, or benefit that he or she chooses not to accept.

Taken together, these provisions are intended to prohibit exclusion and segregation of individuals with disabilities and the denial of equal opportunities enjoyed by others, based on, among other things, presumptions, patronizing attitudes, fears, and stereotypes about individuals with disabilities. Consistent with these standards, public entities are required to ensure that their actions are based on facts applicable to individuals and not on presumptions as to what a class of individuals with disabilities can or cannot do.

Integration is fundamental to the purposes of the Americans with Disabilities Act. Provision of segregated accommodations and services relegates persons with disabilities to second-class status. For example, it would be a violation of this provision to require persons with disabilities to eat in the back room of a government cafeteria or to refuse to allow a person with a disability the full use of recreation or exercise facilities because of stereotypes about the person's ability to participate.

Many commenters objected to proposed paragraphs (b)(1)(iv) and (d) as allowing continued segregation of individuals with disabilities. The Department recognizes that promoting integration of individuals with disabilities into the mainstream of society is an important objective of the ADA and agrees that, in most instances, separate programs for individuals with disabilities will not be permitted. Nevertheless, section 504 does permit separate programs in limited circumstances, and Congress clearly intended the regulations issued under title II to adopt the standards of section 504. Furthermore, Congress included authority for separate programs in the specific requirements of title III of the Act. Section 302(b)(1)(A)(iii) of the Act provides for separate benefits in language similar to that in § 35.130(b)(1)(iv), and section 302(b)(1)(B) includes the same requirement for "the most integrated setting appropriate" as in § 35.130(d).

Even when separate programs are permitted, individuals with disabilities cannot be denied the opportunity to participate in programs that are not separate or different. This is an important and overarching principle of the Americans with Disabilities Act. Separate, special, or different programs that are designed to provide a benefit to persons with disabilities cannot be used to restrict the participation of persons with disabilities in general, integrated activities.

For example, a person who is blind may wish to decline participating in a special museum tour that allows persons to touch sculptures in an exhibit and instead tour the exhibit at his or her own pace with the museum's recorded tour. It is not the intent of this section to require the person who is blind to avail himself or herself of the special tour. Modified participation for persons with disabilities must be a choice, not a requirement.

In addition, it would not be a violation of this section for a public entity to offer recreational programs specifically designed for children with mobility impairments. However, it would be a violation of this section if the entity then excluded these children from other recreational services for which they are qualified to participate when these services are made available to nondisabled children, or if the entity required children with disabilities to attend only designated programs.

Many commenters asked that the Department clarify a public entity's obligations within the integrated program when it offers a separate program but an individual with a disability chooses not to participate in the separate program. It is impossible to make a blanket statement as to what level of auxiliary aids or modifications would be required in the integrated program. Rather, each situation must be assessed individually. The starting point is to question whether the separate program is in fact necessary or appropriate for the individual. Assuming the separate program would be appropriate for a particular individual, the extent to which that individual must be provided with modifications in the integrated program will depend not only on what the individual needs but also on the limitations and defenses of this part. For example, it may constitute an undue burden for a public accommodation, which provides a full-time interpreter in its special guided tour for individuals with hearing impairments, to hire an additional interpreter for those individuals who choose to attend the integrated program. The Department cannot identify categorically the level of assistance or aid required in the integrated program.

Paragraph (b)(1)(v) provides that a public entity may not aid or perpetuate discrimination against a qualified individual with a disability by providing significant assistance to an agency, organization, or person that discriminates on the basis of disability in providing any aid, benefit, or service to beneficiaries of the public entity's program. This paragraph is taken from the regulations implementing section 504 for federally assisted programs.

Paragraph (b)(1)(vi) prohibits the public entity from denying a qualified individual with a disability the opportunity to participate as a member of a planning or advisory board.

Paragraph (b)(1)(vii) prohibits the public entity from limiting a qualified individual with a disability in the enjoyment of any right, privilege, advantage, or opportunity enjoyed by others receiving any aid, benefit, or service.

Paragraph (b)(3) prohibits the public entity from utilizing criteria or methods of administration that deny individuals with disabilities access to the public entity's services, programs, and activities or that perpetuate the discrimination of another public entity, if both public entities are subject to common administrative control or are agencies of the same State. The phrase "criteria or methods of administration" refers to official written policies of the public entity and to the actual practices of the public entity. This paragraph prohibits both blatantly exclusionary policies or practices and nonessential policies and practices that are neutral on their face, but deny individuals with disabilities an effective opportunity to participate. This standard is consistent with the interpretation of section 504 by the U.S. Supreme Court in *Alexander v. Choate,* 469 U.S. 287 (1985). The Court in *Choate* explained that members of Congress made numerous statements during passage of section 504 regarding eliminating architectural barriers, providing access to transportation, and eliminating discriminatory effects of job qualification procedures. The Court then noted: "These statements would ring hollow if the resulting legislation could not rectify the harms resulting from action that discriminated by effect as well as by design." *Id.* at 297 (footnote omitted).

Paragraph (b)(4) specifically applies the prohibition enunciated in § 35.130(b)(3) to the process of selecting sites for construction of new facilities or selecting existing facilities to be used by the public entity. Paragraph (b)(4) does not apply to construction of additional buildings at an existing site.

Paragraph (b)(5) prohibits the public entity, in the selection of procurement contractors, from using criteria that subject qualified individuals with disabilities to discrimination on the basis of disability.

Paragraph (b)(6) prohibits the public entity from discriminating against qualified individuals with disabilities on the basis of disability in the granting of licenses or certification. A person is a "qualified individual with a disability" with respect to licensing or certification if he or she can meet the essential eligibility requirements for receiving the license or certification (see § 35.104).

A number of commenters were troubled by the phrase "essential eligibility requirements" as applied to State licensing requirements, especially those for health care professions. Because of the variety of types of programs to which the definition of "qualified individual with a disability" applies, it is not possible to use more specific language in the definition. The phrase "essential eligibility requirements," however, is taken from the definitions in the regulations implementing section 504, so caselaw under section 504 will be applicable to its interpretation. In *Southeastern Community College v. Davis,* 442 U.S. 397, for example, the Supreme Court held that section 504 does not require an institution to "lower or effect substantial modifications of standards to accommodate a handicapped person," 442 U.S. at 413, and that the school had established that the plaintiff was not "qualified" because she was not able to "serve the nursing profession in all customary ways," *id.* Whether a particular requirement is "essential" will, of course, depend on the facts of the particular case.

In addition, the public entity may not establish requirements for the programs or activities of licensees or certified entities that subject qualified individuals with disabilities to discrimination on the basis of disability. For example, the public entity must comply with this requirement when establishing safety standards for the operations of licensees. In that case the public entity must ensure that standards that it promulgates do not discriminate against the employment of qualified individuals with disabilities in an impermissible manner.

Paragraph (b)(6) does not extend the requirements of the Act or this part directly to the programs or activities of licensees or certified entities themselves. The programs or activities of licensees or certified entities are not themselves programs or activities of the public entity merely by virtue of the license or certificate.

Paragraph (b)(7) is a specific application of the requirement under the general prohibitions of discrimination that public entities make reasonable modifications in policies, practices, or procedures where necessary to avoid discrimination on the basis of disability. Section 302(b)(2)(A)(ii) of the ADA sets out this requirement specifically for public accommodations covered by title III of the Act, and the House Judiciary Committee Report directs the Attorney General to include those specific requirements in the title II regulation to the extent that they do not conflict with the regulations implementing section 504. Judiciary report at 52.

Paragraph (b)(8), a new paragraph not contained in the proposed rule, prohibits the imposition or application of eligibility criteria that screen out or tend to screen out an individual with a disability or any class of individuals with disabilities from fully and equally enjoying any service, program, or activity, unless such criteria can be shown to be necessary for the provision of the service, program, or activity being offered. This prohibition is also a specific application of the general prohibitions of discrimination and is based on section 302(b)(2)(A)(i) of the ADA. It prohibits overt denials of equal treatment of individuals with disabilities, or establishment of exclusive or segregative criteria that would bar individuals with disabilities from participation in services, benefits, or activities.

Paragraph (b)(8) also prohibits policies that unnecessarily impose requirements or burdens on individuals with disabilities that are not placed on others. For example, public entities may not require that a qualified individual with a disability be accompanied by an attendant. A public entity is not, however, required to provide attendant care, or assistance in toileting, eating, or dressing to individuals with disabilities, except in special circumstances, such as where the individual is an inmate of a custodial or correctional institution.

In addition, paragraph (b)(8) prohibits the imposition of criteria that "tend to" screen out an individual with a disability. This concept, which is derived from current regulations under section 504 (see, e.g., 45 CFR 84.13), makes it discriminatory to impose policies or criteria that, while not creating a direct bar to individuals with disabilities, indirectly prevent or limit their ability to participate. For example, requiring presentation of a driver's license as the sole means of identification for purposes of paying by check would violate this section in situations where, for example, individuals with severe vision impairments or developmental disabilities or epilepsy are ineligible to receive a driver's license and the use of an alternative means of identification, such as another photo I.D. or credit card, is feasible.

A public entity may, however, impose neutral rules and criteria that screen out, or tend to screen out, individuals with disabilities if the criteria are necessary for the safe operation of the program in question. Examples of safety qualifications that would be justifiable in appropriate circumstances would include eligibility requirements for drivers' licenses, or a requirement that all participants in a recreational rafting expedition be able to meet a necessary level of swimming proficiency. Safety requirements must be based on actual risks and not on speculation, stereotypes, or generalizations about individuals with disabilities.

Paragraph (c) provides that nothing in this part prohibits a public entity from providing benefits, services, or advantages to individuals with disabilities, or to a particular class of individuals with disabilities, beyond those required by this part. It is derived from a provision in the section 504 regulations that permits programs conducted pursuant to Federal statute or Executive order that are designed to benefit only individuals with disabilities or a given class of individuals with disabilities to be limited to those individuals with disabilities. Section 504 ensures that federally assisted programs are made available to all individuals, without regard to disabilities, unless the Federal program under which the assistance is provided is specifically limited to individuals with disabilities or a particular class of individuals with disabilities. Because coverage under this part is not limited to federally assisted programs, paragraph (c) has been revised to clarify that State and local governments may provide special benefits, beyond those required by the nondiscrimination requirements of this part, that are limited to individuals with disabilities or a particular class of individuals with disabilities, without thereby incurring additional obligations to persons without disabilities or to other classes of individuals with disabilities.

Paragraphs (d) and (e), previously referred to in the discussion of paragraph (b)(1)(iv), provide that the public entity must administer services, programs, and activities in the most integrated setting appropriate to the needs of qualified individuals with disabilities, *i.e.,* in a setting that enables individuals with disabilities to interact with nondisabled persons to the fullest extent possible, and that persons with disabilities must be provided the option of declining to accept a particular accommodation.

Some commenters expressed concern that § 35.130(e), which states that nothing in the rule requires an individual with a disability to accept special accommodations and services provided under the ADA, could be interpreted to allow guardians of infants or older people with disabilities to refuse medical treatment for their wards. Section 35.130(e) has been revised to make it clear that paragraph (e) is inapplicable to the concern of the commenters. A new paragraph (e)(2) has been added stating that nothing in the regulation authorizes the representative or guardian of an individual with a disability to decline food, water, medical treatment, or medical services for that individual. New paragraph (e) clarifies that neither the ADA nor the regulation alters current Federal law ensuring the rights of incompetent individuals with disabilities to receive food, water, and medical treatment. See, *e.g,* Child Abuse Amendments of 1984 (42 U.S.C. 5106a(b)(10), 5106g(10)); Rehabilitation Act of 1973, as amended (29 U.S.C. 794); the Developmentally Disabled Assistance and Bill of Rights Act, (42 U.S.C. 6042).

Sections 35.130(e) (1) and (2) are based on section 501(d) of the ADA. Section 501(d) was designed to clarify that nothing in the ADA requires individuals with disabilities to accept special accommodations and services for individuals with disabilities that may segregate them:

The Committee added this section [501(d)] to clarify that nothing in the ADA is intended to permit discriminatory treatment on the basis of disability, even when such treatment is rendered under the guise of providing an accommodation, service, aid or benefit to the individual with [a] disability. For example, a blind individual may choose not to avail himself or herself of the right to go to the front of a line, even if a particular public accommodation has chosen to offer such a modification of a policy for blind individuals. Or, a blind individual may choose to decline to participate in a special museum tour that allows persons to touch sculptures in an exhibit and instead tour the exhibits at his or her own pace with the museum's recorded tour.

Judiciary report at 71-72. The Act is not to be construed to mean that an individual with disabilities must accept special accommodations and services for individuals with disabilities when that individual can participate in the regular services already offered. Because medical treatment, including treatment for particular conditions, is not a special accommodation or service for individuals with disabilities under section 501(d), neither the Act nor this part provides affirmative authority to suspend such treatment. Section 501(d) is intended to clarify that the Act is not designed to foster discrimination through mandatory acceptance of special services when other alternatives are provided; this concern does not reach to the provision of medical treatment for the disabling condition itself.

Paragraph (f) provides that a public entity may not place a surcharge on a particular individual with a disability, or any group of individuals with disabilities, to cover any costs of measures required to provide that individual or group with the nondiscriminatory treatment required by the Act or this part. Such measures may include the provision of auxiliary aids or of modifications required to provide program accessibility.

Several commenters asked for clarification that the costs of interpreter services may not be assessed as an element of "court costs." The Department has already recognized that imposition of the cost of courtroom interpreter services is impermissible under section 504. The preamble to the Department's section 504 regulation for its federally assisted programs states that where a court system has an obligation to provide qualified interpreters, "it has the corresponding responsibility to pay for the services of the interpreters." (45 FR 37630 (June 3, 1980)). Accordingly, recouping the costs of interpreter services by assessing them as part of court costs would also be prohibited.

Paragraph (g), which prohibits discrimination on the basis of an individual's or entity's known relationship or association with an individual with a disability, is based on sections 102(b)(4) and 302(b)(1)(E) of the ADA. This paragraph was not contained in the proposed rule. The individuals covered under this paragraph are any individuals who are discriminated against because of their known association with an individual with a disability. For example, it would be a violation of this paragraph for a local government to refuse to allow a theater company to use a school auditorium on the grounds that the company had recently performed for an audience of individuals with HIV disease.

This protection is not limited to those who have a familial relationship with the individual who has a disability. Congress considered, and rejected, amendments that would have limited the scope of this provision to specific associations and relationships. Therefore, if a public entity refuses admission to a person with cerebral palsy and his or her companions, the companions have an independent right of action under the ADA and this section.

During the legislative process, the term "entity" was added to section 302(b)(1)(E) to clarify that the scope of the provision is intended to encompass not only persons who have a known association with a person with a disability, but also entities that provide services to or are otherwise associated with such individuals. This provision was intended to ensure that entities such as health care providers, employees of social service agencies, and others who provide professional services to persons with disabilities are not subjected to discrimination because of their professional association with persons with disabilities.

Section 35.131 Illegal Use of Drugs

Section 35.131 effectuates section 510 of the ADA, which clarifies the Act's application to people who use drugs illegally. Paragraph (a) provides that this part does not prohibit discrimination based on an individual's current illegal use of drugs.

The Act and the regulation distinguish between illegal use of drugs and the legal use of substances, whether or not those substances are "controlled substances," as defined in the Controlled Substances Act (21 U.S.C. 812). Some controlled substances are prescription drugs that have legitimate medical uses. Section 35.131 does not affect use of controlled substances pursuant to a valid prescription under supervision by a licensed health care professional, or other use that is authorized by the Controlled Substances Act or any other provision of Federal law. It does apply to illegal use of those substances, as well as to illegal use of controlled substances that are not prescription drugs. The key question is whether the individual's use of the substance is illegal, not whether the substance has recognized legal uses. Alcohol is not a controlled substance, so use of alcohol is not addressed by § 35.131 (although alcoholics are individuals with disabilities, subject to the protections of the statute).

A distinction is also made between the use of a substance and the status of being addicted to that substance. Addiction is a disability, and addicts are individuals with disabilities protected by the Act. The protection, however, does not extend to actions based on the illegal use of the substance. In other words, an addict cannot use the fact of his or her addiction as a defense to an action based on illegal use of drugs. This distinction is not artificial. Congress intended to deny protection to people who engage in the illegal use of drugs, whether or not they are addicted, but to provide protection to addicts so long as they are not currently using drugs.

A third distinction is the difficult one between current use and former use. The definition of "current illegal use of drugs" in § 35.104, which is based on the report of the Conference Committee, H.R. Conf. Rep. No. 596, 101st Cong., 2d Sess. 64 (1990) (hereinafter "Conference report"), is "illegal use of drugs that occurred recently enough to justify a reasonable belief that a person's drug use is current or that continuing use is a real and ongoing problem."

Paragraph (a)(2)(i) specifies that an individual who has successfully completed a supervised drug rehabilitation program or has otherwise been rehabilitated successfully and who is not engaging in current illegal use of drugs is protected. Paragraph (a)(2)(ii) clarifies that an individual who is currently participating in a supervised rehabilitation program and is not engaging in current illegal use of drugs is protected. Paragraph (a)(2)(iii) provides that a person who is erroneously regarded as engaging in current illegal use of drugs, but who is not engaging in such use, is protected.

Paragraph (b) provides a limited exception to the exclusion of current illegal users of drugs from the protections of the Act. It prohibits denial of health services, or services provided in connection with drug rehabilitation to an individual on the basis of current illegal use of drugs, if the individual is otherwise entitled to such services. A health care facility, such as a hospital or clinic, may not refuse treatment to an individual in need of the services it provides on the grounds that the individual is illegally using drugs, but it is not required by this section to provide services that it does not ordinarily provide. For example, a health care facility that specializes in a particular type of treatment, such as care of burn victims, is not required to provide drug rehabilitation services, but it cannot refuse to treat [an] individual's burns on the grounds that the individual is illegally using drugs.

Some commenters pointed out that abstention from the use of drugs is an essential condition of participation in some drug rehabilitation programs, and may be a necessary requirement in inpatient or residential settings. The Department believes that this comment is well-founded. Congress clearly intended to prohibit exclusion from drug treatment programs of the very individuals who need such programs because of their use of drugs, but, once an individual has been admitted to a program, abstention may be a necessary and appropriate condition to continued participation. The final rule therefore provides that a drug rehabilitation or treatment program may prohibit illegal use of drugs by individuals while they are participating in the program.

Paragraph (c) expresses Congress' intention that the Act be neutral with respect to testing for illegal use of drugs. This paragraph implements the provision in section 510(b) of the Act that allows entities "to adopt or administer reasonable policies or procedures, including but not limited to drug testing," that ensure that an individual who is participating in a supervised rehabilitation program, or who has completed such a program or otherwise been rehabilitated successfully is no longer engaging in the illegal use of drugs. The section is not to be "construed to encourage, prohibit, restrict, or authorize the conducting of testing for the illegal use of drugs."

Paragraph 35.131(c) clarifies that it is not a violation of this part to adopt or administer reasonable policies or procedures to ensure that an individual who formerly engaged in the illegal use of drugs is not currently engaging in illegal use of drugs. Any such policies or procedures must, of course, be reasonable, and must be designed to identify accurately the illegal use of drugs. This paragraph does not authorize inquiries, tests, or other procedures that would disclose use of substances that are not controlled substances or are taken under supervision by a licensed health care professional, or other uses authorized by the Controlled Substances Act or other provisions of Federal law, because such uses are not included in the definition of "illegal use of drugs." A commenter argued that the rule should permit testing for lawful use of prescription drugs, but most commenters preferred that tests must be limited to unlawful use in order to avoid revealing the lawful use of prescription medicine used to treat disabilities.

Section 35.132 Smoking

Section 35.132 restates the clarification in section 501(b) of the Act that the Act does not preclude the prohibition of, or imposition of restrictions on, smoking in transportation covered by title II. Some commenters argued that this section is too limited in scope, and that the regulation should prohibit smoking in all facilities used by public entities. The reference to smoking in section 501, however, merely clarifies that the Act does not require public entities to accommodate smokers by permitting them to smoke in transportation facilities.

Section 35.133 Maintenance of Accessible Features

Section 35.133 provides that a public entity shall maintain in operable working condition those features of facilities and equipment that are required to be readily accessible to and usable by persons with disabilities by the Act or this part. The Act requires that, to the maximum extent feasible, facilities must be accessible to, and usable by, individuals with disabilities. This section recognizes that it is not sufficient to provide features such as accessible routes, elevators, or ramps, if those features are not maintained in a manner that enables individuals with disabilities to use them. Inoperable elevators, locked accessible doors, or "accessible" routes that are obstructed by furniture, filing cabinets, or potted plants are neither "accessible to" nor "usable by" individuals with disabilities.

Some commenters objected that this section appeared to establish an absolute requirement and suggested that language from the preamble be included in the text of the regulation. It is, of course, impossible to guarantee that mechanical devices will never fail to operate. Paragraph (b) of the final regulation provides that this section does not prohibit isolated or temporary interruptions in service or access due to maintenance or repairs. This paragraph is intended to clarify that temporary obstructions or isolated instances of mechanical failure would not be considered violations of the Act or this part. However, allowing obstructions or "out of service" equipment to persist beyond a reasonable period of time would violate this part, as would repeated mechanical failures due to improper or inadequate maintenance. Failure of the public entity to ensure that accessible routes are properly maintained and free of obstructions, or failure to arrange prompt repair of inoperable elevators or other equipment intended to provide access would also violate this part.

Other commenters requested that this section be expanded to include specific requirements for inspection and maintenance of equipment, for training staff in the proper operation of equipment, and for maintenance of specific items. The Department believes that this section properly establishes the general requirement for maintaining access and that further details are not necessary.

Section 35.134 Retaliation or Coercion

Section 35.134 implements section 503 of the ADA, which prohibits retaliation against any individual who exercises his or her rights under the Act. This section is unchanged from the proposed rule. Paragraph (a) of § 35.134 provides that no private or public entity shall discriminate against any individual because that individual has exercised his or her right to oppose any act or practice made unlawful by this part, or because that individual made a charge, testified, assisted, or participated in any manner in an investigation, proceeding, or hearing under the Act or this part.

Paragraph (b) provides that no private or public entity shall coerce, intimidate, threaten, or interfere with any individual in the exercise of his or her rights under this part or because that individual aided or encouraged any other individual in the exercise or enjoyment of any right granted or protected by the Act or this part.

This section protects not only individuals who allege a violation of the Act or this part, but also any individuals who support or assist them. This section applies to all investigations or proceedings initiated under the Act or this part without regard to the ultimate resolution of the underlying allegations. Because this section prohibits any act of retaliation or coercion in response to an individual's effort to exercise rights established by the Act and this part (or to support the efforts of another individual), the section applies not only to public entities subject to this part, but also to persons acting in an individual capacity or to private entities. For example, it would be a violation of the Act and this part for a private individual to harass or intimidate an individual with a disability in an effort to prevent that individual from attending a concert in a State-owned park. It would, likewise, be a violation of the Act and this part for a private entity to take adverse action against an employee who appeared as a witness on behalf of an individual who sought to enforce the Act.

Section 35.135 Personal Devices and Services

The final rule includes a new § 35.135, entitled "Personal devices and services," which states that the provision of personal devices and services is not required by title II. This new section, which serves as a limitation on all of the requirements of the regulation, replaces § 35.160(b)(2) of the proposed rule, which addressed the issue of personal devices and services explicitly only in the context of communications. The personal devices and services limitation was intended to have general application in the proposed rule in all contexts where it was relevant. The final rule, therefore, clarifies this point by including a general provision that will explicitly apply not only to auxiliary aids and services but across-the-board to include other relevant areas such as, for example, modifications in policies, practices, and procedures (§ 35.130(b)(7)). The language of § 35.135 parallels an analogous provision in the Department's title III regulations (28 CFR 36.306) but preserves the explicit reference to "readers for personal use or study" in § 35.160(b)(2) of the proposed rule. This section does not preclude the short-term loan of personal receivers that are part of an assistive listening system.

Subpart C—Employment

Section 35.140 Employment Discrimination Prohibited

Title II of the ADA applies to all activities of public entities, including their employment practices. The proposed rule cross-referenced the definitions, requirements, and procedures of title I of the ADA, as established by the Equal Employment Opportunity Commission in 29 CFR part 1630. This proposal would have resulted in use, under § 35.140, of the title I definition of "employer," so that a public entity with 25 or more employees would have become subject to the requirements of § 35.140 on July 26, 1992, one with 15 to 24 employees on July 26, 1994, and one with fewer than 15 employees would have been excluded completely.

The Department received comments objecting to this approach. The commenters asserted that Congress intended to establish nondiscrimination requirements for employment by all public entities, including those that employ fewer than 15 employees; and that Congress intended the employment requirements of title II to become effective at the same time that the other requirements of this regulation become effective, January 26, 1992. The Department has reexamined the statutory language and legislative history of the ADA on this issue and has concluded that Congress intended to cover the employment practices of all public entities and that the applicable effective date is that of title II.

The statutory language of section 204(b) of the ADA requires the Department to issue a regulation that is consistent with the ADA and the Department's coordination regulation under section 504, 28 CFR part 41. The coordination regulation specifically requires nondiscrimination in employment, 28 CFR 41.52-41.55, and does not limit coverage based on size of employer. Moreover, under all section 504 implementing regulations issued in accordance with the Department's coordination regulation, employment coverage under section 504 extends to all employers with federally assisted programs or activities, regardless of size, and the effective date for those employment requirements has always been the same as the effective date for nonemployment requirements established in the same regulations. The Department therefore concludes that § 35.140 must apply to all public entities upon the effective date of this regulation.

In the proposed regulation the Department cross-referenced the regulations implementing title I of the ADA, issued by the Equal Employment Opportunity Commission at 29 CFR part 1630, as a compliance standard for § 35.140 because, as proposed, the scope of coverage and effective date of coverage under title II would have been coextensive with title I. In the final regulation this language is modified slightly. Subparagraph (1) of new paragraph (b) makes it clear that the standards established by the Equal Employment Opportunity Commission in 29 CFR part 1630 will be the applicable compliance standards if the public entity is subject to title I. If the public entity is not covered by title I, or until it is covered by title I, subparagraph (b)(2) cross references section 504 standards for what constitutes employment discrimination, as established by the Department of Justice in 28 CFR part 41. Standards for title I of the ADA and section 504 of the Rehabilitation Act are for the most part identical because title I of the ADA was based on requirements set forth in regulations implementing section 504.

The Department, together with the other Federal agencies responsible for the enforcement of Federal laws prohibiting employment discrimination on the basis of disability, recognizes the potential for jurisdictional overlap that exists with respect to coverage of public entities and the need to avoid problems related to overlapping coverage. The other Federal agencies include the Equal Employment Opportunity Commission, which is the agency primarily responsible for enforcement of title I of the ADA, the Department of Labor, which is the agency responsible for enforcement of section 503 of the Rehabilitation Act of 1973, and 26 Federal agencies with programs of Federal financial assistance, which are responsible for enforcing section 504 in those programs. Section 107 of the ADA requires that coordination mechanisms be developed in connection with the administrative enforcement of complaints alleging discrimination under title I and complaints alleging discrimination in employment in violation of the Rehabilitation Act. Although the ADA does not specifically require inclusion of employment complaints under title II in the coordinating mechanisms required by title I, Federal investigations of title II employment complaints will be coordinated on a government-wide basis also. The Department is currently working with the EEOC and other affected Federal agencies to develop effective coordinating mechanisms, and final regulations on this issue will be issued on or before January 26, 1992.

Subpart D—Program Accessibility

Section 35.149 Discrimination Prohibited

Section 35.149 states the general nondiscrimination principle underlying the program accessibility requirements of § § 35.150 and 35.151.

Section 35.150 Existing Facilities

Consistent with section 204(b) of the Act, this regulation adopts the program accessibility concept found in the section 504 regulations for federally conducted programs or activities (e.g. 28 CFR part 39). The concept of "program accessibility" was first used in the section 504 regulation adopted by the Department of Health, Education, and Welfare for its federally assisted programs and activities in 1977. It allowed recipients to make their federally assisted programs and activities available to individuals with disabilities without extensive retrofitting of their existing buildings and facilities, by offering those programs through alternative methods. Program accessibility has proven to be a useful approach and was adopted in the regulations issued for programs and activities conducted by Federal Executive agencies. The Act provides that the concept of program access will continue to apply with respect to facilities now in existence, because the cost of retrofitting existing facilities is often prohibitive.

Section 35.150 requires that each service, program, or activity conducted by a public entity, when viewed in its entirety, be readily accessible to and usable by individuals with disabilities. The regulation makes clear, however, that a public entity is not required to make each of its existing facilities accessible (§ 35.150(a)(1)). Unlike title III of the Act, which requires public accommodations to remove architectural barriers where such removal is "readily achievable," or to provide goods and services through alternative methods, where those methods are "readily achievable," title II requires a public entity to make its programs accessible in all cases, except where to do so would result in a fundamental alteration in the nature of the program or in undue financial and administrative burdens. Congress intended the "undue burden" standard in title II to be significantly higher than the "readily achievable" standard in title III. Thus, although title II may not require removal of barriers in some cases where removal would be required under title III, the program access requirement of title II should enable individuals with disabilities to participate in and benefit from the services, programs, or activities of public entities in all but the most unusual cases.

Paragraph (a)(2), which establishes a special limitation on the obligation to ensure program accessibility in historic preservation programs, is discussed below in connection with paragraph (b).

Paragraph (a)(3), which is taken from the section 504 regulations for federally conducted programs, generally codifies case law that defines the scope of the public entity's obligation to ensure program accessibility. This paragraph provides that, in meeting the program accessibility requirement, a public entity is not required to take any action that would result in a fundamental alteration in the nature of its service, program, or activity or in undue financial and administrative burdens. A similar limitation is provided in § 35.164.

This paragraph does not establish an absolute defense; it does not relieve a public entity of all obligations to individuals with disabilities. Although a public entity is not required to take actions that would result in a fundamental alteration in the nature of a service, program, or activity or in undue financial and administrative burdens, it nevertheless must take any other steps necessary to ensure that individuals with disabilities receive the benefits or services provided by the public entity.

It is the Department's view that compliance with § 35.150(a), like compliance with the corresponding provisions of the section 504 regulations for federally conducted programs, would in most cases, not result in undue financial and administrative burdens on a public entity. In determining whether financial and administrative burdens are undue, all public entity resources available for use in the funding and operation of the service, program, or activity should be considered. The burden of proving that compliance with paragraph (a) of § 35.150 would fundamentally alter the nature of a service, program, or activity or would result in undue financial and administrative burdens rests with the public entity.

The decision that compliance would result in such alteration or burdens must be made by the head of the public entity or his or her designee and must be accompanied by a written statement of the reasons for reaching that conclusion. The Department recognizes the difficulty of identifying the official responsible for this determination, given the variety of organizational forms that may be taken by public entities and their components. The intention of this paragraph is that the determination must be made by a high level official, no lower than a Department head, having budgetary authority and responsibility for making spending decisions.

Any person who believes that he or she or any specific class of persons has been injured by the public entity head's decision or failure to make a decision may file a complaint under the compliance procedures established in subpart F.

Paragraph (b)(1) sets forth a number of means by which program accessibility may be achieved, including redesign of equipment, reassignment of services to accessible buildings, and provision of aides.

The Department wishes to clarify that, consistent with longstanding interpretation of section 504, carrying an individual with a disability is considered an ineffective and therefore an unacceptable method for achieving program accessibility. Department of Health, Education, and Welfare, Office of Civil Rights, Policy Interpretation No. 4, 43 FR 36035 (August 14, 1978). Carrying will be permitted only in manifestly exceptional cases, and only if all personnel who are permitted to participate in carrying an individual with a disability are formally instructed on the safest and least humiliating means of carrying. "Manifestly exceptional" cases in which carrying would be permitted might include, for example, programs conducted in unique facilities, such as an oceanographic vessel, for which structural changes and devices necessary to adapt the facility for use by individuals with mobility impairments are unavailable or prohibitively expensive. Carrying is not permitted as an alternative to structural modifications such as installation of a ramp or a chairlift.

In choosing among methods, the public entity shall give priority consideration to those that will be consistent with provision of services in the most integrated setting appropriate to the needs of individuals with disabilities. Structural changes in existing facilities are required only when there is no other feasible way to make the public entity's program accessible. (It should be noted that "structural changes" include all physical changes to a facility; the term does not refer only to changes to structural features, such as removal of or alteration to a load-bearing structural member.) The requirements of § 35.151 for alterations apply to structural changes undertaken to comply with this section. The public entity may comply with the program accessibility requirement by delivering services at alternate accessible sites or making home visits as appropriate.

Historic Preservation Programs

In order to avoid possible conflict between the congressional mandates to preserve historic properties, on the one hand, and to eliminate discrimination against individuals with disabilities on the other, paragraph (a)(2) provides that a public entity is not required to take any action that would threaten or destroy the historic significance of an historic property. The special limitation on program accessibility set forth in paragraph (a)(2) is applicable only to historic preservation programs, as defined in § 35.104, that is, programs that have preservation of historic properties as a primary purpose. Narrow application of the special limitation is justified because of the inherent flexibility of the program accessibility requirement. Where historic preservation is not a primary purpose of the program, the public entity is not required to use a particular facility. It can relocate all or part of its program to an accessible facility, make home visits, or use other standard methods of achieving program accessibility without making structural alterations that might threaten or destroy significant historic features of the historic property. Thus, government programs located in historic properties, such as an historic State capitol, are not excused from the requirement for program access.

Paragraph (a)(2), therefore, will apply only to those programs that uniquely concern the preservation and experience of the historic property itself. Because the primary benefit of an historic preservation program is the experience of the historic property, paragraph (b)(2) requires the public entity to give priority to methods of providing program accessibility that permit individuals with disabilities to have physical access to the historic property. This priority on physical access may also be viewed as a specific application of the general requirement that the public entity administer programs in the most integrated setting appropriate to the needs of qualified individuals with disabilities (§ 35.130(d)). Only when providing physical access would threaten or destroy the historic significance of an historic property, or would result in a fundamental alteration in the nature of the program or in undue financial and administrative burdens, may the public entity adopt alternative methods for providing program accessibility that do not ensure physical access. Examples of some alternative methods are provided in paragraph (b)(2).

Time Periods

Paragraphs (c) and (d) establish time periods for complying with the program accessibility requirement. Like the regulations for federally assisted programs (e.g., 28 CFR 41.57(b)), paragraph (c) requires the public entity to make any necessary structural changes in facilities as soon as practicable, but in no event later than three years after the effective date of this regulation.

The proposed rule provided that, aside from structural changes, all other necessary steps to achieve compliance with this part must be taken within sixty days. The sixty day period was taken from regulations implementing section 504, which generally were effective no more than thirty days after publication. Because this regulation will not be effective until January 26, 1992, the Department has concluded that no additional transition period for non-structural changes is necessary, so the sixty day period has been omitted in the final rule. Of course, this section does not reduce or eliminate any obligations that are already applicable to a public entity under section 504.

Where structural modifications are required, paragraph (d) requires that a transition plan be developed by an entity that employs 50 or more persons, within six months of the effective date of this regulation. The legislative history of title II of the ADA makes it clear that, under title II, "local and state governments are required to provide curb cuts on public streets." Education and Labor report at 84. As the rationale for the provision of curb cuts, the House report explains, "The employment, transportation, and public accommodation sections of *** (the ADA) would be meaningless if people who use wheelchairs were not afforded the opportunity to travel on and between the streets." Id. Section 35.151(e), which establishes accessibility requirements for new construction and alterations, requires that all newly constructed or altered streets, roads, or highways must contain curb ramps or other sloped areas at any intersection having curbs or other barriers to entry from a street level pedestrian walkway, and all newly constructed or altered street level pedestrian walkways must have curb ramps or other sloped areas at intersections to streets, roads, or highways. A new paragraph (d)(2) has been added to the final rule to clarify the application of the general requirement for program accessibility to the provision of curb cuts at existing crosswalks. This paragraph requires that the transition plan include a schedule for providing curb ramps or other sloped areas at existing pedestrian walkways, giving priority to walkways serving entities covered by the Act, including State and local government offices and facilities, transportation, public accommodations, and employers, followed by walkways serving other areas. Pedestrian "walkways" include locations where access is required for use of public transportation, such as bus stops that are not located at intersections or crosswalks.

Similarly, a public entity should provide an adequate number of accessible parking spaces in existing parking lots or garages over which it has jurisdiction.

Paragraph (d)(3) provides that, if a public entity has already completed a transition plan required by a regulation implementing section 504, the transition plan required by this part will apply only to those policies and practices that were not covered by the previous transition plan. Some commenters suggested that the transition plan should include all aspects of the public entity's operations, including those that may have been covered by a previous transition plan under section 504. The Department believes that such a duplicative requirement would be inappropriate. Many public entities may find, however, that it will be simpler to include all of their operations in the transition plan than to attempt to identify and exclude specifically those that were addressed in a previous plan. Of course, entities covered under section 504 are not shielded from their obligations under that statute merely because they are included under the transition plan developed under this section.

Section 35.151 New Construction and Alterations

Section 35.151 provides that those buildings that are constructed or altered by, on behalf of, or for the use of a public entity shall be designed, constructed, or altered to be readily accessible to and usable by individuals with disabilities if the construction was commenced after the effective date of this part. Facilities under design on that date will be governed by this section if the date that bids were invited falls after the effective date. This interpretation is consistent with Federal practice under section 504.

Section 35.151(c) establishes two standards for accessible new construction and alteration. Under paragraph (c), design, construction, or alteration of facilities in conformance with the Uniform Federal Accessibility Standards (UFAS) or with the Americans with Disabilities Act Accessibility Guidelines for Buildings and Facilities (hereinafter ADAAG) shall be deemed to comply with the requirements of this section with respect to those facilities except that, if ADAAG is chosen, the elevator exemption contained at § § 36.401(d) and 36.404 does not apply. ADAAG is the standard for private buildings and was issued as guidelines by the Architectural and Transportation Barriers Compliance Board (ATBCB) under title III of the ADA. It has been adopted by the Department of Justice and is published as appendix A to the Department's title III rule in today's FEDERAL REGISTER. Departures from particular requirements of these standards by the use of other methods shall be permitted when it is clearly evident that equivalent access to the facility or part of the facility is thereby provided. Use of two standards is a departure from the proposed rule.

The proposed rule adopted UFAS as the only interim accessibility standard because that standard was referenced by the regulations implementing section 504 of the Rehabilitation Act promulgated by most Federal funding agencies. It is, therefore, familiar to many State and local government entities subject to this rule. The Department, however, received many comments objecting to the adoption of UFAS. Commenters pointed out that, except for the elevator exemption, UFAS is not as stringent as ADAAG. Others suggested that the standard should be the same to lessen confusion.

Section 204(b) of the Act states that title II regulations must be consistent not only with section 504 regulations but also with "this Act." Based on this provision, the Department has determined that a public entity should be entitled to choose to comply either with ADAAG or UFAS.

Public entities who choose to follow ADAAG, however, are not entitled to the elevator exemption contained in title III of the Act and implemented in the title III regulation at § 36.401(d) for new construction and § 36.404 for alterations. Section 303(b) of title III states that, with some exceptions, elevators are not required in facilities that are less than three stories or have less than 3000 square feet per story.

The section 504 standard, UFAS, contains no such exemption. Section 501 of the ADA makes clear that nothing in the Act may be construed to apply a lesser standard to public entities than the standards applied under section 504. Because permitting the elevator exemption would clearly result in application of a lesser standard than that applied under section 504, paragraph (c) states that the elevator exemption does not apply when public entities choose to follow ADAAG. Thus, a two-story courthouse, whether built according to UFAS or ADAAG, must be constructed with an elevator. It should be noted that Congress did not include an elevator exemption for public transit facilities covered by subtitle B of title II, which covers public transportation provided by public entities, providing further evidence that Congress intended that public buildings have elevators.

Section 504 of the ADA requires the ATBCB to issue supplemental Minimum Guidelines and Requirements for Accessible Design of buildings and facilities subject to the Act, including title II. Section 204(e) of the ADA provides that the Attorney General shall promulgate regulations implementing title II that are consistent with the ATBCB's ADA guidelines. The ATBCB has announced its intention to issue title II guidelines in the future. The Department anticipates that, after the ATBCB's title II guidelines have been published, this rule will be amended to adopt new accessibility standards consistent with the ATBCB's rulemaking. Until that time, however, public entities will have a choice of following UFAS or ADAAG, without the elevator exemption.

Existing buildings leased by the public entity after the effective date of this part are not required by the regulation to meet accessibility standards simply by virtue of being leased. They are subject, however, to the program accessibility standard for existing facilities in § 35.150. To the extent the buildings are newly constructed or altered, they must also meet the new construction and alteration requirements of § 35.151.

The Department received many comments urging that the Department require that public entities lease only accessible buildings. Federal practice under section 504 has always treated newly leased buildings as subject to the existing facility program accessibility standard. Section 204(b) of the Act states that, in the area of "program accessibility, existing facilities," the title II regulations must be consistent with section 504 regulations. Thus, the Department has adopted the section 504 principles for these types of leased buildings. Unlike the construction or new buildings where architectural barriers can be avoided at little or no cost, the application of new construction standards to an existing building being leased raises the same prospect of retrofitting buildings as the use of an existing Federal facility, and the same program accessibility standard should apply to both owned and leased existing buildings. Similarly, requiring that public entities only lease accessible space would significantly restrict the options of State and local governments in seeking leased space, which would be particularly burdensome in rural or sparsely populated areas.

On the other hand, the more accessible the leased space is, the fewer structural modifications will be required in the future for particular employees whose disabilities may necessitate barrier removal as a reasonable accommodation. Pursuant to the requirements for leased buildings contained in the Minimum Guidelines and Requirements for Accessible Design published under the Architectural Barriers Act by the ATBCB, 36 CFR 1190.34, the Federal Government may not lease a building unless it contains (1) One accessible route from an accessible entrance to those areas in which the principal activities for which the building is leased are conducted, (2) accessible toilet facilities, and (3) accessible parking facilities, if a parking area is included within the lease (36 CFR 1190.34). Although these requirements are not applicable to buildings leased by public entities covered by this regulation, such entities are encouraged to look for the most accessible space available to lease and to attempt to find space complying at least with these minimum Federal requirements.

Section 35.151(d) gives effect to the intent of Congress, expressed in section 504(c) of the Act, that this part recognize the national interest in preserving significant historic structures. Commenters criticized the Department's use of descriptive terms in the proposed rule that are different from those used in the ADA to describe eligible historic properties. In addition, some commenters criticized the Department's decision to use the concept of "substantially impairing" the historic features of a property, which is a concept employed in regulations implementing section 504 of the Rehabilitation Act of 1973. Those commenters recommended that the Department adopt the criteria of "adverse effect" published by the Advisory Council on Historic Preservation under the National Historic Preservation Act, 36 CFR 800.9, as the standard for determining whether an historic property may be altered.

The Department agrees with these comments to the extent that they suggest that the language of the rule should conform to the language employed by Congress in the ADA. A definition of "historic property," drawn from section 504 of the ADA, has been added to § 35.104 to clarify that the term applies to those properties listed or eligible for listing in the National Register of Historic Places, or properties designated as historic under State or local law.

The Department intends that the exception created by this section be applied only in those very rare situations in which it is not possible to provide access to an historic property using the special access provisions established by UFAS and ADAAG. Therefore, paragraph (d)(1) of § 35.151 has been revised to clearly state that alterations to historic properties shall comply, to the maximum extent feasible, with section 4.1.7 of UFAS or section 4.1.7 of ADAAG. Paragraph (d)(2) has been revised to provide that, if it has been determined under the procedures established in UFAS and ADAAG that it is not feasible to provide physical access to an historic property in a manner that will not threaten or destroy the historic significance of the property, alternative methods of access shall be provided pursuant to the requirements of § 35.150.

In response to comments, the Department has added to the final rule a new paragraph (e) setting out the requirements of § 36.151 as applied to curb ramps. Paragraph (e) is taken from the statement contained in the preamble to the proposed rule that all newly constructed or altered streets, roads, and highways must contain curb ramps at any intersection having curbs or other barriers to entry from a street level pedestrian walkway, and that all newly constructed or altered street level pedestrian walkways must have curb ramps at intersections to streets, roads, or highways.

Subpart E—Communications

Section 35.160 General

Section 35.160 requires the public entity to take such steps as may be necessary to ensure that communications with applicants, participants, and members of the public with disabilities are as effective as communications with others.

Paragraph (b)(1) requires the public entity to furnish appropriate auxiliary aids and services when necessary to afford an individual with a disability an equal opportunity to participate in, and enjoy the benefits of, the public entity's service, program, or activity. The public entity must provide an opportunity for individuals with disabilities to request the auxiliary aids and services of their choice. This expressed choice shall be given primary consideration by the public entity (§ 35.160(b)(2)). The public entity shall honor the choice unless it can demonstrate that another effective means of communication exists or that use of the means chosen would not be required under § 35.164.

Deference to the request of the individual with a disability is desirable because of the range of disabilities, the variety of auxiliary aids and services, and different circumstances requiring effective communication. For instance, some courtrooms are now equipped for "computer-assisted transcripts," which allow virtually instantaneous transcripts of courtroom argument and testimony to appear on displays. Such a system might be an effective auxiliary aid or service for a person who is deaf or has a hearing loss who uses speech to communicate, but may be useless for someone who uses sign language.

Although in some circumstances a notepad and written materials may be sufficient to permit effective communication, in other circumstances they may not be sufficient. For example, a qualified interpreter may be necessary when the information being communicated is complex, or is exchanged for a lengthy period of time. Generally, factors to be considered in determining whether an interpreter is required include the context in which the communication is taking place, the number of people involved, and the importance of the communication.

Several commenters asked that the rule clarify that the provision of readers is sometimes necessary to ensure access to a public entity's services, programs, or activities. Reading devices or readers should be provided when necessary for equal participation and opportunity to benefit from any governmental service, program, or activity, such as reviewing public documents, examining demonstrative evidence, and filling out voter registration forms or forms needed to receive public benefits. The importance of providing qualified readers for examinations administered by public entities is discussed under § 35.130. Reading devices and readers are appropriate auxiliary aids and services where necessary to permit an individual with a disability to participate in or benefit from a service, program, or activity.

Section 35.160(b)(2) of the proposed rule, which provided that a public entity need not furnish individually prescribed devices, readers for personal use or study, or other devices of a personal nature, has been deleted in favor of a new section in the final rule on personal devices and services (see § 35.135).

In response to comments, the term "auxiliary aids and services" is used in place of "auxiliary aids" in the final rule. This phrase better reflects the range of aids and services that may be required under this section.

A number of comments raised questions about the extent of a public entity's obligation to provide access to television programming for persons with hearing impairments. Television and videotape programming produced by public entities are covered by this section. Access to audio portions of such programming may be provided by closed captioning.

Section 35.161 Telecommunication Devices for the Deaf (TDD's)

Section 35.161 requires that, where a public entity communicates with applicants and beneficiaries by telephone, TDD's or equally effective telecommunication systems be used to communicate with individuals with impaired speech or hearing.

Problems arise when a public entity which does not have a TDD needs to communicate with an individual who uses a TDD or vice versa. Title IV of the ADA addresses this problem by requiring establishment of telephone relay services to permit communications between individuals who communicate by TDD and individuals who communicate by the telephone alone. The relay services required by title IV would involve a relay operator using both a standard telephone and a TDD to type the voice messages to the TDD user and read the TDD messages to the standard telephone user.

Section 204(b) of the ADA requires that the regulation implementing title II with respect to communications be consistent with the Department's regulation implementing section 504 for its federally conducted programs and activities at 28 CFR part 39. Section 35.161, which is taken from § 39.160(a)(2) of that regulation, requires the use of TDD's or equally effective telecommunication systems for communication with people who use TDD's. Of course, where relay services, such as those required by title IV of the ADA are available, a public entity may use those services to meet the requirements of this section.

Many commenters were concerned that public entities should not rely heavily on the establishment of relay services. The commenters explained that while relay services would be of vast benefit to both public entities and individuals who use TDD's, the services are not sufficient to provide access to all telephone services. First, relay systems do not provide effective access to the increasingly popular automated systems that require the caller to respond by pushing a button on a touch tone phone. Second, relay systems cannot operate fast enough to convey messages on answering machines, or to permit a TDD user to leave a recorded message. Third, communication through relay systems may not be appropriate in cases of crisis lines pertaining to rape, domestic violence, child abuse, and drugs. The Department believes that it is more appropriate for the Federal Communications Commission to address these issues in its rulemaking under title IV.

Some commenters requested that those entities with frequent contacts with clients who use TDD's have on-site TDD's to provide for direct communication between the entity and the individual. The Department encourages those entities that have extensive telephone contact with the public such as city halls, public libraries, and public aid offices, to have TDD's to insure more immediate access. Where the provision of telephone service is a major function of the entity, TDD's should be available.

Section 35.162 Telephone Emergency Services

Many public entities provide telephone emergency services by which individuals can seek immediate assistance from police, fire, ambulance, and other emergency services. These telephone emergency services—including "911" services—are clearly an important public service whose reliability can be a matter of life or death. The legislative history of title II specifically reflects congressional intent that public entities must ensure that telephone emergency services, including 911 services, be accessible to persons with impaired hearing and speech through telecommunication technology (Conference report at 67; Education and Labor report at 84-85).

Proposed § 35.162 mandated that public entities provide emergency telephone services to persons with disabilities that are "functionally equivalent" to voice services provided to others. Many commenters urged the Department to revise the section to make clear that direct access to telephone emergency services is required by title II of the ADA as indicated by the legislative history (Conference report at 67-68; Education and Labor report at 85). In response, the final rule mandates "direct access," instead of "access that is functionally equivalent" to that provided to all other telephone users. Telephone emergency access through a third party or through a relay service would not satisfy the requirement for direct access.

Several commenters asked about a separate seven-digit emergency call number for the 911 services. The requirement for direct access disallows the use of a separate seven digit number where 911 service is available. Separate seven-digit emergency call numbers would be unfamiliar to many individuals and also more burdensome to use. A standard emergency 911 number is easier to remember and would save valuable time spent in searching in telephone books for a local seven-digit emergency number.

Many commenters requested the establishment of minimum standards of service (e.g., the quantity and location of TDD's and computer modems needed in a given emergency center). Instead of establishing these scoping requirements, the Department has established a performance standard through the mandate for direct access.

Section 35.162 requires public entities to take appropriate steps, including equipping their emergency systems with modern technology, as may be necessary to promptly receive and respond to a call from users of TDD's and computer modems. Entities are allowed the flexibility to determine what is the appropriate technology for their particular needs. In order to avoid mandating use of particular technologies that may become outdated, the Department has eliminated the references to the Baudot and ASCII formats in the proposed rule.

Some commenters requested that the section require the installation of a voice amplification device on the handset of the dispatcher's telephone to amplify the dispatcher's voice. In an emergency, a person who has a hearing loss may be using a telephone that does not have an amplification device. Installation of speech amplification devices on the handsets of the dispatchers' telephones would respond to that situation. The Department encourages their use.

Several commenters emphasized the need for proper maintenance of TDD's used in telephone emergency services. Section 35.133, which mandates maintenance of accessible features, requires public entities to maintain in operable working condition TDD's and other devices that provide direct access to the emergency system.

Section 35.163 Information and Signage

Section 35.163(a) requires the public entity to provide information to individuals with disabilities concerning accessible services, activities, and facilities. Paragraph (b) requires the public entity to provide signage at all inaccessible entrances to each of its facilities that directs users to an accessible entrance or to a location with information about accessible facilities.

Several commenters requested that, where TDD-equipped pay phones or portable TDD's exist, clear signage should be posted indicating the location of the TDD. The Department believes that this is required by paragraph (a). In addition, the Department recommends that, in large buildings that house TDD's, directional signage indicating the location of available TDD's should be placed adjacent to banks of telephones that do not contain a TDD.

Section 35.164 Duties

Section 35.164, like paragraph (a)(3) of § 35.150, is taken from the section 504 regulations for federally conducted programs. Like paragraph (a)(3), it limits the obligation of the public entity to ensure effective communication in accordance with *Davis* and the circuit court opinions interpreting it. It also includes specific requirements for determining the existence of undue financial and administrative burdens. The preamble discussion of § 35.150(a) regarding that determination is applicable to this section and further explains the public entity's obligation to comply with § § 35.160-35.164. Because of the essential nature of the services provided by telephone emergency systems, the Department assumes that § 35.164 will rarely be applied to § 35.162.

Subpart F—Compliance Procedures

Subpart F sets out the procedures for administrative enforcement of this part. Section 203 of the Act provides that the remedies, procedures, and rights set forth in section 505 of the Rehabilitation Act of 1973 (29 U.S.C. 794a) for enforcement of section 504 of the Rehabilitation Act, which prohibits discrimination on the basis of handicap in programs and activities that receive Federal financial assistance, shall be the remedies, procedures, and rights for enforcement of title II. Section 505, in turn, incorporates by reference the remedies, procedures, and rights set forth in title VI of the Civil Rights Act of 1964 (42 U.S.C. 2000d to 2000d-4a). Title VI, which prohibits discrimination on the basis of race, color, or national origin in federally assisted programs, is enforced by the Federal agencies that provide the Federal financial assistance to the covered programs and activities in question. If voluntary compliance cannot be achieved, Federal agencies enforce title VI either by the termination of Federal funds to a program that is found to discriminate, following an administrative hearing, or by a referral to this Department for judicial enforcement.

Title II of the ADA extended the requirements of section 504 to all services, programs, and activities of State and local governments, not only those that receive Federal financial assistance. The House Committee on Education and Labor explained the enforcement provisions as follows:

It is the Committee's intent that administrative enforcement of section 202 of the legislation should closely parallel the Federal government's experience with section 504 of the Rehabilitation Act of 1973. The Attorney General should use section 504 enforcement procedures and the Department's coordination role under Executive Order 12250 as models for regulation in this area.

The Committee envisions that the Department of Justice will identify appropriate Federal agencies to oversee compliance activities for State and local governments. As with section 504, these Federal agencies, including the Department of Justice, will receive, investigate, and where possible, resolve complaints of discrimination. If a Federal agency is unable to resolve a complaint by voluntary means, * * * the major enforcement sanction for the Federal government will be referral of cases by these Federal agencies to the Department of Justice.

The Department of Justice may then proceed to file suits in Federal district court. As with section 504, there is also a private right of action for persons with disabilities, which includes the full panoply of remedies. Again, consistent with section 504, it is not the Committee's intent that persons with disabilities need to exhaust Federal administrative remedies before exercising their private right of action.

Education & Labor report at 98. See also S. Rep. No. 116, 101st Cong., 1st Sess., at 57-58 (1989).

Subpart F effectuates the congressional intent by deferring to section 504 procedures where those procedures are applicable, that is, where a Federal agency has jurisdiction under section 504 by virtue of its provision of Federal financial assistance to the program or activity in which the discrimination is alleged to have occurred. Deferral to the 504 procedures also makes the sanction of fund termination available where necessary to achieve compliance. Because the Civil Rights Restoration Act (Pub. L. 100-259) extended the application of section 504 to all of the operations of the public entity receiving the Federal financial assistance, many activities of State and local governments are already covered by section 504. The procedures in subpart F apply to complaints concerning services, programs, and activities of public entities that are covered by the ADA.

Subpart G designates the Federal agencies responsible for enforcing the ADA with respect to specific components of State and local government. It does not, however, displace existing jurisdiction under section 504 of the various funding agencies. Individuals may still file discrimination complaints against recipients of Federal financial assistance with the agencies that provide that assistance, and the funding agencies will continue to process those complaints under their existing procedures for enforcing section 504. The substantive standards adopted in this part for title II of the ADA are generally the same as those required under section 504 for federally assisted programs, and public entities covered by the ADA are also covered by the requirements of section 504 to the extent that they receive Federal financial assistance. To the extent that title II provides greater protection to the rights of individuals with disabilities, however, the funding agencies will also apply the substantive requirements established under title II and this part in processing complaints covered by both this part and section 504, except that fund termination procedures may be used only for violations of section 504.

Subpart F establishes the procedures to be followed by the agencies designated in subpart G for processing complaints against State and local government entities when the designated agency does not have jurisdiction under section 504.

Section 35.170 Complaints

Section 35.170 provides that any individual who believes that he or she or a specific class of individuals has been subjected to discrimination on the basis of disability by a public entity may, by himself or herself or by an authorized representative, file a complaint under this part within 180 days of the date of the alleged discrimination, unless the time for filing is extended by the agency for good cause. Although § 35.107 requires public entities that employ 50 or more persons to establish grievance procedures for resolution of complaints, exhaustion of those procedures is not a prerequisite to filing a complaint under this section. If a complainant chooses to follow the public entity's grievance procedures, however, any resulting delay may be considered good cause for extending the time allowed for filing a complaint under this part.

Filing the complaint with any Federal agency will satisfy the requirement for timely filing. As explained below, a complaint filed with an agency that has jurisdiction under section 504 will be processed under the agency's procedures for enforcing section 504.

Some commenters objected to the complexity of allowing complaints to be filed with different agencies. The multiplicity of enforcement jurisdiction is the result of following the statutorily mandated enforcement scheme. The Department has, however, attempted to simplify procedures for complainants by making the Federal agency that receives the complaint responsible for referring it to an appropriate agency.

The Department has also added a new paragraph (c) to this section providing that a complaint may be filed with any agency designated under subpart G of this part, or with any agency that provides funding to the public entity that is the subject of the complaint, or with the Department of Justice. Under § 35.171(a)(2), the Department of Justice will refer complaints for which it does not have jurisdiction under section 504 to an agency that does have jurisdiction under section 504, or to the agency designated under subpart G as responsible for complaints filed against the public entity that is the subject of the complaint or in the case of an employment complaint that is also subject to title I of the Act, to the Equal Employment Opportunity Commission. Complaints filed with the Department of Justice may be sent to the Coordination and Review Section, P.O. Box 66118, Civil Rights Division, U.S. Department of Justice, Washington, DC 20035-6118.

Section 35.171 Acceptance of Complaints

Section 35.171 establishes procedures for determining jurisdiction and responsibility for processing complaints against public entities. The final rule provides complainants an opportunity to file with the Federal funding agency of their choice. If that agency does not have jurisdiction under section 504, however, and is not the agency designated under subpart G as responsible for that public entity, the agency must refer the complaint to the Department of Justice, which will be responsible for referring it either to an agency that does have jurisdiction under section 504 or to the appropriate designated agency, or in the case of an employment complaint that is also subject to title I of the Act, to the Equal Employment Opportunity Commission.

Whenever an agency receives a complaint over which it has jurisdiction under section 504, it will process the complaint under its section 504 procedures. When the agency designated under subpart G receives a complaint for which it does not have jurisdiction under section 504, it will treat the complaint as an ADA complaint under the procedures established in this subpart.

Section 35.171 also describes agency responsibilities for the processing of employment complaints. As described in connection with § 35.140, additional procedures regarding the coordination of employment complaints will be established in a coordination regulation issued by DOE and EEOC. Agencies with jurisdiction under section 504 for complaints alleging employment discrimination also covered by title I will follow the procedures established by the coordination regulation for those complaints. Complaints covered by title I but not section 504 will be referred to the EEOC, and complaints covered by this part but not title I will be processed under the procedures in this part.

Section 35.172 Resolution of Complaints

Section 35.172 requires the designated agency to either resolve the complaint or issue to the complainant and the public entity a Letter of Findings containing findings of fact and conclusions of law and a description of a remedy for each violation found.

The Act requires the Department of Justice to establish administrative procedures for resolution of complaints, but does not require complainants to exhaust these administrative remedies. The Committee Reports make clear that Congress intended to provide a private right of action with the full panoply of remedies for individual victims of discrimination. Because the Act does not require exhaustion of administrative remedies, the complainant may elect to proceed with a private suit at any time.

Section 35.173 Voluntary Compliance Agreements

Section 35.173 requires the agency to attempt to resolve all complaints in which it finds noncompliance through voluntary compliance agreements enforceable by the Attorney General.

Section 35.174 Referral

Section 35.174 provides for referral of the matter to the Department of Justice if the agency is unable to obtain voluntary compliance.

Section 35.175 Attorney's Fees

Section 35.175 states that courts are authorized to award attorneys fees, including litigation expenses and costs, as provided in section 505 of the Act. Litigation expenses include items such as expert witness fees, travel expenses, etc. The Judiciary Committee Report specifies that such items are included under the rubric of "attorneys fees" and not "costs" so that such expenses will be assessed against a plaintiff only under the standard set forth in *Christiansburg Garment Co. v. Equal Employment Opportunity Commission,* 434 U.S. 412 (1978), (Judiciary report at 73.)

Section 35.176 Alternative Means of Dispute Resolution

Section 35.176 restates section 513 of the Act, which encourages use of alternative means of dispute resolution.

Section 35.177 Effect of Unavailability of Technical Assistance

Section 35.177 explains that, as provided in section 506(e) of the Act, a public entity is not excused from compliance with the requirements of this part because of any failure to receive technical assistance.

Section 35.178 State Immunity

Section 35.178 restates the provision of section 502 of the Act that a State is not immune under the eleventh amendment to the Constitution of the United States from an action in Federal or State court for violations of the Act, and that the same remedies are available for any such violations as are available in an action against an entity other than a State.

Subpart G—Designated Agencies

Section 35.190 Designated Agencies

Subpart G designates the Federal agencies responsible for investigating complaints under this part. At least 26 agencies currently administer programs of Federal financial assistance that are subject to the nondiscrimination requirements of section 504 as well as other civil rights statutes. A majority of these agencies administer modest programs of Federal financial assistance and/or devote minimal resources exclusively to "external" civil rights enforcement activities. Under Executive Order 12250, the Department of Justice has encouraged the use of delegation agreements under which certain civil rights compliance responsibilities for a class of recipients funded by more than one agency are delegated by an agency or agencies to a "lead" agency. For example, many agencies that fund institutions of higher education have signed agreements that designate the Department of Education as the "lead" agency for this class of recipients.

The use of delegation agreements reduces overlap and duplication of effort, and thereby strengthens overall civil rights enforcement. However, the use of these agreements to date generally has been limited to education and health care recipients. These classes of recipients are funded by numerous agencies and the logical connection to a lead agency is clear (e.g., the Department of Education for colleges and universities, and the Department of Health and Human Services for hospitals).

The ADA's expanded coverage of State and local government operations further complicates the process of establishing Federal agency jurisdiction for the purpose of investigating complaints of discrimination on the basis of disability. Because all operations of public entities now are covered irrespective of the presence or absence of Federal financial assistance, many additional State and local government functions and organizations now are subject to Federal jurisdiction. In some cases, there is no historical or single clear-cut subject matter relationship with a Federal agency as was the case in the education example described above. Further, the 33,000 governmental jurisdictions subject to the ADA differ greatly in their organization, making a detailed and workable division of Federal agency jurisdiction by individual State, county, or municipal entity unrealistic.

This regulation applies the delegation concept to the investigation of complaints of discrimination on the basis of disability by public entities under the ADA. It designates eight agencies, rather than all agencies currently administering programs of Federal financial assistance, as responsible for investigating complaints under this part. These "designated agencies" generally have the largest civil rights compliance staffs, the most experience in complaint investigations and disability issues, and broad yet clear subject area responsibilities. This division of responsibilities is made functionally rather than by public entity type or name designation. For example, all entities (regardless of their title) that exercise responsibilities, regulate, or administer services or programs relating to lands and natural resources fall within the jurisdiction of the Department of Interior.

Complaints under this part will be investigated by the designated agency most closely related to the functions exercised by the governmental component against which the complaint is lodged. For example, a complaint against a State medical board, where such a board is a recognizable entity, will be investigated by the Department of Health and Human Services (the designated agency for regulatory activities relating to the provision of health care), even if the board is part of a general umbrella department of planning and regulation (for which the Department of Justice is the designated agency). If two or more agencies have apparent responsibility over a complaint, § 35.190(c) provides that the Assistant Attorney General shall determine which one of the agencies shall be the designated agency for purposes of that complaint.

Thirteen commenters, including four proposed designated agencies, addressed the Department of Justice's identification in the proposed regulation of nine "designated agencies" to investigate complaints under this part. Most comments addressed the proposed specific delegations to the various individual agencies. The Department of Justice agrees with several commenters who pointed out that responsibility for "historic and cultural preservation" functions appropriately belongs with the Department of Interior rather than the Department of Education. The Department of Justice also agrees with the Department of Education that "museums" more appropriately should be delegated to the Department of Interior, and that "preschool and daycare programs" more appropriately should be assigned to the Department of Health and Human Services, rather than to the Department of Education. The final rule reflects these decisions.

The Department of Commerce opposed its listing as the designated agency for "commerce and industry, including general economic development, banking and finance, consumer protection, insurance, and small business." The Department of Commerce cited its lack of a substantial existing section 504 enforcement program and experience with many of the specific functions to be delegated. The Department of Justice accedes to the Department of Commerce's position, and has assigned itself as the designated agency for these functions.

In response to a comment from the Department of Health and Human Services, the regulation's category of "medical and nursing schools" has been clarified to read "schools of medicine, dentistry, nursing, and other health-related fields." Also in response to a comment from the Department of Health and Human Services, "correctional institutions" have been specifically added to the public safety and administration of justice functions assigned to the Department of Justice.

The regulation also assigns the Department of Justice as the designated agency responsible for all State and local government functions not assigned to other designated agencies. The Department of Justice, under an agreement with the Department of the Treasury, continues to receive and coordinate the investigation of complaints filed under the Revenue Sharing Act. This entitlement program, which was terminated in 1986, provided civil rights compliance jurisdiction for a wide variety of complaints regarding the use of Federal funds to support various general activities of local governments. In the absence of any similar program of Federal financial assistance administered by another Federal agency, placement of designated agency responsibilities for miscellaneous and otherwise undesignated functions with the Department of Justice is an appropriate continuation of current practice.

The Department of Education objected to the proposed rule's inclusion of the functional area of "arts and humanities" within its responsibilities, and the Department of Housing and Urban Development objected to its proposed designation as responsible for activities relating to rent control, the real estate industry, and housing code enforcement. The Department has deleted these areas from the lists assigned to the Departments of Education and Housing and Urban Development, respectively, and has added a new paragraph (c) to § 35.190, which provides that the Department of Justice may assign responsibility for components of State or local governments that exercise responsibilities, regulate, or administer services, programs, or activities relating to functions not assigned to specific designated agencies by paragraph (b) of this section to other appropriate agencies. The Department believes that this approach will provide more flexibility in determining the appropriate agency for investigation of complaints involving those components of State and local governments not specifically addressed by the listings in paragraph (b). As provided in § § 35.170 and 35.171, complaints filed with the Department of Justice will be referred to the appropriate agency.

Several commenters proposed a stronger role for the Department of Justice, especially with respect to the receipt and assignment of complaints, and the overall monitoring of the effectiveness of the enforcement activities of Federal agencies. As discussed above, § § 35.170 and 35.171 have been revised to provide for referral of complaints by the Department of Justice to appropriate enforcement agencies. Also, language has been added to § 35.190(a) of the final regulation stating that the Assistant Attorney General shall provide policy guidance and interpretations to designated agencies to ensure the consistent and effective implementation of this part.

PART THREE

INDIVIDUALS WITH DISABILITIES EDUCATION ACT

Individuals with Disabilities
Education Act Overview

The Individuals With Disabilities Education Act (IDEA) 20 U.S.C. § 1400 *et seq.*, was originally passed into law as the Education of the Handicapped Act of 1970 (EHA) as a response to the findings by Congress that children with disabilities were receiving inadequate services, suffered from improper identification and evaluation, and were often needlessly segregated from regular classes and activities. The EHA was enacted to assist the states in providing children with disabilities with a **free appropriate public education (FAPE)**. The EHA established minimum requirements with which states had to comply in order to be eligible for federal financial assistance. First, each state must have a policy which assures all children with disabilities a free appropriate public education. Also, the states must establish certain procedural safeguards to ensure the proper education of disabled children (20 U.S.C. § 1412(1) and (5)).

To add more effective legal and procedural requirements to the original 1970 act, Congress amended the EHA with the Education for All Handicapped Children Act (EAHCA) in 1975, which contains some of the most important legal protections of the overall legislation. See 20 U.S.C. § 1415. The Handicapped Children's Protection Act of 1986 (HCPA), (P.L. 99-372), specifically authorizes attorney's fee awards to students with disabilities who prevail in IDEA lawsuits. The same legislation provides that disabled students may cumulate available remedies under § 504 of the Rehabilitation Act (29 U.S.C. § 794) and 42 U.S.C. § 1983. The HCPA appears at 20 U.S.C. § 1415(e)(4) and § 1415(f). Unlike the Rehabilitation Act, which is directed to recipients of federal funding, the IDEA is a mandate to states and local educational agencies requiring them to comply with the legislation by meeting minimum educational standards. States are the only entities that directly receive IDEA funds. Failure to comply with the Congressional directives contained in the IDEA results in the loss of funding eligibility. See 20 U.S.C. § 1412.

The IDEA defines **children with disabilities** as children with mental retardation, hearing impairments including deafness, speech or language impairments, visual impairments including blindness, serious emotional disturbance, orthopedic impairments, autism, traumatic brain injury, other health impairments, or specific learning disabilities, and who, by reason thereof, need special education and related services (20 U.S.C. § 1401(a)(1)(A)).

Special education means specially designed instruction, at no cost to the parents or guardians, to meet the unique needs of children with disabilities, including classroom instruction, instruction in physical education, home instruction, and instruction in hospitals and institutions (20 U.S.C. § 1401(a)(16)). **Related Services** means transportation, and such developmental, corrective, and other supportive services as may be required to assist disabled children to benefit from special education, and includes the early identification and assessment of disabling conditions in children (20 U.S.C. § 1401(a)(17)).

The IDEA may be understood as a legislative compromise between two competing special educational goals. The first goal is to integrate students with disabilities into regular classrooms to the greatest extent appropriate. This is the IDEA's **mainstreaming** requirement, which calls for placement of special education students in the **least restrictive environment** (20 U.S.C. § 1412(5)). It was a key finding by Congress in the original enactment of the EHA in 1970 that masses of disabled students were being denied a free appropriate public education by the segregation and exclusion of these students from the general school population. The second goal is to provide an individually tailored educational program, which allows the student to derive some educational benefit from attending school. This is accomplished through the use of an **individualized education program (IEP)**. The IEP is a statement of the special education student's present level of educational performance, the goals, and the methods of attaining those goals through a statement of the educational services to be provided.

Under the IDEA, the individualized education program must be reviewed at least annually (20 U.S.C. § 1401(a)(20)) to determine whether the program is providing the student with a free appropriate public education. Section 1415 of the IDEA is the section which lays out the mandatory procedures to be followed to safeguard the rights of students with disabilities. Under this section, parents must be given notice and an opportunity to participate in the development of their child's special education program. Parents of disabled children must also be given the opportunity to inspect and review all education records with respect to the identification, evaluation, and educational placement of their child so that it can be determined if the child is receiving a free appropriate public education (20 U.S.C. § 1415(b)(1)(A)). Further, § 1415 requires that parents be informed of all available **procedures** and methods by which any grievances or dissatisfaction may be resolved. If a school proposes to change or refuses to initiate a change in a child's educational program, or if the school refuses to perform an initial evaluation and placement of a child, the school must give written notice to the parents (20 U.S.C. § 1415(b)(1)(C)).

Generally, in order to litigate under the IDEA, parents must **exhaust their administrative remedies**. Section 1415 provides for an initial independent review of a contested IEP at the agency level. Parents have the right to an impartial hearing officer who is neither an employee of the school district nor of the state education department. Under this section, an "aggrieved party" may bring a separate civil action in state or federal court to challenge the final decision of a state educational agency. Under circumstances where exhaustion of administrative remedies would be futile, or where irreparable harm would result, exhaustion of remedies will not be required. During the pendency of a dispute over any aspect of a special education program, the disabled child must remain in his or her "then current" educational program (20 U.S.C. § 1415(e)(3)).

According to the U.S. Supreme Court, the IDEA was not enacted to maximize the potential of students with disabilities, but rather to open the door of education to these students. *Board of Education v. Rowley*, 458 U.S. 176, 102 S.Ct. 3034, 73 L.Ed.2d 690 (1982). Thus, unless a state has educational requirements more strict than those in the IDEA, the state will not need to provide the absolute best education to a disabled student, but will merely have to provide some educational benefit. The Supreme Court has also held that indefinite suspensions of students with disabilities is a violation of the **stay put provision** of the IDEA (20 U.S.C. § 1415(e)(3)). *Honig v. Doe*, 484 U.S. 305, 108 S.Ct. 592, 98 L.Ed.2d 686 (1988).

The IDEA vests states with the responsibility of implementing its requirements at 20 U.S.C. § 1412(6). In 1990, Congress passed an amendment renaming the legislation as the IDEA and adding a specific clause which abrogated sovereign immunity and authorized remedies under both legal and equitable theories (see 20 U.S.C. § 1403).

Statutory Text—Chapter 33—Education of Individuals with Disabilities

SUBCHAPTER III— CENTERS AND SERVICES TO MEET SPECIAL NEEDS OF INDIVIDUALS WITH DISABILITIES

SUBCHAPTER IV— TRAINING PERSONNEL FOR THE EDUCATION OF INDIVIDUALS WITH DISABILITIES

SUBCHAPTER V— RESEARCH IN THE EDUCATION OF INDIVIDUALS WITH DISABILITIES

SUBCHAPTER VI— INSTRUCTIONAL MEDIA FOR INDIVIDUALS WITH DISABILITIES

SUBCHAPTER I—GENERAL PROVISIONS

§ 1400. Congressional statements and declarations

(a) Short title

This chapter may be cited as the "Individuals with Disabilities Education Act."

(b) Findings

The Congress finds that—

(1) there are more than eight million children with disabilities in the United States today;

(2) the special educational needs of such children are not being fully met;

(3) more than half of the children with disabilities in the United States do not receive appropriate educational services which would enable them to have full equality of opportunity;

(4) one million of the children with disabilities in the United States are excluded entirely from the public school system and will not go through the educational process with their peers;

(5) there are many children with disabilities throughout the United States participating in regular school programs whose disabilities prevent them from having a successful educational experience because their disabilities are undetected;

(6) because of the lack of adequate services within the public school system, families are often forced to find services outside the public school system, often at great distance from their residence and at their own expense;

(7) developments in the training of teachers and in diagnostic and instructional procedures and methods have advanced to the point that, given appropriate funding, State and local educational agencies can and will provide effective special education and related services to meet the needs of children with disabilities;

(8) State and local educational agencies have a responsibility to provide education for all children with disabilities, but present financial resources are inadequate to meet the special educational needs of children with disabilities; and

(9) it is in the national interest that the Federal Government assist State and local efforts to provide programs to meet the educational needs of children with disabilities in order to assure equal protection of the law.

(c) Purpose

It is the purpose of this chapter to assure that all children with disabilities have available to them, within the time periods specified in section 1412(2)(B) of this title, a free appropriate public education which emphasizes special education and related services designed to meet their unique needs, to assure that the rights of children with disabilities and their parents or guardians are protected, to assist States and localities to provide for the education of all children with disabilities, and to assess and assure the effectiveness of efforts to educate children with disabilities.

(As amended Pub.L. 101-476, Title IX, § 901(a)(1), (b)(1)-(9), Oct. 30, 1990, 104 Stat. 1141, 1142; Pub.L. 102-119, § 25(b), Oct. 7, 1991; 105 Stat. 607.)

§ 1401. Definitions

(a) As used in this chapter—
(1)(A) The term "children with disabilities" means children—
(i) with mental retardation, hearing impairments including deafness, speech or language impairments, visual impairments including blindness, serious emotional disturbance, orthopedic impairments, autism, traumatic brain injury, other health impairments, or specific learning disabilities; and
(ii) who, by reason thereof, need special education and related services.
(B) The term "children with disabilities" for children aged 3 to 5, inclusive, may, at a State's discretion, include children—
(i) experiencing developmental delays, as defined by the State and as measured by appropriate diagnostic instruments and procedures, in one or more of the following areas: physical development, cognitive development, communication development, social or emotional development, or adaptive development; and
(ii) who, by reason thereof, need special education and related services.
(2) Repealed. Pub. L. 98-199, § 2(2), Dec. 2, 1983, 97 Stat. 1357.
(3) Repealed. Pub. L. 100-630, Title I § 101(a)(2), Nov. 7, 1988, 102 Stat. 3289.
(4) The term "construction," except where otherwise specified, means (A) erection of new or expansion of existing structures, and the acquisition and installation of equipment therefor; or (B) acquisition of existing structures not owned by any agency or institution making application for assistance under this chapter; or (C) remodeling or alteration (including the acquisition, installation, modernization, or replacement of equipment) of existing structures; or (D) acquisition of land in connection with activities in clauses (A), (B), and (C); or (E) a combination of any two or more of the foregoing.
(5) The term "equipment" includes machinery, utilities, and built-in equipment and any necessary enclosures or structures to house them, and includes all other items necessary for the functioning of a particular facility as a facility for the provision of educational services, including items such as instructional equipment and necessary furniture, printed, published, and audio-visual instructional materials, telecommunications, sensory, and other technological aids and devices, and books, periodicals, documents, and other related materials.

(6) The term "State" means any of the several States, the District of Columbia, the Commonwealth of Puerto Rico, the Virgin Islands, Guam, American Samoa, the Commonwealth of the Northern Mariana Islands, or Palau (until the compact of Free Association with Palau takes effect pursuant to 101(a) of Public Law 99-658).

(7) The term "State educational agency" means the State board of education or other agency or officer primarily responsible for the State supervision of public elementary and secondary schools, or, if there is no such officer or agency, an officer or agency designated by the Governor or by State law.

(8) The term "local educational agency" means a public board of education or other public authority legally constituted within a State for either administrative control or direction of, or to perform a service function for, public elementary or secondary schools in a city, county, township, school district, or other political subdivision of a State, or such combination of school districts or counties as are recognized in a State as an administrative agency for its public elementary or secondary schools. Such term also includes any other public institution or agency having administrative control and direction of a public elementary or secondary school.

(9) The term "elementary school" means a day or residential school which provides elementary education, as determined under State law.

(10) The term "secondary school" means a day or residential school which provides secondary education, as determined under State law, except that it does not include any education provided beyond grade 12.

(11) The term "institution of higher education" means an educational institution in any State which—

(A) admits as regular students only individuals having a certificate of graduation from a high school, or the recognized equivalent of such a certificate;

(B) is legally authorized within such State to provide a program of education beyond high school;

(C) provides an educational program for which it awards a bachelor's degree, or provides not less than a two-year program which is acceptable for full credit toward such a degree, or offers a two-year program in engineering, mathematics, or the physical or biological sciences which is designed to prepare the student to work as a technician and at a semiprofessional level in engineering, scientific, or other technological fields which require the understanding and application of basic engineering, scientific, or mathematical principles or knowledge;

(D) is a public or other nonprofit institution; and

(E) is accredited by a nationally recognized accrediting agency or association listed by the Secretary pursuant to this paragraph or, if not so accredited, is an institution whose credits are accepted, on transfer, by not less than three institutions which are so accredited, for credit on the same basis as if transferred from an institution so accredited: *Provided, however,* That in the case of an institution offering a two-year program in engineering, mathematics, or the physical or biological sciences which is designed to prepare the student to work as a technician and at a semiprofessional level in engineering, scientific, or technological fields which require the understanding and application of basic engineering, scientific, or mathematical principles or knowledge, if the Secretary determines that there is no nationally recognized accrediting agency or association qualified to accredit such institutions, the Secretary shall appoint an advisory committee, composed of persons specially qualified to evaluate training provided by such institutions, which shall prescribe the standards of content, scope, and quality which must be met in order to qualify such institutions to participate under this Act and shall also determine whether particular institutions meet such standards. For the purposes of this paragraph the Secretary shall publish a list of nationally recognized accrediting agencies or associations which the Secretary determines to be reliable authority as to the quality of education or training offered.

The term includes community colleges receiving funding from the Secretary of the Interior under the Tribally Controlled Community College Assistance Act of 1978. [20 U.S.C. § 1801 *et seq.*]

(12) The term "nonprofit" as applied to a school, agency, organization, or institution means a school, agency, organization, or institution owned and operated by one or more non-profit corporations or associations no part of the net earnings of which inures, or may lawfully inure, to the benefit of any private shareholder or individual.

(13) The term "research and related purposes" means research, research training (including the payment of stipends and allowances), surveys, or demonstrations in the field of education of children with disabilities, or the dissemination of information derived therefrom, including (but without limitation) experimental schools.

(14) The term "Secretary" means the Secretary of Education.

(15) The term "children with specific learning disabilities" means those children who have a disorder in one or more of the basic psychological processes involved in understanding or in using language, spoken or written, which disorder may manifest itself in imperfect ability to listen, think, speak, read, write, spell, or do mathematical calculations. Such disorders include such conditions as perceptual disabilities, brain injury, minimal brain dysfunction, dyslexia, and developmental aphasia. Such term does not include children who have learning problems which are primarily the result of visual, hearing, or motor disabilities, of mental retardation, of emotional disturbance, or of environmental, cultural, or economic disadvantage.

(16) The term "special education" means specially designed instruction, at no cost to parents or guardians, to meet the unique needs of a child with a disability, including—

(A) instruction conducted in the classroom, in the home, in hospitals and institutions, and in other settings; and

(B) instruction in physical education.

(17) The term "related services" means transportation, and such developmental, corrective, and other supportive services (including speech pathology and audiology, psychological services, physical and occupational therapy, recreation, including therapeutic recreation, social work services, counseling services, including rehabilitation counseling, and medical services, except that such medical services shall be for diagnostic and evaluation purposes only) as may be required to assist a child with a disability to benefit from special education, and includes the early identification and assessment of disabling conditions in children.

(18) The term "free appropriate public education" means special education and related services that—

(A) have been provided at public expense, under public supervision and direction, and without charge,

(B) meet the standards of the State educational agency,

(C) include an appropriate preschool, elementary, or secondary school education in the State involved[;] and

(D) are provided in conformity with the individualized education program required under section 1414(a)(5) of this title.

(19) The term "transition services" means a coordinated set of activities for a student, designed within an outcome-oriented process, which promotes movement from school to post-school activities, including post-secondary education, vocational training, integrated employment (including supported employment), continuing and adult education, adult services, independent living, or community participation. The coordinated set of activities shall be based upon the individual student's needs, taking into account the student's preferences and interests, and shall include instruction, community experiences, the development of employment and other post-school adult living objectives, and, when appropriate, acquisition of daily living skills and functional vocational evaluation.

(20) The term "individualized education program" means a written statement for each child with a disability developed in any meeting by a representative of the local educational agency or an intermediate educational unit who shall be qualified to provide, or supervise the provision of, specially designed instruction to meet the unique needs of children with disabilities, the teacher, the parents or guardian of such child, and, whenever appropriate, such child, which statement shall include—

(A) a statement of the present levels of educational performance of such child,

(B) a statement of annual goals, including short-term instructional objectives,

(C) a statement of the specific educational services to be provided to such child, and the extent to which such child will be able to participate in regular educational programs,

(D) a statement of the needed transition services for students beginning no later than age 16 and annually thereafter (and, when determined appropriate for the individual, beginning at age 14 or younger), including, when appropriate, a statement of the interagency responsibilities or linkages (or both) before the student leaves the school setting,

(E) the projected date for initiation and anticipated duration of such services, and

(F) appropriate objective criteria and evaluation procedures and schedules for determining, on at least an annual basis, whether instructional objectives are being achieved.

In the case where a participating agency, other than the educational agency, fails to provide agreed upon services, the educational agency shall reconvene the IEP team to identify alternative strategies to meet the transition objectives.

(21) The term "excess costs" means those costs which are in excess of the average annual per student expenditure in a local educational agency during the preceding school year for an elementary or secondary school student, as may be appropriate, and which shall be computed after deducting—

(A) amounts received—

(i) under this subchapter,

(ii) under chapter 1 of title I of the Elementary and Secondary Education Act of 1965 [20 U.S.C. § 2701 et seq.], or

(iii) under title VII of the Elementary and Secondary Education Act of 1965 [20 U.S.C. § 3281 et seq.], and

(B) any State or local funds expended for programs that would qualify for assistance under such subchapter, chapter, or title.

(22) The term "native language" has the meaning given that term by section 3283(a)(2) of the this title.

(23) The term "intermediate educational unit" means any public authority, other than a local educational agency, which is under the general supervision of a State educational agency, which is established by State law for the purpose of providing free public education on a regional basis, and which provides special education and related services to children with disabilities within that State.

(24)(A) The term "public or private nonprofit agency or organization" includes an Indian tribe and the Bureau of Indian Affairs of the Department of the Interior (when acting on behalf of schools operated by the Bureau for children and students on Indian reservations) and tribally controlled schools funded by the Department of the Interior.

(B) The terms "Indian," "American Indian," and "Indian American" mean an individual who is a member of an Indian tribe.

(C) The term "Indian tribe" means any Federal or State Indian tribe, band, rancheria, pueblo, colony, or community, including any Alaskan native village or regional village corporation (as defined in or established under the Alaska Native Claims Settlement Act [43 U.S.C. § 1601 *et seq.*]).

(25) The term "assistive technology device" means any item, piece of equipment, or product system, whether acquired commercially off the shelf, modified, or customized, that is used to increase, maintain, or improve functional capabilities of individuals with disabilities.

(26) The term "assistive technology service" means any service that directly assists an individual with a disability in the selection, acquisition, or use of an assistive technology device. Such term includes—

(A) the evaluation of the needs of an individual with a disability, including a functional evaluation of the individual in the individual's customary environment;

(B) purchasing, leasing, or otherwise providing for the acquisition of assistive technology devices by individuals with disabilities;

(C) selecting, designing, fitting, customizing, adapting, applying, maintaining, repairing, or replacing of assistive technology devices;

(D) coordinating and using other therapies, interventions, or services with assistive technology devices, such as those associated with existing education and rehabilitation plans and programs;

(E) training or technical assistance for an individual with disabilities, or, where appropriate, the family of an individual with disabilities; and

(F) training or technical assistance for professionals (including individuals providing education and rehabilitation services), employers, or other individuals who provide services to, employ, or are otherwise substantially involved in the major life functions of individuals with disabilities.

(27) The term "underrepresented" means populations such as minorities, the poor, the limited English proficient, and individuals with disabilities.

(b) For purposes of subchapter III of this chapter, "youth with a disability" means any child with a disability (as defined in subsection (a)(1) of this section) who—

(1) is twelve years of age or older; or

(2) is enrolled in the seventh or higher grade in school.

(As amended Pub.L. 101-476, Title I, § 101, Title IX, § 901(b)(10)-(20), Oct. 30, 1990, 104 Stat. 1103, 1142, 1143; Pub.L. 102-73, Title VIII, § 802(d)(1), July 25, 1991, 105 Stat. 361; Pub.L. 102-119, §§ 3, 25(a)(1), (b), Oct. 7, 1991, 105 Stat. 587, 605, 607.)

§ 1402. Office of Special Education Programs

(a) Establishment; purposes.

There shall be, within the Office of Special Education and Rehabilitation Services in the Department of Education, an Office of Special Education Programs which shall be the principal agency in the Department for administering and carrying out this chapter and other programs and activities concerning the education and training of individuals with disabilities.

(b) Deputy Assistant Secretary: selection and supervision, compensation; Associate Deputy Assistant Secretary and minimum number of assistants: establishment, compensation.

(1) The office established under subsection (a) of this section shall be headed by a Deputy Assistant Secretary who shall be selected by the Secretary and shall report directly to the Assistant Secretary for Special Education and Rehabilitative Services. The position of Deputy Assistant Secretary shall be in grade GS-18 of the General Schedule under section 5104 of Title 5 and shall be a Senior Executive Service position for the purposes of section 3132(a)(2) of such Title.

(2) In addition to such Deputy Assistant Secretary, there shall be established in such office not less than six positions for persons to assist the Deputy Assistant Secretary, including the position of the Associate Deputy Assistant Secretary. Each such position shall be in grade GS-15 of the General Schedule under section 5104 of Title 5.

(As amended Pub.L. 101-476, Title IX, § 901(b)(21), Oct. 30, 1990, 104 Stat. 1143; Pub.L. 102-119, § 25(b), Oct. 7, 1991; 105 Stat. 607.)

§ 1403. Abrogation of sovereign immunity

(a) State immunity abrogated

A State shall not be immune under the eleventh amendment to the Constitution of the United States from suit in Federal court for a violation of this chapter.

(b) Availability of remedies

In a suit against a State for a violation of this Act, remedies (including remedies both at law and in equity) are available for such a violation to the same extent as such remedies are available for such a violation in the suit against any public entity other than a State.

(c) Effective date

The provisions of subsections (a) and (b) of this section shall take effect with respect to violations that occur in whole or part after October 30, 1990.

(As amended Pub.L. 91-230, Title VI, § 604, as added Pub.L. 101-476, Title I, Oct. 30, 1990, 104 Stat. 1106.)

§ 1404. Acquisition of equipment and construction of necessary facilities

(a) Authorization for use of funds

In the case of any program authorized by this chapter, if the Secretary determines that such program will be improved by permitting the funds authorized for such program to be used for the acquisition of equipment and the construction of necessary facilities, the Secretary may authorize the use of such funds for such purposes.

(b) Recovery of payments under certain conditions

If, within twenty years after the completion of any construction (except minor remodeling or alteration) for which funds have been paid pursuant to a grant or contract under this chapter, the facility constructed ceases to be used for the purposes for which it was constructed, the United States, unless the Secretary determines that there is good cause for releasing the recipient of the funds from its obligation, shall be entitled to recover from the applicant or other owner of the facility an amount which bears the same ratio to the then value of the facility as the amount of such Federal funds bore to the cost of the portion of the facility financed with such funds. Such value shall be determined by agreement of the parties or by action brought in the United States district court for the district in which the facility is situated.

(As amended Pub.L. 102-119, § 25(a)(2), Oct. 7, 1991, 105 Stat. 605.)

§ 1405. Employment of individuals with disabilities

The Secretary shall assure that each recipient of assistance under this chapter shall make positive efforts to employ and advance in employment qualified individuals with disabilities in programs assisted under this chapter.

(As amended Pub.L. 101-476, Title IX, § 901(b)(22), (23), Oct. 30, 1990, 104 Stat. 1143; Pub.L. 102-119, § 25(b), Oct. 7, 1991; 105 Stat. 607.)

§ 1406. Grants for removal of architectural barriers; authorization of appropriations

(a) The Secretary is authorized to make grants and to enter into cooperative agreements with the Secretary of the Interior and with State educational agencies to assist such agencies in making grants to local educational agencies or intermediate educational units to pay part or all of the cost of altering existing buildings and equipment in accordance with standards promulgated under the Act entitled "An Act to insure that certain buildings financed with Federal funds are so designed and constructed as to be accessible to the physically handicapped," approved August 12, 1968 [42 U.S.C. § 4151 et seq.].

(b) For the purposes of carrying out the provisions of this section, there are authorized to be appropriated such sums as may be necessary.

(As amended Pub.L. 91-230, Title VI, § 607, as added Pub.L. 94-142, § 6(a), Nov. 29, 1975, 89 Stat. 795, and amended Pub.L. 98-199, §§ 3(b), 5, Dec. 2, 1983, 97 Stat.

1358; Pub.L. 99-457, Title IV, § 401, Oct. 8, 1986,100 Stat. 1172; Pub.L. 100-630 Title I, § 101(c), Nov. 7, 1988, 102 Stat. 3290.)

§1407. Regulation requirements

(a) Minimum period for comment before effective date

For purposes of complying with section 1232(b) of this title with respect to regulations promulgated under subchapter II of this chapter, the thirty-day period under such section shall be ninety days.

(b) Lessening of procedural or substantive protections as in effect on July 20, 1983, prohibited

The Secretary may not implement, or publish in final form, any regulation prescribed pursuant to this chapter which would procedurally or substantively lessen the protections provided to children with disabilities under this chapter, as embodied in regulations in effect on July 20, 1983 (particularly as such protections relate to parental consent to initial evaluation or initial placement in special education, least restrictive environment, related services, timeliness, attendance of evaluation personnel at individualized education program meetings, or qualifications of personnel), except to the extent that such regulation reflects the clear and unequivocal intent of the Congress in legislation.

(As amended Pub.L. 101-476, Title IX, § 901(b)(24), Oct. 30, 1990, 104 Stat. 1143; Pub.L. 102-119, § 25(b), Oct. 7, 1991; 105 Stat. 607.)

§ 1408. Eligibility for financial assistance

Effective for fiscal years for which the Secretary may make grants under section 1419(b)(1) of this chapter, no State or local educational agency or intermediate educational unit or other public institution or agency may receive a grant under subchapters III through VII of this chapter which relate exclusively to programs, projects, and activities pertaining to children aged three to five, inclusive, unless the State is eligible to receive a grant under section 1419(b)(1) of this chapter.

(Pub.L. 91-230, Title VI, § 609, as added Pub.L. 99-457, Title II, § 202, Oct. 8, 1986; 100 Stat. 1158.)

§ 1409. Administrative provisions applicable to subchapters III through VII and section 1418

(a) Plan for implementation of authorized programs

The Secretary shall maintain a process for developing a program plan for the implementation of each of the programs authorized under section 1418 of this title and subchapters III through VII of this chapter. The plan shall include program goals, objectives, strategies, and priorities. In conducting the process, the Secretary shall involve individuals with disabilities, parents, professionals, and representatives of

State and local educational agencies, private schools, institutions of higher education, and national organizations who have interest and expertise in the program.

(b) Needs of minority children and youth

In awarding grants, contracts, and cooperative agreements under subchapters III through VII of this chapter, the Secretary, where appropriate, shall require applicants to demonstrate how they will address, in whole or in part, the needs of infants, toddlers, children, and youth with disabilities from minority backgrounds.

(c) Transitions facing children with disabilities during years in school

In awarding grants, contracts, or cooperative agreements under subchapter III through VII of this chapter, the Secretary, where appropriate, may require applicants to address the various transitions that a child with a disability may face throughout such child's years in school, including—

(1) the transition from medical care to special education for those children with disabilities, including chronic health impairments, who may require individualized health-related services to enable such children to participate in, or benefit from, special education;

(2) the transition between residential placement and community-based special education services; and

(3) the transition between a separate educational placement and the regular classroom setting.

(d) Program evaluations

The Secretary shall conduct directly, or by contract or cooperative agreement with appropriate entities, independent evaluations of the programs authorized under section 1418 of this title and under subchapters III through VII of this chapter and may for such purpose use funds appropriated to carry out such provisions. The findings of the evaluators shall be utilized in the planning process under subsection (a) of this section for the purpose of improving the programs. The evaluations shall determine the degree to which the program is being conducted consistent with the program plan and meeting its goals and objectives. The Secretary shall submit to the appropriate committees of the Congress the results of the evaluations required by this subsection.

(e) Report on program plans and evaluations

The Secretary shall report on the program plans required in subsection (a) of this section and findings from the evaluations under subsection (d) of this section in the annual report to the Congress required under section 1418 of this title.

(f) Acquisition and dissemination of information

The Secretary shall develop effective procedures for acquiring and disseminating information derived from programs and projects funded under subchapters III through VII of this chapter, as well as information generated from studies conducted and data collected under section 1418 of this title.

(g) Dissemination of reports to other recipients

The Secretary shall, where appropriate, require recipients of all grants, contracts, and cooperative agreements under subchapters III through VII of this chapter to prepare reports describing their procedures, findings, and other relevant information in a form that will maximize the dissemination and use of such procedures, findings, and information. The Secretary shall require their delivery, as appropriate, to the Regional and Federal Resource Centers, the Clearinghouses, and the Technical Assistance to Parents Programs (TAPP) assisted under subchapters III and IV of this chapter, as well as the National Diffusion Network, the ERIC Clearinghouse on the Handicapped and Gifted, and the Child and Adolescent Service Systems Program (CASSP) under the National Institute of Mental Health, appropriate parent and professional organizations, organizations representing individuals with disabilities and such other networks as the Secretary may determine to be appropriate.

(h) Evaluation panels

(1) The Secretary shall convene, in accordance with paragraph (2), panels of experts who are competent, by virtue of their training or experience, to evaluate proposals under section 1418 of this title and subchapters III through VII of this chapter.

(2) Panels under paragraph (1) shall be composed of individuals with disabilities, parents of such individuals, individuals from the fields of special education, related services, and other relevant disciplines.

(3) The Secretary shall convene panels under paragraph (1) for any application that includes a total funding request exceeding $60,000 and may convene or otherwise appoint panels for applications that include funding requests that are less than such amount.

(4) Panels under paragraph (1) shall include a majority of non-Federal members. Such non-Federal members shall be provided travel and per diem not to exceed the rate provided to other educational consultants used by the Department of Education and shall be provided consultant fees at such a rate.

(5) The Secretary may use funds available under section 618 and parts C through G to pay expenses and fees of non-Federal members of the panels.

(i) Site visits

The Secretary shall conduct at least 1 site visit for each grant, contract, and cooperative agreement receiving $300,000 or more annually under subchapters III through VII of this chapter.

(j) Discretionary programs

(1) With respect to the discretionary programs authorized by subchapters III through VII of this chapter, the Congress finds as follows:

(A)(i) The Federal Government must be responsive to the growing needs of an increasingly more diverse society. A more equitable allocation of resources is essential for the Federal Government to meet its responsibility to provide an equal educational opportunity for all individuals.

(ii) America's racial profile is rapidly changing. While the rate of increase for white Americans is 3.2 percent, the rate of increase for racial and ethnic minorities is much higher: 38.6 percent for Hispanics, 14.6 percent for African-Americans, and 40.1 percent for Asians and other ethnic groups.

(iii) By the year 2000, this Nation will have 260,000,000 people, one of every three of whom will be either African-American, Hispanic, or Asian-American.

(iv) Taken together as a group, it is a more frequent phenomenon for minorities to comprise the majority of public school students. Large city school populations are overwhelmingly minority, e.g., Miami, 71 percent; Philadelphia, 73 percent; Baltimore, 80 percent.

(v) Recruitment efforts within special education at the level of preservice, continuing education, and practice must focus on bringing larger numbers of minorities into the profession in order to provide appropriate practitioner knowledge, role models, and sufficient manpower to address the clearly changing demography of special education.

(vi) The limited English proficient population is the fastest growing in our Nation, and the growth is occurring in many parts of our Nation. In the Nation's 2 largest school districts, limited-English students make up almost half of all students initially entering school at the kindergarten level. Studies have documented apparent discrepancies in the levels of referral and placement of limited-English proficient children in special education. The Department of Education has found that services provided to limited-English proficient students often do not respond primarily to the pupil's academic needs. These trends pose special challenges for special education in the referral, assessment, and services for our Nation's students from non-English language backgrounds.

(B)(i) Greater efforts are needed to prevent the intensification of problems connected with mislabeling and high dropout rates among minority children with disabilities.

(ii) More minority children continue to be served in special education than would be expected from the percentage of minority students in the general school population.

(iii) Poor African-American children are 3.5 times more likely to be identified by their teacher as mentally retarded than their white counterpart.

(iv) Although African-Americans represent 12 percent of elementary and secondary enrollments, they constitute 28 percent of total enrollments in special education.

(v) The drop out rate is 68 percent higher for minorities than for whites.

(vi) More than 50 percent of minority students in large cities drop out of school.

(C)(i) The opportunity for full participation in awards for grants and contracts; boards of organizations receiving funds under this chapter; and peer review panels; and training of professionals in the area of special education by minority individuals, organizations, and historically Black colleges and universities is essential if we are to obtain greater success in the education of minority children with disabilities.

(ii) In 1989, of the 661,000 college and university professors, 4.6 percent were African-American and 3.1 percent were Hispanic. Of the 3,600,000 teachers, prekindergarten through high school, 9.4 percent were African-American and 3.9 percent were Hispanic.

(iii) Students from minority groups comprise more than 50 percent of K-12 public school enrollment in seven States yet minority enrollment in teacher training programs is less than 15 percent in all but six States.

(iv) As the number of African-American and Hispanic students in special education increases, the number of minority teachers and related service personnel produced in our colleges and universities continues to decrease.

(v) Ten years ago, 12.5 percent of the United States teaching force in public elementary and secondary school were members of a minority group. Minorities comprised 21.3 percent of the national population at that time and were clearly underrepresented then among employed teachers. Today, the elementary and secondary teaching force is 3 to 5 percent minority, while one-third of the students in public schools are minority children.

(vi) As recently as 1984-85, Historically Black Colleges and Universities (HBCUs) supplied nearly half of the African-American teachers in the Nation. However, in 1988, HBCUs received only 2 percent of the discretionary funds for special education and related services personnel training.

(vii) While African-American students constitute 28 percent of total enrollment in special education, only 11.2 percent of individuals enrolled in preservice training programs for special education are African-American.

(viii) In 1986-87, of the degrees conferred in education at the B.A., M.A., and Ph.D levels, only 6, 8, and 8 percent, respectively, were awarded to African-American or Hispanic students.

(D) Minorities and underserved persons are socially disadvantaged because of the lack of opportunities in training and educational programs, undergirded by the practices in the private sector that impede their full participation in the mainstream of society.

(2) The Congress further finds that these conditions can be greatly improved by providing opportunities for the full participation of minorities through the implementation of the following recommendation:

(A) Implementation of a policy to mobilize the Nation's resources to prepare minorities for careers in special education and related services.

(B) This policy should focus on—

(i) the recruitment of minorities into teaching; and

(ii) financially assisting HBCUs and other institutions of higher education (whose minority student enrollment is at least 25 percent) to prepare students for special education and related service careers.

(C)(i) The Secretary shall develop a plan for providing outreach services to the entities described in clause (ii) in order to increase the participation of such entities in competitions for grants, contracts, and cooperative agreements under any of subchapters III through VII of this chapter.

(ii) The entities referred to in clause (i) are—

(I) Historically Black Colleges and Universities and other institutions of higher education whose minority student enrollment is at least 25 percent;

(II) eligible institutions as defined in section 1058 of this title;

(III) nonprofit and for-profit agencies at least 51 percent owned or controlled by one or more minority individuals; and

(IV) underrepresented populations.

(iii) For the purpose of implementing the plan required in clause (i), the Secretary shall, for each of the fiscal years 1991 through 1994, expend 1 percent of the funds appropriated for the fiscal year involved for carrying out subchapters III through VII of this chapter.

(3) The Secretary shall exercise his/her utmost authority, resourcefulness, and diligence to meet the requirements of this subsection.

(4) Not later than January 31 of each year, starting with fiscal year 1991, the Secretary shall submit to Congress a final report on the progress toward meeting the goals of this subsection during the preceding fiscal year. The report shall include—

(i) a full explanation of any progress toward meeting the goals of this subsection; and

(ii) a plan to meet the goals, if necessary.

(Pub.L. 91-230, Title VI, § 610, as added Pub.L. 101-476, Title I, § 104, Oct. 30, 1990, 104 Stat. 1106.)

SUBCHAPTER II—ASSISTANCE FOR EDUCATION OF ALL CHILDREN WITH DISABILITIES

§ 1411. Entitlements and allocations

(a) Formula for determining maximum State entitlement

(1) Except as provided in paragraph (5) and in section 1419 of this [title], the maximum amount of the grant to which a State is entitled under this subchapter for any fiscal year shall be equal to—

(A) the number of children with disabilities aged 3-5, inclusive, in a State who are receiving special education and related services as determined under paragraph (3) if the State is eligible for a grant under section 1419 of this title and the number of children with disabilities aged 6-21, inclusive, in a State who are receiving special education and related services as so determined;

multiplied by—

(B)(i) 5 per centum, for the fiscal year ending September 30, 1978, of the average per pupil expenditure in public elementary and secondary schools in the United States;

(ii) 10 per centum, for the fiscal year ending September 30, 1979, of the average per pupil expenditure in public elementary and secondary schools in the United States;

(iii) 20 per centum, for the fiscal year ending September 30, 1980, of the average per pupil expenditure in public elementary and secondary schools in the United States;

(iv) 30 per centum, for the fiscal year ending September 30, 1981, of the average per pupil expenditure in public elementary and secondary schools in the United States; and

(v) 40 per centum, for the fiscal year ending September 30, 1982, and for each fiscal year thereafter, of the average per pupil expenditure in public elementary and secondary schools in the United States:

except that no State shall receive an amount which is less than the amount which such State received under this subchapter for the fiscal year ending September 30, 1977.

(2) For the purpose of this subsection and subsection (b) through subsection (e) of this section, the term "State" does not include Guam, American Samoa, the Virgin Islands, the Commonwealth of the Northern Mariana Islands, the Federated States of Micronesia, the Republic of the Marshall Islands, and Palau.

(3) The number of children with disabilities receiving special education and related services in any fiscal year shall be equal to the number of such children

receiving special education and related services on December 1 of the fiscal year preceding the fiscal year for which the determination is made.

(4) For purposes of paragraph (1)(B), the term "average per pupil expenditure" in the United States, means the aggregate current expenditures, during the second fiscal year preceding the fiscal year for which the computation is made (or, if satisfactory data for such year are not available at the time of computation, then during the most recent preceding fiscal year for which satisfactory data are available) of all local educational agencies in the United States (which, for purposes of this subsection, means the fifty States and the District of Columbia), as the case may be, plus any direct expenditures by the State for operation of such agencies (without regard to the source of funds from which either of such expenditures are made), divided by the aggregate number of children in average daily attendance to whom such agencies provided free public education during such preceding year.

(5) (A) In determining the allotment of each State under paragraph (1), the Secretary may not count—

(i) children with disabilities aged three to seventeen, inclusive, in such State under paragraph (1)(A) to the extent the number of such children is greater than 12 percent of the number of all children aged three to seventeen, inclusive, in such State and the State serves all children with disabilities aged three to five, inclusive, in the State pursuant to State law or practice or the order of any court,

(ii) children with disabilities aged five to seventeen, inclusive, in such State under paragraph (1)(A) to the extent the number of such children is greater than 12 percent of the number of all children aged five to seventeen, inclusive, in such State and the State does not serve all children with disabilities aged three to five, inclusive, in the State pursuant to State law or practice or the order of any court; and

(iii) children with disabilities who are counted under subpart 2 of part D of chapter 1 of title I of the Elementary and Secondary Education Act of 1965 [20 U.S.C. § 2791 *et seq.*].

(B) For purposes of subparagraph (A), the number of children aged three to seventeen inclusive, in any State shall be determined by the Secretary on the basis of the most recent satisfactory data available to the Secretary.

(b) Distribution and use of grant funds by States for fiscal year ending September 30, 1978

(1) Of the funds received under subsection (a) of this section by any State for the fiscal year ending September 30, 1978—

(A) 50 per centum of such funds may be used by such State in accordance with the provisions of paragraph (2); and

(B) 50 per centum of such funds shall be distributed by such State pursuant to subsection (d) of this section to local educational agencies and intermediate educational units in such State, for use in accordance with the priorities established under section 1412(3) of this title.

(2) Of the funds which any State may use under paragraph (1)(A)—

(A) an amount which is equal to the greater of—

(i) 5 per centum of the total amount of funds received under this
   subchapter by such State; or

(ii) $200,000;

may be used by such State for administrative costs related to carrying out sections 1412 and 1413 of this title;

(B) the remainder shall be used by such State to provide support services and direct services, in accordance with the priorities established under section 1412(3) of this title.

(c) Distribution and use of grant funds by States for fiscal years ending September 30, 1979, and thereafter

(1) Of the funds received under subsection (a) of this section by any State for the fiscal year ending September 30, 1979, and for each fiscal year thereafter—

(A) 25 per centum of such funds may be used by such State in accordance with the provisions of paragraph (2); and

(B) except as provided in paragraph (4), 75 per centum of such funds shall be distributed by such State pursuant to subsection (d) of this section to local educational agencies and intermediate educational units in such State, for use in accordance with priorities established under section 1412(3) of this [chapter].

(2) (A) Subject to the provisions of subparagraph (B), of the funds which any State may use under paragraph (1)(A)—

(i) an amount which is equal to the greater of—

(I) 5 per centum of the total amount of funds received under this subchapter by such State; or

(II) $450,000;

may be used by such State for administrative costs related to carrying out the provisions of sections 1412 and 1413 of this title; and

(ii) the part remaining after use in accordance with clause (i) shall be used by the State (I) to provide support services and direct services in accordance with the priorities established under section 1412(3) of this title, and (II) for the administrative costs of monitoring and complaint investigation but only to the extent that such costs exceed the costs of administration incurred during fiscal year 1985.

(B) The amount expended by any State from the funds available to such State under paragraph (1)(A) in any fiscal year for the provision of support services or for the provision of direct services shall be matched on a program basis by such State, from funds other than Federal funds, for the provision of support services or for the provision of direct services for the fiscal year involved.

(3) The provisions of section 1413(a)(9) of this title shall not apply with respect to amounts available for use by any State under paragraph (2).

(4) (A) No funds shall be distributed by any State under this subsection in any fiscal year to any local educational agency or intermediate educational unit in such State if—

(i) such local educational agency or intermediate educational unit is entitled, under subsection (d) of this section, to less than $7,500 for such fiscal year; or

(ii) such local educational agency or intermediate educational unit has not submitted an application for such funds which meets the requirements of section 1414 of this title.

(B) Whenever the provisions of subparagraph (A) apply, the State involved shall use such funds to assure the provision of a free appropriate education to children with disabilities residing in the area served by such local educational agency or such intermediate educational unit. The provisions of paragraph (2)(B) shall not apply to the use of such funds.

(d) Allocation of funds within States to local educational agencies and intermediate educational units

From the total amount of funds available to local educational agencies and intermediate educational units in any State under subsection (b)(1)(B) or subsection (c)(1)(B) of this section, as the case may be, each local educational agency or intermediate educational unit shall be entitled to an amount which bears the same ratio to the total amount available under subsection (b)(1)(B) or subsection (c)(1)(B) of this section, as the case may be, as the number of children with disabilities aged three to twenty-one, inclusive, receiving special education and related services in such local educational agency or intermediate educational unit bears to the aggregate number of children with disabilities aged three to twenty-one, inclusive, receiving special education and related services in all local educational agencies and intermediate educational units which apply to the State educational agency involved for funds under this subchapter.

(e) Territories and possessions

(1) The jurisdictions to which this subsection applies are Guam, American Samoa, the Virgin Islands, the Commonwealth of the Northern Mariana Islands, the Federated States of Micronesia, the Republic of the Marshall Islands, and Palau.

(2) Each jurisdiction to which this subsection applies shall be entitled to a grant for the purposes set forth in section 1400(c) of this title in an amount equal to an amount determined by the Secretary in accordance with criteria based on respective needs, except that the aggregate of the amount to which such jurisdictions are so entitled for any fiscal year shall not exceed an amount equal to 1 per centum of the aggregate of the amounts available to all States under this subchapter for that fiscal year. If the aggregate of the amounts, determined by the Secretary pursuant to the preceding sentence, to be so needed for any fiscal year exceeds an amount equal to such 1 per centum limitation, the entitlement of each such jurisdiction shall be reduced proportionately until such aggregate does not exceed such 1 per centum limitation.

(3) The amount expended for administration by each jurisdiction under this subsection shall not exceed 5 per centum of the amount allotted to such jurisdiction for any fiscal year, or $35,000, whichever is greater.

(f) Indian reservations

(1) The Secretary shall make payments to the Secretary of the Interior to meet the need for assistance for the education of children with disabilities on reservations aged 5-21, inclusive, enrolled in elementary and secondary schools for Indian children operated or funded by the Secretary of the Interior. In the case of Indian students ages 3-5, inclusive, who are enrolled in programs affiliated with Bureau of Indian Affairs (hereafter in this subsection referred to as "BIA") schools and that are required by the States in which such schools are located to attain or maintain State accreditation, and which schools have such accreditation prior to October 7, 1991, the school shall be allowed to count those children for the purpose of distribution of the funds provided under this paragraph to the Secretary of the Interior. The Secretary of the Interior shall be responsible for meeting all of the requirements of this subchapter for these children, in accordance with paragraph (3). The amount of such payment for any fiscal year

shall be 1 percent of the aggregate amounts available for all States under this section for that fiscal year.

(2) With respect to all other children aged 3-21, inclusive, on reservations, the State educational agency shall be responsible for ensuring that all of the requirements of this subchapter are implemented.

(3) The Secretary of the Interior may receive an allotment under paragraph (1) only after submitting to the Secretary of Education an application that—

(A) meets the appropriate requirements, as determined by the Secretary of Education, of sections 1412 (including monitoring and evaluation activities), 1413, and 1414(a) of this title;

(B) includes a description of how the Secretary of the Interior will coordinate the provision of services under this subchapter with local educational agencies, tribes and tribal organizations, and other private and Federal service providers;

(C) includes an assurance that there are public hearings, adequate notice of such hearings, and an opportunity for comment afforded to members of tribes, tribal governing bodies, and affected local school boards before the adoption of the policies, programs, and procedures required under subparagraph (A);

(D) includes an assurance that the Secretary of the Interior will provide such information as the Secretary of Education may require to comply with section 1418(b)(1) of this title, including data on the number of children and youth with disabilities served and the types and amounts of services provided and needed and this information shall be included in the annual report of the Secretary of Education to Congress required in section 1418(g) of this title;

(E) includes an assurance that, by October 1, 1992, the Secretaries of the Interior and Health and Human Services will enter into a memorandum of agreement, to be provided to the Secretary of Education, for the coordination of services, resources, and personnel between their respective Federal, State, and local offices and with State and local educational agencies and other entities to facilitate the provision of services to Indian children with disabilities residing on or near reservations. Such agreement shall provide for the apportionment of responsibilities and costs including, but not limited to, child find, evaluation, diagnosis, remediation or therapeutic measures, and (where appropriate) equipment and medical/personal supplies as needed for a child to remain in school or a program; and

(F) includes an assurance that the Department of the Interior will cooperate with the Department of Education in its exercise of monitoring and oversight of this application, and any agreements entered into between the Secretary of the Interior and other entities under this Act, and will fulfill its duties under this Act.

Section 1416(a) shall apply to any such application.

(4)(A) Beginning with funds appropriated under section 1411(a) for fiscal year 1992, the Secretary shall, subject to this paragraph, make payments to the Secretary of the Interior to be distributed to tribes or tribal organizations (as defined under section 450b of Title 25) or consortiums of the above to provide for the coordination of assistance for special education and related services for children with disabilities aged 3-5, inclusive, on reservations served by elementary and secondary schools for Indian children operated or funded by the Department of the Interior. The amount of such payments under subparagraph (B) for any fiscal year shall be .25 percent of the aggregate amounts available for all States under this section for that fiscal year.

(B) The Secretary of the Interior shall distribute the total amount of the .25 percent under subparagraph (A) in the following manner:

(i) For the first fiscal year, each tribe or tribal organization shall receive an amount proportionate to the amount of weighted student units for special education programs for BIA operated or funded schools serving such reservation generated under the formula established under section 2008 of Title 25 divided by the total number of such students in all BIA operated or funded schools.

(ii) For each fiscal year thereafter, each tribe or tribal organization shall receive an amount based on the number of children with disabilities, ages 3-5, inclusive, residing on reservations as reported annually divided by the total of such children served by all tribes or tribal organizations.

(C) To receive a payment under this paragraph, the tribe or tribal organization shall submit such figures to the Secretary of the Interior as required to determine the amounts to be allocated under subparagraph (B). This information shall be compiled and submitted to the Secretary of Education.

(D) The funds received by a tribe or tribal organization shall be used to assist in child find, screening, and other procedures for the early identification of children aged 3-5, inclusive, parent training, and the provision of direct services. These activities may be carried out directly or through contracts or cooperative agreements with the BIA, local educational agencies, and other public or private non-profit organizations. The tribe or tribal organization is encouraged to involve Indian parents in the development and implementation of these activities. The above entities shall, as appropriate, make referrals to local, State, or Federal entities for the provision of services or further diagnosis.

(E) To be eligible to receive a grant pursuant to subparagraph (A), the tribe or tribal organization shall make a biennial report to the Secretary of the Interior of activities undertaken under this paragraph, including the number of contracts and cooperative agreements entered into, the number of children contacted and receiving services for each year and the estimated number of children needing services during the 2 years following the one in which the report is made. The Secretary of the Interior shall include a summary of this information on a biennial basis in the report to the Secretary of Education required under this subsection. The Secretary of Education may require any additional information from the Secretary of the Interior.

(F) The Secretary of the Interior shall offer and, on request, provide technical assistance (especially in the areas of child find, diagnosis, and referral) to State and local educational agencies (where appropriate, intermediate educational units), and tribes and tribal organizations. Such assistance may be provided through its divisions and offices at the national and local level.

(G) None of the funds allocated under this paragraph can be used by the Secretary of the Interior for administrative purposes, including child count, and the provision of technical assistance.

(5) Before January 1, 1992, the Secretary of the Interior shall submit to the Committee on Education and Labor of the House of Representatives and the Committee on Labor and Human Resources of the Senate a plan for the coordination of services for all Indian children with disabilities residing on reservations covered under this Act. Such plan shall provide for the coordination of services benefiting these children from whatever source, including tribes, the Indian Health Service, other BIA divisions, and other Federal agencies. In developing such a plan, the Secretary of the Interior shall consult with all interested and involved parties. It shall be based upon the needs of the children and the system best suited for meeting those needs, and may involve the establishment of cooperative agreements between the BIA, other Federal agencies, and other entities. Such plan shall also be distributed

upon request to States, State and local educational agencies, and other agencies providing services to infants, toddlers, children, and youth with disabilities, to tribes, and to other interested parties.

(6) To meet the requirements of section 1413(a)(12) of this title, the Secretary of the Interior shall establish, within 6 months of October 7, 1991, under the Bureau of Indian Affairs (BIA), an advisory board composed of individuals involved in or concerned with the education and provision of services to Indian infants, toddlers, children, and youth with disabilities, including Indians with disabilities, Indian parents or guardians of such children, teachers, service providers, State and local educational officials, representatives of tribes or tribal organizations, representatives from State Interagency Coordinating Councils in States having reservations, and other members representing the various divisions and entities of the BIA. The chairperson shall be selected by the Secretary of the Interior. The advisory board shall—

(A) assist in the coordination of services within BIA and with other local, State, and Federal agencies in the provision of education for infants, toddlers, children, and youth with disabilities;

(B) advise and assist the Secretary of the Interior in the performance of the Secretary's responsibilities described in this subsection;

(C) develop and recommend policies concerning effective inter-and intra-agency collaboration, including modifications to regulations, and the elimination of barriers to inter- and intra-agency programs and activities;

(D) provide assistance and disseminate information on best practices, effective program coordination strategies, and recommendations for improved educational programming for Indian infants, toddlers, children, and youth with disabilities; and

(E) provide assistance in the preparation of information required under paragraph (3)(D).

(g) Reductions or increases

(1) If the sums appropriated under subsection (h) of this section for any fiscal year for making payments to States under subsection (a) of this section are not sufficient to pay in full the total amounts which all States are entitled to receive under subsection (a) of this section for such fiscal year, the maximum amounts which all States are entitled to receive under subsection (a) of this section for such fiscal year shall be ratably reduced. In case additional funds become available for making such payments for any fiscal year during which the preceding sentence is applicable, such reduced amounts shall be increased on the same basis as they were reduced.

(2) In the case of any fiscal year in which the maximum amounts for which States are eligible have been reduced under the first sentence of paragraph (1), and in which additional funds have not been made available to pay in full the total of such maximum amounts under the last sentence of such paragraph, the State educational agency shall fix dates before which each local educational agency or intermediate educational unit shall report to the State educational agency on the amount of funds available to the local educational agency or intermediate educational unit, under the provisions of subsection (d) of this section, which it estimates that it will expend in accordance with the provisions of this section. The amounts so available to any local educational agency or intermediate educational unit, or any amount which would be available to any other local educational agency or intermediate educational unit if it were to submit a program meeting the requirements of this subchapter, which the State educational

agency determines will not be used for the period of its availability, shall be available for allocation to those local educational agencies or intermediate educational units, in the manner provided by this section, which the State educational agency determines will need and be able to use additional funds to carry out approved programs.

(h) Authorization of appropriations.

For grants under subsection (a) of this section there are authorized to be appropriated such sums as may be necessary.

(As amended Pub.L. 101-476, Title II, § 201, Title IX, § 901(b)(25)-(32), Oct. 30, 1990, 104 Stat. 1111, 1143; Pub.L. 102-73, Title VIII, § 802(d)(2), (3), July 25, 1991, 105 Stat. 361; Pub.L. 102-119, §§ 4, 25(a)(4), (19), (b), Oct. 7, 1991, 105 Stat. 587, 606, 607.)

§1412. Eligibility requirements

In order to qualify for assistance under this subchapter in any fiscal year, a State shall demonstrate to the Secretary that the following conditions are met:

(1) The State has in effect a policy that assures all children with disabilities the right to a free appropriate public education.

(2) The State has developed a plan pursuant to section 1413(b) of this title in effect prior to November 29, 1975, and submitted not later than August 21, 1975, which will be amended so as to comply with the provisions of this paragraph. Each such amended plan shall set forth in detail the policies and procedures which the State will undertake or has undertaken in order to assure that—

(A) there is established (i) a goal of providing full educational opportunity to all children with disabilities, (ii) a detailed timetable for accomplishing such a goal, and (iii) a description of the kind and number of facilities, personnel, and services necessary throughout the State to meet such a goal;

(B) a free appropriate public education will be available for all children with disabilities between the ages of three and eighteen within the State not later than September 1, 1978, and for all children with disabilities between the ages of three and twenty-one within the State not later than September 1, 1980, except that, with respect to children with disabilities aged three to five and aged eighteen to twenty-one, inclusive, the requirements of this clause shall not be applied in any State if the application of such requirements would be inconsistent with State law or practice, or the order of any court, respecting public education within such age groups in the State;

(C) all children residing in the State who are disabled, regardless of the severity of their disability, and who are in need of special education and related services are identified, located, and evaluated, and that a practical method is developed and implemented to determine which children are currently receiving needed special education and related services and which children are not currently receiving needed special education and related services;

(D) policies and procedures are established in accordance with detailed criteria prescribed under section 1417(c) of this title; and

(E) any amendment to the plan submitted by the State required by this section shall be available to parents, guardians, and other members of the general public at least thirty days prior to the date of submission of the amendment to the Secretary.

(3) The State has established priorities for providing a free appropriate public education to all children with disabilities, which priorities shall meet the timetables set forth in clause (B) of paragraph (2) of this section, first with respect to children with disabilities who are not receiving an education, and second with respect to children with disabilities, within each disability category, with the most severe disabilities who are receiving an inadequate education, and has made adequate progress in meeting the timetables set forth in clause (B) of paragraph (2) of this section.

(4) Each local educational agency in the State will maintain records of the individualized education program for each child with a disability, and such program shall be established, reviewed, and revised as provided in section 1414(a)(5) of this title.

(5) The State has established (A) procedural safeguards as required by section 1415 of this title, (B) procedures to assure that, to the maximum extent appropriate, children with disabilities, including children in public or private institutions or other care facilities, are educated with children who are not disabled, and that special classes, separate schooling, or other removal of children with disabilities from the regular educational environment occurs only when the nature or severity of the disability is such that education in regular classes with the use of supplementary aids and services cannot be achieved satisfactorily, and (C) procedures to assure that testing and evaluation materials and procedures utilized for the purposes of evaluation and placement of children with disabilities will be selected and administered so as not to be racially or culturally discriminatory. Such materials or procedures shall be provided and administered in the child's native language or mode of communication, unless it clearly is not feasible to do so, and no single procedure shall be the sole criterion for determining an appropriate educational program for a child.

(6) The State educational agency shall be responsible for assuring that the requirements of this subchapter are carried out and that all educational programs for children with disabilities within the State, including all such programs administered by any other State or local agency, will be under the general supervision of the persons responsible for educational programs for children with disabilities in the State educational agency and shall meet education standards of the State educational agency. This paragraph shall not be construed to limit the responsibility of agencies other than educational agencies in a State from providing or paying for some or all of the costs of a free appropriate public education to be provided children with disabilities in the State.

(7) The State shall assure that (A) in carrying out the requirements of this section procedures are established for consultation with individuals involved in or concerned with the education of children with disabilities, including individuals with disabilities and parents or guardians of children with disabilities, and (B) there are public hearings, adequate notice of such hearings, and an opportunity for comment available to the general public prior to adoption of the policies, programs, and procedures required pursuant to the provisions of this section and section 1413 of this chapter.

(As amended Pub.L. 101-476, Title IX, § 901(b)(33)-(46), (c), Oct. 30, 1990, 104 Stat. 1143, 1151; Pub.L. 102-119, § 25(a)(5), (b), Oct. 7, 1991, 105 Stat. 606, 607.)

§ 1413. State plans

(a) Requisite features

Any State meeting the eligibility requirements set forth in section 1412 of this title and desiring to participate in the program under this subchapter shall submit to the Secretary, through its State educational agency, a State plan at such time, in such manner, and containing or accompanied by such information, as the Secretary deems necessary. Each such plan shall—

(1) set forth policies and procedures designed to assure that funds paid to the State under this subchapter will be expended in accordance with the provisions of this subchapter, with particular attention given to the provisions of sections 1411(b), 1411(c), 1411(d), 1412(2), and 1412(3) of this title [20 U.S.C. § 2791 *et seq.*];

(2) provide that programs and procedures will be established to assure that funds received by the State or any of its political subdivisions under any other Federal program, including subpart 2 of part D of chapter 1 of title I of the Elementary and Secondary Education Act of 1965, under which there is specific authority for the provision of assistance for the education of children with disabilities, will be utilized by the State, or any of its political subdivisions, only in a manner consistent with the goal of providing a free appropriate public education for all children with disabilities, except that nothing in this clause shall be construed to limit the specific requirements of the laws governing such Federal programs;

(3) describe, consistent with the purposes of this chapter and with the comprehensive system of personnel development described in section 1476(b)(8) of this title, a comprehensive system of personnel development that shall include—

(A) a description of the procedures and activities the State will undertake to ensure an adequate supply of qualified special education and related services personnel, including—

(i) the development and maintenance of a system for determining, on an annual basis—

(I) the number and type of personnel, including leadership personnel, that are employed in the provision of special education and related services, by area of specialization, including the number of such personnel who are employed on an emergency, provisional, or other basis, who do not hold appropriate State certification or licensure; and

(II) the number and type of personnel, including leadership personnel, needed, and a projection of the numbers of such personnel that will be needed in five years, based on projections of individuals to be served, retirement and other leaving of personnel from the field, and other relevant factors;

(ii) the development and maintenance of a system for determining, on an annual basis, the institutions of higher education within the State that are preparing special education and related services personnel, including leadership personnel, by area of specialization, including—

(I) the numbers of students enrolled in such programs, and

(II) the number who graduated with certification or licensure, or with credentials to qualify for certification or licensure, during the past year; and

(iii) the development, updating, and implementation of a plan that—

(I) will address current and projected special education and related services personnel needs, including the need for leadership personnel; and

(II) coordinates and facilitates efforts among State and local educational agencies, institutions of higher education, and professional associations to recruit, prepare, and retain qualified personnel, including personnel from minority backgrounds, and personnel with disabilities; and

(B) a description of the procedures and activities the State will undertake to ensure that all personnel necessary to carry out this subchapter are appropriately and adequately prepared, including—

(i) a system for the continuing education of regular and special education and related services personnel;

(ii) procedures for acquiring and disseminating to teachers, administrators, and related services personnel significant knowledge derived from education research and other sources; and

(iii) procedures for adopting, where appropriate, promising practices, materials, and technology.

(4) set forth policies and procedures to assure—

(A) that, to the extent consistent with the number and location of children with disabilities in the State who are enrolled in private elementary and secondary schools, provision is made for the participation of such children in the program assisted or carried out under this subchapter by providing for such children special education and related services; and

(B) that—

(i) children with disabilities in private schools and facilities will be provided special education and related services (in conformance with an individualized education program as required by this subchapter) at no cost to their parents or guardian, if such children are placed in or referred to such schools or facilities by the State or appropriate local educational agency as the means of carrying out the requirements of this subchapter or any other applicable law requiring the provision of special education and related services to all children with disabilities within such State; and

(ii) in all such instances, the State educational agency shall determine whether such schools and facilities meet standards that apply to State and local educational agencies and that children so served have all the rights they would have if served by such agencies;

(5) set forth policies and procedures which assure that the State shall seek to recover any funds made available under this subchapter for services to any child who is determined to be erroneously classified as eligible to be counted under section 1411(a) or 1411(d) of this title;

(6) provide satisfactory assurance that the control of funds provided under this subchapter, and title to property derived therefrom, shall be in a public agency for the uses and purposes provided in this subchapter, and that a public agency will administer such funds and property;

(7) provide for—

(A) making such reports in such form and containing such information as the Secretary may require to carry out the Secretary's functions under this subchapter, and

(B) keeping such records and affording such access thereto as the Secretary may find necessary to assure the correctness and verification of such reports and proper disbursement of Federal funds under this subchapter;

(8) provide procedures to assure that final action with respect to any application submitted by a local educational agency or an intermediate educational unit shall not be taken without first affording the local educational agency or intermediate educational unit involved reasonable notice and opportunity for a hearing;

(9) provide satisfactory assurance that Federal funds made available under this subchapter—

(A) will not be commingled with State funds, and

(B) will be so used as to supplement and increase the level of Federal, State, and local funds (including funds that are not under the direct control of State or local educational agencies) expended for special education and related services provided to children with disabilities under this subchapter and in no case to supplant such Federal, State, and local funds, except that, where the State provides clear and convincing evidence that all children with disabilities have available to them a free appropriate public education, the Secretary may waive in part the requirement of this subparagraph if the Secretary concurs with the evidence provided by the State;

(10) provide, consistent with procedures prescribed pursuant to section 1417(a)(2) of this title, satisfactory assurance that such fiscal control and fund accounting procedures will be adopted as may be necessary to assure proper disbursement of, and accounting for, Federal funds paid under this subchapter to the State, including any such funds paid by the State to local educational agencies and intermediate educational units;

(11) provide for procedures for evaluation at least annually of the effectiveness of programs in meeting the educational needs of children with disabilities (including evaluation of individualized education programs), in accordance with such criteria that the Secretary shall prescribe pursuant to section 1417 of this chapter;

(12) provide that the State has an advisory panel, appointed by the Governor or any other official authorized under State law to make such appointments, composed of individuals involved in or concerned with the education of children with disabilities, including individuals with disabilities, teachers, parents or guardians of children with disabilities, State and local education officials, and administrators of programs for children with disabilities, which—

(A) advises the State educational agency of unmet needs within the State in the education of children with disabilities,

(B) comments publicly on any rules or regulations proposed for issuance by the State regarding the education of children with disabilities and the procedures for distribution of funds under this subchapter[;] and

(C) assists the State in developing and reporting such data and evaluations as may assist the Secretary in the performance of the responsibilities of the Secretary under section 1418 of this title;

(13) set forth policies and procedures for developing and implementing interagency agreements between the State educational agency and other appropriate State and local agencies to—

(A) define the financial responsibility of each agency for providing children and youth with disabilities with free appropriate public education, and

(B) resolve interagency disputes, including procedures under which local educational agencies may initiate proceedings under the agreement in order to secure reimbursement from other agencies or otherwise implement the provisions of the agreement;

(14) set forth policies and procedures relating to the establishment and maintenance of standards to ensure that personnel necessary to carry out the purposes of this subchapter are appropriately and adequately prepared and trained, including—

(A) the establishment and maintenance of standards which are consistent with any State approved or recognized certification, licensing, registration, or other comparable requirements which apply to the area in which such personnel are providing special education or related services[;] and

(B) to the extent such standards are not based on the highest requirements in the State applicable to a specific profession or discipline, the steps the State is taking to require the retraining or hiring of personnel that meet appropriate professional requirements in the State; and

(15) set forth policies and procedures relating to the smooth transition for those individuals participating in the early intervention program assisted under subchapter VIII of this chapter who will participate in preschool programs assisted under this subchapter, including a method of ensuring that when a child turns age three an individualized education program, or, if consistent with sections 1414(a)(5) and1477(d) of this title, an individualized family service plan, has been developed and is being implemented by such child's third birthday.

(b) Additional assurances

Whenever a State educational agency provides free appropriate public education for children with disabilities, or provides direct services to such children, such State educational agency shall include, as part of the State plan required by subsection (a) of this section, such additional assurances not specified in such subsection (a) of this section as are contained in section 1414(a) of this title, except that funds available for the provision of such education or services may be expended without regard to the provisions relating to excess costs in section 1414(a) of this title.

(c) Notice and hearing prior to disapproval of plan

(1) The Secretary shall approve any State plan and any modification thereof which—

(A) is submitted by a State eligible in accordance with section 1412 of this title; and

(B) meets the requirements of subsection (a) and subsection (b) of this section.

(2) The Secretary shall disapprove any State plan which does not meet the requirements of paragraph (1), but shall not finally disapprove a State plan except after reasonable notice and opportunity for a hearing to the State.

(d) Participation of children with disabilities in private schools; payment of Federal amount; determinations of Secretary: notice and hearing; judicial review: jurisdiction of court of appeals, petition, record, conclusiveness of findings, remand, review by Supreme Court

(1) If, on December 2, 1983, a State educational agency is prohibited by law from providing for the participation in special programs of children with disabilities enrolled in private elementary and secondary schools as required by subsection (a)(4) of this section, the Secretary shall waive such requirement, and shall arrange for the provision of services to such children through arrangements which shall be subject to the requirements of subsection (a)(4) of this section.

(2)(A) When the Secretary arranges for services pursuant to this subsection, the Secretary, after consultation with the appropriate public and private school officials, shall pay to the provider of such services an amount per child which may not exceed the Federal amount provided per child under this subchapter to all children with disabilities enrolled in the State for services for the fiscal year preceding the fiscal year for which the determination is made.

(B) Pending final resolution of any investigation or complaint that could result in a determination under this subsection, the Secretary may withhold from the allocation of the affected State educational agency the amount the Secretary estimates would be necessary to pay the cost of such services.

(C) Any determination by the Secretary under this section shall continue in effect until the Secretary determines that there will no longer be any failure or inability on the part of the State educational agency to meet the requirements of subsection (a)(4) of this section.

(3)(A) The Secretary shall not take any final action under this subsection until the State educational agency affected by such action has had an opportunity, for at least 45 days after receiving written notice thereof, to submit written objections and to appear before the Secretary or the Secretary's designee to show cause why such action should not be taken.

(B) If a State educational agency is dissatisfied with the Secretary's final action after a proceeding under subparagraph (A) of this paragraph, it may, within 60 days after notice of such action, file with the United States court of appeals for the circuit in which such State is located a petition for review of that action. A copy of the petition shall be forthwith transmitted by the clerk of the court to the Secretary. The Secretary thereupon shall file in the court the record of the proceedings on which the Secretary based the Secretary's action, as provided in section 2112 of title 28.

(C) The findings of fact by the Secretary, if supported by substantial evidence, shall be conclusive; but the court, for good cause shown, may remand the case to the Secretary to take further evidence, and the Secretary may thereupon make new or modified findings of fact and may modify the Secretary's previous action, and shall file in the court the record of the further proceedings. Such new or modified findings of fact shall likewise be conclusive if supported by substantial evidence.

(D) Upon the filing of a petition under subparagraph (B), the court shall have jurisdiction to affirm the action of the Secretary or to set it aside, in whole or in part. The judgment of the court shall be subject to review by the Supreme Court of the United States upon certiorari or certification as provided in section 1254 of title 28.

(e) Prohibition on reduction of assistance

This chapter shall not be construed to permit a State to reduce medical and other assistance available or to alter eligibility under titles V and XIX of the Social Security Act with respect to the provision of a free appropriate public education for children with disabilities within the State.

(As amended Pub.L. 101-476, Title II, § 202, Title IX, § 901(b)(47)-(58), Oct. 30, 1990, 104 Stat. 1111, 1144; Pub.L. 102-119, §§ 5, 25(a)(6), (b), Oct. 7, 1991, 105 Stat. 591, 606, 607.)

§ 1414. Application

(a) Requisite features

A local educational agency or an intermediate educational unit which desires to receive payments under section 1411(d) of this chapter for any fiscal year shall submit an application to the appropriate State educational agency. Such application shall—

(1) provide satisfactory assurance that payments under this subchapter will be used for excess costs directly attributable to programs which—

(A) provide that all children residing within the jurisdiction of the local educational agency or the intermediate educational unit who are disabled, regardless of the severity of their disability, and are in need of special education and related services will be identified, located, and evaluated, and provide for the inclusion of a practical method of determining which children are currently receiving needed special education and related services and which children are not currently receiving such education and services;

(B) establish policies and procedures in accordance with detailed criteria prescribed under section 1417(c) of this title;

(C) establish a goal of providing full educational opportunities to all children with disabilities, including—

(i) procedures for the implementation and use of the comprehensive system of personnel development established by the State educational agency under section 1413(a)(3) of this title;

(ii) the provision of, and the establishment of priorities for providing, a free appropriate public education to all children with disabilities, first with respect to children with disabilities who are not receiving an education, and second with respect to children with disabilities, within each disability, with the most severe disabilities who are receiving an inadequate education;

(iii) the participation and consultation of the parents or guardian of such children; and

(iv) to the maximum extent practicable and consistent with the provisions of section 1412(5)(B) of this title, the provision of special services to enable such children to participate in regular educational programs;

(D) establish a detailed timetable for accomplishing the goal described in subclause (C); and

(E) provide a description of the kind and number of facilities, personnel, and services necessary to meet the goal described in subclause (C);

(2) provide satisfactory assurance that—

(A) the control of funds provided under this subchapter, and title to property derived from such funds, shall be in a public agency for the uses and purposes provided in this subchapter, and that a public agency will administer such funds and property;

(B) Federal funds expended by local educational agencies and intermediate educational units for programs under this subchapter—

(i) shall be used to pay only the excess costs directly attributable to the education of children with disabilities; and

(ii) shall be used to supplement and, to the extent practicable, increase the level of State and local funds expended for the education of children with disabilities, and in no case to supplant such State and local funds; and

(C) State and local funds will be used in the jurisdiction of the local educational agency or intermediate educational unit to provide services in program areas that, taken as a whole, are at least comparable to services being provided in areas of such jurisdiction that are not receiving funds under this subchapter;

(3) provide for—

(A) furnishing such information (which, in the case of reports relating to performance, is in accordance with specific performance criteria related to program objectives), as may be necessary to enable the State educational agency to perform its duties under this subchapter, including information relating to the educational achievement of children with disabilities participating in programs carried out under this subchapter; and

(B) keeping such records, and affording such access to such records, as the State educational agency may find necessary to assure the correctness and verification of such information furnished under subparagraph (A);

(4) provide for making the application and all pertinent documents related to such application available to parents, guardians, and other members of the general public, and provide that all evaluations and reports required under clause (3) shall be public information;

(5) provide assurances that the local educational agency or intermediate educational unit will establish or revise, whichever is appropriate, an individualized education program for each child with a disability (or, if consistent with State policy and at the discretion of the local educational agency or intermediate educational unit, and with the concurrence of the parents or guardian, an individualized family service plan described in section 1477(d) of this title for each child with a disability aged 3 to 5, inclusive) at the beginning of each school year and will then review and, if appropriate, revise, its provisions periodically, but not less than annually;

(6) provide satisfactory assurance that policies and programs established and administered by the local educational agency or intermediate educational unit shall be consistent with the provisions of paragraph (1) through paragraph (7) of section 1412 and section 1413(a) of this [title]; and

(7) provide satisfactory assurance that the local educational agency or intermediate educational unit will establish and maintain procedural safeguards in accordance with the provisions of sections 1412(5)(B), 1412(5)(C), and 1415 of this title.

(b) Approval by State educational agencies of applications submitted by local educational agencies or intermediate educational units; notice and hearing

(1) A State educational agency shall approve any application submitted by a local educational agency or an intermediate educational unit under subsection (a) of this section if the State educational agency determines that such application meets the requirements of subsection (a) of this section, except that no such application may be approved until the State plan submitted by such State educational agency under subsection (a) of this section is approved by the Secretary under section 1413(c) of this title. A State educational agency shall disapprove any application submitted by a local educational agency or an intermediate educational unit under subsection (a) of this section if the State educational agency determines that such application does not meet the requirements of subsection (a) of this section.

(2) (A) Whenever a State educational agency, after reasonable notice and opportunity for a hearing, finds that a local educational agency or an intermediate educational unit, in the administration of an application approved by the State educational agency under paragraph (1), has failed to comply with any requirement set forth in such application, the State educational agency, after giving appropriate notice to the local educational agency or the intermediate educational unit, shall—

(i) make no further payments to such local educational agency or such intermediate educational unit under section 1420 of this title until the State educational agency is satisfied that there is no longer any failure to comply with the requirement involved; or

(ii) take such finding into account in its review of any application made by such local educational agency or such intermediate educational unit under subsection (a) of this section.

(B) The provisions of the last sentence of section 1416(a) of this chapter shall apply to any local educational agency or any intermediate educational unit receiving any notification from a State educational agency under this paragraph.

(3) In carrying out its functions under paragraph (1), each State educational agency shall consider any decision made pursuant to a hearing held under section 1415 of this title which is adverse to the local educational agency or intermediate educational unit involved in such decision.

(c) Consolidated applications

(1) A State educational agency may, for purposes of the consideration and approval of applications under this section, require local educational agencies to submit a consolidated application for payments if such State educational agency determines that any individual application submitted by any such local educational agency will be disapproved because such local educational agency is ineligible to receive payments because of the application of section 1411(c)(4)(A)(i) of this title or such local educational agency would be unable to establish and maintain programs of sufficient size and scope to effectively meet the educational needs of children with disabilities.

(2)(A) In any case in which a consolidated application of local educational agencies is approved by a State educational agency under paragraph (1), the payments which such local educational agencies may receive shall be equal to the sum of payments to which each such local educational agency would be entitled under section 1411(d) of this title if an individual application of any such local educational agency had been approved.

(B) The State educational agency shall prescribe rules and regulations with respect to consolidated applications submitted under this subsection which are consistent with the provisions of paragraph (1) through paragraph (7) of section 1412 and section 1413(a) of this title and which provide participating local educational agencies with joint responsibilities for implementing programs receiving payments under this subchapter.

(C) In any case in which an intermediate educational unit is required pursuant to State law to carry out the provisions of this subchapter, the joint responsibilities given to local educational agencies under subparagraph (B) shall not apply to the administration and disbursement of any payments received by such intermediate educational unit. Such responsibilities shall be carried out exclusively by such intermediate educational unit.

(d) Special education and related services provided directly by State educational agencies; regional or State centers

Whenever a State educational agency determines that a local educational agency—

(1) is unable or unwilling to establish and maintain programs of free appropriate public education which meet the requirements established in subsection (a) of this section;

(2) is unable or unwilling to be consolidated with other local educational agencies in order to establish and maintain such programs; or

(3) has one or more children with disabilities who can best be served by a regional or State center designed to meet the needs of such children;

the State educational agency shall use the payments which would have been available to such local educational agency to provide special education and related services directly to children with disabilities residing in the area served by such local educational agency. The State educational agency may provide such education and services in such manner, and at such locations (including regional or State centers), as it considers appropriate, except that the manner in which such education and services are provided shall be consistent with the requirements of this subchapter.

(e) Reallocation of funds

Whenever a State educational agency determines that a local educational agency is adequately providing a free appropriate public education to all children with disabilities residing in the area served by such agency with State and local funds otherwise available to such agency, the State educational agency may reallocate funds (or such portion of those funds as may not be required to provide such education and services) made available to such agency, pursuant to section 1411(d) of this chapter, to such other local educational agencies within the State as are not adequately providing special education and related services to all children with disabilities residing in the areas served by such other local educational agencies.

(f) Programs using State or local funds

Notwithstanding the provisions of subsection (a)(2)(B)(ii) of this section, any local educational agency which is required to carry out any program for the education of children with disabilities pursuant to a State law shall be entitled to receive payments under section 1411(d) of this title for use in carrying out such program, except that such payments may not be used to reduce the level of expenditures for such program made by such local educational agency from State or local funds below the level of such expenditures for the fiscal year prior to the fiscal year for which such local educational agency seeks such payments.

(As amended Pub.L. 101-476, Title IX, § 901(b)(59)-(70), Oct. 30, 1990, 104 Stat. 1144; Pub.L. 102-119, §§ 6, 25(b), Oct. 7, 1991, 105 Stat. 591, 607.)

§ 1415. Procedural safeguards

(a) Establishment and maintenance

Any State educational agency, any local educational agency, and any intermediate educational unit which receives assistance under this subchapter shall establish and maintain procedures in accordance with subsection (b) through subsection (e) of this section to assure that children with disabilities and their parents or guardians are guaranteed procedural safeguards with respect to the provision of free appropriate public education by such agencies and units.

(b) Required procedures; hearing

(1) The procedures required by this section shall include, but shall not be limited to—

(A) an opportunity for the parents or guardian of a child with a disability to examine all relevant records with respect to the identification, evaluation, and educational placement of the child, and the provision of a free appropriate public education to such child, and to obtain an independent educational evaluation of the child;

(B) procedures to protect the rights of the child whenever the parents or guardian of the child are not known, unavailable, or the child is a ward of the State, including the assignment of an individual (who shall not be an employee of the State educational agency, local educational agency, or intermediate educational unit involved in the education or care of the child) to act as a surrogate for the parents or guardian;

(C) written prior notice to the parents or guardian of the child whenever such agency or unit—

(i) proposes to initiate or change, or

(ii) refuses to initiate or change,

the identification, evaluation, or educational placement of the child or the provision of a free appropriate public education to the child;

(D) procedures designed to assure that the notice required by clause (C) fully informs the parents or guardian, in the parents' or guardian's native language, unless it clearly is not feasible to do so, of all procedures available pursuant to this section; and

(E) an opportunity to present complaints with respect to any matter relating to the identification, evaluation, or educational placement of the child, or the provision of a free appropriate public education to such child.

(2) Whenever a complaint has been received under paragraph (1) of this subsection, the parents or guardian shall have an opportunity for an impartial due process hearing which shall be conducted by the State educational agency or by the local educational agency or intermediate educational unit, as determined by State law or by the State educational agency. No hearing conducted pursuant to the requirements of this paragraph shall be conducted by an employee of such agency or unit involved in the education or care of the child.

(c) Review of local decision by State education agency

If the hearing required in paragraph (2) of subsection (b) of this section is conducted by a local educational agency or an intermediate educational unit, any party aggrieved by the findings and decision rendered in such a hearing may appeal to the State educational agency which shall conduct an impartial review of such hearing. The officer conducting such review shall make an independent decision upon completion of such review.

(d) Enumeration of rights accorded parties to hearings

Any party to any hearing conducted pursuant to subsections (b) and (c) of this section shall be accorded—

(1) the right to be accompanied and advised by counsel and by individuals with special knowledge or training with respect to the problems of children with disabilities,

(2) the right to present evidence and confront, cross-examine, and compel the attendance of witnesses,

(3) the right to a written or electronic verbatim record of such hearing, and

(4) the right to written findings of fact and decisions (which findings and decisions shall be made available to the public consistent with the requirements of section 1417(c) of this title and shall also be transmitted to the advisory panel established pursuant to section 1413(a)(12) of this title).

(e) Civil action; jurisdiction; attorney fees

(1) A decision made in a hearing conducted pursuant to paragraph (2) of subsection (b) of this section shall be final, except that any party involved in such hearing may appeal such decision under the provisions of subsection (c) and paragraph (2) of this subsection. A decision made under subsection (c) of this section shall be final, except that any party may bring an action under paragraph (2) of this subsection.

(2) Any party aggrieved by the findings and decision made under subsection (b) of this section who does not have the right to an appeal under subsection (c) of this section, and any party aggrieved by the findings and decision under subsection (c) of this section, shall have the right to bring a civil action with respect to the complaint presented pursuant to this section, which action may be brought in any State court of competent jurisdiction or in a district court of the United States without regard to the amount in controversy. In any action brought under this paragraph the court shall receive the records of the administrative proceedings, shall hear additional evidence at the request of a party, and, basing its decision on the preponderance of the evidence, shall grant such relief as the court determines is appropriate.

(3) During the pendency of any proceedings conducted pursuant to this section, unless the State or local educational agency and the parents or guardian otherwise agree, the child shall remain in the then current educational placement of such child, or, if applying for initial admission to a public school, shall, with the consent of the parents or guardian, be placed in the public school program until all such proceedings have been completed.

(4) (A) The district courts of the United States shall have jurisdiction of actions brought under this subsection without regard to the amount in controversy.

(B) In any action or proceeding brought under this subsection, the court, in its discretion, may award reasonable attorneys' fees as part of the costs to the parents or guardian of a child or youth with a disability who is the prevailing party.

(C) For the purpose of this subsection, fees awarded under this subsection shall be based on rates prevailing in the community in which the action or proceeding arose for the kind and quality of services furnished. No bonus or multiplier may be used in calculating the fees awarded under this subsection.

(D) No award of attorneys' fees and related costs may be made in any action or proceeding under this subsection for services performed subsequent to the time of a written offer of settlement to a parent or guardian, if—

(i) the offer is made within the time prescribed by Rule 68 of the Federal Rules of Civil Procedure or, in the case of an administrative proceeding, at any time more than ten days before the proceeding begins;

(ii) the offer is not accepted within ten days; and

(iii) the court or administrative officer finds that the relief finally obtained by the parents or guardian is not more favorable to the parents or guardian than the offer of settlement.

(E) Notwithstanding the provisions of subparagraph (D), an award of attorneys' fees and related costs may be made to a parent or guardian who is the prevailing party and who was substantially justified in rejecting the settlement offer.

(F) Whenever the court finds that—

(i) the parent or guardian, during the course of the action or proceeding, unreasonably protracted the final resolution of the controversy;

(ii) the amount of the attorneys' fees otherwise authorized to be awarded unreasonably exceeds the hourly rate prevailing in the community for similar services by attorneys of reasonably comparable skill, experience, and reputation; or

(iii) the time spent and legal services furnished were excessive considering the nature of the action or proceeding,

the court shall reduce, accordingly, the amount of the attorneys' fees awarded under this subsection.

(G) The provisions of subparagraph (F) shall not apply in any action or proceeding if the court finds that the State or local educational agency unreasonably protracted the final resolution of the action or proceeding or there was a violation of this section.

(f) Effect on other laws

Nothing in this chapter shall be construed to restrict or limit the rights, procedures, and remedies available under the Constitution, title V of the Rehabilitation Act of 1973 [29 U.S.C. § 701 et seq.], or other Federal statutes protecting the rights of children and youth with disabilities, except that before the filing of a civil action under such laws seeking relief that is also available under this subchapter, the procedures under subsections (b)(2) and (c) of this section shall be exhausted to the same extent as would be required had the action been brought under this subchapter.

(As amended Pub.L. 101-476, Title IX, § 901(b)(71)-(75), Oct. 30, 1990, 104 Stat. 1145; Pub.L. 102-119, § 25(b), Oct. 7, 1991, 105 Stat. 607.)

§ 1416. Withholding of payments

(a) Failure to comply with this subchapter; limitations; public notice

Whenever the Secretary, after reasonable notice and opportunity for hearing to the State educational agency involved (and to any local educational agency or intermediate educational unit affected by any failure described in clause (2)), finds—

(1) that there has been a failure to comply substantially with any provision of section 1412 or section 1413 of this title, or

(2) that in the administration of the State plan there is a failure to comply with any provision of this subchapter or with any requirements set forth in the application of a local educational agency or intermediate educational unit approved by the State educational agency pursuant to the State plan, the Secretary—

(A) shall, after notifying the State educational agency, withhold any further payments to the State under this subchapter, and

(B) may, after notifying the State educational agency, withhold further payments to the State under the Federal programs specified in section 1413(a)(2) of this title within the Secretary's jurisdiction, to the extent that funds under such programs are available for the provision of assistance for the education of children with disabilities.

If the Secretary withholds further payments under clause (A) or clause (B) the Secretary may determine that such withholding will be limited to programs or projects under the State plan, or portions thereof, affected by the failure, or that the State educational agency shall not make further payments under this subchapter to specified local educational agencies or intermediate educational units affected by the failure. Until the Secretary is satisfied that there is no longer any failure to comply with the provisions of this subchapter, as specified in clause (1) or clause (2), no further payments shall be made to the State under this subchapter or under the Federal programs specified in section 1413(a)(2) of this title within the Secretary's jurisdiction to the extent that funds under such programs are available for the provision of assistance for the education of children with disabilities, or payments by the State educational agency under this subchapter shall be limited to local educational agencies and intermediate educational units whose actions did not cause or were not involved in the failure, as the case may be. Any State educational agency, local educational agency, or intermediate educational unit in receipt of a notice pursuant to the first sentence of this subsection shall, by means of a public notice, take such measures as may be necessary to bring the pendency of an action pursuant to this subsection to the attention of the public within the jurisdiction of such agency or unit.

(b) Judicial review

(1) If any State is dissatisfied with the Secretary's final action with respect to its State plan submitted under section 1413 of this title, such State may, within sixty days after notice of such action, file with the United States court of appeals for the circuit in which such State is located a petition for review of that action. A copy of the petition shall be forthwith transmitted by the clerk of the court to the Secretary. The Secretary thereupon shall file in the court the record of the proceedings upon which the Secretary's action was based, as provided in section 2112 of title 28.

(2) The findings of fact by the Secretary, if supported by substantial evidence, shall be conclusive; but the court, for good cause shown, may remand the case to the Secretary to take further evidence, and the Secretary may thereupon make new or modified findings of fact that may modify the Secretary's previous action, and shall file in the court the record of the further proceedings. Such new or modified findings of fact shall likewise be conclusive if supported by substantial evidence.

(3) Upon the filing of such petition, the court shall have jurisdiction to affirm the action of the Secretary or to set it aside, in whole or in part. The judgment of the court shall be subject to review by the Supreme Court of the United States upon certiorari or certification as provided in section 1254 of title 28.

(As amended Pub.L. 101-476, Title IX, § 901(b)(76), Oct. 30, 1990, 104 Stat. 1145; Pub.L. 102-119, § 25(b), Oct. 7, 1991, 105 Stat. 607.)

§ 1417. Administration

(a) Duties of Secretary

(1) In carrying out the Secretary's duties under this subchapter, the Secretary shall—

(A) cooperate with, and furnish all technical assistance necessary, directly or by grant or contract, to the States in matters relating to the education of children with disabilities and the execution of the provisions of this subchapter;

(B) provide such short-term training programs and institutes as are necessary;

(C) disseminate information, and otherwise promote the education of all children with disabilities within the States; and

(D) assure that each State shall, within one year after November 29, 1975 and every year thereafter, provide certification of the actual number of children with disabilities receiving special education and related services in such State.

(2) As soon as practicable after November 29, 1975, the Secretary shall, by regulation, prescribe a uniform financial report to be utilized by State educational agencies in submitting State plans under this subchapter in order to assure equity among the States.

(b) Rules and regulations

In carrying out the provisions of this subchapter, the Secretary shall issue, not later than January 1, 1977, amend, and revoke such rules and regulations as may be necessary. No other less formal method of implementing such provisions is authorized.

(c) Protection of rights and privacy of parents and students

The Secretary shall take appropriate action, in accordance with the provisions of section 1232g of this title, to assure the protection of the confidentiality of any personally identifiable data, information, and records collected or maintained by the Secretary and by State and local educational agencies pursuant to the provisions of this subchapter.

(d) Hiring of qualified personnel

The Secretary is authorized to hire qualified personnel necessary to conduct data collection and evaluation activities required by subsections (b), (c) and (d) of section 1418 of this title and to carry out the Secretary's duties under subsection (a)(1) of this section without regard to the provisions of title 5 relating to appointments in the competitive service and without regard to chapter 51 and subchapter III of chapter 53 of such title relating to classification and general schedule pay rates except that no more than twenty such personnel shall be employed at any time.

(As amended Pub.L. 101-476, Title IX, § 901(b)(77), (78), Oct. 30, 1990, 104 Stat. 1145; Pub.L. 102-119, § 25(a)(7), (b), Oct. 7, 1991, 105 Stat. 606, 607.)

§ 1418. Evaluation and program information.

(a) Duties of Secretary

The Secretary shall, directly or by grant, contract, or cooperative agreement, collect data and conduct studies, investigations, and evaluations—
(1) to assess progress in the implementation of this chapter;
(2) to assess the impact and effectiveness of State and local efforts, and efforts by the Secretary of the Interior, to provide—
(A) free appropriate public education to children and youth with disabilities; and
(B) early intervention services to infants and toddlers with disabilities; and
(3) to provide—
(A) Congress with information relevant to policymaking; and

(B) State, local, and Federal agencies, including the Department of the Interior, with information relevant to program management, administration, delivery, and effectiveness with respect to such education and early intervention services.

(b) Collection of data

(1) In carrying out subsection (a) of this section, the Secretary, on at least an annual basis (except as provided in subparagraph (E)), shall obtain data concerning programs and projects assisted under this chapter and under other Federal laws relating to infants, toddlers, children, and youth with disabilities, and such additional information, from State and local educational agencies, the Secretary of Interior, and other appropriate sources, including designated lead agencies under subchapter VIII of this chapter (except during fiscal year 1992 such entities may not under this subsection be required to provide data regarding traumatic brain injury or autism), including—

(A) the number of infants, toddlers, children, and youth with disabilities in each State receiving a free appropriate public education or early intervention services—

(i) in age groups 0-2 and 3-5, and

(ii) in age groups 6-11, 12-17, and 18-21, by disability category;

(B) the number of children and youth with disabilities in each State, by disability category, who—

(i) are participating in regular educational programs (consistent with the requirements of sections 1412(5)(B) and 1414(a)(1)(C)(iv) of this title);

(ii) are in separate classes, separate schools or facilities, or public or private residential facilities; or

(iii) have been otherwise removed from the regular education environment;

(C) the number of children and youth with disabilities exiting the educational system each year through program completion or otherwise, by disability category, for each year of age from age 14 through 21;

(D) the number and type of personnel that are employed in the provision of—

(i) special education and related services to children and youth with disabilities, by disability category served; and

(ii) early intervention services to infants and toddlers with disabilities; and

(E) at least every three years, using the data collection method the Secretary finds most appropriate, a description of the services expected to be needed, by disability category, for youth with disabilities in age groups 12-17 and 18-21 who have left the educational system.

(2) Beginning with fiscal year 1993, the Secretary shall obtain and report data from the States under section 1413(a)(3)(A) of this title, including data addressing current and projected special education and related services needs, and data on the number of personnel who are employed on an emergency, provisional, or other basis, who do not hold appropriate State certification or licensure, and other data for the purpose of meeting the requirements of this subsection pertaining to special education and related services personnel.

(3) The Secretary shall provide, directly or by grant, contract, or cooperative agreement, technical assistance to State agencies providing the data described in paragraphs (1) and (2) to achieve accurate and comparable information.

(c) Studies and investigations under grants, contracts, or cooperative agreements

(1) The Secretary shall make grants to, or enter into contracts or cooperative agreements with, State or local educational agencies, institutions of higher education, public agencies, and private nonprofit organizations, and, when necessary because of the unique nature of the study, private-for-profit organizations, for the purpose of conducting studies, analyses, syntheses, and investigations for improving program management, administration, delivery, and effectiveness necessary to provide full educational opportunities and early interventions for all children with disabilities from birth through age 21. Such studies and investigations shall gather information necessary for program and system improvements including—

(A) developing effective, appropriate criteria and procedures to identify, evaluate, and serve infants, toddlers, children, and youth with disabilities from minority backgrounds for purposes of program eligibility, program planning, delivery of services, program placement, and parental involvement;

(B) planning and developing effective early intervention services, special education, and related services to meet the complex and changing needs of infants, toddlers, children, and youth with disabilities;

(C) developing and implementing a comprehensive system of personnel development needed to provide qualified personnel in sufficient number to deliver special education, related services, and early intervention services;

(D) developing the capacity to implement practices having the potential to integrate children with disabilities, to the maximum extent appropriate, with children who are not disabled;

(E) effectively allocating and using human and fiscal resources for providing early intervention, special education, and related services;

(F) strengthening programs and services to improve the progress of children and youth with disabilities while in special education, and to effect a successful transition when such children and youth leave special education;

(G) achieving interagency coordination to maximize resource utilization and continuity in services provided to infants, toddlers, children, and youth with disabilities;

(H) strengthening parent-school communication and coordination to improve the effectiveness of planning and delivery of interventions and instruction, thereby enhancing development and educational progress; and

(I) the identification of environmental, organizational, resource, and other conditions necessary for effective professional practice.

(2)(A) The studies and investigations authorized under this subsection may be conducted through surveys, interviews, case studies, program implementation studies, secondary data analyses and syntheses, and other appropriate methodologies.

(B) The studies and investigations conducted under this subsection shall address the information needs of State and local educational agencies for improving program management, administration, delivery, and effectiveness.

(3) The Secretary shall develop and implement a process for the on-going identification of national program information needed for improving the management, administration, delivery, and effectiveness of programs and services provided under this chapter. The process shall identify implementation issues, desired improvements, and information needed by State and local agencies to achieve such improvements, and shall be conducted in cooperation with State educational agencies

that can ensure broad-based statewide input from each cooperating State. The Secretary shall publish for public comment in the Federal Register every 3 years a program information plan describing such information needs. Such program information plan shall be used to determine the priorities for, and activities carried out under, this subsection to produce, organize, and increase utilization of program information. Such program information plan shall be included in the annual report submitted under this section every 3 years.

(4) In providing funds under this subsection, the Secretary shall require recipients to prepare their procedures, findings, and other relevant information in a form that will maximize their dissemination and use, especially through dissemination networks and mechanisms authorized by this chapter, and in a form for inclusion in the annual report to Congress authorized under subsection (g) of this section.

(d) Cooperative agreements with State educational agencies

(1) The Secretary shall enter into cooperative agreements with State educational agencies and other State agencies to carry out studies to assess the impact and effectiveness of programs, policies, and procedures assisted under this chapter.

(2) The agreements referred to in paragraph (1) shall—

(A) provide for the payment of not more than 60 percent of the total cost of studies conducted by a participating State agency to assess the impact and effectiveness of this chapter[;] and

(B) be developed in consultation with the State Advisory Panel established under section 1413(a)(12) of this title, the local educational agencies, and others involved in or concerned with, the education of children and youth with disabilities and the provision of early intervention services to infants and toddlers with disabilities.

(3) The Secretary shall provide technical assistance to participating State agencies in the implementation of the study design, analysis, and reporting procedures.

(e) Studies to assess progress of program

(1) The Secretary shall by grant, contract, or cooperative agreement, provide for special studies to assess progress in the implementation of this chapter, and to assess the impact and effectiveness of State and local efforts and efforts by the Secretary of the Interior to provide free appropriate public education to children and youth with disabilities, and early intervention services to infants and toddlers with disabilities. Reports from such studies shall include recommendations for improving programs and services to such individuals. The Secretary shall, beginning in fiscal year 1993 and for every third year thereafter, submit to the appropriate committees of each House of the Congress and publish in the Federal Register proposed priorities for review and comment.

(2) In selecting priorities for fiscal years 1991 through 1994, the Secretary may give first consideration to—

(A) completing a longitudinal study of a sample of students with disabilities, examining—

(i) the full range of disabling conditions;

(ii) the educational progress of students with disabilities while in special education; and

(iii) the occupational, educational, and independent living status of students with disabilities after graduating from secondary school or otherwise leaving special education.

(B) conducting pursuant to this subsection a nationally representative study focusing on the types, number, and intensity of related services provided to children with disabilities by disability category.

(C) conducting pursuant to this subsection a study that examines the degree of disparity among States with regard to the placement in various educational settings of children and youth with similar disabilities, especially those with mental retardation, and, to the extent that such disparity exists, the factors that lead such children and youth to be educated in significantly different educational settings.

(D) conducting pursuant to this subsection a study that examines the factors that have contributed to the decline in the number of children classified as mentally retarded since the implementation of this chapter, and examines the current disparity among States in the percentage of children so classified.

(E) conducting pursuant to this subsection a study that examines the extent to which out-of-community residential programs are used for children and youth who are seriously emotionally disturbed, the factors that influence the selection of such placements, the degree to which such individuals transition back to education programs in their communities, and the factors that facilitate or impede such transition.

(F) conducting pursuant to this subsection a study that examines (i) the factors that influence the referral and placement decisions and types of placements, by disability category and English language proficiency, of minority children relative to other children, (ii) the extent to which these children are placed in regular education environments, (iii) the extent to which the parents of these children are involved in placement decisions and in the development and implementation of the individualized education program and the results of such participation, and (iv) the type of support provided to parents of these children that enable these parents to understand and participate in the educational process.

(f) Integration of information

The Secretary shall make grants to, or enter into contracts or cooperative agreements with, State or local educational agencies, institutions of higher education, other public agencies, and private nonprofit organizations to support activities that organize, synthesize, interpret, and integrate information obtained under subsections (c) and (e) of this section with relevant knowledge obtained from other sources. Such activities shall include the selection and design of content, formats, and means for communicating such information effectively to specific or general audiences, in order to promote the use of such information in improving program administration and management, and service delivery and effectiveness.

(g) Annual report

(1)(A) The Secretary is authorized to conduct activities, directly or by grant, contract, or cooperative agreement, to prepare an annual report on the progress being made toward the provision of—

(i) a free appropriate public education to all children and youth with disabilities; and

(ii) early intervention services for infants and toddlers with disabilities.

(B) Not later than 120 days after the close of each fiscal year, the Secretary shall transmit a copy of the report authorized under subparagraph (A) to the appropriate committees of each House of Congress. The annual report shall be published and disseminated in sufficient quantities to the education and disability communities and to other interested parties.

(2) The Secretary shall include in each annual report under paragraph (1)—

(A) a compilation and analysis of data gathered under subsection (b) of this section and under subchapter VIII of this chapter; and

(B) a description of findings and determinations resulting from monitoring reviews of State implementation of this chapter.

(3) In the annual report under paragraph (1) for fiscal year 1991 (which is published in 1992) and for every third year thereafter, the Secretary shall include in the annual report—

(A) an index of all current projects funded under subchapters III through VII of this chapter; and

(B) data reported under sections 1422 and 1434 of this title.

(4) The Secretary shall include in each annual report under paragraph (1) the results of research and related activities conducted under subchapter V of this chapter that the Secretary determines are relevant to the effective implementation of this chapter.

(5) The Secretary shall, in consultation with the National Council on Disability and the Bureau of Indian Affairs Advisory Committee for Exceptional Children, include a description of the status of early intervention services for infants and toddlers with disabilities from birth through age 2, and special education and related services to children with disabilities from 3 through 5 years of age (including those receiving services through Head Start, developmental disabilities programs, crippled children's services, mental health/mental retardation agencies, and State child-development centers and private agencies under contract with local schools).

(h) Authorization of appropriations

There are authorized to be appropriated $12,000,000 for fiscal year 1991 and such sums as may be necessary for fiscal years 1992 through 1994 to carry out the purposes of this section and not more than 30 percent may be used to carry out the purposes of subsection (e) of this section.

(As amended Pub.L. 101-476, Title II, § 203, Oct. 30, 1990, 104 Stat. 1112.)

§ 1419. Preschool grants

(a) Grants for fiscal years 1987 through 1989; amount of grants

(1) For fiscal years 1987 through 1989 (or fiscal year 1990 if the Secretary makes a grant under this paragraph for such fiscal year) the Secretary shall make a grant to any State which—

(A) has met the eligibility requirements of section 1412 of this title,

(B) has a State plan approved under section 1413 of this title, and

(C) provides special education and related services to children with disabilities aged three to five, inclusive.

(2) (A) For fiscal year 1987 the amount of a grant to a State under paragraph (1) may not exceed—

(i) $300 per child with a disability aged three to five, inclusive, who received special education and related services in such State as determined under section 1411(a)(3) of this title, or

(ii) if the amount appropriated under subsection (e) of this section exceeds the product of $300 and the total number of children with disabilities aged three to five, inclusive, who received special education and related services as determined under section 1411(a)(3) of this title—

(I) $300 per child with a disability aged three to five, inclusive, who received special education and related services in such State as determined under section 1411(a)(3) of this title, plus

(II) an amount equal to the portion of the appropriation available after allocating funds to all States under subclause (I) (the excess appropriation) divided by the estimated increase, from the preceding fiscal year, in the number of children with disabilities aged three to five, inclusive, who will be receiving special education and related services in all States multiplied by the estimated increase in the number of such children in such State.

(B) For fiscal year 1988, funds shall be distributed in accordance with clause (i) or (ii) of paragraph (2)(A), except that the amount specified therein shall be $400 instead of $300.

(C) For fiscal year 1989, funds shall be distributed in accordance with clause (i) or (ii) of paragraph (2)(A), except that the amount specified therein shall be $500 instead of $300.

(D) If the Secretary makes a grant under paragraph (1) for fiscal year 1990, the amount of a grant to a State under such paragraph may not exceed $1,000 per child with a disability aged three to five, inclusive, who received special education and related services in such State as determined under section 1411(a)(3) of this title.

(E) If the actual number of additional children served in a fiscal year differs from the estimate made under subparagraph (A)(ii)(II), the Secretary shall adjust (upwards or downwards) a State's allotment in the subsequent fiscal year.

(F)(i) The amount of a grant under subparagraph (A), (B), or (C) to any State for a fiscal year may not exceed $3,800 per estimated child with a disability aged three to five, inclusive, who will be receiving, or child with a disability, age three to five, inclusive, who is receiving special education and related services in such State.

(ii) If the amount appropriated under subsection (e) of this section for any fiscal year exceeds the amount of grants which may be made to the States for such fiscal year, the excess amount appropriated shall remain available for obligation under this section for 2 succeeding fiscal years.

(3) To receive a grant under paragraph (1) a State shall make an application to the Secretary at such time, in such manner, and containing or accompanied by such information as the Secretary may reasonably require.

(b) Grants for fiscal year 1990 and thereafter; amount of grants

(1) For fiscal year 1990 (or fiscal year 1991 if required by paragraph (2)) and fiscal years thereafter the Secretary shall make a grant to any State which—

(A) has met the eligibility requirements of section 1412 of this title, and

(B) has a State plan approved under section 1413 of this title which includes policies and procedures that assure the availability under the State law and practice of such State of a free appropriate public education for all children with disabilities aged three to five, inclusive, and for any two-year-old children provided services by the State under subsection(c)(2)(B)(iii) of this section or by a local educational agency or intermediate educational unit under subsection (f)(2) of this section.

(2) The Secretary may make a grant under paragraph (1) only for fiscal year 1990 and fiscal years thereafter, except that if—

(A) the aggregate amount that was appropriated under subsection (e) of this section for fiscal years 1987, 1988, and 1989 was less than $656,000,000, or

(B) the amount appropriated for fiscal year 1990 under subsection (e) of this section is less than $306,000,000,

the Secretary may not make a grant under paragraph (1) until fiscal year 1991 and shall make a grant under subsection (a)(1) of this section for fiscal year 1990.

(3) The amount of any grant to any State under paragraph (1) for any fiscal year may not exceed $1,500 for each child with a disability in such State aged three to five, inclusive.

(4) To receive a grant under paragraph (1) a State shall make an application to the Secretary at such time, in such manner, and containing or accompanied by such information as the Secretary may reasonably require.

(c) Distribution by State of received funds

(1) For fiscal year 1987, a State which receives a grant under subsection (a)(1) of this section shall—

(A) distribute at least 70 percent of such grant to local educational agencies and intermediate educational units in such State in accordance with paragraph (3), except that in applying such section only children with disabilities aged three to five, inclusive, shall be considered,

(B) use not more than 25 percent of such grant for the planning and development of a comprehensive delivery system for which a grant could have been made under section 1423(b) of this title in effect through fiscal year 1987 and for direct and support services for children with disabilities[;] and

(C) use not more than 5 percent of such grant for administrative expenses related to the grant.

(2) For fiscal years beginning after fiscal year 1987, a State which receives a grant under subsection (a)(1) or (b)(1) of this section shall—

(A) distribute at least 75 percent of such grant to local educational agencies and intermediate educational units in such State in accordance with paragraph (3), except that in applying such section only children with disabilities aged three to five, inclusive, shall be considered,

(B) use not more than 20 percent of such grant—

(i) for planning and development of a comprehensive delivery system,

(ii) for direct and support services for children with disabilities, aged 3 to 5, inclusive, and

(iii) at the State's discretion, to provide a free appropriate public education, in accordance with this Act, to 2-year-old children with disabilities who will reach age 3 during the school year, whether or not such children are receiving, or have received, services under subchapter VIII of this chapter[;] and

(C) use not more than 5 percent of such grant for administrative expenses related to the grant.

(3) From the amount of funds available to local educational agencies and intermediate educational units in any State under this section, each local educational agency or intermediate educational unit shall be entitled to—

(A) an amount which bears the same ratio to the amount available under subsection (a)(2)(A)(i) of this section or subsection (a)(2)(A)(ii)(I) of this section, as the case may be, as the number of children with disabilities aged three to five, inclusive, who received special education and related services as determined under section 1411(a)(3) of this title in such local educational agency or intermediate educational unit bears to the aggregate number of children with disabilities aged three to five, inclusive, who received special education and related services in all local educational agencies and intermediate educational units in the State entitled to funds under this section[;] and

(B) to the extent funds are available under subsection (a)(2)(A)(ii)(II) of this section, an amount which bears the same ratio to the amount of such funds of this section as the estimated number of additional children with disabilities aged three to five, inclusive, who will be receiving special education and related services in such local educational agency or intermediate educational unit bears to the aggregate number of such children in all local educational agencies and intermediate educational units in the State entitled to funds under this section.

(d) Insufficiency of appropriated amounts; reduction of maximum amounts receivable by States

If the sums appropriated under subsection (e) of this section for any fiscal year for making payments to States under subsection (a)(1) or (b)(1) of this section are not sufficient to pay in full the maximum amounts which all States may receive under such subsection for such fiscal year, the maximum amounts which all States may receive under such subsection for such fiscal year shall be ratably reduced by first ratably reducing amounts computed under the excess appropriation provision of subsection (a)(2)(A)(ii)(II) of this section. If additional funds become available for making such payments for any fiscal year during which the preceding sentence is applicable, the reduced maximum amounts shall be increased on the same basis as they were reduced.

(e) Authorization of appropriations

For grants under subsections (a)(1) of this section and (b)(1) of this section there are authorized to be appropriated such sums as may be necessary.

(f) Use of appropriated funds

Each local educational agency or intermediate educational unit receiving funds under this section—

(1) shall use such funds to provide special education and related services to children with disabilities aged 3 to 5, inclusive[;] and

(2) may, if consistent with State policy, use such funds to provide a free appropriate public education, in accordance with this part, to 2-year-old children with disabilities who will reach age 3 during the school year, whether or not such children are receiving, or have received, services under subchapter VIII of this chapter.

(g) Nonavailability of assistance under other laws

Subchapter VIII of this chapter does not apply to any child with disabilities receiving a free appropriate public education, in accordance with this subchapter, with funds received under this section.

(As amended Pub.L. 101-476, Title IX, § 901(b)(79)-(93), Oct. 30, 1990, 104 Stat. 1145; Pub.L. 102-119, §§ 7, 25(b), Oct. 7, 1991, 105 Stat. 591, 607.)

§ 1420. Payments

(a) Payments to States; distribution by States to local educational agencies and intermediate educational units

The Secretary shall make payments to each State in amounts which the State educational agency of such State is eligible to receive under this subchapter. Any State educational agency receiving payments under this subsection shall distribute payments to the local educational agencies and intermediate educational units of such State in amounts which such agencies and units are eligible to receive under this subchapter after the State educational agency has approved applications of such agencies or units for payments in accordance with section 1414(b) of this title.

(b) Advances, reimbursements, and installments

Payments under this subchapter may be made in advance or by way of reimbursement and in such installments as the Secretary may determine necessary.

(Pub.L. 91-230, Title VI, § 620, as added Pub.L. 94-142, § 5(a), Nov. 29, 1975, 89 Stat. 793, and amended, Pub.L. 98-199, § 3(b), Dec. 2, 1983, 97 Stat. 1358.)

SUBCHAPTER III—CENTERS AND SERVICES TO MEET SPECIAL NEEDS OF INDIVIDUALS WITH DISABILITIES

§ 1421. Regional resource and Federal centers

(a) Establishment; functions

The Secretary may make grants to, or enter into contracts or cooperative agreements with, institutions of higher education, public agencies, private nonprofit organizations, State educational agencies, or combinations of such agencies or institutions (which combinations may include one or more local educational agencies) within particular regions of the United States, to pay all or part of the cost of the establishment and operation of regional resource centers that focus on special education and related services and early intervention services. Each regional resource center shall provide consultation, technical assistance, and training, as requested, to State educational agencies and through such State educational agencies to local educational agencies and to other appropriate public agencies providing special education and related services and early intervention services. The services provided by a regional resource center shall be consistent with the priority needs identified by the States served by the center. Each regional resource center established or operated under this section shall—

(1) assist in identifying and solving persistent problems in providing quality special education and related services for children and youth with disabilities and early intervention services to infants and toddlers with disabilities and their families,

(2) assist in developing, identifying, and replicating successful programs and practices which will improve special education and related services to children and youth with disabilities and their families and early intervention services to infants and toddlers with disabilities and their families,

(3) gather and disseminate information to all State educational agencies within the region and coordinate activities with other centers assisted under this subsection and other relevant programs and projects conducted under subchapters III through VII of this chapter by the Department of Education.

(4) assist in the improvement of information dissemination to and training activities for professionals and parents of infants, toddlers, children and youth with disabilities[;] and

(5) provide information to and training for agencies, institutions, and organizations, regarding techniques and approaches for submitting applications for grants, contracts, and cooperative agreements under this subchapter and subchapters IV through VII of this chapter.

(b) Considerations governing approval of application

In determining whether to approve an application for a project under subsection (a) of this section, the Secretary shall utilize criteria for setting criteria that are consistent with the needs identified by States within the region served by such center, consistent with requirements established by the Secretary under subsection (f) of this section, and, to the extent appropriate, consistent with requirements under section 1409 of this title, and shall consider the need for such a center in the region to be served by the applicant and the capability of the applicant to fulfill the responsibilities under subsection (a) of this section.

(c) Annual report; summaries

Each regional resource center shall report a summary of materials produced or developed and the summaries reported shall be included in the annual report to Congress required under section 1418 of this title.

(d) Coordinating technical assistance center

The Secretary may establish one coordinating technical assistance center focusing on national priorities established by the Secretary to assist the regional resource centers in the delivery of technical assistance, consistent with such national priorities. Such coordinating technical assistance center is authorized to—

(1) provide information to, and training for, agencies, institutions, and organizations, regarding techniques and approaches for submitting applications for grants, contracts, and cooperative agreements under this subchapter and subchapters IV through VII of this chapter, and shall make such information available to the regional resource centers on request;

(2) give priority to providing technical assistance concerning the education of children with disabilities from minority backgrounds;

(3) exchange information with, and, where appropriate, cooperate with, other centers addressing the needs of children with disabilities from minority backgrounds; and

(4) provide assistance to State educational agencies, through the regional resource centers, for the training of hearing officers.

(e) Amounts available for centers

Before using funds made available in any fiscal year to carry out this section for purposes of subsection (d) of this section, not less than the amount made available in the previous fiscal year for regional resource centers under subsection (a) shall be made available for such centers of this section and in no case shall more than $500,000 be made available for the center under subsection (d) of this section.

(f) Guidelines for resource centers

(1) The Secretary shall develop guidelines and criteria for the operation of Regional and Federal Resource Centers. In developing such criteria and guidelines, the Secretary shall establish a panel representing the Office of Special Education Programs staff, State special education directors, representatives of disability advocates, and, when appropriate, consult with the regional resource center directors.

(2) Such guidelines and criteria shall include—

(A) a description of how the Federal and Regional Resource Centers Program will be administered by the Secretary;

(B) a description of the geographic region each Center is expected to serve;

(C) a description of the role of a Center in terms of expected leadership and dissemination efforts;

(D) a description of expected relationships with State agencies, research and demonstration centers, and with other entities deemed necessary;

(E) a description of how a Center will be evaluated; and

(F) other guidelines and criteria deemed necessary.

(3) The Secretary shall publish in the Federal Register by July 1, 1991, for review and comment, proposed and (then following such review and comment) final guidelines developed by the panel.

(As amended Pub.L. 101-476, Title III, § 301, Title IX, § 901(b)(95)-(99), Oct. 30, 1990, 104 Stat. 1117, 1146; Pub.L. 101-119, § 25(b), Oct. 7, 1991, 105 Stat. 607.)

§ 1422. Services for deaf-blind children and youth

(a) Grant and contract authority; types and scope of programs; governing considerations

(1) The Secretary is authorized to make grants to, or to enter into cooperative agreements or contracts with, public or nonprofit private agencies, institutions, or organizations to assist State educational agencies, local educational agencies, and designated lead agencies under subchapter VIII of this chapter to—

(A) assure deaf-blind infants, toddlers, children and youth provision of special education, early intervention, and related services as well as vocational and transitional services; and

(B) make available to deaf-blind youth (who are in the process of transitioning into adult services) programs, services, and supports to facilitate such transition, including assistance related to independent living and competitive employment.

(2) For purposes of this section, the term "deaf-blind," with respect to children and youth, means having auditory and visual impairments, the combination of which creates such severe communication and other developmental and learning needs that they cannot be appropriately educated in special education programs solely for children and youth with hearing impairments, visual impairments, or severe disabilities, without supplementary assistance to address their educational needs due to these dual, concurrent disabilities.

(3) (A) A grant, cooperative agreement, or contract may be made under paragraph(1)(A) only for programs providing—

(i) technical assistance to agencies, institutions, or organizations providing educational or early intervention services to deaf-blind infants, toddlers, children, or youth;

(ii) preservice or inservice training to paraprofessionals, professionals, or related services personnel preparing to serve, or serving, deaf-blind infants, toddlers, children, or youth;

(iii) replication of successful innovative approaches to providing educational, early intervention, or related services to deaf-blind infants, toddlers, children, and youth;

(iv) pilot projects that are designed to—

(I) expand local educational agency capabilities by providing services to deaf-blind children and youth that supplement services already provided to children and youth through State and local resources; and

(II) encourage eventual assumption of funding responsibility by State and local authorities;

(v) the development, improvement, or demonstration of new or existing methods, approaches, or techniques that contribute to the adjustment and education of deaf-blind infants, toddlers, children, and youth; or

(vi) facilitation of parental involvement in the education of their deaf-blind infants, toddlers, children, and youth.

(B) The programs described in subparagraph (A) may include—

(i) the diagnosis and educational evaluation of infants, toddlers, children, and youth who are likely to be diagnosed as deaf-blind;

(ii) programs of adjustment, education, and orientation for deaf-blind infants, toddlers, children, and youth; and

(iii) consultative, counseling, and training services for the families of deaf-blind infants, toddlers, children, and youth.

(4) A grant, cooperative agreement, or contract pursuant to paragraph (1)(B) may be made only for programs providing (A) technical assistance to agencies, institutions, and organizations that are preparing deaf-blind adolescents for adult placements, or that are preparing to receive deaf-blind young adults into adult living and work environments, or that serve, or propose to serve, deaf-blind individuals; (B) training or inservice training to paraprofessionals or professionals serving, or preparing to serve, such individuals; and (C) assistance in the development or replication of successful innovative approaches to providing rehabilitative, supervised, semisupervised, or independent living programs.

(5) In carrying out this subsection, the Secretary is authorized to enter into a number of grants or cooperative agreements to establish and support single and multi-State centers for the provision of technical assistance and pilot supplementary

services, for the purposes of program development and expansion for children and youth with deaf-blindness and their families.

(b) Contract authority for regional programs of technical assistance

The Secretary is also authorized to enter into a limited number of cooperative agreements or contracts to establish and support regional programs for the provision of technical assistance in the education of deaf-blind children and youth.

(c) Annual report to Secretary; examination of numbers and services and revision of numbers; annual report to Congress; summary of data

(1) Programs supported under this section shall report annually to the Secretary on (A) the numbers of deaf-blind children and youth served by age, severity, sex, and nature of deaf-blindness; (B) the number of paraprofessionals, professionals, and family members directly served by each activity; (C) the types of services provided and the setting in which the services are provided; and (D) student outcomes, where appropriate.

(2) The Secretary shall examine the number of deaf-blind children and youth (A) reported under subparagraph (c)(1)(A) and by the States; (B) served by the programs under subchapter II of this chapter and subpart 2 of part D of chapter1 of title I of the Elementary and Secondary Education Act of 1965 [20 U.S.C. 2791 et seq.]); and (C) the Deaf-Blind Registry of each State. The Secretary shall revise the count of deaf-blind children and youth to reflect the most accurate count.

(3) The Secretary shall summarize these data for submission in the annual report required under section 1418 of this title.

(d) National clearinghouse for children and youth with deaf-blindness

The Secretary shall make a grant, or enter into a contract or cooperative agreement, for a national clearinghouse for children and youth with deaf-blindness—

(1) to identify, coordinate, and disseminate information on deaf-blindness, emphasizing information concerning effective practices in working with deaf-blind infants, toddlers, children, and youth;

(2) to interact with educators, professional groups, and parents to identify areas for programming, materials development, training, and expansion of specific services;

(3) to maintain a computerized data base on local, regional and national resources; and

(4) to respond to information requests from professionals, parents, and members of the community.

(e) Country-wide availability of assistance

In carrying out this section, the Secretary shall take into consideration the availability and quality of existing services for deaf-blind infants, toddlers, children, and youth in the country, and, to the extent practicable, ensure that all parts of the country have an opportunity to receive assistance under this section.

(f) Grants to, or contracts and cooperative agreements with, appropriate organizations and agencies

The Secretary may make grants to, or enter into contracts or cooperative agreements with organizations, or public or nonprofit private agencies, as determined by the Secretary to be appropriate, to address the needs of children and youth with deaf-blindness, for—

(1) research to identify and meet the full range of special needs of such children and youth; and

(2) the development and demonstration of new, or improvements in existing methods, approaches, or techniques that would contribute to the adjustment and education of children and youth with deaf-blindness.

(As amended Pub.L. 101-476, Title III, § 302, Oct. 30, 1990, 104 Stat. 1118; Pub.L. 101-119, § 25(a), (8), Oct. 7, 1991, 105 Stat. 606.)

§ 1423. Early education of children with disabilities

(a) Contracts, grants and cooperative agreements; purpose; coordination with community programs; national dispersion in urban and rural areas; Federal share; non-Federal contributions; arrangements with Indian tribes

(1) The Secretary may arrange by contract, grant, or cooperative agreement with appropriate public and private nonprofit organizations, for the development and operation of experimental, demonstration, and outreach preschool and early intervention programs for children with disabilities, including individuals who are at risk of having substantial developmental delays if early intervention services are not provided, which the Secretary determines show promise of promoting a comprehensive and strengthened approach to the special needs of such children. Such programs shall include activities and services designed to—

(A) facilitate the intellectual, emotional, physical, mental, social, speech or other communication mode, language development, and self-help skills of such children,

(B) provide family education and include a parent or their representative of such child, as well as encourage the participation of the parents of such children in the development and operation of any such program,

(C) acquaint the community to be served by any such program with the special needs and potentialities of such children,

(D) offer training about exemplary models and practices including interdisciplinary models and practices, to State and local personnel who provide services to children with disabilities from birth through age 8 and to the parents of such children,

(E) support the adoption of exemplary models and practices in States and local communities, including the involvement of adult role models with disabilities at all levels of the program,

(F) facilitate and improve the early identification of infants and toddlers with disabilities or those infants and toddlers at risk of having developmental disabilities,

(G) facilitate the transition of infants with disabilities or infants at risk of having developmental delays, from medical care to early intervention services, and the transition from early intervention services to preschool special education or regular education services (especially where the lead agency for early intervention programs under subchapter VIII of this chapter is not the State educational agency),

(H) promote the use of assistive technology devices and assistive technology services, where appropriate, to enhance the development of infants and toddlers with disabilities,

(I) facilitate and improve outreach to low-income, minority, rural, and other underserved populations eligible for assistance under subchapters II and VIII of this chapter,

(J) support statewide projects in conjunction with a State's application under subchapter VIII of this chapter and a State's plan under subchapter II of this chapter, to change the delivery of early intervention services to infants and toddlers with disabilities, and to change the delivery of special education and related services to preschool children with disabilities, from segregated to integrated environments; and

(K) increase the understanding of, and address, the early intervention and preschool needs of children exposed prenatally to maternal substance abuse.

(2) Programs authorized by paragraph (1) shall be coordinated with similar programs in the schools operated or supported by State or local educational agencies of the community to be served and with similar programs operated by other public agencies in such community.

(3) As much as is feasible, programs assisted under paragraph (1) shall be geographically dispersed throughout the Nation in urban as well as rural areas.

(4)(A) Except as provided in subparagraph (B), no arrangement under paragraph (1) shall provide for the payment of more than 90 percent of the total annual costs of development, operation, and evaluation of any program. Non-Federal contributions may be in cash or in kind, fairly evaluated, including plant, equipment, and services.

(B) The Secretary may waive the requirement of subparagraph (A) in the case of an arrangement entered into under paragraph (1) with governing bodies of Indian tribes located on Federal or State reservations and with consortia of such bodies.

(b) Grants for identifying, tracking and referring children at-risk of having developmental delays

The Secretary shall fund up to 5 grants to States for 3 years for the purpose of establishing an inter-agency, multi-disciplinary, and coordinated statewide system for the identification, tracking, and referral to appropriate services for all categories of children who are biologically and/or environmentally at-risk of having developmental delays. To the extent feasible, such grants shall be geographically dispersed throughout the Nation in urban and rural areas. Each grantee must—

(1) create a data system within the first year to document the numbers and types of at-risk children in the State and that develops linkages with all appropriate existing child data and tracking systems that assist in providing information;

(2) coordinate activities with the child find component required under subchapter II and VIII of this chapter;

(3) demonstrate the involvement of the lead agency and the State interagency coordinating council under subchapter VIII of this chapter as well as the State educational agency under subchapter II of this chapter;

(4) coordinate with other relevant prevention activities across appropriate service agencies, organizations, councils, and commissions;

(5) define an appropriate service delivery system based on children with various types of at-risk factors;

(6) document the need for additional services as well as barriers; and

(7) disseminate findings and information in the manner prescribed in section 1409(g) of this title.

(c) Technical assistance development system

The Secretary shall arrange by contract, grant, or cooperative agreement with appropriate public agencies and private nonprofit organizations for the establishment of a technical assistance development system to assist entities operating experimental, demonstration, and outreach programs and to assist State agencies to expand and improve services provided to children with disabilities. This technical assistance development system shall provide assistance to parents of and advocates for infants, toddlers, and children with disabilities, as well as direct service and administrative personnel involved with such children. Information from the system should be aggressively disseminated through established information networks and other mechanisms to ensure both an impact and benefits at the community level. The Secretary shall ensure that the technical assistance provided under this subsection includes assistance to State agencies under subchapter VIII of this chapter on procedures for use by primary referral sources in referring a child to the appropriate agency within the system for evaluation, assessment, or service.

(d) Early childhood research institutes

The Secretary shall arrange by contract, grant, or cooperative agreement with appropriate public agencies and private nonprofit organizations for the establishment of early childhood research institutes to carry on sustained research to generate and disseminate new information on preschool and early intervention for children with disabilities and their families. Such institutes shall disseminate this information in the manner prescribed in section 1409(g) of this title.

(e) Grants or contracts with organizations to identify needs of children with disabilities and for training of personnel

The Secretary may make grants to, or enter into contracts or cooperative agreements under this section with, such organizations or institutions, as are determined by the Secretary to be appropriate, for research to identify and meet the full range of special needs of children with disabilities and for training of personnel for programs specifically designed for children with disabilities, including programs to integrate children with disabilities into regular preschool programs.

(f) Notice in Federal Register of intent to accept applications for grants, contracts, etc.

At least one year before the termination of a grant, contract, or cooperative agreement made or entered into under subsections (c) and (d) of this section, the Secretary shall publish in the Federal Register a notice of intent to accept applications for such a grant, contract, or cooperative agreement contingent on the appropriation of sufficient funds by Congress.

(g) "Children with disabilities" defined

For purposes of this section the term "children with disabilities" includes children from birth through eight years of age including infants and toddlers with disabilities.

(h) Organization, integration, and presentation of developed knowledge

The Secretary may make grants to, or enter into contracts or cooperative agreements with, institutions of higher education and nonprofit private organizations to synthesize the knowledge developed under this section and organize, integrate, and present such knowledge so it can be incorporated and imparted to parents, professionals, and others providing or preparing to provide preschool or early intervention services and to persons designing preschool or early intervention programs.

(As amended Pub.L. 101-476, Title III, § 303, Title IX, § 901(b)(100)-(106), Oct. 30, 1990, 104 Stat. 1121, 1146; Pub.L. 102-119, §§ 8, 25(a) (9), (b), Oct. 7, 1991, 105 Stat. 592, 606, 607.)

§ 1424. Programs for children with severe disabilities

(a) Grant and contract authority

The Secretary may make grants to, or enter into contracts or cooperative agreements with, appropriate public agencies and nonprofit organizations to address the special education, related services, early intervention, and integration needs of infants, toddlers, children, and youth with severe disabilities through—

(1) research to identify and meet the full range of special education, related services, and early intervention needs of such children and youth with disabilities, including their need for transportation to and from school,

(2) the development or demonstration of new, or improvements in existing, methods, approaches, or techniques which would contribute to the adjustment and education of such children and youth with disabilities,

(3) training of special and regular education, related services, and early intervention personnel for programs specifically designed for such infants, toddlers, children and youth, including training of regular teachers, instructors, and administrators in strategies (the goal of which is to serve infants, toddlers, children, and youth with disabilities) that include integrated settings for educating such children along side their nondisabled peers,

(4) dissemination of materials and information about practices found effective in working with such children and youth by utilizing existing networks as prescribed in section 1409(g) of this title[;] and

(5) statewide projects, in conjunction with the State's plan under subchapter II of this chapter, to improve the quality of special education and related services for children and youth with severe disabilities, and to change the delivery of those services from segregated to integrated environments.

(b) Extended school year demonstration programs

The Secretary is authorized to make grants to, or enter into contracts or cooperative agreements with, public or private nonprofit private agencies, institutions, or organizations for the development and operation of extended school year demonstration programs for infants, toddlers, children, and youth with severe disabilities.

(c) Coordination of activities with similar activities under other provisions

In making grants and entering into contracts and cooperative agreements under subsection (a) of this section, the Secretary shall ensure that the activities funded under such grants, contracts, or cooperative agreements will be coordinated with similar activities funded from grants and contracts under other sections of this Act.

(d) National geographic dispersion of programs in urban and rural areas

To the extent feasible, programs authorized by subsection (a) of this section shall be geographically dispersed throughout the Nation in urban and rural areas.

(e) Priority programs

In awarding such grants and contracts under this section, the Secretary shall include a priority on programs that increase the likelihood that these children and youth will be educated with their nondisabled peers.

(As amended Pub.L. 101-476, Title III, § 304, Title IX, § 901(b)(107)-(110), Oct. 30, 1990, 104 Stat. 1122, 1147; Pub.L. 102-119, § 25(a)(10), (b), Oct. 7, 1991, 105 Stat. 606, 607.)

§ 1424a. Postsecondary education

(a)(1) The Secretary may make grants to, or enter into contracts with, State educational agencies, institutions of higher education, junior and community colleges, vocational and technical institutions, and other appropriate nonprofit educational agencies for the development, operation, and dissemination of specially designed model programs of postsecondary, vocational, technical, continuing, or adult education for individuals with disabilities. Such model programs may include joint projects that coordinate with special education and transition services.

(2) In making grants or contracts on a competitive basis under paragraph (1), the Secretary shall give priority consideration to 4 regional centers for the deaf and to model programs for individuals with disabling conditions other than deafness—

(A) for developing and adapting programs of postsecondary, vocational, technical, continuing, or adult education to meet the special needs of individuals with disabilities,

(B) for programs that coordinate, facilitate, and encourage education of individuals with a disability with their nondisabled peers; and

(C) for outreach activities that include the provision of technical assistance to strengthen efforts in the development, operation, and design of model programs that are adapted to the special needs of individuals with disabilities.

(3) Persons operating programs for persons with disabilities under a grant or contract under paragraph (1) must coordinate their efforts with and disseminate information about their activities to the clearinghouse on postsecondary programs established under section 1433(b) of this title.

(4) At least one year before the termination of a grant or contract with any of the 4 regional centers for the deaf, the Secretary shall publish in the Federal Register a notice of intent to accept applications for such grant or contract, contingent on the appropriation of sufficient funds by Congress.

(5) To the extent feasible, programs authorized by paragraph (1) shall be geographically dispersed throughout the Nation in urban and rural areas.

(6) Of the sums made available for programs under paragraph (1), not less than $4,000,000 shall first be available for the 4 regional centers for the deaf. The Secretary shall continue to provide assistance through September 30, 1994, to the current grantees operating the four regional centers for the deaf under subsection (a) of this section. The Secretary shall continue to provide such assistance through September 30, 1995, unless the authorization of appropriations for subchapters III-VII of this chapter is extended by September 30, 1994.

(b) For purposes of subsection (a) of this section, the term "individuals with disabilities" means individuals—

(1) with mental retardation, hearing impairments including deafness, speech or language impairments, visual impairments including blindness, serious emotional disturbance, orthopedic impairments, autism, traumatic brain injury, other health impairments, or specific learning disabilities; and

(2) who, by reason thereof, need special education and related services.

(As amended Pub.L. 101-476, Title III, § 305, Title IX, § 901(b)(111)-(118), Oct. 30, 1990, 104 Stat. 1123, 1147; Pub.L. 102-119, § 25(b), Oct. 7, 1991, 105 Stat. 607; Pub.L. 102-421, Title II, § 201(a), Oct. 16, 1992, 102 Stat. 2164.)

§ 1425. Secondary education and transitional services for youth with disabilities

(a) Grant and contract authority; statement of purposes; national geographic dispersion in urban and rural areas

The Secretary may make grants to, or enter into contracts with, institutions of higher education, State educational agencies, local educational agencies, or other appropriate public and private nonprofit institutions or agencies (including the State job training coordinating councils and service delivery area administrative entities established under the Job Training Partnership Act [29 U.S.C.A. § 1501 et seq.]) to—

(1) strengthen and coordinate special education and related services for youth with disabilities currently in school or who recently left school to assist them in the transition to postsecondary education, vocational training, competitive employment (including supported employment), continuing education, independent and community living, or adult services,

(2) stimulate the improvement and development of programs for secondary special education[;] and

(3) stimulate the improvement of the vocational and life skills of students with disabilities to enable them to be better prepared for transition to adult life and services.

To the extent feasible, such programs shall be geographically dispersed throughout the Nation in urban and rural areas.

(b) Description of specific projects

Projects assisted under subsection (a) of this section may include—

(1) developing strategies and techniques for transition to independent living, vocational training, vocational rehabilitation, postsecondary education, and competitive employment (including supported employment) for youth with disabilities,

(2) establishing demonstration models for services, programs, and individualized education programs, which emphasize vocational training, independent living, transitional services, and placement for youth with disabilities,

(3) conducting demographic studies which provide information on the numbers, age levels, types of disabling conditions, and services required for youth with disabilities in need of transitional programs,

(4) specially designed vocational programs to increase the potential for competitive employment for youth with disabilities,

(5) research and development projects for exemplary service delivery models and the replication and dissemination of successful models,

(6) initiating cooperative models among educational agencies and adult service agencies, including vocational rehabilitation, mental health, mental retardation, and public employment, and employers, which facilitate the planning and developing of transitional services for youth with disabilities to postsecondary education, vocational training, employment, continuing education, and adult services,

(7) developing appropriate procedures for evaluating vocational training, placement, and transitional services for youth with disabilities,

(8) conducting studies which provide information on the numbers, age levels, types of disabling conditions and reasons why some youth with disabilities remain to complete school programs while others drop out,

(9) developing curriculum and instructional techniques in special education and related services that will improve the acquisition of skills by students with disabilities necessary for transition to adult life and services,

(10) specially designed or adapted physical education and therapeutic recreation programs to facilitate the full participation of youths with disabilities in community programs[;] and

(11) developing and disseminating exemplary programs and practices that meet the unique needs of students who utilize assistive technology devices and assistive technology services as such students make the transition to postsecondary education, vocational training, competitive employment (including supported employment), and continuing education or adult services.

(c) Coordination of non-educational-agency applicant with State educational agency

For purposes of paragraphs (1) and (2) of subsection (b) of this section, if an applicant is not an educational agency, such applicant shall coordinate its activities with the State educational agency.

(d) Applications for assistance; contents

Applications for assistance under subsection (a) of this section other than for the purpose of conducting studies or evaluations shall—

(1) describe the procedures to be used for disseminating relevant findings and data to regional resource centers, clearinghouses, and other interested persons, agencies, or organizations,

(2) describe the procedures that will be used for coordinating services among agencies for which youth with a disability are or will be eligible[;] and

(3) provide for the direct participation of students with disabilities and the parents of students with disabilities in the planning, development, and implementation of such projects.

(e) Five-year grants to develop systems to provide transition services

(1) The Secretary shall make one-time, 5-year grants, on a competitive basis, to States in which the State vocational rehabilitation agency and State educational agency submit a joint application to develop, implement, and improve systems to provide transition services for youth with disabilities from age 14 through the age they exit school.

(2) In the case of a State whose vocational rehabilitation agency does not participate regarding a joint application described in paragraph (1), the Secretary may make a grant under such paragraph to the State if a joint application for the grant is submitted by the State educational agency and one other State agency that provides transition services to individuals who are leaving programs under this chapter.

(3) States that receive grants shall use grant funds to:

(A) Increase the availability, access, and quality of transition assistance through the development and improvement of policies, procedures, systems, and other mechanisms for youth with disabilities and their families as such youth prepare for and enter adult life.

(B) Improve the ability of professionals, parents, and advocates to work with such youth in ways that promote the understanding of and the capability to successfully make the transition from "student" to "adult."

(C) Improve working relationships among education personnel, both within LEAs and in postsecondary training programs, relevant State agencies, the private sector (especially employers), rehabilitation personnel, local and State employment agencies, local Private Industry Councils (PICS) authorized by the Job Training Partnership Act (JTPA), and families of students with disabilities and their advocates to identify and achieve consensus on the general nature and specific application of transition services to meet the needs of youth with disabilities.

(D) Create an incentive for accessing and using the expertise and resources of programs, projects, and activities related to transition funded through this section and with other sources.

(4)(A) In order to receive funding under this subsection, a State vocational rehabilitation agency and State educational agency shall describe in their application how they will use the first year, if necessary, to plan how to implement transition services, the second through fourth years to develop and implement transition services, and the fifth year to evaluate transition services. The application shall describe how the grant funds will be used during the planning period and phased out during the evaluation period to ensure the continuation of transition services. Such applications shall also include—

(i) a description of the current availability, access, and quality of transition services for eligible youth and a description of how, over 5 years, the State will improve and expand the availability, access, and quality of transition services for youth with disabilities and their families as such youth prepare for and enter adult life;

(ii) a description of how the State will improve and increase the ability of professionals, parents, and advocates to work with such youth in ways that promote the understanding of and the capability to successfully make the transition from "student" to "adult";

(iii) a description of how the State will improve and increase working relationships among education personnel, both within LEAs and in postsecondary training programs, relevant State agencies, the private sector (especially employers), rehabilitation personnel, local and State employment agencies, local Private Industry Councils (PICS) authorized by the JTPA, and families of students with disabilities and their advocates to identify and achieve consensus on the general nature and specific application of transition services to meet the needs of youth with disabilities; and

(iv) a description of how the State will use grant funds as an incentive for accessing and using the expertise and resources of programs, projects, and activities related to transition funded through this section and with other sources.

(B) The Secretary shall give preference to those applications that, in addition to clearly addressing the requirements under subparagraph (A), describe how the State will—

(i) target resources to school settings, such as providing access to rehabilitation counselors for students with disabilities who are in school settings;

(ii) target a substantial amount of grant funds, received under this subsection, to case management, program evaluation and documentation of, and dissemination of information about, transition services;

(iii) provide incentives for interagency and private sector resource pooling and otherwise investing in transition services, especially in the form of cooperative agreements, particularly with PICS authorized by the JTPA and local branches of State employment agencies;

(iv) provide for early, ongoing information and training for those involved with or who could be involved with transition services—professionals, parents, youth with disabilities, including self-advocacy training for such youth, and advocates for such youth as well as PICS authorized by the JTPA and local branches of State employment agencies;

(v) provide for the early and direct involvement of all relevant parties, including PICS authorized by the JTPA and local branches of State employment agencies, in operating and planning improvements in transition services, and the early and direct involvement of all relevant parties in planning and implementing transition services for individual youth;

(vi) provide access to training for eligible youth that matches labor market needs in their communities;

(vii) integrate transition services with relevant opportunities in communities, including those sponsored by PICS authorized by the JTPA and local employment agencies;

(viii) use a transition services evaluation plan that is outcome oriented and that focuses on individual youth-focused benefits; and

(ix) ensure that, when appropriate and no later than age 22, eligible youth who participate in transition services under this program would be served as appropriate in the State section 110 [29 U.S.C. § 730] and/or title VI, part C program authorized under the Rehabilitation Act of 1973 [29 U.S.C. § 701 *et seq.*].

(f) Development or demonstration of new or improved methods, approaches, or techniques

(1) The Secretary is authorized to make grants to, or to enter into contracts or cooperative agreements with, such organizations or institutions as are determined by the Secretary to be appropriate for the development or demonstration of new or

improvements in existing methods, approaches, or techniques which will contribute to the adjustment and education of children and youth with disabilities and the dissemination of materials and information concerning practices found effective in working with such children and youth. Such organizations and institutions shall disseminate such materials and information as prescribed under section 1409(g) of this title.

(2) The Secretary shall fund one or more demonstration models designed to establish appropriate methods of providing, or continuing to provide, assistive technology devices and services to secondary school students as they make the transition to vocational rehabilitation, employment, postsecondary education, or adult services. Such demonstration models shall include, as appropriate—

(A) cooperative agreements with the Rehabilitation Services Administration and/or State vocational rehabilitation agencies that ensure continuity of funding for assistive technology devices and services to such students; and

(B) methods for dissemination of exemplary practices that can be adapted or adopted by transitional programs for secondary school students with disabilities.

(3)(A) the Secretary shall award one, five-year cooperative agreement through a separate competition to an institution of higher education, or nonprofit public or private organization. The purpose of this agreement will be to evaluate and document the approaches and outcomes of the projects funded under subsection (e) of this section. The results of this agreement shall be disseminated through the appropriate clearinghouses, networks, and through direct communication with Federal, State, and local agencies.

(B) The evaluation carried out pursuant to subparagraph (A) of transition services under subsection (e) of this section shall include an evaluation of—

(i) the outcomes of the transition services provided under such subsection, including the effect of the services regarding postsecondary education, job training, employment, and other appropriate matters;

(ii) the impact of including in the individualized education program a statement of needed transition services (as required under section 1401(a)(20)(D) of this title);

(iii) the extent to which, in the provision of the transition services, agencies are cooperating effectively, including evaluation of the extent of coordination of the staff of the agencies, of procedures regarding confidentiality, assessment of needs and referrals, and coordination regarding data bases and training;

(iv) the extent to which obstacles exist regarding cooperation and coordination among agencies in the provision of the transition services, and the extent to which Federal law creates disincentives to such cooperation and coordination; and

(v) the extent to which the transition services have been provided in a cost-effective manner.

(C) The evaluation carried out pursuant to subparagraph (A) shall include recommendations on the manner in which the program under subsection (e) of this section can be improved.

(D) In the annual report required under section 1418(g) of this title, the Secretary shall include a report of the activities and results associated with the agreement under subparagraph (A).

(g) Coordination of educational programs with vocational rehabilitation projects

The Secretary, as appropriate, shall coordinate programs described under subsection (a) of this section with projects developed under section 777a of Title 29, the Job

Training Partnership Act (JTPA) [29 U.S.C. § 1501 *et seq.*], and the Carl D. Perkins Vocational and Applied Technology Education Act [20 U.S.C. § 2301 *et seq.*].

(As amended Pub.L. 101-476, Title III, § 306, Title IX, § 901(b)(119)-(127), Oct. 30, 1990, 104 Stat. 1124, 1147; Pub.L. 102-119, § 25(a)(11), (b), Oct. 7, 1991, 105 Stat. 606, 607.)

§ 1426. Programs for children and youth with serious emotional disturbance

(a) Grants, contracts, and cooperative agreements to establish projects

The Secretary is authorized to make grants to, or enter into contracts or cooperative agreements with, institutions of higher education, State and local educational agencies, and other appropriate public and private nonprofit institutions or agencies to establish projects for the purpose of improving special education and related services to children and youth with serious emotional disturbance. Such projects may include—

(1) studies regarding the present state of special education and related services to such children and youth and their families, including information and data to enable assessment of the status of such services over time;

(2) developing methodologies and curricula designed to improve special education and related services for these children and youth;

(3) developing and demonstrating strategies and approaches to reduce the use of out-of-community residential programs and the increased use of school district-based programs (which may include day treatment programs, after-school programs, and summer programs);

(4) developing the knowledge, skills, and strategies for effective collaboration among special education, regular education, related services, and other professionals and agencies; or

(5) developing and demonstrating innovative approaches to assist and to prevent children with emotional and behavioral problems from developing serious emotional disturbances that require the provision of special education and related services.

(b) Grants to provide services

(1) The Secretary is authorized to make grants, on a competitive basis, to local educational agencies in collaboration with mental health entities to provide services for children and youth with serious emotional disturbance. Such demonstration projects shall—

(A) increase the availability, access, and quality of community services for such children and youth and their families;

(B) improve working relationships among education, school and community mental health and other relevant personnel, families of such children and youth, and their advocates;

(C) target resources to school settings, such as providing access to school and/or community mental health professionals and other community resources for students with serious emotional disturbance who are in community school settings; and

(D) take into account the needs of minority children and youth in all phases of project activity.

(2) Funds received under this subsection may also be used to facilitate inter-agency and private sector resource pooling to improve services for such children and youth and to provide information and training for those involved with, or who could be involved with, such children and youth.

(c) Application of existing research results; evaluations, reports, dissemination of findings

Each project assisted under this section shall—

(1) apply existing research outcomes from multi-disciplinary fields;

(2) use a grant evaluation plan that is outcome-oriented and that focuses on the benefits to individual children and youth;

(3) report on the effectiveness of such project; and

(4) disseminate the findings of such project, where appropriate, in accordance with section 1409(g) of this title.

(As amended Pub.L. 101-476, Title III, § 307, Oct. 30, 1990, 104 Stat. 1127.)

§ 1427. Authorization of appropriations

(a) There are authorized to be appropriated to carry out section 1421 of this title $8,525,000 for fiscal year 1991, $9,300,000 for fiscal year 1992, $10,140,000 for fiscal year 1993, and $11,052,000 for fiscal year 1994.

(b) There are authorized to be appropriated to carry out section 1422 of this title $21,900,000 for fiscal year 1991, $24,100,000 for fiscal year 1992, $26,500,000 for fiscal year 1993, and $29,200,000 for fiscal year 1994.

(c) There are authorized to be appropriated to carry out section 1423 of this title $31,400,000 for fiscal year 1991, $34,235,000 for fiscal year 1992, $37,325,000 for fiscal year 1993, and $40,705,000 for fiscal year 1994.

(d) There are authorized to be appropriated to carry out section 1424 of this title $9,500,000 for fiscal year 1991, $10,500,000 for fiscal year 1992, $11,600,000 for fiscal year 1993, and $12,700,000 for fiscal year 1994.

(e) There are authorized to be appropriated to carry out section 1424a of this title $9,470,000 for fiscal year 1991, $10,230,000 for fiscal year 1992, $11,050,000 for fiscal year 1993, and $11,930,000 for fiscal year 1994.

(f) There are authorized to be appropriated to carry out section 1425 of this title (except subsection (e)) $9,800,000 for fiscal year 1991, $10,800,000 for fiscal year 1992, $11,900,000 for fiscal year 1993, and $13,050,000 for fiscal year 1994.

(g) There are authorized to be appropriated to carry out section 1425(e) of this title $27,500,000 for fiscal year 1991, $30,250,000 for fiscal year 1992, $33,275,000 for fiscal year 1993, and $36,602,000 for fiscal year 1994.

(h) There are authorized to be appropriated to carry out section 1426 of this title $6,500,000 for fiscal year 1991, $8,000,000 for fiscal year 1992, $9,500,000 for fiscal year 1993, and $11,500,000 for fiscal year 1994.

(As amended Pub.L. 101-476, Title III, § 308, Oct. 30, 1990, 104 Stat. 1128.)

SUBCHAPTER IV—TRAINING PERSONNEL FOR THE EDUCATION OF INDIVIDUALS WITH DISABILITIES

§ 1431. Grants for personnel training

(a) Careers in special education; personnel standards; costs of courses, fellowships and traineeships; contract authority for areas of personnel shortages

(1) The Secretary may make grants, which may include scholarships with necessary stipends and allowances, to institutions of higher education (including university affiliated programs and satellite centers participating in programs under part D of the Developmental Disabilities Assistance and Bill of Rights Act [42 U.S.C. § 6061 *et seq.*]) and other appropriate nonprofit agencies to assist them in training personnel for careers in special education, related services, and early intervention, including—

(A) special education teaching, including speech-language pathology and audiology, and adapted physical education and instructional and assistive technology services,

(B) related services to children and youth with disabilities in educational settings, and other settings,

(C) special education and other careers in preschool and early intervention services for infants and toddlers with disabilities,

(D) special education leadership, including supervision and administration (at the advanced graduate, doctoral, and post-doctoral levels), special education research, and special education personnel preparation (at the doctoral and post-doctoral levels), and

(E) training of special education personnel and other personnel providing special services and pre-school and other early intervention services for children with disabilities.

(2)(A) The Secretary shall base the award of grants under paragraph (1) on information relating to the present and projected need for special education, related services, early intervention, and other personnel to be trained based on identified State, regional, or national shortages, including the need for personnel in the provision of special education to children of limited English proficiency, and the capacity of the institution or agency to train qualified personnel, and other information considered appropriate by the Secretary.

(B) The Secretary shall ensure that grants are only made under paragraph (1) to applicant agencies and institutions that meet State and professionally recognized standards for the preparation of special education and related services personnel unless the grant is for the purpose of assisting the applicant agency institution to meet such standards, and that include in their applications a detailed description of strategies that will be utilized to recruit and train members of minority groups and persons with disabilities.

(3) Grants under paragraph (1) may be used by institutions to assist in covering the cost of courses of training or study for such personnel and for establishing and maintaining fellowships or traineeships with such stipends and allowances as may be determined by the Secretary. Such institutions shall give priority consideration in the selection of qualified recipients of fellowships and traineeships to individuals from disadvantaged backgrounds, including minorities and individuals with disabilities

who are underrepresented in the teaching profession or in the specializations in which they are being trained.

(4) The Secretary in carrying out paragraph (1) may reserve a sum not to exceed 5 percent of the amount available for paragraph (1) in each fiscal year for contracts to prepare personnel in areas where shortages exist when a response to that need has not been adequately addressed by the grant process.

(5) In making grants under subsection (a)(1) of this section, the Secretary may determine that a portion of training supported through such grants shall be conducted on an interdisciplinary basis, and shall be designed to assist special educators in properly coordinating service provision with related services personnel. To the extent feasible, training programs funded under subsection (a)(1)(B) and(a)(1)(E) of this section shall require practica to demonstrate the delivery of related services in an array of regular and special education and community settings.

(6) Nothing in this subsection shall be construed to prevent regular education or special education personnel from benefiting or participating in training activities conducted under this subsection on a preservice or inservice basis.

(7) The Secretary, in carrying out paragraph (1), shall make grants to Historically Black Colleges and Universities, and other institutions of higher education whose minority student enrollment is at least 25 percent.

(8)(A) In making grants under paragraph (1), the Secretary may make grants through a separate competition to institutions of higher education, in partnership with local educational agencies and center schools for students who are deaf, to carry out not less than 4 regional model demonstration training programs on deafness and secondary disabilities.

(B) Such programs shall provide preservice and inservice training to teachers and school administrators, and leadership personnel, in the education of students who are deaf and to related services personnel.

[(9)] In making grants under paragraph (1), the Secretary may provide for the training or retraining of regular education teachers who are involved in providing instruction to individuals who are deaf, but who are not certified as teachers of such individuals, to meet the communications needs of such individuals.

(b) Grants for educational interpreter training programs for personnel educating deaf or deaf-blind students; assurance required; training of regular education teachers

(1) The Secretary may make grants to institutions of higher education, and other appropriate nonprofit agencies or organizations for the establishment or continuation of educational interpreter training programs to train personnel to effectively meet the various communication needs of elementary and secondary students who are deaf or deaf-blind. To the extent feasible, grants shall be geographically dispersed through-out the Nation in urban and rural areas.

(2) The Secretary may make a grant under paragraph (1) only if the applicant for the grant provides an assurance that all interpreters receiving training under the grant will be provided training designed to develop skills necessary for facilitating effective communication for students who are deaf or deaf-blind.

(3) In making grants under paragraph (1), the Secretary may provide for the training or retraining (including short-term and in-service training) of regular educa-tion teachers who are involved in providing instruction to individuals who are deaf,

but who are not certified as teachers of such individuals, and other personnel who work with such individuals, on the role of educational interpreters.

(c) Special projects for preservice training, regular educators, and inservice training of special education personnel.

The Secretary may make grants to institutions of higher education, State agencies, and other appropriate nonprofit agencies and organizations to develop and demonstrate effective ways for preservice training programs to prepare regular educators to work with children and youth with disabilities and their families; for training teachers to work in community and school settings with school students with disabilities and their families; for inservice and preservice training of personnel to work with infants, toddlers, children, and youth with disabilities and their families; for inservice and preservice training of personnel to work with minority infants, toddlers, children, and youth with disabilities and their families; for preservice and inservice training of special education and related services personnel in the use of assistive and instructional technology to benefit infants, toddlers, children, and youth with disabilities; and for the recruitment and retention of special education, related services, and early intervention personnel. Both preservice and inservice training shall include a component that addresses the coordination among all service providers, including regular educators.

(d) Grants for career advancement and competency-based training for current workers

(1) The Secretary shall fund up to 5 grants to States or entities to support the formation of consortia or partnerships of public and private entities for the purpose of providing opportunities for career advancement and/or competency-based training, including but not limited to, certificate or degree granting programs in special education, related services, and early intervention for current workers at public and private agencies that provide services to infants, toddlers, children, and youth with disabilities. Recipients shall meet the requirements of section 1409(g) of this title for the dissemination of information. The purposes for which such a grant may be expended include, but are not limited to, the following:

(A) Establishing a program with colleges and universities to develop creative new programs and coursework options and/or to expand existing programs in the field of special education, related services, or early intervention. Funds may be used to provide release time for faculty and staff for curriculum development, instructional costs, and modest start-up and other program development costs.

(B) Establishing a career development mentoring program using faculty and professional staff members of participating agencies as role models, career sponsors, and academic advisors for experienced State, city, county, and voluntary sector workers who have demonstrated a commitment to working in the above fields and who are enrolled in higher education institution programs relating to these fields.

(C) Supporting a wide range of programmatic and research activities aimed at increasing opportunities for career advancement and competency-based training in the above fields.

(D) Identifying existing public and private agency and labor union personnel policies and benefit programs that may facilitate the ability of workers to take advantage of higher education opportunities such as leave time, tuition reimbursement, etc.

(2) To the extent feasible, projects authorized under paragraph (1) shall be geographically dispersed throughout the Nation in urban and rural areas.

(3) The Secretary shall award, for the purpose of providing technical assistance to States or entities receiving grants under paragraph (1), a cooperative agreement through a separate competition to an entity that has successfully demonstrated the capacity and expertise in the education, training, and retention of workers to serve children and youth with disabilities through the use of consortia or partnerships established for the purpose of retaining the existing workforce and providing opportunities for career enhancement.

(4) The Secretary may conduct an evaluation of projects funded under this subsection.

(5) During the period in which an entity is receiving financial assistance under paragraph (1) or (3), the entity may not receive financial assistance under the other paragraph.

(e) Parent training and information programs

(1) The Secretary may make grants through a separate competition to private nonprofit organizations for the purpose of providing training and information to parents of infants, toddlers, children, and youth with disabilities and persons who work with parents to enable such individuals to participate more effectively with professionals in meeting the educational needs of children with disabilities. Such grants shall be designed to meet the unique training and information needs of parents of infants, toddlers, children, and youth with disabilities living in the area to be served by the grant, particularly those who are members of groups that have been traditionally underrepresented.

(2) In order to receive a grant under paragraph (1) a private nonprofit organization shall—

(A) be governed by a board of directors of which a majority of the members are parents of infants, toddlers, children, and youth with disabilities, particularly minority parents, and that includes members who are professionals, especially minority professionals, in the field of special education, early intervention, and related services, and individuals with disabilities, or, if the nonprofit private organization does not have such a board, such organization shall have a membership that represents the interests of individuals with disabilities, and shall establish a special governing committee of which a majority of the members are parents of infants, toddlers, children, and youth with disabilities, particularly parents of minority children, and which includes members who are professionals, especially minority professionals, in the field of special education, early intervention, and related services, to operate the training and information program under paragraph (1), and parents and professional membership of these boards or special governing committees shall be broadly representative of minority and other individuals and groups having an interest in special education, early intervention, and related services;

(B) serve the parents of infants, toddlers, children, and youth with the full range of disabling conditions under such grant program[;] and

(C) demonstrate the capacity and expertise to conduct effectively the training and information activities for which a grant may be made under paragraph (1), and, for purposes of paragraph (1), network with clearinghouses, including those established under § 1433 of this title and other organizations and agencies, and network with other established national, State, and local parent groups representing the full range of parents of infants, toddlers, children, and youth with disabilities, especially parents of minority children.

Nothing in subparagraph (A) shall be construed to authorize or permit the denial to any person of the due process of law required by the United States Constitution.

(3) The board of directors or special governing committee of a private nonprofit organization receiving a grant under paragraph (1) shall meet at least once in each calendar quarter to review the parent training and information activities for which the grant is made, and each such committee shall advise the governing board directly of its views and recommendations. Whenever a private nonprofit organization requests the renewal of a grant under paragraph (1) for a fiscal year, the board of directors or the special governing committee shall submit to the Secretary a written review of the parent training and information program conducted by that private nonprofit organization during the preceding fiscal year.

(4) The Secretary shall ensure that grants under paragraph (1) will—

(A) be distributed geographically to the greatest extent possible throughout all the States and give priority to grants which involve unserved areas,

(B) be targeted to parents of children with disabilities in both urban and rural areas or on a State or regional basis,

(C) serve parents of minority children with disabilities (including parents served pursuant to paragraph (10)) representative to the proportion of the minority population in the areas being served by requiring that applicants for the grants identify with specificity the special efforts that will be undertaken to involve such parents, including efforts to work with community-based and cultural organizations and the specification of supplementary aids, services, and supports that will be made available, and by specifying budgetary items earmarked to accomplish this subparagraph[;] and

(D) be funded at a sufficient size, scope, and quality to ensure that the program is adequate to serve the parents in the area.

(5) Parent training and information programs assisted under paragraph (1) shall assist parents to—

(A) better understand the nature and needs of the disabling conditions of children,

(B) provide followup support for educational programs of children with disabilities,

(C) communicate more effectively with special and regular educators, administrators, related services personnel, and other relevant professionals,

(D) participate in educational decisionmaking processes, including the development of the individualized education program for a child with a disability,

(E) obtain appropriate information about the range of options, programs, services, and resources available at the national, State, and local levels to assist infants, toddlers, children, and youth with disabilities and their families[;] and

(F) understand the provisions for the education of infants, toddlers, children, and youth with disabilities under this Act.

(6) Parent training and information programs may, at a grant recipient's discretion, include State or local educational personnel where such participation will further an objective of the program assisted by the grant.

(7) Each private nonprofit organization operating a program receiving a grant under paragraph (1) shall consult and network with appropriate national, State, regional, and local agencies and organizations, such as protection and advocacy

agencies, that serve or assist infants, toddlers, children, and youth with disabilities and their families and are located in the jurisdictions served by the program.

(8) The Secretary shall provide technical assistance, by grant or contract, for establishing, developing, and coordinating parent training and information programs.

(9) After the establishment in each State of a parent training and information center, the Secretary shall provide for the establishment of 3 experimental centers to serve large numbers of parents of children with disabilities located in high density areas that do not have such centers and 2 such centers to serve large numbers of parents of children with disabilities located in rural areas.

(10)(A) In the case of a grant under paragraph (1) to a private nonprofit organization for fiscal year 1993 or 1994, the organization, in expending the amounts described in subparagraph (B), shall give priority to providing services under this subsection to parents of children with disabilities aged 0-5.

(B) With respect to a grant under paragraph (1) to a private nonprofit organization for fiscal year 1993 or 1994, the amounts described in this subparagraph are any amounts provided in the grant in excess of the amount of any grant under such paragraph provided to the organization for fiscal year 1992.

(11) Effective for fiscal year 1991 and every year thereafter, the Secretary shall obtain data concerning programs and centers assisted under this subsection on—

(A) the number of parents provided information and training by disability category of their children,

(B) the types and modes of information or training provided,

(C) strategies used to reach and serve parents of minority infants, toddlers, children, and youth with disabilities,

(D) the number of parents served as a result of activities described under subparagraph (C),

(E) activities to network with other information clearinghouses and parent groups as required in subsection (c)(2)(C),

(F) the number of agencies and organizations consulted with at the national, State, regional, and local levels[;] and

(G) the number of parents served under this subsection who are parents of children with disabilities aged 0-5.

The Secretary shall include a summary of this information in the annual report to Congress as required in section 1418(g) of this title.

(As amended Pub.L. 101-476, Title IV, § 401, Title IX, § 901(b)(129)-(142), Oct. 30, 1990, 104 Stat. 1129, 1148; Pub.L. 102-119, §§ 9(a), (b), 25(a)(12), (b), Oct. 7, 1991, 105 Stat. 593, 594, 606, 607; Pub.L. 102-421, Title II, § 202, Oct. 16, 1992, 106 Stat. 2165; Pub.L. 102-569, Title IX, § 912(a), Oct. 29, 1992, 106 Stat. 4486.)

§ 1432. Grants to State educational agencies and institutions for traineeships

(a) Size and scope of grant

The Secretary shall make a grant of sufficient size and scope to each State educational agency for the purposes described in subsection (c) of this section and, in any State in which the State educational agency does not apply for such a grant, to an institution of higher education within such State for such purposes.

(b) Grants on competitive basis

The Secretary may also make a limited number of grants to State educational agencies on a competitive basis for the purposes described in subsection (c) of this section. In any fiscal year, the Secretary may not expend for purposes of this subsection an amount that exceeds 10 percent of the amount expended for purposes of this section in the preceding fiscal year.

(c) Purpose of grants

Grants made under this section shall be for the purpose of assisting States in establishing and maintaining preservice and inservice programs to prepare special and regular education, related services and early intervention personnel to meet the needs of infants, toddlers, children, and youth with disabilities or supervisors of such persons, consistent with the personnel needs identified in the State's comprehensive system of personnel development under section[s] 1413 and 1476(b)(8) of this title, and to assist the State in developing and maintaining such systems and conducting personnel recruitment and retention activities.

(d) Technical assistance to States

The Secretary is authorized to provide directly or by grant, contract, or cooperative agreement, technical assistance to State educational agencies on matters pertaining to the effective implementation of section 1413(a)(3) of this title.

(As amended Pub.L. 101-476, Title IV, § 402, Title IX, § 901(b)(143), Oct. 30, 1990, 104 Stat. 1132, 1148; Pub.L. 102-119, § 25(b), Oct. 7, 1991, 105 Stat. 607.)

§ 1433. Clearinghouses

(a) Establishment of national clearinghouses

The Secretary is authorized to make grants to, or enter into contracts or cooperative agreements with, public agencies or private nonprofit organizations or institutions for the establishment of three national clearinghouses: on children and youth with disabilities; on postsecondary education for individuals with disabilities; and on careers in special education, to—
(1) collect, develop, and disseminate information,
(2) provide technical assistance,
(3) conduct coordinated outreach activities,
(4) provide for the coordination and networking with other relevant national, State, and local organizations and information and referral resources,
(5) respond to individuals and organizations seeking information[;] and
(6) provide for the synthesis of information for its effective utilization by parents, professionals, individuals with disabilities, and other interested parties.

(b) National clearinghouse for children and youth

The national clearinghouse for children and youth with disabilities shall:
(1) Collect and disseminate information (including the development of materials) on characteristics of infants, toddlers, children, and youth with disabilities and on

programs, legislation, and services relating to their education under this chapter and other Federal laws.

(2) Participate in programs and services related to disability issues for providing outreach, technical assistance, collection, and dissemination of information; and promoting networking of individuals with appropriate national, State, and local agencies and organizations.

(3) Establish a coordinated network and conduct outreach activities with relevant Federal, State, and local organizations and other sources for promoting public awareness of disability issues and the availability of information, programs, and services.

(4) Collect, disseminate, and develop information on current and future national, Federal, regional, and State needs for providing information to parents, professionals, individuals with disabilities, and other interested parties relating to the education and related services of individuals with disabilities.

(5) Provide technical assistance to national, Federal, regional, State and local agencies and organizations seeking to establish information and referral services for individuals with disabilities and their families.

(6) In carrying out the activities in this subsection, the clearinghouse will include strategies to disseminate information to underrepresented groups such as those with limited English proficiency.

(c) National clearinghouse on postsecondary education for individuals with disabilities

The national clearinghouse on postsecondary education for individuals with disabilities shall:

(1) Collect and disseminate information nationally on characteristics of individuals entering and participating in education and training programs after high school; legislation affecting such individuals and such programs; policies, procedures, and support services, as well as adaptations, and other resources available or recommended to facilitate the education of individuals with disabilities; available programs and services that include, or can be adapted to include, individuals with disabilities; and sources of financial aid for the education and training of individuals with disabilities.

(2) Identify areas of need for additional information.

(3) Develop new materials (in both print and nonprint form), especially by synthesizing information from a variety of fields affecting disability issues and the education, rehabilitation, and retraining of individuals with disabilities.

(4) Develop a coordinated network of professionals, related organizations and associations, mass media, other clearinghouses, and governmental agencies at the Federal, regional, State, and local level for the purposes of disseminating information and promoting awareness of issues relevant to the education of individuals with disabilities after high school and referring individuals who request information to local resources.

(5) Respond to requests from individuals with disabilities, their parents, and professionals who work with them, for information that will enable them to make appropriate decisions about postsecondary education and training.

(d) National clearinghouse on careers in special education

The national clearinghouse designed to encourage students to seek careers and professional personnel to seek employment in the various fields relating to the education of children and youth with disabilities shall:

(1) Collect and disseminate information on current and future national, regional, and State needs for special education and related services personnel.

(2) Disseminate information to high school counselors and others concerning current career opportunities in special education, location of programs, and various forms of financial assistance (such as scholarships, stipends, and allowances).

(3) Identify training programs available around the country.

(4) Establish a network among local and State educational agencies and institutions of higher education concerning the supply of graduates and available openings.

(5) Provide technical assistance to institutions seeking to meet State and professionally recognized standards.

(e) Priority consideration of applicants

(1) In awarding grants, contracts, and cooperative agreements under this section, the Secretary shall give priority consideration to any applicant with demonstrated, proven effectiveness (at the national level) in performing the functions established in this section; and with the ability to conduct such projects, communicate with intended consumers of information, and maintain the necessary communication with national, regional, State, and local agencies and organizations.

(2) In awarding grants, contracts, and cooperative agreements under this section, the Secretary shall give priority consideration to any applicant with demonstrated, proven effectiveness (at the national level) in providing informational services to minorities and minority organizations.

(f) Annual report to Congress

(1) Beginning in fiscal year 1991, and for each year thereafter, the Secretary shall obtain information on each project assisted under this section, including—

(A) the number of individuals served by disability category, as appropriate, including parents, professionals, students, and individuals with disabilities;

(B) a description of responses utilized;

(C) a listing of new products developed and disseminated; and

(D) a description of strategies and activities utilized for outreach to urban and rural areas with populations of minorities and underrepresented groups.

(2) A summary of the data required by this subsection shall be included in the annual report to Congress required under section 1418 of this title.

(As amended Pub.L. 101-476, Title IV, § 403, Title IX, § 901(b)(144), Oct. 30, 1990, 104 Stat. 1133, 1149; Pub.L. 102-119, § 25(b), Oct. 7, 1991, 105 Stat. 607.)

§ 1434. Reports to the Secretary

(a) Not more than sixty days after the end of any fiscal year, each recipient of a grant or contract under this [subchapter] during such fiscal year shall prepare and submit a report to the Secretary. Each such report shall be in such form and detail as the Secretary determines to be appropriate, and shall include—

(1) the number of individuals trained under the grant or contract, by category of training and level of training;

(2) the number of individuals trained under the grant or contract receiving degrees and certification, by category and level of training[;] and

(3) information described in section 1431(d)(11) of this title and section 1433(f)(1) of this title, as applicable.

(b) A summary of the data required by this section shall be included in the annual report of the Secretary under section 1418 of this title.

(As amended Pub.L. 101-476, Title IV, § 404, Oct. 30, 1990, 104 Stat. 1135; Pub.L. 102-119, § 9(c)(1), Oct. 7, 1991, 105 Stat. 595.)

§ 1435. Authorization of appropriations

(a) In general

(1) There are authorized to be appropriated to carry out this subchapter (other than sections 1431(a)(7), 1431(d), and 1433 of this title) $94,725,000 for fiscal year 1991, $103,255,000 for fiscal year 1992, $113,580,000 for fiscal year 1993, and $123,760,000 for fiscal year 1994.

(2) There are authorized to be appropriated to carry out section 1431(a)(7) of this title $19,250,000 for fiscal year 1991, $21,175,000 for fiscal year 1992, $23,292,500 for fiscal year 1993, and $25,621,750 for fiscal year 1994.

(3) There are authorized to be appropriated to carry out section 1431(d) of this title $11,000,000 for fiscal year 1991, $15,100,000 for fiscal year 1992, $16,300,000 for fiscal year 1993, and $17,600,000 for fiscal year 1994.

(4) There are authorized to be appropriated to carry out section 1433 of this title $2,900,000 for fiscal year 1991, $2,465,000 for fiscal year 1992, $2,710,000 for fiscal year 1993, and $2,960,000 for fiscal year 1994.

(b) Personnel training for careers in special education and early intervention

Of the funds appropriated pursuant to subsection (a) of this section for any fiscal year, the Secretary shall reserve not less than 65 per centum for activities described in subparagraphs (A) through (E) of section 1431(a)(1) of this title.

(As amended Pub.L. 101-476, Title IV, § 405, Oct. 30, 1990, 104 Stat. 1135; Pub.L. 102-119, §§ 9(c)(2), 10, 25(a)(13), Oct. 7, 1991, 105 Stat. 595, 606.)

§ 1436. Authorization of appropriations [For fiscal years 1975-1977; Omitted.]

SUBCHAPTER V—RESEARCH IN THE EDUCATION OF INDIVIDUALS WITH DISABILITIES

§ 1441. Research and related activities

(a) Grants, contracts, and cooperative agreements

The Secretary may make grants to, or enter into contracts or cooperative agreements with, State and local educational agencies, institutions of higher education, other public agencies and nonprofit private organizations for the purpose of advancing and improving the knowledge base and improving the practice of professionals, parents, and others providing early intervention, special education, and related services, including professionals who work with children and youth with disabilities in regular education environments, to provide such children effective instruction and enable them to successfully learn. The activities supported under this section shall support innovation, development, exchange, and use of such advancements in knowledge and practice designed to contribute to the improvement of instruction and learning of infants, toddlers, children, and youth with disabilities. In carrying out this section, the Secretary may support a wide range of research and related activities designed to—

(1) advance knowledge regarding the provision of instruction and other interventions to infants, toddlers, children, and youth with disabilities including—

(A) the organization, synthesis, and interpretation of current knowledge and the identification of knowledge gaps;

(B) the identification of knowledge and skill competencies needed by personnel providing special education, related services, and early intervention services;

(C) the improvement of knowledge regarding the developmental and learning characteristics of infants, toddlers, children, and youth with disabilities in order to improve the design and effectiveness of interventions and instruction;

(D) the evaluation of approaches and interventions;

(E) the development of instructional strategies, techniques, and activities;

(F) the improvement of curricula and instructional tools such as textbooks, media, materials, and technology;

(G) the development of assessment techniques, instruments (including tests, inventories, and scales), and strategies for measurement of progress and the identification, location, and evaluation of infants, toddlers, children, and youth with disabilities for the purpose of determining eligibility, program planning, and placement for special education, related services, and early intervention services. Particular attention should be given to the development of alternative assessment procedures and processes for minority individuals and those with limited English proficiency;

(H) the testing of research findings in practice settings to determine the application, usability, effectiveness, and generalizability of such research findings;

(I) the improvement of knowledge regarding families, minorities, limited English proficiency, and disabling conditions; and

(J) the identification of environmental, organizational, resource, and other conditions necessary for effective professional practice; and

(2) advance the use of knowledge by personnel providing special education, related services, and early intervention services including—

(A) the improvement of knowledge regarding how such individuals learn new knowledge and skills, and strategies for effectively facilitating such learning in preservice, inservice, and continuing education;

(B) the organization, integration, and presentation of knowledge so that such knowledge can be incorporated and imparted in personnel preparation, continuing education programs, and other relevant training and communication vehicles; and

(C) the expansion and improvement of networks that exchange knowledge and practice information.

(b) Qualifications of applicants

In carrying out subsection (a) of this section, the Secretary shall consider the special education, related services, or early intervention and research experience of applicants.

(c) Publication of proposed priorities

The Secretary shall publish proposed priorities under this subchapter in the Federal Register not later than 12 months preceding the fiscal year for which they are being announced, and shall allow a period of 60 days for public comments and suggestions. The Secretary shall, after analyzing and considering the public comments, publish final priorities in the Federal Register not later than 90 days after the close of the comment period.

(d) Index of projects

The Secretary shall provide an index (including the title of each project and the name and address of the funded organization) of all projects conducted under this subchapter in the prior fiscal year in the annual report described under section 1418 of this title.

(e) Coordination with other research; information to other agencies

The Secretary shall—

(1) coordinate the priorities established under subsection (b) of this section with research priorities established by the National Institute for Disability and Rehabilitation Research and other appropriate agencies conducting research pertaining to the education of individuals with disabilities; and

(2) provide information concerning priorities established under subsection (b) of this section to the National Council on Disability and to the Bureau of Indian Affairs Advisory Committee for Exceptional Children.

(f) Attention deficit disorder

(1) The Secretary shall make grants or enter into contracts or cooperative agreements for the establishment of a center or centers designed to organize, synthesize, and disseminate current knowledge relating to children with attention deficit disorder with respect to the following:

(A) Assessment techniques, instruments, and strategies used for identification, location, evaluation and for measurement of progress.

(B) Knowledge and skill competencies needed by professionals providing special and regular education and related services.

(C) Environmental, organizational, resource, and other conditions necessary for effective professional practice.

(D) Developmental and learning characteristics.

(E) Instructional strategies, techniques, and activities.

(F) Curricula and instructional tools such as textbooks, media, materials, and technology.

(G) Strategies, techniques, and activities related to involvement of families.

(2) In awarding grants, contracts, and cooperative agreements under paragraph (1), the Secretary shall give priority consideration to applicants with—

(A) demonstrated knowledge concerning the disorder;

(B) proven effectiveness in performing the functions established in this subsection; and

(C) the ability to—

(i) conduct such projects;

(ii) communicate with intended consumers of information; and

(iii) maintain the necessary communication with national, regional, State, and local agencies.

(g) Model demonstration programs

(1) The Secretary shall make grants, or enter into contracts or cooperative agreements, for the establishment of model demonstration programs, of which some will be school-based models, that provide the services of an ombudsman to assist in resolving problems that are barriers to appropriate educational, related services or other services for children and youth with disabilities.

(2) Programs under paragraph (1) shall provide or identify personnel to assist children and youth with disabilities, their parents or guardians, special and regular education teachers, State and local education administrators, and related services personnel to resolve problems in a timely manner through dispute mediation and other methods, notwithstanding due process procedures, in order to further the delivery of appropriate education and related services. Participation in this program does not preclude or delay due process under subchapter II of this Act.

(3) Ombudsman services for programs under paragraph (1) shall be provided by social workers, parent advocates, psychologists, and persons with similar qualifications designated by the Secretary.

(h) Research grants for unique needs, specialized instruction, and progress measurement; family involvement; adult role models

(1) The Secretary may make grants to institutions of higher education, in partnership with other appropriate agencies and organizations such as local educational agencies and center schools for students who are deaf, to—

(A) conduct research in unique needs of children and youth, including minority children and youth, with disabilities;

(B) develop and evaluate specialized instructional methods, materials, curricula, and technologies for use with such children and youth; and

(C) develop and evaluate assessment techniques, instruments, and strategies used to identify, evaluate, and measure the progress of such children and youth.

(2) Each grantee under this subsection shall provide for the meaningful involvement in its project of parents and family members and adult role models.

(As amended Pub.L. 101-476, Title V, § 501, Oct. 30, 1990, 104 Stat. 1135; Pub.L. 102-421, Title II, § 203, Oct. 16, 1992, 106 Stat. 2165.)

§ 1442. Research and demonstration projects in physical education and recreation for children with disabilities

The Secretary is authorized to make grants to States, State or local educational agencies, institutions of higher education, and other public or nonprofit private educational or research agencies and organizations, and to make contracts with States, State or local educational agencies, institutions of higher education, and other public or private educational or research agencies and organizations, for research and related purposes relating to physical education or recreation for children with disabilities, including therapeutic recreation, and to conduct research, surveys, or demonstrations relating to physical education or recreation for children with disabilities, including therapeutic recreation.

(As amended Pub.L. 101-476, Title V, § 502, Title IX, § 901(b)(145)-(146), Oct. 30, 1990, 104 Stat. 1138, 1149; Pub.L. 101-476, § 901(b), as amended Pub.L. 102-119, § 25(b), Oct. 7, 1991, 105 Stat. 607; Pub.L. 102-119, § 25(a)(14), Oct. 7, 1991, 105 Stat. 606.)

§ 1443. Repealed.

§ 1444. Authorization of appropriations

For purposes of carrying out this subchapter, there are authorized to be appropriated $21,100,000 for fiscal year 1990, $24,650,000 for fiscal year 1991, $27,400,000 for fiscal year 1992, $30,200,000 for fiscal year 1993, and $33,200,000 for fiscal year 1994.

(Pub.L. 91-230, Title VI, § 643, formerly § 644 , Apr. 13, 1970, 84 Stat. 186; Pub.L. 93-380, Title VI, § 619, Aug. 21, 1974, 84 Stat. 585; Pub.L. 95-49, § 5, June 17, 1977, 91 Stat. 231; Pub.L. 98-199, § 12, Dec. 2, 1983 , 97 Stat. 1374; Pub.L. 99-457, Title III, § 314, Oct. 8, 1986, 100 Stat. 1171; renumbered and amended Pub.L. 101-476, Title V, §§ 503, 504, Oct. 30, 1990, 104 Stat. 1138.)

SUBCHAPTER VI— INSTRUCTIONAL MEDIA FOR INDIVIDUALS WITH DISABILITIES

§ 1451. Purposes

The purposes of this subchapter are to promote—
(1) the general welfare of deaf and hard of hearing individuals by—
(A) bringing to such individuals understanding and appreciation of those films and television programs that play such an important part in the general and cultural advancement of hearing individuals;
(B) providing through these films and television programs enriched educational and cultural experiences through which deaf and hard of hearing individuals can be brought into better touch with the realities of their environment;
(C) providing a wholesome and rewarding experience that deaf and hard of hearing individuals may share together; and
(2) the educational advancement of individuals with disabilities by—
(A) carrying on research in the use of educational media for individuals with disabilities;

(B) producing and distributing educational media for the use of individuals with disabilities, their parents, their actual or potential employers, and other individuals directly involved in work for the advancement of individuals with disabilities;

(C) training individuals in the use of educational media for the instruction of individuals with disabilities; and

(D) utilizing educational media to help eliminate illiteracy among individuals with disabilities; and

(3) the general welfare of visually impaired individuals by—

(A) bringing to such individuals an understanding and appreciation of textbooks, films, television programs, video material, and other educational publications and materials that play such an important part in the general and cultural advancement of visually unimpaired individuals; and

(B) ensuring access to television programming and other video materials.

(As amended Pub.L. 101-476, Title VI, § 601, Title IX, § 901(b)(150), Oct. 30, 1990, 104 Stat. 1138, 1149; Pub.L. 101-119, § 25(b), Oct. 7, 1991, 105 Stat. 607.)

§ 1452. Captioned films, television, descriptive video and educational media for individuals with disabilities

(a) Establishment of loan service

The Secretary shall establish a loan service of captioned films, descriptive video and educational media for the purpose of making such materials available, in accordance with regulations, in the United States for nonprofit purposes to individuals with disabilities, parents of individuals with disabilities, and other individuals directly involved in activities for the advancement of individuals with disabilities, including for the purpose of addressing problems of illiteracy among individuals with disabilities.

(b) Authority of Secretary

The Secretary is authorized to—

(1) acquire films (or rights thereto) and other educational media by purchase, lease, or gift;

(2) acquire by lease or purchase equipment necessary for the administration of this subchapter;

(3) provide, by grant or contract, for the captioning for deaf and hard of hearing individuals and video description for the visually impaired, of films, television programs, and video materials;

(4) provide, by grant or contract, for the distribution of captioned and video-described films, video materials, and other educational media and equipment through State schools for [individuals with disabilities], public libraries, and such other agencies or entities as the Secretary may deem appropriate to serve as local or regional centers for such distribution;

(5) provide, by grant or contract, for the conduct of research in the use of educational and training films and other educational media for individuals with disabilities, for the production and distribution of educational and training films and other educational media for individuals with disabilities and the training of individuals in the use of such films and media, including the payment to those individuals of

such stipends (including allowances for travel and other expenses of such individuals and their dependents) as the Secretary may determine, which shall be consistent with prevailing practices under comparable federally supported programs;

(6) utilize the facilities and services of other governmental agencies;

(7) accept gifts, contributions, and voluntary and uncompensated services of individuals and organizations[;] and

(8) provide by grant or contract for educational media and materials for deaf and hard of hearing individuals.

(c) National Theatre of the Deaf

The Secretary may make grants to or enter into contracts or cooperative agreements with the National Theatre of the Deaf, Inc. and other appropriate non-profit organizations for the purpose of providing cultural experiences to—

(1) enrich the lives of deaf and hard of hearing children and adults,

(2) increase public awareness and understanding of deafness and of the artistic and intellectual achievements of deaf and hard of hearing individuals[;] and

(3) promote the integration of hearing and deaf and hard of hearing individuals through shared cultural, educational, and social experiences.

(d) Transcribed tapes and cassettes

(1) The Secretary is authorized to make a grant or enter into a contract for the purpose of providing current, free textbooks and other educational publications and materials to blind and other print-handicapped students in elementary, secondary, postsecondary, and graduate schools and other institutions of higher education through the medium of transcribed tapes and cassettes.

(2) For the purpose of this subsection, the term "print-handicapped" refers to any individual who is blind or severely visually impaired, or who, by reason of a physical or perceptual disability, is unable to read printed material unassisted.

(As amended Pub.L. 101-476, Title VI, § 602, Title IX, § 901(b)(151), (152), Oct. 30, 1990, 104 Stat. 1139, 1149; Pub.L. 102-119, § 25(b), Oct. 7, 1991, 105 Stat. 607.)

§ 1453. Repealed.

§ 1454. Authorization of appropriations

For the purpose of carrying out section 1452 there are authorized to be appropriated $20,010,000 for fiscal year 1991, $22,010,000 for fiscal year 1992, $24,200,000 for fiscal year 1993, and $26,600,000 for fiscal year 1994.

(As amended Pub.L. 101-476, Title VI, § 603, Oct. 30, 1990, 104 Stat. 1140.)

SUBCHAPTER VII—TECHNOLOGY, EDUCATIONAL MEDIA, AND MATERIALS FOR INDIVIDUALS WITH DISABILITIES

§ 1461. Financial assistance

(a) The Secretary may make grants or enter into contracts or cooperative agreements with institutions of higher education, State and local educational agen-

§ 1461. Financial assistance

(a) The Secretary may make grants or enter into contracts or cooperative agreements with institutions of higher education, State and local educational agencies, or other appropriate agencies and organizations for the purpose of advancing the use of new technology, media, and materials in the education of students with disabilities and the provision of related services and early intervention services to infants and toddlers with disabilities. In carrying out this section, the Secretary may fund projects or centers for the purposes of—

(1) determining how technology, assistive technology, media, and materials are being used in the education of individuals with disabilities and how they can be used most effectively, efficiently, and appropriately,

(2) designing and adapting technology, assistive technology, media, and materials to improve the education of students with disabilities,

(3) assisting the public and private sectors in the development and marketing of technology, assistive technology, media, and materials for the education of individuals with disabilities,

(4) disseminating information on the availability and use of technology, assistive technology, media, and materials for the education of individuals with disabilities, where appropriate, to entities described in [20 U.S.C. § 1410(g)],

(5) increasing access to and use of assistive technology devices and assistive technology services in the education of infants, toddlers, children, and youth with disabilities, and other activities authorized under the Technology-Related Assistance for Individuals With Disabilities Act of 1988 [29 U.S.C. § 2201 *et seq.*], as such Act relates to the education of students with disabilities[;] and

(6) examining how these purposes can address the problem of illiteracy among individuals with disabilities.

(b) (1) With respect to new technology, media, and materials utilized with funds under this subchapter to improve the education of students with disabilities, the Secretary shall make efforts to ensure that such instructional materials are closed captioned.

(2) The Secretary may not award a grant, contract, or cooperative agreement under paragraphs (1) through (4) of subsection (a) of this section unless the applicant for such assistance agrees that activities carried out with the assistance will be coordinated, as appropriate, with the State entity receiving funds under title I of [29 U.S.C. § 2201 *et seq.*].

(As amended Pub.L. 101-476, Title VII, § 701, Title IX, § 901(b)(154)-(156), Oct. 30, 1990, 104 Stat. 1140, 1149; Pub.L. 102-119, § 25(a)(15), (b), Oct. 7, 1991, 105 Stat. 606, 607.)

§ 1462. Authorization of appropriations

For the purpose of carrying out this subchapter, there are authorized to be appropriated $11,900,000 for fiscal year 1991, $12,860,000 for fiscal year 1992, $13,890,000 for fiscal year 1993, and $15,000,000 for fiscal year1994.

(As amended Pub.L. 101-476, Title VII, § 702, Oct. 30, 1990, 104 Stat. 1141.)

SUBCHAPTER VIII—INFANTS AND TODDLERS WITH DISABILITIES

§ 1471. Congressional findings and policy

(a) Findings

The Congress finds that there is an urgent and substantial need—
(1) to enhance the development of infants and toddlers with disabilities and to minimize their potential for developmental delay,
(2) to reduce the educational costs to our society, including our Nation's schools, by minimizing the need for special education and related services after infants and toddlers with disabilities reach school age,
(3) to minimize the likelihood of institutionalization of individuals with disabilities and maximize the potential for their independent living in society,
(4) to enhance the capacity of families to meet the special needs of their infants and toddlers with disabilities[;] and
(5) to enhance the capacity of State and local agencies and service providers to identify, evaluate, and meet the needs of historically underrepresented populations, particularly minorities, low-income, inner-city, and rural populations.

(b) Policy

It is therefore the policy of the United States to provide financial assistance to States—
(1) to develop and implement a statewide, comprehensive, coordinated, multidisciplinary, interagency program of early intervention services for infants and toddlers with disabilities and their families,
(2) to facilitate the coordination of payment for early intervention services from Federal, State, local, and private sources (including public and private insurance coverage)[;] and
(3) to enhance their capacity to provide quality early intervention services and expand and improve existing early intervention services being provided to infants and toddlers with disabilities and their families.

(As amended Pub.L. 101-476, Title IX, § 901(b)(158)-(161), Oct. 30, 1990, 104 Stat. 1149; Pub.L. 102-119, §§ 11, 25(a)(16), (b), Oct. 7, 1991, 105 Stat. 595, 606, 607.)

§ 1472. Definitions

As used in this subchapter—
(1) The term "infants and toddlers with disabilities" means individuals from birth to age 2, inclusive, who need early intervention services because they—
(A) are experiencing developmental delays, as measured by appropriate diagnostic instruments and procedures in one or more of the following areas: cognitive development, physical development, language and speech development (hereafter in this subchapter referred to as "communication development"), psychosocial development (hereafter in this subchapter referred to as "social or emotional development"), or self-help skills (hereafter in this subchapter referred to as "adaptive development"), or

(B) have a diagnosed physical or mental condition which has a high probability of resulting in developmental delay.

Such term may also include, at a State's discretion, individuals from birth to age 2, inclusive, who are at risk of having substantial developmental delays if early intervention services are not provided.

(2) The term "early intervention services" are developmental services which—

(A) are provided under public supervision,

(B) are provided at no cost except where Federal or State law provides for a system of payments by families, including a schedule of sliding fees,

(C) are designed to meet the developmental needs of an infant or toddler with a disability in any one or more of the following areas:

(i) physical development,

(ii) cognitive development,

(iii) communication development,

(iv) social or emotional development, or

(v) adaptive development,

(D) meet the standards of the State, including the requirements of this subchapter,

(E) include—

(i) family training, counseling, and home visits,

(ii) special instruction,

(iii) speech pathology and audiology,

(iv) occupational therapy,

(v) physical therapy,

(vi) psychological services,

(vii) case management services (hereafter in this subchapter referred to as "service coordination services"),

(viii) medical services only for diagnostic or evaluation purposes,

(ix) early identification, screening and assessment services,

(x) health services necessary to enable the infant or toddler to benefit from the other early intervention services,

(xi) social work services,

(xii) vision services,

(xiii) assistive technology devices and assistive technology services[;] and

(xiv) transportation and related costs that are necessary to enable an infant or toddler or the infant's or toddler's family to receive early intervention services,

(F) are provided by qualified personnel, including—

(i) special educators,

(ii) speech and language pathologists and audiologists,

(iii) occupational therapists,

(iv) physical therapists,

(v) psychologists,

(vi) social workers,

(vii) nurses,

(viii) nutritionists,

(ix) family therapists,

(x) orientation and mobility specialists[;] and

(xi) pediatricians and other physicians,

(G) to the maximum extent appropriate, are provided in natural environments, including the home, and community settings in which children without disabilities participate, and

(H) are provided in conformity with an individualized family service plan adopted in accordance with section 1477 of this title.

(3) The term "developmental delay" has the meaning given such term by a State under section 1476(b)(1) of this title.

(4) The term "Council" means the State Interagency Coordinating Council established under section 1482 of this title.

(As amended Pub.L. 101-476, Title VIII, § 801, Title IX, § 901(b)(162)-(163), Oct. 30, 1990, 104 Stat. 1141, 1149; Pub.L. 102-119, §§ 12, 25(b), Oct. 7, 1991, 105 Stat. 595, 607.)

(As amended Pub.L. 101-476, Title V, § 502, Title IX, § 901(b)(145)-(146), Oct. 30, 1990, 104 Stat. 1138, 1149; Pub.L. 101-476, § 901(b), as amended Pub.L. 102-119, § 25(b), Oct. 7, 1991, 105 Stat. 607; Pub.L. 102-119, § 25(a)(14), Oct. 7, 1991, 105 Stat. 606.)

§ 1473. General authority

The Secretary shall, in accordance with this subchapter, make grants to States (from their allocations under section 1484 of this title) to assist each State to develop a statewide, comprehensive, coordinated, multidisciplinary, interagency system to provide early intervention services for infants and toddlers with disabilities and their families.

(As amended Pub.L. 101-476, Title IX, § 901(b)(164), Oct. 30, 1990, 104 Stat. 1150; Pub.L. 102-119, § 25(b), Oct. 7, 1991, 105 Stat. 607.)

§ 1474. General eligibility

In order to be eligible for a grant under section 1473 of this title for any fiscal year, a State shall demonstrate to the Secretary (in its application under section 1478 of this title) that the State has established a State Interagency Coordinating Council which meets the requirements of section 1482 of this title.

(Pub.L. 91-230, Title VI, § 674, as added Pub.L. 99-457, Title I, § 101(a), Oct. 8, 1986, 100 Stat. 1147.)

§ 1475. Continuing eligibility

(a) First two years

In order to be eligible for a grant under section 1473 of this title for the first or second year of a State's participation under this subchapter, a State shall include in its application under section 1478 of this title for that year an assurance that funds received under section 1473 of this title shall be used to assist the State to plan, develop, and implement the statewide system required by section 1476 of this title.

(b) Third and fourth year

(1) In order to be eligible for a grant under section 1473 of this title for the third or fourth year of a State's participation under this subchapter, a State shall include in

its application under section 1478 of this title for that year information and assurances demonstrating to the satisfaction of the Secretary that—

(A) the State has adopted a policy which incorporates all of the components of a statewide system in accordance with section 1476 of this title or obtained a waiver from the Secretary under paragraph (2),

(B) funds shall be used to plan, develop, and implement the statewide system required by section 1476 of this title[;] and

(C) such statewide system will be in effect no later than the beginning of the fourth year of the State's participation under section 1473 of this title, except that in order to comply with section 1476(b)(4) of this title, a State need only conduct multidisciplinary assessments, develop individualized family service plans, and make available case management services.

(2) Notwithstanding paragraph (1), the Secretary may permit a State to continue to receive assistance under section 1473 of this title during such third year even if the State has not adopted the policy required by paragraph (1)(A) before receiving assistance if the State demonstrates in its application—

(A) that the State has made a good faith effort to adopt such a policy,

(B) the reasons why it was unable to meet the timeline and the steps remaining before such a policy will be adopted[;] and

(C) an assurance that the policy will be adopted to go into effect before the fourth year of such assistance.

(c) Fifth and succeeding years

In order to be eligible for a grant under section 1473 of this title for a fifth and any succeeding year of a State's participation under this subchapter, a State shall include in its application under section 1478 of this title for that year information and assurances demonstrating to the satisfaction of the Secretary that the State has in effect the statewide system required by section 1476 of this title and a description of services to be provided under section 1476(b)(2) of this title.

(d) Exception

Notwithstanding subsections (a) and (b) of this section, a State which has in effect a State law, enacted before September 1, 1986, that requires the provision of free appropriate public education to children with disabilities from birth through age 2, inclusive, shall be eligible for a grant under section 1473 of this title for the first through fourth years of a State's participation under this subchapter.

(e) Differential funding for fourth or fifth year

(1) In general
Notwithstanding any other provision of this subchapter, a State shall be eligible for a grant under section 1473 of this title for fiscal years 1990, 1991, or 1992 if—

(A) the State satisfies the eligibility criteria described in subsection (b)(1) of this section pertaining to the State's third or fourth year of participation under this subchapter; and

(B) the Governor, on behalf of the State, submits, by a date that the Secretary may establish for each such year, a request for extended participation, including—

(i) information demonstrating to the Secretary's satisfaction that the State is experiencing significant hardships in meeting the requirements of this section for the fourth or fifth year of participation; and

(ii) a plan, including timeliness, for meeting the eligibility criteria described in subsections (b)(1) and (c) of this section for the fourth, fifth, or succeeding years of participation.

(2) Approval of request

(A) First year

The Secretary shall approve a State's request for a first year of extended participation under this subsection if the State meets the requirements of paragraph (1).

(B) Second year

The Secretary shall approve a State's request for a second year of extended participation under this subsection if the State—

(i) meets the requirements of paragraph (1); and

(ii) demonstrates to the Secretary's satisfaction that the State has made reasonable progress in implementing the plan described in paragraph (1)(B)(ii).

(3) Duration

The Secretary may not approve more than two requests from the same State for extended participation under this subsection.

(4) Payment

(A) Fiscal year 1990

Notwithstanding any other provision of law, each State qualifying for extended participation under this subsection for fiscal year 1990 shall receive a payment under this subchapter in an amount equal to such State's payment under this subchapter for fiscal year 1989.

(B) Fiscal year 1991 or 1992

Except as provided in subparagraph (C) and notwithstanding any other provision of law, each State qualifying for extended participation under this subsection for fiscal year 1991 or fiscal year 1992 shall receive a payment under this subchapter for such fiscal years in an amount equal to the payment such State would have received under this subchapter for fiscal year 1990 if such State had met the criteria for the fourth year of participation described in subsection (b)(1) of this section.

(C) Minimum payment for fiscal year 1991 or 1992 for certain States

Notwithstanding any other provision of law, each State qualifying for extended participation under this subsection for fiscal year 1991 or fiscal year 1992 shall receive a payment under this subchapter of not less than $500,000. For purposes of the preceding sentence, the term "State" means each of the 50 States, the District of Columbia, and the Commonwealth of Puerto Rico.

(5) Reallotment

(A) Fiscal year 1990

The amount by which the allotment computed under section 1484 of this title for any State for fiscal year 1990 exceeds the amount that such State may be allotted under paragraph (4)(A) of this subsection (and, notwithstanding section 1484(d) of this title, any fiscal year 1990 funds allotted to any State that such State elects not to receive) shall be reallotted, notwithstanding the percentage limitations set forth in sections 1484(a) and (b) of this title, among those States satisfying the eligibility criteria of subsection (b)(1) of this section for the fourth year of participation that have submitted an application by a date that the Secretary may establish in an amount which bears the same ratio to such amount as the amount of such State's allotment under section 1484 of this title as modified by this subsection in such fiscal year bears to the amount of all such States' allotment under section 1484 of this title as modified by this subsection in such fiscal year.

(B) Fiscal year 1991 or 1992

The amount by which a State's allotment computed under section 1484 of this title for any State for fiscal years 1991 or 1992 exceeds the amount that such State may be allotted for such fiscal year under paragraph (4)(B) of this subsection shall be reallotted, notwithstanding the percentage limitations set forth in section 1484(a) and (b) of this title—

(i) first, among those States satisfying the eligibility criteria of subsection (c) of this section for the fifth year of participation that have submitted applications by a date that the Secretary may establish for each such year in an amount which bears the same ratio to such amount as the amount of such State's allotment under section 1484 of this title as modified by this subsection in such fiscal year bears to the amount of all such States' allotment under section 1484 of this title as modified by this subsection in such fiscal year, except that no such State, by operation of this clause, shall receive an increase of more than 100 percent over the amount such State would have otherwise received under section 1484 of this title for the previous fiscal year;

(ii) second, if funds remain, among those States that have—

(I) satisfied the eligibility criteria of subsection (b)(1) of this section for the fourth year of participation;

(II) qualified for extended participation under this subsection; and

(III) not received a reallotment payment under clause (i),

in an amount which bears the same ratio to such amount as the amount of such State's allotment under section 1484 of this title as modified by this subsection in such fiscal year bears to the amount of all such States' allotment under section 1484 of this title as modified by this subsection in such fiscal year, except that no State, by operation of this clause, shall receive a reallotment payment that is larger than the payment such State would otherwise have received under section 1484 of this title for such year; and

(iii) third, if funds remain, among those States satisfying the eligibility criteria of subsection (c) of this section for the fifth year of participation that did not receive a reallotment payment under clause (ii) in an amount which bears the same ratio to such amount as the amount of such State's allotment under section 1484 of this title as modified by this subsection in such fiscal year bears to the amount of all such States' allotment under section 1484 of this title as modified by this subsection in such fiscal year.

(6) Definitions

For the purposes of this subsection, the term "State," except as provided in paragraph (4)(C), means—

(A) each of the 50 States, the District of Columbia, and the Commonwealth of Puerto Rico;

(B) each of the jurisdictions listed in section 1484(a)[;] and

(C) the Department of the Interior.

(As amended Pub.L. 101-476, Title IX, § 901(b)(165), Oct. 30, 1990, 104 Stat. 1150; Pub.L. 102-52, § 10, June 6, 1991, 105 Stat. 263; Pub.L. 102-119 §§ 19(c), 25(b), Oct. 7, 1991, 105 Stat. 601, 602, 607.)

§ 1476. Requirement for statewide system

(a) In general

A statewide system of coordinated, comprehensive, multidisciplinary, inter-agency programs providing appropriate early intervention services to all infants and toddlers with disabilities and their families, including Indian infants and toddlers with disabilities on reservations, shall include the minimum components under subsection (b) of this section.

(b) Minimum components

The statewide system required by subsection (a) of this section shall include, at a minimum—

(1) a definition of the term "developmentally delayed" that will be used by the State in carrying out programs under this subchapter,

(2) timetables for ensuring that appropriate early intervention services will be available to all infants and toddlers with disabilities in the State, including Indian infants and toddlers with disabilities on reservations, before the beginning of the fifth year of a State's participation under this subchapter,

(3) a timely, comprehensive, multidisciplinary evaluation of the functioning of each infant and toddler with a disability in the State and the needs of the families to appropriately assist in the development of the infant or toddler with a disability,

(4) for each infant and toddler with a disability in the State, an individualized family service plan in accordance with section 1477 of this title, including service coordination services in accordance with such service plan,

(5) a comprehensive child find system, consistent with subchapter II of this chapter, including a system for making referrals to service providers that includes timelines and provides for participation by primary referral sources,

(6) a public awareness program focusing on early identification of infants and toddlers with disabilities, including the preparation and dissemination by the lead agency to all primary referral sources of information materials for parents on the availability of early intervention services, and procedures for determining the extent to which primary referral sources, especially hospitals and physicians, disseminate information on the availability of early intervention services to parents of infants with disabilities,

(7) a central directory which includes early intervention services, resources, and experts available in the State and research and demonstration projects being con-ducted in the State,

(8) a comprehensive system of personnel development, including the training of paraprofessionals and the training of primary referral sources respecting the basic components of early intervention services available in the State, that is consistent with the comprehensive system of personnel development described in section 1413(a)(3) of this title and that may include—

(A) implementing innovative strategies and activities for the recruitment and retention of early intervention service providers,

(B) promoting the preparation of early intervention providers who are fully and appropriately qualified to provide early intervention services under this subchapter,

(C) training personnel to work in rural areas[;] and

(D) training personnel to coordinate transition services for infants and toddlers with disabilities from an early intervention program under this subchapter to a preschool program under section 1419 of this title.

(9) a single line of responsibility in a lead agency designated or established by the Governor for carrying out—

(A) the general administration and supervision of programs and activities receiving assistance under section 1473 of this title, and the monitoring of programs and activities used by the State to carry out this subchapter, whether or not such programs or activities are receiving assistance made available under section 1473 of this title, to ensure that the State complies with this subchapter, of this title to ensure compliance with this subchapter,

(B) the identification and coordination of all available resources within the State from Federal, State, local and private sources,

(C) the assignment of financial responsibility in accordance with 1478(a)(2) of this title to the appropriate agencies,

(D) the development of procedures to ensure that services are provided to infants and toddlers with disabilities and their families in a timely manner pending the resolution of any disputes among public agencies or service providers,

(E) the resolution of intra- and interagency disputes[;] and

(F) the entry into formal interagency agreements that define the financial responsibility of each agency for paying for early intervention services (consistent with State law) and procedures for resolving disputes and that include all additional components necessary to ensure meaningful cooperation and coordination.

(10) a policy pertaining to the contracting or making of other arrangements with service providers to provide early intervention services in the State, consistent with the provisions of this subchapter, including the contents of the application used and the conditions of the contract or other arrangements,

(11) a procedure for securing timely reimbursement of funds used under this subchapter in accordance with section 1481(a) of this title,

(12) procedural safeguards with respect to programs under this subchapter as required by section 1480 of this title,

(13) policies and procedures relating to the establishment and maintenance of standards to ensure that personnel necessary to carry out this subchapter are appropriately and adequately prepared and trained, including—

(A) the establishment and maintenance of standards which are consistent with any State approved or recognized certification, licensing, registration, or other comparable requirements which apply to the area in which such personnel are providing early intervention services[;] and

(B) to the extent such standards are not based on the highest requirements in the State applicable to a specific profession or discipline, the steps the State is taking to require the retraining or hiring of personnel that meet appropriate professional requirements in the State[;] and

(14) a system for compiling data on the numbers of infants and toddlers with disabilities and their families in the State in need of appropriate early intervention services (which may be based on a sampling of data), the numbers of such infants and toddlers and their families served, the types of services provided (which may be based on a sampling of data), and other information required by the Secretary.

(As amended Pub.L. 101-476, Title VIII, § 802, Title IX, § 901(b)(166)-(173), Oct. 30, 1990, 104 Stat. 1141, 1150; Pub.L. 102-119, §§ 13, 19(a)(2), 25(a)(17), (b), Oct. 7, 1991, 105 Stat. 596, 601, 606, 607.)

§ 1477. Individualized family service plan

(a) Assessment and program development

Each infant or toddler with a disability and the infant's or toddler's family shall receive—

(1) a multidisciplinary assessment of the unique strengths and needs of the infant or toddler and the identification of services appropriate to meet such needs,

(2) a family-directed assessment of the resources, priorities, and concerns of the family and the identification of the supports and services necessary to enhance the family's capacity to meet the developmental needs of their infant or toddler with a disability[;] and

(3) a written individualized family service plan developed by a multidisciplinary team, including the parent or guardian, as required by subsection (d) of this section.

(b) Periodic review

The individualized family service plan shall be evaluated once a year and the family shall be provided a review of the plan at 6-month intervals (or more often where appropriate based on infant or toddler and family needs).

(c) Promptness after assessment

The individualized family service plan shall be developed within a reasonable time after the assessment required by subsection (a)(1) of this section is completed. With the parent's consent, early intervention services may commence prior to the completion of such assessment.

(d) Content of plan

The individualized family service plan shall be in writing and contain—

(1) a statement of the infant's or toddler's present levels of physical development, cognitive development, communication development, social or emotional development, and adaptive development, based on acceptable objective criteria,

(2) a statement of the family's resources, priorities, and concerns relating to enhancing the development of the family's infant or toddler with a disability,

(3) a statement of the major outcomes expected to be achieved for the infant or toddler and the family, and the criteria, procedures, and timelines used to determine the degree to which progress toward achieving the outcomes is being made and whether modifications or revisions of the outcomes or services are necessary,

(4) a statement of specific early intervention services necessary to meet the unique needs of the infant or toddler and the family, including the frequency, intensity, and the method of delivering services,

(5) a statement of the natural environments in which early intervention services shall appropriately be provided,

(6) the projected dates for initiation of services and the anticipated duration of such services,

(7) the name of the case manager (hereafter in this subchapter referred to as the "service coordinator") from the profession most immediately relevant to the infant's or toddler's or family's needs (or who is otherwise qualified to carry out all applicable

responsibilities under this subchapter) who will be responsible for the implementation of the plan and coordination with other agencies and persons[;] and

(8) the steps to be taken supporting the transition of the toddler with a disability to services provided under subchapter II of this [chapter, 20 U.S.C. § 1411 *et seq.*] to the extent such services are considered appropriate.

(e) Parental consent.

The contents of the individualized family service plan shall be fully explained to the parents or guardian and informed written consent from such parents or guardian shall be obtained prior to the provision of early intervention services described in such plan. If such parents or guardian do not provide such consent with respect to a particular early intervention service, then the early intervention services to which such consent is obtained shall be provided.

(As amended Pub.L. 101-476, Title IX, § 901(b)(174)-(176), Oct. 30, 1990, 104 Stat. 1150; Pub.L. 102-119, §§ 14, 25(b), Oct. 7, 1991, 105 Stat. 597, 607.)

§ 1478. State application and assurances

(a) Application

Any State desiring to receive a grant under section 1473 of this title for any year shall submit an application to the Secretary at such time and in such manner as the Secretary may reasonably require by regulation. Such an application shall contain—

(1) a designation of the lead agency in the State that will be responsible for the administration of funds provided under section 1473 of this title,

(2) a designation by the State of an individual or entity responsible for assigning financial responsibility among appropriate agencies,

(3) information demonstrating eligibility of the State under section 1474 of this title,

(4) the information or assurances required to demonstrate eligibility of the State for the particular year of participation under section 1475 of this title,

(5)(A) information demonstrating that the State has provided (i) public hearings, (ii) adequate notice of such hearings, and (iii) an opportunity for comment to the general public before the submission of such application and before the adoption by the State of the policies described in such application, and (B) a summary of the public comments and the State's responses,

(6) a description of the uses for which funds will be expended in accordance with this subchapter and, for the fifth and succeeding fiscal years, a description of the services to be provided,

(7) a description of the procedure used to ensure an equitable distribution of resources made available under this subchapter among all geographic areas within the State,

(8) a description of the policies and procedures used to ensure a smooth transition for individuals participating in the early intervention program under this subchapter who are eligible for participation in preschool programs under subchapter II of this chapter, including a description of how the families will be included in the transitional plans and how the lead agency under this subchapter will notify the appropriate local educational agency or intermediate educational unit in which the child resides and

convene, with the approval of the family, a conference between the lead agency, the family, and such agency or unit at least 90 days before such child is eligible for the preschool program under subchapter II of this chapter in accordance with State law, and to review the child's program options, for the period commencing on the day a child turns 3 running through the remainder of the school year, and to establish a transition plan[;] and

(9) such other information and assurances as the Secretary may reasonably require by regulation.

(b) Statement of assurances

Any State desiring to receive a grant under section 1473 of this title shall file with the Secretary a statement at such time and in such manner as the Secretary may reasonably require by regulation. Such statement shall—

(1) assure that funds paid to the State under section 1473 of this title will be expended in accordance with this subchapter,

(2) contain assurances that the State will comply with the requirements of section 1481 of this title,

(3) provide satisfactory assurance that the control of funds provided under section 1473 of this title, and title to property derived therefrom, shall be in a public agency for the uses and purposes provided in this subchapter and that a public agency will administer such funds and property,

(4) provide for (A) making such reports in such form and containing such information as the Secretary may require to carry out the Secretary's functions under this subchapter, and (B) keeping such records and affording such access thereto as the Secretary may find necessary to assure the correctness and verification of such reports and proper disbursement of Federal funds under this subchapter,

(5) provide satisfactory assurance that Federal funds made available under section 1473 of this title (A) will not be commingled with State funds, and (B) will be so used as to supplement and increase the level of State and local funds expended for infants and toddlers with disabilities and their families and in no case to supplant such State and local funds.

(6) provide satisfactory assurance that such fiscal control and fund accounting procedures will be adopted as may be necessary to assure proper disbursement of, and accounting for, Federal funds paid under section 1473 of this title to the State,

(7) beginning in fiscal year 1992, provide satisfactory assurance that policies and practices have been adopted to ensure meaningful involvement of traditionally underserved groups, including minority, low-income, and rural families, in the planning and implementation of all the requirements of this subchapter and to ensure that such families have access to culturally competent services within their local areas[;] and

(8) such other information and assurances as the Secretary may reasonably require by regulation.

(c) Approval of application and assurances required

No State may receive a grant under section 1473 of this title unless the Secretary has approved the application and statement of assurances of that State. The Secretary shall not disapprove such an application or statement of assurances unless the Secretary determines, after notice and opportunity for a hearing, that the application or statement of assurances fails to comply with the requirements of this section.

(As amended Pub.L. 101-476, Title IX, § 901(b)(177), Oct. 30, 1990, 104 Stat. 1150; Pub.L. 102-119, §§ 15, 25(b), Oct. 7, 1991, 105 Stat. 597, 607.)

§ 1479. Uses of funds

In addition to using funds provided under section 1473 of this title to plan, develop, and implement the statewide system required by section 1476 of this title, a State may use such funds—

(1) for direct services for infants and toddlers with disabilities and their families that are not otherwise provided from other public or private sources,

(2) to expand and improve on services for infants and toddlers with disabilities and their families that are otherwise available[;] and

(3) to provide a free appropriate public education, in accordance with subchapter II of this chapter, to children with disabilities from their third birthday to the beginning of the following school year.

(As amended Pub.L. 101-476, Title IX, § 901(b)(178), Oct. 30, 1990, 104 Stat. 1150; Pub.L. 102-119, §§ 16, 25(b), Oct. 7, 1991, 105 Stat. 598, 607.)

§ 1480. Procedural safeguards

The procedural safeguards required to be included in a statewide system under section 1476(b)(12) of this title shall provide, at a minimum, the following:

(1) The timely administrative resolution of complaints by parents. Any party aggrieved by the findings and decision regarding an administrative complaint shall have the right to bring a civil action with respect to the complaint, which action may be brought in any State court of competent jurisdiction or in a district court of the United States without regard to the amount in controversy. In any action brought under this paragraph, the court shall receive the records of the administrative proceedings, shall hear additional evidence at the request of a party, and, basing its decision on the preponderance of the evidence, shall grant such relief as the court determines is appropriate.

(2) The right to confidentiality of personally identifiable information, including the right of parents or guardians to written notice of and written consent to the exchange of such information among agencies consistent with Federal and State law.

(3) The right of the parents or guardian to determine whether they, their infant or toddler, or other family members will accept or decline any early intervention service under this subchapter in accordance with State law without jeopardizing other early intervention services under this subchapter.

(4) The opportunity for parents or a guardian to examine records relating to assessment, screening, eligibility determinations, and the development and implementation of the individualized family service plan.

(5) Procedures to protect the rights of the infant or toddler with a disability whenever the parents or guardian of the child are not known or unavailable or the child is a ward of the State, including the assignment of an individual (who shall not be an employee of the State agency providing services) to act as a surrogate for the parents or guardian.

(6) Written prior notice to the parents or guardian of the infant or toddler with a disability whenever the State agency or service provider proposes to initiate or change or refuses to initiate or change the identification, evaluation, placement, or the

provision of appropriate early intervention services to the infant or toddler with a disability.

(7) Procedures designed to assure that the notice required by paragraph (6) fully informs the parents or guardian, in the parents' or guardian's native language, unless it clearly is not feasible to do so, of all procedures available pursuant to this section.

(8) During the pendency of any proceeding or action involving a complaint, unless the State agency and the parents or guardian otherwise agree, the child shall continue to receive the appropriate early intervention services currently being provided or, if applying for initial services, shall receive the services not in dispute.

(As amended Pub.L. 101-476, Title IX, § 901(b)(179)-(180), Oct. 30, 1990, 104 Stat. 1150; Pub.L. 102-119, §§ 17, 25(b), Oct. 7, 1991, 105 Stat. 598, 607.)

§ 1481. Payor of last resort

(a) Nonsubstitution

Funds provided under section 1473 of this title may not be used to satisfy a financial commitment for services which would have been paid for from another public or private source but for the enactment of this subchapter, except that whenever considered necessary to prevent a delay in the receipt of appropriate early intervention services by the infant or toddler or family in a timely fashion, funds provided under section 1473 of this title may be used to pay the provider of services pending reimbursement from the agency which has ultimate responsibility for the payment.

(b) Reduction of other benefits

Nothing in this subchapter shall be construed to permit the State to reduce medical or other assistance available or to alter eligibility under title V of the Social Security Act [42 U.S.C. § 701 *et seq.*] (relating to maternal and child health) or title XIX of the Social Security Act [42 U.S.C. § 1396 *et seq.*] (relating to medicaid for infants and toddlers with disabilities) within the State.

(As amended Pub.L. 101-476, Title IX, § 901(b)(181), Oct. 30, 1990, 104 Stat. 1150; Pub.L. 102-119, § 25(b), Oct. 7, 1991, 105 Stat. 607.)

§ 1482. State Interagency Coordinating Council

(a) Establishment

(1) Any State which desires to receive financial assistance under section 1473 of this title shall establish a State Interagency Coordinating Council composed of at least 15 members but not more than 25 members, unless the State provides sufficient justification for a greater number of members in the application submitted pursuant to section 1478 of this title.

(2) The Council shall be appointed by the Governor. In making appointments to the Council, the Governor shall ensure that the membership of the Council reasonably represents the population of the State.

(3) The Governor shall designate a member of the Council to serve as the chairperson of the Council, or shall require the Council to so designate such a member.

Any member of the Council who is a representative of the lead agency designated under section 1476(b)(9) of this title may not serve as the chairperson of the Council.

(b) Composition

(1) The Council shall be composed as follows:

(A) At least 20 percent of the members shall be parents, including minority parents, of infants or toddlers with disabilities or children with disabilities aged 12 or younger, with knowledge of, or experience with, programs for infants and toddlers with disabilities. At least one such member shall be a parent of an infant or toddler with a disability or a child with a disability aged 6 or younger.

(B) At least 20 percent of the members shall be public or private providers of early intervention services.

(C) At least one member shall be from the State legislature.

(D) At least one member shall be involved in personnel preparation.

(E) At least one member shall be from each of the State agencies involved in the provision of, or payment for, early intervention services to infants and toddlers with disabilities and their families and shall have sufficient authority to engage in policy planning and implementation on behalf of such agencies.

(F) At least one member shall be from the State educational agency responsible for preschool services to children with disabilities and shall have sufficient authority to engage in policy planning and implementation on behalf of such agency.

(G) At least one member shall be from the agency responsible for the State governance of insurance, especially in the area of health insurance.

(2) The Council may include other members selected by the Governor, including a representative from the Bureau of Indian Affairs, or where there is no BIA operated or funded school, from the Indian Health Service or the tribe/tribal council.

(c) Meetings

The Council shall meet at least quarterly and in such places as it deems necessary. The meetings shall be publicly announced, and, to the extent appropriate, open and accessible to the general public.

(d) Management authority

Subject to the approval of the Governor, the Council may prepare and approve a budget using funds under this subchapter to conduct hearings and forums, to reimburse members of the Council for reasonable and necessary expenses for attending Council meetings and performing Council duties (including child care for parent representatives), to pay compensation to a member of the Council if such member is not employed or must forfeit wages from other employment when performing official Council business, to hire staff, and to obtain services of such professional, technical, and clerical personnel as may be necessary to carry out its functions under this subchapter.

(e) Functions of Council

(1) The Council shall—

(A) advise and assist the lead agency designated or established under section 1476(b)(9) of this title in the performance of the responsibilities set out in such section, particularly the identification of the sources of fiscal and other support for services for early intervention programs, assignment of financial responsibility to the appropriate agency, and the promotion of the interagency agreements,

(B) advise and assist the lead agency in the preparation of applications and amendments thereto,

(C) advise and assist the State educational agency regarding the transition of toddlers with disabilities to services provided under subchapter II of this chapter, to the extent such services are appropriate[;] and

(D) prepare and submit an annual report to the Governor and to the Secretary on the status of early intervention programs for infants and toddlers with disabilities and their families operated within the State.

(2) The Council may advise and assist the lead agency and State educational agency regarding the provision of appropriate services for children aged birth to 5, inclusive.

(f) Conflict of interest

No member of the Council shall cast a vote on any matter which would provide direct financial benefit to that member or otherwise give the appearance of a conflict of interest under State law.

(g) Use of existing Councils

To the extent that a State has established a Council before September 1, 1986, that is comparable to the Council described in this section, such Council shall be considered to be in compliance with this section. Within 4 years after the date the State accepts funds under section 1473 of this title, such State shall establish a council that complies in full with this section.

(As amended Pub.L. 101-476, Title IX, § 901(b)(182), Oct. 30, 1990, 104 Stat. 1150; Pub.L. 102-119, §§ 18, 25(a)(18), (b), Oct. 7, 1991, 105 Stat. 599, 606, 607.)

§ 1483. Federal administration

Sections 1416, 1417 and 1420 of this title shall, to the extent not inconsistent with this subchapter, apply to the program authorized by this subchapter, except that—

(1) any reference to a State educational agency shall be deemed to be a reference to the State agency established or designated under section 1476(b)(9) of this section,

(2) any reference to the education of children with disabilities and the education of all children with disabilities and the provision of free public education to all children with disabilities shall be deemed to be a reference to the provision of services to infants and toddlers with disabilities in accordance with this subchapter[;] and

(3) any reference to local educational agencies and intermediate educational agencies shall be deemed to be a reference to local service providers under this subchapter.

(As amended Pub.L. 101-476, Title IX, § 901(b)(183)-(184), Oct. 30, 1990, 104 Stat. 1151; Pub.L. 102-119, § 25(b), Oct. 7, 1991, 105 Stat. 607.)

§ 1484. Allocation of funds

(a) Territories and insular possessions

From the sums appropriated to carry out this subchapter for any fiscal year, the Secretary may reserve 1 percent for payments to Guam, American Samoa, the Virgin Islands, the Republic of the Marshall Islands, the Federated States of Micronesia, the Republic of Palau, and the Commonwealth of Northern Mariana Islands in accordance with their respective needs.

(b) Payments to Secretary of Interior for assistance to Indians

(1) The Secretary shall, subject to this subsection, make payments to the Secretary of the Interior to be distributed to tribes or tribal organizations (as defined under section 4 of the Indian Self-Determination and Education Assistance Act [25 U.S.C. § 450b]) or consortium of the above entities for the coordination of assistance in the provision of early intervention services by the States to infants and toddlers with disabilities and their families on reservations served by elementary and secondary schools for Indian children operated or funded by the Department of the Interior. The amount of such payment for any fiscal year shall be 1.25 percent of the aggregate of the amount available to all States under this subchapter for that fiscal year.

(2) The Secretary of the Interior shall distribute the total amount of the 1.25 percent under paragraph (1) in the following manner:

(A) For the first fiscal year, each tribe or tribal organization shall receive an amount proportionate to the amount of weighted student units for special education programs for BIA operated or funded schools serving such reservation generated under the formula established under section 1128 of the Education Amendments of 1978 [25 U.S.C. § 2008], divided by the total number of such students in all BIA operated or funded schools.

(B) For each fiscal year thereafter, each tribe or tribal organization shall receive an amount based on the number of infants and toddlers residing on the reservation as determined annually divided by the total of such children served by all tribes or tribal organizations.

(3) To receive a payment under this paragraph, the tribe or tribal organization shall submit such figures to the Secretary of the Interior as are needed to determine the amounts to be allocated under paragraph (2).

(4) The funds received by a tribe or tribal organization shall be used to assist States in child find, screening, and other procedures for the early identification of Indian children aged 0-2, inclusive, and for parent training. Such funds may also be used to provide early intervention services in accordance with this part. These activities may be carried out directly or through contracts or cooperative agreements with the BIA, local educational agencies, and other public or private nonprofit organizations. The tribe and tribal organization is encouraged to involve Indian parents in the development and implementation of these activities. The above entities shall, as appropriate, make referrals to local, State, or Federal entities for the provision of services or further diagnosis.

(5) To be eligible to receive a grant pursuant to paragraph (2), the tribe or tribal organization shall make a biennial report to the Secretary of the Interior of activities undertaken under this subsection, including the number of contracts and cooperative agreements entered into, the number of children contacted and receiving services for

each year, and the estimated number of children needing services during the 2 years following the one in which the report is made. The Secretary of the Interior shall include a summary of this information on a biennial basis to the Secretary of Education along with such other information as required under section 1411(f)(3)(D) of this title. The Secretary of Education may require any additional information from the Secretary of the Interior.

(6) None of the funds under this subsection can be used by the Secretary of the Interior for administrative purposes, including child count, and the provision of technical assistance.

(c) States

(1) For each of the fiscal years 1987 through 1994 from the funds remaining after the reservation and payments under subsections (a) and (b) of this section, the Secretary shall allot to each State an amount which bears the same ratio to the amount of such remainder as the number of infants and toddlers in the State bears to the number of infants and toddlers in all States, except that no State shall receive less than 0.5 percent of such remainder, or $500,000, whichever is greater.

(2) For the purpose of paragraph (1)—

(A) the terms "infants" and "toddlers" mean children from birth to age 2, inclusive[;] and

(B) the term "State" does not include the jurisdictions described in subsection (a) of this section.

(d) Election by State not to receive allotment

If any State elects not to receive its allotment under subsection (c)(1) of this section, the Secretary shall reallot, among the remaining States, amounts from such State in accordance with such subsection.

(As amended Pub.L. 101-476, Title IX, § 901(b)(185), Oct. 30, 1990, 104 Stat. 1151; Pub.L. 102-119, §§ 19(a)(1), (b), 25(b), Oct. 7, 1991, 105 Stat. 600, 601, 607.)

§ 1484a. Federal interagency coordinating council

(a) Establishment and Purpose.

(1) In general

The Secretary shall establish a Federal Interagency Coordinating Council in order to—

(A) minimize duplication of programs and activities relating to early intervention services for infants and toddlers with disabilities and their families, and preschool services for children with disabilities, across Federal, State, and local agencies;

(B) ensure the effective coordination of Federal early intervention and preschool programs and policies across Federal agencies;

(C) coordinate the provision of Federal technical assistance and support activities to States;

(D) identify gaps in Federal agency programs and services; and

(E) identify barriers to Federal interagency cooperation.

(2) Appointments

The council established under paragraph (1) (hereafter in this section referred to as the "Council") and the chairperson of the Council shall be appointed by the Secretary in consultation with other appropriate Federal agencies. In making the appointments, the Secretary shall ensure that each member has sufficient authority to engage in policy planning and implementation on behalf of the department, agency, or program that such member represents.

(b) Composition

The Council shall be composed of—

(1) a representative of the Office of Special Education Programs;

(2) a representative of the National Institute on Disability and Rehabilitation Research;

(3) a representative of the Maternal and Child Health Services Block Grant Program;

(4) a representative of programs assisted under the Developmental Disabilities Assistance and Bill of Rights Act [42 U.S.C. § 6000 *et seq.*];

(5) a representative of the Health Care Financing Administration;

(6) a representative of the Division of Birth Defects and Developmental Disabilities of the Centers for Disease Control;

(7) a representative of the Social Security Administration;

(8) a representative of the Special Supplemental Food Program for Women, Infants and Children of the Department of Agriculture;

(9) a representative of the National Institute of Mental Health;

(10) a representative of the National Institute of Child Health and Human Development;

(11) a representative of the Bureau of Indian Affairs of the Department of the Interior;

(12) a representative of the Indian Health Service;

(13) a representative of the Surgeon General;

(14) a representative of the Department of Defense;

(15) a representative of the Administration for Children and Families;

(16) a representative of the Substance Abuse and Mental Health Services Administration;

(17) a representative of the Pediatric Aids Health Care Demonstration Program in the Public Health Service;

(18) at least 3 parents of children with disabilities age 12 or under, of whom at least one must have a child with a disability under the age of 6;

(19) at least 2 representatives of State lead agencies for early intervention services to infants and toddlers, one of which must be a representative of a State educational agency and the other a representative of a noneducational agency;

(20) other members representing appropriate agencies involved in the provision of, or payment for, early intervention services and special education and related services to infants and toddlers with disabilities and their families and preschool children with disabilities; and

(21) other persons appointed by the Secretary.

(c) Meetings

The Council shall meet at least quarterly and in such places as the Council deems necessary. The meetings shall be publicly announced, and, to the extent appropriate, open and accessible to the general public.

(d) Functions of the Council

The Council shall—
(1) advise and assist the Secretary in the performance of the Secretary's responsibilities described in this subchapter;
(2) conduct policy analyses of Federal programs related to the provision of early intervention services and special educational and related services to infants and toddlers with disabilities and their families, and preschool children with disabilities, in order to determine areas of conflict, overlap, duplication, or inappropriate omission;
(3) identify strategies to address issues described in paragraph (2);
(4) develop and recommend joint policy memoranda concerning effective interagency collaboration, including modifications to regulations, and the elimination of barriers to interagency programs and activities;
(5) coordinate technical assistance and disseminate information on best practices, effective program coordination strategies, and recommendations for improved early intervention programming for infants and toddlers with disabilities and their families and preschool children with disabilities; and
(6) facilitate activities in support of States' interagency coordination efforts.

(e) Conflict of Interest

No member of the Council shall cast a vote on any matter that would provide direct financial benefit to that member or otherwise give the appearance of a conflict of interest under Federal law.

(Pub.L. 91-230, Title VI, § 685, as added Pub.L. 102-119, § 21(2), Oct. 7, 1991, 105 Stat. 602, and amended Pub.L. 102-321, Title I, § 161, July 10, 1992, 106 Stat. 375.)

§ 1485. Authorization of appropriations

There are authorized to be appropriated to carry out this subchapter $220,000,000 for fiscal year 1992, and such sums as may be necessary for each of the fiscal years 1993 and 1994.

(Pub.L. 91-230, Title VI, § 686, formerly 685, as added Pub.L. 99-457, Title I, § 101(a), Oct. 8, 1986, 100 Stat. 1155, and amended and renumbered Pub.L. 102-119, §§ 20-21(1), Oct. 7, 1991, 105 Stat. 602.)

Cases Interpreting the Individuals with Disabilities Education Act
(20 U.S.C. §§ 1400-1485)

A well developed body of law has evolved under the IDEA since the passage of the EAHCA amendments in 1975. Many of the most important recent EHA-IDEA cases are summarized in this section.

A.E. by and through Evans v. Indep. School Dist. No. 25, 936 F.2d 472 (10th Cir.1991). An emotionally disturbed Oklahoma student who had disrupted classes and had attempted suicide was characterized as "socially maladjusted" rather than "seriously disabled" by her school IEP committee, which determined that her **behavioral problems** were **unrelated to** her **learning disability**. This determination was upheld by a federal district court and the U.S. Court of Appeals, 10th Circuit, which noted that a conduct disorder (including socially maladjusted) did not constitute a serious disability within the meaning of the IDEA. [But see *Babb v. Knox County School System*, 965 F.2d 104 (6th Cir.1992), below.]

Amann v. Town of Stow, 991 F.2d 929 (1st Cir.1993). **The IDEA does not have a statute of limitations**, and instead relies upon federal district courts to examine the laws of the states in which they are located to apply the most appropriate statute of limitations. The U.S. Court of Appeals, First Circuit, affirmed a decision by the U.S. District Court for the District of Massachusetts which applied the Massachusetts administrative procedure act's statute of limitations to IDEA cases, requiring the filing of administrative appeals within 30 days in cases of disputed IEPs.

Anderson v. Dist. of Columbia, 877 F.2d 1018 (D.C.Cir.1989). Four students with learning disabilities were placed in schools operated by the District of Columbia Public School (DCPS). The parents unilaterally removed their children from public schools and placed them in fulltime private special education programs, then requested IDEA due process hearings, challenging the original DCPS placements. The U.S. Court of Appeals, District of Columbia Circuit, affirmed the district court decision for DCPS, and did not require it to fund the private school placements **pending appeal from the district court** under the **stay-put provision** of **20 U.S.C. § 1415(e)(3)**. The stay-put provision did not apply following the conclusion of district (trial) court proceedings. [For cases presenting different legal conclusions on this issue, see *Louis M. v. Ambach*, 714 F.Supp. 1276 (N.D.N.Y.1989), and *Grymes v. Madden*, 672 F.2d 321 (3d Cir.1982), below.]

Ash v. Lake Oswego School Dist., 980 F.2d 585 (9th Cir.1992). The U.S. Court of Appeals, Ninth Circuit, held that the parents of an autistic child were entitled to **tuition reimbursement** by their school district because the child was unable to derive educational benefits outside a residential placement. The parents had no right to reimbursement for any time prior to their first request for services, but they were entitled to an award of **attorney's fees**.

Babb v. Knox County School System, 965 F.2d 104 (6th Cir.1992). A Tennessee school district **failed to identify** a student as disabled despite his history of academic and behavior problems. It also failed to **develop an adequate IEP** for him. The U.S. Court of Appeals, Sixth Circuit, ordered the district to pay for the student's **psychological costs** at a private hospital for emotionally disturbed children. [Compare this with *A.E. by and through Evans v. Indep. School Dist. No. 25,* 936 F.2d 472 (10th Cir.1991), above.]

Barnett by Barnett v. Fairfax County School Bd., 927 F.2d 146 (4th Cir.1991), *cert. den.,* — U.S. —, 112 S.Ct. 175, 116 L.Ed.2d 138 (1991). A Virginia student with hearing impairments who was mainstreamed into regular classes progressed well in high school. His school district maintained **cued speech interpreter** services at a centrally-located facility five miles from the student's home. The U.S. Court of Appeals, Fourth Circuit, held that the district was not required to duplicate the service at a school near the student's home. The EHA did not always require placement in the school closest to the disabled student's home and permitted consideration of school district resources.

Bernardsville Bd. of Educ. v. J.H., 817 F.Supp. 14 (D.N.J.1993). The U.S. District Court for the District of New Jersey held that New Jersey's two or six year **statute of limitations** should be applied in an IDEA case, rather than the state administrative procedure act's thirty-day limitation on actions.

Big Beaver Falls Area School Dist. v. Jackson, 615 A.2d 910, (Pa.Cmwlth.1992), *later proceeding,* 624 A.2d 806 (Pa.Cmwlth.1993). A Pennsylvania school district violated the IDEA by failing to allow the parent of a disabled student to fully participate in the IEP process, justifying an award of **compensatory education**. The assignment of more than ten days of **in school suspension** in one school year without prior notice and hearing (as set forth in *Honig v. Doe*, below) violated the IDEA's **stay-put** provision, where the student with a disability voluntarily left school, creating a *de facto* suspension.

Blazejewski v. Bd. of Educ. of Allegheny Cent. School Dist., 560 F.Supp. 701 (W.D.N.Y.1983). The parents of a learning disabled 11th grader obtained an order requiring their local school district to provide him special education services in a resource room. Although the student had been making academic progress, the hearing officer was entitled to rely upon test scores requiring special educational services. The IDEA's **stay-put provision (20 U.S.C. § 1415(e)(3))** required that the student remain in his current placement pending the completion of IDEA appeals.

Bd. of Educ. v. Ambach, 628 F.Supp. 972 (E.D.N.Y.1986). A New York school district was ordered to fund a disabled student's private school tuition due to its many delays. It then developed an appropriate public school IEP which was approved by the state education commissioner. The U.S. District Court for the Eastern District of New York ordered the district to pay the student's private school tuition costs (under the IDEA's **stay-put provision**) up to the time of the commissioner's decision, but the district would not be required to pay for any private school costs after it had developed an appropriate public school IEP.

Bd. of Educ. v. Ambach, 612 F.Supp. 230 (E.D.N.Y.1986). The U.S. District Court for the Eastern District of New York ordered a school district to fund a special educational placement in a private academy due to its failure to make an educational placement within 60 days of identifying a student as disabled. Because the parents had unilaterally placed the student in the academy, it had by then become the student's **current educational placement**.

Bd. of Educ v. Rowley, 458 U.S. 176, 102 S.Ct. 3034, 73 L.Ed.2d 690 (1982). The U.S. Supreme Court held that a New York school board was not required to provide a sign language interpreter to a student with deafness. The EHA required the development of **IEPs** which were **reasonably calculated to enable disabled students to derive some educational benefit**. It creates a minimum floor for the provision of special education services but does not require states to maximize the potential of each disabled child. In this case, the child was advancing through school easily and was not entitled to an interpreter, despite evidence that this would remedy the disparity between her achievement and her potential.

Bd. of Educ. of Cabell County v. Dienelt, 843 F.2d 813 (4th Cir.1988). A school district's failure to conduct a **required multidisciplinary review,** failure to provide an **adequate IEP,** and "grievous procedural defects" resulted in a **tuition reimbursement** award of over $68,000 in a West Virginia disabled student's case.

Bd. of Educ. of Community Consol. School Dist. No. 21 v. Illinois State Bd. of Educ., 938 F.2d 712 (7th Cir.1991). The U.S. Court of Appeals, Seventh Circuit, affirmed a federal district court decision holding that a hearing officer was entitled to consider parental opposition to a disabled student's IEP when assessing the appropriateness of the student's alternative public school placement.

Bd. of Educ., Sacramento City Unif. School Dist. v. Holland, by and through Holland, 786 F.Supp. 874 (E.D.Cal.1992). A federal district court agreed with the parents of a California student with disabilities that a school district should enroll the student in regular classes with **supplementary aids and services** instead of in a special education classroom to comply with the IDEA's **mainstreaming** requirement and to benefit from language and behavior models set by mainstream students.

Bray by Bray v. Hobart City School Corp., 818 F.Supp. 1226 (N.D.Ind.1993). An Indiana state law required the state education department to approve IEPs calling for a residential placement. The residential application review process impermissibly violated the IDEA by **delaying** the **implementation of IEPs** and rendering hearing officer decisions not final. There was no need to exhaust administrative remedies because the administrative procedure itself was being challenged.

Brougham by Brougham v. Town of Yarmouth, 823 F.Supp. 9 (D.Me.1993). The U.S. District Court for the District of Maine affirmed a school district's **IEP** calling for mainstreaming a hearing-impaired student for subjects in which he was progressing, while providing special education instruction for those which were difficult for him. Parental preference alone cannot compel school districts to approve a particular placement.

Brown v. Griggsville Comm. School Dist. No. 4, 817 F.Supp. 734 (C.D.Ill.1993). The parents of an Illinois second-grader objected to an IDEA placement after their son suffered a stroke and became physically disabled. The son began to make significant progress, and the parents withdrew their request for a hearing. The U.S. District Court for the Central District of Illinois ruled that the parents could not be "prevailing parties" under the IDEA's **attorney's fees** provision (**20 U.S.C. § 1415(e)(4)(B)**), because no hearing was ever held.

Burlington School Comm. v. Dept. of Educ. of Massachusetts, 471 U.S. 359, 105 S.Ct. 1996, 85 L.Ed.2d 385 (1985). The U.S. Supreme Court affirmed a decision of the U.S. Court of Appeals, First Circuit, which held that the parents of a learning disabled Massachusetts student had violated the EHA's stay-put provision by unilaterally enrolling him in a private school. The Court held that the parents were not entitled to tuition reimbursement and other costs. Although the proposed IEP had been appropriate, the Court made the further ruling that in some situations, **parents could be reimbursed** even though they **unilaterally placed** a student in a private school. This would be the case where a court later held that the proposed **IEP** was educationally inappropriate. Parents who unilaterally changed their children's placement did so at their own risk, because if (as in this case) the proposed IEP was appropriate, the parents had to pay the private school costs.

Cain v. Yukon Pub. Schools, Dist. I-27, 775 F.2d 15 (10th Cir.1985). The U.S. Court of Appeals, Tenth Circuit, upheld an administrative denial of **tuition reimbursement** to the parents of an Oklahoma student with serious emotional and behavioral problems. The parents had **unilaterally transferred** the student to a private school following a number of disagreements concerning the student's behavior, the methods of instruction to be used, and the hiring of a new teacher. The court held that the school district had provided the student with a **free appropriate public education** and that although a residential facility offered "a superior educational program, an education which maximizes a child's potential is not required by the EHA."

Chris C. by Barbara C. v. Gwinnett County School Dist., 780 F.Supp. 804 (N.D.Ga.1990). The parents of a Georgia student with Down's Syndrome contested the **change in placement** of their son from a program for students with mild disabilities stressing both academics and survival skills to a self-contained class for moderately disabled students. The U.S. District Court for the Northern District of Georgia held that the change in placement was appropriate because he derived "some educational benefit" from the moderate program.

Christopher M. v. Corpus Christi Indep. School Dist., 933 F.2d 1285 (5th Cir.1990). A severely disabled Texas child was provided only four hours of educational services by his school district. The U.S. Court of Appeals, Fifth Circuit, rejected the argument that the child should be entitled to a seven hour school day, affirming a federal district court decision which held that the IDEA does not presume that disabled students must have a school day in conformity with that of regular students.

Clovis Unif. School Dist. v. California Office of Administrative Hearings, 903 F.2d 635 (9th Cir.1990). A California school district was not responsible for **medical and psychological treatment costs** for the placement of a ten-year-old victim of child abuse and neglect in an acute care facility. The U.S. Court of Appeals, Ninth Circuit, ruled that while the IDEA **stay-put provision** required the district to pay for the child's expenses at the facility throughout the course of IDEA proceedings, it was not required to permanently fund the placement there. The child had been hospitalized primarily for **medical and psychological treatment**, and **not for educational purposes**.

Cochran v. Dist. of Columbia, 660 F.Supp. 314 (D.D.C.1987). The District of Columbia Public Schools (DCPS) delayed placing a disabled student, and his parents unilaterally placed him in a private school. The U.S. District Court, District of Columbia, determined that the DCPS's failure to timely develop an adequate IEP rendered the parents' placement the child's **current educational placement** under the IDEA, requiring the DCPS to pay **private school tuition** during the pendency of the litigation under the **stay-put provision** of **20 U.S.C. § 1415(e)(3)**.

Cocores by and through Hughes v. Portsmouth, N.H., School Dist., 779 F.Supp. 203 (D.N.H.1991). A twenty-one year old New Hampshire woman could be entitled to compensatory education if it could be shown that her school district violated the IDEA by depriving her of a **free appropriate public education** when she was between the ages of three and twenty-one.

In re Conklin, 946 F.2d 306 (4th Cir.1991). A dyslexic Maryland student was unilaterally placed in a private school by his parents, who then filed a lawsuit against his school district, challenging a public school placement. The U.S. Court of Appeals, Fourth Circuit, held that the IDEA does not categorically state that students with disabilities who do not advance from grade to grade are deprived of a **free appropriate public education**. The **IDEA creates a minimum floor of educational opportunity** for students with disabilities, which states may voluntarily exceed.

Corbett for Corbett v. Regional Center for East Bay, Inc., 676 F.Supp. 964 (N.D.Cal.1988),*on reconsideration*, 699 F.Supp. 230. A nonprofit residential agency terminated the placement of a California child due to self-abusiveness. A federal district court held that the IDEA's **stay-put provision (20 U.S.C. § 1415(e)(3))** presumes that the current placement is appropriate and permits disabled students to obtain a preliminary injunction without a showing of irreparable harm in order to preserve the status quo during IDEA proceedings. The student need only show that there has been a change in education placement in order to invoke IDEA protection. On rehearing, the court reversed its original decision that it had no jurisdiction. Although the child had been placed by a state welfare agency, the placement could be considered as one for **educational purposes**. When a residential placement is necessary to provide the student with a free appropriate public education, the residential placement is a **related service** under the IDEA.

Cordry v. Eukert, 917 F.2d 1460 (6th Cir.1990), *cert. denied*, 499 U.S. 937, 111 S.Ct. 1391, 113 L.Ed.2d 447 (1991). The U.S. Court of Appeals, Sixth Circuit, held that an Ohio school district did not violate the IDEA's **stay-put provision (20 U.S.C. § 1415(e))** by failing to fund a private school program which was selected by the student's parents but which was not a part of the IEP.

Crocker v. Tennessee Secondary School Athletic Ass'n., 980 F.2d 382 (6th Cir.1992). A learning disabled student who transferred from a private school to a public school was denied a hardship waiver by the state athletic association. A hearing officer held for the student, ruling that he had transferred to take advantage of remedial programs available at the public school. The U.S. Court of Appeals, Sixth Circuit, ruled that the student could participate in varsity contests under a federal district court order, but held that **under the IDEA, general damages for emotional anguish and pain and suffering were unavailable**. The trial court had correctly dismissed a $1.5 million damage claim.

Cronin v. Bd. of Educ., 689 F.Supp. 197 (S.D.N.Y.1991). **Graduation** constitutes a **change in placement** under the IDEA (**20 U.S.C. § 1415(e)(3)**). Accordingly,
it was impermissible for a New York school district to remove a disabled student from
a special education program pending his IDEA administrative appeal.

D. v. Ambach, 694 F.2d 904 (2d Cir.1982). A New York school district's failure
to timely appeal a hearing officer's decision requiring it to fund a special education
student's private school placement did not preclude a finding that the private school
placement was the student's **current educational placement** in a later proceeding.

David D. v. Dartmouth School Comm., 775 F.2d 411 (1st Cir.1985), *cert. den.
sub. nom. Massachusetts Dep't of Educ. v. David D.*, 475 U.S. 1140, 106 S.Ct. 1790,
90 L.Ed.2d 336 (1986). The EHA incorporates state law by defining **free appropriate public education** as special education and related services which "meet the
standards of the State educational agency," under (**20 U.S.C. § 1401(a)(18)(B)**).
Accordingly, a complaint filed under the more stringent provisions of Massachusetts
special education law was susceptible to review by a federal court under federal
question jurisdiction, and was not merely a pendent state law claim barred by the
Eleventh Amendment.

DeLeon v. Susquehanna Comm. School Dist., 747 F.2d 149 (3d Cir.1984.) Minor
changes in a disabled student's transportation routine did not constitute a **change in
placement** under the IDEA.

Dellmuth v. Muth, 491 U.S. 223, 109 S.Ct. 2397, 105 L.Ed.2d 181 (1989). In this
case, the U.S. Supreme Court overruled the Third Circuit Court of Appeals' decision
in *Muth v. Central Bucks School Dist.,* 839 F.2d 113 (3d Cir.1988). The Court held
that Congress did not intend that the EHA permit **monetary damage awards** against
states by federal courts under the doctrine of **sovereign immunity**. This permitted the
Commonwealth of Pennsylvania to avoid liability in an EHA damage suit brought by
a learning disabled student. [In 1990, Congress passed an amendment abrogating
sovereign immunity (see 20 U.S.C. § 1403) in IDEA cases and authorizing both
equitable (injunctive and declaratory) and legal (damage award) remedies under the
IDEA.]

Digre v. Roseville Schools Indep. Dist. No. 623, 893 F.2d 987 (8th Cir.1990).
Following a brief exchange of custody between his separated parents, a Minnesota
student with above-average intelligence and a behavior disorder returned to his
special education classes. His mother sought an order allowing him to attend regular
classes pending a new special educational assessment, claiming that the resumption
of special education constituted a **change in placement**. The U.S. Court of Appeals,
Eighth Circuit, held that the school district could be liable for constitutional violations
under 42 U.S.C. § 1983. This was because **the IDEA does not limit student remedies
under other federal statutes**. However, there was no violation of the IDEA's **stay-
put provision, 20 U.S.C. § 1415(e)(3)**, because the one month of regular classes at
the school in his father's district did not negate the student's special education status
in his mother's district.

Dima v. Macchiarola, 513 F.Supp. 565 (E.D.N.Y.1981). The IDEA's **stay-put
provision** (**20 U.S.C. § 1415(e)(3)**) did not prohibit the New York state education
department from decertifying a private institution following an audit which revealed

financial and educational mismanagement. Offering similar services at other sites did not constitute a **change in placement**.

Doe v. Brookline School Committee, 722 F.2d 910 (1st Cir.1983). The IDEA's **stay-put provision (20 U.S.C. § 1415(e))** does not prevent courts from ordering school districts to reimburse parents for unilateral private school placements.

Doe by and through Doe v. Bd. of Educ. of State of Conn., 753 F.Supp. 65 (D.Conn.1990). A Connecticut school district was not responsible for the costs of institutionalizing a student suffering from depression who exhibited violent behavior. The student was not disabled nor entitled to special education services under the IDEA because his emotional problems did not adversely affect his educational progress.

Doe ex rel. Gonzales v. Maher, 793 F.2d 1470 (9th Cir.1986), later proceeding, 795 F.2d 787, *cert. granted on other grounds,* 479 U.S. 1084, 107 S.Ct. 1284, 94 L.Ed.2d 142 (1987). The IDEA prohibits **expulsion** of a special education student for misbehavior which is linked to a disabling condition. Expulsion procedures designed for regular education students are generally not applicable to students who are enrolled in special education programs under the IDEA. Before a **change in placement**, special education students have the right to avail themselves of the IDEA's procedural protections.

Doe v. Smith, 879 F.2d 1340 (6th Cir.1989), *rehearing den., cert. den.,* 493 U.S. 1024, 110 S.Ct. 730, 107 L.Ed.2d 749 (1990). Parents of a Tennessee student with a language disorder improperly placed him in a private facility and **failed to exhaust** their **administrative remedies**. The U.S. Court of Appeals, Sixth Circuit, remanded the case for a ruling on the appropriateness of the student's proposed IEP by a hearing officer.

Doyle v. Arlington County School Bd., 953 F.2d 100 (4th Cir.1991) *later proceeding,* 806 F.Supp. 1253 (E.D.Va.1992). The U.S. Court of Appeals, Fourth Circuit, held that a federal district court had not given proper deference to the **findings of a hearing officer,** which **are presumed to be valid**. On remand, the district court explained its reasoning with a summary of the hearing officer's many errors.

Ellison v. Bd. of Educ. of Three Village School Dist., 597 N.Y.S.2d 483 (A.D.3d Dept.1993). A New York student required a respirator and the assistance of a specially trained nurse to perform tracheostomy suctioning and catheterization. The New York Supreme Court, Appellate Division, Third Department, affirmed a hearing officer's decision that the provision of a special, full time nurse was not a **related service** under the IDEA. The school district did not need to provide the service, because under the IDEA, **medical services qualify as related services only if they are provided for diagnostic and evaluation purposes**.

Evans v. Dist. 17, Douglas County, Nebraska, 841 F.2d 824 (8th Cir.1988). The U.S. Court of Appeals, Eighth Circuit, ruled that parents of a student with severe behavioral impairments should not be reimbursed for **private school tuition** at the private Kansas school in which they unilaterally placed her because of concerns about the IEP developed by their school district. The parents had failed to give any **written notice** to the school district which would trigger EHA procedural protections.

Fagan v. Dist. of Columbia, 817 F.Supp. 161 (D.D.C.1993). The parents of a disabled student residing in the District of Columbia obtained an administrative ruling that their son's placement was inappropriate because they had been excluded from having input into his **IEP**. However, the parents were not entitled to **tuition reimbursement** because they had unilaterally placed the student in an **unapproved institution**. Under **20 U.S.C. § 1401(a)(18)**, an **appropriate education** consists of "special education and related services that . . . meet the standards of the State Educational Agency."

Felter v. Cape Girardeau School Dist., 810 F.Supp. 1062 (E.D.Mo.1993). A Missouri school district was required to provide a disabled student with **transportation** from the student's parochial school to her public school classes as a **related service** under the IDEA, but was not required to provide transportation to the student's home after school.

Florence County School Dist. Four v. Carter, 114 S.Ct. 361 (1993). The U.S. Supreme Court held that the failure of a school district to propose an appropriate IEP and placement for a learning disabled South Carolina student justified an award of **private school tuition reimbursement** by the district, even though the private school was not on the state list of approved schools. This was because the education provided to the student was appropriate and because South Carolina did not publish a list of approved schools. The IDEA requirement at **20 U.S.C. § 1401(a)(18)** to provide a free appropriate public education did not apply to **parental placements**, so that parents maintained the right to unilaterally place children in private schools. To recover private school tuition costs, parents must show that the placement proposed by the school district violated the IDEA, and that the private school placement is appropriate under the act. Federal courts have broad discretion in granting relief under the IDEA, and may reduce tuition reimbursement awards found to be unreasonably expensive. The Supreme Court upheld the lower court decisions in favor of the parents.

Fuhrmann v. East Hanover Bd. of Educ., 993 F.2d 1031 (3d Cir.1993). IEPs must be reasonably calculated to enable a child to receive educational benefits at the time of the proposed IEP. A New Jersey student with autistic-like behavior was unilaterally placed by his parents in a private school after they disagreed with the proposed IEP. The student's **later educational progress** at the private school was **not relevant to the appropriateness of the proposed IEP**.

Gillette v. Fairland Bd. of Educ., 725 F.Supp. 343 (S.D.Ohio 1989), *aff'd*, 895 F.2d 1413 (6th Cir.1990), *later proceeding*, 932 F.2d 551 (6th Cir.1991). An Ohio school district failed to fully comply with a dyslexic student's IEP, and his parents **unilaterally placed** him in a private school. The student returned to public school after two years, and the parents sued the school district for private school tuition. Meanwhile, the school district delayed development of an IEP for the student and he was returned to private school without district approval. A federal district court noted the initial failure of the parents to request a **due process hearing**, and held that the school district had complied with essential sections of the IDEA during the first two years in issue. It had provided a free appropriate public education for those years and the parents were not entitled to **tuition reimbursement** for that period. However, the parents were entitled to reimbursement for the three years following the student's return to public school because of the district's failure to promptly develop an **adequate IEP**.

Grymes v. Madden, 672 F.2d 321 (3d Cir.1982). A Delaware school district was ordered by a federal district court to fund a private school placement for a disabled student. While the lawsuit was pending, the school district proposed a public school placement which was rejected by the parents. They commenced an administrative appeal and the district withdrew its private school funding. The U.S. Court of Appeals, Third Circuit, affirmed a district court decision for the parents, requiring the school district to pay for **private school tuition** throughout the appellate process. See also *Louis M. v. Ambach*, 714 F.Supp. 1276 (N.D.N.Y.1989). These decisions are contrary to that of the U.S. Court of Appeals, District of Columbia Circuit, in *Anderson v. Dist. of Columbia*, 877 F.2d 1018 (D.C.Cir.1989), above.

Hacienda La Puente School Dist. of Los Angeles v. Honig, 976 F.2d 487 (9th Cir.1992). A California school district failed to diagnose a student's serious emotional disturbance, and expelled him for scaring another student with a starter pistol. The U.S. Court of Appeals, Ninth Circuit, affirmed a federal district court decision finding that the school district violated the IDEA by failing to provide any notice or hearing for the expulsion. **IDEA procedural protections** extend to students not previously identified as disabled.

Hall v. Vance County Bd. of Educ., 774 F.2d 629 (4th Cir.1985). A North Carolina school district permitted a dyslexic student to advance to fifth grade despite his inability to read. The U.S. Court of Appeals, Fourth Circuit, ruled that the school district's failure to fully inform the parents of their IDEA procedural rights and its preparation of an "utterly **inadequate**" **IEP** justified the **unilateral transfer** of the student to a private school. The parents were also entitled to **tuition reimbursement** for the private school costs.

Hampton School Dist. v. Dombrowolski, 976 F.2d 48 (1st Cir.1992). The IDEA requires school districts to develop **IEPs** which are **reasonably calculated to deliver educational benefits** in the **least restrictive environment** for each student with a disability in the district. Although a private school program may have been superior, a New Hampshire school district did not violate the IDEA by proposing a public school placement.

Hayes v. Unified School Dist., 877 F.2d 809 (10th Cir.1989). Parents of a Kansas student with a behavior disorder filed an EHA lawsuit against their school district for use of a **time out room**. The court ruled that the matter had been appropriately filed under the EHA as related to a **free appropriate public education (FAPE)** under **20 U.S.C. § 1415 (b)(1)(E)**, but that the parents had failed to exhaust their administrative remedies.

Hiller v. Bd. of Educ. of Brunswick Cent. School Dist., 753 F.Supp. 65 (D.Conn.1990). A student suffering from handwriting difficulties and a weak attention span was not disabled under the IDEA. The school district's provision of remedial services was adequate for the student, and more appropriate than the special education placement sought by the student's parent.

Helms v. McDaniel, 657 F.2d 800 (5th Cir.1981), *rehearing den.*, 664 F.2d 291 (5th Cir.1982), *cert. den.*, 455 U.S. 946, 102 S.Ct. 1443, 71 L.Ed.2d 658 (1982). The U.S. Court of Appeals, Fifth Circuit, held that a Georgia state law which provided for automatic appeals of local IEP due process hearings to the state level did not violate the EHA. However, the characterization of state-level hearing officer findings as "reports of the special master," subject to review by the state board of education, was inconsistent with both the EHA and § 504 of the Rehabilitation Act. The EHA (**20 U.S.C. § 1415(e)(1)) requires that impartial hearing officer decisions be final**, subject only to appeals to state or federal district courts.

Honig v. Doe, 484 U.S. 305, 108 S.Ct. 592, 98 L.Ed.2d 686 (1988). The U.S. Supreme Court held that the suspension or expulsion of a special education student constitutes a **change in placement**. School authorities may not unilaterally exclude a child from classes pending administrative proceedings. However, the IDEA's **stay-put provision (20 U.S.C. § 1415(e))** does not prevent school districts from imposing temporary suspensions of ten school days or less upon students who present a threat of harm to other persons.

Huldah A. v. Easton Area School Dist., 601 A.2d 860 (Pa.Cmwlth.1992). A Pennsylvania student had outstanding intellectual and creative abilities and was placed in a "pull-out" program, in which gifted students attended enrichment classes rather than regular instruction. The Commonwealth Court of Pennsylvania held that the student was not entitled to an independent evaluation at school district expense and that her father was not entitled to recover an award of **attorney's fees** under the IDEA, because the statute limits such recoveries to cases involving students with disabilities.

Irving Independent School Dist. v. Tatro, 468 U.S. 883, 104 S.Ct. 3371, 82 L.Ed.2d 664 (1984). The U.S. Supreme Court held that a Texas school district was required to provide catheterization services for a disabled student while she attended school as a "supportive service" (**related service**) under the EHA, 20 U.S.C. § 1401(a)(17). The student's parents were also entitled to receive their attorney's fees under § 504 of the Rehabilitation Act.

Jackson v. Franklin County School Bd., 765 F.2d 535 (5th Cir.1985), *later proceeding,* 806 F.2d 623 (5th Cir.1986). The U.S. Court of Appeals, Fifth Circuit, ruled that notwithstanding the EHA's **stay-put provision**, it was permissible to prevent a student with a history of sexual misconduct from returning to his former placement following release from a treatment program, where the return was found to present a **substantial danger** to the student or others. However, in later proceedings, the same court held that the school district had violated the student's procedural rights under the EHA by failing to provide the minimal, informal notice and hearing which is required for even temporary suspensions. The **procedural violations constituted a failure to provide a free appropriate public education**. The court remanded the case to the district court for a determination of the student's damages due to the failure to provide him with any notice and hearing for excluding him from classes.

Johnson v. Lancaster-Lebanon Intermediate Unit 13, 757 F.Supp. 606 (E.D.Pa.1991). A Pennsylvania school district was held to have deprived a hearing impaired student of a **free appropriate public education** because his **IEP** was **not sufficiently individualized**, did not mainstream the student and caused him to fall behind his peers in verbal communication.

Joshua B. v. New Trier Township High School Dist. No. 203, 770 F.Supp. 431 (N.D.Ill.1991). Soon after the U.S. Supreme Court's 1989 decision in *Dellmuth v. Muth,* Congress passed an amendment abrogating **sovereign immunity (20 U.S.C. § 1403)** under the IDEA. The U.S. District Court for the Northern District of Illinois held that the State of Illinois could not claim that it was protected by sovereign immunity in a case involving the alleged deprivation of a free appropriate public education for a student based on facts occurring after October 30, 1990.

Kaelin v. Grubbs, 682 F.2d 595 (6th Cir.1982). A Kentucky student was expelled for refusing to do assigned work, destroying school property and hitting a teacher. The student was expelled without a consideration of the relationship between the student's behavior and his disability. The U.S. Court of Appeals, Sixth Circuit, ruled that the school board must reinstate the student and expunge his expulsion records from board minutes and attendance records. **Expulsion** of special education students constitutes a **change in placement** under the IDEA and the Rehabilitation Act. **Expulsion of a student enrolled in a special education program requires consideration of whether the misconduct is related to the student's disabling condition.**

Kerr Center Parents Ass'n v. Charles, 897 F.2d 1463 (9th Cir.1990). The **placement** of 30 disabled Oregon students for **medical reasons** was sufficiently related to the provision of a **FAPE** for each student to be considered an educational (and not medical) placement. The Oregon legislature could not refuse to appropriate funds to meet the state's obligation to provide each student with a **FAPE,** because under **20 U.S.C. §§ 1412(6)** and **1413(a)(4)(B), states are ultimately responsible for assuring provision of a FAPE.**

Knight v. Dist. of Columbia, 877 F.2d 1025 (D.C.Cir.1989). The U.S. Court of Appeals, District of Columbia Circuit, held that private and public school placements were not inherently dissimilar so as to automatically entitle students to the IDEA's **stay-put procedural protections** when the private placement is no longer available and use of public facilities is required until a new appropriate placement can be made.

Kroot v. Dist. of Columbia, 800 F.Supp. 976 (D.D.C.1992). The U.S. District Court for the District of Columbia held that because **due process hearings are the IDEA's primary procedural protection for special education students,** school districts bear the burden of proof and must provide exhaustive explanations for their decisions.

Lamont X v. Quisenberry, 606 F.Supp. 809 (S.D.Ohio 1984). The modification of two Ohio disabled students' educational programs (by placing them in home-based programs) constituted a **change in placement.** The students were removed from their placements in a severely behaviorally handicapped program following violent incidents. They were prosecuted by the state and adjudicated delinquent. A federal district court granted a motion for a preliminary injunction allowing the students to return to their classroom under the IDEA's **stay-put provision (20 U.S.C. § 1415(e)(3)).**

Lapp v. Reeder Pub. School Dist. No. 3, 491 N.W.2d 65 (N.D.1992). The Supreme Court of North Dakota held that parents of a student with sensori-neural hearing loss should receive boarding care payments from their school district where the family had changed residences solely to obtain education at a school for the deaf.

Leon v. State of Michigan Bd. of Educ, 807 F.Supp. 1278 (E.D.Mich.1992). The State of Michigan did not violate the IDEA or its own administrative procedures act by creating a pool of hearing officers eligible to hear IDEA cases which included school district employees, state university employees and attorneys who represented school districts.

Leonard v. McKenzie, 869 F.2d 1558 (D.C.Cir.1989). The District of Columbia Public Schools (DCPS) was required to fund a student's private school placement because it had violated the student's procedural rights. DCPS then determined that a public school placement was appropriate for the following year. It sent a letter erroneously advising the parents that it would fund the private school placement, but one month later sent a letter of correction describing a public school placement. The U.S. Court of Appeals, District of Columbia Circuit, affirmed the district court's decision approving of the public school placement. The DCPS had given adequate notice that the private school was no longer the student's **current educational placement**, and it was no longer required to fund the private school placement.

Lewis v. School Bd. of Loudoun County, 808 F.Supp. 523 (E.D.Va.1992). The IDEA imposes an obligation upon the states to provide a **free appropriate public education** to each student with a disability, but does not require school districts to provide the best education money can buy. Accordingly, a Virginia school district was not required to reimburse parents of a student with a learning disability who unilaterally placed the student in a private day school when they became disenchanted with the proposed IEP.

Livingston v. DeSoto County School Dist., 782 F.Supp. 1173 (N.D.Miss.1992). A Mississippi school district did not deprive a disabled student of a free appropriate public education by failing to notify parents of their **due process rights**. The student's IEP was educationally appropriate and was calculated to provide meaningful educational benefits.

Logsdon v. Pavillion Cent. School Dist., 765 F.Supp. 66 (W.D.N.Y.1991). The IDEA's **stay-put provision (20 U.S.C. § 1415(e))** requires students to remain in their current placements where they have been placed appropriately under the IDEA. A New York school district did not violate the stay-put requirement by failing to mainstream a disabled student pending an IDEA administrative appeal.

Louis M. v. Ambach, 714 F.Supp. 1276 (N.D.N.Y.1989). Disabled students in New York sued the state education commissioner for implementing a system alleged to be full of **delays**. They specifically complained that delays caused by regional associate review of hearing officer decisions and lack of parental input at that stage violated the IDEA. The U.S. District Court for the Northern District of New York found that the regional associate review caused repeated remands which contravened the IDEA requirement of **promptly placing students with disabilities**. It ordered the commissioner to develop procedures which complied with the IDEA within 180 days. The state was required to fund current private school placements of disabled students throughout the appellate process. [Compare with *Anderson v. Dist. of Columbia*, 877 F.2d 1018 (D.C.Cir.1989), above.]

Manchester School Dist. v. Christopher B., 807 F.Supp. 860 (D.N.H.1992). A New Hampshire school district failed to fully incorporate the findings of an independent evaluator in the **IEP** of a student with disabilities. The U.S. District Court for the District of New Hampshire held that the school district had failed to provide the student with a free appropriate public education and awarded the student **compensatory education** at a private school.

Masotti v. Tustin Unif. School Dist., 806 F.Supp. 221 (C.D.Cal.1992). The IDEA took legal precedence over a California mediation statute which a school district claimed should require the submission of an IDEA case to mediation prior to any district court activity. The parents were entitled to an **attorney's fee award** for work done prior to a hearing, because they were **prevailing parties** under the act.

Matthews v. Davis, 742 F.2d 825 (4th Cir.1984). The parents of a special education student were not entitled to tuition assistance for the residential placement of their profoundly disabled son. The U.S. Court of Appeals, Fourth Circuit, affirmed a district court decision that the child was not likely to receive any educational benefit from the placement, and that the family could best teach him basic living skills at home.

McKenzie v. Smith, 771 F.2d 1527 (D.C.Cir.1985). School districts must provide special education students with "similar" placements pending administrative or judicial approval of eventual plans, where a current educational placement becomes unavailable.

Merrifield v. Lake Cent. School Corp., 770 F.Supp. 468 (N.D.Ind.1991). The IDEA requirement to provide a free appropriate public education does not extend to students beyond the age limit for provision of educational services established by state law.

Militello v. Bd. of Educ. of Union City, 803 F.Supp. 974 (D.N.J.1992). An indigent parent in New Jersey was entitled to a free transcript of IDEA administrative proceedings because they were "other proceedings" within the meaning of federal law.

Moore v. Crestwood Local School Dist., 804 F.Supp. 960 (N.D.Ohio 1992). Parents of a disabled student in Ohio were entitled to over $44,000 in **attorney's fees** as **prevailing parties** under the IDEA because they obtained most of the relief they had sought at the administrative level and were forced to litigate the issue of attorney's fees due to "inflexibility" by the school district.

Mrs. W. v. Tirozzi, 832 F.2d 748 (2d Cir.1987), *later proceeding*, 706 F.Supp. 164 (D.Conn.1989). In one of the first appellate decisions interpreting the Handicapped Children's Protection Act of 1986 (known as the **HCPA**, which amended the EHA at **20 U.S.C. § 1415(e)(4) and § 1415(f)**), the U.S. Court of Appeals, Second Circuit, noted that the amended EHA affirmed the Congressional intent to create an express private right of action which included the **full range of available remedies** to protect the educational rights of students with disabilities. Accordingly, it was appropriate to join an EHA action with a civil rights complaint under 42 U.S.C. § 1983 based upon EHA violations.

Murphy v. Timberlane Reg. School Dist., 973 F.2d 13 (1st Cir.1992), *later proceeding*, 819 F.Supp. 1127 (D.N.H.1993). The parents of a New Hampshire student with disabilities did not delay bringing an IDEA claim against their school district for a period of time which was sufficient to justify application of the legal defense of **laches**. The **five year delay** was not unreasonable as well as prejudicial to the school district.

Norton School Comm. v. Massachusetts Dept. of Educ., 768 F.Supp. 900 (D.Mass.1991). Massachusetts parents unilaterally placed their speech and language impaired son in a private facility when they became convinced that the school district's IEP was inadequate. The U.S. District Court for the District of Massachusetts determined that a federal court may grant appropriate relief when parents unilaterally place students where they can demonstrate (1) that the **proposed IEP** is **inadequate** and (2) that their own choice is appropriate. Having met these requirements, the court held that the parents were entitled to **tuition reimbursement** for the prior school year.

Oberti by Oberti v. Bd. of Educ. of Borough of Clementon School Dist., 789 F.Supp. 1322 (D.N.J.1992), *later proceeding,* 801 F.Supp. 1392 (D.N.J.1992), *aff'd,* 995 F.2d 1204 (3d Cir.1993). A New Jersey school district violated the IDEA by failing to provide adequate supplementary aids and services and failing to develop an **appropriate IEP** for a student with Down's Syndrome. A federal court ordered the school district to formulate a new IEP for the student and to consider a placement in the **least restrictive appropriate environment**. Although the IDEA does not require school districts to provide every possible supplementary aid and service to disabled students, they must provide physical, occupational and speech therapists and supplementary teachers' aides if necessary.

Pink by Crider v. Mt. Diablo Unif. School Dist., 738 F.Supp. 345 (N.D.Cal.1990). The State of California established a standard in excess of the IDEA minimum by requiring education programs to "provide the equal opportunity for each individual with exceptional needs to achieve his or her full potential." This standard was enforceable by the appropriate state agency and the case was remanded for a new administrative hearing.

Rappaport v. Vance, 812 F.Supp. 609 (D.Md.1993). **Prevailing parties in IDEA cases are normally entitled to an award of attorney's fees**. This rule did not apply in the case of a Maryland student enrolled in special education classes who was represented by her father, an attorney, in IDEA litigation with her school district.

Richards v. Fairfax County School Bd., 798 F.Supp. 338 (E.D.Va.1992). A Virginia student with severe learning disabilities was not entitled to relief under the IDEA where her parents delayed action until nearly two years after the student was awarded a high school diploma. The applicable Virginia **statute of limitations** was one year from the time the party learns of an injury.

Roland M. v. Concord School Comm., 910 F.2d 983 (1st Cir.1990), *cert. denied,* 499 U.S. 912, 111 S.Ct. 1122, 113 L.Ed.2d 230 (1991). The U.S. Court of Appeals, First Circuit, held that even though Massachusetts' special education programs were designed to maximize the development of disabled students, there should be no **tuition reimbursement** for parents who **unilaterally placed** their son in a **private school** because of a disagreement over the proposed IEP.

S-1 v. Turlington, 635 F.2d 342 (5th Cir.1981), *cert. denied,* 454 U.S. 1030, 102 S.Ct. 566, 70 L.Ed.2d 473 (1981). Expulsion of students with disabilities constitutes a change in placement that entitles the student to a due process hearing.

School Bd. v. Malone, 762 F.2d 1210 (4th Cir.1985). The **expulsion** of a special education student for distribution of drugs constituted a **change in placement** under the IDEA, because the federal district court determined that the offensive activity was related to the student's learning disability.

Sherri A.D. v. Kirby, 975 F.2d 193 (5th Cir.1992). The U.S. Court of Appeals, Fifth Circuit, held that the moving of a multiply disabled student from a residential school for the visually impaired to a community residence (with educational services provided by the local school district) constituted only a change in housing, not a change in the IEP.

Smith v. Robinson, 468 U.S. 992, 104 S.Ct. 3457, 82 L.Ed.2d 746 (1984). The U.S. Supreme Court held that a disabled Rhode Island student was not entitled to recover attorney's fees despite prevailing in an EHA lawsuit against his school district. The Court ruled that there was no evidence that the school district had violated any of the student's **procedural safeguards** under the EHA. Congress responded to the *Smith* decision by passing the Handicapped Children's Protection Act of 1986 (P.L. 99-372), which specifically authorized **attorney's fee awards** to students with disabilities who prevailed in EHA lawsuits. The same legislation provided that disabled students may cumulate available remedies under § 504 of the Rehabilitation Act (29 U.S.C. § 794) and 42 U.S.C. § 1983. See **20 U.S.C. § 1415(e)(4)** and **§ 1415(f)**.

Sobol v. Burr, 492 U.S. 902, 109 S.Ct. 3209, 106 L.Ed.2d 560 (1989). The U.S. Supreme Court remanded the Second Circuit Court of Appeals' decision in *Burr by Burr v. Sobol,* 888 F.2d 258 (2d Cir.1989), which had awarded a student with blindness a year and a half of **compensatory education**, despite being **over the age of twenty-one**. The court of appeals ruled that the student had been denied a free appropriate public education due to extensive delays by the state administrative appeals process. The Supreme Court vacated the court of appeals' decision and remanded the case in light of its decision in *Dellmuth v. Muth,* above. Congress then passed the 1990 amendments renaming the EHA as the IDEA, specifically abrogating sovereign immunity in IDEA cases.

Sonja C. by and Through Olivas v. Arizona School for the Deaf and Blind, 743 F.Supp. 700 (D.Ariz.1990). The U.S. District Court for the District of Arizona held that the State of Arizona was required to provide special education services for a hearing impaired student who was living within the district for bona fide reasons and whose parents were citizens and residents of Mexico.

Straube v. Florida Union Free School Dist., 778 F.Supp. 774 (S.D.N.Y.1991). In a case involving a **unilateral private school placement** of a dyslexic student by his parents, a federal district court denied a dismissal motion filed by a school district, holding that it would have to determine whether the state's approval process for special education facilities complied with the IDEA. While **the IDEA requires that the placement meet the standards of the state educational agency**, there was no requirement that facilities be on a preapproved list. Under the IDEA, it is inappropriate to require the placement of a disabled student in an unapproved facility. In a later decision, (see 801 F.Supp. 1164 (S.D.N.Y.1992)), the court held that the parents were entitled to a year of **compensatory education** after the student graduated from high school, but the school district was not required to pay for tuition at the unapproved facility.

Swift v. Rapides Parish Pub. School System, 812 F.Supp. 666 (W.D.La.1993). The U.S. District Court for the Western District of Louisiana held that the IDEA does not require provision of optimal services to disabled students; rather, the act was designed to confer upon them some **meaningful educational benefit**.

Timothy W. v. Rochester, New Hampshire School Dist., 875 F.2d 954 (1st Cir.1989), *cert. den.*, 493 U.S. 983, 110 S.Ct. 519, 107 L.Ed.2d 520 (1989). The U.S. Court of Appeals, First Circuit, held that **even severely disabled students are entitled to a free appropriate public education** under the IDEA. The court reversed and remanded a federal district court decision which had ruled that a mutiply disabled New Hampshire student would be unable to benefit from special educational services. Severely disabled students had priority under the IDEA.

W.G. by and through B.G. v. Bd. of Trustees of Target Range School Dist. No. 23, 789 F.Supp. 1070 (D.Mont.1991), *aff'd.*, 960 F.2d 1479 (9th Cir.1992). A Montana school district's failure to formulate a child study team to develop an IEP for two years, and its eventual failure to obtain the input and participation of private school personnel, teachers and the student's parents resulted in the award of **private school tuition** for **failure to provide a free appropriate public education**.

Weil v. Bd. of Elementary & Secondary Educ., 931 F.2d 1069 (5th Cir.1991), *cert. denied,* —U.S.—, 112 S.Ct. 306, 116 L.Ed.2d 249 (1991). The U.S. Court of Appeals, Fifth Circuit, held that it was permissible for a local educational agency to transfer a student during the pendancy of IDEA proceedings where the school in which he was placed was closed. The action did not violate the IDEA's **stay-put provision (20 U.S.C. § 1415(e))**. *See also Concerned Parents & Citizens for Continuing Educ. at Malcolm X v. New York City Bd. of Educ.,* 629 F.2d 751 (2d Cir.1982), *cert. denied,* 449 U.S. 1078, 101 S.Ct. 858, 66 L.Ed.2d 801 (1981); *Tilton v. Jefferson County Bd. of Educ.,* 705 F.2d 800 (6th Cir.1983), *cert. denied,* 465 U.S. 1006, 104 S.Ct. 999, 79 L.Ed.2d 231 (1984).

Williams by and through Wilson v. Gering Pub. Schools, 463 N.W.2d 799, 236 Neb. 722 (1990). A Nebraska school district did not violate the IDEA by changing a developmentally disabled student's **IEP** from one calling for a **residential placement** to one which provided only at-home instruction, because the student would still be able to derive some educational benefits.

Woods v. New Jersey Dept. of Educ., 823 F.Supp. 254 (D.N.J.1993). A federal district court ruled that it was without power to issue an **order to show cause** to vacate an administrative order issued under the IDEA, in a case involving the placement of a twenty-year-old student with a language-based disability and obsessive compulsive disorder.

Yaris v. Special School Dist., 728 F.2d 1055 (8th Cir.1984),*cert. denied,* 476 U.S. 1172, 106 S.Ct. 2896, 90 L.Ed.2d 982 (1986), *later proceeding,* 661 F.Supp. 996 (E.D.Mo.1987). In a case filed under both the EHA and § 504, a Missouri school district was not required to provide extended and summer programs to disabled students and did not discriminate against them by failing to do so.

Zobrest v. Catalina Foothills School Dist., 113 S.Ct. 2462 (1993). The U.S. Supreme Court held that the Establishment Clause of the First Amendment to the U.S. Constitution did not prohibit a public school district from providing a sign language interpreter to an Arizona student who attended a parochial school. Provision of the interpreter was a neutral service which provided only an indirect economic benefit to the parochial school.

Federal Regulations under the Individuals with Disabilities Education Act

DEPARTMENT OF EDUCATION —34 CFR PART 300

PART 300 — ASSISTANCE TO STATES FOR THE EDUCATION OF CHILDREN WITH DISABILITIES

Subpart A—General

Purpose, Applicability, and Regulations that Apply to this Program

Subpart B—State Plans and Local Educational Agency Applications

State Plans —General

State Plans — Contents

Local Educational Agency Applications — General

Local Educational Agency Applications — Contents

Individualized Education Programs

Direct Service by the State Educational Agency

Comprehensive System of Personnel Development

Subpart D—Private Schools

Children with Disabilities in Private Schools Placed or Referred by Public Agencies

Children with Disabilities Enrolled by their Parents in Private Schools

Procedures for By-Pass

Due Process Procedures

300.482 Notice of intent to implement a by-pass.
300.483 Request to show cause.
300.484 Show cause hearing.
300.485 Decision.
300.486 Judicial review.

Subpart E—Procedural Safeguards

Due Process Procedures for Parents and Children

300.500 Definitions of "consent," "evaluation," and "personally identifiable."
300.501 General responsibility of public agencies.
300.502 Opportunity to examine records.
300.503 Independent educational evaluation.
300.504 Prior notice; parent consent.
300.505 Content of notice.
300.506 Impartial due process hearing.
300.507 Impartial hearing officer.
300.508 Hearing rights.
300.509 Hearing decision; appeal.
300.510 Administrative appeal; impartial review.
300.511 Civil action.
300.512 Timeliness and convenience of hearings and reviews.
300.513 Child's status during proceedings.
300.514 Surrogate parents.
300.515 Attorney's fees.

Protection in Evaluation Procedures

300.530 General.
300.531 Preplacement evaluation.
300.532 Evaluation procedures.
300.533 Placement procedures.
300.534 Reevaluation.

Additional Procedures for Evaluating Children with Specific Learning Disabilities

300.540 Additional team members.
300.541 Criteria for determining the existence of a specific learning disability.
300.542 Observation.
300.543 Written report.

Least Restrictive Environment

300.550 General.
300.551 Continuum of alternative placements.
300.552 Placements.
300.553 Nonacademic settings.

Confidentiality of Information

Department Procedures

Subpart F-State Administration

General

Use of Funds

State Advisory Panel

State Complaint Procedures

Subpart G-Allocation of funds; Reports

Allocations

Reports

Authority: 20 U.S.C. 1411-1420, unless otherwise noted.
Source: 57 FR 44798, Sept. 29, 1992, unless otherwise noted.

Subpart A-General

Purpose, Applicability, and Regulations That Apply to this Program

§ 300.1 Purpose.
The purpose of this part is:

(a) To ensure that all children with disabilities have available to them a free appropriate public education that includes special education and related services to meet their unique needs;

(b) To ensure that the rights of children with disabilities and their parents are protected;

(c) To assist States and localities to provide for the education of all children with disabilities; and

(d) To assess and ensure the effectiveness of efforts to educate those children.

(Authority: 20 U.S.C. 1401 Note)

§ 300.2 Applicability to State, local, and private agencies.
(a) *States.* This part applies to each state that receives payments under Part B of the Act.

(b) *Public agencies within the State.* The State plan is submitted by the State educational agency on behalf of the State as a whole. Therefore, the provisions of this part apply to all political subdivisions of the State that are involved in the education of children with disabilities. These would include:

(1) The State educational agency;

(2) Local educational agencies and intermediate educational units;

(3) Other State agencies and schools such as Departments of Mental Health and Welfare and State schools for students with deafness or students with blindness; and

(4) State correctional facilities.

(c) *Private schools and facilities.*

Each public agency in the State is responsible for ensuring that the rights and protections under this part are given to children referred to or placed in private schools and facilities by that public agency. (See §§ 300.400-300.402)

(Authority: 20 U.S.C. 1412(1), (6); 1413(a); 1413(a)(4)(B))

Note: The requirements of this part are binding on each public agency that has direct or delegated authority to provide special education and related services in a State that receives funds under Part B of the Act, regardless of whether that agency is receiving funds under Part B.

§ 300.3 Regulations that apply.
The following regulations apply to this program:

(a) 34 CFR part 76 (State-Administered Programs) except for §§ 76.780-76.782.

(b) 34 CFR part 77 (Definitions).

(c) 34 CFR part 79 (Intergovernmental Review of Department of Education Programs and Activities).

(d) 34 CFR part 80 (Uniform Administrative Requirements for Grants and Cooperative Agreements to State and Local Governments).

(e) 34 CFR part 81 (General Education Provisions Act —Enforcement).

(f) 34 CFR part 82 (New Restrictions on Lobbying).

(g) 34 CFR part 85 (Governmentwide Debarment and Suspension (Nonprocurement) and Governmentwide Requirements for Drug-Free Workplace (Grants)).

(h) 34 CFR part 86 (Drug-Free Schools and Campuses).

(i) The regulations in this part—34 CFR part 300 (Assistance to States for Education of Children with Disabilities).

(Authority: 20 U.S.C. 1221e-3(a)(1))

Definitions

Note 1: Definitions of terms that are used throughout these regulations are included in this subpart. Other terms are defined in the specific subparts in which they are used. Below is a list of those terms and the specific sections in which they are defined:

Appropriate professional requirements in the State (§ 300.153(a)(1))

Average per pupil expenditure in public elementary and secondary schools in the United States (§ 300.701(c))

Consent (§ 300.500)

Destruction (§ 300.560)

Direct services (§ 300.370(b)(1))

Education records (§ 300.560)

Evaluation (§ 300.500)

First priority children (§ 300.320(a))

Highest requirements in the State applicable to a specific profession or discipline (§ 300.153(a)(2))

Independent educational evaluation (§ 300.503(a)(3)(i))

Individualized education program (§ 300.340)

Participating agency, as used in the IEP requirements in §§ 300.346 and 300.347 (§ 300.340(b))

Participating agency, as used in the confidentiality requirements in §§ 300.560-300.576 (§ 300.560)

Party or parties (§ 300.584(a))

Personally identifiable (§ 300.500)

Private school children with disabilities (§ 300.450)

Profession or discipline (§ 300.153(a)(3))

Public expense (§ 300.503(a)(3)(ii))

Second priority children (§ 300.320(b))

Special definition of "State" (§ 300.700)

State-approved or recognized certification, licensing, registration, or other comparable requirements (§ 300.153(a)(4))

Support services (§ 300.370(b)(2))

Note 2: Below are abbreviations for selected terms that are used throughout these regulations:

"FAPE" means "free appropriate public education."

"IEP" means "individualized education program."

"IEU" means "intermediate educational unit."

"LEA" means "local educational agency."

"LRE" means "least restrictive environment."

"SEA" means "State educational agency."

As appropriate, each abbreviation is used interchangeably with its nonabbreviated term.

§ 300.4 Act.

As used in this part, "Act" means the Individuals with Disabilities Education Act, formerly the Education of the Handicapped Act.

(Authority: 20 U.S.C. 1400)

§ 300.5 Assistive technology device.

As used in this part, "assistive technology device" means any item, piece of equipment, or product system, whether acquired commercially off the shelf, modified, or customized, that is used to increase, maintain, or improve the functional capabilities of children with disabilities.

(Authority: 20 U.S.C. 1401(a)(25))

§ 300.6 Assistive technology service.

As used in this part, "assistive technology service" means any service that directly assists a child with a disability in the selection, acquisition, or use of an assistive technology device.

The term includes—

(a) The evaluation of the needs of a child with a disability, including a functional evaluation of the child in the child's customary environment;

(b) Purchasing, leasing, or otherwise providing for the acquisition of assistive technology devices by children with disabilities;

(c) Selecting, designing, fitting, customizing, adapting, applying, retaining, repairing, or replacing assistive technology devices;

(d) Coordinating and using other therapies, interventions, or services with assistive technology devices, such as those associated with existing education and rehabilitation plans and programs;

(e) Training or technical assistance for a child with a disability or, if appropriate, that child's family; and

(f) Training or technical assistance for professionals (including individuals providing education or rehabilitation services), employers, or other individuals who provide services to, employ, or are otherwise substantially involved in the major life functions of children with disabilities.

(Authority: 20 U.S.C. 1401(a)(26))

Note: The definitions of "assistive technology device" and "assistive technology service" used in this part are taken directly from section 602(a)(25)-(26) of the Act, but in accordance with Part B, the statutory reference to "individual with a disability" has been replaced with "child with a disability." The Act's definitions of "assistive technology device" and "assistive technology service" incorporate verbatim the definitions of these terms used in the Technology-Related Assistance for Individuals with Disabilities Act of 1988.

§ 300.7 Children with Disabilities.

(a)(1) As used in this part, the term "children with disabilities" means those children evaluated in accordance with §§ 300.530-300.534 as having mental retardation, hearing impairments including deafness, speech or language impairments, visual impairments including blindness, serious emotional disturbance, orthopedic impairments, autism, traumatic brain injury, other health impairments, specific learning disabilities, deaf-blindness, or multiple disabilities, and who because of those impairments need special education and related services.

(2) The term "children with disabilities" for children ages 3 through 5 may, at a State's discretion, include children—

(i) Who are experiencing developmental delays, as defined by the State and measured by appropriate diagnostic instruments and procedures, in one or more of the following areas: physical development, cognitive development, communication development, social or emotional development, or adaptive development; and

(ii) Who, for that reason, need special education and related services.

(b) The terms used in this definition are defined as follows:

(1) "Autism" means a developmental disability significantly affecting verbal and nonverbal communication and social interaction, generally evident before age 3, that adversely affects a child's educational performance. Other characteristics often associated with autism are engagement in repetitive activities and stereotyped movements, resistance to environmental change or change in daily routines, and unusual responses to sensory experiences. The term does not apply if a child's educational performance is adversely affected primarily because the child has a serious emotional disturbance, as defined in paragraph (b)(9) of this section.

(2) "Deaf-blindness" means concomitant hearing and visual impairments, the combination of which causes such severe communication and other developmental and educational problems that they cannot be accommodated in special education programs solely for children with deafness or children with blindness.

(3) "Deafness" means hearing impairment that is so severe that the child is impaired in processing linguistic information through hearing, with or without amplification, that adversely affects a child's educational performance.

(4) "Hearing impairment" means an impairment in hearing, whether permanent or fluctuating, that adversely affects a child's educational performance but which is not included under the definition of deafness in this section.

(5) "Mental retardation" means significantly subaverage general intellectual functioning existing concurrently with deficits in adaptive behavior and manifested during the developmental period, which adversely affects a child's educational performance.

(6) "Multiple disabilities" means concomitant impairments (such as mental retardation-blindness, mental retardation-orthopedic impairment, etc.), the combination of which causes such severe educational problems that they cannot be accommodated in special education programs solely for one of the impairments. The term does not include deaf-blindness.

(7) "Orthopedic impairment" means a severe orthopedic impairment that adversely affects a child's educational performance. The term includes impairments caused by congenital anomaly (e.g., clubfoot, absence of some member, etc.), impairments caused by disease (e.g. poliomyelitis, bone tuberculosis, etc.), and impairments from other causes (e.g., cerebral palsy, amputations, and fractures or burns, which cause contractures).

(8) "Other health impairment" means having limited strength, vitality or alertness, due to chronic or acute health problems such as a heart condition, tuberculosis, rheumatic fever, nephritis, asthma, sickle cell anemia, hemophilia, epilepsy, lead poisoning, leukemia, or diabetes that adversely affects a child's educational performance.

(9) "Serious emotional disturbance" is defined as follows:

(i) The term means a condition exhibiting one or more of the following characteristics over a long period of time and to a marked degree, that adversely affects a child's educational performance:

(A) An inability to learn which cannot be explained by intellectual, sensory, or health factors;

(B) An inability to build or maintain satisfactory interpersonal relationships with peers and teachers;

(C) Inappropriate types of behavior or feelings under normal circumstances;

(D) A general pervasive mood of unhappiness or depression; or

(E) A tendency to develop physical symptoms or fears associated with personal or school problems.

(ii) The term includes schizophrenia. The term does not apply to children who are socially maladjusted, unless it is determined that they have a serious emotional disturbance.

(10) "Specific learning disability" means a disorder in one or more of the basic psychological processes involved in understanding or in using language, spoken or written, which may manifest itself in an imperfect ability to listen, think, speak, read, write, spell, or to do mathematical calculations. The term includes such conditions as perceptual disabilities, brain injury, minimal brain dysfunction, dyslexia, and developmental aphasia. The term does not apply to children who have learning problems that are primarily the result of visual, hearing, or motor disabilities, of mental retardation of emotional disturbance, or of environmental, cultural, or economic disadvantage.

(11) "Speech or language impairment" means a communication disorder such as stuttering, impaired articulation, a language impairment, or a voice impairment, that adversely affects a child's educational performance.

(12) "Traumatic brain injury" means an acquired injury to the brain caused by an external physical force, resulting in total or partial functional disability or psychosocial impairment, or both, that adversely affects a child's educational performance. The term applies to open or closed head injuries resulting in impairments in one or more areas, such as cognition; language; memory; attention; reasoning; abstract thinking; judgment; problem-solving; sensory, perceptual and motor abilities; psychosocial behavior; physical functions; information processing; and speech. The term does not apply to brain injuries that are congenital or degenerative, or brain injuries induced by birth trauma.

(13) "Visual impairment including blindness" means an impairment in vision that, even with correction, adversely affects a child's educational performance. The term includes both partial sight and blindness.

(Authority: 20 U.S.C. 1401(a)(1))

Note: If a child manifests characteristics of the disability category "autism" after age 3, that child still could be diagnosed as having "autism" if the criteria in paragraph (b)(1) of this section are satisfied.

§ 300.8 Free appropriate public education.

As used in this part, the term "free appropriate public education" means special education and related services that—

(a) Are provided at public expense, under public supervision and direction, and without charge;

(b) Meet the standards of the SEA, including the requirements of this part;

(c) Include preschool, elementary school, or secondary school education in the State involved; and

(d) Are provided in conformity with an IEP that meets the requirements of §§ 300.340-300.350.

(Authority: 20 U.S.C. 1401(a)(18))

§ 300.9 Include.

As used in this part, the term "include" means that the items named are not all of the possible items that are covered, whether like or unlike the ones named.

(Authority: 20 U.S.C. 1417(b))

§ 300.10 Intermediate educational unit.

As used in this part, the term "intermediate educational unit" means any public authority, other than an LEA, that—

(a) Is under the general supervision of an SEA;

(b) Is established by State law for the purpose of providing free public education on a regional basis; and

(c) Provides special education and related services to children with disabilities within that State.

(Authority: 20 U.S.C. 1401(a)(23))

§ 300.11 Local educational agency.

(a) [Reserved]

(b) For the purposes of this part, the term "local educational agency" also includes intermediate educational units.

(Authority: 20 U.S.C. 1401(a)(8))

§ 300.12 Native language.

As used in this part, the term "native language" has the meaning given that term by section 703(a)(2) of the Bilingual Education Act, which provides as follows:

The term "native language," when used with reference to an individual of limited English proficiency, means the language normally used by that individual, or in the case of a child, the language normally used by the parents of the child.

(Authority: 20 U.S.C. 3283(a)(2); 1401(a)(22))

Note. Section 602(a)(22) of the Act states that the term "native language" has the same meaning as the definition from section 703(a)(2) of the Bilingual Education Act. (The term is used in the prior notice and evaluation sections under § 300.505(b)(2) and § 300.532(a)(1).) In using the term, the Act does not prevent the following means of communication:

(1) In all direct contact with a child (including evaluation of the child), communication would be in the language normally used by the child and not that of the parents, if there is a difference between the two.

(2) For individuals with deafness or blindness, or for individuals with no written language, the mode of communication would be that normally used by the individual (such as sign language, braille, or oral communication).

§ 300.13 Parent.

As used in this part, the term "parent" means a parent, a guardian, a person acting as a parent of a child, or a surrogate parent who has been appointed in accordance with § 300.514. The term does not include the State if the child is a ward of the State.

(Authority: 20 U.S.C. 1415)

Note. The term "parent" is defined to include persons acting in the place of a parent, such as a grandmother or stepparent with whom a child lives, as well as persons who are legally responsible for a child's welfare.

§ 300.14 Public agency.

As used in this part, the term "public agency" includes the SEA, LEAs, IEUs, and any other political subdivisions of the State that are responsible for providing education to children with disabilities.

(Authority: 20 U.S.C. 1412(2)(B); 1412(6); 1413(a))

§ 300.15 Qualified.

As used in this part, the term "qualified" means that a person has met SEA approved or recognized certification, licensing, registration, or other comparable requirements that apply to the area in which he or she is providing special education or related services.

(Authority: 20 U.S.C. 1417(b))

§ 300.16 Related services.

(a) As used in this part, the term "related services" means transportation and such developmental, corrective, and other supportive services as are required to assist a child with a disability to benefit from special education, and includes speech pathology and audiology, psychological services, physical and occupational therapy, recreation, including therapeutic recreation, early identification and assessment of disabilities in children, counseling services, including rehabilitation counseling, and medical services for diagnostic or evaluation purposes. The term also includes school health services, social work services in schools, and parent counseling and training.

(b) The terms used in this definition are defined as follows—

(1) "Audiology" includes:

(i) Identification of children with hearing loss;

(ii) Determination of the range, nature, and degree of hearing loss, including referral for medical or other professional attention for the habilitation of hearing;

(iii) Provision of habilitative activities, such as language habilitation, auditory training, speech reading (lip-reading), hearing evaluation, and speech conservation;

(iv) Creation and administration of programs for prevention of hearing loss;

(v) Counseling and guidance of pupils, parents, and teachers regarding hearing loss; and

(vi) Determination of the child's need for group and individual amplification, selecting and fitting an appropriate aid, and evaluating the effectiveness of amplification.

(2) "Counseling services" means services provided by qualified social workers, psychologists, guidance counselors, or other qualified personnel.

(3) "Early identification and assessment of disabilities in children" means the implementation of a formal plan for identifying a disability as early as possible in a child's life.

(4) "Medical services" means services provided by a licensed physician to determine a child's medically related disability that results in the child's need for special education and related services.

(5) "Occupational therapy" includes:

(i) Improving, developing or restoring functions impaired or lost through illness, injury, or deprivation;

(ii) Improving ability to perform tasks for independent functioning when functions are impaired or lost; and

(iii) Preventing, through early intervention, initial or further impairment or loss of function.

(6) "Parent counseling and training" means assisting parents in understanding the special needs of their child and providing parents with information about child development.

(7) "Physical therapy" means services provided by a qualified physical therapist.

(8) "Psychological services" includes—

(i) Administering psychological and educational tests and other assessment procedures;

(ii) Interpreting assessment results;

(iii) Obtaining, integrating, and interpreting information about child behavior and conditions relating to learning.

(iv) Consulting with other staff members in planning school programs to meet the special needs of children as indicated by psychological tests, interviews, and behavioral evaluations; and

(v) Planning and managing a program of psychological services, including psychological counseling for children and parents.

(9) "Recreation" includes:

(i) Assessment of leisure function;

(ii) Therapeutic recreation services;

(iii) Recreation programs in school and community agencies; and

(iv) Leisure education.

(10) "Rehabilitation counseling services" means services provided by qualified personnel in individual or group sessions that focus specifically on career development, employment preparation, achieving independence, and integration in the workplace and community of a student with a disability. The term also includes vocational rehabilitation services provided to students with disabilities by vocational rehabilitation programs funded under the Rehabilitation Act of 1973, as amended.

(11) "School health services" means services provided by a qualified school nurse or other qualified person.

(12) "Social work services in schools" includes—

(i) Preparing a social or developmental history on a child with a disability;

(ii) Group and individual counseling with the child and family;

(iii) Working with those problems in a child's living situation (home, school, and community) that affect the child's adjustment in school; and

(iv) Mobilizing school and community resources to enable the child to learn as effectively as possible in his or her educational program.

(13) "Speech pathology" includes—

(i) Identification of children with speech or language impairments;

(ii) Diagnosis and appraisal of specific speech or language impairments;

(iii) Referral for medical or other professional attention necessary for the habilitation of speech or language impairments;

(iv) Provision of speech and language services for the habilitation or prevention of communicative impairments; and

(v) Counseling and guidance of parents, children, and teachers regarding speech and language impairments.

(13) "Transportation" includes—

(i) Travel to and from school and between schools;

(ii) Travel in and around school buildings; and

(iii) Specialized equipment (such as special or adapted buses, lifts, and ramps), if required to provide special transportation for a child with a disability.

(Authority 20 U.S.C. 1401(a)(17))

Note. With respect to related services, the Senate Report states: The Committee bill provides a definition of related services, making clear that all such related services may not be required for each individual child and that such term includes early identification and assessment of handicapping conditions and the provision of services to minimize the effects of such conditions.

(S.Rep.No. 94-168, p.12 (1975))

The list of related services is not exhaustive and may include other developmental, corrective, or supportive services (such as artistic and cultural programs, and art, music, and dance therapy), if they are required to assist a child with a disability to benefit from special education.

There are certain kinds of services which might be provided by persons from varying professional backgrounds and with a variety of operational titles, depending upon requirements in individual States. For example, counseling services might be provided by social workers, psychologists, or guidance counselors, and psychological testing might be done by qualified psychological examiners, psychometrists, or psychologists, depending upon State standards.

Each related service defined under this part may include appropriate administrative and supervisory activities that are necessary for program planning, management, and evaluation.

§ 300.17 Special education.

(a) (1) As used in this part, the term "special education" means specially designed instruction, at no cost to the parents, to meet the unique needs of a child with a disability, including—

(i) Instruction conducted in the classroom, in the home, in hospitals and institutions, and in other settings; and

(ii) Instruction in physical education.

(2) The term includes speech pathology, or any other related service, if the service consists of specially designed instruction, at no cost to the parents, to meet the unique needs of a child with a disability, and is considered special education rather than a related service under State standards.

(3) The term also includes vocational education if it consists of specially designed instruction, at no cost to the parents, to meet the unique needs of a child with a disability.

(b) The terms in this definition are defined as follows:

(1) "At no cost" means that all specially designed instruction is provided without charge, but does not preclude incidental fees which are normally charged to nondisabled students or their parents as a part of the regular education program.

(2) "Physical education" is defined as follows:

(i) The term means the development of—

(A) Physical and motor fitness;

(B) Fundamental motor skills and patterns; and

(C) Skills in aquatics, dance, and individual and group games and sports (including intramural and lifetime sports).

(ii) The term includes special physical education, adaptive physical education, movement education, and motor development.

(Authority: 20 U.S.C. 1401(a)(16))

(3) "Vocational education" means organized educational programs that are directly related to the preparation of individuals for paid or unpaid employment, or for additional preparation for a career requiring other than a baccalaureate or advanced degree.

(Authority: 20 U.S.C. 1401(16))

Note 1: The definition of special education is a particularly important one under these regulations, since a child does not have a disbility under this part unless he or she needs special education. (See the definition of children with disabilities in § 300.7.) The definition of related services (§ 300.16) also depends on this definition, since a related service must be necessary for a child to benefit from special education. Therefore, if a child does not need special education, there can be no related services, and the child is not a child with a disability and is therefore not covered under the Act.

Note 2: The above definition of vocational education is taken from the Vocational Education Act of 1963, as amended by Pub.L. 94-482. Under that Act, "vocational education" includes industrial arts and consumer and homemaking education programs.

[57 FR 44798, Sept. 29, 1992; 57 FR 48694, Oct. 27, 1992]

§ 300.18 Transition services.

(a) As used in this part, "transition services" means a coordinated set of activities for a student, designed within an outcome-oriented process, that promotes movement from school to post-school activities, including postsecondary education, vocational training, integrated employment (including supported employment), continuing and adult education, adult services, independent living, or community participation.

(b) The coordinated set of activities described in paragraph (a) of this section must—

(1) Be based on the individual student's needs, taking into account the student's preferences and interests; and

(2) Include—

(i) Instruction;

(ii) Community experiences;

(iii) The development of employment and other post-school adult living objectives; and

(iv) If appropriate, acquisition of daily living skills and functional vocational evaluation.

(Authority: 20 U.S.C. 1401(a)(19))

Note: Transition services for students with disabilities may be special education, if they are provided as specially designed instruction, or related services, if they are required to assist a student with a disability to benefit from special education. The list of activities in paragraph (b) is not intended to be exhaustive.

[57 FR 44798, Sept. 29, 1992; 57 FR 48694, Oct. 27, 1992]

Subpart B—State Plans and Local Educational Agency Applications

State Plans—General

§ 300.110 Condition of assistance.

In order to receive funds under Part B of the Act for any fiscal year, a State must submit a State plan to the Secretary through its SEA, which plan shall be effective for a period of 3 fiscal years.

(Authority: 20 U.S.C. 1231g, 1412, 1413)

(Approved by the Office of Management and Budget under control number 1820-0030)

[57 FR 44798, Sept. 29, 1992, as amended at 58 FR 13528, Mar. 11, 1993]

§ 300.111 Content of plan.

Each State plan must contain the provisions required in §§ 300.121-300.154.

(Authority: 20 U.S.C. 1412, 1413)

[57 FR 48694, Oct. 27, 1992]

State Plans— Contents

§ 300.121 Right to a free appropriate public education.

(a) Each State plan must include information that shows that the State has in effect a policy that ensures that all children with disabilities have the right to FAPE within the age ranges and timelines under § 300.122.

(b) The information must include a copy of each State statute, court order, State Attorney General opinion, and other State document that shows the source of the policy.

(c) The information must show that the policy—

(1) Applies to all public agencies in the State;

(2) Applies to all children with disabilities;

(3) Implements the priorities established under §§ 300.320- 300.324; and

(4) Establishes timelines for implementing the policy, in accordance with § 300.122.

(Authority: 20 U.S.C. 1412(1), (2)(B), (6); 1413(a)(1))

(Approved by the Office of Management and Budget under control number 1820-0030)

[57 FR 44798, Sept. 29, 1992, as amended at 58 FR 13528, Mar. 11, 1993]

§ 300.122 Timelines and ages for free appropriate public education.

(a) *General.* Each State plan must include in detail the policies and procedures that the State will undertake or has undertaken in order to ensure that FAPE is available for all children with disabilities aged 3 through 18 within the State not later than September 1, 1978, and for all children with disabilities aged 3 through 21 within the State not later than September 1, 1980.

(b) *Documents relating to timelines.* Each State plan must include a copy of each statute, court order, attorney general decision, and other State documents that demonstrate that the State has established timelines in accordance with paragraph (a) of this section.

(c) *Exception.* The requirement in paragraph (a) of this section does not apply to a State with respect to children with disabilities aged 3, 4, 5, 18, 19, 20, or 21 to the extent that the requirement would be inconsistent with State law or practice, or the order of any court, respecting public education for one or more of those age groups in the State.

(d) *Documents relating to exceptions.* Each State plan must—

(1) Describe in detail the extent that the exception in paragraph (c) of this section applies to the State; and

(2) Include a copy of each State law, court order, and other documents that provide a basis for the exception.

(Authority: 20 U.S.C. 1412(2)(B))

(Approved by the Office of Management and Budget under control number 1820-0030)

[57 FR 44798, Sept. 29, 1992, as amended at 58 FR 13528, Mar. 11, 1993]

§ 300.123 Full educational opportunity goal.

Each State plan must include in detail the policies and procedures that the State will undertake, or has undertaken, in order to ensure that the State has a goal of providing full educational opportunity to all children with disabilities aged birth through 21.

(Authority: 20 U.S.C. 1412(2)(A))

(Approved by the Office of Management and Budget under control number 1820-0030)

[57 FR 44798, Sept. 29, 1992, as amended at 58 FR 13528, Mar. 11, 1993]

§ 300.124 [Reserved]

§ 300.125 Full educational opportunity goal—timetable.

Each State plan must contain a detailed timetable for accomplishing the goal of providing full educational opportunity for all children with disabilities.

(Authority: 20 U.S.C. 1412(2)(A))

(Approved by the Office of Management and Budget under control number 1820-0030)

[57 FR 44798, Sept. 29, 1992, as amended at 58 FR 13528, Mar. 11, 1993]

§ 300.126 Full educational opportunity goal—facilities, personnel, and services.

Each State plan must include a description of the kind and number of facilities, personnel, and services necessary throughout the State to meet the goal of providing full educational opportunity for all children with disabilities.

(Authority: 20 U.S.C. 1412(2)(A))
(Approved by the Office of Management and Budget under control number 1820-0030)
[57 FR 44798, Sept. 29, 1992, as amended at 58 FR 13528, Mar. 11, 1993]

§ 300.127 Priorities.

Each State plan must include information that shows that—
(a) The State has established priorities that meet the requirements under §§ 300.320-300.324;
(b) The State priorities meet the timelines under § 300.122; and
(c) The State has made progress in meeting those timelines.

(Authority: 20 U.S.C. 1412(3))
(Approved by the Office of Management and Budget under control number 1820-0030)
[57 FR 44798, Sept. 29, 1992, as amended at 58 FR 13528, Mar. 11, 1993]

§ 300.128 Identification, location, and evaluation of children with disabilities.

(a) *General requirement.* Each State plan must include in detail the policies and procedures that the State will undertake or has undertaken to ensure that—
(1) All children with disabilities, regardless of the severity of their disability, and who are in need of special education and related services are identified, located, and evaluated; and
(2) A practical method is developed and implemented to determine which children are currently receiving needed special education and related services and which children are not currently receiving needed special education and related services.
(b) *Information.* Each State plan must:
(1) Designate the State agency (if other than the SEA) responsible for coordinating the planning and implementation of the policies and procedures under paragraph (a) of this section.
(2) Name each agency that participates in the planning and implementation and describe the nature and extent of its participation.
(3) Describe the extent that—
(i) The activities described in paragraph (a) of this section have been achieved under the current State plan; and
(ii) The resources named for these activities in that plan have been used.
(4) Describe each type of activity to be carried out during the next school year, including the role of the agency named under paragraph (b)(1) of this section, timelines for completing those activities, resources that will be used, and expected outcomes.
(5) Describe how the policies and procedures under paragraph (a) of this section will be monitored to ensure that the SEA obtains—

(i) The number of children with disabilities within each disability category that have been identified, located, and evaluated; and

(ii) Information adequate to evaluate the effectiveness of those policies and procedures.

(6) Describe the method the State uses to determine which children are currently receiving special education and related services and which children are not receiving special education and related services.

(Authority: 20 U.S.C. 1412(2)(C))

Note 1: The State is responsible for ensuring that all children with disabilities are identified, located, and evaluated, including children in all public and private agencies and institutions in the State. Collection and use of data are subject to the confidentiality requirements in §§ 300.560-300.576.

Note 2: Under both Parts B and H of the Act, States are responsible for identifying, locating, and evaluating infants and toddlers from birth through 2 years of age who have disabilities or who are suspected of having disabilities. In States where the SEA and the State's lead agency for the Part H program are different and the Part H lead agency will be participating in the child find activities described in paragraph (a) of this section, the nature and extent of the Part H lead agency's participation must, under paragraph (b)(2) of this section, be included in the State plan. With the SEA's agreement, the Part H lead agency's participation may include the actual implementation of child find activities for infants and toddlers. The use of an interagency agreement or other mechanism for providing for the Part H lead agency's participation would not alter or diminish the responsibility of the SEA to ensure compliance with all child find requirements, including the requirements in paragraph (a)(1) of this section that all children with disabilities who are in need of special education and related services are evaluated.

(Approved by the Office of Management and Budget under control number 1820-0030)

[57 FR 44798, Sept. 29, 1992, as amended at 58 FR 13528, Mar. 11, 1993]

§ 300.129 Confidentiality of personally identifiable information.

(a) Each State plan must include in detail the policies and procedures which the State will undertake, or has undertaken, in order to ensure the protection of the confidentiality of any personally identifiable information collected, used, or maintained under this part.

(b) The Secretary shall use the criteria in §§ 300.560-300.576 of Subpart E to evaluate the policies and procedures of the State under paragraph (a) of the section.

(Authority: 20 U.S.C. 1412(2)(D); 1417(c))

Note: The confidentiality regulations were published in the FEDERAL REGISTER in final form on February 27, 1976 (41 FR 8603-8610), and met the requirements of Part B of the Act. Those regulations are incorporated in §§ 300.560-300.576.

(Approved by the Office of Management and Budget under control number 1820-0030)

[57 FR 44798, Sept. 29, 1992, as amended at 58 FR 13528, Mar. 11, 1993]

§ 300.130 Individualized education programs.

(a) Each State plan must include information that shows that each public agency in the State maintains records of the IEP for each child with disabilities, and each public agency establishes, reviews, and revises each program as provided in §§ 300.340-300.350.

(b) Each State plan must include—

(1) A copy of each State statute, policy, and standard that regulates the manner in which IEPs are developed, implemented, reviewed, and revised; and

(2) The procedures that the SEA follows in monitoring and evaluating those programs.

(Authority: 20 U.S.C. 1412(4) 1413(a)(1))

(Approved by the Office of Management and Budget under control number 1820-0030)

[57 FR 44798, Sept. 29, 1992, as amended at 58 FR 13528, Mar. 11, 1993]

§ 300.131 Procedural safeguards.

Each State plan must include procedural safeguards that ensure that the requirements of §§ 300.500-300.514 are met.

(Authority: 20 U.S.C. 1412(5)(A))

(Approved by the Office of Management and Budget under control number 1820-0030)

[57 FR 44798, Sept. 29, 1992, as amended at 58 FR 13528, Mar. 11, 1993]

§ 300.132 Least restrictive environment.

(a) Each State plan must include procedures that ensure that the requirements of §§ 300.550-300.556 are met.

(b) Each State plan must include the following information:

(1) The number of children with disabilities in the State, within each disability category, who are participating in regular education programs, consistent with §§ 300.550-300.556.

(2) The number of children with disabilities who are in separate classes or separate school facilities, or who are otherwise removed from the regular education environment.

(Authority: 20 U.S.C. 1412(5)(A))

(Approved by the Office of Management and Budget under control number 1820-0030)

[57 FR 44798, Sept. 29, 1992, as amended at 58 FR 13528, Mar. 11, 1993]

§ 300.133 Protection in evaluation procedures.

Each State plan must include procedures which ensure that the requirements in §§ 300.530-300.534 are met.

(Authority: 20 U.S.C. 1412(5)(C))

(Approved by the Office of Management and Budget under control number 1820-0030)

[57 FR 44798, Sept. 29, 1992, as amended at 58 FR 13528, Mar. 11, 1993]

§ 300.134 Responsibility of State educational agency for all educational programs.

(a) Each State plan must include information that shows that the requirements of § 300.600 are met.

(b) The information under paragraph (a) of this section must include a copy of each State statute, State regulation, signed agreement between respective agency officials, and any other document that shows compliance with that paragraph.

(Authority: 20 U.S.C. 1412(6))
(Approved by the Office of Management and Budget under control number 1820-0030)
[57 FR 44798, Sept. 29, 1992, as amended at 58 FR 13528, Mar. 11, 1993]

§ 300.135 [Reserved]

§ 300.136 Implementation procedures—State educational agency.
Each State plan must describe the procedures the SEA follows to inform each public agency of its responsibility for insuring effective implementation of procedural safeguards for the children with disabilities served by that public agency.

(Authority: 20 U.S.C. 1412(6))
(Approved by the Office of Management and Budget under control number 1820-0030)
[57 FR 44798, Sept. 29, 1992, as amended at 58 FR 13528, Mar. 11, 1993]

§ 300.137 Procedures for consultation.
Each State plan must include an assurance that in carrying out the requirements of section 612 of the Act, procedures are established for consultation with individuals involved in or concerned with the education of children with disabilities, including individuals with disabilities and parents of children with disabilities.

(Authority: 20 U.S.C. 1412(7)(A))

§ 300.138 Other Federal programs.
Each State plan must provide that programs and procedures are established to ensure that funds received by the State or any public agency in the State under any other Federal program, including subpart 2 of Part D of chapter 1 of title I of the Elementary and Secondary Education Act of 1965, under which there is specific authority for assistance for the education of children with disabilities, are used by the State, or any public agency in the State, only in a manner consistent with the goal of providing FAPE for all children with disabilities, except that nothing in this section limits the specific requirements of the laws governing those Federal programs.

(Authority: 20 U.S.C. 1413(a)(2))
(Approved by the Office of Management and Budget under control number 1820-0030)
[57 FR 44798, Sept. 29, 1992, as amended at 58 FR 13528, Mar. 11, 1993]

§ 300.139 Comprehensive system of personnel development.
Each State plan must include the procedures required under §§ 300.380-300.383.

(Authority: 20 U.S.C. 1413(a)(3))
(Approved by the Office of Management and Budget under control number 1820-0030)
[57 FR 44798, Sept. 29, 1992, as amended at 58 FR 13528, Mar. 11, 1993]

§ 300.140 Private schools.

Each State plan must include policies and procedures that ensure that the requirements of §§ 300.400-300.403 and §§ 300.450-300.452 are met.

(Authority: 20 U.S.C. 1413(a)(4))
(Approved by the Office of Management and Budget under control number 1820-0030)
[57 FR 44798, Sept. 29, 1992, as amended at 58 FR 13528, Mar. 11, 1993]

§ 300.141 Recovery of funds for misclassified children.

Each State plan must include policies and procedures that ensure that the State seeks to recover any funds provided under Part B of the Act for services to a child who is determined to be erroneously classified as eligible to be counted under section 611 (a) or (d) of the Act.

(Authority: 20 U.S.C. 1413(a)(5))
(Approved by the Office of Management and Budget under control number 1820-0030)
[57 FR 44798, Sept. 29, 1992, as amended at 58 FR 13528, Mar. 11, 1993]

§§ 300.142-300.143 [Reserved]

§ 300.144 Hearing on application.

Each State plan must include procedures to ensure that the SEA does not take any final action with respect to an application submitted by an LEA before giving the LEA reasonable notice and an opportunity for a hearing under § 76.401(d) of this title.

(Authority: 20 U.S.C. 1413(a)(8))
(Approved by the Office of Management and Budget under control number 1820-0030)
[57 FR 44798, Sept. 29, 1992, as amended at 58 FR 13528, Mar. 11, 1993]

§ 300.145 Prohibition of commingling.

Each State plan must provide assurance satisfactory to the Secretary that funds provided under Part B of the Act are not commingled with State funds.

(Authority: 20 U.S.C. 1413(a)(9))
Note: This assurance is satisfied by the use of a separate accounting system that includes an audit trail of the expenditure of the Part B Funds. Separate bank accounts are not required. (See 34 CFR 76.702 (Fiscal control and fund accounting procedures).)

§ 300.146 Annual evaluation.

Each State plan must include procedures for evaluation at least annually of the effectiveness of programs in meeting the educational needs of children with disabilities, including evaluation of IEPs.

(Authority: 20 U.S.C. 1413(a)(11))
(Approved by the Office of Management and Budget under control number 1820-0030)
[57 FR 44798, Sept. 29, 1992, as amended at 58 FR 13528, Mar. 11, 1993]

§ 300.147 Statutory advisory panel.

Each State plan must provide that the requirements of §§ 300.650-300.653 are met.

(Authority: 20 U.S.C. 1413(a)(12))

§ 300.148 Policies and procedures for use of Part B funds.

Each State plan must set forth policies and procedures designed to ensure that funds paid to the State under Part B of the Act are spent in accordance with the provisions of Part B, with particular attention given to sections 611(b), 611(c), 611(d), 612(2), and 612(3) of the Act.

(Authority: 20 U.S.C. 1413(a)(1))

(Approved by the Office of Management and Budget under control number 1820-0030)

[57 FR 44798, Sept. 29, 1992, as amended at 58 FR 13528, Mar. 11, 1993]

§ 300.149 Description of use of Part B Funds.

(a) State allocation. Each State plan must include the following information about the State's use of funds under § 300.370 and § 300.620:

(1) A list of administrative positions, and a description of duties for each person whose salary is paid in whole or in part with those funds.

(2) For each position, the percentage of salary paid with those funds.

(3) A description of each administrative activity the SEA will carry out during the next school year with those funds.

(4) A description of each direct service and each support service that the SEA will provide during the next period covered by the State plan with those funds, and the activities the State advisory panel will undertake during that period with those funds.

(b) Local educational agency allocation. Each State plan must include—

(1) An estimate of the number and percent of LEAs in the State that will receive an allocation, under this part (other than LEAs which submit a consolidated application);

(2) An estimate of the number of LEAs that will receive an allocation under a consolidated application;

(3) An estimate of the number of consolidated applications and the average number of LEAs per application; and

(4) A description of direct services the SEA will provide under § 300.360.

(Authority: 20 U.S.C. 1412(6))

(Approved by the Office of Management and Budget under control number 1820-0030)

[57 FR 44798, Sept. 29, 1992, as amended at 58 FR 13528, Mar. 11, 1993]

§ 300.150 State-level nonsupplanting.

Each State plan must provide assurance satisfactory to the Secretary that funds provided under this part will be used so as to supplement and increase the level of Federal (other than funds available under this part), State, and local funds—including funds that are not under the direct control of the SEA or LEAs—expended for special education and related services provided to children with disabilities under this part and in no case to supplant those Federal (other than funds available under this part), State, and local funds unless a waiver is granted in accordance with § 300.589.

(Authority: 20 U.S.C. 1413(a)(9))

Note: This requirement is distinct from the LEA nonsupplanting provision already contained in these regulations at § 300.230. Under this State-level provision, the State must assure that Part B funds distributed to LEAs and IEUs will be used to supplement and not supplant other Federal, State, and local funds (including funds not under the control of educational agencies) that would have been expended for special education and related services provided to children with disabilities in the absence of the Part B funds. The portion of Part B funds that are not distributed to LEAs or IEUs under the statutory formula (20 U.S.C. 1411(d)) are not subject to this nonsupplanting provision. See 20 U.S.C. 1411(c)(3). States may not permit LEAs or IEUs to use Part B funds to satisfy a financial commitment for services that would have been paid for by a health or other agency pursuant to policy or practice but for the fact that these services are now included in the IEPs of children with disabilities.

(H. R. Rep. No. 860, 99th Cong., 21-22 (1986))

§ 300.151 Additional information if the State educational agency provides direct services.

If an SEA provides FAPE for children with disabilities or provides them with direct services, its State plan must include the information required under §§ 300.226, 300.227, 300.231, and 300.235.

(Authority: 20 U.S.C. 1413(b))

§ 300.152 Interagency agreements.

(a) Each State plan must set forth policies and procedures for developing and implementing interagency agreements between—

(1) The SEA; and

(2) All other State and local agencies that provide or pay for services required under this part for children with disabilities.

(b) The policies and procedures referred to in paragraph (a) of this section must—

(1) Describe the role that each of those agencies plays in providing or paying for services required under this part for children with disabilities; and

(2) Provide for the development and implementation of interagency agreements that—

(i) Define the financial responsibility of each agency for providing children with disabilities with FAPE;

(ii) Establish procedures for resolving interagency disputes among agencies that are parties to the agreements; and

(iii) Establish procedures under which LEAs may initiate proceedings in order to secure reimbursement from agencies that are parties to the agreement or otherwise implement the provisions of the agreements.

(Authority: 20 U.S.C. 1413(a)(13))

(Approved by the Office of Management and Budget under control number 1820-0030)

[57 FR 44798, Sept. 29, 1992, as amended at 58 FR 13528, Mar. 11, 1993]

§ 300.153 Personnel standards.

(a) As used in this part:

(1) "Appropriate professional requirements in the State" means entry level requirements that—

(i) Are based on the highest requirements in the State applicable to the profession or discipline in which a person is providing special education or related services; and

(ii) Establish suitable qualifications for personnel providing special education and related services under this part to children and youth with disabilities who are served by State, local, and private agencies (see § 300.2).

(2) "Highest requirements in the State applicable to a specific profession or discipline" means the highest entry-level academic degree needed for any State approved or recognized certification, licensing, registration, or other comparable requirements that apply to that profession or discipline;

(3) "Profession or discipline" means a specific occupational category that—

(i) Provides special education and related services to children with disabilities under this part;

(ii) Has been established or designated by the State; and

(iii) Has a required scope of responsibility and degree of supervision.

(4) "State approved or recognized certification, licensing, registration, or other comparable requirements" means the requirements that a State legislature either has enacted or has authorized a State agency to promulgate through rules to establish the entry-level standards for employment in a specific profession or discipline in that State.

(b)(1) Each State plan must include policies and procedures relating to the establishment and maintenance of standards to ensure that personnel necessary to carry out the purposes of this part are appropriately and adequately prepared and trained.

(2) The policies and procedures required in paragraph (b)(1) of this section must provide for the establishment and maintenance of standards that are consistent with any State approved or recognized certification, licensing, registration, or other comparable requirements that apply to the profession or discipline in which a person is providing special education or related services.

(c) To the extent that a State's standards for a profession or discipline, including standards for temporary or emergency certification, are not based on the highest requirements in the State applicable to a specific profession or discipline, the State plan must include the steps the State is taking and the procedures for notifying public agencies and personnel of those steps and the timelines it has established for the retraining or hiring of personnel to meet appropriate professional requirements in the State.

(d)(1) In meeting the requirements in paragraphs (b) and (c) of this section, a determination must be made about the status of personnel standards in the State. That determination must be based on current information that accurately describes, for each profession or discipline in which personnel are providing special education or related services, whether the applicable standards are consistent with the highest requirements in the State for that profession or discipline.

(2) The information required in paragraph (d)(1) of this section must be on file in the SEA, and available to the public.

(e) In identifying the highest requirements in the State for purposes of this section, the requirements of all State statutes and the rules of all State agencies applicable to serving children and youth with disabilities must be considered.

(Authority: 20 U.S.C. 1413(a)(14))

Note: The regulations require that the State use its own existing highest requirements to determine the standards appropriate to personnel who provide special education and related services under this part. The regulations do not require States to set any specified training standard, such as a master's degree, for employment of personnel who provide services under this part. In some instances, States will be required to show that they are taking steps to retrain or to hire personnel to meet the standards adopted by the SEA that are based on requirements for practice in a specific profession or discipline that were established by other State agencies. States in this position need not, however, require personnel providing services under this part to apply for and obtain the license, registration, or other comparable credential required by other agencies of individuals in that profession or discipline. The regulations permit each State to determine the specific occupational categories required to provide special education and related services and to revise or expand these categories as needed. The professions or disciplines defined by the State need not be limited to traditional occupational categories.

(Approved by the Office of Management and Budget under control number 1820-0030)

[57 FR 44798, Sept. 29, 1992, as amended at 58 FR 13528, Mar. 11, 1993]

§ 300.154 Transition of individuals from Part H to Part B

Each State plan must set forth policies and procedures relating to the smooth transition for those individuals participating in the early intervention program under Part H of the Act who will participate in preschool programs assisted under this part, including a method of ensuring that when a child turns age 3 an IEP, or, if consistent with sections 614(a)(5) and 677(d) of the Act, an individualized family service plan, has been developed and implemented by the child's third birthday.

(Authority: 20 U.S.C. 1413(a)(15))

Local Educational Agency Applications— General

§ 300.180 Submission of application.

In order to receive payments under Part B of the Act for any fiscal year, an LEA must submit an application to the SEA.

(Authority: 20 U.S.C. 1414(a))

(Approved by the Office of Management and Budget under control number 1820-0600)

[57 FR 44798, Sept. 29, 1992, as amended at 58 FR 13528, Mar. 11, 1993]

§ 300.181 [Reserved]

§ 300.182 The excess cost requirement.

An LEA may only use funds under part B of the Act for the excess costs of providing special education and related services for children with disabilities.

(Authority: 20 U.S.C. 1414(a)(1), (a)(2)(B)(i))

§ 300.183 Meeting the excess cost requirement.

(a) An LEA meets the excess cost requirement if it has on the average spent at least the amount determined under § 300.184 for the education of each of its children with disabilities. This amount may not include capital outlay or debt service.

(Authority: 20 U.S.C. 1402(20); 1414(a)(1))

Note: The excess cost requirement means that the LEA must spend a certain minimum amount for the education of its children with disabilities before Part B funds are used. This ensures that children served with part B funds have at least the same average amount spent on them, from sources other than Part B, as do the children in the school district taken as a whole.

The minimum amount that must be spent for the education of children with disabilities is computed under a statutory formula. Section 300.184 implements this formula and gives a step-by-step method to determine the minimum amount. Excess costs are those costs of special education and related services that exceed the minimum amount. Therefore, if an LEA can show that it has (on the average) spent the minimum amount for the education of each of its children with disabilities, it has met the excess cost requirement, and all additional costs are excess costs. Part B funds can then be used to pay for these additional costs, subject to the other requirements of Part B (priorities, etc.). In the Note under § 300.184, there is an example of how the minimum amount is computed.

§ 300.184 Excess costs—computation of minimum amount.

The minimum average amount that an LEA must spend under § 300.183 for the education of each of its children with disabilities is computed as follows:

(a) Add all expenditures of the LEA in the preceding school year, except capital outlay and debt service—

(1) For elementary school students, if the child with a disability is an elementary school student; or

(2) For secondary school students, if the child with a disability is a secondary school student.

(b) From this amount, subtract the total of the following amounts spent for elementary school students or for secondary school students, as the case may be—

(1) Amounts the agency spent in the preceding school year from funds awarded under part B of the Act and Titles I and VII of the Elementary and Secondary Education Act of 1965; and

(2) Amounts from State and local funds that the agency spent in the preceding school year for—

(i) Programs for children with disabilities;

(ii) Programs to meet the special educational needs of educationally deprived children; and

(iii) Programs of bilingual education for limited English proficient children.

(c) Divide the result under paragraph (b) of this section by the average number of students enrolled in the agency in the preceding school year—

(1) In its elementary schools, if the child with a disability is an elementary school student, or,

(2) In its secondary schools, if the child with a disability is a secondary school student.

(Authority: 20 U.S.C. 1414(a)(1))

Note: The following is an example of how an LEA might compute the average minimum amount it must spend for the education of each of its children with disabilities, under § 300.183. This example follows the formula in § 300.184. Under the statute and regulations, the LEA must make one computation for children with disabilities in its elementary schools and a separate computation for children with disabilities in its secondary schools. The computation for elementary school students with disabilities would be done as follows:

a. First, the LEA must determine its total amount of expenditures for elementary school students from all sources— local, State, and Federal (including Part B)—in the preceding school year. Only capital outlay and debt service are excluded.

Example: An LEA spent the following amounts last year for elementary school students (including its elementary school students with disabilities):

(1) From local tax funds.......................$2,750,000
(2) From State Funds............................7,000,000
(3) From Federal funds......................... 750,000
                                                10,500,000

Of this total, $500,000 was for capital outlay and debt service relating to the education of elementary school students. This must be subtracted from total expenditures:

                                        $10,500,000
              -500,000
Total expenditures for elementary
school students (less capital outlay
and debt service)...............................$10,000,000

b. Next, the LEA must subtract amounts spent for:
(1) Programs for children with disabilities;
(2) Programs to meet the special educational needs of educationally deprived children; and
(3) Programs of bilingual education for limited English proficient children.

These are funds that the LEA actually spent, not funds received last year but carried over for the current school year.

Example: The LEA spent the following amounts for elementary school students last year:

(1) From funds under Chapter 1 of
title I of the Elementary and
Secondary Education Act of 1965..........$300,000
(2) From a special State program
for educationally deprived children 200,000
(3) From a grant under Part B....................200,000
(4) From State funds for the education
of children with disabilities........................500,000
(5) From a locally-funded program for
children with disabilities...........................250,000

(6) From a grant for a bilingual
education program under Title VII
of the Elementary and Secondary
Education Act of 1965...............................150,000

Total..1,600,000

(An LEA would also include any other funds it spent from Federal, State, or local sources for the three basic purposes: Children with disabilities, educationally deprived children, and bilingual education for limited English proficient children.)

This amount is subtracted from the LEA's total expenditure for elementary school students computed above:

$10,000,000
-1,600,000
8,400,000

c. The LEA next must divide by the average number of students enrolled in the elementary schools of the agency last year (including its students with disabilities).

Example: Last year, an average of 7,000 students were enrolled in the agency's elementary schools. This must be divided into the amount computed under the above paragraph: $8,400,000/7,000 students = $1,200/student.

This figure is in the minimum amount the LEA must spend (on the average) for the education of each of its students with disabilities. Funds under Part B may be used only for costs over and above this minimum. In this example, if the LEA has 100 elementary school students with disabilities, it must keep records adequate to show that it has spent at least $120,000 for the education of those students, (100 students times $1,200/student), not including capital outlay and debt service.

This $120,000 may come from any funds except funds under Part B, subject to any legal requirements that govern the use of those other funds.

If the LEA has secondary school students with disabilities, it must do the same computation for them. However the amounts used in the computation would be those the LEA spent last year for the education of secondary school students, rather than for elementary school students.

§ 300.185 Computation of excess costs— consolidated application.

The minimum average amount under § 300.183; if two or more LEAs submit a consolidated application, is the average of the combined minimum average amounts determined under § 300.184 in those agencies for elementary or secondary school students, as the case may be.

(Authority: 20 U.S.C. 1414(a)(1))

§ 300.186 Excess costs—limitation on use of Part B funds.

(a) The excess cost requirement prevents an LEA from using funds provided under Part B of the Act to pay for all of the costs directly attributable to the education of a child with a disability, subject to paragraph (b) of this section.

(b) The excess cost requirement does not prevent an LEA from using Part B funds to pay for all of the costs directly attributable to the education of a child with a disability in any of the age ranges three, four, five, eighteen, nineteen, twenty, or twenty-one, if no local or State funds are available for nondisabled children in that age

range. However, the LEA must comply with the nonsupplanting and other requirements of this part in providing the education and services.

(Authority: 20 U.S.C. 1402(20); 1414(a)(1))

§§ 300.187-300.189 [Reserved]

§ 300.190 Consolidated applications.
(a) [Reserved]

(b) *Required applications.* An SEA may require LEAs to submit a consolidated
application for payments under Part B of the Act if the SEA determines that an
individual application submitted by an LEA will be disapproved because—

(1) The agency's entitlement is less than the $7,500 minimum required by
section 611(c)(4)(A)(i) of the Act (§ 300.360(a)(1)); or

(2) The agency is unable to establish and maintain programs of sufficient size
and scope to effectively meet the educational needs of children with disabilities.

(c) *Size and scope of program.* The SEA shall establish standards and procedures
for determinations under paragraph (b)(2) of this section.

(Authority: 20 U.S.C. 1414(c)(1))

§ 300.191 [Reserved]

§ 300.192 State regulation of consolidated applications.
(a) The SEA shall issue regulations with respect to consolidated applications
submitted under this part.

(b) The SEA's regulations must—

(1) Be consistent with sections 612(1)-(7) and 613(a) of the Act; and

(2) Provide participating LEAs with joint responsibilities for implementing
programs receiving payments under this part.

(Authority: 20 U.S.C. 1414(c)(2)(B))

(c) If an IEU is required under State law to carry out this part, the joint
responsibilities given to LEAs under paragraph (b)(2) of this section do not apply to
the administration and disbursement of any payments received by the IEU. Those
administrative responsibilities must be carried out exclusively by the IEU.

(Authority: 20 U.S.C. 1414(c)(2)(C))

(Approved by the Office of Management and Budget under control number
1820-0600)

[57 FR 44798, Sept. 29, 1992, as amended at 58 FR 13528, Mar. 11, 1993]

§ 300.193 State educational agency approval; disapproval.
(a)-(b) [Reserved]

(c) In carrying out its functions under this section, each SEA shall consider any
decision resulting from a hearing under §§ 300.506-300.513 that is adverse to the LEA
involved in the decision.

(Authority: 20 U.S.C. 1414(b)(3))

§ 300.194 Withholding.

(a) If an SEA, after giving reasonable notice and an opportunity for a hearing to an LEA, decides that the LEA in the administration of an application approved by the SEA has failed to comply with any requirement in the application, the SEA, after giving notice to the LEA, shall—

(1) Make no further payments to the LEA until the SEA is satisfied that there is no longer any failure to comply with the requirement; or

(2) Consider its decision in its review of any application made by the LEA under § 300.180; or

(3) Both.

(b) [Reserved]

(Authority: 20 U.S.C. 1414(b)(2))

Local Educational Agency Applications— Contents

§ 300.220 Child identification.

Each application must include procedures that ensure that all children residing within the jurisdiction of the LEA who have disabilities, regardless of the severity of their disability, and who are in need of special education and related services, are identified, located, and evaluated, including a practical method of determining which children are currently receiving needed special education and related services and which children are not currently receiving needed special education and related services.

(Authority: 20 U.S.C. 1414(a)(1)(A))

Note: The LEA is responsible for ensuring that all children with disabilities within its jurisdiction are identified, located, and evaluated, including children in all public and private agencies and institutions within that jurisdiction. Collection and use of data are subject to the confidentiality requirements in §§ 300.560-300.576.

(Approved by the Office of Management and Budget under control number 1820-0600)

[57 FR 44798, Sept. 29, 1992, as amended at 58 FR 13528, Mar. 11, 1993]

§ 300.221 Confidentiality of personally identifiable information.

Each application must include policies and procedures that ensure that the criteria in §§ 300.560-300.574 are met.

(Authority: 20 U.S.C. 1414(a)(1)(B))

§ 300.222 Full educational opportunity goal—timetable.

Each application must—(a) Include a goal of providing full educational opportunity to all children with disabilities, aged birth through 21; and

(b) Include a detailed timetable for accomplishing the goal.

(Authority: 20 U.S.C. 1414(a)(1)(C), (D))

(Approved by the Office of Management and Budget under control number 1820-0600)

[57 FR 44798, Sept. 29, 1992, as amended at 58 FR 13528, Mar. 11, 1993]

§ 300.223 Facilities, personnel, and services

Each application must provide a description of the kind and number of facilities, personnel, and services necessary to meet the goal in § 300.222.

(Authority: 20 U.S.C. 1414(a)(1)(E))
(Approved by the Office of Management and Budget under control number 1820-0600)
[57 FR 44798, Sept. 29, 1992, as amended at 58 FR 13528, Mar. 11, 1993]

§ 300.224 Personnel development.

Each application must include procedures for the implementation and use of the comprehensive system of personnel development established by the SEA under § 300.139.

(Authority: 20 U.S.C. 1414(a)(1)(C)(i))
(Approved by the Office of Management and Budget under control number 1820-0600)
[57 FR 44798, Sept. 29, 1992, as amended at 58 FR 13528, Mar. 11, 1993]

§ 300.225 Priorities.

Each application must include priorities that meet the requirements of §§ 300.320-300.324.

(Authority: 20 U.S.C. 1414(a)(1)(C)(ii))
(Approved by the Office of Management and Budget under control number 1820-0600)
[57 FR 44798, Sept. 29, 1992, as amended at 58 FR 13528, Mar. 11, 1993]

§ 300.226 Parent involvement.

Each application must include procedures to ensure that, in meeting the goal under § 300.222, the LEA makes provision for participation of and consultation with parents or guardians of children with disabilities.

(Authority: 20 U.S.C. 1414(a)(1)(C)(iii))
(Approved by the Office of Management and Budget under control number 1820-0600)
[57 FR 44798, Sept. 29, 1992, as amended at 58 FR 13528, Mar. 11, 1993]

§ 300.227 Participation in regular education programs.

(a) Each application must include procedures to ensure that to the maximum extent practicable, and consistent with §§ 300.550-300.553, the LEA provides special services to enable children with disabilities to participate in regular educational programs.

(b) Each application must describe—

(1) The types of alternative placements that are available for children with disabilities[;] and

(2) The number of children with disabilities within each disability category who are served in each type of placement.

(Authority: 20 U.S.C. 1414(a)(1)(C)(iv))

(Approved by the Office of Management and Budget under control number 1820-0600)

[57 FR 44798, Sept. 29, 1992, as amended at 58 FR 13528, Mar. 11, 1993]

§ 300.228 [Reserved]

§ 300.229 Excess cost.

Each application must provide assurance satisfactory to the SEA that the LEA uses funds provided under Part B of the Act only for costs that exceed the amount computed under § 300.184 and that are directly attributable to the education of children with disabilities.

(Authority: 20 U.S.C. 1414(a)(2)(B))

§ 300.230 Nonsupplanting.

(a) Each application must provide assurance satisfactory to the SEA that the LEA uses funds provided under Part B of the Act to supplement and, to the extent practicable, increase the level of State and local funds expended for the education of children with disabilities, and in no case to supplant those State and local funds.

(b) To meet the requirement in paragraph (a) of this section, the total amount or average per capita amount of State and local school funds budgeted by the LEA for expenditures in the current fiscal year for the education of children with disabilities must be at least equal to the total amount or average per capita amount of State and local school funds actually expended for the education of children with disabilities in the most recent preceding fiscal year for which the information is available. Allowance may be made for—

(1) Decreases in enrollment of children with disabilities; and

(2) Unusually large amounts of funds expended for such long-term purposes as the acquisition of equipment and the construction of school facilities.

(Authority: 20 U.S.C. 1414(a)(2)(B))

§ 300.231 Comparable services.

(a) Each application must provide assurance satisfactory to the SEA that the LEA meets the requirements of this section.

(b) An LEA may not use funds under Part B of the Act to provide services to children with disabilities unless the agency uses State and local funds to provide services to those children that, taken as a whole, are at least comparable to services provided to other children with disabilities in that LEA.

(c) Each LEA shall maintain records that show that the LEA meets the requirement in paragraph (b) of this section.

(Authority: 20 U.S.C. 1414(a)(2)(C))

Note: Under the "comparability" requirement, if State and local funds are used to provide certain services, those services must be provided with State and local funds to all children with disabilities in the LEA who need them. Part B funds may then be used to supplement existing services, or to provide additional services to meet special needs. This, of course, is subject to the other requirements of the Act, including the priorities under §§ 300.320-300.324.

(Approved by the Office of Management and Budget under control number 1820-0600)

[57 FR 44798, Sept. 29, 1992, as amended at 58 FR 13528, Mar. 11, 1993]

§§ 300.232-300.234 [Reserved]

§ 300.235 Individualized education program.

Each application must include procedures to assure that the LEA complies with §§ 300.340-300.350.

(Authority: 20 U.S.C. 1414(a)(5))

§ 300.236 [Reserved]

§ 300.237 Procedural safeguards.

Each application must provide assurance satisfactory to the SEA that the LEA has procedural safeguards that meet the requirements of §§ 300.500-300.515.

(Authority: 20 U.S.C. 1414(a)(7))

§ 300.238 Use of Part B funds.

Each application must describe how the LEA will use the funds under Part B of the Act during the next school year.

(Authority: 20 U.S.C. 1414(a))
(Approved by the Office of Management and Budget under control number 1820-0600)
[57 FR 44798, Sept. 29, 1992, as amended at 58 FR 13528, Mar. 11, 1993]

§ 300.239 [Reserved]

§ 300.240 Other requirements.

Each local application must include additional procedures and information that the SEA may require in order to meet the State plan requirements of §§ 300.121-300.153.

(Authority: 20 U.S.C. 1414(a)(6))
(Approved by the Office of Management and Budget under control number 1820-0600)
[57 FR 44798, Sept. 29, 1992, as amended at 58 FR 13528, Mar. 11, 1993]

Application From Secretary of the Interior

§ 300.260 Submission of application; approval.

(a) In order to receive a grant under this part, the Secretary of the Interior shall submit an application that—

(1) Meets the requirements of section 612(1), 612(2)(C)-(E), 612(4), 612(5), 612(6), and 612(7) of the Act (including monitoring and evaluating activities);

(2) Meets the requirements of section 613(a), (2), (3), (4)(B), (5), (6), (7), (10), (11), (12), (13), (14), and (15), 613(b), and 613(e) of the Act;

(3) Meets the requirements of section 614(a)(1)(A)-(B), (2)(A), (C), (3), (4), (5), and (7) of the Act;

(4) Meets the requirements of this part that implement the sections of the Act listed in paragraphs (a)(1)-(3) of this section.

(5) Includes a description of how the Secretary of the Interior will coordinate the provision of services under this part with LEAs, tribes and tribal organizations, and other private and Federal service providers;

(6) Includes an assurance that there have been public hearings, adequate notice of such hearings, and an opportunity for comment afforded to members of tribes, tribal governing bodies, and affected local school boards before the adoption of the policies, programs, and procedures required under paragraphs (a)(1)-(3) of this section;

(7) Includes an assurance that the Secretary of the Interior will provide such information as the Secretary may require to comply with section 618(b)(1) of the Act, including data on the number of children and youth with disabilities served and the types and amounts of services provided and needed;

(8) Includes an assurance that, by October 1, 1992, the Secretaries of the Interior and Health and Human Services will enter into a memorandum of agreement, to be provided to the Secretary, for the coordination of services, resources, and personnel between their respective Federal, State, and local offices and with SEAs and LEAs and other entities to facilitate the provision of services to Indian children with disabilities residing on or near reservations. That agreement must provide for the apportionment of responsibilities and costs, including, but not limited to, those related to child find, evaluation, diagnosis, remediation or therapeutic measures, and (where appropriate) equipment and medical or personal supplies, or both, as needed for a child to remain in school or a program; and

(9) Includes an assurance that the Department of the Interior will cooperate with the Department of Education in the latter's exercise of monitoring and oversight of this application, and any agreements entered into between the Secretary of the Interior and other entities under the Act and will fulfill its duties under the Act.

(b) Sections 300.581-300.585 apply to grants available to the Secretary of the Interior under this part.

(Authority: 20 U.S.C. 1411(f))

§ 300.261 Public participation.

In the development of the application for the Department of the Interior, the Secretary of the Interior shall provide for public participation consistent with §§ 300.280-300.284.

(Authority: 20 U.S.C. 1411(f))

§ 300.262 Use of Part B funds.

(a)(1) The Department of the Interior may use five percent of its payment under § 300.709 in any fiscal year, or $350,000, whichever is greater, for administrative costs in carrying out the provisions of this part.

(2) The remainder of the payments to the Secretary of the Interior under § 300.709 in any fiscal year must be used in accordance with the priorities under §§ 300.320-300.324.

(b) Payments to the Secretary of the Interior under § 300.710 must be used in accordance with that section.

(Authority: 20 U.S.C. 1411(f))

§ 300.263 Applicable regulations

The Secretary of the Interior shall comply with the requirements of §§ 300.301-300.303, §§ 300.305-300.307, and §§ 300.340-300.347, § 300.350, §§ 300.360-300.383, §§ 300.400-300.402, §§ 300.500-300.585, §§ 300.600-300.621, and §§ 300.660-300.662.

(Authority: 20 U.S.C. 1411(f)(2))

Public Participation

§ 300.280 Public hearings before adopting a State plan.

Prior to its adoption of a State plan, the SEA shall—
(a) Make the plan available to the general public;
(b) Hold public hearings; and
(c) Provide an opportunity for comment by the general public on the plan.

(Authority: 20 U.S.C. 1412(7))
(Approved by the Office of Management and Budget under control number 1820-0600)
[57 FR 44798, Sept. 29, 1992, as amended at 58 FR 13528, Mar. 11, 1993]

§ 300.281 Notice.

(a) The SEA shall provide notice to the general public of the public hearings.
(b) The notice must be in sufficient detail to inform the general public about—
(1) The purpose and scope of the State plan and its relation to Part B of the Act;
(2) The availability of the State plan;
(3) The date, time, and location of each public hearing;
(4) The procedures for submitting written comments about the plan; and
(5) The timetable for developing the final plan and submitting it to the Secretary for approval.
(c) The notice must be published or announced—
(1) In newspapers or other media, or both, with circulation adequate to notify the general public about the hearings; and
(2) Enough in advance of the date of the hearings to afford interested parties throughout the State a reasonable opportunity to participate.

(Authority: 20 U.S.C. 1412(7))
(Approved by the Office of Management and Budget under control number 1820-0600)
[57 FR 44798, Sept. 29, 1992, as amended at 58 FR 13528, Mar. 11, 1993]

§ 300.282 Opportunity to participate; comment period.

(a) The SEA shall conduct the public hearings at times and places that afford interested parties throughout the State a reasonable opportunity to participate.
(b) The plan must be available for comment for a period of at least 30 days following the date of the notice under § 300.281.

(Authority: 20 U.S.C. 1412(7))

§ 300.283 Review of public comments before adopting plan.
Before adopting its State plan, the SEA shall—
(a) Review and consider all public comments; and
(b) Make any necessary modifications in the plan.

(Authority: 20 U.S.C. 1412(7))

§ 300.284 Publication and availability of approved plan.
After the Secretary approves a State plan, the SEA shall give notice in newspapers or other media, or both, that the plan is approved. The notice must name places throughout the State where the plan is available for access by any interested person.

(Authority: 20 U.S.C. 1412(7))

Subpart C—Services

Free Appropriate Public Education

§ 300.300 Timelines for free appropriate public education.
(a) *General.* Each State shall ensure that FAPE is available to all children with disabilities aged 3 through 18 within the State not later than September 1, 1978, and to all children with disabilities aged 3 through 21 within the State not later than September 1, 1980.
(b) *Age ranges 3-5 and 18-21.* This paragraph provides rules for applying the requirement in paragraph (a) of this section to children with disabilities aged 3, 4, 5, 18, 19, 20, and 21:
(1) If State law or a court order requires the State to provide education for children with disabilities in any disability category in any of these age groups, the State must make FAPE available to all children with disabilities of the same age who have that disability.
(2) If a public agency provides education to nondisabled children in any of these age groups it must make FAPE available to at least a proportionate number of children with disabilities of the same age.
(3) If a public agency provides education to 50 percent or more of its children with disabilities in any disability category in any of these age groups, it must make FAPE available to all its children with disabilities of the same age who have that disability. This provision does not apply to children aged 3 through 5 for any fiscal year for which the State receives a grant under section 619(a)(1) of the Act.
(4) If a public agency provides education to a child with a disability in any of these age groups, it must make FAPE available to that child and provide that child and his or her parents all of the rights under Part B of the Act and this part.
(5) A State is not required to make FAPE available to a child with a disability in one of these age groups if:
(i) State law expressly prohibits, or does not authorize, the expenditure of public funds to provide education to nondisabled children in that age group; or
(ii) The requirement is inconsistent with a court order that governs the provision of free public education to children with disabilities in that State.
(c) *Children aged 3 through 21 on reservations.* With the exception of children identified in § 300.709(a)(1) and (2), the SEA shall be responsible for ensuring that all of the requirements of Part B of the Act are implemented for all children aged 3 through 21 on reservations.

(Authority: 20 U.S.C. 1411(f), 1412(2)(B); S. Rep. No. 94-168 p. 19 (1975))

Note 1: The requirement to make FAPE available applies to all children with disabilities within the State who are in the age ranges required under § 300.300 and who need special education and related services. This includes children with disabilities already in school and children with less severe disabilities, who are not covered under the priorities under § 300.321.

Note 2: In order to be in compliance with §300.300, each State must ensure that the requirement to identify, locate, and evaluate all children with disabilities is fully implemented by public agencies throughout the State. This means that before September 1, 1978, every child who has been referred or is on a waiting list for evaluation (including children in school as well as those not receiving an education) must be evaluated in accordance with §§ 300.530-300.533. If, as a result of the evaluation, it is determined that a child needs special education and related services, an IEP must be developed for the child by September 1, 1978, and all other applicable requirements of this part must be met.

Note 3. The requirement to identify, locate, and evaluate children with disabilities (commonly referred to as the "child find system") was enacted on August 21, 1974, under Pub. L. 93-380. While each State needed time to establish and implement its child find system, the four year period between August 21, 1974, and September 1, 1978, is considered to be sufficient to ensure that the system is fully operational and effective on a State-wide basis.

Under the statute, the age range for the child find requirement (0-21) is greater than the mandated age range for providing FAPE. One reason for the broader age requirement under "child find" is to enable States to be aware of and plan for younger children who will require special education and related services. It also ties in with the full educational opportunity goal requirement, that has the same age range as child find. Moreover, while a State is not required to provide FAPE to children with disabilities below the age ranges mandated under § 300.300, the State may, at its discretion, extend services to those children, subject to the priority requirements of §§ 300.320-300.324.

§ 300.301 Free appropriate public education— methods and payments.

(a) Each State may use whatever State, local, Federal, and private sources of support are available in the State to meet the requirements of this part. For example, when it is necessary to place a child with a disability in a residential facility, a State could use joint agreements between the agencies involved for sharing the cost of that placement.

(b) Nothing in this part relieves an insurer or similar third party from an otherwise valid obligation to provide or to pay for services provided to a child with a disability.

(Authority: 20 U.S.C. 1401(18); 1412(2)(B))

§ 300.302 Residential placement.

If placement in a public or private residential program is necessary to provide special education and related services to a child with a disability, the program, including non-medical care and room and board, must be at no cost to the parents of the child.

(Authority: 20 U.S.C. 1412(2)(B); 1413(a)(4)(B))

Note: This requirement applies to placements which are made by public agencies for educational purposes, and includes placements in State-operated schools for children with disabilities, such as a State school for students with deafness or students with blindness.

§ 300.303 Proper functioning of hearing aids.

Each public agency shall ensure that the hearing aids worn by children with hearing impairments including deafness in school are functioning properly.

(Authority: 20 U.S.C. 1412(2)(B))

Note: The report of the House of Representatives on the 1978 appropriation bill includes the following statement regarding hearing aids:

In its report on the 1976 appropriation bill the Committee expressed concern about the condition of hearing aids worn by children in public schools. A study done at the Committee's direction by the Bureau of Education for the Handicapped reveals that up to one-third of the hearing aids are malfunctioning. Obviously, the Committee expects the Office of Education will ensure that hearing impaired school children are receiving adequate professional assessment, follow-up and services.

(Authority: House Report No. 95-381, p. 67 (1977))

§ 300.304 Full educational opportunity goal.

(a) Each SEA shall ensure that each public agency establishes and implements a goal of providing full educational opportunity to all children with disabilities in the area served by the public agency.

(b) Subject to the priority requirements of §§ 300.320-300.324, an SEA or LEA may use Part B funds to provide facilities, personnel, and services necessary to meet the full educational opportunity goal.

(Authority: 20 U.S.C. 1412(2)(A); 1414(a)(1)(C))

Note: In meeting the full educational opportunity goal, the Congress also encouraged LEAs to include artistic and cultural activities in programs supported under this part, subject to the priority requirements of §§ 300.320-300.324. This point is addressed in the following statements from the Senate Report on Public Law 94-142:

The use of the arts as a teaching tool for the handicapped has long been recognized as a viable, effective way not only of teaching special skills, but also of reaching youngsters who had otherwise been unteachable. The Committee envisions that programs under this bill could well include an arts component and, indeed, urges that local educational agencies include the arts in programs for the handicapped funded under this Act. Such a program could cover both appreciation of the arts by the handicapped youngsters, and the utilization of the arts as a teaching tool per se.

Museum settings have often been another effective tool in the teaching of handicapped children. For example, the Brooklyn Museum has been a leader in developing exhibits utilizing the heightened tactile sensory skill of the blind. Therefore, in light of the national policy concerning the use of museums in federally supported education programs enunciated in the Education Amendments of 1974, the Committee also urges local educational agencies to include museums in programs for the handicapped funded under this Act.

(Authority: Sen. Rep. No. 94-168. p. 13 (1975))

§ 300.305 Program options.

Each public agency shall take steps to ensure that its children with disabilities have available to them the variety of educational programs and services available to nondisabled children in the area served by the agency, including art, music, industrial arts, consumer and homemaking education, and vocational education.

(Authority: 20 U.S.C. 1412(2)(A); 1414(a)(l)(C))

Note: The above list of program options is not exhaustive, and could include any program or activity in which nondisabled students participate.

§ 300.306 Nonacademic services.

(a) Each public agency shall take steps to provide nonacademic and extracurricular services and activities in such manner as is necessary to afford children with disabilities an equal opportunity for participation in those services and activities.

(b) Nonacademic and extracurricular services and activities may include counseling services, athletics, transportation, health services, recreational activities, special interest groups or clubs sponsored by the public agency, referrals to agencies that provide assistance to individuals with disabilities, and employment of students, including both employment by the public agency and assistance in making outside employment available.

(Authority: 20 U.S.C. 1412(2)(A); 1414(a)(1)(C))

§ 300.307 Physical education.

(a) *General.* Physical education services, specially designed if necessary, must be made available to every child with a disability receiving FAPE.

(b) *Regular physical education.* Each child with a disability must be afforded the opportunity to participate in the regular physical education program available to nondisabled children unless—

(1) The child is enrolled full time in a separate facility; or

(2) The child needs specially designed physical education, as prescribed in the child's IEP.

(c) *Special physical education.* If specially designed physical education is prescribed in a child's IEP, the public agency responsible for the education of that child shall provide the services directly, or make arrangements for those services to be provided through other public or private programs.

(d) *Education in separate facilities.* The public agency responsible for the education of a child with a disability who is enrolled in a separate facility shall ensure that the child receives appropriate physical education services in compliance with paragraphs (a) and (c) of this section.

(Authority: 20 U.S.C. 1401(a)(16); 1412(5)(B); 1414(a)(6))

Note: The Report of the House of Representatives on Public Law 94-142 includes the following statement regarding physical education:

Special education as set forth in the Committee bill includes instruction in physical education, which is provided as a matter of course to all non-handicapped children enrolled in public elementary and secondary schools. The Committee is concerned that although these services are available to and required of all children in our school systems, they are often viewed as a luxury for handicapped children.

*   *   *   *   *

The Committee expects the Commissioner of Education to take whatever action is necessary to assure that physical education services are available to all handicapped children, and has specifically included physical education within the definition of special education to make clear that the Committee expects such services, specially designed where necessary, to be provided as an integral part of the educational program of every handicapped child.

(Authority: H. R. Rep. No. 94-332, p. 9 (1975))

§ 300.308 Assistive Technology.

Each public agency shall ensure that assistive technology devices or assistive technology services, or both, as those terms are defined in §§ 300.5-300.6, are made available to a child with a disability if required as a part of the child's—

(a) Special education under § 300.17;

(b) Related services under § 300.16; or

(c) Supplementary aids and services under § 300.550(b)(2).

(Authority: 20 U.S.C. 1412(2), (5)(B))

Priorities in the Use of Part B Funds

§ 300.320 Definitions of first priority children and second priority children.

For the purposes of §§ 300.321-300.324, the term:

(a) "First priority children" means children with disabilities who—

(1) Are in an age group for which the State must make FAPE available under § 300.300; and

(2) Are not receiving any education.

(b) "Second priority children" means children with disabilities, within each disability category, with the most severe disabilities who are receiving an inadequate education.

(Authority: 20 U.S.C. 1412(3))

Note 1: After September 1, 1978, there should be no second priority children, since States must ensure, as a condition of receiving Part B funds for fiscal year 1979, that all children with disabilities will have FAPE available by that date.

Note 2: The term "free appropriate public education," as defined in § 300.8, means special education and related services that *** "are provided in conformity with an IEP" ***.

New first priority children will continue to be found by the State after September 1, 1978 through on-going efforts to identify, locate, and evaluate all children with disabilities.

§ 300.321 Priorities.

(a) Each SEA and LEA shall use funds provided under Part B of the Act in the following order of priorities:

(1) To provide FAPE to first priority children, including the identification, location, and evaluation of first priority children.

(2) To provide FAPE to second priority children, including the identification, location, and evaluation of second priority children.

(3) To meet the other requirements of this part.

(b) The requirements of paragraph (a) of this section do not apply to funds that the State uses for administration under § 300.620.

(Authority: 20 U.S.C. 1411(b)(1)(B), (b)(2)(B), (c)(1)(B), (c)(2)(A)(ii))

Note: SEAs as well as LEAs must use Part B funds (except the portion used for State administration) for the priorities. A State may have to set aside a portion of its Part B allotment to be able to serve newly identified first priority children.

After September 1, 1978, Part B funds may be used—

(1) To continue supporting child identification, location, and evaluation activities;

(2) To provide FAPE to newly identified first priority children;

(3) To meet the full educational opportunity goal required under § 300.304, including employing additional personnel and providing inservice training, in order to increase the level, intensity and quality of services provided to individual children with disabilities; and

(4) To meet the other requirements of Part B.

§ 300.322 [Reserved]

§ 300.323 Services to other children.

If an SEA or an LEA is providing FAPE to all of its first priority children, that State or LEA may use funds provided under Part B of the Act—

(a) To provide FAPE to children with disabilities who are not receiving any education and who are in the age groups not covered under § 300.300 in that State; or

(b) To provide FAPE to second priority children; or

(c) Both.

(Authority: 20 U.S.C. 1411(b)(1)(B), (b)(2)(B), (c)(2)(A)(ii))

§ 300.324 Application of local educational agency to use funds for the second priority.

An LEA may use funds provided under Part B of the Act for second priority children, if it provides assurance satisfactory to the SEA in its application (or an amendment to its application)—

(a) That all first priority children have FAPE available to them;

(b) That the LEA has a system for the identification, location, and evaluation of children with disabilities, as described in its application; and

(c) That whenever a first priority child is identified, located, and evaluated, the LEA makes FAPE available to the child.

(Authority: 20 U.S.C. 1411 (b)(1)(B), (c)(1)(B); 1414(a)(1)(C)(ii))

Individualized Education Programs

§ 300.340 Definitions.

(a) As used in this part, the term "individualized education program" means a written statement for a child with a disability that is developed and implemented in accordance with §§ 300.341-300.350.

(b) As used in §§ 300.346 and 300.347, "participating agency" means a State or local agency, other than the public agency responsible for a student's education, that is financially and legally responsible for providing transition services to the student.

(Authority: 20 U.S.C. 1401(a)(20))

§ 300.341 State educational agency responsibility.

(a) *Public agencies.* The SEA shall ensure that each public agency develops and implements an IEP for each of its children with disabilities.

(b) *Private schools and facilities.* The SEA shall ensure that an IEP is developed and implemented for each child with a disability who—

(1) Is placed in or referred to a private school or facility by a public agency; or

(2) Is enrolled in a parochial or other private school and receives special education or related services from a public agency.

(Authority: 20 U.S.C. 1412(4), (6); 1413(a)(4))

Note: This section applies to all public agencies, including other State agencies (e.g., departments of mental health and welfare), that provide special education to a child with a disability either directly, by contract or through other arrangements. Thus, if a State welfare agency contracts with a private school or facility to provide special education to a child with a disability, that agency would be responsible for ensuring that an IEP is developed for the child.

(Approved by the Office of Management and Budget under control number 1820-0030)

[57 FR 44798, Sept. 29, 1992, as amended at 58 FR 13528, Mar. 11, 1993]

§ 300.342 When individualized education programs must be in effect.

(a) At the beginning of each school year, each public agency shall have in effect an IEP for every child with a disability who is receiving special education from that agency.

(b) An IEP must—

(1) Be in effect before special education and related services are provided to a child; and

(2) Be implemented as soon as possible following the meetings under § 300.343.

(Authority: 20 U.S.C. 1412 (2)(B), (4), (6); 1414(a)(5); Pub. L. 94-142, sec. 8(c) (1975))

Note: Under paragraph (b)(2) of this section, it is expected that the IEP of a child with a disability will be implemented immediately following the meetings under § 300.343. An exception to this would be (1) when the meetings occur during the summer or a vacation period, or (2) where there are circumstances that require a short delay (e.g., working out transportation arrangements). However, there can be no undue delay in providing special education and related services to the child.

§ 300.343 Meetings.

(a) *General.* Each public agency is responsible for initiating and conducting meetings for the purpose of developing, reviewing, and revising the IEP of a child with a disability (or, if consistent with State policy and at the discretion of the LEA, and with the concurrence of the parents, an individualized family service plan described in section 677(d) of the Act for each child with a disability, aged 3 through 5).

(b) [Reserved]

(c) *Timeline.* A meeting to develop an IEP for a child must be held within 30 calendar days of a determination that the child needs special education and related services.

(d) *Review.* Each public agency shall initiate and conduct meetings to review each child's IEP periodically and, if appropriate, revise its provisions. A meeting must be held for this purpose at least once a year.

(Authority: 20 U.S.C. 1412(2)(B), (4), (6); 1414(a)(5))

Note: The dates on which agencies must have IEPs in effect are specified in § 300.342 (the beginning of each school year). However, except for new children with disabilities (i.e., those evaluated and determined to need special education and related services for the first time), the timing of meetings to develop, review, and revise IEPs is left to the discretion of each agency.

In order to have IEPs in effect at the beginning of the school year, agencies could hold meetings at the end of the preceding school year or during the summer prior to the next school year. Meetings may be held any time throughout the year, as long as IEPs are in effect at the beginning of each school year.

The statute requires agencies to hold a meeting at least once each year in order to review and, if appropriate, revise each child's IEP. The timing of those meetings could be on the anniversary date of the child's last IEP meeting, but this is left to the discretion of the agency.

§ 300.344 Participants in meetings.

(a) *General.* The public agency shall ensure that each meeting includes the following participants:

(1) A representative of the public agency, other than the child's teacher, who is qualified to provide, or supervise the provision of, special education.

(2) The child's teacher.

(3) One or both of the child's parents, subject to § 300.345.

(4) The child, if appropriate.

(5) Other individuals at the discretion of the parent or agency.

(b) *Evaluation personnel.* For a child with a disability who has been evaluated for the first time, the public agency shall ensure—

(1) That a member of the evaluation team participates in the meeting; or

(2) That the representative of the public agency, the child's teacher, or some other person is present at the meeting, who is knowledgeable about the evaluation procedures used with the child and is familiar with the results of the evaluation.

(c) *Transition services participants.* (1) If a purpose of the meeting is the consideration of transition services for a student, the public agency shall invite—

(i) The student; and

(ii) A representative of any other agency that is likely to be responsible for providing or paying for transition services.

(2) If the student does not attend, the public agency shall take other steps to ensure that the student's preferences and interests are considered; and

(3) If an agency invited to send a representative to a meeting does not do so, the public agency shall take other steps to obtain the participation of the other agency in the planning of any transition services.

(Authority: 20 U.S.C. 1401(a)(19), (a)(20); 1412(2)(B), (4), (6); 1414(a)(5))

Note 1: In deciding which teacher will participate in meetings on a child's IEP, the agency may wish to consider the following possibilities:

(a) For a child with a disability who is receiving special education, the teacher could be the child's special education teacher. If the child's disability is a speech impairment, the teacher could be the speech-language pathologist.

(b) For a child with a disability who is being considered for placement in special education, the teacher could be the child's regular teacher, or a teacher qualified to provide education in the type of program in which the child may be placed, or both.

(c) If the child is not in school or has more than one teacher, the agency may designate which teacher will participate in the meeting.

Either the teacher or the agency representative should be qualified in the area of the child's suspected disability.

For a child whose primary disability is a speech or language impairment, the evaluation personnel participating under paragraph (b)(1) of this section would normally be the speech-language pathologist.

Note 2: Under paragraph (c) of this section, the public agency is required to invite each student to participate in his or her IEP meeting, if a purpose of the meeting is the consideration of transition services for the student. For all students who are 16 years of age or older, one of the purposes of the annual meeting will always be the planning of transition services, since transition services are a required component of the IEP for these students.

For a student younger than age 16, if transition services are initially discussed at a meeting that does not include the student, the public agency is responsible for ensuring that, before a decision about transition services for the student is made, a subsequent IEP meeting is conducted for that purpose, and the student is invited to the meeting.

§ 300.345 Parent participation.

(a) Each public agency shall take steps to ensure that one or both of the parents of the child with a disability are present at each meeting or are afforded the opportunity to participate, including—

(1) Notifying parents of the meeting early enough to ensure that they will have an opportunity to attend; and

(2) Scheduling the meeting at a mutually agreed on time and place.

(b)(1) The notice under paragraph (a)(1) of this section must indicate the purpose, time, and location of the meeting, and who will be in attendance.

(2) If a purpose of the meeting is the consideration of transition services for a student, the notice must also—

(i) Indicate this purpose;

(ii) Indicate that the agency will invite the student; and

(iii) Identify any other agency that will be invited to send a representative.

(c) If neither parent can attend, the public agency shall use other methods to ensure parent participation, including individual or conference telephone calls.

(d) A meeting may be conducted without a parent in attendance if the public agency is unable to convince the parents that they should attend. In this case the public agency must have a record of its attempts to arrange a mutually agreed on time and place such as—

(1) Detailed records of telephone calls made or attempted and the results of those calls;

(2) Copies of correspondence sent to the parents and any responses received; and

(3) Detailed records of visits made to the parent's home or place of employment and the results of those visits.

(e) The public agency shall take whatever action is necessary to ensure that the parent understands the proceedings at a meeting, including arranging for an interpreter for parents with deafness or whose native language is other than English.

(f) The public agency shall give the parent, on request, a copy of the IEP.

(Authority: 20 U.S.C. 1401(a)(20); 1412(2)(B), (4), (6); 1414(a)(5))

Note: The notice in paragraph (a) could also inform parents that they may bring other people to the meeting. As indicated in paragraph (c) of this section, the procedure used to notify parents (whether oral or written or both) is left to the discretion of the agency, but the agency must keep a record of its efforts to contact parents.

(Approved by the Office of Management and Budget under control number 1820-0030)

[57 FR 44798, Sept. 29, 1992, as amended at 58 FR 13528, Mar. 11, 1993]

§ 300.346 Content of individualized education program.

(a) *General.* The IEP for each child must include—

(1) A statement of the child's present levels of educational performance;

(2) A statement of annual goals, including short term instructional objectives;

(3) A statement of the specific special education and related services to be provided to the child and the extent that the child will be able to participate in regular educational programs;

(4) The projected dates for initiation of services and the anticipated duration of the services; and

(5) Appropriate objective criteria and evaluation procedures and schedules for determining, on at least an annual basis, whether the short term instructional objectives are being achieved.

(b) *Transition services.* (1) The IEP for each student, beginning no later than age 16 (and at a younger age, if determined appropriate), must include a statement of the needed transition services as defined in § 300.18, including, if appropriate, a statement of each public agency's and each participating agency's responsibilities or linkages, or both, before the student leaves the school setting.

(2) If the IEP team determines that services are not needed in one or more of the areas specified in § 300.18 (b)(2)(i) through (b)(2)(iii), the IEP must include a statement to that effect and the basis upon which the determination was made.

(Authority: 20 U.S.C. 1401(a)(19), (a)(20); 1412(2)(B), (4), (6); 1414(a)(5))

Note 1: The legislative history of the transition services provisions of the Act suggests that the statement of needed transition services referred to in paragraph (b) of this section should include a commitment by any participating agency to meet any financial responsibility it may have in the provision of transition services. See House Report No. 101-544, p. 11 (1990).

Note 2: With respect to the provisions of paragraph (b) of this section, it is generally expected that the statement of needed transition services will include the areas listed in § 300.18 (b)(2)(i) through (b)(2)(iii). If the IEP team determines that services are not needed in one of those areas, the public agency must implement the requirements in paragraph (b)(2) of this section. Since it is a part of the IEP, the IEP team must reconsider its determination at least annually.

Note 3: Section 602(a)(20) of the Act provides that IEPs must include a statement of needed transition services for students beginning no later than age 16, but permits transition services to students below age 16 (i.e., "* * * and, when determined appropriate for the individual, beginning at age 14 or younger.") Although the statute does not mandate transition services for all students beginning at age 14 or younger, the provision of these services could have a significantly positive effect on the employment and independent living outcomes for many of these students in the future, especially for students who are likely to drop out before age 16. With respect to the provision of transition services to students below age 16, the Report of the House Committee on Education and Labor on Public Law 101-476 includes the following statement:

Although this language leaves the final determination of when to initiate transition services for students under age 16 to the IEP process, it nevertheless makes clear that Congress expects consideration to be given to the need for transition services for some students by age 14 or younger. The Committee encourages that approach because of their concern that age 16 may be too late for many students, particularly those at risk of dropping out of school and those with the most severe disabilities. Even for those students who stay in school until age 18, many will need more than two years of transitional services. Students with disabilities are now dropping out of school before age 16, feeling that the education system has little to offer them. Initiating services at a younger age will be critical.

(House Report No. 101-544, 10 (1990).)

(Approved by the Office of Management and Budget under control number 1820-0030)

[57 FR 44798, Sept. 29, 1992, as amended at 58 FR 13528, Mar. 11, 1993]

§ 300.347 Agency responsibilities for transition services.

(a) If a participating agency fails to provide agreed-upon transition services contained in the IEP of a student with a disability, the public agency responsible for the student's education shall, as soon as possible, initiate a meeting for the purpose of identifying alternative strategies to meet the transition objectives and, if necessary, revising the student's IEP.

(b) Nothing in this part relieves any participating agency, including a State vocational rehabilitation agency, of the responsibility to provide or pay for any transition service that the agency would otherwise provide to students with disabilities who meet the eligibility criteria of that agency.

(Authority: 20 U.S.C. 1401(a)(18), (a)(19), (a)(20); 1412(2)(B))

§ 300.348 Private school placements.

(a) *Developing individualized education programs.* (1) Before a public agency places a child with a disability in, or refers a child to, a private school or facility, the agency shall initiate and conduct a meeting to develop an IEP for the child in accordance with § 300.343.

(2) The agency shall ensure that a representative of the private school or facility attends the meeting. If the representative cannot attend, the agency shall use other methods to ensure participation by the private school or facility, including individual or conference telephone calls.

(3) [Reserved]

(b) *Reviewing and revising individualized education programs.* (1) After a child with a disability enters a private school or facility, any meetings to review and revise the child's IEP may be initiated and conducted by the private school or facility at the discretion of the public agency.

(2) If the private school or facility initiates and conducts these meetings, the public agency shall ensure that the parents and an agency representative:

(i) Are involved in any decision about the child's IEP; and

(ii) Agree to any proposed changes in the program before those changes are implemented.

(c) *Responsibility*. Even if a private school or facility implements a child's IEP, responsibility for compliance with this part remains with the public agency and the SEA.

(Authority: 20 U.S.C. 1413(a)(4)(B))

§ 300.349 Children with disabilities in parochial or other private schools.

If a child with a disability is enrolled in a parochial or other private school and receives special education or related services from a public agency, the public agency shall—

(a) Initiate and conduct meetings to develop, review, and revise an IEP for the child, in accordance with § 300.343; and

(b) Ensure that a representative of the parochial or other private school attends each meeting. If the representative cannot attend, the agency shall use other methods to ensure participation by the private school, including individual or conference telephone calls.

(Authority: 20 U.S.C. 1413(a)(4)(A))
(Approved by the Office of Management and Budget under control number 1820-0600)
[57 FR 44798, Sept. 29, 1992, as amended at 58 FR 13528, Mar. 11, 1993]

§ 300.350 Individualized education program— accountability.

Each public agency must provide special education and related services to a child with a disability in accordance with an IEP. However, Part B of the Act does not require that any agency, teacher, or other person be held accountable if a child does not achieve the growth projected in the annual goals and objectives.

(Authority: 20 U.S.C. 1412(2)(B); 1414(a) (5), (6); Cong. Rec. at H7152 (daily ed., July 21, 1975))
Note: This section is intended to relieve concerns that the IEP constitutes a guarantee by the public agency and the teacher that a child will progress at a specified rate. However, this section does not relieve agencies and teachers from making good faith efforts to assist the child in achieving the goals and objectives listed in the IEP. Further, the section does not limit a parent's right to complain and ask for revisions of the child's program, or to invoke due process procedures, if the parent feels that these efforts are not being made.

Direct Service by the State Educational Agency

§ 300.360 Use of local educational agency allocation for direct services.

(a) An SEA may not distribute funds to an LEA, and shall use those funds to ensure the provision of FAPE to children with disabilities residing in the area served by the LEA, if the LEA, in any fiscal year—

(1) Is entitled to less than $7,500 for that fiscal year (beginning with fiscal year 1979);

(2) Does not submit an application that meets the requirements of §§ 300.220-300.240;

(3) Is unable or unwilling to establish and maintain programs of FAPE;

(4) Is unable or unwilling to be consolidated with other LEAs in order to establish and maintain those programs; or

(5) Has one or more children with disabilities who can best be served by a regional or State center designed to meet the needs of those children.

(b) In meeting the requirements of paragraph (a) of this section, the SEA may provide special education and related services directly, by contract, or through other arrangements.

(c) The excess cost requirements of §§ 300.182-300.186 do not apply to the SEA.

(Authority: 20 U.S.C. 1411(c)(4); 1413(b); 1414(d))

Note: Section 300.360 is a combination of three provisions in the statute (Sections 611(c)(4), 613(b), and 614(d)). This section focuses mainly on the State's administration and use of local entitlements under Part B.

The SEA, as a recipient of Part B funds, is responsible for ensuring that all public agencies in the State comply with the provisions of the Act, regardless of whether they receive Part B funds. If an LEA elects not to apply for its Part B entitlement, the State would be required to use those funds to ensure that FAPE is made available to children residing in the area served by that local agency. However, if the local entitlement is not sufficient for this purpose, additional State or local funds would have to be expended in order to ensure that FAPE and the other requirements of the Act are met.

Moreover, if the LEA is the recipient of any other Federal funds, it would have to be in compliance with 34 CFR §§ 104.31-104.39 of the regulations implementing section 504 of the Rehabilitation Act of 1973. It should be noted that the term "FAPE" has different meanings under Part B and section 504. For Example, under Part B, "FAPE" is a statutory term that requires special education and related services to be provided in accordance with an IEP. However, under section 504, each recipient must provide an education that includes services that are "designed to meet individual educational needs of handicapped persons as adequately as the needs of nonhandicapped persons are met***" Those regulations state that implementation of an IEP, in accordance with Part B, is one means of meeting the FAPE requirement.

§ 300.361 Nature and location of services.

The SEA may provide special education and related services under § 300.360(a) in the manner and at the location it considers appropriate. However, the manner in which the education and services are provided must be consistent with the requirements of this part (including the LRE provisions of §§ 300.550-300.556).

(Authority: 20 U.S.C. 1414(d))

§ 300.370 Use of State agency allocations.

(a) The State may use the portion of its allocation that it does not use for administration under §§ 300.620-300.621—

(1) For support services and direct services in accordance with the priority requirements of §§ 300.320-300.324; and

(2) For the administrative costs of the State's monitoring activities and complaint investigations, to the extent that these costs exceed the administrative costs for monitoring and complaint investigations incurred during fiscal year 1985.

(b) For the purposes of paragraph (a) of this section—

(1) "Direct services" means services provided to a child with a disability by the State directly, by contract, or through other arrangements; and

(2) "Support services" includes implementing the comprehensive system of personnel development of §§ 300.380-300.383, recruitment and training of hearing officers and surrogate parents, and public information and parent training activities relating to FAPE for children with disabilities.

(Authority: 20 U.S.C. 1411(b)(2), (c)(2))

§ 300.371 State matching.
Beginning with the period July 1, 1978-June 30, 1979, and for each following fiscal year, the funds that a State uses for direct and support services under § 300.370 must be matched on a program basis by the State from funds other than Federal funds. This requirement does not apply to funds that the State uses under § 300.360.

(Authority: 20 U.S.C. 1411(c)(2)(B), (c)(4)(B))
Note: The requirement in § 300.371 would be satisfied if the State can document that the amount of State funds expended for each major program area (e.g., the comprehensive system of personnel development) is at least equal to the expenditure of Federal funds in that program area.

§ 300.372 Applicability of nonsupplanting requirement.
Beginning with funds appropriated for Fiscal Year 1979 and for each following fiscal year, the requirement in section 613(a)(9) of the Act, which prohibits supplanting with Federal funds, does not apply to funds that the State uses from its allocation under § 300.706(a) of Subpart G for administration, direct services, or support services.

(Authority: 20 U.S.C. 1411(c)(3))

Comprehensive System of Personnel Development

§ 300.380 General.
Each State shall—
(a) Develop and implement a comprehensive system of personnel development that—
　　(1) Is consistent with the purposes of the Act and with the comprehensive system of personnel development described in 34 CFR § 300.360;
　　(2) Meets the requirements in §§ 300.381-300.383; and
　　(3) Is consistent with the provisions on personnel standards in § 300.153; and
(b) Include in its State plan a description of the personnel development system required in paragraph (a)(1) of this section

(Authority: 20 U.S.C. 1413(a)(3), (a)(14))
(Approved by the Office of Management and Budget under control number 1820-0030)
[57 FR 44798, Sept. 29, 1992, as amended at 58 FR 13528, Mar. 11, 1993]

§ 300.381 Adequate supply of qualified personnel.
Each State plan must include a description of the procedures and activities the State will undertake to ensure an adequate supply of qualified personnel (as the term "qualified" is defined at § 300.15), including special education and related services

personnel and leadership personnel, necessary to carry out the purposes of this part. The procedures and activities must include the development, updating, and implementation of a plan that—

(a) Addresses current and projected special education and related services personnel needs, including the need for leadership personnel; and

(b) Coordinates and facilitates efforts among SEA and LEAs, institutions of higher education, and professional associations to recruit, prepare, and retain qualified personnel, including personnel from minority backgrounds, and personnel with disabilities.

(Authority: 20 U.S.C. 1413(a)(3)(A))
(Approved by the Office of Management and Budget under control number 1820-0600)
[57 FR 44798, Sept. 29, 1992, as amended at 58 FR 13528, Mar. 11, 1993]

§ 300.382 Personnel preparation and continuing education.
Each State plan must include a description of the procedures and activities the State will undertake to ensure that all personnel necessary to carry out this part are appropriately and adequately prepared. The procedures and activities must include—

(a) A system for the continuing education of regular and special education and related services personnel to enable these personnel to meet the needs of children with disabilities under this part;

(b) Procedures for acquiring and disseminating to teachers, administrators, and related services personnel significant knowledge derived from education research and other sources; and

(c) Procedures for adopting, if appropriate, promising practices, materials, and technology, proven effective through research and demonstration.

(Authority: 20 U.S.C. 1413(a)(3)(B))
(Approved by the Office of Management and Budget under control number 1820-0600)
[57 FR 44798, Sept. 29, 1992, as amended at 58 FR 13528, Mar. 11, 1993]

§ 300.383 Data system on personnel and personnel development.
(a) *General.* The procedures and activities required in §§ 300.381 and 300.382 must include the development and maintenance of a system for determining, on an annual basis, the data required in paragraphs (b) and (c) of this section.

(b) *Data on qualified personnel.* (1) The system required by paragraph (a) of this section must enable each State to determine, on an annual basis—

(i) The number and type of personnel, including leadership personnel, employed in the provision of special education and related services, by profession or discipline;

(ii) The number and type of personnel who are employed with emergency, provisional, or temporary certification in each profession or discipline who do not hold appropriate State certification, licensure, or other credentials comparable to certification or licensure for that profession or discipline; and

(iii) The number and type of personnel, including leadership personnel, in each profession or discipline needed, and a projection of the numbers of those personnel that will be needed in five years, based on projections of individuals to be served, retirement and other departures of personnel from the field, and other relevant factors.

(2) The data on special education and related services personnel required in paragraph (b)(1) of this section must include audiologists, counselors, diagnostic and evaluation personnel, home-hospital teachers, interpreters for students with hearing impairments including deafness, occupational therapists, physical education teachers, physical therapists, psychologists, rehabilitation counselors, social workers, speech-language pathologists, teacher aides, recreation and therapeutic recreation specialists, vocational education teachers, work-study coordinators, and other instructional and noninstructional staff.

(3) The data on leadership personnel required by paragraph (b)(1) of this section must include administrators and supervisors of State or local agencies who are involved in the provision or supervision of services or activities necessary to carry out the purposes of this part.

(c) *Data on personnel development.* The system required in paragraph (a) of this section must enable each State to determine, on an annual basis, the institutions of higher education within the State that are preparing special education and related services personnel, including leadership personnel, by area of specialization, including—

(1) The numbers of students enrolled in programs for the preparation of special education and related services personnel administered by these institutions of higher education; and

(2) The number of students who graduated during the past year with certification or licensure, or with credentials to qualify for certification or licensure, from programs for the preparation of special education and related services personnel administered by institutions of higher education.

(Authority: 20 U.S.C. 1413(a)(3)(A))

(Approved by the Office of Management and Budget under control number 1820-0030)

[57 FR 44798, Sept. 29, 1992, as amended at 58 FR 13528, Mar. 11, 1993]

§ 300.384-300.387 [Reserved]

Subpart D—Private Schools

Children with Disabilities in Private Schools
Placed or Referred by Public Agencies

§ 300.400 Applicability of §§ 300.400-300.402.

Sections 300.401-300.402 apply only to children with disabilities who are or have been placed in or referred to a private school or facility by a public agency as a means of providing special education and related services.

(Authority: 20 U.S.C. 1413(a)(4)(B))

§ 300.401 Responsibility of State educational agency.

Each SEA shall ensure that a child with a disability who is placed in or referred to a private school or facility by a public agency:

(a) Is provided special education and related services—

(1) In conformance with an IEP that meets the requirements under §§ 300.340-300.350;

(2) At no cost to the parents; and

(3) At a school or facility that meets the standards that apply to the SEA and LEAs (including the requirements in this part); and

(b) Has all of the rights of a child with a disability who is served by a public agency.

(Authority: 20 U.S.C. 1413(a)(4)(B))

§ 300.402 Implementation by State educational agency.

In implementing § 300.401, the SEA shall—

(a) Monitor compliance through procedures such as written reports, on-site visits, and parent questionnaires;

(b) Disseminate copies of applicable standards to each private school and facility to which a public agency has referred or placed a child with a disability; and

(c) Provide an opportunity for those private schools and facilities to participate in the development and revision of State standards that apply to them.

(Authority: 20 U.S.C. 1413(a)(4)(B))

(Approved by the Office of Management and Budget under control number 1820-0030)

[57 FR 44798, Sept. 29, 1992, as amended at 58 FR 13528, Mar. 11, 1993]

§ 300.403 Placement of children by parents.

(a) If a child with a disability has FAPE available and the parents choose to place the child in a private school or facility, the public agency is not required by this part to pay for the child's education at the private school or facility. However, the public agency shall make services available to the child as provided under §§ 300.450-300.452.

(b) Disagreements between a parent and a public agency regarding the availability of a program appropriate for the child, and the question of financial responsibility, are subject to the due process procedures under §§ 300.500-300.515.

(Authority: 20 U.S.C. 1412(2)(B); 1415)

Children with Disabilities Enrolled by their Parents in Private Schools

§ 300.450 Definition of "private school children with disabilities."

As used in this part, "private school children with disabilities" means children with disabilities enrolled by their parents in private schools or facilities other than children with disabilities covered under §§ 300.400-300.402.

(Authority: 20 U.S.C. 1413(a)(4)(A))

§ 300.451 State educational agency responsibility.

The SEA shall ensure that—

(a) To the extent consistent with their number and location in the State, provision is made for the participation of private school children with disabilities in the program assisted or carried out under this part by providing them with special education and related services; and

(b) The requirements of 34 CFR §§ 76.651-76.662 are met.

(Authority: 20 U.S.C. 1413(a)(4)(A))

§ 300.452 Local educational agency responsibility.
Each LEA shall provide special education and related services designed to meet the needs of private school children with disabilities residing in the jurisdiction of the agency.

(Authority: Sec. 1413(a)(4)(A); 1414(a)(6))

Procedures for By-Pass

§ 300.480 By-pass—general.
(a) The Secretary implements a by-pass if an SEA is, and was on December 2, 1983, prohibited by law from providing for the participation of private school children with disabilities in the program assisted or carried out under this part, as required by section 613(a)(4)(A) of the Act and by §§ 300.451-300.452.

(b) The Secretary waives the requirement of section 613(a)(4)(A) of the Act and of §§ 300.451-300.452 if the Secretary implements a by-pass.

(Authority: 20 U.S.C. 1413(d)(1))

§ 300.481 Provisions for services under a by-pass.
(a) Before implementing a by-pass, the Secretary consults with appropriate public and private school officials, including SEA officials, in the affected State to consider matters such as—

(1) The prohibition imposed by State law that results in the need for a by-pass;

(2) The scope and nature of the services required by private school children with disabilities in the State, and the number of children to be served under the by-pass; and

(3) The establishment of policies and procedures to ensure that private school children with disabilities receive services consistent with the requirements of section 613(a)(4)(A) of the Act, §§ 300.451-300.452, and 34 CFR §§ 76.651-76.662.

(b) After determining that a by-pass is required, the Secretary arranges for the provision of services to private school children with disabilities in the State in a manner consistent with the requirements of section 613(a)(4)(A) of the Act and §§ 300.451-300.452 by providing services through one or more agreements with appropriate parties.

(c) For any fiscal year that a by-pass is implemented, the Secretary determines the maximum amount to be paid to the providers of services by multiplying—

(1) A per child amount that may not exceed the amount per child provided by the Secretary under this part for all children with disabilities in the State for the preceding fiscal year; by

(2) The number of private school children with disabilities (as defined by §§ 300.7(a) and 300.450) in the State, as determined by the Secretary on the basis of the most recent satisfactory data available, which may include an estimate of the number of those children with disabilities.

(d) The Secretary deducts from the State's allocation under this part the amount the Secretary determines is necessary to implement a by-pass and pays that amount to the provider of services. The Secretary may withhold this amount from the State's allocation pending final resolution of any investigation or complaint that could result in a determination that a by-pass must be implemented.

(Authority: 20 U.S.C. 1413(d)(2))

Due Process Procedures

§ 300.482 Notice of intent to implement a by-pass

(a) Before taking any final action to implement a by-pass, the Secretary provides the affected SEA with written notice.

(b) In the written notice, the Secretary—

(1) States the reasons for the proposed by-pass in sufficient detail to allow the SEA to respond; and

(2) Advises the SEA that it has a specific period of time (at least 45 days) from receipt of the written notice to submit written objections to the proposed by-pass and that it may request in writing the opportunity for a hearing to show cause why a by-pass should not be implemented.

(c) The Secretary sends the notice to the SEA by certified mail with return receipt requested.

(Authority: 20 U.S.C. 1413(d)(3)(A))
(Approved by the Office of Management and Budget under control number 1820-0030)
[57 FR 44798, Sept. 29, 1992, as amended at 58 FR 13528, Mar. 11, 1993]

§ 300.483 Request to show cause.

An SEA seeking an opportunity to show cause why a by-pass should not be implemented shall submit a written request for a show cause hearing to the Secretary.

(Authority: 20 U.S.C. 1413(d)(3)(A))
(Approved by the Office of Management and Budget under control number 1820-0030)
[57 FR 44798, Sept. 29, 1992, as amended at 58 FR 13528, Mar. 11, 1993]

§ 300.484 Show cause hearing.

(a) If a show cause hearing is requested, the Secretary—

(1) Notifies the SEA and other appropriate public and private school officials of the time and place for the hearing; and

(2) Designates a person to conduct the show cause hearing. The designee must not have had any responsibility for the matter brought for a hearing.

(b) At the show cause hearing, the designee considers matters such as—

(1) The necessity for implementing a by-pass;

(2) Possible factual errors in the written notice of intent to implement a by-pass; and

(3) The objections raised by public and private school representatives.

(c) The designee may regulate the course of the proceedings and the conduct of parties during the pendency of the proceedings. The designee takes all steps necessary to conduct a fair and impartial proceeding, to avoid delay, and to maintain order.

(d) The designee may interpret applicable statutes and regulations, but may not waive them or rule on their validity.

(e) The designee arranges for the preparation, retention, and, if appropriate, dissemination of the record of the hearing.

(Authority: 20 U.S.C. 1413(d)(3)(A))

§ 300.485 Decision.

(a) The designee who conducts the show cause hearing—

(1) Issues a written decision that includes a statement of findings; and

(2) Submits a copy of the decision to the Secretary and sends a copy to each party by certified mail with return receipt requested.

(b) Each party may submit comments and recommendations on the designee's decision to the Secretary within 15 days of the date the party receives the designee's decision.

(c) The Secretary adopts, reverses, or modifies the designee's decision and notifies the SEA of the Secretary's final action. That notice is sent by certified mail with return receipt requested.

(Authority: 20 U.S.C. 1413(d)(3)(A))

§ 300.486 Filing requirements.

(a) Any written submission under §§ 300.482-300.485 must be filed by hand-delivery, by mail, or by facsimile transmission. The Secretary discourages the use of facsimile transmission for documents longer than five pages.

(b) The filing date under paragraph (a) of this section is the date the document is—

(1) Hand-delivered;

(2) Mailed; or

(3) Sent by facsimile transmission.

(c) A party filing by facsimile transmission is responsible for confirming that a complete and legible copy of the document was received by the Department.

(d) If a document is filed by facsimile transmission, the Secretary or the hearing officer, as applicable, may require the filing of a follow-up hard copy by hand-delivery or by mail within a reasonable period of time.

(e) If agreed upon by the parties, service of a document may be made upon the other party by facsimile transmission.

(Authority: 20 U.S.C. 1413(d)(3)(A))
[57 FR 56796, Nov. 30, 1992]

§ 300.487 Judicial review.

If dissatisfied with the Secretary's final action, the SEA may, within 60 days after notice of that action, file a petition for review with the United States court of appeals for the circuit in which the State is located. The procedures for judicial review are described in section 613(d)(3)(B)-(D) of the Act.

(Authority: 20 U.S.C. 1413(d)(3)(B)-(D))
[57 FR 56796, Nov. 30, 1992]

Subpart E—Procedural Safeguards

Due Process Procedures for Parents and Children

§ 300.500 Definitions of "consent," "evaluation," and "personally identifiable."

(a) As used in this part: "Consent" means that—

(1) The parent has been fully informed of all information relevant to the activity for which consent is sought, in his or her native language, or other mode of communication;

(2) The parent understands and agrees in writing to the carrying out of the activity for which his or her consent is sought, and the consent describes that activity and lists the records (if any) that will be released and to whom; and

(3) The parent understands that the granting of consent is voluntary on the part of the parent and may be revoked at any time.

(b) "Evaluation" means procedures used in accordance with §§ 300.530-300.534 to determine whether a child has a disability and the nature and extent of the special education and related services that the child needs. The term means procedures used selectively with an individual child and does not include basic tests administered to or procedures used with all children in a school, grade, or class.

(c) "Personally identifiable" means that information includes—

(1) The name of the child, the child's parent, or other family member;

(2) The address of the child;

(3) A personal identifier, such as the child's social security number or student number; or

(4) A list of personal characteristics or other information that would make it possible to identify the child with reasonable certainty.

(Authority: 20 U.S.C. 1415, 1417(c))

§ 300.501 General responsibility of public agencies.

Each SEA shall ensure that each public agency establishes and implements procedural safeguards that meet the requirements of §§ 300.500-300.515.

(Authority: 20 U.S.C. 1415(a))

§ 300.502 Opportunity to examine records.

The parents of a child with a disability shall be afforded, in accordance with the procedures in §§ 300.562-300.569 an opportunity to inspect and review all education records with respect to—

(a) The identification, evaluation, and educational placement of the child, and

(b) The provision of FAPE to the child.

(Authority: 20 U.S.C. 1415(b)(1)(A))

§ 300.503 Independent educational evaluation.

(a) *General.* (1) The parents of a child with a disability have the right under this part to obtain an independent educational evaluation of the child, subject to paragraphs (b) through (e) of this section.

(2) Each public agency shall provide to parents, on request, information about where an independent educational evaluation may be obtained.

(3) For the purposes of this part:

(i) "Independent educational evaluation" means an evaluation conducted by a qualified examiner who is not employed by the public agency responsible for the education of the child in question.

(ii) "Public expense" means that the public agency either pays for the full cost of the evaluation or ensures that the evaluation is otherwise provided at no cost to the parent, consistent with § 300.301.

(b) *Parent right to evaluation at public expense.* A parent has the right to an independent educational evaluation at public expense if the parent disagrees with an evaluation obtained by the public agency. However, the public agency may initiate a hearing under § 300.506 to show that its evaluation is appropriate. If the final decision is that the evaluation is appropriate, the parent still has the right to an independent educational evaluation, but not at public expense.

(c) *Parent initiated evaluations.* If the parent obtains an independent educational evaluation at private expense, the results of the evaluation—

(1) Must be considered by the public agency in any decision made with respect to the provision of FAPE to the child; and

(2) May be presented as evidence at a hearing under this subpart regarding that child.

(d) *Requests for evaluations by hearing officers.* If a hearing officer requests an independent educational evaluation as part of a hearing, the cost of the evaluation must be at public expense.

(e) *Agency criteria.* Whenever an independent evaluation is at public expense, the criteria under which the evaluation is obtained, including the location of the evaluation and the qualifications of the examiner, must be the same as the criteria which the public agency uses when it initiates an evaluation.

(Authority: 20 U.S.C. 1415(b)(1)(A))

§ 300.504 Prior notice; parent consent.

(a) *Notice.* Written notice that meets the requirements of § 300.505 must be given to the parents of a child with a disability a reasonable time before the public agency—

(1) Proposes to initiate or change the identification, evaluation, or educational placement of the child or the provision of FAPE to the child; or

(2) Refuses to initiate or change the identification, evaluation, or educational placement of the child or the provision of FAPE to the child.

(b) *Consent; procedures if a parent refuses consent.* (1) Parental consent must be obtained before—

(i) Conducting a preplacement evaluation; and

(ii) Initial placement of a child with a disability in a program providing special education and related services.

(2) If State law requires parental consent before a child with a disability is evaluated or initially provided special education and related services, State procedures govern the public agency in overriding a parent's refusal to consent.

(3) If there is no State law requiring consent before a child with a disability is evaluated or initially provided special education and related services, the public agency may use the hearing procedures in §§ 300.506-300.508 to determine if the child may be evaluated or initially provided special education and related services without parental consent. If it does so and the hearing officer upholds the agency, the agency may evaluate or initially provide special education and related services to the

child without the parent's consent, subject to the parent's rights under §§ 300.510-300.513.

(c) *Additional State consent requirements.* In addition to the parental consent requirements described in paragraph (b) of this section, a State may require parental consent for other services and activities under this part if it ensures that each public agency in the State establishes and implements effective procedures to ensure that a parent's refusal to consent does not result in a failure to provide the child with FAPE.

(d) *Limitation.* A public agency may not require parental consent as a condition of any benefit to the parent or the child except for the service or activity for which consent is required under paragraphs (b) or (c) of this section.

(Authority: 20 U.S.C. 1415(b)(1)(C), (D); 1412(2), (6))

Note 1: Any changes in a child's special education program, after the initial placement, are not subject to the parental consent requirements in paragraph (b)(1) of this section, but are subject to the prior notice requirement in paragraph (a) of this section and the IEP requirements of §§ 300.340-300.350.

Note 2: Paragraph (b)(2) of this section means that if State law requires parental consent before evaluation or before special education and related services are initially provided, and the parent refuses (or otherwise withholds) consent, State procedures, such as obtaining a court order authorizing the public agency to conduct the evaluation or provide the education and related services, must be followed.

If, however, there is no legal requirement for consent outside of these regulations, the public agency may use the due process procedures of §§ 300.506-300.508 to obtain a decision to allow the evaluation or services without parental consent. The agency must notify the parent of its actions, and the parent has appeal rights as well as rights at the hearing itself.

Note 3: If a State adopts a consent requirement in addition to those described in paragraph (b) of this section and consent is refused, paragraph (d) of this section requires that the public agency must nevertheless provide the services and activities that are not in dispute. For example, if a State requires parental consent to the provision of all services identified in an IEP and the parent refuses to consent to physical therapy services included in the IEP, the agency is not relieved of its obligation to implement those portions of the IEP to which the parent consents.

If the parent refuses to consent and the public agency determines that the service or activity in dispute is necessary to provide FAPE to the child, paragraph (c) of this section requires that the agency must implement its procedures to override the refusal. This section does not preclude the agency from reconsidering its proposal if it believes that circumstances warrant.

§ 300.505 Content of notice.

(a) The notice under § 300.504 must include—

(1) A full explanation of all of the procedural safeguards available to the parents under § 300.500, §§ 300.502-300.515, and §§ 300.562-300.569;

(2) A description of the action proposed or refused by the agency, an explanation of why the agency proposes or refuses to take the action, and a description of any options the agency considered and the reasons why those options were rejected;

(3) A description of each evaluation procedure, test, record, or report the agency uses as a basis for the proposal or refusal; and

(4) A description of any other factors that are relevant to the agency's proposal or refusal.

(b) The notice must be—

(1) Written in language understandable to the general public; and

(2) Provided in the native language of the parent or other mode of communication used by the parent, unless it is clearly not feasible to do so.

(c) If the native language or other mode of communication of the parent is not a written language, the SEA or LEA shall take steps to ensure—

(1) That the notice is translated orally or by other means to the parent in his or her native language or other mode of communication;

(2) That the parent understands the content of the notice; and

(3) That there is written evidence that the requirements in paragraphs (c)(1) and (2) of this section have been met.

(Authority: 20 U.S.C. 1415(b)(1)(D))

(Approved by the Office of Management and Budget under control number 1820-0030)

[57 FR 44798, Sept. 29, 1992, as amended at 58 FR 13528, Mar. 11, 1993]

§ 300.506 Impartial due process hearing.

(a) A parent or a public educational agency may initiate a hearing on any of the matters described in § 300.504(a)(1) and (2).

(b) The hearing must be conducted by the SEA or the public agency directly responsible for the education of the child, as determined under State statute, State regulation, or a written policy of the SEA.

(c) The public agency shall inform the parent of any free or low-cost legal and other relevant services available in the area if—

(1) The parent requests the information; or

(2) The parent or the agency initiates a hearing under this section.

(Authority: 20 U.S.C. 1415(b)(2))

Note: Many States have pointed to the success of using mediation as an intervening step prior to conducting a formal due process hearing. Although the process of mediation is not required by the statute or these regulations, an agency may wish to suggest mediation in disputes concerning the identification, evaluation, and educational placement of children with disabilities, and the provision of FAPE to those children. Mediations have been conducted by members of SEAs or LEA personnel who were not previously involved in the particular case. In many cases, mediation leads to resolution of differences between parents and agencies without the development of an adversarial relationship and with minimum emotional stress. However, mediation may not be used to deny or delay a parent's rights under §§ 300.500-300.515.

§ 300.507 Impartial hearing officer.

(a) A hearing may not be conducted—

(1) By a person who is an employee of a public agency that is involved in the education or care of the child; or

(2) By any person having a personal or professional interest that would conflict with his or her objectivity in the hearing.

(b) A person who otherwise qualifies to conduct a hearing under paragraph (a) of this section is not an employee of the agency solely because he or she is paid by the agency to serve as a hearing officer.

(c) Each public agency shall keep a list of the persons who serve as hearing officers. The list must include a statement of the qualifications of each of those persons.

(Authority: 20 U.S.C. 1414(b)(2))

§ 300.508 Hearing rights.
(a) Any party to a hearing has the right to:
(1) Be accompanied and advised by counsel and by individuals with special knowledge or training with respect to the problems of children with disabilities.
(2) Present evidence and confront, cross-examine, and compel the attendance of witnesses.
(3) Prohibit the introduction of any evidence at the hearing that has not been disclosed to that party at least five days before the hearing.
(4) Obtain a written or electronic verbatim record of the hearing.
(5) Obtain written findings of fact and decisions. The public agency, after deleting any personally identifiable information shall—
(i) Transmit those findings and decisions to the State advisory panel established under § 300.650; and
(ii) Make those findings and decisions available to the public.
(b) Parents involved in hearings must be given the right to—
(1) Have the child who is the subject of the hearing present; and
(2) Open the hearing to the public.

(Authority: 20 U.S.C. 1415(d))

§ 300.509 Hearing decision; appeal.
A decision made in a hearing conducted under § 300.506 is final, unless a party to the hearing appeals the decision under § 300.510 or § 300.511.

(Authority: 20 U.S.C. 1415(c))

§ 300.510 Administrative appeal; impartial review.
(a) If the hearing is conducted by a public agency other than the SEA, any party aggrieved by the findings and decision in the hearing may appeal to the SEA.
(b) If there is an appeal, the SEA shall conduct an impartial review of the hearing. The official conducting the review shall:
(1) Examine the entire hearing record.
(2) Ensure that the procedures at the hearing were consistent with the requirements of due process.
(3) Seek additional evidence if necessary. If a hearing is held to receive additional evidence, the rights in § 300.508 apply.
(4) Afford the parties an opportunity for oral or written argument, or both, at the discretion of the review official.
(5) Make an independent decision on completion of the review.
(6) Give a copy of written findings and the decision to the parties.
(c) The SEA, after deleting any personally identifiable information, shall—
(1) Transmit the findings and decisions referred to in paragraph (b)(6) of this section to the State advisory panel established under § 300.650; and
(2) Make those findings and decisions available to the public.

(d) The decision made by the reviewing official is final, unless a party brings a civil action under § 300.511.

(Authority: 20 U.S.C. 1415(c), (d); H. R. Rep. No. 94-664, at p. 49 (1975))

Note 1: The SEA may conduct its review either directly or through another State agency acting on its behalf. However, the SEA remains responsible for the final decision on review.

Note 2. All parties have the right to continue to be represented by counsel at the State administrative review level, whether or not the reviewing official determines that a further hearing is necessary. If the reviewing official decides to hold a hearing to receive additional evidence, the other rights in § 300.508 relating to hearings also apply.

(Approved by the Office of Management and Budget under control number 1820-0030)

[57 FR 44798, Sept. 29, 1992, as amended at 58 FR 13528, Mar. 11, 1993]

§ 300.511 Civil action.

Any party aggrieved by the findings and decision made in a hearing who does not have the right to appeal under § 300.510, and any party aggrieved by the decision of a reviewing officer under § 300.510 has the right to bring a civil action under section 615(e)(2) of the Act.

(Authority: 20 U.S.C. 1415)

§ 300.512 Timelines and convenience of hearings and reviews.

(a) The public agency shall ensure that not later than 45 days after the receipt of a request for a hearing—

(1) A final decision is reached in the hearing; and

(2) A copy of the decision is mailed to each of the parties.

(b) The SEA shall ensure that not later than 30 days after the receipt of a request for a review—

(1) A final decision is reached in the review; and

(2) A copy of the decision is mailed to each of the parties.

(c) A hearing or reviewing officer may grant specific extensions of time beyond the periods set out in paragraphs (a) and (b) of this section at the request of either party.

(d) Each hearing and each review involving oral arguments must be conducted at a time and place that is reasonably convenient to the parents and child involved.

(Authority: 20 U.S.C. 1415)

(Approved by the Office of Management and Budget under control number 1820-0030)

[57 FR 44798, Sept. 29, 1992, as amended at 58 FR 13528, Mar. 11, 1993]

§ 300.513 Child's status during proceedings.

(a) During the pendency of any administrative or judicial proceeding regarding a complaint, unless the public agency and the parents of the child agree otherwise, the child involved in the complaint must remain in his or her present educational placement.

(b) If the complaint involves an application for initial admission to public school, the child, with the consent of the parents, must be placed in the public school program until the completion of all the proceedings.

(Authority: 20 U.S.C. 1415(e)(3))

Note: Section 300.513 does not permit a child's placement to be changed during a complaint proceeding, unless the parents and agency agree otherwise. While the placement may not be changed, this does not preclude the agency from using its normal procedures for dealing with children who are endangering themselves or others.

§ 300.514 Surrogate parents.

(a) *General.* Each public agency shall ensure that the rights of a child are protected when—

(1) No parent (as defined in § 300.13) can be identified;

(2) The public agency, after reasonable efforts, cannot discover the whereabouts of a parent; or

(3) The child is a ward of the State under the laws of that State.

(b) *Duty of public agency.* The duty of a public agency under paragraph (a) of this section includes the assignment of an individual to act as a surrogate for the parents. This must include a method: (1) for determining whether a child needs a surrogate parent, and (2) for assigning a surrogate parent to the child.

(c) *Criteria for selection of surrogates.* (1) The public agency may select a surrogate parent in any way permitted under State law.

(2) Public agencies shall ensure that a person selected as a surrogate—

(i) Has no interest that conflicts with the interest of the child he or she represents; and

(ii) Has knowledge and skills that ensure adequate representation of the child.

(d) *Non-employee requirement; compensation.* (1) A person assigned as a surrogate may not be an employee of a public agency which is involved in the education or care of the child.

(2) A person who otherwise qualifies to be a surrogate parent under paragraphs (c) and (d)(1) of this section, is not an employee of the agency solely because he or she is paid by the agency to serve as a surrogate parent.

(e) *Responsibilities.* The surrogate parent may represent the child in all matters relating to—

(1) The identification, evaluation, and educational placement of the child; and

(2) The provision of FAPE to the child.

(Authority: 20 U.S.C. 1415(b)(1)(B))

§ 300.515 Attorney's fees.

Each public agency shall inform parents that in any action or proceeding under section 615 of the Act, courts may award parents reasonable attorney's fees under the circumstances described in section 615(e)(4) of the Act.

(Authority: 20 U.S.C. 1415(b)(1)(D); 1415(e)(4))

Protection in Evaluation Procedures

§ 300.530 General.

(a) Each SEA shall ensure that each public agency establishes and implements procedures that meet the requirements of §§ 300.530-300.534.

(b) Testing and evaluation materials and procedures used for the purposes of evaluation and placement of children with disabilities must be selected and administered so as not to be racially or culturally discriminatory.

(Authority: 20 U.S.C. 1412(5)(C))

§ 300.531 Preplacement evaluation.

Before any action is taken with respect to the initial placement of a child with a disability in a program providing special education and related services, a full and individual evaluation of the child's educational needs must be conducted in accordance with the requirements of § 300.532.

(Authority: 20 U.S.C. 1412(5)(C))

§ 300.532 Evaluation procedures.

State educational agencies and LEAs shall ensure, at a minimum, that:

(a) Tests and other evaluation materials—

  (1) Are provided and administered in the child' native language or other mode of communication, unless it is clearly not feasible to do so;

  (2) Have been validated for the specific purpose for which they are used; and

  (3) Are administered by trained personnel in conformance with the instructions provided by their producer.

(b) Tests and other evaluation materials include those tailored to assess specific areas of educational need and not merely those that are designed to provide a single general intelligence quotient.

(c) Tests are selected and administered so as best to ensure that when a test is administered to a child with impaired sensory, manual, or speaking skills, the test results accurately reflect the child's aptitude or achievement level or whatever other factors the test purports to measure, rather than reflecting the child's impaired sensory, manual, or speaking skills (except where those skills are the factors that the test purports to measure).

(d) No single procedure is used as the sole criterion for determining an appropriate educational program for a child.

(e) The evaluation is made by a multidisciplinary team or group of persons, including at least one teacher or other specialist with knowledge in the area of suspected disability.

(f) The child is assessed in all areas related to the suspected disability, including, if appropriate, health, vision, hearing, social and emotional status, general intelligence, academic performance, communicative status, and motor abilities.

(Authority: 20 U.S.C. 1412(5)(C))

Note: Children who have a speech or language impairment as their primary disability may not need a complete battery of assessments (e.g., psychological, physical, or adaptive behavior). However, a qualified speech-language pathologist would: (1) evaluate each child with a speech or language impairment using procedures that are appropriate for the diagnosis and appraisal of speech and language impairments, and (2) if necessary, make referrals for additional assessments needed to make an appropriate placement decision.

(Approved by the Office of Management and Budget under control number 1820-0030)

[57 FR 44798, Sept. 29, 1992, as amended at 58 FR 13528, Mar. 11, 1993]

§ 300.533 Placement procedures.

(a) In interpreting evaluation data and in making placement decisions, each public agency shall—

(1) Draw upon information from a variety of sources, including aptitude and achievement tests, teacher recommendations, physical condition, social or cultural background, and adaptive behavior;

(2) Ensure that information obtained from all of these sources is documented and carefully considered;

(3) Ensure that the placement decision is made by a group of persons, including persons knowledgeable about the child, the meaning of the evaluation data, and the placement options; and

(4) Ensure that the placement decision is made in conformity with the LRE rules in §§ 300.550-300.554.

(b) If a determination is made that a child has a disability and needs special education and related services, an IEP must be developed for the child in accordance with §§ 300.340-300.350.

(Authority: 20 U.S.C. 1412(5)(C); 1414(a)(5))

Note: Paragraph (a)(1) of this section includes a list of examples of sources that may be used by a public agency in making placement decisions. The agency would not have to use all the sources in every instance. The point of the requirement is to ensure that more than one source is used in interpreting evaluation data and in making placement decisions. For example, while all of the named sources would have to be used for a child whose suspected disability is mental retardation, they would not be necessary for certain other children with disabilities, such as a child who has a severe articulation impairment as his primary disability. For such a child, the speech-language pathologist, in complying with the multiple source requirement, might use: (1) A standardized test of articulation, and (2) observation of the child's articulation behavior in conversational speech.

(Approved by the Office of Management and Budget under control number 1820-0030)

[57 FR 44798, Sept. 29, 1992, as amended at 58 FR 13528, Mar. 11, 1993]

§ 300.534 Reevaluation.

Each SEA and LEA shall ensure—

(a) That the IEP of each child with a disability is reviewed in accordance with §§ 300.340-300.350; and

(b) That an evaluation of the child, based on procedures that meet the requirements of § 300.532, is conducted every three years, or more frequently if conditions warrant, or if the child's parent or teacher requests an evaluation.

(Authority: 20 U.S.C. 1412(5)(c))

Additional Procedures for Evaluating
Children with Specific Learning Disabilities

§ 300.540 Additional team members.

In evaluating a child suspected of having a specific learning disability, in addition to the requirements of § 300.532, each public agency shall include on the multidisciplinary evaluation team—

(a) (1) The child's regular teacher; or

(2) If the child does not have a regular teacher, a regular classroom teacher qualified to teach a child of his or her age; or

(3) For a child of less than school age, an individual qualified by the SEA to teach a child of his or her age; and

(b) At least one person qualified to conduct individual diagnostic examinations of children, such as a school psychologist, speech-language pathologist, or remedial reading teacher.

(Authority: 20 U.S.C. 1411 note)

§ 300.541 Criteria for determining the existence of a specific learning disability.

(a) A team may determine that a child has a specific learning disability if—

(1) The child does not achieve commensurate with his or her age and ability levels in one or more of the areas listed in paragraph (a)(2) of this section, when provided with learning experiences appropriate for the child's age and ability levels; and

(2) The team finds that a child has a severe discrepancy between achievement and intellectual ability in one or more of the following areas—

(i) Oral expression;

(ii) Listening comprehension;

(iii) Written expression;

(iv) Basic reading skill;

(v) Reading comprehension;

(vi) Mathematics calculation; or

(vii) Mathematics reasoning.

(b) The team may not identify a child as having a specific learning disability if the severe discrepancy between ability and achievement is primarily the result of—

(1) A visual, hearing, or motor impairment;

(2) Mental retardation;

(3) Emotional disturbance;

(4) Environmental, cultural or economic disadvantage.

(Authority: 20 U.S.C. 1411 note)

§ 300.542 Observation.

(a) At least one team member other than the child's regular teacher shall observe the child's academic performance in the regular classroom setting.

(b) In the case of a child of less than school age or out of school, a team member shall observe the child in an environment appropriate for a child of that age.

(Authority: 20 U.S.C. 1411 note)

§ 300.543 Written report.
(a) The team shall prepare a written report of the results of the evaluation.
(b) The report must include a statement of—
    (1) Whether the child has a specific learning disability;
    (2) The basis for making the determination;
    (3) The relevant behavior noted during the observation of the child;
    (4) The relationship of that behavior to the child's academic functioning;
    (5) The educationally relevant medical findings, if any;
    (6) Whether there is a severe discrepancy between achievement and ability which is not correctable without special education and related services; and
    (7) The determination of the team concerning the effects of environmental, cultural, or economic disadvantage.
(c) Each team member shall certify in writing whether the report reflects his or her conclusion. If it does not reflect his or her conclusion, the team member must submit a separate statement presenting his or her conclusions.

(Authority: 20 U.S.C. 1411 note)
(Approved by the Office of Management and Budget under control number 1820-0030)
[57 FR 44798, Sept. 29, 1992, as amended at 58 FR 13528, Mar. 11, 1993]

Least Restrictive Environment

§ 300.550 General
(a) Each SEA shall ensure that each public agency establishes and implements procedures that meet the requirements of §§ 300.550-300.556.
(b) Each public agency shall ensure—
    (1) That to the maximum extent appropriate, children with disabilities, including children in public or private institutions or other care facilities, are educated with children who are nondisabled; and
    (2) That special classes, separate schooling or other removal of children with disabilities from the regular educational environment occurs only when the nature or severity of the disability is such that education in regular classes with the use of supplementary aids and services cannot be achieved satisfactorily.

(Authority: 20 U.S.C. 1412(5)(B); 1414(a)(1)(C)(iv))
(Approved by the Office of Management and Budget under control number 1820-0030)
[57 FR 44798, Sept. 29, 1992, as amended at 58 FR 13528, Mar. 11, 1993]

§ 300.551 Continuum of alternative placements.
(a) Each public agency shall ensure that a continuum of alternative placements is available to meet the needs of children with disabilities for special education and related services.
(b) The continuum required under paragraph (a) of this section must—
    (1) Include the alternative placements listed in the definition of special education under § 300.17 (instruction in regular classes, special classes, special schools, home instruction, and instruction in hospitals and institutions); and
    (2) Make provision for supplementary services (such as resource room or itinerant instruction) to be provided in conjunction with regular class placement.

(Authority: 20 U.S.C. 1412(5)(B))

§ 300.552 Placements.

Each public agency shall ensure that:

(a) The educational placement of each child with a disability—

    (1) Is determined at least annually;

    (2) Is based on his or her IEP; and

    (3) Is as close as possible to the child's home.

(b) The various alternative placements included at § 300.551 are available to the extent necessary to implement the IEP for each child with a disability.

(c) Unless the IEP of a child with a disability requires some other arrangement, the child is educated in the school that he or she would attend if nondisabled.

(d) In selecting the LRE, consideration is given to any potential harmful effect on the child or on the quality of services that he or she needs.

(Authority: 20 U.S.C. 1412(5)(B))

Note: Section 300.552 includes some of the main factors that must be considered in determining the extent to which a child with a disability can be educated with children who are nondisabled. The overriding rule in this section is that placement decisions must be made on an individual basis. The section also requires each agency to have various alternative placements available in order to ensure that each child with a disability receives an education that is appropriate to his or her individual needs.

The requirements of § 300.552, as well as the other requirements of §§ 300.550-300.556, apply to all preschool children with disabilities who are entitled to receive FAPE. Public agencies that provide preschool programs for nondisabled preschool children must ensure that the requirements of § 300.552(c) are met. Public agencies that do not operate programs for nondisabled preschool children are not required to initiate such programs solely to satisfy the requirements regarding placement in the LRE embodied in §§ 300.550-300.556. For these public agencies, some alternative methods for meeting the requirements of §§ 300.550-300.556 include:

(1) Providing opportunities for the participation (even part-time) of preschool children with disabilities in other preschool programs operated by public agencies (such as Head Start);

(2) Placing children with disabilities in private school programs for nondisabled preschool children or private school preschool programs that integrate children with disabilities and nondisabled children; and

(3) Locating classes for preschool children with disabilities in regular elementary schools.

In each case the public agency must ensure that each child's placement is in the LRE in which the unique needs of that child can be met, based upon the child's IEP, and meets all of the other requirements of §§ 300.340-300.350 and §§ 300.550-300.556.

The analysis of the regulations for Section 504 of the Rehabilitation Act of 1973 (34 CFR part 104-Appendix, Paragraph 24) includes several points regarding educational placements of children with disabilities that are pertinent to this section:

1. With respect to determining proper placements, the analysis states: "*** it should be stressed that, where a handicapped child is so disruptive in a regular classroom that the education of other students is significantly impaired, the needs of the handicapped child cannot be met in that environment. Therefore regular placement would not be appropriate to his or her needs ***."

2. With respect to placing a child with a disability in an alternate setting, the analysis states that among the factors to be considered in placing a child is the need to place the child as close to home as possible. Recipients are required to take this factor into account in making placement decisions. The parent's right to challenge the placement of their child extends not only to placement in special classes or separate schools, but also to placement in a distant school, particularly in a residential program. An equally appropriate education program may exist closer to home; and this issue may be raised by the parent under the due process provisions of this subpart.

§ 300.553 Nonacademic settings.

In providing or arranging for the provision of nonacademic and extracurricular services and activities, including meals, recess periods, and the services and activities set forth in § 300.306, each public agency shall ensure that each child with a disability participates with nondisabled children in those services and activities to the maximum extent appropriate to the needs of that child.

(Authority: 20 U.S.C. 1412(5)(B))

Note: Section 300.553 is taken from a requirement in the final regulations for Section 504 of the Rehabilitation Act of 1973. With respect to this requirement, the analysis of the Section 504 Regulations includes the following statement: "[This paragraph] specifies that [children with disabilities] must also be provided nonacademic services in as integrated a setting as possible. This requirement is especially important for children whose educational needs necessitate their being solely with other handicapped children during most of each day. To the maximum extent appropriate, children in residential settings are also to be provided opportunities for participation with other children." (34 CFR part 104— Appendix, Paragraph 24.)

§ 300.554 Children in public or private institutions.

Each SEA shall make arrangements with public and private institutions, (such as a memorandum of agreement or special implementation procedures) as may be necessary to ensure that §300.550 is effectively implemented.

(Authority: 20 U.S.C. 1412(5)(B))

Note: Under section 612(5)(B) of the statute, the requirement to educate children with disabilities with nondisabled children also applies to children in public and private institutions or other care facilities. Each SEA must ensure that each applicable agency and institution in the State implements this requirement. Regardless of other reasons for institutional placement, no child in an institution who is capable of education in a regular public school setting may be denied access to an education in that setting.

§ 300.555 Technical assistance and training activities.

Each SEA shall carry out activities to ensure that teachers and administrators in all public agencies—

(a) Are fully informed about their responsibilities for implementing § 300.550; and

(b) Are provided with technical assistance and training necessary to assist them in this effort.

(Authority: 20 U.S.C. 1412(5)(B))

§ 300.556 Monitoring activities.

(a) The SEA shall carry out activities to ensure that § 300.550 is implemented by each public agency.

(b) If there is evidence that a public agency makes placements that are inconsistent with § 300.550, the SEA shall—

(1) Review the public agency's justification for its actions, and

(2) Assist in planning and implementing any necessary corrective action.

(Authority: 20 U.S.C. 1412(5)(B))

Confidentiality of Information

§ 300.560 Definitions.

As used in §§ 300.560-300.576—

Destruction means physical destruction or removal of personal identifiers from information so that the information is no longer personally identifiable.

Education records means the type of records covered under the definition of education records in part 99 of this title (the regulations implementing the Family Educational Rights and Privacy Act of 1974).

Participating agency means any agency or institution that collects, maintains, or uses personally identifiable information, or from which information is obtained, under this part.

(Authority: 20 U.S.C. 1412(2)(D); 1417(c))

§ 300.561 Notice to parents.

(a) The SEA shall give notice that is adequate to fully inform parents about the requirements of § 300.128, including—

(1) A description of the extent that the notice is given in the native languages of the various population groups in the State;

(2) A description of the children on whom personally identifiable information is maintained, the types of information sought, the methods the State intends to use in gathering the information (including the sources from whom information is gathered), and the uses to be made of the information;

(3) A summary of the policies and procedures that participating agencies must follow regarding storage, disclosure to third parties, retention, and destruction of personally identifiable information; and

(4) A description of all of the rights of parents and children regarding this information, including the rights under the Family Educational Rights and Privacy Act of 1974 and implementing regulations in part 99 of this title.

(b) Before any major identification, location, or evaluation activity, the notice must be published or announced in newspapers or other media, or both, with circulation adequate to notify parents throughout the State of the activity.

(Authority: 20 U.S.C. 1412(2)(D); 1417(c))

(Approved by the Office of Management and Budget under control number 1820-0030)

[57 FR 44798, Sept. 29, 1992, as amended at 58 FR 13528, Mar. 11, 1993]

§ 300.562 Access rights.

(a) Each participating agency shall permit parents to inspect and review any education records relating to their children that are collected, maintained, or used by the agency under this part. The agency shall comply with a request without unnecessary delay and before any meeting regarding an IEP or any hearing relating to the identification, evaluation, or educational placement of the child, or the provision of FAPE to the child, and in no case more than 45 days after the request has been made.

(b) The right to inspect and review education records under this section includes—

(1) The right to a response from the participating agency to reasonable requests for explanations and interpretations of the records;

(2) The right to request that the agency provide copies of the records containing the information if failure to provide those copies would effectively prevent the parent from exercising the right to inspect and review the records; and

(3) The right to have a representative of the parent inspect and review the records.

(c) An agency may presume that the parent has authority to inspect and review records relating to his or her child unless the agency has been advised that the parent does not have the authority under applicable State law governing such matters as guardianship, separation, and divorce.

(Authority: 20 U.S.C. 1412(2)(D); 1417(c))

(Approved by the Office of Management and Budget under control number 1820-0030)

[57 FR 44798, Sept. 29, 1992, as amended at 58 FR 13528, Mar. 11, 1993]

§ 300.563 Record of access.

Each participating agency shall keep a record of parties obtaining access to education records collected, maintained, or used under this part (except access by parents and authorized employees of the participating agency), including the name of the party, the date access was given, and the purpose for which the party is authorized to use the records.

(Authority: 20 U.S.C. 1412(2)(D); 1417(c))

(Approved by the Office of Management and Budget under control number 1820-0030)

[57 FR 44798, Sept. 29, 1992, as amended at 58 FR 13528, Mar. 11, 1993]

§ 300.564 Records on more than one child.

If any education record includes information on more than one child, the parents of those children shall have the right to inspect and review only the information relating to their child or to be informed of that specific information.

(Authority: 20 U.S.C. 1412(2)(D); 1417(c))

§ 300.565 List of types and locations of information.

Each participating agency shall provide parents on request a list of the types and locations of education records collected, maintained, or used by the agency.

(Authority: 20 U.S.C. 1412(2)(D); 1417(c))

(Approved by the Office of Management and Budget under control number 1820-0030)

[57 FR 44798, Sept. 29, 1992, as amended at 58 FR 13528, Mar. 11, 1993]

§ 300.566 Fees.

(a) Each participating education agency may charge a fee for copies of records that are made for parents under this part if the fee does not effectively prevent the parents from exercising their right to inspect and review those records.

(b) A participating agency may not charge a fee to search for or to retrieve information under this part.

(Authority: 20 U.S.C. 1412(2)(D); 1417(c))

§ 300.567 Amendment of records at parent's request.

(a) A parent who believes that information in education records collected, maintained, or used under this part is inaccurate or misleading or violates the privacy or other rights of the child may request the participating agency that maintains the information to amend the information.

(b) The agency shall decide whether to amend the information in accordance with the request within a reasonable period of time of receipt of the request.

(c) If the agency decides to refuse to amend the information in accordance with the request, it shall inform the parent of the refusal, and advise the parent of the right to a hearing under § 300.568.

(Authority: 20 U.S.C. 1412(2)(D); 1417(c))

§ 300.568 Opportunity for a hearing.

The agency shall, on request, provide an opportunity for a hearing to challenge information in education records to ensure that it is not inaccurate, misleading, or otherwise in violation of the privacy or other rights of the child.

(Authority: 20 U.S.C. 1412(2)(D); 1417(c))

§ 300.569 Result of hearing.

(a) If, as a result of the hearing, the agency decides that the information is inaccurate, misleading, or otherwise in violation of the privacy or other rights of the child, it shall amend the information accordingly and so inform the parent in writing.

(b) If, as a result of the hearing, the agency decides that the information is not inaccurate, misleading, or otherwise in violation of the privacy or other rights of the child, it shall inform the parent of the right to place in the records it maintains on the child a statement commenting on the information or setting forth any reasons for disagreeing with the decision of the agency.

(c) Any explanation placed in the records of the child under this section must—
(1) Be maintained by the agency as part of the records of the child as long as the record or contested portion is maintained by the agency; and
(2) If the records of the child or the contested portion is disclosed by the agency to any party, the explanation must also be disclosed to the party.

(Authority: 20 U.S.C. 1412(2)(D); 1417(c))

(Approved by the Office of Management and Budget under control number 1820-0030)

[57 FR 44798, Sept. 29, 1992, as amended at 58 FR 13528, Mar. 11, 1993]

§ 300.570 Hearing procedures.
(1) A hearing held under § 300.568 must be conducted according to the procedures under § 99.22 of this title.

[57 FR 48694, Oct. 27, 1992]

§ 300.571 Consent.
(a) Parental consent must be obtained before personally identifiable information is—
(1) Disclosed to anyone other than officials of participating agencies collecting or using the information under this part, subject to paragraph (b) of this section; or
(2) Used for any purpose other than meeting a requirement of this part.
(b) An educational agency or institution subject to part 99 of this title may not release information from education records to participating agencies without parental consent unless authorized to do so under part 99 of this title.
(c) The SEA shall include policies and procedures in its State plan that are used in the event that a parent refuses to provide consent under this section.

(Authority: 20 U.S.C. 1412(2)(D); 1417(c))
(Approved by the Office of Management and Budget under control number 1820-0030)
[57 FR 44798, Sept. 29, 1992, as amended at 58 FR 13528, Mar. 11, 1993]

§ 300.572 Safeguards.
(a) Each participating agency shall protect the confidentiality of personally identifiable information at collection, storage, disclosure, and destruction stages.
(b) One official at each participating agency shall assume responsibility for ensuring the confidentiality of any personally identifiable information.
(c) All persons collecting or using personally identifiable information must receive training or instruction regarding the State's policies and procedures under § 300.129 and part 99 of this title.
(d) Each participating agency shall maintain, for public inspection, a current listing of the names and positions of those employees within the agency who may have access to personally identifiable information.

(Authority: 20 U.S.C. 1412(2)(D); 1417(c))
(Approved by the Office of Management and Budget under control number 1820-0030)
[57 FR 44798, Sept. 29, 1992, as amended at 58 FR 13528, Mar. 11, 1993]

§ 300.573 Destruction of information.
(a) The public agency shall inform parents when personally identifiable information collected, maintained, or used under this part is no longer needed to provide educational services to the child.
(b) The information must be destroyed at the request of the parents. However, a permanent record of a student's name, address, and phone number, his or her grades, attendance record, classes attended, grade level completed, and year completed may be maintained without time limitation.

(Authority: 20 U.S.C. 1412(2)(D); 1417(c))

Note: Under § 300.573, the personally identifiable information on a child with a disability may be retained permanently unless the parents request that it be destroyed. Destruction of records is the best protection against improper and unauthorized disclosure. However, the records may be needed for other purposes. In informing parents about their rights under this section, the agency should remind them that the records may be needed by the child or the parents for social security benefits or other purposes. If the parents request that the information be destroyed, the agency may retain the information in paragraph (b) of this section.

§ 300.574 Children's rights.

The SEA shall include policies and procedures in its State plan regarding the extent to which children are afforded rights of privacy similar to those afforded to parents, taking into consideration the age of the child and type or severity of disability.

(Authority: 20 U.S.C. 1412(2)(D); 1417(c))

Note: Under the regulations for the Family Educational Rights and Privacy Act (34 [also 45] CFR [Part] 99.5(a)), the rights of parents regarding education records are transferred to the student at age 18.

(Approved by the Office of Management and Budget under control number 1820-0030)

[57 FR 44798, Sept. 29, 1992, as amended at 58 FR 13528, Mar. 11, 1993]

§ 300.575 Enforcement.

The SEA shall describe in its State plan the policies and procedures, including sanctions, that the State uses to ensure that its policies and procedures are followed and that the requirements of the Act and the regulations in this part are met.

(Authority: 20 U.S.C. 1412(2)(D); 1417(c))

(Approved by the Office of Management and Budget under control number 1820-0030)

[57 FR 44798, Sept. 29, 1992, as amended at 58 FR 13528, Mar. 11, 1993]

§ 300.576 Department.

If the Department or its authorized representatives collect any personally identifiable information regarding children with disabilities that is not subject to 5 U.S.C. 552a (The Privacy Act of 1974), the Secretary shall apply the requirements of 5 U.S.C. section 552a (b) (1)-(2), (4)-(11); (c); (d); (e)(1); (2); (3)(A), (B), and (D), (5)-(10); (h); (m); and (n), and the regulations implementing those provisions in part 5b of this title.

(Authority: 20 U.S.C. 1412(2)(D); 1417(c))

Department Procedures

§ 300.580 [Reserved]

§ 300.581 Disapproval of a State plan.

Before disapproving a State plan, the Secretary gives the SEA written notice and an opportunity for a hearing.

(Authority: 20 U.S.C. 1413(c))

§ 300.582 Content of notice.

(a) In the written notice, the Secretary—

(1) States the basis on which the Secretary proposes to disapprove the State plan;

(2) May describe possible options for resolving the issues;

(3) Advises the SEA that it may request a hearing and that the request for a hearing must be made not later than 30 calendar days after it receives the notice of proposed disapproval; and

(4) Provides information about the procedures followed for a hearing.

(b) The Secretary sends the written notice to the SEA by certified mail with return receipt requested.

(Authority: 20 U.S.C. 1413(c))

§ 300.583 Hearing official or panel.

(a) If the SEA requests a hearing, the Secretary designates one or more individuals, either from the Department or elsewhere, not responsible for or connected with the administration of this program, to conduct a hearing.

(b) If more than one individual is designated, the Secretary designates one of those individuals as the Chief Hearing Official of the Hearing Panel. If one individual is designated, that individual is the Hearing Official.

(Authority: 20 U.S.C. 1413(c))

§ 300.584 Hearing procedures.

(a) As used in §§ 300.581-300.586 the term *party* or *parties* means the following:

(1) An SEA that requests a hearing regarding the proposed disapproval of its State plan under this part.

(2) The Department of Education official who administers the program of financial assistance under this part.

(3) A person, group or agency with an interest in and having relevant information about the case who has applied for and been granted leave to intervene by the Hearing Official or Panel.

(b) Within 15 calendar days after receiving a request for a hearing, the Secretary designates a Hearing Official or Panel and notifies the parties.

(c) The Hearing Official or Panel may regulate the course of proceedings and the conduct of the parties during the proceedings. The Hearing Official or Panel takes all steps necessary to conduct a fair and impartial proceeding, to avoid delay, and to maintain order, including the following:

(1) The Hearing Official or Panel may hold conferences or other types of appropriate proceedings to clarify, simplify, or define the issues or to consider other matters that may aid in the disposition of the case.

(2) The Hearing Official or Panel may schedule a prehearing conference of the Hearing Official or Panel and parties.

(3) Any party may request the Hearing Official or Panel to schedule a prehearing or other conference. The Hearing Official or Panel decides whether a conference is necessary and notifies all parties.

(4) At a prehearing or other conference, the Hearing Official or Panel and the parties may consider subjects such as—

(i) Narrowing and clarifying issues;

(ii) Assisting the parties in reaching agreements and stipulations;

(iii) Clarifying the positions of the parties;

(iv) Determining whether an evidentiary hearing or oral argument should be held; and

(v) Setting dates for—

(A) The exchange of written documents;

(B) The receipt of comments from the parties on the need for oral argument or evidentiary hearing;

(C) Further proceedings before the Hearing Official or Panel (including an evidentiary hearing or oral argument, if either is scheduled);

(D) Requesting the names of witnesses each party wishes to present at an evidentiary hearing and estimation of time for each presentation; or

(E) Completion of the review and the initial decision of the Hearing Official or Panel.

(5) A prehearing or other conference held under paragraph (b)(4) of this section may be conducted by telephone conference call.

(6) At a prehearing or other conference, the parties shall be prepared to discuss the subjects listed in paragraph (b)(4) of this section.

(7) Following a prehearing or other conference the Hearing Official or Panel may issue a written statement describing the issues raised, the action taken, and the stipulations and agreements reached by the parties.

(d) The Hearing Official or Panel may require parties to state their positions and to provide all or part of the evidence in writing.

(e) The Hearing Official or Panel may require parties to present testimony through affidavits and to conduct cross-examination through interrogatories.

(f) The Hearing Official or Panel may direct the parties to exchange relevant documents or information and lists of witnesses, and to send copies to the Hearing Official or Panel.

(g) The Hearing Official or Panel may receive, rule on, exclude, or limit evidence at any stage of the proceedings.

(h) The Hearing Official or Panel may rule on motions and other issues at any stage of the proceedings.

(i) The Hearing Official or Panel may examine witnesses.

(j) The Hearing Official or Panel may set reasonable time limits for submission of written documents.

(k) The Hearing Official or Panel may refuse to consider documents or other submissions if they are not submitted in a timely manner unless good cause is shown.

(l) The Hearing Official or Panel may interpret applicable statutes and regulations but may not waive them or rule on their validity.

(m)(1) The parties shall present their positions through briefs and the submission of other documents and may request an oral argument or evidentiary hearing. The Hearing Official or Panel shall determine whether an oral argument or an evidentiary hearing is needed to clarify the positions of the parties.

(2) The Hearing Official or Panel gives each party an opportunity to be represented by counsel.

(n) If the Hearing Official or Panel determines that an evidentiary hearing would materially assist the resolution of the matter, the Hearing Official or Panel gives each party, in addition to the opportunity to be represented by counsel—

(1) An opportunity to present witnesses on the party's behalf; and

(2) An opportunity to cross-examine witnesses either orally or with written questions.

(o) The Hearing Official or Panel accepts any evidence that it finds is relevant and material to the proceedings and is not unduly repetitious.

(p)(1) The Hearing Official or Panel—

(i) Arranges for the preparation of a transcript of each hearing;

(ii) Retains the original transcript as part of the record of the hearing; and

(iii) Provides one copy of the transcript to each party.

(2) Additional copies of the transcript are available on request and with payment of the reproduction fee.

(q) Each party shall file with the Hearing Official or Panel all written motions, briefs, and other documents and shall at the same time provide a copy to the other parties to the proceedings.

(Authority: 20 U.S.C. 1413(c))

§ 300.585 Initial decision; final decision.

(a) The Hearing Official or Panel prepares an initial written decision that addresses each of the points in the notice sent by the Secretary to the SEA under § 300.582.

(b) The initial decision of a Panel is made by a majority of Panel members.

(c) The Hearing Official or Panel mails by certified mail with return receipt requested a copy of the initial decision to each party (or to the party's counsel) and to the Secretary, with a notice stating that each party has an opportunity to submit written comments regarding the decision to the Secretary.

(d) Each party may file comments and recommendations on the initial decision with the Hearing Official or Panel within 15 calendar days of the date the party receives the Panel's decision.

(e) The Hearing Official or Panel sends a copy of a party's initial comments and recommendations to the other parties by certified mail with return receipt requested. Each party may file responsive comments and recommendations with the Hearing Official or Panel within seven calendar days of the date the party receives the initial comments and recommendations.

(f) The Hearing Official or Panel forwards the parties' initial and responsive comments on the initial decision to the Secretary who reviews the initial decision and issues a final decision.

(g) The initial decision of the Hearing Official or Panel becomes the final decision of the Secretary unless, within 25 calendar days after the end of the time for receipt of written comments, the Secretary informs the Hearing Official or Panel and the parties to a hearing in writing that the decision is being further reviewed for possible modification.

(h) The Secretary may reject or modify the initial decision of the Hearing Official or Panel if the Secretary finds that it is clearly erroneous.

(i) The Secretary conducts the review based on the initial decision, the written record, the Hearing Official's or Panel's proceedings, and written comments. The Secretary may remand the matter for further proceedings.

(j) The Secretary issues the final decision within 30 calendar days after notifying the Hearing Official or Panel that the initial decision is being further reviewed.

§ 300.586 Filing requirements.

(a) Any written submission under §§ 300.582-300.585 must be filed by hand-delivery, by mail, or by facsimile transmission. The Secretary discourages the use of facsimile transmission for documents longer than five pages.

(b) The filing date under paragraph (a) of this section is the date the document is—

(1) Hand-delivered;

(2) Mailed; or

(3) Sent by facsimile transmission.

(c) A party filing by facsimile transmission is responsible for confirming that a complete and legible copy of the document was received by the Department.

(d) If a document is filed by facsimile transmission, the Secretary, the Hearing Official, or the Panel, as applicable, may require the filing of a follow-up hard copy by hand-delivery or by mail within a reasonable period of time.

(e) If agreed upon by the parties, service of a document may be made upon the other party by facsimile transmission.

(Authority: 20 U.S.C. 1413(c))
[57 FR 56796, Non. 30, 1992]

§ 300.587 Judicial review.

If a State is dissatisfied with the Secretary's final action with respect to its State plan, the State may, within 60 calendar days after notice of that action, file a petition for review with the United States court of appeals for the circuit in which the State is located.

(Authority: 20 U.S.C. 1416(b)(1))
[57 FR 44798, Sept. 29, 1992. Redesignated at 57 FR 56796, Nov. 30, 1992]

§§ 300.588 [Reserved]

§ 300.589 Waiver of requirement regarding supplementing and supplanting with Part B funds.

(a) Under sections 613(a)(9)(B) and 614(a)(2)(B)(ii) of the Act, SEAs and LEAs must ensure that Federal funds provided under this part are used to supplement and increase the level of Federal, State, and local funds (including funds that are not under the direct control of SEAs or LEAs) expended for special education and related services provided to children with disabilities under this part and in no case to supplant those Federal, State, and local funds. The nonsupplanting requirement applies only to funds allocated to LEAs (See § 300.372).

(b) If the State provides clear and convincing evidence that all children with disabilities have FAPE available to them, the Secretary may waive in part the requirement under sections 613(a)(9)(B) and 614(a)(2)(B)(ii) of the Act if the Secretary concurs with the evidence provided by the State.

(c) If a State wishes to request a waiver, it must inform the secretary in writing. The Secretary then provides the State with a finance and membership report form that provides the basis for the request.

(d) In its request for a waiver, the State shall include the results of a special study made by the State to obtain evidence of the availability of FAPE to all children with disabilities. The special study must include statements by a representative sample of organizations that deal with children with disabilities, and parents and teachers of children with disabilities, relating to the following areas—

(1) The adequacy and comprehensiveness of the State's system for identifying, locating, and evaluating children with disabilities;

(2) The cost to parents, if any, for education for children enrolled in public and private day schools, and in public and private residential schools and institutions; and

(3) The adequacy of the State's due process procedures.

(e) In its request for a waiver, the State shall include finance data relating to the availability of FAPE for all children with disabilities, including—

(1) The total current expenditures for regular education programs and special education programs by function and by source of funds (State, local, and Federal) for the previous school year; and

(2) The full-time equivalent membership of students enrolled in regular programs and in special programs in the previous school year.

(f) The Secretary considers the information that the State provides under paragraphs (d) and (e) of this section, along with any additional information he may request, or obtain through on-site reviews of the State's education programs and records, to determine if all children have FAPE available to them, and if so, the extent of the waiver.

(g) The State may request a hearing with regard to any final action by the Secretary under this section.

(Authority: 20 U.S.C. 1411(c)(3); 1413(a)(9)(B))

(Approved by the Office of Management and Budget under control number 1820-0030)

[57 FR 44798, Sept. 29, 1992, as amended at 58 FR 13528, Mar. 11, 1993]

Subpart F—State Administration

General

§ 300.600 Responsibility for all educational programs.

(a) The SEA is responsible for ensuring—

(1) That the requirements of this part are carried out; and

(2) That each educational program for children with disabilities administered within the State, including each program administered by any other public agency—

(i) Is under the general supervision of the persons responsible for educational programs for children with disabilities in the SEA; and

(ii) Meets the education standards of the SEA (including the requirements of this part).

(b) The State must comply with paragraph (a) of this section through State statute, State regulation, signed agreement between respective agency officials, or other documents.

(c) This part may not be construed to limit the responsibility of agencies other than educational agencies for providing or paying some or all of the costs of FAPE to children with disabilities in the State.

(Authority: 20 U.S.C. 1412(6))

Note: The requirement in § 300.600(a) is taken essentially verbatim from section 612(6) of the statute and reflects the desire of the Congress for a central point of responsibility and accountability in the education of children with disabilities within each State. With respect to SEA responsibility, the Senate Report on Pub. L. 94-142 includes the following statements:

This provision is included specifically to assure a single line of responsibility with regard to the education of [children with disabilities], and to assure that in the implementation of all provisions of this Act and in carrying out the right to education for [children with disabilities], the State educational agency shall be the responsible agency***.

Without this requirement, there is an abdication of responsibility for the education of [children with disabilities]. Presently, in many States, responsibility is divided, depending upon the age of the handicapped child, sources of funding, and type of services delivered. While the Committee understands that different agencies may, in fact, deliver services, the responsibility must remain in a central agency overseeing the education of handicapped children, so that failure to deliver services or the violation of the rights of handicapped children is squarely the responsibility of one agency. (S. Rep. No. 94-168, p. 24 (1975))

In meeting the requirements of this section, there are a number of acceptable options that may be adopted, including the following:

(1) Written agreements are developed between respective State agencies concerning SEA standards and monitoring. These agreements are binding on the local or regional counterparts of each State agency.

(2) The Governor's Office issues an administrative directive establishing the SEA responsibility.

(3) State law, regulation, or policy designates the SEA as responsible for establishing standards for all educational programs for individuals with disabilities, and includes responsibility for monitoring.

(4) State law mandates that the SEA is responsible for all educational programs.

(Approved by the Office of Management and Budget under control number 1820-0030)

[57 FR 44798, Sept. 29, 1992, as amended at 58 FR 13528, Mar. 11, 1993]

§ 300.601 Relation of Part B to other Federal programs.

This part may not be construed to permit a State to reduce medical and other assistance available to children with disabilities, or to alter the eligibility of a child with a disability under Title V (Maternal and Child Health) or Title XIX (Medicaid) of the Social Security Act, to receive services that are also part of FAPE.

(Authority: 20 U.S.C. 1413(e))

Use of Funds

§ 300.620 Federal funds for State administration.

A State may use five percent of the total State allotment in any fiscal year under Part B of the Act, or $450,000, whichever is greater, for administrative costs related to carrying out sections 612 and 613 of the Act. However, this amount cannot be greater than twenty-five percent of the State's total allotment for the fiscal year under Part B of the Act.

(Authority: 20 U.S.C. 1411(b),(c))

§ 300.621 Allowable costs.

(a) The SEA may use funds under § 300.620 for—

(1) Administration of the State plan and for planning at the State level, including planning, or assisting in the planning, of programs or projects for the education of children with disabilities;

(2) Approval, supervision, monitoring, and evaluation of the effectiveness of local programs and projects for the education of children with disabilities;

(3) Technical assistance to LEAs with respect to the requirements of this part;

(4) Leadership services for the program supervision and management of special education activities for children with disabilities; and

(5) Other State leadership activities, and consultative services.

(b) The SEA shall use the remainder of its funds under § 300.620 in accordance with § 300.370.

(Authority: 20 U.S.C. 1411(b), (c))

State Advisory Panel

§ 300.650 Establishment.

(a) Each State shall establish, in accordance with the provisions of §§ 300.650-300.653, a State advisory panel on the education of children with disabilities.

(b) The advisory panel must be appointed by the Governor or any other official authorized under State law to make those appointments.

(c) If a State has an existing advisory panel that can perform the functions in § 300.652, the State may modify the existing panel so that it fulfills all of the requirements of §§ 300.650-300.653, instead of establishing a new advisory panel.

(Authority: 20 U.S.C. 1413(a)(12))

§ 300.651 Membership.

(a) The membership of the State advisory panel must be composed of persons involved in or concerned with the education of children with disabilities. The membership must include at least one person representative of each of the following groups—

(1) Individuals with disabilities;

(2) Teachers of children with disabilities;

(3) Parents of children with disabilities;

(4) State and local educational officials;

(5) Special education program administrators;

(b) The State may expand the advisory panel to include additional persons in the groups listed in paragraph (a) of this section and representatives of other groups not listed.

(Authority: 20 U.S.C. 1413(a)(12))

Note: The membership of the State advisory panel, as listed in paragraphs (a)(1)-(5) of this section, is required in section 613(a)(12) of the Act. As indicated in paragraph (b) of this section, the composition of the panel and the number of members may be expanded at the discretion of the State. In adding to the membership, consideration could be given to having—

(1) An appropriate balance between professional groups and consumers (i.e., parents, advocates, and individuals with disabilities);

(2) Broad representation within the consumer-advocate groups, to ensure that the interests and points of view of various parents, advocates and individuals with disabilities are appropriately represented;

(3) Broad representation within professional groups (e.g., regular education personnel: special educators, including teachers, teacher trainers, and administrators, who can properly represent various dimensions in the education of children with disabilities; and appropriate related services personnel); and

(4) Representatives from other State advisory panels (such as vocational education).

If a State elects to maintain a small advisory panel (e.g., 10-15 members), the panel itself could take steps to ensure that it (1) consults with and receives inputs from various consumer and special interest professional groups, and (2) establishes committees for particular short-term purposes composed of representatives from those input groups.

§ 300.652 Advisory panel functions.

The State advisory panel shall—

(a) Advise the SEA of unmet needs within the State in the education of children with disabilities;

(b) Comment publicly on the State plan and rules or regulations proposed for issuance by the State regarding the education of children with disabilities and the procedures for distribution of funds under this part; and

(c) Assist the State in developing and reporting such information and evaluations as may assist the Secretary in the performance of his responsibilities under section 618 of the Act.

(Authority: 20 U.S.C. 1413(a)(12))

§ 300.653 Advisory panel procedures.

(a) The advisory panel shall meet as often as necessary to conduct its business.

(b) By July 1 of each year, the advisory panel shall submit an annual report of panel activities and suggestions to the SEA. This report must be made available to the public in a manner consistent with other public reporting requirements of this part.

(c) Official minutes must be kept on all panel meetings and shall be made available to the public on request.

(d) All advisory panel meetings and agenda items must be publicly announced prior to the meeting, and meetings must be open to the public.

(e) Interpreters and other necessary services must be provided at panel meetings for panel members or participants. The State may pay for these services from funds under § 300.620.

(f) The advisory panel shall serve without compensation but the State must reimburse the panel for reasonable and necessary expenses for attending meetings and performing duties. The State may use funds under § 300.620 for this purpose.

(Authority: 20 U.S.C. 1413(a)(12))

(Approved by the Office of Management and Budget under control number 1820-0030)

[57 FR 44798, Sept. 29, 1992, as amended at 58 FR 13528, Mar. 11, 1993]

State Complaint Procedures

§ 300.660 Adoption of State complaint procedures.

Each SEA shall adopt written procedures for:

(a) Resolving any complaint that meets the requirements of § 300.662 by—

(1) Providing for the filing of a complaint with the SEA; and

(2) At the SEA's discretion, providing for the filing of a complaint with a public agency and the right to have the SEA review the public agency's decision on the complaint.

(b) Informing parents and other interested individuals about the procedures in §§ 300.660-300.662.

(Authority: 20 U.S.C. 2831(a))

(Approved by the Office of Management and Budget under control number 1820-0599)

[57 FR 44798, Sept. 29, 1992, as amended at 58 FR 13528, Mar. 11, 1993]

§ 300.661 Minimum State complaint procedures.

Each SEA shall include the following in its complaint procedures:

(a) A time limit of 60 calendar days after a complaint is filed under § 300.660(a) to—

(1) Carry out an independent on-site investigation, if the SEA determines that such an investigation is necessary;

(2) Give the complainant the opportunity to submit additional information, either orally or in writing, about the allegations in the complaint;

(3) Review all relevant information and make an independent determination as to whether the public agency is violating a requirement of part B of the Act or of this part; and

(4) Issue a written decision to the complainant that addresses each allegation in the complaint and contains—

(i) Findings of fact and conclusions; and

(ii) The reasons for the SEA's final decision.

(b) An extension of the time limit under paragraph (a) of this section only if exceptional circumstances exist with respect to a particular complaint.

(c) Procedures for effective implementation of the SEA's final decision, if needed, including technical assistance activities, negotiations, and corrective actions to achieve compliance.

(d) The right of the complainant or the public agency to request the Secretary to review the SEA's final decision.

(Authority: 20 U.S.C. 2831(a))

(Approved by the Office of Management and Budget under control number 1820-0599)

[57 FR 44798, Sept. 29, 1992, as amended at 58 FR 13528, Mar. 11, 1993]

§ 300.662 Filing a complaint.

An organization or individual may file a signed written complaint under the procedures described in §§ 300.600-300.661. The complaint must include—

(a) A statement that a public agency has violated a requirement of part B of the Act or of this part; and

(b) The facts on which the statement is based.

(Authority: 20 U.S.C. 2831(a))
(Approved by the Office of Management and Budget under control number 1820-0599)
[57 FR 44798, Sept. 29, 1992, as amended at 58 FR 13528, Mar. 11, 1993]

Subpart G—Allocation of Funds; Reports

Allocations

§ 300.700 Special definition of the term "State."
For the purposes of § 300.701, § 300.702, and §§ 300.704-300.708, the term "State" does not include Guam, American Samoa, the Virgin Islands, the Commonwealth of the Northern Mariana Islands, the Federated States of Micronesia, the Republic of the Marshall Islands, or Palau.

(Authority: 20 U.S.C. 1411(a)(2))

§ 300.701 State entitlement; formula
(a) The Secretary calculates the maximum amount of the grant to which a State is entitled under section 611 of the Act in any fiscal year as follows:

(1) If the State is eligible for a grant under section 619 of the Act, the maximum entitlement is equal to the number of children with disabilities aged 3 through 21 in the State who are receiving special education and related services, multiplied by 40 percent of the average per pupil expenditure in public elementary and secondary schools in the United States.

(2) If the State is not eligible for a grant under section 619 of the Act, the maximum entitlement is equal to the number of children with disabilities aged 6 through 21 in the State who are receiving special education and related services, multiplied by 40 percent of the average per pupil expenditure in public elementary and secondary schools in the United States.

(Authority: 20 U.S.C. 1411(a)(1))

(b) [Reserved]
(c) For the purposes of this section, the *average per pupil expenditure in public elementary and secondary schools in the United States*, means the aggregate expenditures during the second fiscal year preceding the fiscal year for which the computation is made (or if satisfactory data for that year are not available at the time of computation, then during the most recent preceding fiscal year for which satisfactory data are available) of all LEAs in the United States (which, for the purpose of this section, means the 50 States and the District of Columbia), plus any direct expenditures by the State for operation of those agencies (without regard to the source of funds from which either of those expenditures are made), divided by the aggregate number of children in average daily attendance to whom those agencies provided free public education during that preceding year.

(Authority: 20 U.S.C. 1411(a)(4))

§ 300.702 Limitations and exclusions.

(a) In determining the amount of a grant under § 300.701:

(1) If a State serves all children with disabilities aged 3 through 5 in the State, the Secretary does not count children with disabilities aged 3 through 17 in the State to the extent that the number of those children is greater than 12 percent of the number of all children aged 3 through 17 in the State.

(2) If a State does not serve all children with disabilities aged 3 through 5 in the State, the Secretary does not count children with disabilities aged 5 through 17 to the extent that the number of those children is greater than 12 percent of the number of all children aged 5 through 17 in the State.

(3) The Secretary does not count children with disabilities who are counted under Subpart 2 of Part D of Chapter 1 of Title I of the Elementary and Secondary School Education Act of 1965.

(b) For the purposes of paragraph (a) of this section, the number of children aged 3 through 17 and 5 through 17 in any State is determined by the Secretary on the basis of the most recent satisfactory data available.

(Authority: 20 U.S.C. 1413(a)(5))

§ 300.703 Ratable reductions.

(a) *General.* If the sums appropriated for any fiscal year for making payments to States under section 611 of the Act are not sufficient to pay in full the total amounts that all States are entitled to receive for that fiscal year, the maximum amount that all States are entitled to receive for that fiscal year shall be ratably reduced. In case additional funds become available for making payments for any fiscal year during which the preceding sentence is applicable, those reduced amounts shall be increased on the same basis they were reduced.

(Authority: 20 U.S.C. 1411(g)(1))

(b) *Reporting dates for Local educational agencies and reallocations.* (1) In any fiscal year in which the State entitlements have been ratably reduced, and in which additional funds have not been made available to pay in full the total of the amounts under paragraph (a) of this section, the SEA shall fix dates before which each LEA shall report to the State the amount of funds available to it under this part which it estimates it will expend.

(2) The amounts available under paragraph (a)(1) of this section, or any amount which would be available to any other LEA agency if it were to submit an application meeting the requirements of this part, which the SEA determines will not be used for the period of its availability, shall be available for allocation to those LEAs, in the manner provided in § 300.707, that the SEA determines will need and be able to use additional funds to carry out approved programs.

(Authority: 20 U.S.C. 1411(g)(2))

§ 300.704 Hold harmless provision.

No State shall receive less than the amount it received under Part B of the Act for fiscal year 1977.

(Authority: 20 U.S.C. 1411(a)(1))

§ 300.705 Allocation for State in which bypass is implemented for private school children with disabilities.

In determining the allocation under §§ 300.700-300.703 of a State in which the Secretary will implement a by-pass for private school children with disabilities under §§ 300.451-300.486, the Secretary includes in the State's child count—

(a) For the first year of a by-pass, the actual or estimated number of private school children with disabilities (as defined in §§ 300.7(a) and 300.450) in the State, as of the preceding December 1; and

(b) For succeeding years of a by-pass, the number of private school children with disabilities who received special education and related services under the by-pass in the preceding year.

(Authority: 20 U.S.C. 1411(a)(1)(A), 1411(a)(3), 1413(d))

§ 300.706 Within-State distribution: Fiscal year 1979 and after.

Of the funds received under § 300.701 by any State for fiscal year 1979, and for each fiscal year after fiscal year 1979—

(a) 25 percent may be used by the State in accordance with § 300.620 and §300.370; and

(b) 75 percent shall be distributed to the LEAs in the State in accordance with § 300.707.

(Authority: 20 U.S.C. 1411(c)(1))

§ 300.707 Local educational agency entitlement; formula.

From the total amount of funds available to all LEAs, each LEA is entitled to an amount that bears the same ratio to the total amount as the number of children with disabilities aged 3 through 21 in that agency who are receiving special education and related services bears to the aggregate number of children with disabilities aged 3 through 21 receiving special education and related services in all LEAs that apply to the SEA for funds under Part B of the Act.

(Authority: 20 U.S.C. 1411(d))

§ 300.708 Reallocation of local educational agency funds.

If an SEA determines that an LEA is adequately providing FAPE to all children with disabilities residing in the area served by the local agency with State and local funds otherwise available to the local agency, the SEA may reallocate funds (or portions of those funds that are not required to provide special education and related services) made available to the local agency under § 300.707, to other LEAs within the State that are not adequately providing special education and related services to all children with disabilities residing in the areas served by the other LEAs.

(Authority: 20 U.S.C. 1414(e))

§ 300.709 Payments to Secretary of Interior for the Education of Indian Children.

(a) *General.* (1) The Secretary makes payments to the Secretary of the Interior to meet the need for assistance for the education of children with disabilities on reservations, aged 5 through 21, who are enrolled in elementary and secondary schools for Indian children operated by or funded by the Secretary of the Interior.

(2) In the case of Indian students aged 3 through 5 who are enrolled in programs affiliated with Bureau of Indian Affairs (BIA) schools that are required by States in which the schools are located to attain or maintain State accreditation and had State accreditation prior to October 7, 1991, the schools may count those children for the purpose of distribution of the funds provided under paragraph (a)(1) of this section to the Secretary of the Interior.

(3) The amount of payment under paragraph (a)(1) of this section for any fiscal year is one percent of the aggregate amounts available to all States under this part for that fiscal year.

(b) *Responsibilities for meeting the requirements of part B.* The Secretary of the Interior shall be responsible for meeting all of the requirements of part B of the Act for the children described in paragraph (a) of this section, in accordance with § 300.260.

(Authority: 20 U.S.C. 1411(f))

§ 300.710 Payments to the Secretary of the Interior for Indian tribes or tribal organizations.

(a) *General.* (1) Beginning with funds appropriated under part B of the Act for fiscal year 1992, the Secretary, subject to this section, makes payments to the Secretary of the Interior to be distributed to tribes or tribal organizations (as defined under section 4 of the Indian Self-Determination and Education Assistance Act) or consortiums of those tribes or tribal organizations to provide for the coordination of assistance for special education and related services for children with disabilities, aged 3 through 5, on reservations served by elementary and secondary schools for Indian children operated or funded by the Department of the Interior.

(2) The amount of the payment under paragraph (b)(1) of this section for any fiscal year is .25 percent of the aggregate amounts available for all States under this part for that fiscal year.

(3) None of the funds allocated under this section may be used by the Secretary of the Interior for administrative purposes, including child count, and the provision of technical assistance.

(b) *Distribution of funds.* The Secretary of the Interior shall distribute the total amount of the .25 percent under paragraph (a) of this section in accordance with section 611(f)(4) of the Act.

(Authority: 20 U.S.C. 1411(f))

§ 300.711 Entitlements to jurisdictions.

(a) The jurisdictions to which this section applies are Guam, American Samoa, the Virgin Islands, the Commonwealth of the Northern Mariana Islands, the Federated States of Micronesia, the Republic of the Marshall Islands, and Palau, (until the Compact of Free Association with Palau takes effect pursuant to section 101(a) of Pub. L. 99-658).

(b) Each jurisdiction under paragraph (a) of this section is entitled to a grant for the purposes set forth in section 601(c) of the Act. The amount to which those jurisdictions are so entitled for any fiscal year shall not exceed an amount equal to 1 percent of the aggregate of the amounts available to all States under this part for that fiscal year. Funds appropriated for those jurisdictions shall be allocated proportionately among them on the basis of the number of children aged 3 through 21 in each jurisdiction. However, no jurisdiction shall receive less than $150,000, and other allocations shall be ratably reduced if necessary to ensure that each jurisdiction receives at least that amount.

(c) The amount expended for administration by each jurisdiction under this section shall not exceed 5 percent of the amount allotted to the jurisdiction for any fiscal year, or $35,000, whichever is greater.

(Authority: 20 U.S.C. 1411(e))

Reports

§ 300.750 Annual report of children served— report requirement.

(a) The SEA shall report to the Secretary no later than February 1 of each year the number of children with disabilities aged 3 through 21 residing in the State who are receiving special education and related services.

(Authority: 20 U.S.C. 1411(a)(3))

(b) The SEA shall submit the report on forms provided by the Secretary.

(Authority: 20 U.S.C. 1411(a)(3))

Note: It is very important to understand that this report and the requirements that relate to it are solely for allocation purposes. The population of children the State may count for allocation purposes may differ from the population of children to whom the State must make FAPE available. For example, while section 611(a)(5) of the Act limits the number of children who may be counted for allocation purposes to 12 percent of the general school population aged 3 through 17 (in States that serve all children with disabilities aged 3 through 5) or 5 through 17 (in States that do not serve all children with disabilities aged 3 through 5), a State might find that 14 percent (or some other percentage) of its children have disabilities. In that case, the State must make FAPE available to all of those children with disabilities.

(Approved by the Office of Management and Budget under control number 1820-0043)

[57 FR 44798, Sept. 29, 1992, as amended at 58 FR 13528, Mar. 11, 1993]

§ 300.751 Annual report of children served—information required in the report.

(a) In its report, the SEA shall include a table that shows—

(1) The number of children with disabilities receiving special education and related services on December 1 of that school year;

(2) The number of children with disabilities aged 3 through 5 who are receiving FAPE;

(3) The number of those children with disabilities aged 6 through 21 within each disability category, as defined in the definition of "children with disabilities" in § 300.7; and

(4) The number of those children with disabilities aged 3 through 21 for each year of age (3, 4, 5, etc.).

(b) For the purpose of this part, a child's age is the child's actual age on the date of the child count: December 1.

(c) The SEA may not report a child aged 6 through 21 under more than one disability category.

(d) If a child with a disability aged 6 through 21 has more than one disability, the SEA shall report that child in accordance with the following procedure:

(1) A child with deaf-blindness must be reported under the category "deaf-blindness."

(2) A child who has more than one disability (other than deaf-blindness) must be reported under the category "multiple disabilities."

(Authority: 20 U.S.C. 1411(a)(3); (5)(A)(ii); 1418(b))

(Approved by the Office of Management and Budget under control number 1820-0043)

[57 FR 44798, Sept. 29, 1992, as amended at 58 FR 13528, Mar. 11, 1993]

§ 300.752 Annual report of children served— certification.

The SEA shall include in its report a certification signed by an authorized official of the agency that the information provided is an accurate and unduplicated count of children with disabilities receiving special education and related services on the dates in question.

(Authority: 20 U.S.C. 1411(a)(3); 1417(b))

§ 300.753 Annual report of children served— criteria for counting children.

(a) The SEA may include in its report children with disabilities who are enrolled in a school or program that is operated or supported by a public agency, and that either—

(1) Provides them with both special education and related services; or

(2) Provides them only with special education if they do not need related services to assist them in benefiting from that special education.

(b) The SEA may not include children with disabilities in its report who—

(1) Are not enrolled in a school or program operated or supported by a public agency;

(2) Are not provided special education that meets State standards;

(3) Are not provided with a related service that they need to assist them in benefiting from special education;

(4) Are counted by a State agency under Subpart 2 of Part D of Chapter 1 of Title I of the Elementary and Secondary Education Act of 1965; or

(5) Are receiving special education funded solely by the Federal Government. However, the State may count children covered under 300.186(b).

(Authority: 20 U.S.C. 1411(a)(3); 1417(b))

Note 1: Under paragraph (a) of this section, the State may count children with disabilities in a Head Start or other preschool program operated or supported by a public agency if those children are provided special education that meets State standards.

Note 2: Special education, by statutory definition, must be at no cost to parents. As of September 1, 1978, under the FAPE requirement, both special education and related services must be at no cost to parents.

There may be some situations, however, where a child receives special education from a public source at no cost, but whose parents pay for the basic or regular education. This child may be counted. The Department expects that there would only be limited situations where special education would be clearly separate from regular education—generally, where speech services is the only special education required by the child. For example, the child's parents may have enrolled the child in a regular program in a private school, but the child might be receiving speech services in a program funded by the LEA. Allowing these children to be counted will provide incentives (in addition to complying with the legal requirement in section 613(a)(4)(A) of the Act regarding private schools) to public agencies to provide services to children enrolled by parents in private schools, since funds are generated in part on the basis of the number of children provided special education and related services. Agencies should understand, however, that if a public agency places or refers a child with a disability to a public or private school for educational purposes, special education includes the entire educational program provided to the child. In that case, parents may not be charged for any part of the child's education.

A State may not count Indian children on or near reservations and children on military facilities if it provides them no special education. If an SEA or LEA is responsible for serving these children, and does provide them special education and related services, they may be counted.

§ 300.754 Annual report of children served— other responsibilities of the State educational agency.

In addition to meeting the other requirements of §§ 300.750-300.753, the SEA shall:

(a) Establish procedures to be used by LEAs and other educational institutions in counting the number of children with disabilities receiving special education and related services;

(b) Set dates by which those agencies and institutions must report to the SEA to ensure that the State complies with § 300.750(a);

(c) Obtain certification from each agency and institution that an unduplicated and accurate count has been made;

(d) Aggregate the data from the count obtained from each agency and institution, and prepare the reports required under §§ 300.750-300.753; and

(e) Ensure that documentation is maintained that enables the State and the Secretary to audit the accuracy of the count.

(Authority: 20 U.S.C. 1411(a)(3); 1417(b))

Note: States should note that the data required in the annual report of children served are not to be transmitted to the Secretary in personally identifiable form. States are encouraged to collect these data in non-personally identifiable form.

(Approved by the Office of Management and Budget under control number 1820-0043)

[57 FR 44798, Sept. 29, 1992, as amended at 58 FR 13528, Mar. 11, 1993]

APPENDIX A TO PART 300—[RESERVED]
APPENDIX B TO PART 300—[RESERVED]

APPENDIX C TO PART 300—NOTICE OF INTERPRETATION

I. Purpose of the IEP
II. IEP Requirements

***

AUTHORITY: Part B of the Individuals with Disabilities Education Act (20 U.S.C. 1411-1420, unless otherwise noted.

INDIVIDUALIZED EDUCATION PROGRAMS (IEPs)

Interpretation of Requirements of Part B of the Individuals with Disabilities Education Act

I. Purpose of the IEP

There are two main parts of the IEP requirement, as described in the Act and regulations: (1) The IEP meeting(s), where parents and school personnel jointly make decisions about an educational program for a child with a disability, and (2) the IEP document itself, that is, a written record of the decisions reached at the meeting. The overall IEP requirement, comprised of these two parts, has a number of purposes and functions:

a. The IEP meeting serves as a communication vehicle between parents and school personnel, and enables them, as equal participants, to jointly decide what the child's needs are, what services will be provided to meet those needs, and what the anticipated outcomes may be.

b. The IEP process provides an opportunity for resolving any differences between the parents and the agency concerning the special education needs of a child with a disability; first, through the IEP meeting, and second, if necessary, through the procedural protections that are available to the parents.

c. The IEP sets forth in writing a commitment of resources necessary to enable a child with a disability to receive needed special education and related services.

d. The IEP is a management tool that is used to ensure that each child with a disability is provided special education and related services appropriate to the child's special learning needs.

e. The IEP is a compliance/monitoring document which may be used by authorized monitoring personnel from each governmental level to determine whether a child with a disability is actually receiving the FAPE agreed to by the parents and the school.

f. The IEP serves as an evaluation device for use in determining the extent of the child's progress toward meeting the projected outcomes.

NOTE: The Act does not require that teachers or other school personnel be held accountable if a child with a disability does not achieve the goals and objectives set forth in the IEP. See § 300.350, Individualized education program—accountability.

II. IEP Requirements

This part (1) repeats the IEP requirements in § § 300.340-300.350 of the regulations (boxed material) [The regulations are noted in this version, but not reprinted as in the original CFR part. Please refer to the regulations for the full text.], (2) provides additional clarification, as necessary, on sections or paragraphs of the regulations on which such clarification is needed, and (3) answers some questions regarding implementation of the IEP requirements that are not expressly addressed in the regulations. These questions and clarifying information are presented in a question and answer format immediately after the particular section of the regulations that is presented.

****

§ 300.340 Definition. [See text of regulation, above.]

****
****

§ 300.341 State educational agency responsibility. [See text of regulation, above.]

****

1. Who is responsible for ensuring the development of IEPs for children with disabilities served by a public agency other than an LEA?

The answer will vary from State to State, depending upon State law, policy, or practice. In each State, however, the SEA is ultimately responsible for ensuring that each agency in the State is in compliance with the IEP requirements and the other provisions of the Act and regulations. (See § 300.600 regarding SEA responsibility for all education programs.)

The SEA must ensure that every child with a disability in the State has FAPE available, regardless of which agency, State or local, is responsible for the child. While the SEA has flexibility in deciding the best means to meet this obligation (e.g., through interagency agreements), there can be no failure to provide FAPE due to jurisdictional disputes among agencies.

NOTE: Section 300.2(b) states that the requirements of the Act and regulations apply to all political subdivisions of the State that are involved in the education of children with disabilities, including (1) the SEA, (2) LEAs, (3) other State agencies (such as Departments of Mental Health and Welfare, and State schools for students with deafness or students with blindness), and (4) State correctional facilities.

The following paragraphs outline (1) some of the SEA's responsibilities for developing policies or agreements under a variety of interagency situations, and (2) some of the responsibilities of an LEA when it initiates the placement of a child with a disability in a school or program operated by another State agency:

a. SEA POLICIES OR INTERAGENCY AGREEMENTS. The SEA, through its written policies or agreements, must ensure that IEPs are properly written and implemented for all children with disabilities in the State. This applies to each interagency situation that exists in the State, including any of the following:

(1) When an LEA initiates the placement of a child in a school or program operated by another State agency (see "LEA-Initiated Placements" in paragraph "b", below); (2) when a State or local agency other than the SEA or LEA places a child in a residential facility or other program; (3) when parents initiate placements in public institutions; and (4) when the courts make placements in correctional facilities.

NOTE: This is not an exhaustive list. The SEA's policies must cover any other interagency situation that is applicable in the State, including placements that are made for both educational and for non-educational purposes.

Frequently, more than one agency is involved in developing or implementing an IEP of a child with a disability (e.g., when the LEA remains responsible for the child, even though another public agency provides the special education and related services, or when there are shared cost arrangements). It is important that SEA policies or agreements define the role of each agency involved in the situations described above, in order to resolve any jurisdictional problems that could delay the provision of FAPE to a child with a disability. For example, if a child is placed in a residential facility, any one or all of the following agencies might be involved in the development and/or implementation of the child's IEP: The child's LEA, the SEA, another State agency, an institution or school under that agency, and the LEA where the institution is located.

NOTE: The SEA must also ensure that any agency involved in the education of a child with a disability is in compliance with the LRE provisions of the Act and regulations, and, specifically, with the requirement that the placement of each child with a disability (1) be determined at least annually, (2) be based on the child's IEP, and (3) be as close as possible to the child's home (§ 300.552(a), Placements.)

b. LEA-INITIATED PLACEMENTS. When an LEA is responsible for the education of a child with a disability, the LEA is also responsible for developing the child's IEP. The LEA has this responsibility even if development of the IEP results in placement in a State-operated school or program.

NOTE: The IEP must be developed before the child is placed. (See Question 5, below.) When placement in a State-operated school is necessary, the affected State agency or agencies must be involved by the LEA in the development of the IEP. (See response to Question 59, below, regarding participation of a private school representative at the IEP meeting.)

After the child enters the State school, meetings to review or revise the child's IEP could be conducted by either the LEA or the State school, depending upon State law, policy, or practice. However, both agencies should be involved in any decisions made about the child's IEP (either by attending the IEP meetings, or through correspondence or telephone calls). There must be a clear decision, based on State law, as to whether responsibility for the child's education is transferred to the State school or remains with the LEA, since this decision determines which agency is responsible for reviewing or revising the child's IEP.

2. For a child placed out of State by a public agency, is the placing or receiving State responsible for the child's IEP?

The "placing" State is responsible for developing the child's IEP and ensuring that it is implemented. The determination of the specific agency in the placing State that is responsible for the child's IEP would be based on State law, policy, or practice. However, as indicated in Question 1, above, the SEA in the placing State is responsible for ensuring that the child has FAPE available.

****

§ 300.342 When individualized education programs must be in effect.
[See text of regulation, above.]
****

3. In requiring that an IEP be in effect before special education and related services are provided, what does "be in effect" mean?

As used in the regulations, the term "be in effect" means that the IEP (1) has been developed properly (i.e., at a meeting(s) involving all of the participants specified in the Act (parent, teacher, agency representative, and, if appropriate, the child)); (2) is regarded by both the parents and agency as appropriate in terms of the child's needs, specified goals and objectives, and the services to be provided; and (3) will be implemented as written.

4. How much of a delay is permissible between the time an IEP of a child with a disability is finalized and when special education is provided?

In general, no delay is permissible. It is expected that the special education and related services set out in a child's IEP will be provided by the agency beginning immediately after the IEP is finalized. The note following § 300.342 identifies some exceptions ((1) when the meetings occur during the summer or other vacation period, or (2) when there are circumstances that require a short delay, such as working out transportation arrangements). However, unless otherwise specified in the IEP, the IEP services must be provided as soon as possible following the meeting.

NOTE: Section 300.346(a)(4) requires that the IEP include the projected dates for initiation of services.

5. For a child with a disability receiving special education for the first time, when must an IEP be developed—before placement or after placement?

An IEP must be in effect before special education and related services are provided to a child. (§ 300.342(b)(1), emphasis added.) The appropriate placement for a given child with a disability cannot be determined until after decisions have been made about what the child's needs are and what will be provided. Since these decisions are made at the IEP meeting, it would not be permissible to first place the child and then develop the IEP. Therefore, the IEP must be developed before placement. The above requirement does not preclude temporarily placing an eligible child with a disability in a program as part of the evaluation process—before the IEP is finalized—to aid in determining the most appropriate placement for the child. It is essential that the temporary placement not become the final placement before the IEP is finalized. In order to ensure that this does not happen, the State might consider requiring LEAs to take the following actions:

a. Develop an interim IEP for the child, that sets out the specific conditions and timelines for the trial placement. (See paragraph "c", below.)

b. Ensure that the parents agree to the interim placement before it is carried out, and that they are involved throughout the process of developing, reviewing, and revising the child's IEP.

c. Set a specific timeline (e.g., 30 days) for completing the evaluation and making judgments about the most appropriate placement for the child.

d. Conduct an IEP meeting at the end of the trial period in order to finalize the child's IEP.

NOTE: Once the IEP of a child with a disability is in effect and the child is placed in a special education program, the teacher might develop detailed lesson plans or objectives *based* on the IEP. However, these lesson plans and objectives are not required to be a part of the IEP itself. (See Questions 37-43, below, regarding IEP goals and objectives.)

6. If a child with a disability has been receiving special education in one LEA and moves to another community, must the new LEA hold an IEP meeting before the child is placed in a special education program?

It would not be necessary for the new LEA to conduct an IEP meeting if:

(1) A copy of the child's current IEP is available; (2) the parents indicate that they are satisfied with the current IEP; and (3) the new LEA determines that the current IEP is appropriate and can be implemented as written.

If the child's current IEP is not available, or if either the LEA or the parent believes that it is not appropriate, an IEP meeting would have to be conducted. This meeting should take place within a short time after the child enrolls in the new LEA (normally, within one week).

NOTE: The child must be placed in a special education program immediately after the IEP is finalized. See Question 4, above.

If the LEA or the parents believe that additional information is needed (e.g., the school records from the former LEA) or that a new evaluation is necessary before a final placement decision can be made, it would be permissible to temporarily place the child in an interim program before the IEP is finalized. (See Question 5, above.)

****

§ 300.343 Meetings. [See text of regulation, above.]
****

7. What is the purpose of the 30 day timeline in § 300.343(c)?

The 30 day timeline in § 300.343(c) ensures that there will not be a significant delay between the time a child is evaluated and when the child begins to receive special education. Once it is determined—through the evaluation—that a child has a disability, the public agency has up to 30 days to hold an IEP meeting.

NOTE: See Questions 4 and 5, above, regarding finalization of IEP and placement of the child.

8. Must the agency hold a separate meeting to determine a child's eligibility for special education and related services, or can this step be combined with the IEP meeting?

Paragraph (e) of § 300.532 (Evaluation procedures) provides that the evaluation of each child with a disability must be "made by a multidisciplinary team or group of persons ***". The decisions regarding (1) whether the team members actually meet together, and (2) whether such meetings are separate from the IEP meeting are matters that are left to the discretion of State or local agencies.

In practice, some agencies hold separate eligibility meetings with the multidisciplinary team before the IEP meeting.

NOTE: When separate meetings are conducted, placement decisions would be made at the IEP meeting. However, placement options could be discussed at the eligibility meeting.

Other agencies combine the two steps into one. If a combined meeting is conducted, the public agency must include the parents as participants at the meeting. (See § 300.345 for requirements on parent participation.)

NOTE: If, at a separate eligibility meeting, a decision is made that a child is not eligible for special education, the parents should be notified about the decision.

9. Must IEPs be reviewed or revised at the beginning of each school year?

No. The basic requirement in the regulations is that IEPs must be in effect at the beginning of each school year. Meetings must be conducted at least once each year to review and, if necessary, revise the IEP of each child with a disability. However, the meetings may be held anytime during the year, including (1) at the end of the school year, (2) during the summer, before the new school year begins, or (3) on the anniversary date of the last IEP meeting on the child.

10. How frequently must IEP meetings be held and how long should they be?

Section 614(a)(5) of the Act provides that each public agency must hold meetings periodically, but not less than annually, to review each child's IEP and, if appropriate, revise its provisions. The legislative history of the Act makes it clear that there should be as many meetings a year as any one child may need. (121 Cong. Rec. S20428-29 (Nov. 19, 1975) (remarks of Senator Stafford))

There is no prescribed length for IEP meetings. In general, meetings (1) will be longer for initial placements and for children who require a variety of complex services, and (2) will be shorter for continuing placements and for children who require only a minimum amount of services. In any event, however, it is expected that agencies will allow sufficient time at the meetings to ensure meaningful parent participation.

11. Who can initiate IEP meetings?

IEP meetings are initiated and conducted at the discretion of the public agency. However, if the parents of a child with a disability believe that the child is not progressing satisfactorily or that there is a problem with the child's current IEP, it would be appropriate for the parents to request an IEP meeting. The public agency should grant any reasonable request for such a meeting.

NOTE: Under § 300.506(a), the parents or agency may initiate a due process hearing at any time regarding any matter related to the child's IEP.

If a child's teacher(s) feels that the child's placement or IEP services are not appropriate to the child, the teacher(s) should follow agency procedures with respect to (1) calling or meeting with the parents and/or (2) requesting the agency to hold another meeting to review the child's IEP.

12. May IEP meetings be tape-recorded? The use of tape recorders at IEP meetings is not addressed by either the Act or the regulations. Although taping is clearly not required, it is permissible at the option of either the parents or the agency. However, if the recording is maintained by the agency, it is an education record, within the meaning of the Family Educational Rights and Privacy Act ("FERPA"; 20 U.S.C. 1232g), and would, therefore, be subject to the confidentiality requirements of the regulations under both FERPA (34 CFR part 99) and Part B (34 CFR 300.560-300.575).

****

§ 300.344 Participants in meetings. [See text of regulation, above.]
****

13. Who can serve as the representative of the public agency at an IEP meeting?

The representative of the public agency could be any member of the school staff, other than the child's teacher, who is qualified to provide, or supervise the provision of, specially designed instruction to meet the unique needs of children with disabilities. (Section 602(20) of the Act.) Thus, the agency representative could be (1) a qualified special education administrator, supervisor, or teacher (including a speech-language pathologist), or (2) a school principal or other administrator—if the person is qualified to provide, or supervise the provision of, special education.

Each State or local agency may determine which specific staff member will serve as the agency representative. However, the representative should be able to ensure that whatever services are set out in the IEP will actually be provided and that the IEP will not be vetoed at a higher administrative level within the agency. Thus, the person selected should have the authority to commit agency resources (i.e., to make decisions about the specific special education and related services that the agency will provide to a particular child).

For a child with a disability who requires only a limited amount of special education, the agency representative able to commit appropriate resources could be a special education teacher, or a speech-language pathologist, other than the child's teacher. For a child who requires extensive special education and related services, the agency representative might need to be a key administrator in the agency.

NOTE: IEP meetings for continuing placements could be more routine than those for initial placements, and, thus, might not require the participation of a key administrator.

14. Who is the representative of the public agency if a child with a disability is served by a public agency other than the SEA or LEA?

The answer depends on which agency is responsible, under State law, policy, or practice, for any one or all of the following:

(1) The child's education, (2) placing the child, and (3) providing (or paying for the provision of) special education and related services to the child.

In general, the agency representative at the IEP meeting would be a member of the agency or institution that is responsible for the child's education. For example, if a State agency (1) places a child in an institution, (2) is responsible under State law for the child's education, and (3) has a qualified special education staff at the institution, then a member of the institution's staff would be the agency representative at the IEP meetings.

Sometimes there is no special education staff at the institution, and the children are served by special education personnel from the LEA where the institution is located. In this situation, a member of the LEA staff would usually serve as the agency representative.

NOTE: In situations where the LEA places a child in an institution, paragraph "b" of the response to Question 1, above, would apply.

15. For a child with a disability being considered for initial placement in special education, which teacher should attend the IEP meeting?

The teacher could be either (1) a teacher qualified to provide special education in the child's area of suspected disability, or (2) the child's regular teacher. At the option of the agency, both teachers could attend. In any event, there should be at least one member of the school staff at the meeting (e.g., the agency representative or the teacher) who is qualified in the child's area of suspected disability.

NOTE: Sometimes more than one meeting is necessary in order to finalize a child's IEP. If, in this process, the special education teacher who will be working with the child is identified, it would be useful to have that teacher participate in the meeting with the parents and other members of the IEP team in finalizing the IEP. When this is not possible, the agency should ensure that the teacher is given a copy of the child's IEP as soon as possible after the IEP is finalized and before the teacher begins working with the child.

16. If a child with a disability is enrolled in both regular and special education classes, which teacher should attend the IEP meeting?

In general, the teacher at the IEP meeting should be the child's special education teacher. At the option of the agency or the parent, the child's regular teacher also might attend. If the regular teacher does not attend, the agency should either provide the regular teacher with a copy of the IEP or inform the regular teacher of its contents. Moreover, the agency should ensure that the special education teacher, or other appropriate support person, is able, as necessary, to consult with and be a resource to the child's regular teacher.

17. If a child with a disability in high school attends several regular classes, must all of the child's regular teachers attend the IEP meeting?

No. Only one teacher must attend. However, at the option of the LEA, additional teachers of the child may attend. The following points should be considered in making this decision:

a. Generally, the number of participants at IEP meetings should be small. Small meetings have several advantages over large ones. For example, they (1) allow for more open, active parent involvement, (2) are less costly, (3) are easier to arrange and conduct, and (4) are usually more productive.

b. While large meetings are generally inappropriate, there may be specific circumstances where the participation of additional staff would be beneficial. When the participation of the regular teachers is considered by the agency or the parents to be beneficial to the child's success in school (e.g., terms of the child's participation in the regular education program), it would be appropriate for them to attend the meeting.

c. Although the child's regular teachers would not routinely attend IEP meetings, they should either (1) be informed about the child's IEP by the special education teacher or agency representative, and/or (2) receive a copy of the IEP itself.

18. If a child's primary disability is a speech impairment, must the child's regular teacher attend the IEP meeting?

No. A speech-language pathologist would usually serve as the child's teacher for purposes of the IEP meeting. The regular teacher could also attend at the option of the school.

19. If a child is enrolled in a special education class because of a primary disability, and also receives speech-language pathology services, must both specialists attend the IEP meeting?

No. It is not required that both attend. The special education teacher would attend the meeting as the child's teacher. The speech-language pathologist could either (1) participate in the meeting itself, or (2) provide a written recommendation concerning the nature, frequency, and amount of services to be provided to the child.

20. When may representatives of teacher organizations attend IEP meetings?

Under the Family Educational Rights and Privacy Act ("FERPA"; 20 U.S.C. 1232g) and implementing regulations (34 CFR part 99) and the confidentiality requirements of Part B, officials of teacher organizations may not attend IEP meetings if personally identifiable information from the student's education records is discussed—except with the prior written consent of the parents. (See 34 CFR 99.30(a) and 300.571 (a)(1).)

In addition, Part B does not provide for the participation of representatives of teacher organizations at IEP meetings. The legislative history of the Act makes it clear that attendance at IEP meetings should be limited to those who have an intense interest in the child. (121 Cong. Rec. S10974 (June 18, 1975) (remarks of Sen. Randolph).) Since a representative of a teacher organization would be concerned with the interests of the teacher rather than the interests of the child, it would be inappropriate for such an official to attend an IEP meeting.

21. When may a child with a disability attend an IEP meeting?

Generally, a child with a disability should attend the IEP meeting whenever the parent decides that it is appropriate for the child to do so. Whenever possible, the agency and parents should discuss the appropriateness of the child's participation before a decision is made, in order to help the parents determine whether or not the child's attendance will be (1) helpful in developing the IEP and/or (2) directly beneficial to the child. The agency should inform the parents before each IEP meeting—as part of the notice of meeting required under § 300.345(b)—that they may invite their child to participate.

NOTE: The parents and agency should encourage older children with disabilities (particularly those at the secondary school level) to participate in their IEP meetings.

22. Do the parents of a student with a disability retain the right to attend the IEP meeting when the student reaches the age of majority?

The Act is silent concerning any modification of the rights of the parents of a student with a disability when the student reaches the age of majority.

23. Must related services personnel attend IEP meetings?

No. It is not required that they attend. However, if a child with a disability has an identified need for related services, it would be appropriate for the related services personnel to attend the meeting or otherwise be involved in developing the IEP. For example, when the child's evaluation indicates the need for a specific related service (e.g., physical therapy, occupational therapy, or counseling), the agency should ensure that a qualified provider of that service either (1) attends the IEP meeting, or (2) provides a written recommendation concerning the nature, frequency, and amount of service to be provided to the child.

NOTE: This written recommendation could be a part of the evaluation report.

24. Are agencies required to use a case manager in the development of the IEP of a child with a disability?

No. However, some agencies have found it helpful to have a special educator or some other school staff member (e.g., a social worker, counselor, or psychologist) serve as coordinator or case manager of the IEP process for an individual child or for all children with disabilities served by the agency. Examples of the kinds of activities that case managers might carry out are (1) coordinating the multidisciplinary evaluation; (2) collecting and synthesizing the evaluation reports and other relevant information about a child that might be needed at the IEP meeting; (3) communicating with the parents; and (4) participating in, or conducting, the IEP meeting itself.

25. For a child with a suspected speech impairment, who must represent the evaluation team at the IEP meeting?

No specific person must represent the evaluation team. However, a speech-language pathologist would normally be the most appropriate representative. For many children whose primary disability is a speech impairment, there may be no other evaluation personnel involved. The comment following § 300.532 (Evaluation procedures) states:

Children who have a speech impairment as their primary disability may not need a complete battery of assessments (e.g., psychological, physical, or adaptive behavior). However, a qualified speech-language pathologist would (1) evaluate each child with a speech impairment using procedures that are appropriate for the diagnosis and appraisal of speech and language impairments, and (2) if necessary, make referrals for additional assessments needed to make an appropriate placement decision.

****

§ 300.345 Parent participation. [See text of regulation, above.]
****

26. What is the role of the parents at an IEP meeting?

The parents of a child with a disability are expected to be equal participants along with school personnel, in developing, reviewing, and revising the child's IEP. This is an active role in which the parents (1) participate in the discussion about the child's need for special education and related services, and (2) join with the other participants in deciding what services the agency will provide to the child.

NOTE: In some instances, parents might elect to bring another participant to the meeting, e.g., a friend or neighbor, someone outside of the agency who is familiar with applicable laws and with the child's needs, or a specialist who conducted an independent evaluation of the child.)

27. What is the role of a surrogate parent at an IEP meeting?

A surrogate parent is a person appointed to represent the interests of a child with a disability in the educational decision-making process when that child has no other parent[al] representation. The surrogate has all of the rights and responsibilities of a parent under Part B. Thus, the surrogate parent is entitled to (1) participate in the child's IEP meeting, (2) see the child's education records, and (3) receive notice, grant consent, and invoke due process to resolve differences. (See § 300.514, Surrogate parents.)

28. Must the public agency let the parents know who will be at the IEP meeting?

Yes. In notifying parents about the meeting, the agency "must indicate the purpose, time, and location of the meeting, and *who will be in attendance*. (§ 300.345(b), emphasis added.) If possible, the agency should give the name and position of each person who will attend. In addition, the agency should inform the parents of their right to bring other participants to the meeting. (See Question 21, above, regarding participation of the child.) It is also appropriate for the agency to ask whether the parents intend to bring a participant to the meeting.

29. Are parents required to sign IEPs?

Parent signatures are not required by either the Act or regulations. However, having such signatures is considered by parents, advocates, and public agency personnel to be useful.

The following are some of the ways that IEPs signed by parents and/or agency personnel might be used:

a. A signed IEP is one way to document who attended the meeting.

NOTE: This is useful for monitoring and compliance purposes.

If signatures are not used, the agency must document attendance in some other way.

b. An IEP signed by the parents is one way to indicate that the parents approved the child's special education program.

NOTE: If, after signing, the parents feel that a change is needed in the IEP, it would be appropriate for them to request another meeting. See Question 11, above.

c. An IEP signed by an agency representative provides the parents a signed record of the services that the agency has agreed to provide.

NOTE: Even if the school personnel do not sign, the agency still must provide, or ensure the provision of, the services called for in the IEP.

30. If the parent signs the IEP, does the signature indicate consent for initial placement?

The parent's signature on the IEP would satisfy the consent requirement concerning initial placement of the child (§ 300.504(b)(1)(ii)) only if the IEP includes a statement on initial placement that meets the definition of consent in § 300.500:

Consent means that: (a) the parent has been fully informed of all information relevant to the activity for which consent is sought * * *

(b) The parent understands and agrees in writing to the carrying out of the activity for which his or her consent is sought, and the consent describes that activity and lists the records (if any) which will be released and to whom; and

(c) The parent understands that the granting of consent is voluntary * * * and may be revoked at any time.

31. Do parents have the right to a copy of their child's IEP?

Yes. Section 300.345(f) states that the public agency shall give the parent, on request, a copy of the IEP. In order that parents may know about this provision, it is recommended that they be informed about it at the IEP meeting and/or receive a copy of the IEP itself within a reasonable time following the meeting.

32. Must parents be informed at the IEP meeting of their right to appeal?

If the agency has already informed the parents of their right to appeal, as it is required to do under the prior notice provisions of the regulations (§§ 300.504-300.505), it would not be necessary for the agency to do so again at the IEP meeting.

Section 300.504(a) of the regulations states that "written notice that meets the requirements under § 300.505 must be given to parents a reasonable time" before the public agency proposes or refuses "to initiate or change the identification, evaluation, or educational placement of the child or the provision of FAPE to the child."

Section 300.505(a) states that the notice must include "(1) A full explanation of all of the procedural safeguards available to parents under § 300.500, §§ 300.502-300.515, and §§ 300.562-300.569)."

The IEP meeting serves as a communication vehicle between parents and school personnel, and enables them, as equal participants, to jointly decide upon what the child's needs are, what will be provided, and what the anticipated outcomes may be. If, during the IEP meeting, parents and school staff are unable to reach agreement, the agency should remind the parents that they may seek to resolve their differences though the due process procedures under the Act.

NOTE: Section 300.506(a) states that "a parent or public educational agency may initiate a hearing on any matters described in § 300.504(a)(1) and (2)."

Every effort should be made to resolve differences between parents and school staff without resort to a due process hearing (i.e., through voluntary mediation or some other informal step). However, mediation or other informal procedures may not be used to deny or delay a parent's right to a due process hearing. (See § 300.506. Impartial due process hearing.)

33. Does the IEP include ways for parents to check the progress of their children?

In general, the answer is yes. The IEP document is a written record of decisions jointly made by parents and school personnel at the IEP meeting regarding the special education program of a child with a disability. That record includes agreed upon items, such as goals and objectives, and the specific special education and related services to be provided to the child.

The goals and objectives in the IEP should be helpful to both parents and school personnel, in a general way, in checking on a child's progress in the special education program. (See Questions 37-43, below, regarding goals and objectives in the IEP.) However, since the IEP is not intended to include the specifics about a child's total educational program that are found in daily, weekly, or monthly instructional plans, parents will often need to obtain more specific, on-going information about the child's progress—through parent-teacher conferences, report cards and other reporting procedures ordinarily used by the agency.

34. Must IEPs include specific checkpoint intervals for parents to confer with teachers and to revise or update their children's IEPs?

No. The IEP of a child with a disability is not required to include specific "checkpoint intervals" (i.e., meeting dates) for reviewing the child's progress. However, in individual situations, specific meeting dates could be designated in the IEP, if the parents and school personnel believe that it would be helpful to do so.

Although meeting dates are not required to be set out in the IEP itself, there are specific provisions in the regulations and in this document regarding agency responsibilities in initiating IEP meetings including the following:

(1) Public agencies must hold meetings periodically, but not less than annually, to review, and if appropriate, revise, each child's IEP (§ 300.343(d)); (2) there should be as many meetings a year as the child needs (see Question 10, above); and (3) agencies should grant any reasonable parental request for an IEP meeting (see Question 11, above).

In addition to the above provisions, it is expected that, through an agency's general reporting procedures for all children in school, there will be specific designated times for parents to review their children's progress (e.g., through periodic parent teacher conferences, and/or the use of report cards, letters, or other reporting devices).

35. If the parents and agency are unable to reach agreement at an IEP meeting, what steps should be followed until agreement is reached?

As a general rule, the agency and parents would agree to an interim course of action for serving the child (i.e., in terms of placement and/or services) to be followed until the area of disagreement over the IEP is resolved. The manner in which this interim measure is developed and agreed to by both parties is left to the discretion of the individual State or local agency. However, if the parents and agency cannot agree on an interim measure, the child's last agreed upon IEP would remain in effect in the areas of disagreement until the disagreement is resolved. The following may be helpful to agencies when there are disagreements:

a. There may be instances where the parent and agency are in agreement about the basic IEP services (e.g., the child's placement and/or the special education services), but disagree about the provision of a particular related service (i.e., whether the service is needed and/or the amount to be provided). In such cases, it is recommended (1) that the IEP be implemented in all areas in which there is agreement, (2) that the document indicate the points of disagreement, and (3) that procedures be initiated to resolve the disagreement.

b. Sometimes the disagreement is with the placement or kind of special education to be provided (e.g., one party proposes a self-contained placement, and the other proposes resource room services). In such cases, the agency might, for example, carry out any one or all of the following steps:

(1) Remind the parents that they may resolve their differences through the due process procedures under Part B; (2) work with the parents to develop an interim course of action (in terms of placement and/or services) that both parties can agree to until resolution is reached: and (3) recommend the use of mediation or some other informal procedure for resolving the differences without going to a due process hearing. (See Question 32, above, regarding the right to appeal.)

c. If, because of the disagreement over the IEP, a hearing is initiated by either the parents or agency, the agency may not change the child's placement unless the parents and agency agree otherwise. (See § 300.513, Child's status during proceedings.) The following two examples are related to this requirement:

(1) A child in the regular fourth grade has been evaluated and found to be eligible for special education. The agency and parents agree that the child has a specific learning disability. However, one party proposes placement in a self-contained program, and the other proposes placement in a resource room. Agreement cannot be reached, and a due process hearing is initiated. Unless the parents and agency agree otherwise, the child would remain in the regular fourth grade until the issue is resolved.

On the other hand, since the child's need for special education is not in question, both parties might agree—as an interim measure—(1) to temporarily place the child in either one of the programs proposed at the meeting (self-contained program or resource room), or (2) to serve the child through some other temporary arrangement.

(2) A child with a disability is currently receiving special education under an existing IEP. A due process hearing has been initiated regarding an alternative special education placement for the child. Unless the parents and agency agree otherwise, the child would remain in the current placement. In this situation, the child's IEP could be revised, as necessary, and implemented in all of the areas agreed to by the parents and agency, while the area of disagreement (i.e., the child's placement) is being settled through due process.

NOTE: If the due process hearing concerns whether or not a particular service should continue to be provided under the IEP (e.g., physical therapy), that service would continue to be provided to the child under the IEP that was in effect at the time the hearing was initiated, (1) unless the parents and agency agree to a change in the services, or (2) until the issue is resolved.

****

§ 300.346 Content of individualized education program. [See text of regulation, above.]

****

36. What should be included in the statement of the child's present levels of educational performance?

The statement of present levels of educational performance will be different for each child with a disability. Thus, determinations about the content of the statement for an individual child are matters that are left to the discretion of participants in the IEP meetings. However, the following are some points that should be taken into account in writing this part of the IEP:

a. The statement should accurately describe the effect of the child's disability on the child's performance in any area of education that is affected, including (1) academic areas (reading, math, communication, etc.), and (2) non-academic areas (daily life activities, mobility, etc.).

NOTE: Labels such as mental retardation or deafness may not be used as a substitute for the description of present levels of educational performance.)

b. The statement should be written in objective measurable terms, to the extent possible. Data from the child's evaluation would be a good source of such information. Test scores that are pertinent to the child's diagnosis might be included, if appropriate. However, the scores should be (1) self-explanatory (i.e., they can be interpreted by all participants without the use of test manuals or other aids), or (2) an explanation should be included. Whatever test results are used should reflect the impact of the disability on the child's performance. Thus, raw scores would not usually be sufficient.

c. There should be a direct relationship between the present levels of educational performance and the other components of the IEP. Thus, if the statement describes a problem with the child's reading level and points to a deficiency in a specific reading skill, this problem should be addressed under both (1) goals and objectives, and (2) specific special education and related services to be provided to the child.

37. Why are goals and objectives required in the IEP?

The statutory requirements for including annual goals and short term instructional objectives (Section 602(19)(B)), and for having at least an annual review of the IEP of a child with a disability (Section 614(a)(5)) provide a mechanism for determining (1) whether the anticipated outcomes for the child are being met (i.e., whether the child is progressing in the special education program) and (2) whether the placement and services are appropriate to the child's special learning needs. In effect, these requirements provide a way for the child's teacher(s) and parents to be able to track the child's progress in special education. However, the goals and objectives in the IEP are not intended to be as specific as the goals and objectives that are normally found in daily, weekly, or monthly instructional plans.

38. What are annual goals in an IEP?

The annual goals in the IEP are statements which describe what a child with a disability can reasonably be expected to accomplish within a twelve month period in the child's special education program. As indicated under Question 36, above, there should be a direct relationship between the annual goals and the present levels of educational performance.

39. What are short term instructional objectives in an IEP?

Short term instructional objectives (also called IEP objectives) are measurable, intermediate steps between the present levels of educational performance of a child with a disability and the annual goals that are established for the child. The objectives are developed based on a logical breakdown of the major components of the annual goals, and can serve as milestones for measuring progress toward meeting the goals.

In some respects, IEP objectives are similar to objectives used in daily classroom instructional plans. For example, both kinds of objectives are used (1) to describe what a given child is expected to accomplish in a particular area within some specified time period, and (2) to determine the extent that the child is progressing toward those accomplishments.

In other respects, objectives in IEPs are different from those used in instructional plans, primarily in the amount of detail they provide. IEP objectives provide general benchmarks for determining progress toward meeting the annual goals. These objectives should be projected to be accomplished over an extended period of time (e.g., an entire school quarter or semester). On the other hand, the objectives in classroom instructional plans deal with more specific outcomes that are to be accomplished on a daily, weekly, or monthly basis. Classroom instructional plans generally include details not required in an IEP, such as the specific methods, activities, and materials (e.g., use of flash cards) that will be used in accomplishing the objectives.

40. Should the IEP goals and objectives focus only on special education and related services, or should they relate to the total education of the child?

IEP goals and objectives are concerned primarily with meeting the needs of a child with a disability for special education and related services, and are not required to cover other areas of the child's education. Stated another way, the goals and objectives in the IEP should focus on offsetting or reducing the problems resulting from the child's disability that interfere with learning and educational performance in school. For example, if a child with a learning disability is functioning several grades below the child's indicated ability in reading and has a specific problem with word recognition, the IEP goals and objectives would be directed toward (1) closing the gap between the child's indicated ability and current level of functioning, and (2) helping the child increase the ability to use word attack skills effectively (or to find some other approach to increase independence in reading).

For a child with a mild speech impairment, the IEP objectives would focus on improving the child's communication skills, by either (1) correcting the impairment, or (2) minimizing its effect on the child's ability to communicate. On the other hand, the goals and objectives for a child with severe mental retardation would be more comprehensive and cover more of the child's school program than if the child has only a mild disability.

41. Should there be a relationship between the goals and objectives in the IEP and those that are in instructional plans of special education personnel?

Yes. There should be a direct relationship between the IEP goals and objectives for a given child with a disability and the goals and objectives that are in the special education instructional plans for the child. However, the IEP is not intended to be detailed enough to be used as an instructional plan. The IEP, through its goals and objectives, (1) sets the general direction to be taken by those who will implement the IEP, and (2) serves as the basis for developing a detailed instructional plan for the child.

NOTE: See Question 56, below, regarding the length of IEPs.

42. When must IEP objectives be written—before placement or after placement?

IEP objectives must be written before placement. Once a child with a disability is placed in a special education program, the teacher might develop lesson plans or more detailed objectives based on the IEP; however, such plans and objectives are not required to be a part of the IEP itself.

43. Can short term instructional objectives be changed without initiating another IEP meeting?

No. Section 300.343(a) provides that the agency "is responsible for initiating and conducting meetings for the purpose of developing, reviewing, and *revising* the IEP of a child with a disability" (emphasis added). Since a change in short term instructional objectives constitutes a revision of the child's IEP, the agency must (1) notify the parents of the proposed change (see § 300.504(a)(1)), and (2) initiate an IEP meeting. Note, however, that if the parents are unable or unwilling to attend such a meeting, their participation in the revision of the IEP objectives can be obtained through other means, including individual or conference telephone calls (see § 300.345(c)).

44. Must the IEP include all special education and related services needed by the child or only those available from the public agency?

Each public agency must provide a FAPE to all children with disabilities under its jurisdiction. Therefore, the IEP for a child with a disability must include all of the specific special education and related services needed by the child—as determined by the child's current evaluation. This means that the services must be listed in the IEP even if they are not directly available from the local agency, and must be provided by the agency through contract or other arrangements.

45. Is the IEP a commitment to provide services—i.e., must a public agency provide all of the services listed in the IEP?

Yes. The IEP of each child with a disability must include all services necessary to meet the child's identified special education and related services needs; and all services in the IEP must be provided in order for the agency to be in compliance with the Act.

46. Must the public agency itself directly provide the services set out in the IEP?

The public agency responsible for the education of a child with a disability could provide IEP services to the child (1) directly, through the agency's own staff resources, or (2) indirectly, by contracting with another public or private agency, or through other arrangements. In providing the services, the agency may use whatever State, local, Federal, and private sources of support are available for those purposes (see § 300.301(a)). However, the services must be at no cost to the parents, and responsibility for ensuring that the IEP services are provided remains with the public agency.

47. Does the IEP include only special education and related services or does it describe the total education of the child?

The IEP is required to include only those matters concerning the provision of special education and related services and the extent that the child can participate in regular education programs. (NOTE: The regulations define special education as specially designed instruction to meet the unique needs of a child with a disability, and related services as those services that are necessary to assist the child to benefit from special education.) (See §§ 300.17 and 300.16, respectively.)

For some children with disabilities, the IEP will only address a very limited part of their education (e.g., for a child with a speech impairment, the IEP would generally be limited to the child's speech impairment). For other children (e.g., those with profound mental retardation), the IEP might cover their total education. An IEP for a child with a physical disability with no mental or emotional disability might consist only of specially designed physical education. However, if the child also has a mental or emotional disability, the IEP might cover most of the child's education.

NOTE: The IEP is not intended to be detailed enough to be used as an instructional plan. See Question 41, above.

48. If modifications are necessary for a child with a disability to participate in a regular education program, must they be included in the IEP?

Yes. If modifications (supplementary aids and services) to the regular education program are necessary to ensure the child's participation in that program, those modifications must be described in the child's IEP (e.g., for a child with a hearing impairment, special seating arrangements or the provision of assignments in writing). This applies to any regular education program in which the student may participate, including physical education, art, music, and vocational education.

49. When must physical education (PE) be described or referred to in the IEP?

Section 300.307(a) provides that physical education services, specially designed if necessary, must be made available to every child with a disability receiving FAPE. The following paragraphs (1) set out some of the different PE program arrangements for students with disabilities, and (2) indicate whether, and to what extent, PE must be described or referred to in an IEP:

a. Regular PE with nondisabled students. If a student with a disability can participate fully in the regular PE program without any special modifications to compensate for the student's disability, it would not be necessary to describe or refer to PE in the IEP. On the other hand, if some modifications to the regular PE program are necessary for the student to be able to participate in that program, those modifications must be described in the IEP.

b. Specially designed PE. If a student with a disability needs a specially designed PE program, that program must be addressed in all applicable areas of the IEP (e.g., present levels of educational performance, goals and objectives, and services to be provided). However, these statements would not have to be presented in any more detail than the other special education services included in the student's IEP.

c. PE in separate facilities. If a student with a disability is educated in a separate facility, the PE program for that student must be described or referred to in the IEP. However, the kind and amount of information to be included in the IEP would depend on the physical-motor needs of the student and the type of PE program that is to be provided.

Thus, if a student is in a separate facility that has a standard PE program (e.g., a residential school for students with deafness), and if it is determined—on the basis of the student's most recent evaluation—that the student is able to participate in that program without any modifications, then the IEP need only note such participation. On the other hand, if special modifications to the PE program are needed for the student to participate, those modifications must be described in the IEP. Moreover, if the student needs an individually designed PE program, that program must be addressed under all applicable parts of the IEP. (See paragraph "b", above.)

50. If a student with a disability is to receive vocational education, must it be described or referred to in the student's IEP?

The answer depends on the kind of vocational education program to be provided. If a student with a disability is able to participate in the regular vocational education program without any modifications to compensate for the student's disability, it would not be necessary to include vocational education in the student's IEP. On the other hand, if modifications to the regular vocational education program are necessary in order for the student to participate in that program, those modifications must be included in the IEP. Moreover, if the student needs a specially designed vocational education program, then vocational education must be described in all applicable areas of the student's IEP (e.g., present levels of educational performance, goals and objectives, and specific services to be provided). However, these statements would not have to be presented in any more detail than the other special education services included in the IEP.

51. Must the IEP specify the amount of services or may it simply list the services to be provided?

The amount of services to be provided must be stated in the IEP, so that the level of the agency's commitment of resources will be clear to parents and other IEP team members. The amount of time to be committed to each of the various services to be provided must be (1) appropriate to that specific service, and (2) stated in the IEP in a manner that is clear to all who are involved in both the development and implementation of the IEP.

Changes in the amount of services listed in the IEP cannot be made without holding another IEP meeting. However, as long as there is no change in the overall amount, some adjustments in scheduling the services should be possible (based on the professional judgment of the service provider) without holding another IEP meeting.

NOTE: The parents should be notified whenever this occurs.

52. Must the IEP of a child with a disability indicate the extent that the child will be educated in the regular educational program?

Yes. Section 300.346(c) provides that the IEP for each child with a disability must include a "statement of * * * the extent that the child will be able to participate in regular educational programs." One way of meeting this requirement is to indicate the percent of time the child will be spending in the regular education program with nondisabled students. Another way is to list the specific regular education classes the child will be attending.

NOTE: If a child with a severe disability, for example, is expected to be in a special classroom setting most of the time, it is recommended that, in meeting the above requirement, the IEP include any non-curricular activities in which the child will be participating with non-handicapped students (e.g.. lunch, assembly periods, club activities, and other special events).

53. Can the anticipated duration of services be for more than twelve months?

In general, the anticipated duration of services would be up to twelve months. There is a direct relationship between the anticipated duration of services and the other parts of the IEP (e.g., annual goals and short term objectives), and each part of the IEP would be addressed whenever there is a review of the child's program. If it is anticipated that the child will need a particular service for more than one year, the duration of that service could be projected beyond that time in the IEP. However, the duration of each service must be reconsidered whenever the IEP is reviewed.

54. Must the evaluation procedures and schedules be included as a separate item in the IEP?

No. The evaluation procedures and schedules need not be included as a separate item in the IEP, but they must be presented in a recognizable form and be clearly linked to the short term instructional objectives.

NOTE: In many instances, these components are incorporated directly into the objectives.

OTHER QUESTIONS ABOUT THE CONTENT OF AN IEP

55. Is it permissible for an agency to have the IEP completed when the IEP meeting begins?

No. It is not permissible for an agency to present a completed IEP to parents for their approval before there has been a full discussion with the parents of (1) the child's need for special education and related services, and (2) what services the agency will provide to the child. Section 602(20) of the Act defines the IEP as a written statement developed in any meeting with the agency representative, the teacher, the parent, and, whenever appropriate, the child.

It would be appropriate for agency staff to come prepared with evaluation findings, statements of present levels of educational performance, and a recommendation regarding annual goals, short term instructional objectives, and the kind of special education and related services to be provided. However, the agency must make it clear to the parents at the outset of the meeting that the services proposed by the agency are only recommendations for review and discussion with the parents. The legislative history of Pub. L. 94-142 makes it clear that parents must be given the opportunity to be active participants in all major decisions affecting the education of their children with disabilities. (See. e.g., S. Rep. No. 168, 94th Cong. 1st Sess. 13 (1975); S. Rep. No. 455 (Conference Report), 94th Cong. 1st Sess. 47-50 (1975).)

56. Is there a prescribed format or length for an IEP?

No. The format and length of an IEP are matters left to the discretion of State and local agencies. The IEP should be as long as necessary to adequately describe a child's program. However, as indicated in Question 41, above, the IEP is not intended to be a detailed instructional plan. The Federal IEP requirements can usually be met in a one to three page form.

NOTE: In a national survey conducted under contract with the Department, it was found that 47% of the IEPs reviewed were 3 pages or less in length.

57. Is it permissible to consolidate the IEP with an individualized service plan developed under another Federal program?

Yes. In instances where a handicapped child must have both an IEP and an individualized service plan under another Federal program, it may be possible to develop a single, consolidated document only if: (1) It contains all of the information required in an IEP, and (2) all of the necessary parties participate in its development.

Examples of individualized service plans that might be consolidated with the IEP are: (1) The Individualized Care Plan (Title XIX of the Social Security Act (Medicaid)), (2) the individualized Program Plan (Title XX of the Social Security Act (Social Services)), (3) the Individualized Service Plan (Title XVI of the Social Security Act (Supplemental Security Income)), and (4) the Individualized Written Rehabilitation Plan (Rehabilitation Act of 1973).

58. What provisions on confidentiality of information apply to IEPs?

IEPs are subject to the confidentiality provisions of both (1) Part B (Section 617(c) of the Act; §§ 300.560-300.576 of the regulations), and (2) the Family Educational

Rights and Privacy Act ("FERPA"' 20 U.S.C. 1232g) and implementing regulations in 34 CFR Part 99. An IEP is an education record as that term is used in the FERPA and implementing regulations (34 CFR [Part] 99.3) and is, therefore, subject to the same protections as other education records relating to the student.

NOTE: Under Section 99.31(a) of the FERPA regulations, an educational agency may disclose personally identifiable information from the education records of a student without the written consent of the parents "(1) The disclosure is to other school officials, including teachers, within the agency or institution whom the agency or institution has determined to have legitimate educational interests * * *" in that information.

****

§ 300.348 Private school placements by public agencies.
[See text of regulation, above.]
****

59. If placement decisions are made at the time the IEP is developed, how can a private school representative attend the meeting?

Generally, a child who requires placement in either a public or private residential school has already been receiving special education, and the parents and school personnel have often jointly been involved over a prolonged period of time in attempting to find the most appropriate placement for the child. At some point in this process (e.g., at a meeting where the child's current IEP is being reviewed), the possibility of residential school placement might be proposed—by either the parents or school personnel. If both agree, then the matter would be explored with the residential school. A subsequent meeting would then be conducted to finalize the IEP. At this meeting, the public agency must ensure that a representative of the residential school either (1) attends the meeting, or (2) participates through individual or conference telephone calls, or by other means.

****

§ 300.349 Children with disabilities in parochial or other private schools.
[See text of regulation, above.]
****

****

§ 300.350 Individualized education program—accountability.
[See text of regulation, above.]
****

60. Is the IEP a performance contract?

No. Section 300.350 makes it clear that the IEP is not a performance contract that imposes liability on a teacher or public agency if a child with a disability does not meet the IEP objectives. While the agency must provide special education and related services in accordance with the IEP of a child with a disability, the Act does not require that the agency, the teacher, or other persons be held accountable if the child does not achieve the growth projected in the written statement.

AUTHORITY 20 U.S.C. 1411-1420
(Catalog of Federal Domestic Assistance number 84.027, Assistance to States for Education of Children with Disabilities; 84.173 Preschool Grants Program)
[57 FR 48694, Oct. 27, 1992]

Cases Interpreting the Individuals with
Disabilities Education Act Regulations (34 CFR Part 300)

IDEA regulations published by the Department of Education provide interpretive guidance to IDEA principles. The following cases provide case law guidance to the regulations and statute.

A.E. by and through Evans v. Indep. School Dist. 25, 936 F.2d 472 (10th Cir.1991). An Oklahoma student who was learning disabled in math also had a conduct disorder. Her parents sought to have her labeled as seriously disturbed. The U.S. Court of Appeals, Tenth Circuit, determined that just because a student was socially maladjusted did not automatically qualify her as **seriously emotionally disturbed** under **34 CFR Part 300.5(b)(8)**. The court ruled that she would have to show that the **emotional disorder affected her ability to benefit from education**.

Anderson v. Dist. of Columbia., 877 F.2d 1018 (D.C.Cir.1989). The U.S. Court of Appeals, District of Columbia Circuit, did not require a public school district to fund the private school placement of learning disabled students pending appeal from a federal district court under the stay-put provision of 20 U.S.C. § 1415(e)(3). The stay-put provision did not apply following the conclusion of district (trial) court proceedings. Special education placements must be based upon the student's **IEP** under **34 CFR Part 300.552(a)(2)**. Hearing officers are required to make **written findings of fact** under **34 CFR Part 300.508(a)(5)**.

Angela L. v. Pasadena Indep. School Dist., 918 F.2d 1188 (5th Cir.1990). After a Texas child failed all of her fifth grade classes, her parents sought to have her classified as disabled. The school district refused and a due process hearing was held. The parties entered into a settlement agreement. The parents sued for attorney's fees. The U.S. Court of Appeals, Fourth Circuit, determined that the parents were the prevailing party because the student received **occupational therapy** which is authorized under **34 CFR Part 300.13**.

Angevine v. Smith, 959 F.2d 292 (D.C.Cir.1992). The U.S. Court of Appeals, District of Columbia Circuit, ruled that under **34 CFR Part 300.403(a)** the school district was not required to pay for a **private placement** if it offered an appropriate public school placement. The appellate court also noted that the lower court erred by considering the progress of the student at the private school because it was suggestive of potential maximizing.

Ash v. Lake Oswego School Dist No. 7J, 766 F.Supp. 852 (D.Or.1991). An Oregon child was diagnosed with infantile autism and his parents placed him in a residential school for autistic children. After four years, the parents contacted the school district about tuition reimbursement. The school district evaluated the child and offered to place him in a self-contained classroom at a nearby school. The parents appealed this decision and a federal district court found that under **34 CFR Part 300.302** the state was required to pay for the autistic child's **residential placement** because he needed a 24 hour consistent enrollment in order to benefit from his education. However, the court determined that the school district's obligation did not arise until the parents had contacted the school about placing their son.

Babb v. Knox City School System, 965 F.2d 104 (6th Cir.1992). The parents of an emotionally disturbed child sought reimbursement for expenses paid for a residential placement. The court ordered reimbursement and ruled that the student should have been classified as **seriously emotionally disturbed** under **34 CFR Part 300.5(b)(8)** due to physical abuse of siblings and classmates, torture of animals, and property destruction. Thus, the appropriate placement was a residential facility where the student would receive psychiatric care. The court also found that the school district had violated **34 CFR Parts 300.531 and 300.532(f)** by failing to provide a **"full and individual evaluation."** The school district failed to consult the student's academic record, personal psychologist or his parents. Since the school district did not comply with the procedural requirements under the IDEA, the parents were not required to exhaust their **administrative remedies** as required under **CFR Parts 300.550 to 300.552**.

Barnett v. Fairfax Cty School Board, 927 F.2d 146 (4th Cir.1991). The parents of a hearing impaired student objected to their son's placement at a school five miles away from home. They wished to send their son to a nearby school with a cued speech interpreter. **34 CFR Parts 300.522 and 300.552** provide that a student should be placed **as close to home as possible** in the school the child would attend if not handicapped. However, the U.S. Court of Appeals, Fourth Circuit, ruled that it was acceptable to **consider the financial strain** on the school district in determining an appropriate placement.

Block v. Dist. of Columbia, 748 F.Supp. 891 (D.D.C.1990). After a school district failed to implement an IEP at the beginning of the school year, the mother unilaterally placed the student in a private school. The school district then developed an IEP which provided for a public school placement. The court ruled that although the public placement was appropriate, the school district would have to pay for the private school because a switch in the middle of the school year would be harmful to the student. See **34 CFR Parts 300.132, 300.227, 300.307(b), and 300.347**. The court also found the school district's 11-day delay in providing an official decision was significant and had violated **34 CFR Part 300.512(a)** which states that an official decision be made within 45 days after receipt of a request for a hearing.

Board of Educ., Sacramento Cty School Dist. v. Holland, 786 F.Supp. 874 (E.D.Cal.1992). A federal district court determined that the appropriate placement of a moderately mentally retarded student was in a full regular classroom with supportive services to comport with the **mainstreaming requirement** of the IDEA. See **34 CFR Part 300.550**.

Bow School Dist. v. Quentin W., 750 F.Supp. 546 (D.N.H.1990). After the state department of education ordered reimbursement and development of a new IEP for a learning and emotionally disabled child, the school district appealed. The court found that the school district's appeal was time barred because the statute of limitations for appeal was 30 days. See **34 CFR Part 300.512(a)**.

Brown v. Wilson County School Board, 747 F.Supp. 436 (M.D.Tenn.1990). A federal district court determined that a brain damaged student with the inability to control her behavior or conform her conduct rendered her disabled within the meaning of **34 CFR Part 300.5(b)(8)** because the disabilities affected her ability to **benefit from education** and were not exclusively **medical in nature**. The parents sought reimbursement for placing the student in a residential facility for brain injury victims and the school district refused. On appeal, the court ordered reimbursement and determined that the program was not medical in nature but offered special education and related services allowed under the IDEA. Further, the court determined that the **amount of available insurance coverage had no bearing on the educational distinction**. See **34 CFR Part 300.301(b)**.

Burke County Board of Educ. v. Denton, 895 F.2d 973 (4th Cir.1990). **34 CFR Part 300.302** states that where home instruction or residential placement is necessary to allow a child to benefit educationally, the local education agency must pay for the costs. The U.S. Court of Appeals, Fourth Circuit, determined that a home habilitation plan that helped conform the student's behavior at home, but was not necessary to allow her to benefit educationally, was not covered as a related service under the IDEA. Further, the court found that the requirements of **34 CFR Part 300.342(b)(2) and 300.343(c)** (that an IEP be developed within 30 days of a determination that the child needs special education) were met when the IEP was developed 4 days after receiving the evaluation even though it was not developed within 30 days of the determination that she needed special education.

Caroline T. v. Hudson School Dist., 915 F.2d 752 (1st Cir.1990). Parents sought to enjoin school district from using a court reporter during a special education proceeding. The court allowed the court reporter under **34 CFR Part 300.508(a)** which states that any party has the right to a **written verbatim recording**.

Carter v. Florence County School Dist. Four, 950 F.2d 156 (4th Cir.1991). A school district implemented an IEP which called for the student's reading to progress from grade level 5.4 to 5.8. The parents were dissatisfied with the progress projection and placed the student in a private school. The parents then brought suit for a violation of the IDEA and reimbursement of private school expenses. The U.S. Court of Appeals, Fourth Circuit, awarded reimbursement because the school district failed to provide an IEP that called for more than **minimal or trivial progress**. Further, the court ordered reimbursement even though the private school was not approved by the state because **federal regulations only apply to a private school when the child is placed there by a state agency**. See **34 CFR Part 300.400 to 300.403**.

Chester County Intern. Unit v. Pennsylvania Shield, 896 F.2d 808 (3rd Cir.1988). The U.S. Court of Appeals, Third Circuit, cited **34 CFR Part 300.301** as the justification for ruling that **the IDEA does not preclude companies offering medical and hospital insurance from excluding those services from coverage which are provided free of charge** under the IDEA. **Section 301** provides that each state may use whatever state, local, federal, and **private sources** available to provide adequate educational services to its disabled students.

Chris D. v. Montgomery Cty Board of Education, 743 F.Supp. 1524 (M.D.Ala.1990). The school board was required to place an emotionally disabled 12-year-old in a residential school after several public and private placements did not meet his behavioral needs. The court found that home instruction was too isolated to **mainstream him to the maximum extent possible**. See **34 CFR Part 300.302**.

Chris D. v. Montgomery Cty Board of Educ., 753 F.Supp. 922 (M.D.Ala.1990). The court found that the school board did not satisfy requirements of the IDEA in developing a program for an emotionally disabled student. Therefore, the court granted the parents' request to adopt the outside consultant's IEP which called for **parent counseling**. The court noted that counseling of parents was a related service under **34 CFR Part 300.13(a)** if needed to allow a student to benefit from his education. The court also found that the school district had violated **34 CFR Part 300.13(b)(6)** by failing to provide information to the parents about the developmental and educational needs of their child.

Christopher P. by Norma P. v. Marcus, 915 F.2d 794 (2d Cir.1990). After a disabled student was discharged from a medical facility and affiliated special school, his parents filed suit against the facility protesting that the discharge violated their procedural rights. The court noted that the IDEA only applies to state and **local educational agencies**, intermediate educational units, and schools and state correctional facilities. See **34 CFR Part 300.2**. The court determined that the medical facility was not the local education agency. Thus, the facility was not required to provide due process to the student.

Clovis Unified v. Office of Administration Hearings, 903 F.2d 635 (9th Cir.1990). A California student's behavior deteriorated to the point where she was hospitalized at an **acute care facility**. Her parents sued for reimbursement of the costs of the facility. The court denied reimbursement under **34 CFR Parts 300.13** and **34 CFR Part 300.302** because the placement was mostly for medical reasons and the school district was not obligated to pay for the costs.

Cordrey v. Euckert, 917 F.2d 1460 (6th Cir.1990). An Ohio student's parents sought to revise their son's IEP. They wished to have an **extended school year program** permanently placed in his IEP. He had been attending a summer program for the last 2 years. During the IEP meeting, the student's teacher was not present as required under **34 CFR Part 300.343(d)**. After the parents refused the offer of another IEP meeting with the teacher present, the school district held an IEP meeting without the parents present. The parents claimed a **procedural violation**. However, the court found that the parents waived their right to a properly constituted IEP meeting when they refused the offer to reschedule (with the benefit of counsel). Further, they could not show that another meeting would have been futile. The court held that although the school district held the meeting without the parents present, it was in **substantial compliance** with the IDEA. The court also ruled that the **stay put** provision (**34 CFR Part 300.513**) had not been violated when the student's extended year program was canceled because the ESY (extended school year) was never officially part of his IEP.

Doe v. Alabama State Dept. of Educ., 915 F.2d 651 (11th Cir.1990). Georgia parents filed an action under the IDEA concerning placement of their child who suffered from manic-depressive illness. The school district and parents had been trying for years to find an appropriate placement for the student. The court determined that a violation of the **parental notification requirement** did not require relief because no damage was incurred. Further, the U.S. Court of Appeals, Eleventh Circuit, found that while some procedural deficiencies existed, the school district was in **substantial compliance** because it maintained close contact with the parents, gave actual notice, and the deficiency had no impact on the parents' decision. See **34 CFR**

Parts 300.504(a), 300.504(b) and 300.505(a). Further, **34 CFR Part 300.532** requires that a **multidisciplinary team test specific areas of educational needs and be tailored to the student**. However, the court found no violation because the child's **fragile emotional state** did not allow testing. The court also found no violation of **34 CFR Part 300.551** (which requires the school district to consider residential placement) because it did not have an inflexible policy that all children with a similar handicapping condition are never provided a residential placement.

Doe v. Board of Educ. of State of Conn., 753 F.Supp. 65 (D.Conn. 1990). Connecticut parents sought to have their disabled child educated under the IDEA. He had severe behavioral problems. However, he was able to do exceptionally well academically. The definition of **seriously emotionally disturbed** is a "condition over a long time and to a marked degree which affects **educational performance**." Thus, the court determined that the student was not disabled under **34 CFR Part 300.5(b)(8)** where his emotional and behavioral problems did not adversely affect his educational performance.

Doe v. Maher, 793 F.2d 1470 (9th Cir.1986), later proceeding, 795 F.2d 787, *cert. granted on other grounds*, 479 U.S. 1084, 107 S.Ct. 1284, 94 L.Ed.2d 142 (1987). Although IDEA regulations at **34 CFR Part 300.513** allow educational agencies to use normal disciplinary procedures where students with disabilities present a risk of harm to themselves and others, the IDEA prohibits expulsion of a special education student for misbehavior which is linked to a disabling condition. Before any **change in placement**, such as an **expulsion**, special education students have the right to avail themselves of the IDEA's procedural protections.

Doe by and through Doe v. Defendant I, 898 F.2d 1186 (6th Cir.1990). No IEP was implemented at the beginning of the school year because a student's father requested that the student be given a chance to attend regular class. After the student failed all subjects, an IEP meeting was held. The parents rejected the IEP and appealed the decision. On appeal, the parents claimed that the school district violated the IDEA by not providing an IEP at the beginning of the school year as required under **34 CFR Part 300.342**. The U.S. Court of Appeals, Sixth Circuit, determined that there was no need for an IEP until a **§ 343** meeting had taken place which did not occur until November. Further, the court found that the father's request that nothing be done until November was given great weight as parents are supposed to be involved in the IEP process. See **34 CFR Part 300.345**.

Edwards-White v. Dist. of Columbia, 785 F.Supp. 1022 (D.D.C.1992). Parent's request for due process hearing obligated school district to review and possibly revise child's IEP under **34 CFR Parts 300.343(a) and 300.343(d)** which require the school district to review and revise the IEP **at least** once a year.

E.H. v. Tirozzi, 735 F.Supp. 53 (D.Conn.1990). Parents wanted to tape record placement meeting so that the mother, who was Danish, could better understand the proceedings. The court determined that she could under **34 CFR Part 300.345** which emphasizes parental participation.

Eva N. v. Brock, 741 F.Supp. 626 (E.D.Ky.1990). Parents of a mentally retarded child who was also blind challenged the refusal to admit the student to the state school for the blind. The court found that the school could be required to accept **blind students who have other disabilities** even if they would not meet the **admission requirements**, if the placement was called for in their IEP. The court found that the school was not separate from the state and thus, if the state's placement decision was to place the student in the school then it must accept the student. See **34 CFR Part 300.344**.

Evans v. Evans, 818 F.Supp. 1215 (N.D.Ind.1993). **34 CFR Part 300.343 requires school districts to implement IEPs immediately** and to commence provision of special education services without undue delay. An Indiana statute which added an additional layer of administrative activity to the provisions of the IDEA caused a delay of nearly 200 days for many Indiana students who required residential placement. The U.S. District Court for the Northern District of Indiana held that the Indiana statute violated the IDEA and denied a summary judgment motion filed by state officials in a class action suit.

Fagan v. Dist. of Columbia, 817 F.Supp. 161 (D.D.C.1993). **34 CFR Part 300.345 requires school districts to include parents in the development of IEPs** for disabled students. The parents of a disabled student residing in the District of Columbia obtained an administrative ruling that their son's placement was inappropriate because the parents had been excluded from the IEP development process. However, the parents were not entitled to tuition reimbursement because they had unilaterally placed the student in an unapproved institution.

Field v. Haddonfield Board of Education, 769 F.Supp. 1313 (D.N.J.1991). A federal district court ruled that parents would be responsible for the costs of a **drug treatment program** because under **34 CFR Part 300.302**, the drug treatment would be for mostly **medical reasons** and not necessary to allow the student to benefit educationally. The only medical services provided for under the IDEA are those services provided by licensed physicians to determine medically related disabling conditions. See **34 CFR Part 300.16(b)(4)**.

Frutiger v. Hamilton Central School Dist., 928 F.2d 68 (5th Cir.1990). Parents of a learning disabled student brought suit raising issues concerning the student's IEP. The court found that the parents must exhaust their **administrative remedies** first. **34 CFR Parts 300.506 and 300.512** set out a two tier administrative review of a child's IEP which must be exhausted unless the parents can show that it would be futile to continue through the process.

G.P. v. Westmoreland Dist., 930 F.2d 1490 (1st Cir.1991). **34 CFR Part 300.503(c)(1)** states that the results of an **independent education evaluation** must be considered by the school district with regard to placement of a disabled student. The U.S. Court of Appeals, First Circuit, ruled that the parents' argument that the school district did not sufficiently consider their evaluation as required under § **503(c)(1)** failed because the hearing officer had specifically mentioned the evaluation in his decision.

Granite School Dist. v. Shannon M. by Myrna M., 787 F.Supp. 1020 (D.Utah 1990). Parents sought to have their child who required constant **tracheostomy care** educated at school. The court found that services which could be performed by a school nurse must be provided at school. See **34 CFR Part 300.13(b)(10)**. However, the court found that the burden of the cost of the medical services should not be shifted to the school district under the guise of related services. The court **allowed the school district to consider the cost of the service in development of an IEP**. Thus, the school district's home placement was upheld as meeting the requirements of the IDEA.

Greer v. Rome City School Dist., 762 F.Supp. 936 (N.D.Ga.1990). A Georgia father sought to have his son's IEP invalidated. The federal district court found that the IEP failed to properly mainstream and thus was not the **least restrictive environment**. The court opined that under **34 CFR Parts 300.340 to 300.349** the question to ask was: **Can education in a regular class be achieved satisfactorily with the aid of supplements? If not, then is the child mainstreamed to the maximum extent possible?** Further, the court determined that the school district did not comply with **34 CFR Part 300.551(a)** which requires the school district to provide a **continuum of alternate placements** — the school district did not make provisions for supplemental services to be provided in conjunction with a regular class placement.

Hall v. Knott Cty Board of Educ., 941 F.2d 402 (6th Cir.1991). A blind high school graduate sought damages from the school district for failure to follow statutorily mandated procedural rights. Specifically, she alleged that the school district should not be able to use the **statute of limitations** defense because it failed to advise her parents of their procedural rights. See **34 CFR Parts 300.504 to 300.506**. The court disagreed and stated that the parents had missed their "**window of opportunity**." A dissenting judge opined that it was unreasonable to expect the parents to assert rights that they were not aware existed.

Heldman v. Sobol, 962 F.2d 148 (2d Cir.1992). Father brought an action under the IDEA challenging the authority of the board of education to appoint a hearing officer. The court noted that under **34 CFR Parts 300.506 and 300.507** the parents have a **right to an impartial hearing officer** whose "personal and professional interests do not conflict with the ability to make an impartial decision." Thus, the father had a right to bring the action and was not required to exhaust his administrative remedies.

Helms v. McDaniel, 657 F.2d 800 (5th Cir.1981), *rehearing den.*, 664 F.2d 291, *cert. den.*, 455 U.S. 946, 102 S.Ct. 1443, 71 L.Ed.2d 658 (1982). Compliance with the EHA (now IDEA) also satisfies the Rehabilitation Act § 504. See **34 CFR Part 104.36**.

Hiller v. Board of Education of Brunswick Central School Dist., 743 F.Supp. 958 (N.D.N.Y.1990). A federal district court ruled that **a student who exhibited a weak attention span and poor handwriting was not learning disabled** within the meaning of the IDEA. **34 CFR part 300.541(a)** states that to be learning disabled the student must have a **severe discrepancy** between achievement and intellectual ability in one or more areas: listening comprehension, oral expression, written expression, basic reading, reading comprehension, or math comprehension. Further, the court found that the procedural violation **34 CFR Part 300.543** (the school district did not file a written report of the evaluation) did not violate the **spirit of the IDEA**.

Honig v. Doe, 484 U.S. 305, 108 S.Ct. 592, 98 L.Ed.2d 686 (1987). The U.S. Supreme Court determined that a **student's inability to conform conduct to socially acceptable norms rendered him disabled** within the meaning of the IDEA and satisfied the regulations set out in **34 CFR Part 300.5(b)(8)**. Further, the court ruled that the school district must comport with the **stay-put** provision of the IDEA when the expulsion or suspension is the result of behavior related to the student's disability. However, the ruling does not preclude the school district from carrying out the **normal suspension procedure** when the child is a **danger to himself or others** and thus, would not violate **34 CFR Part 300.513**.

Howey by Howey v. Tippecanoe School Corp., 734 F.Supp. 1485 (N.D.Ind.1990). Parents sought to have their own physical therapist work with their daughter instead of school district personnel. The parents would not give **medical consent** for the therapist to work with the child. The court found that under **34 CFR Part 300.500(c)** medical consent is voluntary and may be revoked at any time but could not be used to throw up road blocks for evaluation of the child. The school district then argued that it should not have to pay for the benefit if it did not have the parents' medical consent. However, the court found that except for placement, consent may not be required as a condition for any benefit. See **34 CFR Part 300.504(b)(2)**. Thus, the court ordered the school district to pay the costs of the parents' physical therapist.

Jerkins v. Squillarote, 935 F.2d 303 (D.C.Cir.1991). A Washington, D.C., school superintendent appealed a hearing examiner's finding that the notice to the parents was insufficient. The court dismissed the suit as moot because the student had graduated. However, the Federal Circuit reversed the dismissal stating that there was still a controversy because the **school district could still be aggrieved by a similar application** of the IDEA in the future. See **34 CFR Part 300.505(a)**.

Jenkins by and through Jenkins v. State of Florida, 931 F.2d 1469 (11th Cir.1991). A class action suit was brought by a disabled student who required residential placement. The court ruled that under **34 CFR Part 300.302**, maintenance fees are prohibited if the residential placement is required for educational purposes.

Johnson v. Indep. School Dist. No.4 of Bixby, Oklahoma, 921 F.2d 1022 (10th Cir.1990). The court found that to determine whether a structured summer program was appropriate required consideration of both retrospective data and predictive data. See **34 CFR Parts 300.1** through **300.754**. The court also dismissed the center that provided the special services from suit stating that it was the responsibility of the local education agency to provide education to the student. See **34 CFR Part 300.8**.

Kerkam v. Superintendent, D.C. Public Schools, 931 F.2d 84 (D.C.Cir.1991). A severely retarded student's IEP provided an extended day program to meet the requirements of the IDEA. The court noted that even though the student could have increased educational progress through a residential placement, the school district need not **maximize** the student's potential and the school district met the requirements of **34 CFR Part 300.552**.

Kerr Center Parents Ass'n v. Charles, 897 F.2d 1463 (9th Cir.1990). **Placement** of disabled Oregon students for **medical reasons** was sufficiently related to the provision of **FAPE** for each student. The Oregon legislature could not refuse to appropriate funds to meet the state's obligation to provide each student with **FAPE**. Under **34 CFR Parts 300.401 and 300.600, states are** ultimately **responsible for assuring provision of FAPE.**

Lamont X v. Quisenberry, 606 F.Supp. 809 (S.D.Ohio 1984). The modification of two Ohio disabled students' educational programs after violent incidents (by placing them in home-based situations) constituted a change of placement. A federal district court granted a motion for a preliminary injunction allowing the students to return to their classroom under the IDEA, noting that under **34 CFR Part 300.551**, home-based tutoring was in the continuum of alternative placements, and therefore a **change of placement**.

Lester H. by Octavia P. v. Gilhoul, 916 F.2d 869 (9th Cir.1990). Court awards **compensatory education** to 12-year-old under **34 CFR Parts 300.340 to 300.346**. However, the form of the instructional program was deferred until the child reached the age of 21.

Liscio v. Woodland Hills School Dist., 734 F.Supp. 689 (W.D.Pa.1989). A Pennsylvania mother objected to her mentally retarded son's placement because it did not provide for any interaction between the student and his nondisabled peers. The court determined that the student's IEP should include academic subjects with disabled students and nonacademic subjects with nondisabled students without unduly affecting the entire 5th grade schedule. This placement would comport with **34 CFR Part 300.551** (which requires the school district to offer a **continuum of services** to disabled students).

Livingston v. DeSota Cty School Dist., 782 F.Supp. 1173 (N.D.Mass.1992). Parents sought to have a hearing officer's decision reversed because a Massachusetts school district failed to provide the parents with a **written notice of their procedural safeguards**. See **34 CFR Part 300.505**. However, the court noted that the procedural error did not warrant reversal of the hearing officer's decision that the placement was appropriate because the parents were active in the special education decisions of their son and a local education advocate had explained the entire process to them. The court further noted that under **34 CFR Part 300.347** the formality of an IEP is not required when the parents unilaterally place the child in a private school.

Merrifield v. Lake Central School Corp., 770 F.Supp. 468 (N.D.Ind.1991). **34 CFR Part 300.300(b)(2)** requires the state to provide services to disabled children aged 18 to 21 if the state offers educational services to nondisabled children in the same age group. Parents sought **compensatory education** for child who had reached age 23. However, the court determined that the case was **moot** because the child reached the maximum age of public education.

Mrs. C. v. Wheaton, 916 F.2d 69 (2d Cir.1990). A functionally retarded student's mother challenged the **termination of her son's placement** as a violation of the IDEA. Neither she nor the boy's surrogate parent were advised of the discharge. The U.S. Court of Appeals, Second Circuit, determined that under **34 CFR Part 300.300(b)(4)** a functionally retarded 20-year-old may not terminate his educational placement himself. The school district must have the **approval of the parent or surrogate parent**.

Myles S. v. Montgomery County Bd. of Educ., 824 F.Supp. 1549 (M.D.Ala.1993). IDEA regulations at **34 CFR Part 300.343** require school districts to convene IEP meetings during the summer in order to be in place by the start of the school year. Another regulation, **300.307** states that physical education programs need only be included in an IEP if found to be necessary by the IEP team. School officials are required to notify parents in writing whenever there is a change in placement (**34 CFR Part 300.504**), and must also provide written notice of the refusal to change an IEP when requested by parents (**34 CFR Part 300.505**).

Oberti v. Board of Education, 789 F.Supp. 1322 (D.N.J.1992). Parents challenged the decision to place their son in a school outside the school district rather than a regular classroom in their neighborhood school. The court reversed the placement decision and determined that the school district erred when it considered the difficulties experienced by the kindergarten teacher because she did not have the skills or resources to cope with the student. See **34 CFR Parts 300.343 to 300.346**. The court noted that under **34 CFR Parts 300.531, 300.532, 300.551, and 300.552**, the school district was required to provide a **full evaluation**, and choose from the placement options that provide a **continuum of services** from full mainstreaming to completely segregated and must consider the **least restrictive environment** first. Further, the placement must be as close to home as possible.

P.C. v. McLaughlin, 913 F.2d 1033 (2d Cir.1990). A mildly retarded young man brought suit under **34 CFR Part 300.534** against state officials employed at the residential facility where he was placed. He had been placed at the facility under an emergency admission policy but stayed for two years without the benefit of an IEP. **Section 534** states that a disabled student has a right to a **comprehensive evaluation prior to any significant change in placement**. The court determined that the officials were entitled to qualified immunity because they did not have a **clearly established duty** to provide an appropriate education.

P.J. by and through W.J. v. Conn. Board of Educ., 788 F.Supp. 673 (D.Conn.1992). A 4-year-old child with Down's Syndrome sought to attend a regular kindergarten class. The school district refused and the parents challenged that decision in a federal district court. The court found that the school district's failure to write an IEP and recommendation of placement even before evaluation was a violation of **34 CFR Part 300.342** which states that **placement must be in the least restrictive environment and unique to the child**. See also **34 CFR Parts 300.340 to 300.349**.

Remis v. New Jersey Dept. of Human Serv., 815 F.Supp. 1410 (D.N.J.1993). Parents of a New Jersey student prevailed in an IDEA case because their school district placed the student in a Delaware facility even though a **residential placement** in their home town offered comparable services. Because the home town facility was comparable to the one selected by the school district, it was the appropriate placement under IDEA regulations at **34 CFR Part 300.552(a)(3)**, which requires school districts to take into account the location of residential placements.

Roland M. v. Concord School Committee, 910 F.2d 983 (1st Cir.1990). The court found that under **34 CFR Part 300.13, the need for related services for fine motor control and visual tracking must be balanced with other academic needs**. The parents of a disabled child had unilaterally placed their child in a private school. The court found that the private school placement did not properly mainstream under **34**

CFR Part 300.552(d) and thus the parents could not receive reimbursement for their costs.

Schuldt v. Mankato School Dist. No. 77, 937 F.2d 1357 (8th Cir.1991). Parents of a Minnesota child with spina bifida challenged the school district's placement of their son four miles away from home. The court upheld the placement and noted that although IDEA regulations at **34 CFR Part 300.552** required placement "**as close as possible**" to the home of a disabled student, **the IDEA does not require school districts to duplicate accessible facilities throughout the district.**

Sean R. by Dwight R. v. Bd. of Educ. of Town of Woodbridge, 794 F.Supp. 467 (D.Conn.1992). IDEA regulations published at **34 CFR Parts 300.571** and **300.572 prohibit school officials from releasing personally identifiable information** about special education students without parental consent.

Seneca Falls School Dist. v. Liverpool School District, 728 F.Supp. 910 (W.D.N.Y.1990). A federal district court ruled that **only parents have a right to sue under 34 CFR Part 300.506.** A school district had attempted to sue a neighborhood school district for a change in placement of a disabled student who attended school at the neighborhood school.

Smith v. Henson, 786 F.Supp. 43 (D.D.C. 1992). A federal district court ruled that the **notice** to the parents of a change in placement that also included a time limit on the parents' right to request a due process hearing had violated the IDEA. See **34 CFR Part 300.347**.

Smith v. Squillacote, 800 F.Supp. 993 (D.D.C.1992). A federal district court reversed the decision of a hearing officer which penalized the District of Columbia Public Schools because of an allegedly deficient notice. IDEA regulations at **34 CFR Part 300.505(a)** require school districts to provide parents with notice including "**a description of the action proposed or refused by the agency, an explanation of why the agency proposes or refuses to take the action, and a description of any option the agency considered and the reasons why those options were rejected.**"

State of Washington v. U.S. Dept. of Educ., 905 F.2d 274 (9th Cir.1990). To receive any money at all, a state must spend a "**minimum average amount.**" **34 CFR Part 300.230** requires that federal funds supplement rather than displace local funds. It further requires spending at an equal level to the previous year. There are two exceptions: a decrease in enrollment of disabled students and an unusually large amount paid out in the previous year. To determine the number of disabled students the state properly looked at the number of students and not the number of full-time equivalent students. See **34 CFR Part 300.184**.

Taylor by and through Taylor v. Honig, 910 F.2d 627 (9th Cir.1990). The U.S. Court of Appeals, Ninth Circuit, ordered the school district to pay the out-of-state tuition costs for a psychiatric care facility and school. It was the only appropriate placement for a student who was **seriously emotionally disturbed** under **34 CFR Part 300.13** due to his aggressive behavior toward his family and the fact that in-home psychotherapy had not worked.

Thomas v. Cincinnati Board of Educ., 918 F.2d 618 (6th Cir.1990). **34 CFR Part 300.544(a)(12)** provides for written notice to the parents or guardians of a change in placement of a student. The court found that **although there was no written notice given, the violation was harmless because oral notice was received**.

Todd D. by Robert D. v. Andrews, 933 F.2d 1576 (11th Cir.1991). After a student came home for a visit from an out of state residential facility, his parents became aware that he was not receiving basic care — he lost 65 lbs, had a temperature of 104ºF, and was unclean. His parents challenged the decision to place their son in the out-of-state facility. The court remanded the case to determine if the local education agency was able to provide the **least restrictive environment** under **34 CFR Part 300.552** and whether the state agency should be given the responsibility of the child.

T.S. v. Ridgefield Bd. of Educ., 808 F.Supp. 926 (D.Conn.1992). IDEA regulations published at **34 CFR Part 503** require school officials to "consider" evaluator reports in determining the appropriate placement of special education students. A Connecticut school district had no obligation to pay private school tuition for a learning disabled student whose parents accused the district of violating their due process rights by making a public school placement contrary to that recommended by an independent evaluator.

Tribble v. Montgomery County Bd. of Educ., 798 F.Supp. 668 (M.D.Ala.1992). IDEA regulations published at **34 CFR Part 403** do not require school districts to pay for private school tuition if they can provide a free appropriate public education using their own facilities. The school district in this case was required only to make services available under the same regulation, and the school board was required to provide transportation services to a private school.

Valerie J. v. Derry Co-op School Dist., 771 F.Supp. 483 (D.N.H.1991). A federal district court ruled that a school district had violated the IDEA when it suspended a student for being disruptive but did not reconvene to develop a new IEP as required under **34 CFR Parts 300.342(a) and 300.343(d)**. Thus, the student was entitled to 7 and 1/2 months of **compensatory education** after high school or to age 21.

W.G. v. Board of Trustees of Target Range School Dist., 960 F.2d 1479 (9th Cir.1992). Court found that parents were entitled to reimbursement for private tutoring for school district's failure to comply with procedures for preparing an IEP. The school had failed to ensure the participation of the private school teacher in violation of **34 CFR Parts 300.345, 300.348 and 300.533**.

Webster Groves School Dist. v. Pulitzer Pub. Co., 898 F.2d 1371 (8th Cir.1990). The U.S. Court of Appeals, Eighth Circuit, determined that **34 CFR Part 300.508(d)** which provides for open hearings could not be used to obtain court files about a disabled student. The court found that under **34 CFR Parts 300.571, 300.572 and 300.573** the parents have the right to prevent the school district from revealing **confidential information about a disabled student**. Thus, the court stated that "when courts become involved it is necessary to restrict access to court files to prevent disclosure of the information."

Weil v. Board of Elementary and Secondary Education, 931 F.2d 1069 (5th Cir.1991). Transfer of child from one school to another without notice did not violate

34 CFR Parts 300.504, 300.505 or 300.506 because both schools were under the control of the local school district and they implemented the same IEP in the same type of classroom.

Zobrest v. Catalina Foothills School Dist., 113 S.Ct. 2462 (1993). The U.S. Supreme Court held that the Establishment Clause of the First Amendment to the U.S. Constitution did not prohibit a public school district from providing a **sign language interpreter** to an Arizona student who attended a parochial school. Provision of the interpreter was a neutral service which did not violate IDEA regulations found at **34 CFR Parts 300.5, 300.13 and 300.532(a)(1)**.

APPENDIX

GLOSSARY

ADA - see Americans with Disabilities Act.

ADAAG - Americans with Disabilities Act Accessibility Guidelines for Buildings and Facilities is the accessibility standard for public accommodations and commercial facilities under ADA Title III.

ALJ - Administrative law judge. See **hearing officer**.

alcoholism - see also **drug addiction**. Under the ADA, at 42 U.S.C. § 12114(b)(4), an employer may hold an alcoholic employee to the same performance standards as other employees. However, alcoholism may be a disability under the ADA, where the employee seeks treatment. Alcoholism may also be a handicapping condition under the Rehabilitation Act § 501, which applies to federal government employees. See *National Treasury Employees Union v. Reagan*, 685 F.Supp. 1346 (E.D.La.1988), *Callicotte v. Carlucci*, 731 F.Supp. 1119 (D.D.C.1990). Where alcohol abuse results in poor performance, there is no Rehabilitation Act protection because the individual is not an **otherwise qualified** handicapped individual. See *Traynor v. Turnage*, 485 U.S. 535, 108 S.Ct. 1372, 99 L.Ed.2d 618 (1988), *Anderson v. Univ. of Wisconsin*, 841 F.2d 737 (7th Cir.1988).

Americans With Disabilities Act (ADA) - The ADA, at 42 U.S.C. § 12101 *et seq.*, went into effect on July 26, 1992. Among other things, it prohibits discrimination against a qualified individual with a disability because of that person's disability with respect to job application procedures, the hiring, advancement or discharge of employees, employee compensation, job training, and other terms, conditions and privileges of employment.

attorney's fees- Under the Rehabilitation Act, IDEA, (20 U.S.C. § 1415(e)(4)(B)), and ADA, (42 U.S.C. § 12205), courts may award reasonable attorneys' fees and costs to the prevailing party in the litigation or administrative proceeding.

auxiliary aids and services - Under the ADA § 3(1), (42 U.S.C. § 12102(1)), qualified interpreters, readers, equipment or devices are auxiliary aids and services. See also 28 CFR Part 35.104(1). Under IDEA, see **related services**.

bona fide - Latin term for good faith.

business necessity - Under Rehabilitation Act § 504 and the ADA, if a test or other selection criterion excludes an individual with a disability because of the disability and does not relate to the essential functions of a job, it is inconsistent with business necessity. Unlike Title VII of the 1964 Civil Rights Act, the business necessity test does not require statistical comparisons between groups of persons to determine whether an employer has discriminated against disabled persons. For an interpretation of the "business necessity" defense under the Rehabilitation Act, see *Davis v. Frank*, 711 F.Supp. 447 (N.D.Ill.1989) and *Davis v. Meese*, 692 F.Supp. 505 (E.D.Pa.1988), *aff'd,* 865 F.2d 592.

change in placement - Under the IDEA (20 U.S.C. § 1415(b)(1)(c)), school districts must provide parents with written notice of any proposed change in placement. The long-term suspension or expulsion of a student with a disability constitutes a change in placement under the act and entitles the student and parents to full procedural protections.

children with disabilities - As defined in the IDEA, 20 U.S.C. § 1401(a)(1)(A), children with disabilities means children who by reason of a disabling condition need special education and related services. Disabilities that are specified in the statute include: mental retardation, hearing impairments including deafness, speech or language impairments, visual impairments including blindness, serious emotional disturbance, orthopedic impairments, autism, traumatic brain injury, other health impairments, or specific learning disabilities. Under 20 U.S.C. § 1401(a)(1)(B), children with disabilities for children aged 3 to 5, inclusive, may, at a State's discretion, include children with developmental delays in physical development, cognitive development, communication development, social or emotional development, or adaptive development who require special education and related services.

contagious diseases - see **direct threat**; see also 29 CFR Part 1630.2(r), *School Board of Nassau County v. Arline*, 480 U.S. 273, 107 S.Ct. 1123, 94 L.Ed.2d 307 (1986), *Carter v. Casa Cent.*, 849 F.2d 1048, 1056 (7th Cir.1988), *Chalk v. U.S. Dist. Court, Central Dist. of California*, 840 F.2d 701, 705 (9th Cir.1988).

covered entity - A covered entity is a public or private employer, employment agency, labor organization or joint labor-management committee that is subject to ADA coverage. See 42 U.S.C. § 12111(2), and 29 CFR Part 1630.2 (b).

DOJ - The U.S. Department of Justice, the federal agency which enforces the accessibility requirements of ADA Titles II and III and many other federal civil and criminal statutes.

DOT - The U.S. Department of Transportation, the federal agency which enforces the accessibility requirements of ADA Title II, Subtitle B.

damage awards - These are recoverable under the Rehabilitation Act and ADA (see *Coleman v. Zatechka,* 824 F.Supp. 1360, 1373 (D.Neb.1993)), but there is no provision for an award of damages under the IDEA.

defenses - Defenses to charges of discrimination under ADA Title I include undue hardship (42 U.S.C. § 12111(10)), direct threat to health or safety (42 U.S.C. § 12111(10)) qualification standards, preference by religious employers for persons of the same faith, and risk of transmitting an infectious or communicable disease (42 U.S.C. § 12113). See 29 CFR Parts 1630.15-16.

direct threat - Under the ADA (42 U.S.C. § 12111(10)), no covered entity is required to hire or retain an employee who presents a direct threat to the health or safety of the individual or others. The employee presents a significant risk of substantial harm, which is identified, and is not remote. The assessment of risk must be based on objective medical or other factual evidence about the individual. Even if a significant risk of substantial harm exists, the employer must consider whether the risk can be eliminated by reasonable accommodation. Employers must make an individualized assessment that relies on current medical evidence to assess the nature, duration and severity of the risk, the probability that actual harm will occur and whether reasonable modification of employment policies, practice or procedures will eliminate the risk. See factors to be considered under ADA Title I regulations at 29 CFR Part 1630.2(r).

disability - see also **mental impairment, physical impairment, handicapped person**. Under the ADA § 3(2) (42 U.S.C. § 12102(2), and regulations at 29 CFR Part 1630.2(g) and 28 CFR Part 35.104(4), disability means a physical or mental impairment that substantially limits one or more major life activities of an individual, or a record of such an impairment, or being regarded as having such an impairment. Under Rehabilitation Act regulations, the term handicapped was still in use, but for legal and practical purposes, the terms are identical. See *School Board of Nassau County v Arline*, 480 U.S. 273, 107 S.Ct. 1123, 94 L.Ed.2d 307 (1986).

disabilities, children with - Under the IDEA (20 U.S.C. § 1401 (a)) and 34 CFR Part 300.7), children with disabilities include those evaluated under the act as having mental retardation, visual, hearing and speech impairments, specific learning disabilities, multiple disabilities, orthopedic and other health impairments and serious emotional disturbance, who need special education and related services because of their disabilities.

disabilities, persons with - Any person who has a physical or mental impairment that substantially limits one or more major life activities, has a record of such an impairment, or is regarded as having such an impairment. ADA § 3(2) (42 U.S.C. § 12102(2)); 29 CFR Part 1630.2 (g); 29 CFR Part 1613.702(a). The term has the same legal meaning as **handicapped person** under the Rehabilitation Act. See 34 CFR Part 104.3(j) and 45 CFR Part 84.3(j). For IDEA definition, see **disabilities, children with.**

discrimination - Under ADA Title I (42 U.S.C. § 12112) and its regulations (29 CFR Parts 1630.4-5), discrimination includes limiting, segregating, or classifying job applicants in a manner that adversely affects employment opportunity because of disability. It also refers to using standards that perpetuate discrimination on the basis of disability, using tests that screen out persons with disabilities, failing to reasonably accommodate a person with a disability, and denying employment opportunities to otherwise qualified individuals with disabilities. See also ADA Title II (42 U.S.C. § 12132, 28 CFR Parts 35.130 and 140), which prohibits the exclusion of a qualified individual with a disability from participation in the programs of a public entity on the basis of the disability. The Title III definition, applicable to places of public accommodation and services, at 42 U.S.C. § 12182(b)(2), prohibits the denial of the opportunity to participate or derive benefits from public services, facilities and other accommodations.

drug addiction - Under the ADA, drug addiction may be an impairment which substantially limits major life activities and may invoke ADA protection if the individual undertakes or completes a rehabilitation program. See 42 U.S.C. § 12110(b). However, 42 U.S.C. §§ 12114(a) and 12210(a) specifically exclude individuals who currently use drugs illegally from being considered individuals with disabilities under the ADA. See also **alcoholism.**

drug testing - Drug testing by employers is specifically allowed under ADA Title I (see 42 U.S.C. § 12114(d)(2), (e) and 29 CFR Part 1630.16(c)).

drugs - Under the ADA (42 U.S.C. §§ 12111(6)(B) and 12210(d)(2)), a drug is a controlled substance according to schedules I through V of the Controlled Substances Act (21 U.S.C. § 812). See also 42 U.S.C. §§ 12114 and 12210(d)(1), illegal use of drugs. Employers are not restricted by the ADA from prohibiting the illegal employee use of drugs and alcohol in the workplace.

due process - Due process is "fair play" in the government's application of laws to its citizens, guaranteed by the Fifth and Fourteenth Amendments. The process which may be due a particular party generally corresponds to the importance of the legal or administrative proceeding. There is a range of due process protections available to persons bringing suit under the statutes presented in this volume, going from simple notice and an opportunity to respond, to trial-type hearings and other protections. For instance, under the IDEA, school districts are required to provide notice to parents of students with disabilities of all their substantive rights, including the right to appeal school board decisions. (See due process procedures codified at 20 U.S.C. § 1415, 34 CFR Parts 300.500-515.) For Rehabilitation Act due process procedures, see 45 CFR Part 84.36 [34 CFR Part 104.36]. The ADA requires the development and application of uniform due process protections as set forth in Rehabilitation Act procedures. See 42 U.S.C. § 12117(b).

due process hearing - Under the IDEA (20 U.S.C. § 1415(b)-(d)), the statutory right of students and parents to review school district placement decisions, including an opportunity for the parents to examine relevant records and to obtain an independent educational evaluation of the child; written prior notice to the parents whenever there is a proposed change in placement, or identification, evaluation, or educational placement of the child or other issue concerning the provision of a free appropriate public education; and an opportunity to present complaints.

EEOC - Equal Employment Opportunity Commission, the federal agency that enforces the employment provisions of ADA Title I as well as many other federal employment discrimination statutes, such as Title VII of the Civil Rights Act of 1964. Persons alleging discrimination must pursue their administrative remedies within the EEOC before they are allowed to file suit under ADA Title I and Civil Rights Act Title VII.

EAHCA - The **Education for All Handicapped Children Act** of 1975. An amendment to the Education of the Handicapped Act of 1970 (EHA) which enacted many of the most important procedural due process rights of the present-day IDEA. (See 20 U.S.C. § 1415).

EHA - The **Education of the Handicapped Act**, now known as the Individuals with Disabilities Education Act (IDEA), was enacted in 1970 and became an effective enforcement statute for the rights of disabled students with the passage of the Education for All Handicapped Children Act of 1975 (EAHCA).

employer - Under ADA Title I (42 U.S.C. § 12111(5)), a person engaged in an industry affecting commerce that is under ADA coverage and must comply with the act. A covered entity has 25 or more employees, or, as of 1994, 15 or more employees. See also **covered entity**, ADA § 101(5) (42 U.S.C. § 12111(2)) and 29 CFR 1630.2(e).

employment agency - Includes private and public employment agencies, university placement services and other organizations that regularly place employees. Employment agencies are "covered entities," under the ADA § 101(7) (42 U.S.C. § 12111(7)), 29 CFR 1630.2(c). Both the employer and employment agency come under ADA coverage where the employer uses the agency to recruit, screen and refer applicants.

Equal Protection Clause - The U.S. Constitution's Fourteenth Amendment prohibits a *state* from denying any person within its jurisdiction equal protection of its laws. Also, the Due Process Clause of the Fifth Amendment which pertains to the *federal government* has been interpreted by the Supreme Court to grant equal protection even though there is no explicit grant in the Constitution.

essential functions - The essential functions of a job are those that are fundamental and not marginal. The employer's judgment as to what aspects are essential is important. See EEOC regulations under the ADA, at 29 CFR 1630.2(n).

exhaustion of administrative remedies, doctrine of - Requires that persons follow administrative appeal processes to their conclusion before resorting to the courts. Exceptions apply where administrative appeal would be futile, or where the administrative procedures themselves are being challenged. Rehabilitation Act see *Doe v. Garrett*, 903 F.2d 1455 (11th Cir.1990),*cert. den.*, 111 S.Ct. 1102, 113 L.Ed.2d 213.

expulsion constitutes a change in placement - Expulsion of students with disabilities is a change in placement under the IDEA, because it alters the placement status quo. See *Honig v. Doe*, 484 U.S. 305, 108 S.Ct. 592, 98 L.Ed.2d 686 (1988).

FAPE - see **free appropriate public education.**

federal financial assistance - Under the Rehabilitation Act, any grant, loan, contract or other provision of funds, services or federal property or personnel, including sale proceeds, transfers and leases for less than fair market value. An entity must receive federal funding to be within Rehabilitation Act coverage. See 45 CFR Part 84.3(h) [34 CFR Part 104.3(h)]. The IDEA requires states to comply with its mandate under 20 U.S.C. § 1412 in order to be eligible for federal funds.

42 U.S.C. §§ 1981, 1983 - Also referred to as §§ 1981 and 1983 of the Civil Rights Act. Section 1983 prohibits any person acting under color of state law from depriving any other person of rights protected by the Constitution or by federal laws. The majority of lawsuits claiming constitutional violations are brought under § 1983. Section 1981 provides that all persons enjoy the same right to make and enforce contracts as white citizens. Section 1981 applies to employment contracts.

free appropriate public education (FAPE) - Under the IDEA, 20 U.S.C. § 1401(a)(18) and 34 CFR Part 300.8, the term free appropriate public education (FAPE) means special education and related services that have been provided at public expense, under public supervision and direction, without charge, that meet the standards of the State educational agency, include an appropriate preschool, elementary, or secondary school education, and conform with the student's IEP. FAPE is also mandated by Rehabilitation Act regulations at 34 CFR Part 104.33 (45 CFR Part 84.33).

HCPA - The **Handicapped Children's Protection Act** of 1986, P.L. 99-372, amended the EHA (now IDEA) by authorizing courts to award attorney's fees to prevailing parties in IDEA actions and expressly authorized disabled students and parents to combine available remedies under the IDEA, the Civil Rights Act of 1964 and the Rehabilitation Act.

handicapped children - Under the Rehabilitation Act, see handicapped person. Under the IDEA, please see **disabilities, children with.**

handicapped person - Under Rehabilitation Act regulations at 29 CFR Part 1613.702(a), 34 CFR Part 104.3(j) and 45 CFR Part 84.3(j), a handicapped person is any person who has a physical or mental impairment that substantially limits one or more major life activities, has a record of such an impairment, or is regarded as having such an impairment. The term has the same legal meaning as **person with a disability** under the ADA. See 29 CFR 1630.2(g).

has a record of such impairment - Under the ADA, this means a history (even if merely a misclassification) of having a mental or physical impairment that substantially limits one or more major life activities. See 29 CFR Part 1630.2(k).

hearing officer - Also known as an administrative law judge (ALJ). Hearing officers decide disputes that arise at the administrative level, and have powers to administer oaths, take testimony, rule on evidentiary questions, and make determinations of law and fact.

IDEA - The **Individuals with Disabilities Education Act**, 20 U.S.C. § 1400 *et seq.,* formerly known as the Education of the Handicapped Act. The IDEA is the major federal legislation that protects the rights of students with disabilities.

IEP - see Individualized Education Program.

illegal use of drugs - and alcohol. Persons who currently use drugs illegally are not protected under the ADA. See ADA § 101(6) (42 U.S.C. § 12114), and 29 CFR 1630.3(a)-(c). Persons who have completed a rehabilitation program or are currently enrolled in a rehabilitation program may be qualified disabled persons under the ADA. See 29 CFR Part 1630.3(a)(2), 28 CFR Parts 35.104(4), and 35.131.

immunity - see state immunity.

impairment, physical or mental - Under Rehabilitation Act regulations at 45 CFR Part 84.3(j)(2)(i) [34 CFR Part 104.3(j)(2)(i)] and ADA regulations at 29 CFR Part 1630.2(h) and 28 CFR Part 35.104(1)(i), "impairment" means any physiological disorder or condition, cosmetic disfigurement, or anatomical loss affecting one or more of the following body systems: neurological; musculoskeletal; special sense organs; respiratory, including speech organs; cardiovascular; reproductive; digestive; genitourinary; hemic and lymphatic; skin; and endocrine. It also means any mental or psychological disorder, such as mental retardation, organic brain syndrome, emotional or mental illness, and specific learning disabilities. To obtain legal redress under either the ADA or the Rehabilitation Act, the impairment must be one that "substantially limits a **major life activity**."

individual with a disability - Under the ADA and the Rehabilitation Act (29 U.S.C. § 706(2)(8)(B)), an individual who has a physical or mental impairment that substantially limits one or more of his or her major life activities, has a record of such an impairment, or is regarded as having such an impairment. See 28 CFR 35.104, 28 CFR 36.104. See also "**qualified individual with a disability**."

individual with handicaps - Under the Rehabilitation Act, 29 U.S.C. § 706(8)(B), any person who "(i) has a physical or mental impairment which substantially limits one or more of such person's major life activities, (ii) has a record of such impairment, or (iii) is regarded as having such an impairment."

individualized educational program (IEP) - Under the IDEA (§ 1401(a)(20)) and 34 CFR Parts 300.340-350, the term "individualized education program" (IEP) means a written statement for each child with a disability developed in a meeting by a representative of the LEA or a qualified intermediate educational unit, describing a specially designed program of instruction to meet the unique needs of children with disabilities. IEPs must include a statement of the present levels of educational performance of the child, annual goals, including short-term instructional objectives, the specific educational services to be provided, the child's ability to participate in regular educational programs, and a statement of needed transition services. IEPs must also include the projected date for initiation and anticipated duration of such services, and appropriate objective criteria and evaluation procedures and schedules for determining whether instructional objectives are being achieved. See also 20 U.S.C. § 1414(a)(5).

Individuals with Disabilities Education Act (IDEA) - 20 U.S.C. § 1400 *et seq.*, also known as the Education of the Handicapped Act (EHA), includes the Education for All Handicapped Children Act (EAHCA), and the Handicapped Children's Protection Act (HCPA). Originally enacted in 1970 as the EHA, the IDEA is the federal law that requires states to provide a free appropriate public education to all children with disabilities.

injunction- An equitable remedy in which a court orders a party to do or to refrain from doing some particular action.

insurance - The insurance industry is generally unrestricted by the ADA under 42 U.S.C. § 12201(c), so long as the insurer, hospital, health maintenance organization, agent, plan or underwriter does not act inconsistently with state laws. See 29 CFR Part 1630.16(f).

intermediate educational unit - Under the IDEA, 20 U.S.C. § 1401(a)(23), "intermediate educational unit" means any public authority, other than a local educational agency, that is under the general supervision of a State educational agency established by State law for the purpose of providing free public education on a regional basis, and which provides special education and related services to children with disabilities within that State.

is regarded as having such an impairment - Under ADA and Rehabilitation Act regulations, persons who are not substantially limited in a major life activity but who are perceived to be substantially limited may be entitled to protection if they are treated as having an impairment. See 29 CFR 1630.2(l), 28 CFR 35.104, 28 CFR 36.104; and 29 CFR Part 1613.702(e).

job restructuring - The transfer of marginal job duties that cannot be performed by a person with a disability to other employees who are capable of performing the duties. Employers are not required to transfer essential job duties to other employees in order to reasonably accommodate a person with a disability.

jurisdiction - The power of a court to determine cases and controversies. The U.S. Supreme Court's jurisdiction generally extends to cases arising under the Constitution and under federal law. Federal courts have the power to hear cases where there is diversity of citizenship or where a federal question is involved. Jurisdiction also refers to the territorial limits of a particular court.

LEA - see local educational agency.

labor organization - An entity that is not exempt from ADA coverage, see ADA § 101(7) (42 U.S.C. § 12111(7)) and 29 CFR 1630.2(c).

least restrictive environment - Also known as **mainstreaming**. This is the desegregation requirement of the IDEA, found at 20 U.S.C. § 1412(5)(B) and 34 CFR Part 300.550(b)(1). The IDEA requires school districts to provide FAPE to students with disabilities in the same classes with children who are not disabled "to the maximum extent appropriate."

local educational agency (LEA) - Under the IDEA, 20 U.S.C. § 1401(a)(8), "local educational agency" means a public board of education or other public authority legally constituted within a State for either administrative control or direction of public elementary or secondary schools, or a combination of school districts or counties recognized in a State as an administrative agency for its public elementary or secondary schools. The term includes any other public institution or agency having administrative control and direction of a public elementary or secondary school. See also 34 CFR Part 300.8.

mainstreaming - Under the IDEA, a major component of a free appropriate public education is that each child with a disability be educated in the **least restrictive environment** that is educationally appropriate for the child. See 20 U.S.C. § 1412 (5)(B) and 34 CFR Part 300.550(b)(1). When disabled children are educated with nondisabled children in regular education classes, they are being mainstreamed.

major life activity - Activities such as caring for one's self, performing manual tasks, walking, seeing, hearing, speaking, breathing, learning, and working. Under the Rehabilitation Act and ADA, major life activities are those that an average person can perform without difficulty. See 29 CFR 1630.2(i), 29 CFR Part 1613.702(c), *Santiago v. Temple Univ.*, 739 F.Supp. 974 (E.D.Pa.1990).

medical examinations, preemployment - Are prohibited prior to an offer of employment under ADA Title I. See 42 U.S.C. § 12112(a), (d)(1)-(3), and 29 CFR Parts 1630.13-14. However, post-offer medical examinations prior to the first day of work are permitted. See 29 CFR Part 1630.14(b).

medical services - Under the IDEA (§ 1401(a)(17)), medical services must be only for diagnostic and evaluation purposes to be considered as related services which the public school district must provide to each child with a disability as a part of its obligation to provide FAPE to all students with disabilities.

mental impairment - Under the ADA, "Any mental or psychological disorder, such as mental retardation, organic brain syndrome, emotional or mental illness, and specific learning disabilities." The term mental impairment does not extend to sexual orientation or behavior. Drug addiction is a mental impairment under the ADA, but current illegal usage of drugs precludes ADA coverage. See 29 CFR 1630.2(h), 28 CFR Part 35.104(4).

monetary damages - Limited under § 504 to "retrospective equitable damages" in cases in which there is a finding of intentional discrimination. Punitive damages, and damages for emotional distress and mental suffering are unavailable under § 504. *Shinault v. American Airlines, Inc.*, 738 F.Supp. 193, 198 (S.D.Miss.1990), *aff'd in part, rev'd in part*, 936 F.2d 796 (5th Cir.1991). Case law concerning the availability of monetary damages under the ADA is undeveloped, but see *Coleman v. Zatechka*, 824 F.Supp. 1360 (D.Neb.1993), 824 F.Supp. at 1373, n. 29.

nondiscrimination, employment - Under the ADA, nondiscriminatory employment practices are those that provide equal access to employment opportunities to similarly situated individuals who do not have disabilities.

otherwise qualified individual with a handicap - Not fully defined in the Rehabilitation Act, the term refers to individuals with disabilities who are able to perform the essential functions of a job. Described by the U.S. Supreme Court in *Southeastern Community College v. Davis*, 442 U.S. 397, 99 S.Ct. 2361, 60 L.Ed.2d 980 (1979) as "one who meets *all* of a program's requirements in spite of his handicap." The Supreme Court definition was further discussed in *Alexander v. Choate*, 469 U.S. 287, 107 S.Ct. 1123, 94 L.Ed.2d 307 (1985): "an otherwise qualified handicapped individual must be provided with meaningful access to the benefit that the grantee offers...." Otherwise qualified individual with a handicap is equivalent to the ADA's qualified individual with a disability. See *School Board of Nassau County, Florida v. Arline*, 480 U.S. 273 (1987), *Anderson v. Univ. of Wisconsin*, 841 F.2d 737 (7th Cir.1988), *Langon v. U.S. Dept. of Health and Human Services*, 749 F.Supp. 1 (D.D.C.1990), *Gilbert v. Frank*, 949 F.2d 637 (2d Cir.1991).

physical impairment - Under the ADA, "Any physiological disorder, or condition, cosmetic disfigurement, or anatomical loss affecting one or more of the following body systems: neurological, musculoskeletal, special sense organs, respiratory (including speech organs), cardiovascular, reproductive, digestive, genitourinary, hemic and lymphatic, skin and endocrine." See 29 CFR 1630.2(h).

placement - A special education student's placement must be appropriate (as well as responsive to the particular child's needs). Under the IDEA's "stay-put" provision, school officials may not remove a special education child from his or her "then current placement" over the parents' objections until the completion of administrative or judicial proceedings.

prevailing party - see also **attorney's fees.** Under the IDEA (20 U.S.C. § 1415(e)(4)(B)), ADA and Rehabilitation Act, courts may award reasonable attorneys' fees to individuals with disabilities, and the parents or guardian of a child with a disability who is the prevailing party. A prevailing party is one who has succeeded in changing the legal relationship between the parties by gaining at least some part of the relief requested in an administrative hearing or lawsuit.

private club - One of the few entities exempt from ADA coverage, see 28 CFR 36.104.

private schools - see **tuition reimbursement.**

procedural protections - see **due process.**

program accessibility - Under ADA Title II, a public entity's services, programs and activities must be readily accessible and usable to individuals with disabilities. See 28 CFR Parts 35.149-150.

program or activity receiving Federal financial assistance - Under § 504 of the Rehabilitation Act, a department, agency or other instrumentality of a state or local government to which federal assistance is extended, including colleges, universities, local educational agencies, corporations, partnerships, and other private organizations and entities. See *Consolidated Rail Corp. v. Darrone*, 465 U.S. 624, 104 S.Ct. 1248, 79 L.Ed.2d 568 (1984).

pro se - A party representing his or her own interests in court, without the benefit of an attorney, appears *pro se*.

public entity - Under ADA Title II, (42 U.S.C. § 12131(1)), any state or local government, or department, agency, special purpose district or instrumentality of a state or local government is within ADA coverage. Under Subtitle B of ADA Title II, this term extends to Amtrak and other public commuter services. While Title II applies broadly to all state and local programs, activities and services, it does not apply to the federal government, which is covered under the Rehabilitation Act §§ 501 and 504. See ADA § 201(1) (42 U.S.C. § 12115(1)), 28 CFR 35.104.

qualified handicapped person - The Rehabilitation Act equivalent of the ADA's **qualified individual with a disability**. See 45 CFR Part 84.3(k) [34 CFR Part 104.3(k)], 29 CFR Part 1613.702(f). The terms have the same legal meaning.

qualified individual with a disability - Under ADA Title I (at 42 U.S.C. § 12111(8)), an individual with a disability who satisfies the job-related requirements of a position, and who, with or without reasonable accommodation, can perform the essential functions of the job. Protected individuals are those with a physical or mental impairment that substantially limits one or more major life activities, individuals who have a record of physical or mental impairment that substantially limits major life activities, or are *regarded* as having such an impairment, regardless of whether they are actually impaired. Under ADA Title II (42 U.S.C. § 12131(1)), **qualified individual with a disability** refers to an individual with a disability who, with or without reasonable accommodation, meets the essential eligibility requirements to participate in programs or activities of a public entity. See also regulatory definitions at 29 CFR Part 1630.2(m) and 28 CFR Part 35.104.

readily achievable - Under ADA Title III, barriers must be removed from places of public accommodation where the removal is readily achievable, regardless of whether the accommodation being offered can be made accessible by other methods. ADA § 301(9), (42 U.S.C. § 12181(9)). See also 28 CFR Part 36.104.

reasonable accommodation - Under the ADA (at 42 U.S.C. § 12111(9)) and § 504 of the Rehabilitation Act, a change in the work environment or course of business which brings about equal employment opportunities for individuals with disabilities. The ADA requires employers to consider making reasonable accommodations in determining whether an individual with a disability is qualified to perform a particular job. See also **undue hardship**. Reasonable accommodation encompasses a range of actions such as job restructuring, making facilities accessible, providing readers and interpreters and other alterations. Courts may not order entities to "fundamentally alter" their programs to accommodate disabled persons. See Rehabilitation Act regulations at 45 CFR Part 84.12 [34 CFR Part 104.12], and ADA regulations at 29 CFR Part 1630.2(o), *Kohl by Kohl v. Woodhaven Learning Center*, 865 F.2d 930 (8th Cir.1989), *cert. den.* 493 U.S. 892, 110 S.Ct. 239, 107 L.Ed.2d 189; *Doherty v.*

Southern College of Optometry, 862 F.2d 570 (6th Cir.1988), *cert. den.* 493 U.S. 810, 110 S.Ct. 53, 107 L.Ed.2d 22.

recipient - Under the Rehabilitation Act, a recipient is a state, state political subdivision or instrumentality, public or private agency, institution, entity or person that receives federal financial assistance either directly or through another recipient. An entity must be determined to be a recipient of federal funding to be within the act's coverage. See 45 CFR Part 84.3(f) [34 CFR Part 104.3(f)], and Appendix B to 34 CFR Part 100, part B-C.

Rehabilitation Act of 1973 - (29 U.S.C. § 701 *et seq.*), the Rehabilitation Act prohibits employers who receive federal financial assistance from discriminating against otherwise qualified individuals with handicaps solely on the basis of their handicap. Section 501 of the act prohibits federal agencies from discrimination against persons with handicaps.

related services - Under the IDEA (§ 1401(a)(17)), the term "related services" means transportation, developmental, corrective, and other supportive services (including speech pathology and audiology, psychological services, physical and occupational therapy, recreation, including therapeutic recreation, social work services, counseling services, including rehabilitation counseling, and medical services, except that such medical services shall be for diagnostic and evaluation purposes only) as may be required to assist a child with a disability to benefit from special education, and includes the early identification and assessment of disabling conditions in children.

religious entities - Are subject to ADA coverage, but may grant nondiscriminatory preferential treatment to persons within the faith.

remand - The act of an appellate court in returning a case to the court from which it came for further action.

remedies - There are two general categories of remedies: legal remedies, which consist of money damages, and equitable remedies, which consist of a court mandate (injunction) that a specific action be prohibited or required. Legal and equitable remedies are available under the Rehabilitation Act and ADA Titles I and II (42 U.S.C. §§ 12117 and 12133). The IDEA permits students with disabilities to cumulate available remedies (see **HCPA**), but does not permit damage awards. The remedies of the Civil Rights Act of 1964 are available under ADA Title I, at 42 U.S.C. § 12117.

SEA - see State educational agency.

Section 501 - Rehabilitation Act § 501 prohibits discrimination on the basis of disability by federal employers.

Section 503 - Rehabilitation Act § 503 prohibits private entities contracting with the federal government from discriminating on the basis of disability. This section permits contractors and their subcontractors who perform work for the federal government to invite individuals with disabilities to identify themselves on job applications for affirmative action compliance.

Section 504 - The most important section of the Rehabilitation Act of 1973, 29 U.S.C. § 794, which broadly protects individuals from discrimination on the basis of disability in all programs receiving federal financial assistance. It requires that an otherwise qualified individual cannot be denied employment based on his or her handicap. An otherwise qualified individual is one who can perform the "essential functions" of the job with "reasonable accommodation."

Section 1981 & Section 1983 - (see 42 U.S.C. §§ 1981, 1983).

significant risk of substantial harm - Permits an employer to invoke the business necessity defense. Where an applicant presents a significant risk of substantial harm, the individual is unprotected by the ADA. A significant risk is a high probability of substantial harm and must be identified, not based on mere speculation, but must be a current and not a remote or future risk. A risk assessment may not be based on speculation that an individual will become unable to perform a job in the future, or that the individual will increase health insurance or workers' compensation claims or absenteeism.

smoking - Covered entities may prohibit, or impose restrictions on, smoking in the workplace under ADA Title I. See 29 CFR Part 1630.16(d).

sovereign immunity - The legal doctrine that the government cannot be sued without its own consent, has been abrogated under the IDEA (20 U.S.C. § 1403), ADA (42 U.S.C. § 12202), and Rehabilitation Act (29 U.S.C. § 794a).

special education - Under the IDEA, § 20 U.S.C. § 1401(a)(16), special education means specially designed instruction, at no cost to parents or guardians, to meet the unique needs of a child with a disability, including instruction conducted in classrooms, homes, hospitals and institutions, including physical education.

standing - A judicial doctrine which states that in order to maintain a lawsuit a party must have some real interest at stake in the outcome of the trial.

state - Under the IDEA (§ 1401(a)(6)), any of the several States, the District of Columbia, the Commonwealth of Puerto Rico, the Virgin Islands, Guam, American Samoa, the Commonwealth of the Northern Mariana Islands, or the Trust Territory of the Pacific Islands. See the similar definition at ADA § 3(3), (42 U.S.C. § 12102(3)), 29 CFR 1630.2(d), 28 CFR 35.104 and 28 CFR 36.104.

State educational agency (SEA) - Under the IDEA, 20 U.S.C. § 1401(a)(7), SEA means the State board of education or other agency or officer primarily responsible for the State supervision of public elementary and secondary schools, or, if there is no such officer or agency, an officer or agency designated by the governor or by State law.

state immunity - The legal doctrine that the government cannot be sued without its own consent. State (also known as sovereign) immunity has been abrogated under the acts contained in this volume, so that government entities are subject to suit under them. See 20 U.S.C. § 1403, 42 U.S.C. § 12202, and 29 U.S.C. § 794a.

statutes of limitation - Provide the time period in which an action may be brought. Under the Rehabilitation Act and IDEA, there is no explicit statute of limitations, and courts are required to use and apply the most appropriate or analogous statute of limitations from the jurisdiction in which the court is located. This leads to different results among jurisdictions.

stay put provision - A procedural protection of the IDEA, found at 20 U.S.C. § 1415(e)(3), which requires preservation of the status quo of a child's placement during the pendency of any IDEA proceeding. The child must remain in his or her "then current educational placement" until all hearings and proceedings have been completed. See 34 CFR Part 300.513.

substantially limits - Under the ADA, an impairment is deemed a disability if it "substantially limits" one or more major life activities, according to the following criteria: the nature and severity of the impairment, the duration of the impairment, and its expected long-term or permanent impact. See 29 CFR Part 1630.2(j).

summary judgment - Federal Rule of Civil Procedure 56 provides for the summary adjudication of a case if either party can show that there is no genuine issue as to any material fact and that, given the facts agreed upon, the party is entitled to judgment as a matter of law. In general, summary judgment is used to dispose of claims which do not support a legally recognized claim.

Supremacy Clause - Clause in Article VI of the Constitution which states that federal legislation is the supreme law of the land. Under this doctrine, the federal statutes in this volume take legal precedence over the contrary provisions of any state laws, regulations or policies.

surrogate parent - Under IDEA regulations at 34 CFR Part 300.515, surrogate parents may be appointed to ensure the rights of a child with a disability where no parent may be identified or located, or where the child is a ward of the state.

TDD - Telecommunication devices for the deaf. See 28 CFR Part 31.161.

Title I, ADA - Sections 101-108, 42 U.S.C. § 12111-12117, the ADA section governing private employers. See federal labor regulations at 29 CFR Part 1630.1-.16.

Title II, ADA - Sections 201-246, at 42 U.S.C. §§ 12131-12165. Title II Subtitle A, protects qualified individuals with disabilities from discrimination in state and local government services, programs and activities. Enforced by the Department of Justice, Title II Subtitle B governs private providers of public services, including public transit and railroads. See regulations at 28 CFR Part 35.102-104.

Title III, ADA - Sections 301-310, 42 U.S.C. §§ 12181-12189, which governs public accommodations and services that are operated by private entities, such as hotels, restaurants, theaters, stores, auditoriums, laundromats, museums, libraries, private schools, daycare centers, gymnasiums, golf courses and other recreational facilities.

Title IV, ADA - Sections 401-402, 47 U.S.C. § 201 *et seq.*, amends Title II of the Communications Act of 1934 by adding a section governing telecommunications services for hearing-impaired and speech-impaired individuals.

Title V, ADA - Sections 501-514, 42 U.S.C. §§ 12201-12213. This general provision includes definitions, rules of construction and coverage, an attorney's fees provision and amendments to the Rehabilitation Act (29 U.S.C. § 706(8)).

Title VII, Civil Rights Act of 1964 - (42 U.S.C. § 2000e) Prohibits employment discrimination on the basis of race, color, sex, national origin, or religion by any employer having fifteen or more employees. Under Title VII, where an employer intentionally discriminates, employees may obtain money damages unless the claim is for race discrimination. The EEOC enforces Title VII, as well as ADA Title I and § 503.

transition services - Under the IDEA, 20 U.S.C. § 1401(a)(19), a coordinated set of activities for a student, that promotes movement from school to post-school activities, based upon the individual student's needs, including instruction, community experiences, development of employment and other adult living objectives.

tuition reimbursement - Reimbursement for private school tuition must be paid by public school districts if they do not have the facilities to provide FAPE to a student with a disability in the district.

UFAS - The Uniform Federal Accessibility Standards

undue hardship - A defense to the general requirements of ADA Title I and the Rehabilitation Act by entities seeking to avoid reasonably accommodating persons with disabilities. An action by a covered entity that is unduly costly, extensive, substantial or disruptive that would fundamentally alter the nature or operation of a business, or that causes significant difficulty or expense, may impose an undue hardship on the entity. The term takes into account the financial resources and number of other employees of a covered entity. See ADA § 101(10) (42 U.S.C. § 12111(10)), and ADA regulations at 29 CFR Part 1630.2(p). For a federal district court's interpretation of undue hardship under Rehabilitation Act § 501, see *Johnson v.*

Sullivan, 764 F.Supp. 1053 (D.Md.1991). See also *Guice-Mills v. Derwinski*, 778 F.Supp. 188 (S.D.N.Y.1991), *aff'd*, 967 F.2d 794 (2d Cir.1992).

unilateral transfer or placement by parent - This has been authorized by the U.S. Supreme Court where the school district disobeys the IDEA by failing to provide FAPE, by making an inappropriate placement or by violating procedural protections of the IDEA. See *Burlington School Comm. v. Dept. of Educ. of Massachusetts*, 471 U.S. 359, 105 S.Ct. 1996, 85 L.Ed.2d 385 (1985), *Florence County School Dist. Four v. Carter*, 114 S.Ct. 361(1993). See also 34 CFR Parts 300.403, 300.450-452.

vacate - The annulment of a court's judgment by an appellate court or by the court itself.

INDEX